CONTENTS

World mythology is a vast subject, one that encompasses the cultural dreams of the human race. A fully comprehensive book on world mythology would fill many volumes and would involve a seemingly infinite number of highly subjective choices of stories, characters, and themes. What we think of as Greece is a cultural entity made up of many cultures over time. Native American mythology is, in fact, made up of the mythologies of hundreds of tribes. The same can be said of African mythology, Germanic mythology, Indonesian mythology, Mesopotamian mythology, or any other large cultural grouping of myths. And there is the question of boundaries in connection with the definition of "myth." Often it is difficult to say definitively, for instance, that a particular story is a myth rather than a legend or other type of folk tale.

In this book, I do not pretend to have covered every corner of world mythology. I have attempted to be inclusive and reasonably comprehensive. Not surprisingly, the majority of entries are products of the best known of the world's mythological systems. There are more entries related to Greek, Egyptian, East Indian, Mesopotamian, Celtic, and Norse myths here than those pertaining to Ainu or Island Arawak myths. To a great extent, of course, this type of imbalance is a reflection of existing information and scholarship.

As for the distinction of myth versus legend or other type of folklore, I have taken a somewhat relaxed approach. It might well be argued that the Brer Rabbit story, for instance, is not really a myth. Without commenting on that question, I have chosen to include the story (and other folk stories that are perhaps not technically myths) because it has mythic aspects and can be usefully compared with a similar, perhaps more evidently mythic story from another culture.

Finally, I have not avoided the sensitive area of myth and religion. I have treated the sacred narratives of the "great religions," including the monotheistic Abrahamic religions, as myths, not to deprecate those religions, but simply because to a believer in one religion the stories—especially the supernatural ones—of another religion tend to be seen as myth rather than history.

The lists at the beginning of the book, after the introduction, categorize entries according to both large (e.g., Asian, European) and narrower (e.g., Irish) cultural groups and in some cases according to themes (e.g., Arthurian myths) and general subjects (e.g., mythic themes). Included in these lists are all of the entries in the text, as well as (in brackets) some of the categories themselves (e.g., the "Celtic" category includes in its list "[Arthurian myths]," referring to all of the entries listed under the category "Arthurian myths"). Specific thematic categories are indicated by cross-referencing in the text (e.g., "descent," "hero," "miraculous conception").

The articles themselves are arranged alphabetically. There are entries on the major religion-based and ethnicity-based mythologies, as well as entries on major mythological characters and themes and on other topics related to mythology. References, by author name (and year, if necessary), to items in the general bibliography at the end of the book are placed after particular articles in brackets to suggest further reading and to recognize significant source material.

To make names of individuals and places more easily pronounceable for English-speaking readers, I have, in most cases, avoided using the diacriticals that are often applied to transliterations of, for example, Greek, Sanskrit, Celtic, ancient Mesopotamian, and Semitic words. Thus, for instance, the name of the great Hindu destroyer and yogic god is spelled Shiva in the admittedly old-fashioned Anglicized manner, rather than Siva in the more academic manner, and the Hindu elephant-headed god is represented as Ganesh rather than Gane´sa.

The Oxford
ILLUSTRATED COMPANION TO
WORLD MYTHOLOGY

DAVID LEEMING

Tess Press

Published by Tess Press, an imprint of
Black Dog & Leventhal Publishers, Inc.
151 West 19th Street
New York, NY 10011

PHOTOGRAPHIC CREDITS

All images courtesy of **Getty Images** including the following which have additional attributions:

Agence France Presse: vii,35,48,69,109,140; **Altrendo:**193; **Asia Images:** 295; **Aurora:**178; **Axiom:** 223; **Bridgeman Art Library:** front cover (2L)/ Deir el-Medina,Thebes, (3L)/The De Morgan Centre, London, (2R)/ Bradford Art Galleries & Museums, West Yorkshire,UK, (BL)/ Simon Marsden, Belvoir Castle, Leicestershire,UK , (BR)/ Private Collection; back cover: (2L)/ Private Collection, (3L)/Victoria & Albert Museum, London, (2R)/ Bibliotheque Nationale, Paris, (1R)/ Musee des Beaux-Arts, Rennes, (BL)/Private Collection, (BR)/ Museo Archaeologico Nazionale, Naples; spine:Private Collection; iii/Museo Archeologico Nazionale,Naples; viii/Private Collection; xi/Musee National de Phnom Penh,Cambodia; xii/Musee des Beaux-Arts,Rennes; xv/Private Collection; 1/Palais du Luxembourg, Paris; 3/Musee des Beaux-Arts, Pau; 4/Rubenhuis, Antwerp; 6/Hamburger Kunsthalle, Hamburg; 7/Private Collection; 8/Bibliotheque Nationale, Paris; 9/Villa Valmarana,Vicenza; 10/Bibliotheque des Arts Decoratifs, Paris; 18/Private Collection; 19/Duomo, Orvieto; 20/Deir el-Medina,Thebes; 21/ Private Collection; 23/Ma'rib,Yemen; 27/The De Morgan Centre, London; 29/Galleria degli Uffizi, Florence; 31/Private Collection; 32/ Museo Archaeologico Nazionale, Naples; 33/Valley of the Queens, Thebes; 36/Museo Nacional de Antropologia, Mexico City; 44/Trustees of the Chester Beatty Library, Dublin; 47/India Office Library; 53/Louvre, Paris; 56/Chapel of the Planets,Tempo Malatestiano, Rimini; 57/ Museum of Antiquities,Newcastle upon Tyne, UK; 58/Museo Archeologico Nazionale, Naples; 61/Bibliotheque Nationale, Paris; 64/Private Collection; 65/Private Collection; 73/Bible Society, London; 74/Galleria dell'Accademia, Venice; 75/Czartoryski Museum, Cracow; 77/Cecil Higgins Art Gallery,Bedford,UK; 78/Palazzo Farnese, Rome; 79/Palazzo Farnese, Rome; 82/Bibliotheque Nationale, Paris; 83/Museo Regional de Oaxaca, Mexico; 85/The De Morgan Centre, London; 86/Private Collection; 88/Museo Archeologico Nazionale, Naples; 92/Louvre, Paris; 94/Valley of the Queens, Thebes; 97/British Museum, London; 98, 100/Louvre, Paris; 106/British Museum, London; 110/St Peter's, Vatican City; 113/British Library, London; 114/Walker Art Gallery, National Museums, Liverpool; 123/Egyptian National Museum, Cairo; 124/Private Collection; 125/Louvre, Paris; 127/National Museum, Aleppo, Syria; 128/British Museum, London; 131/Tretyakov Gallery, Moscow; 135/ Musee de la Chartreuse, Douai; 136/Wien Museum, Karlsplatz, Vienna; 143/Private Collection; 145/Musee Marmottan, Paris; 148/National Gallery, London; 149/Private Collection; 151/Hamburger Kunsthalle, Hamburg; 152/Kunsthaus, Zurich; 153/Museo Capitolino, Rome; 156/Yazilikaya,Turkey; 159/Musee d'Art Thomas Henry, Cherbourg; 162/Iraq Museum, Baghdad; 163/Trustees of the Chester Beatty Library, Dublin; 164/Racchi, near Cuzco, Peru; 165/Bibliotheque de l'Opera, Paris; 166/Deogarh, Uttar Pradesh,India; 168/Private Collection; 171/Hermitage, St Petersburg; 172/University Library, Istanbul; 173/Private Collection; 174/Musee Conde,Chantilly; 177/Bibliotheque Nationale, Paris; 179/Private Collection; 180/Galleria degli Uffizi, Florence; 184/Victoria & Albert Museum, London; 187/Bradford Art Galleries & Museums, West Yorkshire,UK; 190/Victoria & Albert Museum, London; 195/Musee des Beaux-Arts, Chambery, Savoie; 197/Musee Guimet, Paris; 198/Private Collection; 199/British Museum, London; 203/Surya Temple,Somnath,Bombay; 207/Prado, Madrid; 209/Simon Marsden, Belvoir Castle, Leicestershire,UK; 212/Galleria Borghese,Rome; 216/Bibliotheque des Arts Decoratifs, Paris; 220/Mycenae, Greece; 225/Egyptian National Museum, Cairo; 228/Musee des Beaux-Arts, Valenciennes; 229/Private Collection; 230/Lund, Sweden; 233/Musee de l'Hotel Sandelin, Saint-Omer; 234/Louvre, Paris; 236/Private Collection; 238/Kunsthistorisches Museum, Vienna; 240/Johnny van Haeften Gallery,London; 241/Trustees of the Royal Watercolour Society, London; 245/Musee des Beaux-Arts, Rennes; 246/Vatican Museums & Galleries, Vatican City;248/Kremlin Museum, Moscow; 251/Naturhistorisches Museum, Vienna; 253/Hermitage, St Petersburg; 254/Vatican Museums & Galleries, Vatican City; 255/Louvre, Paris; 258/Valley of the Kings, Thebes; 260/Institute of Oriental Studies, St Petersburg; 261/ Victoria & Albert Museum, London; 262/National Museum of India, New Delhi; 265/Vatican Museums & Galleries, Vatican City; 268/Louvre, Paris; 270/Prado, Madrid; 271/Musee des Beaux-Arts, Caen; 275/Southampton City Art Gallery, Hampshire, UK; 277/Private Collection; 278/Oriental Museum, Durham University, UK; 280/Trustees of the Royal Watercolour Society, London; 281/Victoria & Albert Museum, London; 285/Musee National de Phnom Penh, Cambodia; 287/Kunsthistorisches Museum, Vienna; 288/Louvre, Paris; 290/Private Collection; 296/Musee des Beaux-Arts, Rouen; 298/Private Collection; 299/Private Collection; 304/Museu Calouste Gulbenkian, Lisbon; 305/Private Collection; 306/Musee Guimet, Paris; 308/Tirgoviste Park, Wallachia, Romania; 309/Government Museum & National Art Gallery, Madras; 312/Galleria dell'Accademia, Venice; 315/Private Collection; 319/British Museum, London; 323/Archaeological Museum, Athens; **China Span:** 139; **Dorling Kindersley:** 154; **Gallo Images:** 132; **Imagno:** front cover (1L),5,17,25,43,51,55,63,89,90,110,134,160,242,266,267,272,302,317; **Lonely Planet:** 316; **Library of Congress:** 222, 292; **National Geographic Society:** 40,42,45,189,237,273,276; **Purestock:** 313; **Robert Harding World Imagery:** 324; **Roger Viollet:** 68,87; **Time and Life Pictures:** 11,12,28,37,52,71,91,94,103,105,126,181,196,213,218,219,221,239,243,257,259,300,322

Jacket Design by Lindsay Wolff
Interior Design by Red Herring Design

ISBN: 978-1-60376-035-5

Printed in China

h g f e d c b a

The Nature and Dimensions of Myth

It is through symbol that man finds his way out of his particular situation and opens himself to the general and universal.

Mircea Eliade

Myths are for the most part religious narratives that transcend the possibilities of common experience and that express any given culture's literal or metaphorical understanding of various aspects of reality. To the extent that a religion is a system that lends authority to myths, a religion is a mythological system. This is so whether we are speaking of so-called primitive animistic cults or the equally arbitrarily defined "great world religions." Religious stories are "holy scripture" to believers—narratives used to support, explain, or justify a particular system's rituals, theology, and ethics—and are myths to people of other cultures or belief systems. Inevitably, what begins as metaphor grows for some into divine word that is literal and absolute truth. Just as inevitably, many humans have insisted on confusing the logic of history and science with the quite different mytho-logic or mythology.

The parting of the Sea of Reeds and the resurrection of Jesus are myths for Hindus and Taoists. They are myths because they describe phenomena too far outside of our experience to be believed. By the same token, the Christian sees the stories of the elephant god Ganesh or the resurrection of the ancient Egyptian god-man Osiris as perhaps "religious," perhaps even beautiful, but certainly bizarre and definitely mythological rather than literally true. Seas do not part; humans are not resurrected. Religious myths, however, are very different from the merely superstitious "myths" that abound in popular usage. We commonly use the word "myth" to mean a generally held belief or concept that is clearly not true, but merely fanciful. It is a myth that crime never pays, that George Washington never told a lie, that all women are intuitive, or that walking under a ladder brings bad luck. This definition of myth as false belief or superstition develops naturally enough from the more accurate understanding of the word as describing a fabulous and obviously untrue narrative of the deeds of heroes and gods—characters such as Odin or Pallas Athena or the Native American trickster. But whereas common-usage myths of the "under the ladder" sort are for the most part products of the secular world, mythic narratives are the sacred stories that are central to cultural identity because, for the cultures to which they belong, these religious myths convey some significant truth about the relationship between human beings and the source of being.

Furthermore, for many it is reasonable to believe that just as myths are literally or symbolically true to particular cultures, they may also contain elements in which outsiders can discern some kind of truth. In this latter sense, myths can be said to be elements of a larger world mythology, the cultural vehicles for understandings that people in all corners of the world have shared. I may not believe that King Arthur pulled the sword from the rock or that Athena was born from Zeus 's head, and my Zoroastrian friend might not believe that Jesus was born of a virgin, but we can both recognize a universal significance in these stories, all of which point to the importance of crossing initiatory boundaries and of nurturing a higher state of being within ourselves. In terms of history, the myth of Thor's hammer, or that of the travels of Gilgamesh, or the Passover are, to say the least, questionable as literal truth; but when we think of these stories mytho-logically, they take on an importance, a truth, without which we would lose our very identity as cultures and as humans. Thor's hammer conveys a Scandinavian and ultimately a human sense of a terrible and wonderful power of fertility in the universe that is difficult to explain in any historical or scientific sense. The travels of Gilgamesh express the ancient Sumerian-Babylonian search for meaning, a search that metaphorically is still very much ours. The Passover story speaks to the sense that a culture (but also humanity itself) is somehow unique and that humans do best when they make proper use of that uniqueness in relation to the larger mysteries of the universe.

Whereas, then, for so-called fundamentalists of any given religion the stories of that religion are literally true and the stories of other cultures and religions mere folklore—what in common usage we in fact mean by "myth"—there are people both within given cultures and outside of them who see myths as important metaphorical constructs reflecting understandings that cannot be expressed in any other way. Surely both definitions of myths, as illusory stories and as containers of eternal truth, are valid simultaneously. The sacred products of the human imagination are in some sense true in ways that history cannot be. Myths might be considered the most basic expressions of a defining aspect of the human species—the need and ability to understand and to tell stories to reflect our understanding, whether or not we know the real facts. Humans, unlike other animals, are blessed or cursed with consciousness and specifically with the consciousness of plot—of beginnings, middles, and ends. We wonder individually, culturally, and as a species about our origins and about the significance of our present time, and we think continually of the future. We are always aware of the journey aspect of our existence. So it has always been that adults have told stories to children to describe our journey, and leaders have told their people stories for the same reason.

In this sense, myths may be thought of as universal metaphors or dreams, what mythologist William Doty calls "projective psyche models"). Doty, in defining the words "myth" and "mythology," suggests a connection between the universal ma, the sound a baby makes at its mother's breast, as well as the Indo-European root for mother, and the root sound mu, out of which emerges the Greek word mythos, literally "to make a sound with the mouth" or "word." This ma-mu connection he calls "mother-myth," which we might also call the beginning word, the first stage in the articulation of creation. Doty traces the development of the word mythos to its Homeric meaning first as style and then as the arrangement of words in story form, then to Plato as a metaphorical tale used to explain realities beyond the power of simple logic—such as the famous myth of the cave—and finally to Aristotle's use of the term as that most important of dramatic elements, "plot," the significant arrangement of events for the ritual process that was Greek tragedy. Mythology or mythologia is a combination of mythos and logos, or informing principle, and later the "Word" of the Christian creation myth of John, which begins "In the beginning was the Word." To study mythology is to study mytho-logic in general, or the defining myths of cultures in particular, or the cultural and collective inner life of the human quest for self-identity that stretches back at least to the Paleolithic cave paintings, themselves expressions of our defining drive to make

a metaphor, to "tell a story," a drive that continues to characterize the human species.

But it must be emphasized that myths require cultural clothes to take on life, to become concrete. Any set of cultural clothes is usually insufficient, however, to convey completely and ultimately such archetypal concepts as Supreme Deity, Creation, and the Hero Journey. By taking into consideration the metaphors and dreams of all cultures, we come closer to a sense of the real nature and significance of those concepts. In short, considered from a non-exclusionary perspective, other people's religious narratives can be seen both as tribe-defining cultural dreams and as significant metaphors that can speak truthfully to people across cultural and sectarian boundaries. Slavic goddess myths, for instance, will tell us a great deal about the priorities and characteristics of the Slavic people, and when we compare the Slavic goddess myth with goddess myths of various other cultures, the Slavic myth stands as a version of a universal goddess concept that expresses an aspect of the human psyche or, some would say, soul. Once again, it is useful, then, to think of myths as cultural and universal human dreams. By studying the many myth-dreams of our world culturally and at the same time collecting them comparatively, we hope to better understand human culture as a whole. The term "mythology" refers specifically both to the study of myth—that is, myth as a subject—and to the collected myths of a culture. Thus we speak of Greek mythology or Norse mythology, or, even less specifically, African mythology or Asian mythology, both of which, of course, contain many mythologies—Vedic, Shinto, Yoruba, and Bantu, for instance. And we speak of world mythology, a term that, if it is meaningful, must inevitably imply the comparison of cultural constructs in the interest of discovering a larger, collective one.

CULTURAL LISTINGS OF ENTRIES

Note: Bracketed items refer to entries under the corresponding heading in this list. Entries in italics refer to titles of works or collections of works.

African Mythology

Abuk
African mythology
Ala
Amma
Ananse
Animism
Asase Ya
Bintu
Carthage
Chibinda Ilunga
Chinawezi
Chitimukulu
Dido
Dikithi
Dogon creation
Dxui
Egyptian mythology
Elegba
Eshu
Faro
Fu
Garang
Gla
Gu
Heitsi-Eibib
Ifa
Kalala Ilunga
Kigwa
Kintu
Kyazimba
Legba
Lueji
Mantis
Mboom and Ngaan
Minia
Mwari
Mwetsi
Mwindo
Nambi
Nkongolo
Nommo
Nummo twins
Nyambe
Nyame
Nyikang
Pale Fox
Shango
Tricksters
Voodoo mythology
Wanjiru
Woot
Wulbari

Ainu Mythology

Bear myths and cults

Kotan Utunnai
Woman of Poi Soya
Woman's Epic: Repunnot-un-kur

American Myths and Legends

American myths
Brer Rabbit
Camelot
Carribean mythology
[Native North American mythology]
Mormon mythology
Tall tale
Voodoo mythology

Anatolian Mythology

Anatolian mythology
Armenian mythology
çatal Hüyük
[Greek mythology]
[Hattian-Hittite-Hurrian mythology]
[Phrygian mythology]

Anglo-Saxon Mythology

Beowulf
Grendel
Tiw
Woden

Animistic Mythology

[African mythology]
Animism
[Native North American mythology]
Sacred Earth
Spirits

Arabian Mythology

Arabian mythology
Arabian Nights, The
[Islamic mythology]
Sindbad the Sailor
Thousand and One Nights, The

Aramean Mythology

Aramean mythology
Hadad

Arthurian Myths

Annwn
Arthurian mythology
Caliburn
Camelot

Chrétien de Troyes
Excalibur
Fisher King
Galahad, Sir
Gawain, Sir
Green Knight
Guinevere
Holy Grail
Igraine
King Arthur
Lady of the Lake
Lancelot, Sir
Mabinogion
Mabon
Malory, Sir Thomas
Merlin
Mordred
Morgan Le Fay
Morgause
Otherworld
Parsifal
Percival
Peredur
Round Table
Tristan and Iseult
Welsh mythology

Asian Mythology

Asian mythology
[Central Asian mythology]
[East Asian mythology]
[Middle Eastern mythology]
[Southeast Asian mythology]

Assyrian Mythology

Adad
Ashur
Assyrian mythology
[Babylonian mythology]
[Mesopotamian mythology]

Australian Aboriginal Mythology

Argula
Australian mythology
Biljara and Wagu
Djanggawul
Djungunn
Dreaming, the
Kunapipi
Mimi
Mudungkala
Namorodo
Nganda-Ngandjala
Seven Sisters
Wagu

Wandjina
Wawilak sisters
Yurlunggur

Aztec Mythology

Aztec mythology
Centeotl and Chicomecoatl
Centzon Totochtin
Chalchiuhtlicue
Coatlicue
Ehecatl
Emergence creation
Five Suns
Huehueteotl
Huitzilopochtli
Jaguar
[Mesoamerican mythology]
Mictlan
Ometeotl
Quetzalcoatl
Tezcatlipoca
Tlaloc
Tonantzin
Xilonen
Xipe Totec
Xochipilli and Xochiquetzal

Babylonian Mythology

Akkadian mythology
Allata
Anu
Apsu
[Assyrian mythology]
Atrahasis
Ea
Enuma elish
Gilgamesh
Humbaba
Ishtar
Marduk
[Mesopotamian mythology]
Sumerian mythology
[Sumero-Akkadian mythology]
Tiamat
Utnapishtim

Balinese Mythology

Agung
Balinese mythology
Barong
Basuki
Batara Kala
Bedawang
[Indian and Hindu mythology]
Rangda Rice Mother Semara

Tintiya
Wayang theater and myths

Balkan Mythology

Balkan mythology
Illyrian mythology
Thracian mythology

Baltic Mythology

Asvinai
Baltic mythology
Dieves
Patollo
Pecullus
Perkuno
Potrimpo
Saules

Buddhist Mythology

Ananda
Arhat
Avalokiteshvara
Bodhi Tree
Bodhisattva
Buddha
Buddha Sakyamuni
Buddhacarita
Buddhas
Buddhism and Buddhist
    mythology
Ch'an
[Chinese mythology]
Dhyani buddhas and
    bodhisattvas
[East Asian mythology]
Enlightenment
Gautama Buddha
Hinayana Buddhism
[Indian and Hindu
    mythology]
Japanese Buddhism
[Japanese mythology]
Jataka tales
Kunda
Lalitavistara
Mahavamsa
Mahavastu
Mahayana Buddhism
Maitreya
Mara
Marichi
Maya
Nagas
Nirvana
Pali
Sakyamuni
Siddahrtha
[Southeast Asian mythology]
Sutras
Svastika
Tathagata
Theravada Buddhism

Three Worlds
[Tibetan mythology]
Trikaya
Triloka
Vessantra
Yama
Zen Buddhism

Canaanite Mythology

Anat
Aqhat (Ahat)
Asherah
Astarte
Athirat
Baal
Bulls
Canaanite mythology
Cow
Dagan
Danel
Danel and Aquat
El
Kirta
Mot
Philistine mythology
[Phoenician mythology]
Shapash
Ugaritic mythology
Yam
Yarikh

Celtic Mythology

Albion
[Arthurian mythis]
Belenus
Celtic mythology
Cernunnos
Decapitation
Dis Pater
Druids
Epona
[Irish mythology]
Lugus
Maponos
Matrona
Nehalenia
Taranis
[Welsh mythology]

Central Asian Mythology

Altaic mythology
Buryat mythology
Central Asian mythology
Erlik
Jahangir
Khori Tumed
Mangi
North Caucasus mythology
Secret History of the Mongols
Siberian mythology
Tengri
Tu'chueh

Turko-Mongol mythology
Ulgen
Umai
Xargi
Xeglun
Zong Belegt Baatar

Chinese Mythology

Ancestor Cults
Cao Guojiu
Ch'an
Ch'ang O
Chinese emperor myths
Chinese mythology
Chiyou
Chu tzu
Chuangzi
Confucius
Dao
Daode Jing
Daoism
Daoist mythology
Di Jun
Dragon King
Dragons
Eight Immortals
Emperor God myths
Emperor Yu the Great
Excellent Archer
Fuxi
Gonggong
Gourd Children
Guandi
Guanyin
Gun
Han Xiang
Han Zhongi
He Xiangu
Heavenly Weaver Girl
Hou Ji
Hsi-tsu
Hsuan-tsang
Huangdi
I Ching
Jade Emperor
Journey to the West
Kong Fuzi
Lan Caihe
Laozi
Li Xuan
Lu Dongbin
Monkey
Monkey King
Mo-ti
Nuwa
Pangu
Radish
Shang-ti
Shih-Ching
Shun
Sun Wu-k'ung
T'ai-i

Tai-hao
Tao
Ti
Tian
Tiandi
Tripitaka
Xihe
Xuanzang
Yao
Yi
Yin-yang
Yu
Zhang Guo
Zhurong

Christian Mythology

Adam and Eve
Angels
Annunciation
Antichrist
Apocalypse
Apocryphal Gospels
Armageddon
Arthurian mythology
[Arthurian myths]
Ascension
Assumption
Bible
Black Madonna
Christ
Christian mythology
Christmas
Crucifixion
Day of Judgment
Devil
Easter
[Gnostic mythology]
God
Halloween
Heaven
[Hebrew and Judaic
    mythology]
Hell
Holy Grail
Holy Spirit
Immaculate Conception
Jehovah
John the Baptist
Jonah and the Whale
Joseph of Nazareth
Last Judgment
Last Supper
Logos
Mary
Massacre of the innocents
Messiah
Milton and myth
Mormon mythology
New Testament
Old Testament
Paradise
Paul

Pentacost
Purgatory
Resurrection
Revelation of St. John the
    Divine
Stan
Second Coming
Sophia
Soul
Tree
Trinity
Virgin birth
Virgin Mary
Virgin of Guadalupe
Water of Life

East Asian Mythology

[Ainu mythology]
[Chinese mythology]
[Japanese mythology]
[Korean mythology]

Egyptian Mythology

Akhenaton
Amun (Amon)
Amun Re (Ra)
Anubis
Apis
Apopis
Aton
Atum
Atum-Re
Bastet
Bes
Book of Going Forth by Day
Book of the Dead
Coffin texts
Egyptian flood
Egyptian Goddesses
Egyptian mythology
Ennead
Eye
Geb and Nut
Gnostic mythology
Hathor
Horus
Isis
Kek and Keket
Khepry
Khnum
Khonsu
Maat
Mut
Naunet
Neith
Nekhbet
Nephtys
Nun
Nut
Ogdoad
Osiris and Isis
Ptah

Pyramid Texts
Ra
Re
Re-Atum
Sekhmet
Serapis
Seth
Shu and Tefnut
Sobek
Sphinx
Tefnut
Thoth

European Mythology

[Arthurian myths]
[Balkan mythology]
[Baltic mythology]
Basque mythology
[Celtic mythology]
[Christian mythology]
Cid, the
Etruscan mythology
European mythology
Faust
Finno-Urgic mythology
[Germanic mythology]
[Greek mythology]
Green Man
Iberian mythology
Indo-European mythology
Medieval mythology
Roland
[Roman mythology]
[Slavic mythology]
Tartessian, Turdetan, and
    Iberian mythology
Tristan and Iseult

Finno-Ugric Mythology

Finnish mythology
Finno-Ugric mythology
Hungarian mythology
Ilmarinen
Kalevala
Lapp mythology
Lemminkainen
Louhi
Vainamoinen

German Mythology

Brunhild
Donar
Dwarfs
Faust
Friia
German mythology
[Germanic mythology]
Nibelungenlied
Siegfried
Tiwaz
Wodan
Water of Life

Germanic Mythology

[Anglo-Saxon mythology]
[German mythology]
Germanic mythology
Nehalennia
Nerthus
[Norse mythology]

Gnostic Mythology

Gnostic mythology
Ophis
Sophia
Thoth

Greek Mythology

Achaians
Acheron
Achilles
Acteon
Admetus
Adonis
Adrasteia
Adrastus
Aeetes
Aegean mythology
Aegeus
Aegisthos
Aeolus
Aeschylus
Aesop
Agamemnon
Ajax
Alcestis
Alexander the Great
Alkmene
Amalthea
Amazons
Ambrosia
Amphion
Amphitrite
Amphitryon
Andromache
Andromeda
Antaeus
Antigone
Antiope
Aphrodite
Apollo
Apollodorus
Apollonius of Rhodes
Apples of the Hesperides
Arachne
Arcadian Stag
Ares
Argonautica
Argonauts
Argos
Ariadne
Aristotle
Artemis
Asklepios
Astyanax

Atalanta
Atlantis
Atlas
Atreus
Augean stables
Bacchae
Baucis and Philemon
Bellerophon
Cadmus
Callisto
Calypso
Cassandra
Castor and Polydeuces
Cattle of Geryones
Centaurs
Cephalus and Procris
Cerebus
Cerynean Hind
Chaos
Charioteers
Charon
Charybdis
Chimera
Chiron
Circe
Clytemnestra
Cornucopia
Creon
Cretan mythology
Cycladic mythology
Cyclops
Daedalus and Icarus
Danae
Danaides
Danaus
Daphne
Deianeira
Delphi
Demeter and Persephone
Descent of Herakles
Deucalion and Pyrrha
Diomedes
Dionysos
Dioskouri
Echidne
Echo
Elektra
Eleusinian mysteries
Elysian Fields
Elysium
Endymion
Eos
Epimetheus
Erebos
Ericthonius
Erinyes
Eros
Eros and Psyche
Erymanthian Boar
Eteocles
Eumenides
Euripides

Mountain mythology
Noah and the flood
Old Testament
Passover
Salome
Samson and Delilah
Sarah
Satan
[Semitic mythology]
Shem
Song of Songs
Torah
Tower of Babel
Yahweh

Incan Mythology

Cochamama
Cuichu
Ilyap'a
Incan mythology
Inti
Mamacocha
Mamakilya
Mamapacha
Manco Capac
Pacariqtambo
Pachacamac
Pachamama
Viracocha

Indian and Hindu Mythology

Aditi and the Adityas
Advaita Vedanta
Agastya
Agni
Ahalya
Ananta
Annanmar
Antaragattamma
Aranyakas
Arjuna
Aryaman
Aryans
Ashvins
Asuras
Athara Veda
Atman
Aurobindo Ghose
Avatar
Avatars of Vishnu
Balarama
Balinese mythology
Banaras
Bhaga
Bhagavadgita
Bhakti
Bhima
Birhor mythology
Boar
Brahma
Brahman

Brahmanas
Brahmanism
Brahmans
Brhaspati
[Buddhist mythology]
Candaini epic
Catakantaravanan
Charioteers
Churning of the Ocean of Milk
Daksha
Dance of Shiva
Dasharatha
Descent of the Ganges
Devaki
Devas
Devayana
Devi
Devnarayan
Dharma
Dhola epic
Diti and the Daityas
Draupadi
Dravidians
Durga
Durvasas
Dwarf
Dyaus
Fish and the Flood
Four ages of man
Ganesh
Ganges
Garuda
Gitagovinda
Go
Gond mythology
Gopis
Govinda
Hanuman
Hara
Hare Krishna
Hari
Hari-Hara
Harivamsha
Hindu mythology
Indian flood
Indo-Iranian mythology
Indra
Indus Valley mythology
Jain mythology
Jalamdhara
Jayadeva
Jiva
Kalakacaryakatha
Kali
Kaliya
Kalkin
Kama
Kamadhenu
Kamamma Katha
Kamsa
Kanyaka Amavari Katha

Karman
Karna
Karttikeya
Katamaraju Katha
Kauravas
Krishna
Kunda
Kunti
Kurma
Lakshama
Lakshmi
Laws of Manu
Lila
Linga
Lingal
Loka
Mahabharata
Mahadevi
Mahashakti
Mahisha
Manasa Devi
Mandalas
Manimekhalai
Mankanaka
Manu
ManuSmirti
Mara
Markandeya
Matsya
Maya
Meru
Minashki
Mitra
Moksha
Murugan
Nagas
Nanda
Narada
Narasimha
Narayana
Nataraja
Om
Pabuji epic
Pancaratra
Pancatantra
Pandavas
Panis
Parade of Ants
Parashurama
Parsis
Parvati
Prajapati
Prakriti
Prahlada
Pritha
Prthivi
Puranas
Purusa
Radha
Rama
Ramayana
Ravana

Rig Veda
Rishi
Rudra
Rukmini
Sacred Circle
Sadhana
Sama Veda
Samsara
Sanskrit
Sarasvati
Sati
Savitri
Shaivas
Shakat Katha
Shakka
Shaktas
Shakti
Shesha
Seven sages
Shalakapurusha
Shiva
Shri
Shruti and Smirti
Sikh mythology
Sisupala
Sita
Skanda
Smirti
Soma
Sugriva
Surabhi
Surya
Svastika
Tamil mythology
Tantric mythology
Three Worlds
Triloka
Trimurti
Trisiras
Tvashtir
Uma
Upanishads
Ushas
Vairocana
Vaishnavism
Vaishravana
Valmiki
Vamana
Varaha
Varuna
Vasudeva
Vasuki
Vayu
Vedas
Vedanta
Vedic mythology
Vedism
Virtra
Vishnu
Vishnu Purana
Vishvakarman
Vyasa

Yama-no-kami
Yamato-takeru
Yomi-no-kuni
Yorimitsu
Zen Buddhism

Korean Mythology
Cumong
Korean mythology
Samguk Sagi and *Samguk Yusa*

Mayan Mythology
Ah Mun
Ahau Kin
Bacab
Chac
Hunaphu and Xbalanque
Itzamma
Ix Chei
Jaguar
Kukulkan
Mayan mythology
[Mesoamerican mythology]
Pauahtun
Popol Vuh
Xbalanque and Hunahpu
Xibalba

Melanesian Mythology
Honoyeta
Karaperamun
Malaveyovo
Melanesian mythology
[Oceanic mythology]
Qat
Sida
Tiv'r

Mesoamerican Mythology
[Aztec mythology]
Caribbean mythology
Emergence creation
Jaguar
[Mayan mythology]
Mesoamerican mythology
Olmec mythology
Quetzalcoatl
Teotihuacan mythology
Tezcatlipoca
Tlaloc
Toltec mythology
Xipe Totec
Zapotec mythology

Mesopotamian Mythology
Amorites
[Assyrian mythology]
[Babylonian mythology]
[Hattian-Hittite-Hurrian mythology]

Mesopotamian mythology
[Sumero-Akkadian mythology]
Ziggurats

Micronesian Mythology
Areop-Enap
Iolofath
Micronesian mythology
Nareau
[Oceanic mythology]

Middle Eastern Mythology
[Anatolian mythology]
[Arabian mythology]
Aramean mythology
[Canaanite mythology]
Çatal Hüyük
[Christian mythology]
[Egyptian mythology]
[Hattite-Hittite-Hurrian mythology]
[Hebrew and Judaic mythology]
[Indo-Iranian mythology]
[Iranian mythology]
[Islamic mythology]
Judaism and its Abrahamic relatives
[Mesopotamian mythology]
Middle Eastern mythology
Philistine mythology
[Prehistoric mythology]
[Semitic mythology]

Minoan Mythology
Ariadne
Cretan Bull
Cretan Goddess
Cretan mythology
Daedalus and Icarus
Dionysos
[Greek mythology]
Labyrinth
Linear A and B
Minos
Minotaur
Pasiphae
Phaedre
Rhadamanthus
Sarpedon
Theseus

Myth Theory, Mythologists, and Mythic Motifs and Types
Abandonment
Abduction
Afterlife
Androgynes
Animal myths

Animism
Apocalypse
Apotheosis
Archetypes
Aristotle
Art and creation
Astrology and myth
Astronomy and myth
Axis Mundi
Bards
Biogenetic structuralism
Bullroarer
Bulls Call, the
Campbell, Joseph
Cassirer
Charioteers
Cities
Cosmic egg
Cosmogonic and cosmological myths
Creation
Culture heroes
Dark Night of the Soul
Death
Decapitation
Deity concept
Deluge
Demons
Descent to the underworld
Deus faber creation
Devils
Diffusion and parallelism
Disappearing god
Dismemberment
Divine child
Doty, William
Douglas, Mary
Dragons
Dreams and myth
Dualism
Dumézil, Georges
Durkheim, Emile
Dwarfs
Dying god
Earth
Earth Goddess
Earth-diver creation
Eliade, Mircea
Emergence creation
Eschatology
Eternal return
Etiological myth
Etymology of "myth"
Ex nihilo creation
Fairy tale and myth
Father god
Femme fatale
Fertility myths
Fire
First man and woman
First parents
Flood

Frazer, Sir James
Freud, Sigmund
Frye, Northrop
Gaia hypothesis
Gardens, groves, caves, and hidden shelters
Gate guardians
Genital myths and symbols
Giants and giant killers
Gimbutas, Marija
God Goddess Gods and goddesses
Golden Bough, The
Graves, Robert
Great Goddess
Great Mother
Harrison, Jane
Heaven
Hell
Hero quest
Heroes
Heroic monomyth
Heroines
High god
Hillman, James
Human body and cosmology
Indo-European mythology
Initiation
Ithyphallic gods
Jung, C. G.
Language and myth
Last Judgment
Levi-Strauss, Claude
Liminality
Lincoln, Bruce
Literary analysis and myth
Mandalas
Massacre of the innocents
Miraculous conception
Modernism and mythology
Monism
Monomyth
Monotheism
Monster slayer
Monsters
Moon goddesses
Moon myths
Mother Earth
Mother Goddess
Mountain mythology
Myth and Ritual School
Mythic origins of drama
Mythical beasts
New Mythology
Night Journey
Ontological myths
Origin myths
Paradise myths
Phallic myths
Philosophical myths
Plato
Polytheism

AARON Aaron was the older brother and sometimes spokesman for the Hebrew hero Moses in the Hebrew Bible (*Torah*). Although head of the ancient priesthood established by God (Yahweh) in the Book of Exodus, he makes the mistake of creating a golden calf for the restless Israelites to worship while Moses is receiving divine instruction on Mount Sinai about the Ark of the Covenant and other matters of what would become Jewish law.

ABANDONMENT An important stage of the universal hero myth or monomyth is that of the abandonment of the infant hero to the elements. Sargon, Moses, Oedipus, Siegfried, Karna, and Hau Ki are only a few of the many examples of this theme. Besides adding to the drama of the stories, the theme of the separation of the hero from his or her biological parents and the abandonment in a river or a wilderness suggests the idea that the hero belongs to the larger community or the world rather than to a single family.

ABDUCTION The abduction motif in myth usually involves the malicious capture of a girl or young woman by an evil force or lustful deity or hero. In Greek mythology Persephone is abducted and raped by the underworld god Hades; Helen of Troy is abducted by Paris, leading to the Trojan War; and Zeus in the form of a bull abducts Europa. Sita, the wife of the Vishnu avatar Rama, is abducted by the demon Ravana in the Indian epic the *Ramayana*. The hero Lemminkainen abducts Kylliki in the Finnish epic the *Kalevala*. A clue to a partial meaning of this motif might be found in the fact that mock abductions are common in various marriage traditions. Marriage can perhaps be seen as an abduction from the mother by the patriarchal powers that see their relationship with women in terms of ownership. The abduction of women in any context suggests the idea of the female as a valuable commodity in a male-dominated world. It might be argued, too, that abduction represents an innate resentment of innocence and a desire to own what clearly belongs to another.

ABRAHAM Abraham or Avraham (at first Abram, or Ibrahim in Arabic) is a central figure in Hebrew mythology as developed in the biblical Book of Genesis. Abraham was the

Zeus assumes the form of the bull in order to abduct Europa

mythical hero and "father" of all three of the monotheistic "Abrahamic" religions—Judaism, Christianity, and Islam. Genesis 11–50 is a combination of several versions of the story of Abraham and his immediate descendants, told by the so-called Yahwist contributor to the Bible (*Torah*), who was writing in Judah in about 950 B.C.E. under the early monarchy; the so-called Elohist author, writing in about 850 B.C.E.; and the writers of the priestly tradition of c. 550–400 B.C.E. The story takes us up to the myth of Moses and the Exodus.

A man called Tehar, who had several sons, including Abram, was said to have decided to move from Ur, the ancient city in Mesopotamia, to Canaan. Tehar was accompanied by his grandson Lot and by Abram and Abram's wife, Sara'i (the name of an Arabian great goddess), who was childless and barren. The group traveled northeast and stopped in Haran, where Tehar, now 205 years old, died. It was in Haran that Abram's god, Yahweh, came to the 75-year-old Abram and urged him to move on to Canaan, where "I shall make you into a great nation" (12:2). So Abram journeyed down to Shechem, where there was a sacred tree (probably sacred to the Canaanite goddess Asherah), at which point Abram built an altar to Yahweh. He did the same thing in Bethel, as he moved south, following a tradition of building altars to his tribal god on sites sacred to others.

Famine caused the group to move to Egypt, but after some time they returned to Canaan with a great deal of wealth and livestock. As the land could not support the people of both Abram and Lot, Lot moved to the Jordan plain near Sodom. Yahweh again spoke to Abram, giving him the land of Canaan, and Abram moved around in the land and eventually erected an altar to Yahweh in Hebron. After Abram had assisted an alliance of tribes in a successful war and accepted no booty, Yahweh once again appeared to him and promised that after 400 years of oppression his descendants would possess all of the land of Canaan from the Nile to the Euphrates.

As Sara'i was childless and knew that Abram required a son, she gave him her Egyptian slave girl Hagar as a concubine, and soon a son, Ishmael (Ismail), was born. When Sara'i, now jealous, mistreated Hagar, Yahweh promised the slave that her son would be "like the wild ass . . . at odds with all his kin" (16:12).

According to the priestly authors of Genesis, Yahweh came to Abram when the patriarch was 99 years old and announced that Abram was now to be called Abraham, the "father of many nations." Yahweh would be his and his descendants' god. This was a solemn covenant between Yahweh and his people, whose sign of having accepted the covenant would be circumcision, a sign of community and of exclusivity, as the uncircumcised would be "cut off from the kin of his father" (17:14). Both Abraham and Ishmael immediately had themselves circumcised.

Yahweh told Abraham that Sara'i was now to be called Sarah ("princess") and that in spite of her old age she would give birth to a child, Isaac. As for Ishmael, he too would be fruitful and would father a great nation. Three men—presumably angels—appeared to Abraham and confirmed that Sarah would soon give birth to a son.

For a while Abraham lived in Gerar, among the Philistines, and there Sarah gave birth to Isaac. Sarah demanded that Abraham expel Hagar and Ishmael from his entourage. This he did, since Yahweh informed him that although Ishmael would be the father of a great nation, Isaac would be his true heir.

When Isaac was still a boy, Yahweh tested Abraham's loyalty by demanding that he sacrifice his son to him. Abraham agreed, but at the last minute Yahweh provided a sheep as a substitute for the child.

Sarah died in Hebron at the age of 127. Abraham died there at the age of 175. He was buried by Isaac and Ishmael in a cave in Hebron bought previously from its Hittite owners.

In the Jewish *aggadah* and *midrash* (literature that elaborates on canonical sources) and elsewhere, myths and legends about Abraham's life suggest his connection to the heroic monomyth, the universal hero-type. As in the story of Jesus, legends hold that Abraham was born in a hidden place—in this case a cave—where he was watched over by angels. The child was abandoned by his fearful mother, but the angel Gabriel brought him milk from God. As in the Christian story, Abraham's birth had been prophesied to a jealous king, who feared the boy's power, and a massacre of boy children was ordered. Like many heroes, such as the Buddha, the legendary Abraham was able to walk about and speak almost immediately after his birth.

Abraham's son Isaac, through whom Yahweh renewed the covenant with the Hebrews, would marry Rebekah, and she would give birth to Jacob and Esau. The promise of the land of Canaan for the Hebrews was again made to Jacob, he having been renamed Israel by God. Jacob's most famous son, by his wife Rachel, was Joseph of the many-colored coat. Isaac, Jacob, and Joseph all possessed heroic qualities and were much favored by their god.

The whole Abrahamic myth serves as a bridge between ancient times and the actual presence of the Hebrews in Canaan and as a mythological justification for the particular role of Israel and the Jews in history. It serves particularly as a justification for the belief in monotheism and for claims of exclusivity and land rights that by extension and mythical adjustment have been taken up at various times by Christians and Muslims as well. These myth-fed claims on the part of the Abrahamic religions are very much alive in the turmoil that characterizes the Middle East today.

ABUK The Dinka people of Sudan in Africa have a story of the first parents that is reminiscent of the story of Adam and Eve. Abuk, the first woman, broke the High God's command that she and her mate, Garang, plant one seed of grain a day to meet their needs. Selfishly, Abuk decided to plant more, and as she did so she disturbed and infuriated God, who moved away from earth and cut the rope that tied earth to his home in Heaven. Since that time humans have been plagued by work, sickness, and death. And women have all too often been regarded as both dangerous and inferior to men.

ACHAIANS The Achaians were Greek peoples who were believed to have been descended from the son of Hellen, who gave his name to the Hellenes. Homer uses the term "Achaians" as, like "Hellenes," a synonym for the Greeks, who fought against the Trojans in the *Iliad*. He uses the terms "Argives" (*see* Argos) and "Danaans" (*see* Danaides) in the same way.

ACHERON In the Greek mythology of the Homeric period, the boundary between this world and the underworld was the river named Acheron, the "River of Sadness." It was crossed after death with the help of the boatman Charon.

ACHILLES Achilles is the primary hero of Homer's epic the *Iliad*. His father was King Peleus of the Myrmidones in Thessaly. His mother was Thetis, a sea divinity who had been raised by Hera, the wife of Zeus. Achilles was tutored in his youth by Phoenix and by the great centaur Chiron. Thetis attempted to make her son immortal by dipping him in the river Styx, but as she held the child by his right heel, that part of his body remained vulnerable. Thetis understood that her son would either live a long but uneventful life or die young as a glorious hero. The boy had already revealed his heroic qualities by killing his first boar at the age of six, several years before Odysseus and other envoys of Agamemnon came to recruit him for the Trojan War. In a desperate attempt to save Achilles from what she knew would be an early death, Thetis disguised her boy, still a beardless teenager, as a girl and hid him in the women's quarter of the Lycomedes of Scyros. Living among the girls of the palace, however, Achilles impregnated one and eventually was discovered by the sly Odysseus. In any case, he more than willingly left the confines of the palace for the heroic opportunities presented by a great war.

Quickly Achilles, fiery by nature, distinguished himself as a warrior and became a crucial element of the Greek forces before the walls of Troy. His importance became evident when Agamemnon made the mistake of wrongly taking possession of the younger man's mistress, Briseis—a woman won in a peripheral battle in the Trojan territories. Insulted and humiliated, Achilles withdrew to his tent and refused to continue fighting. Without their greatest warrior the Greeks faltered and were forced to beg the sulking hero to return

to battle. Achilles refused but allowed his dearest friend, Patraklos, to lead the Myrmidones into battle. When Patraklos was killed, Achilles returned, driven by a combination of rage and deep sorrow, and newly armed by the smith god Hephaistos. He put the Trojans to rout and killed their great hero Hector, desecrating his body by dragging it three times around the walls of Troy. Later Achilles was himself killed by an arrow shot by Paris (assisted by Apollo), which pierced his vulnerable right heel.

ACTAEON Actaeon, a grandson of King Cadmus of Thebes in Greece, was out hunting when he happened to come upon the virgin goddess Artemis bathing in a stream. The goddess was furious at having been seen naked, and she turned poor Actaeon into a stag, which was then hunted and torn apart by Actaeon's own dogs.

ADAD Adad was perhaps the same as or a counterpart of Hadad, a Semitic weather or storm god. Adad was particularly important in Assyria.

ADAM AND EVE A central story in Hebrew mythology contained in the first chapter of the biblical book of Genesis, sacred to Jews and Christians and to some extent Muslims, tells how the creator made humans, male and female, in his image (1:27). Genesis 5:1 tells us that after God (Elohim) created "them" he named "them" "man" (*adam*). The second chapter, probably an earlier version and written by a different author, tells us that God (Yahweh) created a *man* (adam) out of dust (earth), breathed life into

Achilles fights Hector in front of the walls of Troy

Adam and Eve in the Garden of Eden

myth that exists in the collective Christian psyche. For Jews and Muslims the "fall" of Adam and Eve is less catastrophic than in Christianity, where the doctrine of the "original sin" in Eden infecting the whole world until the coming of Christ (the "New Adam") is emphasized. In fact, in Islam, Adam repents, travels about the earth, and goes, accompanied by Hawwa (Eve), on a *hajj* (pilgrimage) to Mecca, where he is said to have built the first Ka'bah and to have become, in effect, not only the father of humanity but the first prophet.

The first children of Adam and Eve were the famous brothers Cain and Abel. Genesis 5 says that Adam, who lived to be 930 years old, begot a son named Seth when he was 130.

ADITI AND THE ADITYAS In Indian Vedic mythology, Aditi is "infinity," the source of all forms of consciousness, even of the divine characteristics of the gods themselves. Aditi is also unity, whereas her sister Diti or Danu is the force that separates things. Aditi is the source of the divine within mankind. Diti reflects the flawed aspect of humanity. Vedic mythology celebrates Aditi as Earth, the goddess who is the source of all living things. She is the mother by the sage Kasyapa of the dityas, the "sons of Aditi," who are gods of the sun (one name for which is Aditya) and are the formative principles of the universe. Among the personified dityas are Surya, Mitra, Varuna, Aryaman, and, perhaps most important, the great Vedic King of the gods, Indra. In Buddhism, ditya is a name sometimes applied to the Buddha.

ADMETUS Apollo was forced by Zeus to serve this king of Pherae in Thessaly as a punishment for his having killed the Cyclops. Later Admetus, with Apollo's help, succeeded in marrying Alcestis.

ADONIS The best known of the Canaanite dying gods was the young spring god Adonai ("my lord"), who was particularly favored by the Phoenicians and also became popular in Greece and Rome as a human with whom Aphrodite/Venus fell in love. In his Greco-Roman form he was a symbol more of youthful sexuality than of spring. The Roman poet Ovid tells the story in his *Metamorphoses* (10) of how the Greek Kinyras, son of Pygmalion and Galatea, was the object of his daughter Myrrha's erotic love. To prevent the girl from committing suicide, her nurse arranged for her to sleep with her father without, in the darkness, revealing her identity. When, after some time, the ruse was exposed to Kinyras, he attempted to destroy his daughter, now pregnant with his child, but Myrrha was changed into a myrrh tree. Adonis was born from that tree. As he grew up, he became an exceedingly handsome young man known for his hunting abilities, and Aphrodite/Venus fell in love with him. Ovid tells us that Venus warned her beloved to beware of certain wild animals. But soon the boy was gored in the groin by a wild boar and left to die. Hearing his groans, Venus flew to him and in her grief performed a ritual that resulted in the boy's blood giving birth to the flower we call the anemone. This myth is clearly an accompaniment to fertility rites associated with Adonis and Venus, who in Phoenicia would have been Astarte. Related myths and rituals are those of Attis and Cybele in Phrygia and Inanna/Ishtar and Dumuzi/Tammuz in Mesopotamia. These are stories of death and resurrection that were particularly popular in the Middle East, where the resurrection myths of Osiris and Jesus also have their origins.

him, and placed him in the Garden of Eden (2:7). After the man had named the creatures of God's creation, God decided to make a suitable partner for him. He put the man to sleep and removed one of his ribs, out of which he made the first woman, that name having been given to her by the man because "from man she was taken" (2:20–23). Adam's name comes from the Hebrew meaning "man" and perhaps from the Hebrew *adamah*, meaning "earth." Adam named his partner Eve (Havvah), the "Mother of All Living Beings." The name suggests a connection to the old Middle Eastern mother goddesses, who, like mother goddesses in much of the world, were often associated with trees and snakes. As is evident from the Genesis story, Eve had a close speaking relationship with the serpent (3:1–6). All was well in the Garden of Eden, until Eve, tempted in a conversation with the serpent (traditionally Satan, Arabic Shaytan, in the *form* of a serpent), ate fruit from a tree forbidden to the couple by God and convinced Adam to eat as well. This was the Tree of Knowledge of Good and Evil. The couple now knew about good and evil, and they became guilty about their sexual desires and covered their genitals with leaves. God punished Adam and Eve for disobeying him by exiling them from Paradise and by introducing work, pain, and death into their lives. Women forever after were condemned to be subservient to men. Because of her "weakness" in relation to the serpent, Eve has been used in varying degrees over the centuries by the Abrahamic religions—perhaps especially by Christianity—as the model of female inferiority and as a justification for the dominance of men. This is clearly a simplistic understanding of Genesis in the intellectual sense, but it is essentially the version of the

ADRASTEIA In the Orphic tradition in Greece, Adrasteia ("Necessity") was present with Kronos ("Time") at the beginning of existence.

ADRASTUS Adrastus, King of Argos, was the only hero of seven who survived the disastrous attempt, led by him, to place his son-in-law and Oedipus's son Polynices on the throne of Thebes. Much of this Greek myth is told in the play *Seven Against Thebes* by Aeschylus.

ADVAITA VEDANTA One of several interpretations of Vedanta Hinduism, Advaita Vedanta was developed probably in the eighth and ninth centuries C.E. by the philosopher Sankara. For followers of this branch of the religion, the closest concept to a supreme deity is Brahman, the absolute undifferentiated principle underlying all apparent reality. Even the differentiation between the individual, or self, and Brahman is ultimately illusory. The proper path for humans is to discover the oneness of the self (Atman)—what some in other cultures might call the "god within"—and Brahman. With this realization the individual achieves *Moksha*, or release from *samsara*, the illusory state of worldly entanglements.

AEETES This king of Colchis on the Black Sea was the guardian of the Golden Fleece sought by the Greek hero Jason and the Argonauts.

AEGEUS The man recognized by the Greek hero Theseus as his father—some say Theseus's father was the god Poseidon—Aegeus was king of Athens. Theseus went to Crete to put an end to the human tribute the Athenians had been forced to pay to Minos there, but he forgot his promise to his father to hoist white sails to signify his safety upon returning home. When Aegeus saw the black sails on his son's returning ship, he assumed that the boy was dead and threw himself in despair from the cliff at Sounium into the sea which from then on took his name, the Aegean. Earlier, Aegeus had married the sorceress Medea, former wife of Jason. But when Medea tried to trick Aegeus into poisoning the young Theseus, the king banished her from his kingdom.

AEGISTHOS According to the Greek dramatist Aeschylus in his *Oresteia*, when King Agamemnon of Argos went off to the Trojan War, his cousin Aegisthos had a love affair with his queen, Clytemnestra, and the lovers conspired in the murder of the king when he returned to Argos. Later Aegisthos, having usurped Agamemnon's throne, was killed along with Clytemnestra by Agamemnon and Clytemnestra's son Orestes. Aegisthos was the result of an incestuous relationship between his father and his father's daughter. The nephew and stepson of King Atreus of Argos-Mycenae, he is one of many members of the House of Atreus to experience the curse originally laid upon his brother, Atreus.

AENEAS According to the tradition utilized by the Roman poet Virgil in his epic, the *Aeneid*, Aeneas was a Trojan hero (see *Iliad*). The son of Venus by Anchises, he led various followers out of the ruins of Troy on a long journey that would culminate in the founding of the "new Troy," or Rome.

AENEID The Roman emperor Augustus commissioned the poet Virgil to write an epic that would serve the purposes of Rome just as he might have considered the *Iliad* and the *Odyssey* of Homer to have served those of Greece. The *Aeneid*, composed between 29 and 19 B.C.E., is considered a literary rather than a primary epic because it was the result of the emperor's commission and because the poet clearly had the Greek epics in mind as models. Virgil did, however, make extensive use of myths and legends that had emerged over the centuries in Roman religion and folklore. The first half of the epic calls to mind the post-Trojan War wanderings of Odysseus in the *Odyssey*, although the epic's hero, Aeneas, demonstrates Roman characteristics of stoicism and respect for rules that differentiate him from the wily Greek hero, whose personality reflects a less orderly pre-classical age. The battles of the second half of the *Aeneid* are reminiscent of the Trojan War, but in this case the epic hero is a Roman who is less concerned with his personal reputation than in succeeding through a "just" war in laying the foundations of the new Troy, Rome.

The *Aeneid* is made up of twelve sections or books. Book One describes the flight of Aeneas and his family from Troy after the city's fall to the Greeks. Commanded by the ghost of his dead wife to head west, Aeneas and his party are shipwrecked at Carthage, where they are treated hospitably by Queen Dido. Book Two finds Aeneas telling his story, as

Venus embraces her beloved Adonis

A

Aesop's fables are still used to illustrate morals to children

Lavinia, and founds Lavinium. Later, according to Roman tradition, Aeneas's son Ascanius or Iulius, the ancestor of Julius Caesar, would build Alba Longa near what would become Rome.

AEOLUS In the *Odyssey* Homer depicted Aeolus as the hospitable keeper of the winds who lived on the floating island of Aeolia. Aeolus gave Odysseus a bag containing the winds and told him how to make use of the winds to get home. Unfortunately, while their leader was sleeping, Odysseus's men, thinking the bag contained gold, opened it, releasing a chaos of winds that blew the ship back to Aeolia. Angered, Aeolus refused to be of further help.

AESCHYLUS This great Greek tragic dramatist was born in Eleusis in 525 B.C.E. As was almost always the case with the Greek tragedians—his Persians being the only extant exception—Aeschylus took his subjects from mythology. Of the ninety plays he is said to have written, only seven are extant. These include *The Persians, Seven Against Thebes, The Suppliants, Prometheus*, and the three plays—*Agamemnon, Choephori* ("The Libation-Bearers"), and *Eumenides* ("Kindly-Ones" or "Furies")—that form the trilogy known as the *Oresteia*, one of the masterpieces of world literature. The *Oresteia* spawned many later dramatic representations, particularly of the deeds of Elektra, the daughter of Agamemnon and Clytemnestra, and the sister of Orestes, whose name is the basis for the trilogy's title. Aeschylus contributed significantly to the technical development of Greek drama and the movement away from pure ritual to theater as we know it. He did so especially by introducing the concept of two actors in dialogue and by somewhat limiting the role of the chorus.

A myth adds drama to Aeschylus's death at Gela in 456 B.C.E. Tradition has it that an eagle thought the old man's bald head was a stone and dropped a turtle on it in order to break the shell. Instead it was Aeschylus's head that was broken, fulfilling an oracle predicting that the poet would be struck dead by a force from the heavens.

AESIR In Norse mythology, the Germanic mythology native to Scandinavia and the Vikings, the Aesir were warrior deities of the sky who lived in Asgard. They were opposed in the overall pantheon by perhaps older deities, the Vanir, who were associated with the earth and fertility. The major Aesir were Odin, the Aesir king; his consort Frigg; Freya, the goddess of love; Thor, the powerful thunder god; Tyr, the god of war; Heimdall, who guarded the bridge that led to Asgard; and Balder, the much beloved dying god.

AESOP Aesop was the legendary sixth-century B.C.E. composer of Greek fables, some actually dating from as early as the seventh century B.C.E. A figure whose life comes down to us only in popular myth, Aesop is said to have been a dark-skinned hunchback, a slave of Phrygian origin who could not speak until the Egyptian goddess Isis gave him the art of speech and storytelling. Condemned unjustly by the people of Delphi for supposed sacrilege, Aesop administered an eventually effective curse on the Delphians as he was thrown over a cliff to his death.

AFRICAN MYTHOLOGY As in the case of Asian or European mythology, to speak of African mythology is to speak of many mythologies, reflecting the understandings and

Odysseus had told his to the Phaiakians in the *Odyssey*. He describes how the Greeks entered the city in the famous Wooden Horse and how he lost his wife. Book Three is the story of the trip from Troy to Carthage and the death of Aeneas's father, Anchises, in Sicily. Dido and Aeneas fall in love in Book Four, and it takes a warning from the gods to make the hero continue on toward the "new Troy." Full of resentment and despair, Dido commits suicide when her lover leaves. As if pointing back to Achilles' funeral games for Patroklos in the *Iliad*, Aeneas holds funeral games for his father in Sicily in Book Five, and in Book Six he visits his father in the underworld. There Anchises reveals in some detail the future Rome to its founder. Book Seven tells how Latinus, a king in Italy, offered the hero his daughter Lavinia as a wife. The offer leads to war, as the young woman's fiancè Tumus, understandably, objects to the marriage. Aeneas prepares for war in Book Eight and visits Latium. Two of Aeneas's friends spy on the enemy in Book Nine and are captured and killed. The war itself is described in Books Ten and Eleven. It has its formative model in Homer's *Iliad* and is a version of the great Indo-European Armageddon, which we find, for instance, not only in the Trojan War but also in the Indian *Mahabharata*, the Irish *Book of Invasions*, and the Norse *Eddas*. Finally, in Book Twelve, Aeneas confronts and kills Tumus, marries

priorities of various social groups, tribes, or races. At the same time, it must be said that geographical proximity and the effects of long years of colonialism make the term "African mythology" at least initially valid. It is possible to say, for example, that animism (the cult of spirits, especially animal spirits), the somewhat withdrawn presence of a creator high god with the earth usually personified as the high god's wife, the mediating and sometimes disruptive activities of culture hero–tricksters, and the influence of or suppression by European and Middle Eastern religions are all ubiquitous in the mythologies of the sub-Saharan African continent.

The Pygmies of the central equatorial region have their sky god Khonvum, who once was on earth as an animal master but who now lives above and concerns himself with the stars and solar system. He deals with humans through intermediary animal spirits. Animal spirits are particularly prominent among the neighboring Bushmen, whose Praying Mantis Kaggen (Cagn) is married to the Antelope or some other animal spirit. This god is also a resurrection trickster, whose bones and body reform after he is killed by enemies and stripped of his flesh by ants. The Hottentot sky god of the equatorial region is a trickster–sky god combination known as Tsui-Goab. He is also a storm god who struggles against a devil character in a "black sky." The Hottentot culture hero–trickster–first man is Heitsi-Eibib, whose mother, a cow, conceived him miraculously by eating a special grass, which suggests that this hero has archetypal connections with other world heroes of the monomyth.

Many other groups have supreme creator beings who have long since retreated to the sky and associate with humans only by way of intermediaries. For the Shilluk people of the Nilotic tribes, Juck is such a god, and Nyikang, son of a crocodile mother, is the intermediary. It was he who turned animals into the Shillucks. The Dinkas have a creator, Nyalitch, and an incarnation of the creator called Deng ("Rain"), who, with the goddess Abuk, is the intercessory route to the high god. For the Dogon the creator god is Amma; his intermediaries with humans are the Nummo twins, who, with the help of various culture heroes, participate in an ongoing creation.

The Bantu tribes further south have several versions of a supreme deity, who is usually seen as a distant creator and is also a storm god. The southern Bantu Tilo is such a god. Another Bantu high god is Kurunga. Still others are Ndyami and Kalunga. The characteristics of these gods sometimes suggest the influence of the Christian colonizers, who attached elements of their monotheistic concept of God to African high gods, thus obliterating earlier stories of those gods. In any case, more important to most Bantus than the supreme deity concept seems to be the first man–culture hero figure. The Kaffir-Zulus, for instance, have Unkulunkulu, made in the image of the supreme being, who was born miraculously from the earth—that is from the goddess associated with earth—and who teaches humans what they need to know. Like many Native North American trickster–culture heroes—Raven and Coyote, for example—he also introduces death. Hlakanaya is another version of the Kaffir trickster.

In the Masai area of southeast Africa there is the storm-fertility high god Ngai, whose daughter long ago fell in love with the Masai first man Kintu, who traveled to the heav-

A Yoruba depiction of the African trickster, Eshu

ens and who, after satisfactorily completing tests set by Ngai, was given the god's daughter. Kintu and the god's daughter are the culture heroes of the Masai; they teach the domestic and agricultural arts. But Kintu also introduces Death, a son of Ngai, who follows Kintu to earth after the hero, in spite of the warnings of Ngai, returns to the sky to retrieve grain he had forgotten to bring down to earth.

The Bantu high god of the Congo region is the sky god Nzambe or Nzame. It was Nzambe who created a first man, Fam, who revolted against the god and was buried by him in a hole in the ground. Then Nzame created a second first man, Sekume, who created his own mate from a tree. But Fam rose from his hole and undermined Sekume and his wife and the human race to which she gave birth. A frequent theme of the people of the Congo area is that of the supreme deity's son, who becomes a teaching culture hero and sometimes is rejected by his father. Bingo is such a hero, as is Nyiko in the Cameroons. The first man figure in Africa is frequently a trickster who plays tricks on or steals from the high god. Whether the Sudanese Bele, Tule, or Mba, or the Spiders—the Ashanti Ananse or the Manja Seto—they help the people, stealing such important gifts as storytelling power, fire, or water. A Bantu transformer-trickster is Dikithi, a highly accomplished thief.

Perhaps the best-known African mythologies are those of the west African Ashanti, Fon, and Yoruba peoples. Nyame is the Ashanti sky and fertility god, the rain source for his wife Asase Ya, the earth itself. It is the culture hero–trickster Ananse the Spider who acts as the god's connection to human beings. Essentially, Ananse corrects the mistakes of Nyame's creation, convincing the god to send rain to counteract the extreme heat of the new sun, and river and ocean banks to contain the water that would otherwise have flooded the world. Ananse also lives up to his trickster reputation by succeeding in marrying the high god's daughter. Another important west African

trickster is Legba, who so exasperated the high god with his tricks that the god retreated from the earth and remained in the heavens. Still another cognate is Eshu.

Among the Fon the supreme deity is Nana Buluku; his twin children Mahu and Lisa—female and male, earth and sky, fertility and virility—establish balance in the world. Their son, Dan, maintains life by controlling the deities who embody aspects of nature.

The Yoruba sky god is the aloof Olorun, who had children by the primordial waters, Olokun. These were Obatala of the sky and Odudua of the earth. From their union came dry and wet land, which produced Orungan, who made love to his mother, producing the later Yoruba pantheon. The gods of this pantheon represent various phenomena and human activities. [Abrahams; Beier; Grimal; Okpewho; Soyinka, Zuesse]

AFTERLIFE Myths of the afterlife exist in most cultures. Many peoples have myths of a specific underworld to which heroes descend for various reasons and where the dead reside. The nature of afterlife myths and the concept of the afterlife itself depend, of course, on the given culture's myths of divinity and the understood nature of the relationship between humans and that divinity. If the deity myths suggest an anthropomorphic god, the afterlife is apt to be physical. The Christian God lives in "Heaven above," to which Christians are beckoned after leading good lives. The Vedanta-Hindu Brahman, the source of all being, is a principle or concept rather than a being, and therefore the Vedantic afterlife is philosophical rather than geographical.

If divinity is associated with the judgment of human actions, the afterlife is likely to be associated with judgment. So it is that Zoroastrianism, for example, preaches the idea that death is the work of the evil Angra Mainyu. The religion also asserts the existence of the soul (*fravarti*) and the resurrection of the body at the time of the "Great Renewal," which will come one day. The soul, created by Ahura Mazda, is immortal and will be judged immediately after the death of the body. At the time of death, the soul must pass over a narrow bridge. At the entrance to the bridge stands the *daena*, or conscience, a maiden who becomes identified with the individual soul. The good souls see a beautiful and dignified woman, while the evil souls see a witch. The good, led by the maiden, will pass over to the "House of Songs," or Paradise, as angel-like beings who will serve as guardians of the living good people. The souls of those who have lived evil lives will be attacked by the witch and will fall as demons into the dark, cold ravine, or "House of Lies" that is Hell. According to some sources, it is the bridge itself, Chinvat, that decides the fate of souls. Other sources say Ahura Mazda himself makes the judgment, and still others say that Mithra presides over an actual trial of the individual, who must plead his or her own case.

Christians and Muslims also tend to associate the afterlife and its geography with judgment. For some, Hell is a place "below" where the fallen angel Lucifer reigns as the Devil or Satan. Hell is opposed to Heaven, the former being the place where sinners suffer after death, and the latter being the eternal home of the good—in popular culture a place of pearly gates and saints in white reigned over by God. For some Christians, God is literally enthroned and is accompanied by angels; by his son, Jesus; and, some believe, by Jesus' mother, the Virgin Mary. According to canonical writings, Jesus ascended bodily to God after his death and resurrection. Later tradition and Catholic dogma hold that Mary, too, was bodily "assumed" by God (the Assumption). Again, depending on the tradition and the level of

The poet Dante, guided by Virgil, explores the afterlife in Hell

Minerva prevents Achilles from killing Agamemnon

fundamentalism, Christians believe that they will join God and the others in Heaven, perhaps even in bodily form.

Jews have the ancient concept of Sheol, an underworld of sorts that is perhaps best seen as a metaphor for the emptiness of death. In the Book of Psalms (55:15), Sheol seems, like Hell, to be a place of punishment for sins. The Norse people have both Hel, an unpleasant place, and Valhalla, a great hall in Asgard, the home of the gods, where dead warriors feast and enjoy battling as they wait for the final end of the world (Ragnarok). The ancient Greeks had a pleasant land, the Elysian Fields, for good heroes to go without actually dying. For the Romans these fields were Elysium, where the good shades lived. Aeneas visits his father, Anchises, there in Virgil's *Aeneid*.

The Greeks also had the myth of Hades, where the god of that name reigned. This was a dreary, dull, and dark place where the dead lived. After he abducted her, Hades took Persephone there and she reigned with him as a perhaps reluctant queen.

In Asian religions and mythologies, too, there are specific underworld geographies. In Siberia, for example, the underworld exists below the domain of the Great Mother Goddess and is ruled by a king, Mangi or Xargi. The period of death in the underworld is seen as one of gestation leading to rebirth, as is the case, for instance, with some Hindu concepts of afterlife. In Japan we find an afterlife geography in the pre-Buddhist Shinto story of Izanagi and Izanami. In the *Kojiki* we are told that Izanagi visits his wife Izanami in *Yomi no kuni*, a place of darkness and impurity inhabited by furies. The passage to it is blocked by a boulder, and the putrefied Izanami reigns there as queen in a palace. There is no indication of judgment in this afterlife setting, but gloom decidedly prevails. In other stories

Yomi is less gloomy, and there is a tradition that the dead live in the sky or on mountaintops (where they are often buried). During the annual rites of the Buddhist-originated *Bon* festival, the dead ancestors are said to return to visit their families.

But often the Asian afterlife is more a philosophical state than a physical place. In these cases the afterlife is a state in which the individual develops into another being or is absorbed into the eternal flow or all-encompassing void, the nothingness that is, for example, the Buddhist nirvana, a state of freedom from the endless cycles of existence, *samsara*.

The ubiquitous quality of the afterlife motif suggests that human beings are unwilling or unable to accept the idea of the loss of self or consciousness after death. Of all species, only humans appear to be capable of conceiving of life as a whole process involving birth, living, and death. Consciousness of that process—that plot, with its beginning, middle, and end—and consciousness itself are perhaps our ultimate defining characteristics. Even if we do not go so far as to believe in the eternal physical restoration of our lives after death, we seem to be unable to conceive of existence without the miracle of the consciousness by which we perceive existence.

AGAMEMNON Perhaps a real king of ancient Argos, with his capital at Mycenae in about 1300 B.C.E., Agamemnon was believed in ancient Greece to have led the alliance of Greeks that fought against the Trojans in the Trojan War, as depicted in Homer's *Iliad*. According to that story, Agamemnon, heir of the famous House of Atreus of Argos, was the brother of the Spartan king Menelaus, whose wife Helen had been abducted by the Trojan prince Paris, causing the Greeks to attack Troy to retrieve her (*see* abduction,

Atreus). Our experience of the myth of Agamemnon is continued in the *Oresteia* of Aeschylus. In the play we learn of his prewar sacrifice of his daughter Iphigenia, and we follow the story that includes his murder by his wife Clytemnestra and her lover, and the revenge taken by his children Elektra and Orestes.

AGASTYA Agastya was the greatest sage of mythical South India. Sometimes known as Kumbhayoni, he was a dwarf and was said to have been born in a jar. By means of his ascetic powers he defeated and controlled the monstrous Raksasas of his region so that other creatures could thrive there. As a teacher of Vishnu's avatar, Rama, he presented that hero with the great god's ever-true bow and endless quiver of arrows.

AGNI A major Vedic god who appears originally in the *Rig Veda* as one of the asuras or Adityas—along with Mitra, Varuna, Aryaman, Rudra, Ushas, and Indra—at the most obvious level, Agni is the god of fire. He is often opposed to Varuna, the god of waters, in philosophical dialogues. Sacrifice is associated with Agni; he carries sacrificial offerings to the gods. In a deeper sense he is the divine will without which nothing can happen in the universe. He is a hidden god—the divine fire in plants, in the earth, in animals, in the elements, in humans; he is the divine light by which we see, by which we are conscious. The sacrifice, of which Agni is at once the priest and the flame and the offering itself, is central to Hindu life. Thus, when he is depicted, it is as a red man out of whose mouth shoot flames. He has three legs and seven arms and rides on a ram.

Many myths of Agni are related to his hidden aspect. In the *Mahabharata*, the gods roamed the world looking for Agni, who had hidden in the elemental waters. His hiding place was revealed by a frog, who had been burned by the god's heat. Agni was furious at the frog and decreed that he would no longer possess the sensation of taste. He then

The "Wise Lord," Ahura Mazda, confronts his evil opposite, Angra Mainyu

hid himself in a fig tree but was betrayed by the elephant, whose tongue he bent backward as a punishment. After hiding in several other places and being betrayed by several other animals, whom he cursed, Agni was discovered in the *sami* tree, the wood of which is still used to create the fire of sacrifice. The gods asked Agni to father Skanda (Karttikeya, sometimes said to have been fathered by Shiva), whose six heads represent what the Hindus see as the six seasons of the year.

AGUNG Agung is the volcanic mountain sacred to Balinese Hindus and represented in their temples and shrines. According to Balinese myth, the Hindu gods moved to the mountain—the true center of the world—when neighboring Java converted to Islam.

AH MUN Ah Mun is a Mayan maize god from whose head a cob of corn grows.

AHALYA In the Hindu epic the *Ramayana*, Ahalya practiced asceticism and abstinence with her partner, the sage Gautama. But the god Indra lusted after the beautiful Ahalya and, disguised as Gautama, seduced her. Ahalya recognized Indra behind the disguise but was flattered by the god's attention. After this act of adultery, the sage returned and recognized the departure of the god and realized what had happened. In a rage he used his powers to make Indra impotent. In fact, the god's testicles dropped off. Turning to his offending wife, Gautama condemned her to lie for thousands of years on a bed of ashes with no food. Only when the great Rama came to purify her would Ahalya's curse be lifted. As for Indra's testicles, they were replaced by those of a ram, and to this day the gods are offered castrated lambs in sacrifice.

AHAU KIN The Mayan sun god, Ahau Kin was usually depicted as a jaguar, in which form he roamed the underworld at night.

AHURA MAZDA The chief god of the ancient Iranians (*see* Mazdaism) and later the Zoroastrians, Ahura Mazda (Oromazdes or Ohrmazd) first came to Iran during the Aryan (Indo-Iranian) invasions of the second millennium B.C.E. as one of the *ahura* gods whose roots were in the ancient Indo-European past. His equivalent among the Aryans who invaded India at about the same time would perhaps have been Indra, as revealed in the *Rig Veda*. It seems likely, too, that Ahura Mazda's nature owes something to the Vedic Varuna. In both India and Iran the old gods were either *asuras* (*ahuras* in Iran) or *devas* (*daevas* in Iran). In the *Avesta*, the holy book of Zoroaster (Zarathustra), who lived perhaps as early as the middle of the second millennium B.C.E. but probably not until the later part of that millennium, the *daevas* had become demons and a supreme god had emerged as Ahura Mazda. Ahura Mazda was the "Wise Lord," the sky god organizer of the sun and the stars, the epitome of the true order of the universe. He was placed in opposition to an evil principle called Angra Mainyu (Ahriman). According to one version of the myth—a heretical one for most Zoroastrians—Ahura Mazda and Angra Mainyu were both born of Zurvan, or Time. When the evil principle escaped from the primeval womb into the world, Zurvan was forced to divide Time in the world between good and evil until a time in the distant future when goodness would prevail. In fourth- and fifth-century bas reliefs, Ahura Mazda is depicted as a bearded male on a winged disk, which seems to associate this supreme god with the sun—an appropriate association, since light and fire were central factors in Zoroastrian ritual and dogma.

AHURAS Ahura, meaning "lord," is an ancient Iranian term that is equivalent to the Vedic term *asura*. The *ahuras* are three principal deities, Ahura Mazda, Mithra, and Apam Napat.

AINU MYTHOLOGY Early non-Mongoloid inhabitants of the islands now called Japan, the non–Japanese-speaking Ainu were subjugated by the Japanese beginning in the early ninth century. The few Ainu who remain live in the northern islands. The essential dualism of Ainu mythology is expressed by a supreme deity in Heaven and evil deities who live in the world below. There is a fire goddess who presides over a kind of Last Judgment and a creation story that resembles the one in the Japanese *Nihongi*. In this story a bird is sent down to earth to dry out some of the mud in the primordial slush so that islands can be formed for the Ainu. In one Ainu myth the creator is said to have sent a couple down to earth who gave birth to the first Ainu. The word "ainu" means human. Other myths say that the Ainu, who tend to have a great deal of body hair, are descended from the polar bear or a Bear god. A bear sacrifice ritual is still practiced by the Ainu in which the sacrificed bear is sent "home" to the ancestors. The Ainu have a flood myth in which a very few people escape to a mountaintop. Many Ainu myths are contained in several heroic narratives (see *Kotan Utunnai*, *Kutune Shirka*, and *The Woman of Poi-Soya*), some as long as 15,000 lines, which are often sung by female shamans. [Ohnuki-Tierney]

AIZEN-MYO-O One of the *myo-o* or *Vidja-raja* class of Japanese Buddhist deities, Aizen-myo-o is a god of love. In fact, his name means love, and he represents the idea of love changed into the Buddhist desire for enlightenment. Aizen is usually depicted with a red body possessing eight arms and three eyes on an angry face. A lion's head rests in his hair, symbolizing passion. He carries bows and arrows, which symbolize love as well as his role as a destroyer of evil.

AJAX Ajax, or Aias, is described by Homer in the *Iliad* as one of the strongest and bravest of the Greek heroes who fought in the Trojan War. In a contest for the armor of the slain Achilles, he lost to Odysseus, which, according to Sophocles in his tragedy *Ajax*, led to his madness. During one of his outbursts he is said to have destroyed all the sheep belonging to the Greek armies, mistaking them for enemy soldiers. His response to this mistake was suicide.

AKHENATON The successor to King Amunhotep III of Egypt was his son Amunhotep IV (1353–1336 B.C.E.). Amunhotep IV disassociated himself from the dominant Amun-Re religion, allying himself with a Sun god, Aton (Aten), with himself and his wife Nefertiti as the principal intermediaries between that divinity and mortals. Aton was represented as a sun disk, the rays of which reached down to the earth as hands. The pharaoh renamed himself Akhen*aton* (Akhenaten) in honor of the god and in about 1349 created a new capital city, Akhetaton (el Amarna), north of Thebes, beginning what is known as the Amarna period of Egyptian history. Although it has been fashionable over the centuries

Statue of Pharoah Akhenaton (Amenhotep IV)

to consider Aton a sole god and to claim Akhenaton as the founder of monotheism, it seems more likely that Aton was a manifestation of Re and was one among several gods worshipped at the time. Still, it is true that the pharaoh greatly favored the god from whom he took his new name and the name of his new capital. Under Akhenaton's son or son-in-law Tutankh*aton* ("King Tut"), the old Amun religion with Thebes as its capital was restored, and the pharaoh changed his name to Tutankh*amun* to reflect that restoration.

AKKADIAN MYTHOLOGY King Sargon I of Akkad captured the southern region of Mesopotamia from the Sumerians sometime between 2390 and 2330 B.C.E., establishing a capital, Agade (Akkad), near Kish. The Akkadians adapted their own Semitic language to Sumerian cuneiform, and that language became the lingua franca of the region for centuries to come. The Akkadian dynasty controlled what was now, in effect, Sumer-Akkad, only until about 2254, however, when the old Sumerian area regained independence, beginning what is sometimes

King Sargon I, Akkadian conqueror of Sumer

called the neo-Sumerian period. King Naram-Sin of Akkad regained control of all of Mesopotamia soon after that, desecrating the holy city of Nippur, and he extended his territory to include the ancient Semitic kingdom of Ebla (perhaps the land of the original Amorites), which had flourished in what is now northern Syria from c. 2700 B.C.E. Ebla is near Aleppo and not far from Haran, where Abram (Abraham) is said to have lived for a while on his way to Canaan. At Tell Mardikh, the site of Elba's center, archeologists have found important materials, including what might be called the first bilingual dictionary, cuneiform tablets combining words in several languages.

Naram-Sin was deified by the Akkadians for his successes in Ebla and elsewhere, but eventually he lost power to invading Gutian tribes from the mountains of western Iran, who were in turn confronted by Utuhegal of Uruk and by Lagash, powerful again for a brief period under its leader Gudea. Much of Akkadian mythology is essentially similar to that of the Sumerians and Babylonians.

ALA Among the Ibo people of Africa, Ala is a goddess whose life-size image sits on the porches of little wooden houses built in her honor. Ala is synonymous with earth and as such is an Earth Mother. It is she who is said to make the seed grow in the womb and in the soil. And just as she gives life, in death she takes us back into herself.

ALALU In the Hittite myths known as the Kumarbi cycle, Alalu was the first high god. After a short reign he was overcome by Anu and condemned to live in the underworld.

ALBION Ancient Celts referred to Britain—not including Ireland—as Albion and only later as Britannia. The Romans connected Albion through their word *albus*, meaning "white," with the white cliffs of Dover. Geoffrey of Monmouth reported that the Celts believed a certain Albion who ruled the island was a giant fathered by a god of the sea. Others believe the island was named for a princess who came to the island with fifty women who in their former home had killed their husbands.

ALCESTIS The heroine of the *Alcestis* by Sophocles, Alcestis was a daughter of King Pelias of Iolcus, better known for his connection with the story of Jason and the Golden Fleece. Her husband was Admetus, much favored of the god Apollo. Apollo arranged with the Fates that Admetus would not have to die if someone would die for him. When Admetus's father and mother refused to be sacrificed, Alcestis offered herself. After she did so and died, however, she was brought back from the dead by Herakles.

ALEXANDER THE GREAT The biography of this great Macedonian king, Alexander (356–323 B.C.E.), the student of Aristotle and the conqueror of Persia and, in fact, most of the ancient world, is a mixture of fact and mythology. Early in his series of conquests he was said to have cut the Gordian knot of Phrygia with his sword. According to a Phrygian myth, the people were plagued by dissension, and an oracle predicted that only a man arriving in a wagon would solve their problems. When a man named Gordius did, in fact, arrive in a wagon, the Phrygians made him their king. The grateful Gordius thanked the people and honored Zeus in the temple square by dedicating his vehicle to the god and tying its pole to its yoke by means of a complex knot. An oracle claimed that the one who could untie that knot would rule in Asia. When Alexander came to Phrygia, he cut the knot with his sword and proclaimed himself the conqueror named by the oracle. When in 331 he made a pilgrimage to a great temple of the god Amon-Ra in Egypt—a god the Greeks thought of as a version of Zeus—he decided that, like the old Egyptian pharaohs, he was a son of the god. Near the end of his life he commanded that he be worshipped as a god himself, justifying the command by his supposedly divine origin.

ALKMENE The mother of the Greek hero Herakles by Zeus, Alkmene (Alcmene) was married to Amphitryon, who was wrongly supposed to be Herakles' father, much as Aegeus was thought to be Theseus's father. In fact, while Amphitryon was off fighting a war, Zeus came to Alkmene in the form of Amphitryon, and the result was Herakles. This story brings to mind the Arthurian tale in which the wizard Merlin magically disguises Uther Pendragon as Igraine 's husband while the latter is at war, making possible a nighttime visit by Uther to Igraine and the conception of Arthur. Alkmene was much revered at her cult center at Thebes.

ALLAH Derived from the Arabic *al* (the) and *Lah* (god), or *al ilah*—*ilah* coming from the old Semitic *el* indicating divinity—Allah was the name of the dominant god of the old Arabic-Meccan pantheon and the name taken by Muslims for God. This was the same god worshipped by Jews and Christians, said to be the God of Abraham, whose name had been given as Elohim or Yahweh or simply God. It should be noted that the Muslim Allah is not the same as the old pre-Muslim Meccan chief deity. The Muslim Allah is the sole god, the Creator who determines all things; he is absolute, the only being to be worshipped. "There is no god other than Allah" is the central Islamic belief. He is the perfect one, the unknowable one of the "ninety-nine beautiful names." The Quaranic Sura (Chapter) 112, the *Tawhid*, or Sura of Unity, says: "He is God, One, the ever self-sufficing, God the Eternal. He does not beget and he was not begotten, and there is not anyone like him."

AMA NO UZUME In the Shinto mythology of Japan, Ama no Uzume is the beautiful goddess whose erotic dance delights the gods and causes the emergence of the sun goddess Amaterasu from hiding and, therefore, the return of the sun to the world.

AMAIRGEN The great warrior and bard-prophet of Irish mythology, Amairgen, in his song to Ireland in the *Book of Invasions*, literally contains reality and history within himself. His Welsh counterpart is Taliesen. Both have possible Indo-European roots in the mysterious being of Krishna, the "poet" of the Hindu *Bhagavadgita*, who contains the universe within himself.

AMALTHEA Amalthea was the infant Zeus's nurse on the island of Crete. She was either a nymph or a she-goat, and she gave the child goat's milk. Some accounts say that Zeus broke off one horn of the goat that was suckling him and gave it the power always to be filled with good things for its possessor. Thus we have the term "Horn of Plenty," or cornucopia.

AMATERASU AND SUSANOWO Considered to be the prime ancestor of the Japanese emperor, the Sun Goddess Amaterasu Omikami, queen of the *kami*, or the Shinto forces of Nature, is honored especially at her temple at Ise, Japan. As the Rising Sun, she gives spiritual power to her people. Amaterasu has a brother, the storm god Susanowo.

One day when Susanowo was visiting his sister in Heaven, he produced five gods by biting Amaterasu's necklaces and blowing a cloud over them. Meanwhile, Amaterasu had created three goddesses by breaking her brother's sword, chewing on the pieces, and blowing a cloud over them. When later, in a drunken fury, Susanowo disrupted and destroyed much of Heaven and earth and Amaterasu's home, the goddess hid in a cave, depriving the world of her light and warmth and causing the death of plants and animals. The gods and goddesses, after several failed attempts to lure Amaterasu back into the world, asked the goddess Ama no Uzume to dance in front of the cave. She did so lasciviously, dropping her clothes in the process, so that the gods were overcome with such loud laughter that Amaterasu became curious and opened the door to her cave. In so doing she noticed the reflection of herself in a mirror that the gods had hung outside her door. Overcome by her own beauty, she left her cave to examine herself more closely, allowing the gods to rope off the door. Thus the world was bright and warm again, and life returned to it. It is said that in later years Amaterasu gave her jewels and mirror to her grandson Ninigi, who went down to earth as the first ruler. Her brother Susanowo was banished from the heavens (see Izumo). Amaterasu never disappeared again.

AMAZONS The Amazons (Amazones or Amazonides, "breastless ones") of Greek mythology were a race of warrior women led by a queen. They fought against the Greeks, for instance, during the Trojan War. Procreation for them took place only by way of men from other races. Boy children

Shinto priests perform a ceremony at the Ise Shrine, dedicated to Amaterasu

were disposed of; girls had their right breasts removed so as not to impede the use of bows. The hero, Theseus, had significant relations with the Amazons. There are many versions of these relations. The most popular involves his abduction of and marriage to the Amazon queen Hippolyta, who gave birth to his son Hippolytus. Some say that Theseus abducted Hippolyta's sister Antiope and that he defeated the Amazon army led by Hippolyta, which invaded Attica in a rescue attempt. Some say that Hippolyta and Antiope are different names for the same Amazon. Still others say that Herakles killed Hippolyta during the course of his ninth labor, which involved the taking of her sacred belt or "girdle."

AMBROSIA Ambrosia was the food of the Greek gods. With their drink, nectar, it ensured immortality, much as soma did for the Vedic gods of India.

AMERICAN MYTHS As a young culture anxious in some ways to distance itself from its roots, European America had to create its own mythological stories and heroes. Technically, these stories and heroes fall under the rubric of folktale or legend rather than myth, but they do, like myth, serve to express certain cultural values and priorities—America's sense of its place in the world. Some of the American myths were totally fabricated stories meant to extol American strength and the hugeness of things American. The Paul Bunyan stories are examples. Bunyan was the giant backwoods-man who formed the Grand Canyon by dragging his pick along the ground. A similar hero was Joe Magarac, a steelworker

who made rails for the railroad by squeezing white-hot steel with his bare hands.

Sometimes the "tall tales," as they are called, were exaggerations of the deeds of real people, again to emphasize American values. John Henry was an African American railroad worker, a modern-day Herakles who was said to have won a drilling race against a steam drill at the cost of his life. Daniel Boone and Davy Crockett were real people whose lives were turned into tall tales. Crockett, a sometime congressman who died at the Alamo, was said to have planned to tear the tail off of Halley's Comet in 1835. Boone was known for various impossible woodland exploits. Real western outlaws were admired for their individualism and supposed bravery; Billy the Kid and especially Jesse James took on characteristics of Robin Hood. An African American "bad" man who achieved mythical status was Stagolee, who shared characteristics with African tricksters.

Furthermore, the frontier and the immigration process generated their own American philosophical myths, such as the Melting Pot and Manifest Destiny. America was a nation that in theory could transcend the national, ethnic, and religious barriers that plagued Europe, and our relentless conquering of the continent was our God-given or "Manifest Destiny." America's movement away from the European class system was reflected in the myth perpetrated by writer Horatio Alger and others of the "self-made man."

Several well-known American "myths" are really patriotic legends intended to raise certain popular political figures to the level of iconic heroes. There is the story of George Washington and the cherry tree, a product of the imagina-

The American frontier hero, Daniel Boone, leads the settlers westward

tion of one Mason Locke Weems, an Anglican priest turned bookseller who wrote "biographies" of famous Americans. Weems tells, for instance, about young George—age six—cutting down one of his father's prize cherry trees. Asked whether he knew what had happened to the tree, George rushed into his father's arms, admitting his guilt and crying that he could never tell a lie. [Leeming and Page (1999)]

AMESA SPENTAS In Iranian mythology the Amesa Spentas are the beneficent immortals or mortal saints (they also take human form by way of the qualities they represent) who, with Ahura Mazda (the Wise Lord) or within the prophet Zoroaster (Zarathustra) or other humans who adhere to divine truth (*asha*), form a spiritual pantheon of sorts in Zoroastrianism. These are the Yazata, or "Venerables," gods created by the supreme god, Ahura Mazda. However analyzed, they are crucial to Zoroastrian thought. Specifically, they are Vohu Manah ("Good Thought"), Asha Vahishta ("Best Truth"), Khshathra ("Desirable Dominion"), Armaiti ("Beneficent Devotion"), Haurvatat ("Wholeness"), and Amretat ("Immortality"). Sometimes Ahura Mazda himself is seen as the first of seven Amesa Spentas. Other Iranian deities, who have equivalents in India, are Hoama, Anahita, Mithra, Vayu, and Verethraghna, all representing moral values or natural phenomena.

AMIDA BUDDHA Amida nyorai (the Buddha Amitabha), the Buddha of Pure Light, is the closest entity to the Western idea of God that we find in Japanese Buddhism. Statues of Amida abound in Japan. Amida promises salvation to all who invoke his name. In the tenth century a monk named Genshin developed the idea of rebirth into Amida's paradise or "Pure Land." Thus Pure Land Buddhism was born and was developed further by the monks Honen and then Shinran in the twelfth and thirteenth centuries with emphasis on salvation through Amida's grace. There is a close association between Amida Buddha and the great Tibetan bodhisattva Avalokiteshvara.

AMMA Amma is the creator and father god of the Dogon people of Mali in Africa. He is sometimes seen as the cosmic egg that precedes creation. In reaction to an act of the trickster Pale Fox, he instituted agriculture in Mali.

AMPHITRITE The Nereid or Oceanid wife of the Greek god Poseidon, Amphitrite was the mother of Triton, the male version of the mermaid. Amphitrite turned her rival Scylla into a monster.

AMPHITRYON Amphitryon was the husband of Alcmene and the "foster father" of Herakles.

AMRETAT Representing immortality, Amretat is one of the Persian (Iranian) Zoroastrian deities, the Amesa Spentas. She is particularly associated with Haurvatat, or prosperity, and with the earth patroness Armaiti.

AMUN In Egyptian mythology as developed at the cult center of Hermopolis, Amun (Amon) and his female aspect, Amaunet, represented the hidden aspect of pre-creation and were responsible, with the other Hermopolitan gods, collectively known as the Ogdoad, for the existence of the primal egg of creation. Later Amun became associated with the Old Kingdom high god Re (Ra), and the result was Amun-Re.

AMUN-RE (Amun Ra) Derived from an assimilation of Amun and Re, Amun-Re was the Middle and New Kingdom high god of ancient Egyptian Thebes, with a cult center at Karnak. Married to Mut, he was a solar god with a ram's head and was perhaps the most important high god in Egyptian mythology. It was he who was for a time briefly superseded during the reign of Akhenaton by the solar disk god the Aton.

ANAHITA The only important goddess of Iranian Zoroastrianism, Ardva Sura Anahita (Anahid, "the High, Powerful, and Immaculate One") is depicted as a beautiful young woman with full breasts. She is dressed in elaborate clothing, complete with jewels and a halo-crown of starry light. Anahita began as a goddess of the primal waters. As such she is associated with all bodily secretions as well as bodies of water. Later she taught Zoroaster (Zarathustra) how to perform sacrifices and fight for justice among humans. Anahita aided Ahura Mazda in his work as Creator.

ANANDA The cousin of Gautama Buddha, Ananda became his primary companion and disciple. After his master's death he became an arhat and was called the Dhammabhandagarika, or "treasurer of the teachings." It is said that Ananda convinced the Buddha to admit women to the "priesthood" of his followers, thus establishing the concept of Buddhist nuns.

ANANSE Ananse, the Spider, is a trickster god of the Ashanti in west Africa who, like many tricksters (such as Erlik, Coyote, Raven, and the west African Legba and Eshu), plays a role in creation. The Ashanti people tell how Ananse created the first people, into whom the sky god Nyame (Nyankopon) breathed life. He sometimes worked behind Nyame's back, disguising himself (tricksters are always shape shifters) as a bird and creating the sun, moon, and stars and differentiating night from day. Like most tricksters, Ananse had a rapacious appetite for pleasure; he even succeeded in stealing away the high god's daughter.

There is a Krachi tale in which the sky god was Wulbari. Wulbari overheard Ananse bragging about how clever he was, even cleverer than Wulbari himself. Thinking he would teach the trickster a lesson, Wulbari sent him on a mission to the earth to find something, but he refused to tell him what that something was. "If you're so clever, you should know what I want," he laughed. Undaunted, Ananse went down to earth and borrowed feathers from all the different birds, attached the feathers to himself, and returned to Heaven disguised as one of them. When Wulbari came out of his house and found the mysterious and beautiful multicolored bird perched on a tree nearby, he asked the animals what it was called. Naturally, the animals did not know but suggested that Ananase might know. "But I've sent him away to find something," said the god. When the animals asked what that something was, Ananse, of course, overheard. "I didn't tell him," said Wulbari, "but in fact I hoped he would find the sun, the moon, and darkness." Everyone laughed and, realizing the impossibility of such a task, praised the god for outsmarting the trickster. Now, however, Ananse knew what Wulbari wanted and at least had a fair chance of succeeding. In fact, he managed somehow to gather the sun, the moon, and darkness into a sack, and he returned to the god. First he pulled darkness out of the bag, and no one could see anything. Next he took out the moon, and everyone could see a little bit. Finally he brought out the sun. Those who looked at it went blind, those who turned partly away lost the sight of one eye, but those who blinked kept their full sight. So it is that Ananse outsmarted Wulbari, but so it is also that blindness came into the world. Tricksters are clever and creative, but they often stir up trouble.

Ananse, like other tricksters, is an intermediary between humans and the sky god. The Abure people believe, for instance, that it was Nyame who created the hot sun and that Ananse acted in the interest of humans to get the sky god to send rain to cool them off.

According to an Ashanti myth, it was Ananse who stole storytelling ability from Nyame. The mysterious transforming power of language is an important part of the trickster's repertoire.

Ananse decided he must learn the stories known only to the sky god, so he offered to pay Nyame for them. "Why should I sell them to you?" said the god. "Even the wealthiest villages haven't been able to come up with the selling price." When asked what the price was, Nyame said it was the Python, the Leopard, the Fairy, and the Hornets. Ananse said he would pay this price and went off to consult with his wife, Aso, who told him what he would need to do.

Following Aso's advice, Ananse went with a stick and a string of vines down to a stream, where he found Python. "My wife and I have been arguing about how long you are," the trickster told the snake. "Well, place that stick next to me and measure," said Python. Ananse did just that and then quickly used the vine to tie the stretched-out serpent to the stick. He delivered his captive to Nyame.

Then, following Aso's suggestion, he took a gourd full of water and poured some of it over a swarm of the Hornets and some of it over himself before covering his head with a plantain leaf. "Look," he cried to the Hornets, "the rains have come; get into my gourd so you'll stay safe." The Hornets did as they were told, and Ananse closed the gourd and took the Hornets off to Nyame.

Again following Aso's advice, the Spider dug a hole in the ground on the Leopard's trail and disguised it with sticks. Later the Leopard came along and, of course, fell into the trap. Ananse pretended to help the Leopard escape by making a ladder for him, but when the great beast put his head out of the top of the hole, Ananse slashed him with his knife and then hauled the disabled animal off to the sky god.

Finally, helped by Aso, Ananse carved a little doll (an *akua*) and covered it with sticky resin. Then he made some yam mash, which he placed in the doll's hands. He placed the doll under the Odum tree, where the Fairies enjoyed playing, and attached a string to its head. When one of the Fairies asked if she could have some of the mash, Ananse used the string to make the doll nod. The Fairy ate and then thanked the doll; but when the doll did not answer, the Fairy, thinking the doll was rude, slapped its face and pushed it with her stomach. Now she found herself stuck to the doll—an African version of the American "tar baby." All Ananse had to do was pick up the captured Fairy and carry her off to Nyame. Ananse also threw in his old mother as a bonus for the sky god, and Nyame was forced to hand over the stories. He proclaimed that they would now be called Spider stories.

ANANTA The serpent Ananta, or Shesha, on whom the god Vishnu sleeps in Indian Vedic cosmogony, represents eternity or infinity. Sometimes Vishnu himself is called Ananta.

ANAT The daughter of the goddess Asherah/ Athirat and the god El in Western Semitic, especially Canaanite, mythology and sometimes the daughter of the sun god Re (Ra) in Egypt, Anat (Anath) is thought by some to be identical to Astarte. Anat was known primarily as a goddess of the hunt but sometimes also as a goddess of war. As the latter, she has a Kali-like or Sekhmet-like bloodthirstiness. As "Lady of the Mountain" she reminds us both of the Indian Parvati and the Sumerian Ninhursag. Anat descends to the underworld to retrieve her brother and mate Baal from his gloomy brother Mot, an act tying her to such figures as the Sumerian/Babylonian Inanna/Ishtar and the Egyptian Isis. The descents of all of these goddesses are related to the fertility of the land, the sprouting forth of grain from the seed planted in the dark earth. By her descent into the underworld, Anat released the spring rains and the fruit of the "planted" seed that was the captured Baal. Anat, in her form as a heifer fertilized by Baal as the Great Bull, gave birth to a fierce bull child, the bull itself being a strong fertility symbol in the Middle East. The story of the mating of goddess and god as cow and bull suggests more serious and ancient connotations for the popular comic story of Pasiphae and the bull and their Minotaur child in Crete (*see* Aqhat).

ANCESTOR CULTS In many cosmogonies of Asia, as in similar myths in other parts of the world, the creation of the world is followed by the creation of beings who become the ancestors of the human race, couples such as Adam and Eve. In Laos, for example, New Year celebrations feature the return of the first ancestors decked in elaborate masks. The veneration of ancestors of particular clans or families is particularly important in Hinduism and Buddhism, as well as in Shinto and Confucianism and even Daoism. In China there is a belief that individuals have two souls. One is the spiritual one (*hun*), made of *yang*. At the time of death the *hun* goes to Heaven. The second soul is the physical one (*p'o*) and is made up of *yin*. At death this soul accompanies the body to earth. It is generally believed that proper ritual sacrifices and filial loyalty to the ancestors will ensure that they will become benevolent protective spirits rather than malevolent destructive ghosts.

Often monarchies justify their existence by claiming descent from divine ancestors. Traditionally, the Japanese trace their emperor's family back to the sun goddess Amaterasu.

ANDHRIMNIR Andhrimnir was Odin's cook at the Norse Valhalla, where each day he boiled up the great boar, which by magic becomes whole again to be cooked up the next day.

ANDROGYNES Androgynes (from the Greek *andros*, meaning "man," and *gune*, meaning "woman") are half male and half female. In mythology they can appear as hermaphrodites—usually with female breasts and male genitalia, as in the case of the Greek Hermaphroditus, who was a blending of his beautiful parents, Hermes and Aphrodite. It could be argued that all original creator gods—that is, those who create alone and *ex nihilo*—are, by definition, androgynes. Sometimes original beings contain both genders and must be separated so that the vitality and differentiation necessary to creation can come into being. Geb and Nut in Egypt, Prajapati in India, or any number of creation myths involving the separation of earth and sky are examples of myths in which the universe itself is an androgyne that must be differentiated into male and female in order for life to evolve.

The primal parents can be seen as androgynous. The Jewish *midrash*, or commentary on Genesis 1, assumes that the implicitly androgynous God created the first human as an androgyne in God's "image," from which being, Adam, later came Eve.

Philosophically and psychologically, the androgyne has sometimes stood for wholeness or true fusion, individuations and integration. In Jungian psychology individuation can be symbolized by the androgyne.

Plato, in his *Symposium* (189–191), attributes one of his philosophical myths to the dramatist Aristophanes, reporting that at first there were three kinds of beings—male, female, and androgyne, each possessing four legs and four arms. When these beings became arrogant and too strong vis-à-vis the gods, Zeus split them each into two parts. From the males came homosexuals, and from the females came lesbians. From the original androgynes came heterosexual males and females, who are intent on sex—that is, on coupling and in so doing restoring the primeval androgynous state.

ANDROMACHE The wife of Hector in Homer's *Iliad*, Andromache begged Hector not to go to battle. She had a son named Scamandrius, or Astyanax, who was thrown to his death by the Greeks from the walls of defeated Troy. Andromache was taken off to Epirus by Achilles' son Neoptolemus.

ANDROMEDA Andromeda was the daughter of the Ethiopian king Cepheus, whose wife, Cassiopeia, angered the Greek sea god Poseidon by claiming to be more beautiful than the sea nymphs known as the Nereids. Poseidon caused a massive flood in Ethiopia and sent a dragon to destroy everything in its path. The king was told by an oracle that only the sacrifice of his daughter Andromeda could save his kingdom. So it was that Cepheus had the girl chained naked to a rock so that the dragon could eat her. Fortunately, however, the great hero Perseus happened by on his winged sandals (some say on the winged horse Pegasus) and offered to save Andromeda in return for her hand in marriage. His magic helmet (some say cloak) rendering him invisible, Perseus was able to decapitate the monster and free and marry Andromeda. Because Andomeda had previously been promised to Phineus, the latter fought with Perseus at the wedding, only to be slain along with all of his followers. After her death, Andromeda was turned into a constellation of stars.

ANGELS Angels are messengers (Greek *angelos*, "messenger") of God in the Abrahamic mythologies. Not surprisingly, then, in popular tradition they came to have wings. An angel intervenes in the sacrifice of Isaac in the Hebrew *Torah*. In the New Testament the angel Gabriel announces to the Virgin Mary that she will become the mother of Jesus and announces Jesus' birth. Angels speak to Mary's husband, Joseph, in dreams. The most famous angels are the archangels. Besides Gabriel there are Raphael, Uriel, and Michael, who led God's forces in the War in Heaven against the bad angels of Satan. But a whole host of angels traditionally exist in various ranks. In Islam Gabriel is Jibril, an impor-

Hermaphroditus, the androgynous offspring of Hermes and Aphrodite

tant revealer of Allah's word and will. "Guardian angels" are said to watch protectively over individuals.

ANGKOR A collection of impressive ruins in Cambodia, Angkor was the center of Khmer civilization in Southeast Asia. There are several myths surrounding its origins. It is said that five goddesses came down to earth from the god Indra's Heaven. One remained behind for six years, on Indra's order, as the wife of a simple gardener. By weaving wonderful clothes to sell, the goddess (*devi*) brought riches to her husband, and they had a son who became the great architect Vishvakarman, as he is called in Sanskrit in India, or Brah Bisnukar, an aspect of Vishnu, as he is called in Cambodia. It seems that as a youth Brah Bisnukar set off to find his mother after she returned to Heaven. In Heaven he was introduced to Indra, who enrolled him in his heavenly workshops. There he learned to be the master of all human architects. When Indra named his own son, Brah Khet Mala, king of Cambodia, he sent Brah Biskunar down to create Angkor so that the son could be reminded of the heavenly Paradise of his father.

ANGRA MAINYU Sometimes called Ahriman in Zoroastrian mythology, Angra Mainyu is the twin brother of Spenta Mainyu ("Holy Spirit") or Vohu Mainyu (the spirit of "Right Thought") or, according to some, of Ahura Mazda (the "Wise Lord") himself. As such, he is the source of the dualism peculiar to Zoroastrianism—the evil force that opposes the good which is Ahura Mazda. (Zoroaster) Zarathustra calls on his followers to concern themselves with this duality in the universe and to make the right choices accordingly.

A Blackfoot medicine man as the sacred White Buffalo

ANIMALS IN MYTHOLOGY Animals in mythology typically belong to an age when humans and animals could communicate directly. In many cases they are totem figures related to particular individuals, tribes, or cultures. Native American religions and social structures are, for instance, often based around animal clans—the bear clan, the beaver clan, the antelope clan, to name a few. In these cases the animals are more than mere mascots; they represent the sacredness of the animal world in creation and the gifts of food and clothing that animals give humans. Many Native American myths reflect this sense of the animal world. The myth of White Buffalo Woman is an example, as is that of the Cherokee Bear Man.

In earth-diver creation myths in Native North America, Central Asia, and elsewhere, it is animals who are sent into the primordial waters by the creator to find the material with which to create the earth. Often that creation takes place on the back of an animal such as the turtle.

Animals take on specifically sacred functions in mythologies such as the Egyptian, in which particular gods are depicted with particular animal heads. As early as the Paleolithic period, animal costumes were used to carry shaman-like humans into the mythic world of spirits.

Monstrous animals and combinations of animal and human forms appear frequently in mythologies all over the world. Dragons and other ferocious beasts stand as barriers that must be overcome by the hero on his quest. In Greek mythology especially there are monstrous combinations such as the centaurs and the Minotaur.

Gods sometimes take on animal forms. All tricksters—the Norse Loki and the Native American Coyote are good examples—have that shape-shifting ability. The Greek god Zeus used animal forms on certain lascivious adventures that he wished to hide from his wife. He impregnated Leda in his form as a swan and abducted Europa as a bull.

ANIMISM Animism is the belief that all things are given life—that is, animated—by spirits. The word often refers specifically to the idea that aspects of nature—rivers, mountain, trees, and so forth—were originally parts of immortal beings and thus suffused with the spirit world. Animism plays an important role in many creation stories in Asia, Native North America, and elsewhere. (*see*, e.g., Bon, Korean mythology, Phi, Tiamat, Corn Mother).

ANNANMAR This folk epic of the Tamil Nadu region of India has been sung by professional storytellers at festivals since the fifteenth century. The narrative tells of a grandfather who leaves his famine-struck home in search of work. When the man succeeds in doing farm work for a Chola king, the king rewards him and his brothers with gifts of land. The brothers become jealous of their older brother and try to cheat him of his land—especially as his oldest son is childless and therefore vulnerable. Although Shiva and Vishnu provide a son for the childless man to adopt, the evil uncles eventually deprive the boy of his grandfather's and father's land. The boy spends time in the wilderness protected by Vishnu until he marries a woman named Tamarai and returns to reclaim his land in spite of the antagonism of his cousins. After twenty-one years, Tamarai gives birth magically to twin boys. She is protected by Vishnu against the evil cousins, who try to prevent the birth. The twins are hidden from the evil ones and fed on tiger's milk by the goddess Cellatta. Because the twins are hidden, Tamarai and her husband, who also have a daughter, appear to be sonless. Once more, the cousins take away the land and send the old couple into exile. Eventually the twins join them and lead them in an epic battle to regain their birthright. After the death of their parents and the defeat of their cousins, the twins rule all of the land in question. When the twins become involved in wars with certain hunters, many of their followers are killed, and in despair they kill themselves, only to be briefly revived by their sister. When all three finally die, they are carried off to the home of the gods by Shiva's representative.

ANNUNCIATION In Christianity the term "Annunciation" refers to the angel Gabriel's announcement to the Virgin Mary that she will become the mother of Jesus.

ANNWN Annwn (Caer Feddwid) is a name for the Welsh Otherworld, where a magic cauldron exists. In a medieval Arthurian tale, *Preiddeu Annwn* (*The Spoils of Annwn*), Arthur and his knights go to Annwn to obtain the cauldron, which, as indicated by the possession of the Cauldron of Plenty by the Dagda, the father god of the Irish Tuatha Dè Danaan, was a symbol of sacred kingship. Arthur and the few of his men that remained return empty-handed. The tale is seen as a prototype for the story of the Holy Grail.

ANTAEUS The giant Antaeus was the ruler of Libya and was slain by Herakles on his way to the Garden of Hesperides to perform the twelfth of his Labors. Antaeus was the son of the god Poseidon and Mother Earth (Gaia or Ge) and was invincible as long as he could maintain contact with his mother—that is, with earth. Herakles killed him by holding him up off the ground and literally squeezing him to death.

ANTARAGATTAMMA This epic of Dravidian India is of the type that is told in homes rather than at religious festivals. It concerns the whole question of caste. In the story a brahman girl is left in the wilderness by her parents because she has her first period before she has been promised in marriage. A man finds her and adopts her until a member of the "Untouchable" caste, who has seen her and fallen in love with her, disguises himself as a brahman and succeeds in winning her hand. The couple has two children, who eventually discover their father doing the work of the Untouchables and tell their mother. Realizing that she has been deceived into marrying improperly and that she is, therefore, corrupted, the brahman wife becomes so enraged that she turns into a Mari—a Kali-like goddess called Antaragattamma (she of the lolling tongue)—hungry for revenge. The many victims of her anger include her two sons and her husband, whose blood she drinks.

ANTICHRIST Mentioned several times in the Christian Bible, or New Testament, in the epistle of John, the antichrist is the person who denies the divinity of Jesus as the Christ or Messiah. According to John, antichrists, who will come to power before the Last Judgment, are already in the world, attempting to thwart the inevitable coming of God's "kingdom" under the Christ. The ultimate antichrist would be Satan, symbolized as a beast in the last book of the Bible, the Apocalypse, or Book of Revelation, by the writer known as Saint John the Divine. Tradition says that before the coming of the kingdom, a final War in Heaven, or Armageddon, will take place between the forces of good and those of evil. This idea owes much to similar traditions among the Babylonians, Iranians, and Jews.

ANTIGONE Antigone was the daughter of King Oedipus of Thebes and his mother-wife Jocaste. When her father had blinded himself and been exiled from Thebes after being revealed as the husband of his mother, the killer of his father, and the half brother of his children, Antigone accompanied her unfortunate father to Colonus, where he died. Sophocles tells of these events in his plays *Oedipus the King* and *Oedipus at Colonus*. Antigone is best known, however, for her deeds described in Sophocles's play *Antigone*.

After her father's death, Antigone returned to Thebes to find her two brothers Eteocles and Polynices fighting over the throne. When the brothers had succeeded in killing each other, Creon, who had taken over the crown and had supported Eteocles, refused to allow Polynices a proper burial. For Antigone this was sacrilege, and unaided by her much more passive sister Ismene, she defied the king and buried her brother. In the interest of public order, Creon felt obligated to punish his unrepentant niece and ordered her confined to a subterranean place, where she committed suicide. What Creon did not realize was that his son Haemon loved Antigone sufficiently to go to his own death at her side.

ANTIOPE This Theban woman was impregnated by the Greek god Zeus, who had taken the form of a satyr. She gave birth to future kings of Thebes, Amphion and Zetheus. There is some confusion between this Antiope and the sister of the Amazon queen Hippolyta. According to some sources, either Antiope or Hippolyta was the mother, by Theseus, of the tragic Hippolytus.

ANU Anu (Sumerian An) was a major god of the Sumerians, Akkadians, Babylonians, and Hittite-Hurrians of Mesopotamia. Originally, the cuneiform sign for An simply meant divinity, much as El or *il* or *ilah* (*al-ilah* _ Allah) signifies divinity in Semitic languages. An took on a specific personal nature, probably at Sumerian Uruk, by at least the middle of the second millennium B.C.E. In the Sumerian creation An is the son of the primeval waters and the goddess Nammu represents the heavens. He mates with his sister Ki (Earth), forming the universe, or An-Ki, and they produce the Sumerian pantheon. For the Akkadians, it was the primeval waters—Apsu, the sweet waters, and Tiamat, the salt waters—that produced Anu and other members of the pantheon. In Hittite-Hurrian mythology Anu plays a significant role in the leadership conflict described in the Kumarbi cycle. The Babylonians worshiped Anu as one of the major sky gods.

Satan (the Antichrist) attempts to influence Jesus

ANUBIS Anubis (Anpu) was the jackal-headed Egyptian funerary god. He is above all the god of embalming and in prehistoric times had probably been responsible, given his jackal nature, for the destruction of corpses. He played an important role in the Egyptian concept of life after death, serving as an assistant in the underworld to the god-king Osiris, whom he had embalmed and thus made the first mummy. He not only conducted souls to the afterlife realm of Osiris; he served there as a judge of souls. It was said by some that Anubis was the son of Osiris and Osiris's sister Nephtys. Priest-embalmers representing Anubis presided over ancient Egyptian ceremonies meant to revive the dead in the underworld.

ANUNNAKI The Anunnaki (Anunna, Anukki, Enunaki) are the Sumerian deities of the old primordial time; they are chthonic deities of fertility, associated eventually with the underworld, where they became judges. They take their name from the old sky god An (Anu).

AONGHUS Aonghus Og (Oenghus), son of the Dagda and Boann, and foster father to Diarmuid, was the beautiful love god of Irish mythology. Many stories are told of

him. In one known as "The Dream of Aonghus" he fell in love with Caer Ibormeith of Connacht. Aonghus asked the help of the rulers of Connacht, Ailill and Medb, to persuade Caer's father, Ethal Anubhail, to allow a marriage. But the girl's father said the marriage would probably not be possible because his daughter took the form of a swan among 150 other swans on Loch Bel Dragon. Only if the love god could identify his beloved and she agreed to the match would the marriage be possible. As it turned out, Aonghus did identify Caer, and they lived together at his palace by the Boyne River.

APHRODITE Although Aphrodite was said by the Greeks to be the daughter of Zeus and the nymph Dione, recent scholars believe she was a late, post-Mycenaean arrival in Greece from Phoenicia via Cyprus, a version of the Semitic fertility goddess Astarte. The Roman Venus, like her Greek counterpart, may have non–Greco-Roman and more generally Indo-European roots, too. Her name perhaps looks back to the neuter Vedic term for "desire," but under the Greek influence of Aphrodite she becomes distinctly feminine. Still, as the mother of Aeneas and, therefore, a patroness of Rome, she takes on the kind of stature

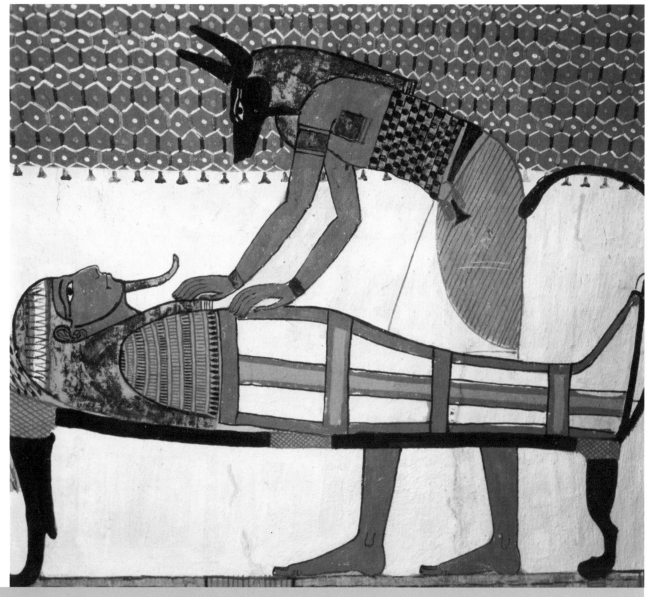

The Egyptian funerary god, Anubis, prepares King Tut for the afterlife

that Athenians gave to Pallas Athena rather than to Aphrodite, who in Greece was something of a spoiled daughter and a vamp.

When Ouranos's (Uranus, Uranos) genitals were cut off by Kronos, they were said to have landed in the ocean near Cyprus, the "foam" (semen) within them producing Aphrodite. The birth of this goddess, attended by Eros (later called her son), does not signify a return of goddess power. Just as goddesses like Artemis and Athena would be masculinized by the highly patriarchal, Zeus-dominated Olympian mythology, stripped of their earth-centered activities as goddesses of fertility and removed to the sky god home of Mount Olympus as virginal Amazon-like warriors or huntresses, Aphrodite would be associated in Greece not with the Indo-European ideal of sovereign power but with irrational passion. Her gift to the world is the madness called *aphrodisia*. Hesiod tells us that her role was to stimulate the joys of love and the guiles that women employ to seduce men. Aphrodite was married to the lame smith god Hephaistos, but she was known to stray. Not only did she love the young Adonis, but she had a well-publicized affair with her fellow Olympian Ares.

Homer has the blind bard Demodokos tell a wonderfully comic story of this affair. In Book 8 of the *Odyssey* he tells how the powerful Ares and the beautiful Aphrodite made love in the bed of Aphrodite 's lame husband, and how the wronged husband prepared a trap for the lovers when he discovered their treachery. He created a netting of chains around his bed and waited hidden until the lovers were at the very height of the act of love. Then he pulled a rope that released the trap, and the bed with the entwined lovers was raised to the ceiling, preventing either separation or escape. Hephaistos then called the gods together to mock the naked pair caught in their indecency.

APIS Sometimes worshipped as the Golden Calf, Apis was the bull god of Egypt. This was perhaps the idol wrongly worshipped by the biblical Hebrews in Exodus 32.

APOCALYPSE In religious studies the Apocalypse has a specific meaning relating to the meaning of the word in Greek, that is, "revelation," referring to a revealed future, usually eschatological, or having to do with the "last days." In the Judaic tradition there are the stories of the *Apocalypse of Abraham*, the *Life of Adam and Eve*, and the *Apocalypse of Baruch*. In Christianity the Apocalypse is synonymous with the final book of the Bible, the Book of Revelation, attributed to St. John the Divine. This book is perhaps the most obviously mythical work in the Christian canon, as well as the most mystical and the most allegorical. Revelation is a book of prophetic visions in which John sees such things as the destruction of the "harlot" Babylon, representing pagan Rome, and the seven-headed dragon, representing Satan, perhaps a Christian version of the ancient Mesopotamian Tiamat, destroyed by Marduk. It is the archangel Michael here (Revelation 12:9) who defeats the primal chaos. John also sees the marriage banquet of the Lamb, clearly the ultimate triumph of Christ in union with the Church. In John's view the clear choice is between worship of the Lamb and worship of the Beast (the Antichrist), that is, between Christ and Satan. The great Battle of Armageddon, echoing final battles in Babylonian, Iranian, and Jewish traditions, will be the climactic event in the struggle between good and evil. John ends his visions with the

Death, Famine, Pestilence, and War. Durer's Four Horsemen of the Apocalypse from the New Testament Book of Revelations

new Jerusalem, a metaphorical city representing the final perfection of God, and he hears the Christ calling the unified peoples to drink of the "water of life."

The word "apocalypse" has tended in mythological parlance to be synonomous with any end-of-the-world or eschatological myth, much as Armageddon has taken on the meaning of any great final struggle. The great battle at the end of the Hindu *Mahabharata* is certainly apocalyptic, and so is the Norse myth of the end of the world, *Ragnarok*.

APOLLO One of the most important of the Greek gods, Apollo (Apollon) was the son of Zeus and Leto (Roman Latona), the daughter of a Titan. The pregnant Leto, faced with the jealous anger of Zeus's wife, Hera, fled to the island of Delos in the Cyclades, where she gave birth to Apollo and his sister Artemis. Apollo was worshipped as the guardian of young men, Artemis as the guardian of young women.

Apollo was a complex god of many aspects. He was a god of light and sometimes specifically the sun; to the Romans, especially, he was Phoebus Apollo, the "pure shining" one. A great musician and divinity of the arts, he played the lyre to the delight of the other Olympians. He was also an archer and was sometimes depicted as a warrior. He decimated the Greek army at Troy with his fatal arrows.

Apollo, the Greek god of patriarchal law and moral order

Thus, Apollo is a healer, and the healer Asclepius is usually seen as his son. When Asclepius is killed by Zeus as punishment for his having raised a man from the dead, Apollo kills Zeus's followers the Cyclopes, and is in turn punished by his father by being made to serve Admetus in Thessaly as a herdsman for a year.

Like the other male Olympians, Apollo treated women casually. After kidnapping and raping the Athenian princess Creusa, he deserted both her and their child. Because he desired King Priam's daughter Cassandra, he gave her the gift of prophecy, but when she rejected him, he decreed that no one would ever believe her prophecies. Apollo was beautiful, but he could be dangerous.

APOLLODORUS Apollodorus is the second-century B.C.E. Athenian scholar to whom a primary compilation of Greek mythology, the *Bibliotheca* ("Library"), is perhaps falsely attributed.

APOLLONIUS OF RHODES Apollonios Rhodios lived in Alexandria in the third and second centuries B.C.E. and eventually became head of the great library there. He wrote the story of the voyage of the Argonauts and the Golden Fleece, the *Argonautica*.

APOPIS Apopis (Apophis, Apep) was the Egyptian serpent that attempted every night to overcome the barque of the sun god as it made its nightly passage through the Duat, the underworld of the sky, to the horizon, where it rose again in glory.

APOTHEOSIS Derived from the Greek *apo* ("from") and *theoun* ("to deify"), a mythical hero or heroine's apotheosis marks the raising of a human from the level of a mortal to that of a god. Often the gods make humans with whom they have had relations stars, as in the cases of the Greeks Andromeda and Ariadne or Callisto in the Artemis myth. Ascension is a means by which heroes are clearly recognized as divinities. Herakles at the end of his mortal life is raised to the heavens. And so the resurrected Jesus is taken up to Heaven, as is his mother, Mary, in the tradition of the Assumption.

APPLES OF THE HESPERIDES For the eleventh of his Twelve Labors, Herakles was sent to fetch the golden apples of the Hesperides, which had been a wedding gift to Hera from the Greek earth goddess Gaia. The apples were cared for by the seven Hesperides on Mount Atlas, daughters of the Titan Atlas and Hesperus. Their helper in guarding the apples was the dragon Ladon, which Herakles probably killed when he finally discovered where the apples were. After almost being tricked by Atlas into holding up the world for him forever, Herakles managed to get the apples.

APSU Apsu (Sumerian Abzu) referred to the extensive underground sweet waters that produced the southern marshlands of Mesopotamia (southern Iraq). The Sumerians saw Abzu as the home of the wise god Enki (Akkadian Ea). Some Sumerians held that Nammu, the goddess who may be said to be a personification of Abzu, created the first humans from the sweet waters. The Babylonians made Apsu into a personal deity who, with the female salt-water primeval being Tiamat, generated the Babylonian pantheon. In this myth cycle, contained in the Babylonian creation epic, the *Enuma elish*, Ea (Enki) eventually kills Apsu in the strug-

Perhaps most important, he was associated with the great prophetic center of Delphi. His motto, made so poignantly relevant in the tragic story of Oedipus, is "Know thyself." Apollo is a version, like the Vedic Indra and Rudra (later Shiva) and the Babylonian Marduk, of the god-hero who defeats the primeval, chaotic monster—in this case, the Python at the foot of Mount Parnassus near Delphi. Thus Apollo is Pythian Apollo, and Delphi was the center of his oracular cult, where Greeks from very ancient times went for divine direction. Almost always the monster-dragon-serpent is associated with the chthonic powers of the ancient Great Mother, whose powers are then taken over by the Indo-European patriarchy. In the case of the Greeks, this takeover is indicated not only by the replacement of the Goddess cult at Delphi—originally Delphi was the sacred precinct of Gaia—with that of Apollo, but also by the myth of the trial of Orestes at Athens for the revenge killing of his mother, Clytemnestra. At that trial, as depicted by Aeschylus in the *Eumenides*, the final portion of the *Oresteia*, Apollo absolves Orestes on the grounds that the mother is not the real parent, only the vessel of the seed placed there by the father.

Apollo, then, is the god of patriarchal law and moral order. Whereas Dionysos, in a sense his opposite, personifies ecstasy, Apollo is Greek moderation, balance, and form. Both Dionysian and Apollonian qualities, of course, are necessary for great art, and both gods are associated with the arts; the Muses were among Apollo's companions. Law and order, balance and form, apply to the body as well.

gle between the old, primitive deities and the new order led by Marduk.

ARA AND IRIK Ara and Irik are the first beings in the creation myth of the Iban people in Borneo. In the form of birds they plucked two primal eggs from the primeval waters, and Ara made the sky from his egg while Irik made the earth from hers. The first pair also created the first humans.

ARABIAN MYTHOLOGY Muslims consider the pre-Islamic age as the *Jahiliyah*, or "Age of Ignorance"—that is, the time before the revelations of Allah (al-Lah, "the god") to his prophet Muhammad. The Arabs were Semitic peoples of the Arabian Peninsula who spoke a language closely related to the languages of the Palestinian and Mesopotamian Semites, including, of course, the Hebrews. Arab culture, like that of the early Hebrews, would have been centered in kinship, clans, and tribes. Their presence as organized groups in the peninsula has been dated as early as 1200 B.C.E. The Queen of Saba's visit to King Solomon in Jerusalem would have been early in the first millennium B.C.E. Sabaeans are listed in Assyrian documents by the eighth century B.C.E. Inscriptions describe an outpost in Ethiopia in the fifth century B.C.E., and Sabaeans are mentioned by classical writers beginning in the fourth century B.C.E. The fertile land of the southern peninsula, known in ancient times as Arabia Felix, in what is now Yemen, gave rise to several centers of commerce, trade, and culture in addition to Saba, which gradually gained ascendancy over the other centers. These were city-states ruled by priest-kings (*mukarribs*) or kings (*maliks*). Among the more important states were Ma'in, Qataban, and Hadhramat.

Intertribal warfare and religions with many idols would have been characteristic of the earliest history of the Arabs. The Bedouin tribes of the mid-peninsula—around the regions of Hijaz (containing Mecca and Medina) and Najd (containing Riyhad)—were constantly at war. But even early on there appears to have been a sense of pan-Arabism, as indicated by a tradition of annual gatherings of tribes for poetry competitions—a kind of poetic Olympic Games—and the development of a common way of life based on the concept of *muruwah*. *Muruwah* obligated a man to obey his overlord, or *sayyid*, and to accept the communal ideal of the blood feud, in which revenge for murder could be taken on any member of the murderer's tribe as a substitute for the murderer himself. In general, *muruwah* also provided a sense of the importance of community as opposed to the individual, of generosity as opposed to material need. All of

Remains of the 5th century B.C.E. Temple of the Arabian Moon god at Marib in the Kingdom of Saba (Sheba, Yemen)

these concepts would be important to the later emergence of Islam.

By the time of Muhammad, Arabia had long been taken advantage of by various powers. Persians from an early date had controlled the area around Saba. Although there had been Arab kingdoms as far north as Syria and Iraq—one was led by Queen Zenobia—they were annexed by the Romans in the second and third centuries C.E. Later Byzantine Christians would establish Christian Arab kingdoms in Syria and Iraq and elsewhere in the Middle East. Not long before Muhammad's birth, Christian Abyssinians had come up from Yemen and invaded Mecca.

Pre-Islamic Arabia—before it was influenced through various conquests by Judaism, Christianity, and perhaps Zoroastrianism—was polytheistic in its religion. Jinn (spirits) were worshipped, and various tribal groups worshipped their own, often astral, deities. Cult centers were marked by temples and by holy stones (*baetyls*) representing these and other tribal deities. Also, sacred trees could serve as cult centers. Muhammad's tribe, the Quraysh, for instance, worshipped a great tree called the *Dhat Anwat* on the road between Mecca and Medina.

Given the nomadic nature of many of the tribes, objects—especially stones—in any given place could be invested temporarily with the sacred and used as a focus of worship. An ancient, permanent sacred stone cult center for the tribes of the Hijaz (western Arabia), the land of Muhammad's tribe, as well as of other Arabs, was the Ka'bah in Mecca, with its mysterious Black Stone. Even in pre-Islamic times the Ka'bah was a pilgrimage center and sanctuary surrounded by some 360 idols, but there are indications that some Meccans even before the time of Muhammad were moving toward a concept of a single divine power, *al-ilah* or *al-lah* ("the god"), a supreme divinity behind the tribal gods of Arabia, such as Wadd, Suwa, Yaghuth, Ya'uq, and Nasr in southern Arabia—several of whom, according to the *Qur'an* (71:23), were worshipped in the days of Nuh (Noah). Some Meccans had perhaps even worshipped Allah as their high god. Scholars have pointed out that when Muhammad began his preaching, the Quraysh already believed in al-Lah and that many "believed him to be the God worshipped by the Jews and Christians," with whom they had frequent contacts. These Meccans apparently believed that the Ka'bah had, in the beginning, been dedicated to this deity, in spite of the supreme presence there of the Nabatean warrior rain god Hubal, the tutelary deity of Mecca.

Goddesses played an important role in pre-Islamic Arabian religion and mythology. Manat, Allat (al-Lat, the "Goddess"), and al-Uzza are all mentioned in the *Qur'an* (53:19–22). Manat was worshipped in Qudayd, near Mecca, and in northern Arabia. She was a goddess of rain, health, victory, and destiny and was particularly honored during the pre-Islamic pilgrimages to the Ka'bah. Allat was popular in Taif, also close to Mecca. There she was represented by a large, flat stone and smaller precious stones kept in a wooden box. Called the Mother of the Gods and Mother of the Sun, she protected travelers. Al-Uzza was the primary goddess of the Quraysh. She seems to have been a love goddess whose worship took place in a sanctuary made up of three trees, a fact that associates her with the Canaanite-Hebrew Asherah. Together these Arabic goddesses were the *banat al-Lah* (the "Daughters of God") and were much revered by the Meccans at various stone shrines.

ARACHNE The Lydian maiden Arachne was so proud of her abilities as a weaver that she challenged the goddess Athena to a weaving competition. Arachne's finished work depicted the love affairs of the gods. Athena was so impressed that she tore the cloth to pieces in a rage of envy. Poor, despairing Arachne hanged herself but was released by the goddess, who turned the hanging rope into a web and the girl into a spider, a primary member of a class of beings to which we apply the name *arachnid*, after the Greek word for spider (*arakhne*).

ARAMEAN MYTHOLOGY The Arameans were one of many Semitic-speaking peoples of the area that includes what was once known as the land of Canaan. By the eleventh century B.C.E. the Arameans, who had been in the area at least since the third millennium B.C.E., controlled northern Syria with their capital at Damascus and were a major force in the Middle East until their defeat by the Assyrians in the eighth and seventh centuries B.C.E. Even after their defeat, however, the Arameans retained significant cultural influence through their language and mythology. Because of the efficiency of the Aramaic alphabet as opposed to cuneiform, Aramaic became the diplomatic and commercial lingua franca of the neo-Assyrian Empire. Population exchanges after the Assyrians defeated Israel in 722 B.C.E. made Aramaic the common language of the Samaria and Galilee areas of that country. Later it served as the vernacular language of the exiles in Babylon and of the returnees to Israel in the sixth century. The position of the language was solidified by the arrival in the sixth century of the Persians, who used Aramaic as their administrative language. Although Hebrew remained the literary language of the Jews, their common language for some time was Aramaic. This was so much the case that in the fifth century B.C.E. Aramaic translations of the *Torah* (*targumin*) were deemed necessary. Jesus spoke Aramaic, and later Syriac, an eastern Aramaic dialect, became an important liturgical and literary language of Middle Eastern Christians.

Although little is known of it, Aramean mythology, dominated by the benevolent weather-storm-fertility god Hadad, seems at first to have been significantly different from that of either the Mesopotamians or the Canaanites, Israelites, and other tribes in the area. Gradually, however, under Assyrian dominance, much of Mesopotamian religion was assimilated by the Arameans; and still later, during the fourth century B.C.E., under the Seleucids, there are strong Phoenician and Greek influences. In addition to their storm god with a strong fertility aspect, the Arameans assimilated several goddesses from Mesopotamia and Phoenicia.

The Aramean high god, Hadad, was the counterpart of the Mesopotamian-Assyrian weather-storm-fertility god Adad. He was sometimes combined with or displaced by the Canaanite Baal—as Baal-Hadad or at least as the *baal*, or "lord," in his form as the moon god Sin or Sahar—and later he was associated with the Greek Zeus and Roman Jupiter.

ARANRHOD The daughter of the Welsh Mother Goddess Don, Aranrhod was the sister of Gwydion. The best-known story of Aranrhod has to do with Gwydion and Math, son of Mathonwy, who had to sleep with his feet on the lap of a virgin. When Math's foot holder was abducted by Gilfaethwy, Gwydion suggested that his sister Aranrhod could take her place. But as she steps over Math's magic wand to prove her virginity, two baby boys drop from her womb. The first child, who was ever after known as Dylan Eil Ton ("Dylan, Son of the Wave"), leapt into the sea, like Balarama, the brother of the Hindu Vishnu avatar Lord Krishna. The second child was quickly whisked up by Gwydion and hidden in a chest. He was later named Lleu Llaw Gyffes.

ARANYAKAS *Aranyakas* are Vedic texts in Hindu India meant to comment on the earlier sacred texts, the *Brahmanas.*

ARCADIAN STAG A great beast with golden antlers and brazen hooves, this animal, taken alive, was the objective of the third of the Twelve Labors of Herakles. After pursuing it for a year, the hero wounded it and carried it back to his taskmaster Eurystheus on his back.

ARCHETYPES Many thinkers have used the term "archetype" in slightly different ways in connection with mythology. The two modern myth scholars who have made the most use of it are Carl Jung and Mircea Eliade. Although he used the term somewhat differently at various stages of his life, Jung thought of archetypes as universal psychic tendencies or "primordial images" of a "collective unconscious" that, when given individual or cultural form—in dreams, art, or literary expressions such as myths and fairy tales, and later, literature—became universally familiar human motifs. These motifs, then—the trickster, the father god, the hero and his monomyth, the flood, and so many more—wear various individual and cultural masks but strike a familiar chord in people everywhere. Ananse is clearly a trickster, and an African will recognize Coyote and Raven, for instance, as Ananse 's archetypal Native North American relatives. The reader of the Osiris and Jesus resurrection myths will recognize in these heroes' overcoming of death a common human concern or "thought."

Eliade 's use of "archetype" is more religious and less psychological than Jung's. For him archetypes are "sacred paradigms" or "exemplary models" that characterize the sacred or transcendent aspect of life that springs from primordial "myth time"—archetypal time—as opposed to the profane aspect of life, that which is dominated by material things and linear time. Eliade believes, however, that the sacred can appear to the archetypally oriented person in the world of the profane through various revelations or hierophanies.

AREOP-ENAP Areop-Enap was the spider god of the Nauru people of Micronesia, who created the heavens and the earth in a way that resembles the process in the earth-diver creation myths of several North American Indian and Central Asian peoples. The creator found a clamshell and asked various animals to help him open it. Finally, a caterpillar succeeded but died in the process. Still, his sweat in the bottom shell became the sea and he became the sun. The top of the clamshell became the sky.

ARES One of the Greek Olympians, Ares was the god of war. The son of Zeus and Hera, he participated enthusiastically with other gods in the Trojan War, as described by Homer in the *Iliad*. A comic story is told of his affair with Aphrodite, who, according to some, was his sister and who was married at the time to their brother or half brother, the smith god Hephaistos. Homer has the blind bard Demodokos—per-

haps a self-portrait—tell the story of the affair. He tells how the powerful Ares and the beautiful Aphrodite made love in the bed of Aphrodite 's lame husband, and how the wronged husband prepared a trap for the lovers when he discovered their treachery. He created a netting of chains around his bed and waited hidden until the lovers began making love. Then he pulled a rope that released the trap, and the bed with the entwined lovers was raised to the ceiling, preventing either separation or escape and causing humiliation.

ARGONAUTICA This third-century B.C.E. epic poem, usually translated as the *Voyage of the Argonauts*, by Apollonius Rhodius (Apollonius of Rhodes) tells the story of Jason, Medea, Jason's companions (the Argonauts), and the quest for the Golden Fleece of a ram, a story that was well known at least as early as Homer's time. Many events in the Apollonian epic are reminiscent of the *Odyssey*.

King Pelias of Iolcus in Greece, a son of the god Poseidon by a mortal woman, wished to rid himself of his nephew Jason, the rightful heir to the throne he had usurped. Pelias promised to give up the throne to Jason only in return for the achievement of what he thought was an

Jason, hero of the *Argonautica*, wins the Golden Fleece

impossible task. He required that Jason go to Aea (Colchis) to retrieve the Golden Fleece, which was hanging from an oak tree in a grove sacred to Ares and which was protected by a dragon.

Jason sailed away on his mission on a ship named *Argo*, after Argus, its builder. Jason's fifty companions on his great adventure were known as the Argonauts (sailors of the *Argo*). They included, among others, the heroes Herakles, Castor and Pollux, Orpheus, Admetus, and Theseus.

The Argonauts had many adventures on their way to Colchis. They spent a pleasant time with the women of Lemnos, who had killed their husbands the year before and were starved for love. Later they were entertained by the Doliones, but after they left that land they were blown back to it and attacked by the Doliones, who did not recognize them. In the ensuing battle Jason killed their king. While staying with the people of Bebryces, the hero Polydeuces killed their king in a boxing match. In Salmydessus the Argonauts saved Phineus, the blind king of that land, from the Harpies. The grateful Phineus told them how to avoid being destroyed between the clashing Cyanean rocks by sending a dove between them, waiting while the rocks clashed, and then rushing through as the rocks moved apart. After driving away attacking birds of Ares, the heroes rescued the shipwrecked sons of Jason's cousin Phrixus, who once, when about to be sacrificed to Zeus, had been saved by Hermes' ram of the Golden Fleece.

The sons of Phrixus led the Argonauts to Colchis, where King Aeetes agreed to give up the Golden Fleece only if Jason succeeded in harnessing two fire-spouting bulls to plow a field. With the help of Aeetes' sorcerer daughter Medea, who had fallen hopelessly in love with him, Jason accomplished this seemingly impossible task and, after sowing the field with dragon teeth, overcame the armed men who sprung from the sown teeth. But Aeetes reneged on his promise, and Jason once again had to depend on help from Medea. The witch put the guardian dragon to sleep with her magic, and Jason obtained the fleece and escaped with it and Medea from Colchis. When the men of Colchis gave chase, Medea killed her own brother and scattered his dismembered body in the path of the pursuers to slow them down.

This horrendous murder deeply angered Zeus, who placed many difficulties before the Argonauts on their way home. After being purged by Aeetes' sister Circe of the murder of Medea's brother, the Argonauts were helped through the dangerous Wandering Rocks by Achilles' mother, Thetis. Then Orpheus disarmed the Sirens by outsinging them. And after Medea overcame the bronze giant Tolus of Crete with her magic, preventing him from destroying the *Argo*, the Argonauts arrived home at Iolcus.

According to many sequels to the *Argonautica*, the adventures of Jason and Medea did not end here. Wherever they went, sorcery and devious acts went with them.

ARGONAUTS The heroes of the *Argonautica*.

ARGOS As a place name, Argos is used in various ways in Greek mythology. Homer uses it to refer sometimes to the kingdom of Agamemnon, with its capital at Mycenae, and sometimes to the whole of the Peloponnesus, making the Greeks the "Argives." He also mentions the specific town of Argos, of which the hero Diomedes was the leader.

ARGULA Argula is a trickster among the aboriginal people of western Kimberley in Australia. Traditionally,

he paints ritual pictures of people who have committed wrongs, and who will die when insulting songs are sung to the pictures.

ARHAT In Buddhism, the arhat is literally one who is at the final stage before enlightenment. He is, therefore, worthy of special respect. Usually the arhat is an ascetic. He is no longer attached to the world of form and the senses. For Hinayana and Theravada Buddhists there can be only one Buddha in any era, and in our era Gautama Buddha, "*the* Buddha," has already existed. Therefore, the state of the arhat is the highest achievable for others. The reformist Mahayana Buddhists consider the arhat idea a self-centered concept and have generally substituted for it the ideal of the bodhisattva, who could become a buddha but chooses rather to work with compassion in this world for the enlightenment of others.

ARIADNE The daughter of King Minos and Queen Pasiphae of Crete, Ariadne fell in love with the young Theseus when he came to Crete intending to put an end to the forced annual tribute-sacrifice of Athenian youths to the Minotaur. Ariadne betrayed her father by helping Theseus to escape the Minotaur's Labyrinth by way of a thread that followed the hero's path through what was, in fact, a maze, after he had succeeded in slaying the monster. Theseus had promised marriage in return for Ariadne's help, and he took the girl with him when he left Crete. According to Homer, she was killed by Artemis on the island of Naxos, but more often it is said that Theseus deserted Ariadne on Naxos and that she either died giving birth to a child or was taken up by Dionysos as his wife and placed forever among the stars. Later Theseus would marry Ariadne's sister Phaedra, who, in earlier Minoan mythology, may have been a Cretan goddess.

ARJUNA The third of the five Pandava brothers, who struggle against their Kaurava cousins in the Hindu epic the *Mahabharata*, Arjuna is the recipient of Lord Krishna's teachings in the part of the epic called the *Bhagavadgita*.

ARK In Genesis 6 the story is told of Noah, who built an ark to save his family and pairs of animals from the great flood sent by Yahweh (God).

ARK OF THE COVENANT The Ark of the Covenant (*aron haberith*) was given to the Israelites by Yahweh (God) during their wanderings in the wilderness. It was intended to contain the tablets of the covenant given by God to Moses. The Ark was captured by the Philistines, but later recovered and placed in the Holy of Holies, the sanctuary of the Temple at Jerusalem. When the first temple was destroyed in 586 B.C.E. by the Babylonians, the Ark was lost. Since then many stories have circulated as to its whereabouts. Some even say it rests in a small church in Ethiopia.

ARMAGEDDON Armageddon is the place in the New Testament Book of Revelation (16:16) where the final battle will be fought between the forces of good and those of evil. The word has come to have general apocalyptic, eschatological significance, referring to any ultimate or final battle or struggle. One could say, for instance, that Ragnarok is the Norse Armageddon. In the Hebrew Bible, Armageddon is *Haer Megiddon*, a famous battlefield in the Old Testament books of Judges and Kings.

ARMAITI One of the Amesa Spentas or major deities associated with the Zoroastrian supreme god Ahura Mazda, Spenta Armaiti, or Spendarmat in Pahlavi, is the goddess of the earth and is the essence of devotion and fidelity. Tradition says that she once appeared to Zoroaster.

ARMENIAN MYTHOLOGY The mythology of the Indo-European Armenian (Hay) people, who came to Anatolia as early as the middle of the second millennium B.C.E., was probably a mixture of assimilated proto-Greek and Middle Eastern elements, such as the god Tork, based in all likelihood on a Hittite deity and who for the Armeneans was probably an underworld god, and the Mithra-like Mher. The name Hay is derived from the story of the eponymous hero Hayk, who lived in Babylon and led a rebellion against the Babylonian king, Bel, supposedly sometime in the first millennium B.C.E. Contained in a work known as the *Primary History*, probably written down sometime between the fifth and seventh centuries C.E., the story tells how Hayk led his people to Armenia. Included in the history is the story of Hayk's descendant Ara, who died and was in a sense resurrected.

Conquered by the Medes in the sixth century B.C.E. and later by the Persians, the Armenians assimilated aspects of the mythologies of these peoples, especially Zoroastrianism, including the supreme deity, Aramazd (Ahura Mazda). Vahagn was another name for the supreme deity. They also assimilated the Phrygian goddess Cybele, whom they worshipped as Nane.

The conversion of the Armenians from what was essentially a monotheistic-leaning Zoroastrianism to Christianity took place in the fourth century C.E. [Russell]

ARTEMIS One of the major Olympian goddesses of Greece, Artemis was the sister of Apollo, born of Leto by Zeus. Zeus loved her dearly and gave her many special gifts, especially a silver bow made by the Cyclopes. Artemis put the bow to good use as a huntress. She was also a militant virgin, as a young man named Acteon discovered. After purely by chance coming upon her bathing in the forest, poor Acteon was changed into a stag and hunted down by Artemis's dogs for his "sin." Artemis was sometimes associated with the moon, as her brother was with the sun. Artemis's real sources are probably in the Middle East, where she would have been a much more sexual goddess associated with fecundity and birth. The famous Artemis of Ephesus is depicted with many breasts, and even in Greece she is the goddess of childbirth, an aspect indicated by the fact that Leto gave birth to her without the usual pains associated with the process.

Artemis, like the other Olympians, could cause great pain to humans. She played an important role in the story of the sacrifice of Iphigenia and in that of the ruthless killing of the children of Niobe, who had made the mistake of boasting that they were more beautiful than the children of Leto. When one of her own followers, the nymph Callisto, had an affair with Zeus, Artemis became so angry that she turned the girl into a bear and set her hounds on her. Zeus plucked up the bear and flung her into the sky to become the constellation Ursa Major (the Great Bear).

ARYAMAN Aryaman is one of the Vedic Indian Adityas. He is associated with rulership.

Ariadne deserted and alone on the Island of Naxos

Artemis, the goddess of hunting, fights a group of giants

ARYANS The so-called Aryans (Sanskrit *arya*, Old Iranian *airya*) were Indo-European tribes who migrated from Eastern Europe to Central Asia and beyond in the third millennium B.C.E. They were patriarchal warriors who brought powerful male gods with them as they migrated eventually into Greece, Anatolia, the Fertile Crescent, Iran, and India. For some time (c. 2200–2000 B.C.E.), the Aryan ancestors of the later Indians and Iranians (Persians) lived in the same region—probably around Balkh—and developed the Vedic (after the *Vedas*) and Avestan (after the *Avesta*) traditions that were the source for later Zoroastrianism and Hinduism. Thus we have the term "Indo-Iranian," which is often used synonymously with "Aryan." The Indo-Iranian gods were divided into Asura (Ahura in Iran) and Deva (Daeva in Iran). The proto-religion was based on a universal law that became the Vedic *rta* and the Avestan *asa*. The Vedic supervisor of the law was Varuna and the Avestan head god was Ahura Mazda. During the migration to India and the wars involved with it, the cult of Indra as king of the gods developed. Fire worship was central to the Aryans and to their Vedic and Avestan expressions, as was the tradition of the holy drink—the Vedic *soma* and the Avestan *haoma*. Powerful sacred verses, or *mantras*, and hymns were important to both groups. There was the hope of an afterlife and there were sacrificial rituals. Aryans generally looked down on the darker-skinned "barbarian" peoples they conquered—especially in India. The mytho-religious system of the Indo-Aryans is revealed by what we now call the Vedic texts, the best known of which is the *Rig Veda*. Hinduism developed from the Vedic tradition in India and

Zoroastrianism out of the early Aryan religion and mythology expressed eventually in the *Avesta* in Iran.

ASASE YA The earth goddess of the Ashanti people in Africa, Asase Ya is the wife of the sky god Nyame. She is the mother of the storm and river god Tano.

ASCANIUS The son of the Roman hero Aeneas of Virgil's *Aeneid*, and sometimes known as Iulus, Ascanius was traditionally the ancestor of Julius Caesar and the builder of the city Alba Longa, the forerunner of Rome. See *Aeneid* and Roman mythology.

ASCENSION According to Christian scripture (Acts 1:9), Jesus ascended to Heaven to join God, his father, forty days after the Resurrection. Traditionally this happened at the Mount of Olives, near Jerusalem. Islam also celebrates an ascension (*Miraj*), Muhammad's ascent to heaven from the Al-Aqsa Mosque, also in Jerusalem. In myths such as that of Herakles, the raising up of the hero to the heavens is an apotheosis, an elevation to the level of divinity. It can be said reasonably that ascension is always closely related to apotheosis.

ASCLEPIUS A Greek physician and sometimes god, Asclepius (Aesculapius) was fathered by Apollo and taught healing and hunting by the centaur Chiron. Asclepius became so good at healing—he could even raise the dead—that the jealous Zeus killed him with a thunderbolt. Upset by this, Apollo convinced Zeus to revive the master physician and place him in the heavens as a star. Asclepius's cult center was at Epidaurus. He was also popular in Rome. Because they were symbols of regeneration, serpents were associated with him.

ASGARD The Norse gods known as the Aesir lived in a heavenly realm ruled by Odin called Asgard. This place, which contained the great hall known as Valhalla, was separated from Jotunheim below, the place of the gods known as the Vanir, by a bridge, Bifrost (perhaps the Milky Way), guarded by Heimdall.

ASHA One of the Ameshas of Iranian Zoroastrianism, Asha (Arta or Ashavahisht) was the guardian of fire and of moral and physical order.

ASHERAH Originally a Canaanite mother goddess—perhaps Athirat—Asherah was sometimes seen as the wife of the father god El or Sumerian An (Anu). As a mother goddess associated with moisture—she is "Lady of the Sea" as well as "Mother of the Gods"—she has similarities to the Sumerian goddesses Ninhursag and Nammu and even the Egyptian Isis. Asherah was associated with the Tree of Life and was worshipped in groves. At times it is difficult to tell, in the Hebrew scriptures, for instance, whether Asherah is a goddess or a carved image. Such images, *asherim*, were placed on altars and in groves and even in the Jerusalem Temple of the Israelites. It is believed that Asherah became a figure of Hebrew worship through a Canaanite wife of King Solomon. Under King Ahab and his Canaanite wife Jezebel, Asherah was worshipped with her son Baal. In spite of frequent and determined efforts of the Hebrew prophets to stamp out Asherah worship, the veneration of Asherah persisted among the Hebrews. It is likely that some believed that, as she had been the wife of El, she was the wife of Elohim/ Yahweh.

The biblical book of Jeremiah (44:1–28) contains a confrontation between the prophet and the people of Judea. Jeremiah scolds the people for their idol worship. The people answer him:

> We are not going to listen to what you tell us in the name of the Lord. We intend to fulfill all the vows by which we have bound ourselves: we shall burn sacrifices to the queen of heaven and pour drink-offerings to her as we used to do, we and our forefathers, our kings and leaders, in the towns of Judah and in the streets of Jerusalem. Then we had food in plenty and were content; no disaster touched us. But from the time we left off burning sacrifices to the queen of heaven and pouring drink offerings to her, we have been in great want, and we have fallen victim to sword and famine.

We learn in 2 Kings 23:15 that the King of Judah "burned Asherah" in the late seventh century B.C.E., perhaps putting an end to her worship.

ASHUR The eponymous Ashur was the leading Assyrian deity. His Semitic roots were in northern Mesopotamia. Ashur assimilated the characteristics of many chief gods of the region. Enlil, Anu, Samas, and even Marduk, whose son Nabu was particularly popular among the Assyrians, were all mythological relatives. It was believed that Ashur was married to Ishtar (as Ishtar Ashuritum) or Ninlil (called Mullissu in Assyria). His emblem, like that of Marduk, was the ser-

pent-dragon. His horned cap was like those of Anu and Enlil.

ASHVINS The Ashvins are twin horse gods, sons of the sun and a mare, who father the Pandava twins Nakula and Sahadeva with Pandu's wife, Madri, in the Hindu epic the *Mahabharata*.

ASSUMPTION In Catholic Christian tradition, the Assumption is the bodily taking up (assuming) of the Virgin Mary to Heaven after her death. It resembles the Ascension of Jesus.

ASSYRIAN MYTHOLOGY In about 1170 B.C.E. Hittite Hattusa fell to invaders, probably the so-called Sea People, an Indo-European group probably of Aegean/south European origin from the west, and the Hittite time in history essentially came to an end. When the Hittites abandoned Babylonia, the Kassites, other Indo-Europeans from the eastern mountains, moved in and ruled for some

Jesus ascends to Heaven in the presence of his disciples

time, but they were always challenged by the Assyrians, a Semitic people who had established trading colonies in the north of Mesopotamia late in the third millennium, and who by 2300 B.C.E. had become a small kingdom of which the capital was Ashur. Ashur had been conquered by Sargon of Akkad in 2300 but had regained independence with the fall of the Ur III dynasty, only to be reconquered by the Amorites and Hurrians. But when the Hurrian Empire collapsed in about 1360, the Assyrians once again became independent and maintained that independence in wars against not only the Hurrians but also the Kassites. In 1225 B.C.E. the Assyrians, under King Tukulti-Ninurta (Nimrod) defeated the Kassites and briefly took over Babylon. A rebellion and a series of invasions by the Sea People led to the withdrawal of the Assyrians back to the north and the return of the Kassites to Babylon before they in turn were defeated by the Elamites, who took the much-fought-over statue of the Babylonian city god Marduk as booty to Elam. At the end of the millennium King Nebuchadrezzar I of Isin liberated Babylonia from Elam and brought back the Marduk statue.

For some time, beginning at the turn of the millennium, the Assyrians had been a potent force in the Middle East. In fact, the first half of the first millennium is usually referred to as the neo-Assyrian period. Assyrian power became particularly formidable under a self-proclaimed king, Tiglath-Pileser III, who took power in Ashur in 745. With an advanced Iron Age army, including huge battering devices and a cavalry of archers, the Assyrians defeated the Arameans of Syria and in 721 Israel. According to their custom, as a way of preventing future rebellions or the reestablishment of defeated nations, the Assyrians took away thousands of Israelites as slaves. Judah, too, was besieged, but Jerusalem was spared in return for a large ransom. Soon the Assyrians had conquered Egypt, which had weakened after internal struggles. In 671 they captured Memphis, and in 663 Ashurbanipal conquered and sacked Thebes. By 640 B.C.E. the Assyrian Empire covered Mesopotamia, Egypt, Palestine, Syria, and much of Asia Minor. Judah survived as a puppet state under King Manasseh. During his reign the Yahweh religion shared space with that of the Assyrians and Canaanites.

The later years of the Assyrian Empire saw the building of roads, bridges, and complex water systems as well as the development of law courts and great cultural centers such as the library at Nineveh. The empire suffered at the end, however, from a civil war between the brothers Ashurbanipal, whose base was Nineveh, and Shamash-sum-ukin, who ruled the area around Babylon.

The Assyrians tended to assimilate the mythologies of their neighbors and conquered subjects. One seemingly local Assyrian god in Ashur was Adad, the Thor of Assyria, whose name probably means "thunder." Like other thunder gods he was also a warrior god who could devastate the land of Assyria's enemies. Another Assyrian war god was the old Sumerian Ninurta. The most important of the Assyrian gods, however, was the eponymous Ashur.

ASTARTE This important goddess in ancient Canaan was called Ashtoreth in Hebrew and was possibly identical to the goddess named Anath. Like the Sumerian/Babylonian Inanna/Ishtar, with whom Anath has connections, Astarte is the "Queen of Heaven." It was said that she was either the child of Asherah, like Anath, or simply an aspect of Asherah. In some Ugaritic texts, Astarte rather than Asherah is

mentioned as El's wife and "Mother of the Gods," and she was known in some places as "Lady Asherah of the Sea." She was assimilated in Babylon as Asratu, wife of Amurru, who was the son of the god Anu. Whatever her form or true origins, Astarte was a particularly important figure in the Middle East, with palace-temples at places such as Sidon and Byblos. She is associated not only with the sea but with the moon and the morning and evening stars. Astarte had mythological "sisters" not only in such diverse fertility figures as Inanna/Ishtar and Asratu but also in Aphrodite and Artemis in Greece, Cybele in Phrygia, and Isis and Hathor in Egypt.

ASTROLOGY AND MYTH Astrology assumes a synchronicity between the psychic lives of people and the positions of the planets and stars in the heavens at the time of birth. Thus certain characteristics are associated with various celestial archetypes represented by the planets, themselves named after Greco-Roman deities, and certain related signs of the zodiac from Pisces to Aries. For example, the archetype of Neptune (Poseidon), Pisces, is associated with the primordial waters of chaos and the eternal mysteries of the soul; that of Ouranos (Uranos), Aquarius, is the light of the heavens, born, like Ouranos, of the primordial chaos. The sign of Capricorn is centered in the Saturn (Kronos) archetype associated with time and its constant passing toward fate. Sagittarius is the archetype of Jupiter (Zeus), born of Saturn, and is tied to the idea of the sacred king. Jupiter's brother Pluto (Hades) gives his name to Scorpio and the sense of the hidden inner world. Libra is the archetype of Jupiter's son Vulcan (Hephaistos), who, as the master smith, stands for culture. Various mythological figures other than the Greco-Roman ones have been associated with the signs of the zodiac. The chaotic Babylonian mother goddess Tiamat is a natural Pisces. All of the Indo-European sky gods are Aquarius figures. The sacred kings of ancient Mesopotamia are Sagittarius figures.

ASTRONOMY AND MYTH Cultures at least as early as the Sumerians attached mythological animals to various constellations—the bull and the lion, for example. Later Homer found even more mythological significance in the stars. When in the *Iliad* he describes the shield made by Hephaistos for Achilles, he mentions the existence on it of depictions of the constellations, including the Pleiades, Orion, and the Bear, which take their names from mythological tales. Later, in fifth-century Athens, the whole sky was essentially mapped in mythological terms. In many cases the stars were seen as divine bodies placed in the sky by Zeus. Europa and Ganymede are such bodies. Several modern thinkers, most especially Girgio de Santillana and Hertha von Dechend in their *Hamlet's Mill* (1969), have posited a common origin of myths in the human study of the celestial bodies. For them, mythology was an astronomical language.

ASTYANAX The son of Hector and Andromache in Homer's *Iliad*, Astyanax (Scamandrius) was hurled by the Greeks to his death from the walls of defeated Troy.

ASURAS In a sense, asuras are demons in Hindu mythology. That is, they oppose the devas—the celestial gods. But taken individually they are of equal status with the devas, and a great god such as Varuna can be an asura. In the Vedic tradition, devas and asuras are both offspring of the Creator Prajapati, or later of Brahma. But the constant struggle between these two forces is a theme of later Hindu mythology, in which the devas occupy Heaven, humans the earth, and asuras the dark depths.

ASVINAI The Asvinai, or Dievas Deli, were the divine twins and horse gods, sons of the solar god Dievs, of the Baltic tradition. Their name, close to that of the Indian Ashvins, points to the Indo-European tradition out of which they emerge.

ATALANTA A Greek myth tells how, as a baby, the girl child Atalanta was abandoned by her father, who had hoped for a boy child. But Atalanta, following in the heroic monomythic tradition of others, was adopted—in this case, by hunters, who brought her up as a huntress. She became famous for her speed as a runner. When Meleager, a prince, hunted the monstrous boar that was plaguing Calydon, he asked Atalanta to join in the hunt and fell in love with her. After the successful hunt, Meleager gave the boar's hide to his beloved, but his uncles took it away from her, and in a rage, Meleager killed them, an act that would lead to his own death. Later Atalanta was received back by her father, who decreed that she should marry. Atalanta agreed to marry only the man who could defeat her in a race and announced that she would kill anyone who lost to her. She was defeated by Milanion, who won the race when Aphrodite gave him three golden apples to drop during the race. Atalanta picked up one and Milanion, her future husband, was able to pass her.

ATHARVA VEDA The fourth *Veda* of India, probably later than the *Rig Veda*, the *Sama Veda*, and the *Yaj ur Veda*, the *Atharva Veda* is made up of myths, magical formulae, spells, prayers, verses, and hymns and is named after Atharavan, a priest in charge of the worship of fire and *soma*.

ATHENE The patroness of Athens, Pallas ("Maiden") Athene (Athena) or Athene Partheneia ("the Virgin"), whose Athenian temple was the Parthenon, was one of the most important of the Greek Olympians. Athene's animal is the owl, the symbol of wisdom, which is the goddess's particular quality. Her roots go back to the Old European Great Goddess, the Neolithic Bird Goddess, and her descendents, the Great Goddesses of the Minoans and the Mycenaeans. Like those goddesses, she is associated with snakes, which, especially in her archaic depictions, are wound about her head or attached to her cloak. A hint of her pre-classical association with what may have been a goddess religion there is the story that the rock around which Athens was built—the Acropolis—was originally called Athene because it was the goddess herself, much as the Phrygian Mother Goddess Cybele was the Agdos Rock on which the father god Pappas spilled his procreative seed. In fact, the story goes that the smith god Hephaistos assaulted Athene and managed to spill semen on her thigh, only to have her wipe it off and fling it to the ground. The semen engendered the first Athenian king. Athene also gave Athens the gift of the olive tree.

A 17th century astrological chart with signs of the Zodiac

The Titan, Atlas, holds up the world

Athene was the daughter of Zeus and the Titaness Metis, the great god's first wife, and the personification of essential intelligence. Metis was the daughter of Oceanus and Tethys, who, according to Homer, were the primal couple of creation, like the Mesopotamian Apsu and Tiamat. When Zeus learned from an oracle of the Earth Mother that Metis's child would be wiser than he was, he ate his pregnant wife, hoping to preserve his superiority. Athene, however, was determined to be born. One day Zeus had such a headache that he begged Hephaistos to split his head open with an axe. Out sprang his fully armed daughter Athene.

In classical Greece Athene gave up some of her old Great Goddess characteristics to a more masculinized worldview. She was both a warrior and a virgin, the protector of Athens and of heroes, as she had been the protector of Odysseus in the archaic period. She was said to have helped construct the famous Wooden Horse of Troy. With Apollo she established the new patriarchal order of Olympian Greece at the trial of Orestes in the *Eumenides*, the final segment of the *Oresteia* of Aeschylus. As the story of Arachne indicates, Athene shared with her Olympian family a tendency toward a bad temper.

ATHIRAT An Ugaritic-Canaanite goddess who is close to the high god El—perhaps his consort—Athirat may be a version of several other Western Semitic goddesses, such as Asherah and Astarte, with ties to the Mesopotamian Ishtar.

ATLANTIS In the *Timaeus* Plato tells the story of the island of Atlantis, supposedly told originally to the seventh-century B.C.E. Athenian statesman Solon by Egyptian priests. According to the myth, there was once a large island west of the Pillars of Herakles opposite Mt. Atlas. After the island's defeat by the Athenians and others, its people turned against morality and the gods and they, along with their whole island, were swallowed up by the sea. Ever since, people have searched for the lost city of Atlantis.

ATLAS The Titan Atlas, after the failed war with the Greek Olympians, was made by Zeus to hold up the world. Later the hero Perseus turned him to stone with the Medusa's head, and he became the Atlas Mountains of present-day Morocco.

ATMAN In Advaita Vedanta and other branches of Hinduism, Brahman is the absolute that is transcendent—nowhere—but immanent—everywhere—as the self or Atman within all things. In the *Upanishads*, Brahman is the ultimate whole while Atman is the individual soul that can merge with Brahman in mystical oneness, a state of ultimate consciousness or identity.

ATON The Aton (Aten), represented by the solar disk, was the already existing aspect of the sun cult taken up by the Egyptian pharaoh Amenhotep IV, who renamed himself Akhen*aton* (Akhenaten) after the primary object of his religious devotion. Because he, with his queen Nefertiti, apparently worshipped the Aton above all other gods, including the high god Amun-Re, he is sometimes called the father of monotheism. In support of this contention are the facts that Akhenaton had the word "gods" removed from religious monuments and wrote a hymn in which he referred to his favorite god as "sole god, without another beside you."

ATRAHASIS An Akkadian-Babylonian version of the ancient Mesopotamian flood myth, which influenced the Noah story of the *Torah*, features the flood hero Atrahasis. In the earlier Sumerian version the hero had been Ziasudra. The most popular form of the flood myth is the one told in the various versions of the epic of Gilgamesh, in which the Noah-like flood hero is Utnapishtim (in some versions of the story Atrahasis was Utnapishtim's father). In the best-known Atrahasis version, the noise being made by an overpopulation of humans, who had been created to work so that the gods would not have to, so disturbed the divine community that the god Enlil planned a great flood to cut down the population. The trickster god Enki warned King Atrahasis of Shurupak of the impending disaster. He did so by an indirect means, thus avoiding the wrath of Enlil, who had decreed that the flood be kept secret—especially from humans. Atrahasis, thanks to Enki, was able to build a boat for himself and his family. Of all humans, only these people survived. Although he was angry that Atrahasis had escaped the divine wrath, Enlil allowed him to exist and procreate, since the gods already missed human labor. Eventually Atrahasis was made immortal.

ATREUS The father of the Trojan War Greek heroes Agamemnon and Menelaus by Aerope, the widow of one of his sons, Atreus was the son of Pelops and the grandson of Tantalus. Atreus and his brother Thyestes murdered their half brother and were forced to leave their homeland. The brothers fled to Mycenae (Argos), where Atreus was eventually made king. When Thyestes seduced Aerope, Atreus banished him. Thyestes sent Plisthenes, a son of Atreus whom Thyestes had brought up as his own, to kill the king; but Atreus killed Plisthenes, not realizing he was his own son. Once he discovered what he had done, Atreus pretended to reconcile with his brother, but in fact he killed Thyestes' two sons and served them up to their father as dinner. Thyestes fled in horror, and the gods cursed the House of Atreus, leading to many disasters, including, according to some, Atreus's marriage to the daughter of Thyestes, who was pregnant by her own father and whose son, Aegisthos, would kill Atreus himself. The curse also affected Atreus's son Agamemnon. As Aeschylus reveals in the *Oresteia*, Aegisthos seduced Agamemnon's wife Clytemnestra while the king was off fighting the Trojan War and helped her murder him when he returned home.

ATTIS A central figure in the mythology of the Phrygians in Asia Minor, Attis was a dying god who experienced some sort of resurrection, depending on the particular version of the myth. Mythologically and archetypally, then, Attis, as first indicated by Sir James Frazer in his *Golden Bough*, is a relative of Adonis and Osiris and an ancestor of Jesus. The myth itself was the basis for a ritual that developed in Phrygia and became popular later in Rome. Attis, a vegetation god whose death and resurrection were celebrated in the spring, was closely associated with the Phrygian Great Mother goddess, Cybele. In some sense Attis was both the goddess's son and lover.

One myth of Attis's birth is a virgin birth story in which the Great Goddess, in her form as the virgin Nana, placed a pomegranate on her lap only to have a seed enter her and result in the birth of Attis.

Many stories of Attis's death exist. Some say he was killed by a boar, like Adonis. Others say he was attacked sexually by a brute called Agdistis, who had been conceived by Cybele as she slept on the Agdos Rock and semen from the sky god Pappas fell on her. According to that story, Attis had grown into a beautiful boy who was much loved by Cybele, and rather than commit an act of infidelity to the goddess with the monstrous Agdidtis, Attis castrated himself and died. A tree with an effigy of Attis played a part in the enactment of Attis's death, tying him to both Adonis and Jesus. Rituals that took place both in Phrygia and Rome suggest that Attis returned to life in an Easter-like resurrection. In Rome the celebration of Attis 's resurrection took place on March 25 in a saturnalia of sorts known as the *Hilaria*, or "Holiday of Joy."

ATUM In the Egyptian mythology of the cult center Heleopolis, Atum was the high god, who created the world with his own bodily fluids. He is also the primal androgyne, the container of the potential for male and female and the progenitor of Geb and Nut, earth and sky. He is the ancestor of Osiris, Isis, Seth, and Nephtys. Assimilated with the sun god Re, he became in the Old Kingdom the dominant high god Re-Atum or Atum-Re.

ATUM-RE Atum-Re is one of the many combinations of high gods in Egyptian mythology. For some Egyptians the mutual assimilation of Atum and the solar god Re (Ra) represented the setting sun.

AUDUMLA As the de facto mother of the gods in Norse mythology, the primal cow Audumla reminds us of the Egyptian cow mother-goddess Hathor. Created from the primal ice, Audumla suckled the first giant, Ymir, whose body became the earth. She licked ice into the form of Buri, the forefather of the gods.

AUGEAN STABLES These were the stables containing thirty years worth of manure belonging to the 3000 oxen of King Augeas of Elis. Herakles was ordered to clean them in a day as the fifth of his Twelve Labors. He did so by re-routing the rivers Alpheus and Peneus through them. Later Herakles would kill Augeas, and then he is said to have founded the Olympic Games.

AUROBINDO GHOSE The founder of Integral Yoga, a system combining older forms of yoga that works toward a consciousness change in the cosmos, Aurobindo (1872–1950) was also an expert on Indian mythology and religion.

AURORA Aurora was the Roman version of the Greek goddess of dawn, Eos.

AVALOKITESHVARA Perhaps the most popular figure in Mahayana Buddhism, Avalokiteshvara is a bodhisattva of compassion who originated in northern India. He is concerned especially with the needs of those who suffer. With his eleven heads, thousand eyes, and thousand arms, he is all-knowing, all-seeing, and able to respond simultaneously to suffering everywhere. It can be said that this bodhisattva is a de facto deification of the compassionate aspect of the Buddha himself. As such, he is, in fact, worshipped. Avalokiteshvara has close associations with the Amida (Amitabha) Buddha of esoteric Japanese Pure Land Buddhism. In that form he is the guardian of the world between the Buddha Sakyamuni and the Buddha to come. The worship of Avalokiteshvara as Guanyin (Kuan-yin, Kannon in Japan) was introduced in China as early as the first century C.E., and here this bodhisattva is sometimes male, sometimes female. In Tibet, where he was introduced in the twelfth century, Avalokiteshvara

Underworld King, Osiris (left), and Creator Atum, guarding the tomb of Queen Nefertiti.

Rama, the hero of the Ramayana; the great avatar of Vishnu

cosmic order. The first avatar was the great horned fish who saved Manu, the first human, from the deluge that took place at the beginning of this world. The second avatar was the great horned boar who saved the goddess Prthivi ("Earth") from the demon Hiranyaksa. As the Tortoise, Vishnu is the cosmic foundation on which rests the churning stick used by the gods and demons in their act of creation in the ocean of milk (*see* Ananta). As the man-lion, Vishnu was able to defeat Hiranyakasipu, who was invulnerable to humans and animals but, apparently, not to a combination of the two. Hiranyakasipu was no favorite of Vishnu since he persecuted his own son, Prahlada, a devotee of the god. When the asura, Bali, took over the world from the gods, he agreed that Vishnu, who had taken the form of a dwarf, could own whatever he could cover in three strides. The dwarf, Vamana, immediately took on his real being as Vishnu and in three steps encompassed the whole world for the gods. When the ksatriya (warrior) class persecuted the brahman class, Vishnu became the ax-wielding Parashurama and defeated the ksatriyas, thus establishing the theological and social dominance of the brahmans. The two most famous avatars of Vishnu are Rama, the hero of the Hindu epic the *Ramayana*, and Krishna, who appears in, among many other places, the epic the *Mahabharata* as a supporter of Arjuna and his Pandava brothers against their Kaurava cousins. Krishna is particularly known for his preaching to Arjuna as his charioteer in the *Bhagavadgita*. Krishna and Rama have become, in effect, popular Hindu deities. It is said that the Buddha was also an avatar of Vishnu, coming to preach gentleness, and that Vishnu will appear at the end of this age as a human, Kalki, riding on a white horse.

AVESTA The *Avesta* is the Bible of Zoroastrianism. Most of the original *Avesta*, much of which predates the Zoroastrian reforms of the old Iranian religion, based on earlier Aryan roots, has been lost. The most important part of the *Avesta* is the *Yasna* ("Sacrifice") verses, meant to be used by priests during sacrifice rituals. Contained in the *Yasna* are the *Gathas*, "songs" said to have been written by Zoroaster (Zarathustra), containing the essence of the prophet's philosophy. Also important in the *Avesta* are the *Yasts*, hymns that tell us much of what we know of Zoroastrian mythology.

AZTEC MYTHOLOGY In the mid-thirteenth century a wandering Nahuatl-speaking group known as the Mexica came into the Valley of Mexico and in 1325 founded the city of Tenochtitlan on two islands of Lake Texoco. By 1428, in alliance with the city states of Texoco and Tlacopan, the Mexica defeated the Tepaneca and—under Itzcoatl, Montezuma I, and Netzahualcoyotl—founded and expanded the last of the great pre-Columbian Mesoamerican empires, that of the Aztecs. When the Spanish arrived in the sixteenth century, the Venice-like capital city, Tenochtitlan, was one of the great cities of the world, probably exceeding the major European capitals in size, appointments, and beauty. In 1521 the conquering Spanish filled in the canals with the rubble left by their siege of ninety-one days. The main square of present-day Mexico City lies over the center of what was once the Aztec capital. Aztec religion, filtered down from the Olmecs, Teotihuacan, Monte Alban, Mayan, and especially the fellow Nahuatl-speaking Toltec peoples, was typically Mesoamerican in terms of cosmology, the

(sPyan-ras-gzigs or Chenrei—"He with the look of Pity") is the most popular of deities. Tibetan mythology holds that Avalokiteshvara was the progenitor of the Tibetans and was the first Tibetan sovereign. So it is that he is reincarnated in each Dalai Lama, who traditionally lives, like Avalokiteshvara himself, on a mountaintop (Potala) from which the cries of suffering humanity can be heard. In Mongolia Avalokiteshvara is "The One Who Watches." In Southeast Asia he is "Lord of the World." The bodhisattva has a female counterpart, or *Shakti*, in Tara, who is particularly popular in Tibet as a savior goddess. One myth says that Tara was born from a compassionate tear shed by Avalokiteshvara.

AVALON Avalon (Avallon), another name for Annwn, was the Welsh Otherworld—and sometimes the Land of the Dead, a paradise where fallen heroes live as immortals. For some, Avalon was a mysterious island, also called the "Isle of Apples" by Geoffrey of Monmouth and the "Isle of Women" in older Celtic tradition. King Arthur was taken to Avalon after his defeat. It was from Avalon that he was to one day return to save Britain.

AVATAR The idea of the avatar or avatara is central to Hindu mythology, especially to the concept of the god Vishnu (*see* Avatars of Vishnu). An avatara is the earthly form taken by a deity.

AVATARS OF VISHNU The Hindu god Vishnu takes various earthly forms in Hindu mythology in order to restore

A

emphasis on the sun, and even particular deities. It was, however, in something of a state of flux and development when the Spanish put an end to the empire and imposed Christianity. On one hand there were the deities of an old fertility- and earth-based religion, perhaps brought from the north by the original Mexica migrants. Tlaloc, the rain and moisture god, and various other gods and goddesses who personified aspects of plant growth and fertility were part of an important cult. Among these fertility deities were Xilonen, a maize goddess; Xochipilli and Xochiquetzal, male and female deities representing flower growth; and the Centzon Totochtin ("the 400 Rabbits"). A Tlaloc shrine stood at the top of the great pyramid-temple of Tenochtitlan.

Human sacrifice, representing death and rebirth and the "feeding" of the earth and the sun, represented by the warrior god Tonatiuh, also apparently had ancient roots. Sacrifice was justified on the basis of the concept of the process by which various worlds or "suns" die and are resurrected as new suns. Suns were fed blood to keep them alive. One of the ancient pre-Aztec gods of fecundity was Xipe Totec, during whose festivals the skins of sacrificed victims were worn by the god's followers. Xipe Totec was associated with Tezacatlipoca, the lord of the first of the five "suns," or world eras. Unlike the Mayans, the Aztecs believed their "sun," the fifth, was the last and that eventually eternal chaos would envelop it. That chaos had to be delayed by the blood feeding of the present sun.

Several creation stories exist in Aztec mythology, some coming from the early Mexica, some from other Mesoamericans. According to some, a primal goddess, Omeciuatl, gave birth to a sacrificial knife, which fell to earth on the land of the Mexica and itself produced people and gods. Another myth says that originally there was a dual-gendered deity, Ometeotl (the male Ometecuhtli and the female Omechuatl, also known as Tonacatecuhtli and Tonacacihuatl). The male and female aspects of this self-created deity coupled to produce the most important and familiar Mesoamerican solar deities, blue Huitzilopochtli, white Quetzalcoatl, black Tezcatlipoca, and red Xipe Totec. In one sense these four are really aspects of one, Tezcatlipoca; they are sometimes called the "Four Tezcatlipocas." Thus, for example, Huitzilpochtli is also the "Blue Tezcatlipoca, and Quetzalcoatl is the "White Tezcatlipoca." Some have seen this concept as a movement toward a kind of philosophical monotheism or monism.

The creation myth of the "Five Suns" has echoes in the emergence myths of the Native North American pueblos, where world history is divided into various states of emergence from the earth. The Aztecs believed that the first "sun" was ruled by Tezcatlipoca, god of the north and darkness. This sun was devoured by tigers. The second sun was that of Quetzalcoatl, god of the west and magic. Winds destroyed that world, and human survivors became monkeys. The third sun, that of Tlaloc, here the god of fire as well as rain, was destroyed by a rain of fire, and humans

An Aztec calendar

A

became birds. The fourth sun belonged to the goddess of the east and water, Chalchihuitlicue, Tlaloc's consort. It was destroyed by a flood survived by one man and one woman. The present sun, the fifth, is that of the fire god Xiuhtecuhtli. It will end in earthquakes. It was believed in some quarters that Quetzalcoatl ("Feathered Serpent") and his opposite, Tezcatlipoca ("Smoking Mirror"), created this world, which was ruled by Huitzilopochtli. The beginnings and ends of the various sun-worlds are specifically noted and based on a complex numerological system and "Divine Calendar" (tonalamatl).

The image that gives life to this complex sense of creation is the struggle of the sun itself against the forces of darkness. The early sun god Tonatiuh typically sticks his tongue out, waiting for blood. The sun is threatened by its negative force, the dark Tezcatlipoca. The setting sun is Quetzalcoatl, an old man heading back to the west. The bright sun is the head of the Aztec pantheon, Huitzilopochtli ("Hummingbird of the South"), depicted as the victorious, bright young warrior. Huitzilopochtli in some ways was a cognate of Tonatiuh.

Huitzilopochtli, like Quetzalcoatl, may once have been a hero rather than a god. He displays many characteristics of the heroic monomyth, including a miraculous conception and a quest for new land. Huitzilopochtli's mother was Coatlicue ("Serpent-Petticoated"). It was Huitzilo-pochtli who was said to have led his people to Lake Texoco. His shrine was at the very top of the great temple of Tenochtitlan; it was here that human sacrifices to the sun took place.

The most popular of the Aztec gods, who came directly from the Toltecs, was Quetzalcoatl, the "Feathered-Serpent" or "Precious Twin." For many Mesoamericans, the serpent was a central and positive figure; it comes from the depths of earth, it supports the world on its back, it is the sea surrounding the world, it is lightning, it is the rivers that fertilize. Like Huitzilopochtli, Quetzalcoatl may have had heroic rather than divine roots. For the Toltecs he was the morning and evening star. He was said to have disapproved of human sacrifice. He descended to the underworld to steal the bones with which to make humans. A Toltec-Aztec story says that he was defeated in a ritual ball game by his enemy Tezcatlipoca, who became a jaguar and chased him out of Tollan. Perhaps Quetzalcoatl, in effect the culture hero of the Toltec and Aztecs, died, but it was believed he would return one day, like the rising sun.

The Aztec calendar said that Quetzalcoatl would return during the year whose sign was "One Reed" (Ce Acatl), a sign associated with the hero-god. The Spaniard Cortes arrived during the year Ce Acatl, and it is said that the Aztecs unfortunately thought he was Quetzalcoatl. [Carrasco, Grimal]

Huitzilopochtli: Sun god and war god of the Aztecs

BAAL In Canaanite mythology, Baal was the most important god. His name, like that of Adonis, means "Lord." His father was either Dagan, a weather or storm god, or the patriarchal high god El. He has mythological brothers in such gods as the Norse Thor, the Aramean and Babylonian Hadad, the Assyrian Adad, and the Hebrew Yahweh, as well as in all the Middle Eastern and Indo-European younger gods who wrested authority from earlier, more primitive divinities. Zeus defeating Kronos is an example. The transfer of power in the Hittite-Hurrian Kumarbi cycle is another.

Baal is sometimes directly assimilated with related gods. He is, for instance Baal-Hadad in some of the Ugaritic texts. Baal-Karmelos was the storm god of Mount Carmel in Palestine, and Baal-Hammon was important in Dido's Carthage. Perhaps more important, Baal must be seen in relation to the Babylonian god Marduk, who, like him, gained his dominant position among the gods by defeating the primal powers of water—in the case of Marduk, the sweet waters personified by Apsu and the sea waters which were Tiamat. Baal defeats the sea as the god Yamm, sometimes called Lotan the serpent, reminding us of Yahweh's defeat of Leviathan.

Whatever his form, Baal's defeat of the water powers is clearly tied to the climatic and agricultural processes of the Middle Eastern year. By defeating the monster Yamm, Baal was able to determine the flow of waters—that is, rain.

Baal's greatest battle was with Mot, Death himself, who had entered the god's new palace by way of a foolishly placed window. At one point Mot seems to have defeated his rival, as Baal is condemned to descend to the depths of Death's throat, taking the rains, clouds, and other storm god characteristics with him. The result in the world was horrendous drought and devastation.

But Baal's sister Anat saved the day, descending, like the Mesopotamian Inanna/ Ishtar to Death, splitting him in two, grinding him up, and sowing him as seed. The result of the planting was the resurrection of Baal and the return of life to the earth. The defeat of death and periods of prosperity and fertility are never permanent, however, and in time Mot would challenge and probably defeat Baal again. Thus the Baal cycle is a continuous story of life, death, and rebirth.

BABA YAGA In Slavic mythology Baba Yaga (Iaga) is a famous Kali-like witch whose large body fills a turning hut resting on chicken legs and surrounded by a fence of human bones in a dark forest near a river of fire. The keyhole of the hut's front door contains teeth. Some have traced Baba Yaga to a prehistoric European goddess of death. Like the ancient goddess, she has clear associations with birds and snakes. Baba Yaga can change her appearance at will—sometimes appearing to be young, sometimes old. She can fly; her vehicle is a mortar with a pestle used as a rudder. She often carries a broomstick.

BABYLONIAN MYTHOLOGY The second millennium B.C.E. saw many changes in Mesopotamia and the Middle East. Early in the millennium, Amorites ("Westerners"), Semites who had begun to migrate to the Fertile Crescent in the middle of the previous millennium, perhaps from the Arabian Peninsula, became powerful in Mesopotamia, Egypt, and the Levant (now Lebanon, Syria, Jordan, Israel, and Palestine). In Syria they established the city of Mari, and in Mesopotamia a capital, Babylon, in what had once been Akkad. Under Hammurabi (c. 1792–1750 B.C.E.), who ruled over a land populated by a variety of races, they developed a unifying code of laws and printed it on the famous column at Susa for all to see. Old Babylonia, as it is now called, was constantly threatened from

The Babylonian king before the Sun God on the tablet-inscribed Laws of Hammurabi

B

Babylon and the Tower of Babel

within and from Elamites and others from outside its borders. Much of the area that had once been Sumer declared its independence during the rule of Hammurabi's son, and that area's kings stressed cultural descendancy from Sumer, even though the people who actually spoke Sumerian were now essentially extinct. But the decisive blow came in 1600 B.C.E., when Old Babylonia was invaded and defeated by the Hittites, Indo-Europeans from the northwest.

In 612 the Assyrians, in alliance with the Egyptians, were defeated by Semitic Medes from Persia and Babylonians. Nineveh was destroyed, and under King Nebuchadnezzar II (605–562 B.C.E.) of the Chaldean dynasty, Babylon once again dominated the Middle East during an era known as the neo-Babylonian. This was the period of the Hanging Gardens of Babylon and of great astronomical advancement, as well as of a revival of Babylonian religion and mythology that reached back to the ancient Sumerians. It was also the period of the Babylonian Captivity, or Exile of the Hebrews.

Babylonian mythology was deeply influenced by that of ancient Sumer and Akkad. In fact, the most ancient Babylonian myths were written in Akkadian during the second millennium B.C.E. and saved on tablets preserved in the neo-Assyrian and neo-Babylonian archives—particularly those of Nineveh and Babylon itself. The myth of Ishtar's (Inanna's) descent to the underworld is a good example,

as is the reworking of the Sumerian tale of Gilgamesh. Babylonian mythology maintained connections with the old deities of Mesopotamia, but the emphasis was decidedly different. Nowhere is that difference clearer than in the great Babylonian creation epic, the *Enuma elish*, in effect a celebration of the rise of the once-minor Sumerian god Marduk to chief god of the Babylonian pantheon during the reign of Nebuchadnezzar I in the twelfth century B.C.E.

The rise of Marduk (and Ashur) marks a significant change in the mythology of Mesopotamia, reflecting a movement from cultural principles centered on fertility and the balance of male and female roles, to a much more patriarchal and hierarchical perspective such as that which was emerging, for instance, among the Hebrews and that has equivalents in the predominance of Zeus, Odin, and other Indo-European sky gods over earlier primal powers.

BACAB Bacab was one of the four Mayan wind gods who held up the sky.

BACCHAE The Roman (Latin) word for the Greek Maenads.

BACCHAE The Greek playwright Euripides relates an aspect of the myth of the god Dionysos (sometimes

Bacchus) in the fifth-century B.C.E. play known as the *Bacchae* or *Bacchantes*. The title refers to the bacchae (bacchantes), or maenades (meneads) or thyiades, the female votaries of the god, who became intoxicated by his powers and his presence and who celebrated him with frenzied festival dances in fields and forests, wearing fawn skins and vine leaves.

In Euripides' play, Dionysos has come to Thebes, where he joins his worshippers on Mount Cithearon. The blind prophet Tiresias and Cadmus are about to join the revelers, but the young King Pentheus enters and argues against what he considers their foolish superstitious allegiance to Dionysos. To prove his point, he orders the arrest of the god, who is disguised as a prophet. In spite of warnings from the chorus about the pride of disbelief, Pentheus persists in his persecution of the visiting god, insults him in an interrogation, and imprisons him. Enraged, Dionysos calls down destruction. Pentheus's prison cannot hold him and, in fact, he overpowers the king's reason, having him disguise himself as a bacchante and leading him to the scene of the revels. There the revelers, led by Pentheus's own mother, Agave, tear him apart.

BACCHUS Bacchus is the Roman equivalent of the Greek god Dionysos. He has come to be associated particularly with drunkenness and lascivious behavior. Thus, even today people speak of having "bacchic rites," referring back to ecstatic and frenzied Dionysian or bacchic festivals such as those that take place in Euripides' play the *Bacchae*.

BADB Badb (Badhbh, Bodhbh) was a triune Celtic goddess of sorcery, war, and death in the Irish tradition. Often taking the form of a screaming raven or crow, she terrifies and demoralizes warriors in battle. Her husband is the war god Net. Badb, with Nemain and Macha, is an aspect of or one and the same with the triune goddess Morrigan.

BALARAMA The son of Vasudeva, the Hindu "Lord of Wealth," and Rohini or "Red Cow," both of whom are associated with the moon, Balarama ("lover of power") is Lord Krishna's older brother and companion. Always a complement to his brother, Balarama is white whereas Krishna is black. As Krishna is an avatar of Vishnu, Balarama is an incarnation of the world serpent Shesha (Ananta), on whom Vishnu sleeps. Like Krishna, he is placed in the care of Nanda ("Joy"), the cowherd. Balarama's birth was extraordinary. He was conceived in Devaki, whose children her brother, the demon Kamsa, had threatened to kill. But by the power of Vishnu, Balarama was moved to Rohini's womb for birth. Eventually, Balarama would help Krishna kill Kamsa.

BALDER The Balder (Baldr) myth comes down to us by way of the *Prose Edda* of Snorri Sturluson and the work of Saxo Grammaticus When Balder the Beautiful, son of the Germanic Norse high god Odin, had dreams foreshadowing his destruction, the gods intervened to save him. His mother, Frigg, convinced everything on earth to swear not to harm her son. Only one small plant, the mistletoe, was overlooked. Believing Balder was now immune to any threat, the gods enjoyed throwing things at him for fun. But the trickster Loki, in female disguise, learned from Frigg of the neglected mistletoe. He plucked it out of the earth and convinced the blind god Hod (Hodr) to throw the plant at his brother Balder. Loki guided the god's hand, and the mistletoe struck its victim in the heart, causing instant death.

The gods were bitterly sad at the loss of so wonderful a companion, and Odin realized that Balder's death foreshadowed the death of all the gods. Frigg called on a volunteer to travel to Hel to bring her son back. Another of her sons, Hermod, agreed to go. He rode to Hel, found Balder seated in a place of honor, and learned that the god could return to earth only if all things, living and dead, would weep for him. When Odin learned the news of his son, he called on all things to weep. And all things did weep—all but a giantess, the disguised Loki, who snarled, "Let Hel keep her own." And so Balder was to remain in the land of the dead. With the death of Balder, Ragnarok, the end of the world, was inevitable.

But it was believed that the earth would rise from the depths again one day, green and blossoming, that a new sun would arise, and that a number of gods would return to the ancient ruins of Asgard, led by Balder.

Certain similarities exist between the myths of King Arthur and those of the Norse Balder, suggesting a possible common source for both stories. As Arthur was slain by his son or nephew, Balder was killed by his brother, and as the wounded Arthur was cared for by women, Balder was sometimes associated with the supernatural warrior-women called the Valkyries. Like Arthur, he partook of magical food. Furthermore, his death, like Arthur's, with its promise of return, can be tied to the idea of fertility.

Scholars have long sought Balder's origins in the fertility gods of the Middle East—gods such as Attis, Baal, Adonis, and Osiris, who died and returned with the plants of spring. Balder's particular plant, the mistletoe—the one Snorri tells us killed him—attaches itself to the oak, a sacred tree not only to the Celts but to Indo-Europeans in general. Later, northern Christians would see in Balder a prophecy of the new Christian god, who, after his return from the dead, as we learn from the Anglo-Saxon *Dream of the Rood*—"surrounded by the mighty host of souls He had freed from the torments of Hell—returned to the City of God crowned with victory and glory." The Balder myth may well have been influenced by the Christian tradition, but it seems to have existed in some form that predates that influence.

BALINESE MYTHOLOGY A visitor to Bali will be struck by the importance of the stories from the Hindu epic the *Ramayana* in various rituals. In fact, Bali is the only Hindu-Buddhist civilization in Indonesia. The official religion is Bali Hinduism. Old Balinese and Sanskrit texts on the island indicate Indian influence from perhaps as early as the first millennium B.C.E. These texts reveal the presence in Old Balinese mythology and religion of such familiar Hindu figures as Ganesh, Durga, various Buddhas, Vishnu, and Shiva. All the sacred texts of Bali are dedicated to the goddess of speech and wisdom, Sarasvati, who is the wife of Brahma. The Balinese say that the Hindu world center, Mount Meru, or Mandara, is in fact their own sacred mountain, Gunung Agung. The Balinese also have Anantaboga, their own version of the primeval Indian serpent Ananta. There are also remnants in Balinese mythology of pre-Hindu gods such as the popular

B

Gunung Agung, the highest mountain on Bali, is the historic dwelling place of the Balinese Gods

trickster-like Twalen, who is assimilated into Hinduism as a brother of the great god Siwa (Shiva). Balinese dance ceremonies often celebrate not only the major events from the *Ramayana* but popular stories such as the one involving the struggle between the sorceress Rangda and the dragon king, the Barong. [Lansing]

BALKAN MYTHOLOGY In what are the present-day Balkans, ancient Slavic migrants encountered and at least partly assimilated Albanian-speaking Indo-Europeans, whose linguistic and cultural ancestors are possibly the Illyrians, an ancient people mentioned by Homer as allies of the Trojans against the Greeks. Other Indo-European Balkan tribes were the Thracians and their relatives the Geto-Dacians, a version of whose language still exists in Romania. Herodotus claimed that the Thracians were the second largest tribe on earth. They too are listed among the enemies of the Greeks at Troy. The Greeks believed that both Dionysos and Orpheus came from Thrace. In telling the story that was a possible source for Euripides' the *Bacchae*, Homer reports in the *Iliad* (Book 5) on the struggle between Dionysos—perhaps synonymous with Sabazios—and the Thracian king Lykurgos, who was probably the source for Pentheus in Euripides' work. Other Thracian divinities known to the Greeks included two goddesses whose origins are perhaps pre–Indo-European. These were the goddesses Bendis and Cotys. The Greeks associated both with their Artemis. Cotys, whose cult involved men dressing as women, would seem to be related, like the Thracian Dionysos, to the Euripidean story of the demise of the feminized Pentheus at the hands of the orgiastic maenads, who punished the king for denying their god. As for the Geto-Dacians, their mythology was dominated by Zalmoxis, a divine king whose Pythagorean philosophy promised immortality to his followers, making him, like Dionysos, a natural forerunner to the Christian man-god who would eventually come to dominate Europe. [Mallory, Leeming (2003)]

BALOR In Irish myth, Balor (Balar) was one of the most powerful of the Fomorians, a war-like race defeated finally by the Tuatha Dè Danaan, the race of gods in pre-Christian Ireland. Balor was a giant known for his single evil eye, a mere glance from which could defeat whole armies. It was foretold that Balor would be killed by his grandson, so he locked his daughter Ethlinn in a tower on Tory Island so that she could never become pregnant. Unfortunately for Balor, however, Birog managed to enter the tower and impregnate Ethlinn. The couple's child, Lugh Lamhfada, killed Balor with a slingshot at the Second Battle of Magh Tuiread. His stone hit the giant in his evil eye. There are obvious parallels between this story and that of David and Goliath in Hebrew mythology. After slaying the Philistine giant, David became the Israelite king, just as Lugh became the Tuatha Dè Danaan king.

BALTIC MYTHOLOGY Baltic peoples included Latvians, Lithuanians—not Christianized until the early fifteenth century—and Old Prussians, who inhabited what is now eastern Germany and the Baltics and land extending as far east as Moscow, beginning in about the middle of the second millennium B.C.E. By the first millennium the Balts, whose languages are closer to the ancient Indo-European Vedic language than to any other European language group, had developed from a hunter-gatherer culture into an agricultural one. Not surprisingly, then, what little we know of Baltic mythology is a combination of perhaps very ancient nature deities and deities closely associated with farming and fertility.

Baltic mythology has not received the scholarly attention devoted to other Indo-European mythologies, partly because of the continuous subjugation of Balts by their neighbors over the centuries and the consequent "contamination" of the old religion by Christianity and other mythologies—particularly Germanic and Slavic. In recent years, however, more concentrated scholarly work has been done by Marija Gimbutas, Harold Biezais, Jaan Puhvel, and others.

It is mainly through folklore, contained primarily in folk songs (Latvian *dainas*, Lithuanian *dainos*), typically sung at significant rites of passage, and Russian and German chronicles of the tenth through seventeenth centuries that we discover the remnants of the old Baltic religion and its pantheon. In about 1520 Simon Grunau in his *Prussian Chronicle* revealed something of the Old Prussian aspect of Baltic mythology, at the center of which was a typically Indo-European triad. The triad, somewhat resembling the king-priest god, warrior god- thunder god, fertility god triad represented by the Norse Odin-Thor-Freyr, was made up of Patollo (Pecullus, Pikoulis), Perkuno, and Potrimpo. All were associated with a sacred oak tree. The triad had its earthly brahmanic-type priests—equivalents of the Celtic druids or the Roman flamines—called in German *waidolotten*.

A sky god creator, who in all likelihood preceded the rise of Perkuno to divine dominance in the Baltics and remained important especially in Lithuania, was Dievs in Latvia, or Dievas in Lithuania and Old Prussia. He is clearly related, like the Greek Zeus, to the Vedic Dyaus (Indo-European root dyeu = "heavens") and probably began his existence as a personification of the sky.

The goddess Saule, whose name points to her solar nature (or Saules Mate, "Mother Sun"), like Dievs, must have begun as the natural phenomenon itself, become a personification, and eventually achieved a personal nature. According to some, Saule is constantly pursued by a would-be lover, the moon god Menuo. In other stories she is the wife of Dievs.

Another version of the fertility goddess is Zeme (Zemyna in Lithuanian). She was originally earth itself and then a personification and personal goddess with seventy sisters who represent various aspects of nature—fields, mushrooms, elk, and so forth. Still other fertility deities are Ceroklis and Jumis. These and the Baltic gods in general have survived in the modern Baltic states in folkloric tradition even though they were officially replaced by the Christian god, whose fertility is spiritual, and later by political systems that for many years rejected both mythologies. [Gimbutas (1963), Biezais]

BANARAS Banaras (also Kasi or Varanasi) is a *tirtha*, a spiritual pilgrimage city on the sacred Ganges River in northern India. Pilgrims come from all over India to bathe in the river at Banaras. The Buddha preached near Banaras in the Anandavana (the "forest of Bliss"), and deities have always been worshipped there. The god Shiva is the dominant god at Banaras. The *Skanda Purana* tells how Shiva's linga, or sacred phallus of light, arose from the earth itself to pierce the skies above Banaras. It is also said that Shiva sent all the gods to his sacred city, which he entered in glory after Vishnu had helped him rid it of its king, Divodasa.

BARDO THOTROL The title *Bardo Thotrol* (*Bar-do'i-thos-grol*), or *Tibetan Book of the Dead*, refers to the brief period between death and rebirth, the intermediate state (*bardo*) during which the soul remains near the body seeking release into a form of enlightenment and/ or moves along a path toward rebirth. The book says that a person's last thought affects his or her future birth and presents the opportunity for enlightenment. If the soul fails to achieve enlightenment, as is the case with most people, it remains in the physical world as an unhappy ghost of sorts until it passes into a second, intermediate state, in which it comes face to face with peaceful and angry deities who represent aspects of the person's own mind. Enlightenment is still possible at this stage. Having failed to achieve enlightenment, the dead person moves to a third bardo, that of the search for rebirth. Here the individual's past life is assessed. This process is represented by the Lord of the Otherworld weighing the person's good deeds as white pebbles against the bad deeds as black pebbles. The dead person tries to reestablish contact with family members but fails and is led by karma to an appropriate womb for rebirth.

BARDS In certain mythologies bards, or possessors of the divine ability to reveal the essence of truth through words, play significant roles in leading their people. Bards could be poet-prophets like the Celtic Amairgen and Taliesen, literally singing reality or history into life, or Hindu Brahmins who do something of the same thing. Or bards can be lesser figures who simply reveal the myths—the "true" stories of the given cultures. These are the *filidh* of Ireland and the *skalds* of the north. Bards, are sometimes blind, like the legendary Homer, which suggests the importance of their *in*sight.

BARONG A popular figure in Balinese mythology, the Barong is a dragon-like king whose primary purpose is to defeat the powers of evil represented by the witch-queen Rangda. The myth is ritualized in an important form of Balinese theater called the Barong play. There are variations to the performances, but generally the Barong is first defeated by the witch. Then the villagers attack Rangda, who uses her

The Barong against the powers of evil in the Balinese ritual play

magical powers to turn the villagers' daggers upon themselves. A death orgy follows. But a resurrection of sorts takes place when the Barong returns and revives the dead villagers. Rangda disappears.

BASQUE MYTHOLOGY The mythology of the non–Indo-European Basques, whose language and culture have survived defiantly into the present era and who inhabit the mountainous region between Spain and France, was greatly influenced by the mythologies of the Celts and the Romans, but also developed patterns familiar to students of the prehistoric Neolithic period. The existence of *lamniaks*, female figures with bird or fish characteristics, points back to the goddesses of Old Europe. An important Basque goddess is Mari, a rain deity associated, like many ancient goddesses, with a serpent husband. The Basque blacksmith-grain god Basajaun has been compared to the Roman Silvanus, a nature deity. [Blazquez (1987a, 1987b)]

BASTET One of many Egyptian goddesses, Bastet is the feline-headed love-sex-fertility counterpart to her sister, the lion-headed and more violent Sekhmet.

BASUKI The serpent Basuki—perhaps a version of the Vedic Ananta or the Sumatran Padoha—lives in the Balinese underworld described in the myth of Batara Guru.

BATARA GURU In the pre-Islamic mythology of the Indonesian island of Sumatra, Batara Guru was the primal being, the creator of earth and the first ancestor of humans. The Batara Guru myth is of particular interest as an earth-diver creation story, one with many analogues, especially in Central Asia and Native North America. The story contains the particular element of the young woman falling from the sky, which is found in many Native American earth-diver creations—for example, in several Cherokee and Iroquoian versions.

In the Sumatran myth Batara Guru's daughter Boru Deak Parudjar dives from the heavens into the primal sea, causing the god to send a bird down with soil to make land for his daughter and to serve as a place to plant the seeds of creation. Batara then dispatches a young hero, an avatar of himself, down to earth to defeat Padoha, the primal serpent of the underworld and to marry his daughter, and with her to populate the earth with the first humans.

BATARA KALA The Balinese cosmology includes an underworld ruled by the god Batara Kala, creator of light and earth, and his wife Setesuyara.

BAUCIS AND PHILEMON The Roman poet Ovid tells the story of how, when the gods Jupiter and Mercury paid a visit to earth disguised as poor travelers, they were not treated well by humans. Only the aged and poor Phrygian couple Baucis and her husband Philemon were hospitable. For this they were richly rewarded.

BEAR MYTHS AND CULTS In what are possibly Neanderthal cave "sanctuaries" high in the Alps, skulls are set into "altar" niches, suggesting a worshipping of animal spirits and an early belief in the willing participation of animals in the life-giving process of killing and eating. Although the hunt itself was a source of survival for these hunter-gatherers, the special treatment of animal bones and dead human bodies was not and can reasonably be attributed to the peculiarly human realm of *myth-o*logic. Joseph Campbell sees the Neanderthal bear sanctuaries as the "earliest evidence anywhere on earth of the veneration of a divine being" and as an indication of ritual sacrifice (1983, p. 147). For Campbell the bear sanctuaries were the source for bear cults that would spread across northern Europe and Asia into Native North America. In connection with these cults, particularly in light of the fact that hibernation was a mystery for early humans—one augmented by the ability of the bear to stand and even walk upright like us—the question arises as to whether this bear "god" was the first of many who seemed to die only to return later to life, and who, if treated properly in a ritual context, would allow himself to be killed for the good of all.

The modern existence of bear ceremonies and stories—especially among the Ainu of Japan and several Native American groups—may give us at least a partial sense of the nature of the early bear cult and its myths. Among the Ainu, a black bear, raised from an early age in a cage, is sacrificed and its pelt is ritually served a stew made of its own flesh. The Cherokee Indians tell the story of a young hunter who was adopted by a bear after the bear proved magically invincible before his arrows. When a year had passed and the man had grown bear-like fur, the host informed him that the Indians would return and would succeed in killing him, but that if the "bear man" followed certain instructions, all would be well. When the hunters arrived, they killed the bear and discovered their long-lost—now furry—cohort in the cave. After skinning the bear the hunters watched as the bear man performed the ritual over the bear's remains. As the men left, they looked back to see the bear rising from the bones.

Representations of the goddess Bastet often had feline characteristics

Bellerophon on Pegasus fights the Chimera

BEDAWANG Bedawang is the Great Turtle of the Balinese creation. He was created through the meditation of the cosmic serpent Antaboga (Ananta) and carried on his back the snakes that were the earth and the Black Stone that covered the entrance to the underworld.

BELENUS Also known in Celtic Ireland and Britain by various names—Bel, Belinos, Beli, Bile—Belenus is a god of Celtic Gaul whom Julius Caesar compared to the Greco-Roman Apollo as a solar god of light and reason. He carries a solar disk on the chariot that he presumably uses to travel daily across the sky. His British name is the source for Billingsgate in London. Fires in honor of the god were lit for Celtic festivals of Beltaine ("Bel's Fires") on May 1.

BELL BIRD BROTHERS The two Bell Bird brothers of the Australian Dreaming mythology were out hunting an emu who was drinking from a pool near the rock of Uluru when a young woman lost control of a dish she was carrying on her head. The fall of the object frightened the emu, who ran off. To this day a rock pool in Uluru is said to be the one from which the emu was drinking, and the indentation near the rock is attributed to the object that fell from the girl's head.

BELLEROPHON The son of King Glaucus and Queen Eurynome of Corinth, Bellerophon was so named for having killed Belerus. When Antea, the wife of King Proteus of Argos, fell in love with him, he refused her advances. Enraged by this rejection, Antea claimed to her husband that Bellerophon had tried to seduce her. Proteus's reaction was to send the young man off to Iobates, Antea's father

and the king of Lycia in Asia Minor, with a letter containing instructions to kill the bearer. Iobates thought a good way of killing Bellerophon would be to send him off to fight the monster known as the Chimaera. But Bellerophon took possession of the winged horse Pegasus and managed to kill the monster from the air with his arrows. Still hoping to end Bellerophon's life, Iobates sent him on more impossible missions—for instance, against the Amazons—but the hero always succeeded in accomplishing the Heraklean tasks set before him. After Bellerophon killed all the brave Lycians that had attempted to kill him in ambush, he succeeded in convincing Iobates that he was invincible, and the king gave the hero his daughter in marriage and made him his heir.

Later, however, Bellerophon became arrogant and attempted to fly on Pegasus to the top of Mount Olympus. This angered Zeus, who sent a gadfly to sting the winged horse, causing the animal to throw Bellerophon, who fell to the earth and became a disillusioned, lame wanderer.

BENZAITEN A transplant to Japan of the Hindu Sarasvati—the sacred river personified as the goddess of speech and wisdom and wife of Brahma—Benten, as she is most often known, is the Japanese Buddhist and Shinto goddess of good speech and music. Sometimes she is depicted with two arms, sometimes with eight. She always carries objects symbolic of her meaning—for example, the lute for music, and the sword and jewel for wisdom and sacred vows. She is one of the Seven Deities of Good Fortune.

BEOWULF The hero of the eighth-century Anglo-Saxon epic poem named for him, Beowulf represents a combina-

A page from the Bhagavad Gita shows Krishna and Arjuna preparing for battle

tion of the Christian values of the monks who compiled the epic and the older Germanic mythology from which the story springs.

The young Beowulf, with several Swedish (specifically Geat) followers, arrives in Denmark to support King Hrothgar in his struggle against the monster Grendel, who periodically comes at night into the king's meadehall to eat his men. In a terrifying battle Beowulf succeeds in killing Grendel, only to be faced with the task of defeating the monster's horrible mother in her underwater lair.

In his later years Beowulf, now king of the Geats, has to defend his own kingdom from a dragon. In a final battle, the king and his loyal friend Wiglaf succeed in killing the dragon, but Beowulf dies as a result of his heroic effort.

BES A relatively late Egyptian god particularly popular in Greco-Roman times, Bes was in all likelihood imported from Libya (Punt). Unlike the much more formal gods of the various orthodox pantheons, Bes had trickster qualities; he was a coarse and bearded dwarf with a gleam in his bulging eyes and a feather stuck in his messy hair, and he was sometimes ithyphallic. Bes was popular among the lower and middle classes, a protective deity, a tutelary god of childbirth, and later a protector of the dead as well. Above all, he was a god of pleasure and joviality.

BHAGA One of the Vedic Adityas, Bhaga is the dispenser of wealth and the brother of the Dawn (Ushas).

BHAGAVADGITA "The Blessed Lord's Song," the *Bhagavadgita* was composed about two thousand years ago and is generally considered to be the most beautiful religious writing in India. Since it is part of the epic the *Mahabharata*, the *Gita* is technically *Smirti*, or traditional literature, rather than *Shruti*, or revealed sacramental text. In effect, however, the *Bhagavadgita* has attained the level of *Shruti*. More than any other Hindu text, it is consulted as a source of truth and wisdom. The poem itself, which is placed in Book VI of the *Mahabharata*, is made up of seven hundred Sanskrit verses divided into eighteen sections. The source of the wisdom contained in these verses is the Lord Krishna, who, as an avatar of the god Vishnu, teaches the Pandava hero Arjuna. The sermon takes place in the middle of the battlefield. Krishna is at first in his form as mortal ally and charioteer of Arjuna. The Pandava hero has suddenly been overcome by inner questions about the mass killing that the battle will entail. Krishna answers that Arjuna must follow his proper social role, or dharma, as a member of the warrior caste without considering the outcome. Sometimes becoming Vishnu himself, Krishna tells Arjuna that, in any case, the individual is immortal, only appearing to control his destiny. The essence of Krishna's teaching is that the individual is ultimately linked to an ultimate divine reality. In terms of the mythology contained in the *Gita*, Krishna-Vishnu reveals himself as the personal embodiment of supreme primal power—of the impersonal Brahman. He appears to Arjuna as the container of every kind of place and being, of the gods themselves, even as time and the universe itself. He is the universal bard who contains the whole story of existence within himself. In the epic poem, therefore, the relationship of Arjuna to Krishna stands as a metaphor for the real relationship between humanity and divinity in the world.

BHAKTI The Sanskrit word for something approximating "devotion" or "reverence," *bhakti* is expressed traditionally through Hindu ritual sacrifices, ascetic practices, and hymns and prayers. Different kinds of *bhakti* apply to the worship of particular deities. Thus Shaivas, followers of Shiva, have one kind of *bhakti* and Shaktas, devotees of Devi (Shakti), have another. Worshippers following a *bhaktimarga*, a *bhakti* path, generally believe in only one personal god or *Isvara*. The goal of the *bhakta* is union of some sort with the deity in question.

BIBLE, THE The collection called the Bible (Greek *biblia*, "books") is made up of what Christians call the Old Testament, or Jewish scripture, consisting of the *Torah* ("Law"), the first five books, as well as Prophets, and Writings; and the New Testament, composed of the four Gospels, or biographies of Jesus, and the interpretive writings of various followers of Jesus, dominated by Saul of Tarsus, who became Paul. The Bible contains the canonical myths—the generally accepted sacred stories of Judaism and of Christianity, with Christians subscribing to all of the biblical stories and Jews accepting only those of the Old Testament.

BIBLICAL CREATION See Genesis

BILJARA AND WAGU Two southeast Australian aboriginal tricksters, Biljara (Hawk) and Wagu (Crow) use their shapeshifting magic in attempts to get the best of each other. In this aspect, they somewhat resemble Native North American trickster pairs such as Coyote and Iktome. Wagu sometimes teams up with other animal tricksters such as Crab. He is said to have introduced death to the world, much as Coyote did in North America. It was Wagu and Biljara who instituted marriage among the people.

B

BINTU In the western Sahara region of Africa, Bintu is the sacred antelope from whose skull the smith god made the first hoe. With this hoe the smith god taught humans how to farm.

BIOGENETIC STRUCTURALISM Advocates of biogenetic structuralism, such as Eugene d'Aquili and Charles Laughlin, are influenced by Jean Piaget. They see myths as a phenomenon tied to evolutionary survival, as concrete expressions of neurophysical development. Myths and rituals are the way we communicate our relationship to our environment.

BIRHOR MYTHOLOGY The Birhors are a central Indian tribe who do not subscribe to the classical Hindu caste and religious system but, like most of the non-classical tribes of the region, sometimes make use of Hindu deities and heroes in their myths. The Birhors tell their own version of the *Ramayana* epic, for example, in which the Monkey hero Hanuman has a Birhor uncle. The Birhor creation myth is of particular interest because it is an earth-diver story such as those found in Central Asia and Native North America. In the Birhor version, the creator, Singbonga, arises from the depths of the primal waters through the stem of a lone lotus. Sitting on the lotus, he decides to create the world and sends a series of animals into the depths to find mud with which to work. It is the leech who succeeds in this task after other creatures fail. The leech swallows some mud and spits it into the creator's hand. Out of this mud Singbonga makes various animals and, after several false tries, the human being.

BISHAMON Sometimes known as Tamon-tenno, Bishamon is the Japanese Buddhist-Shinto equivalent of the Indian god-king Vaisramana, one of the four guardians of the world's directions. The four god-kings were adopted by Japanese Buddhism as protectors of the law. By the ninth century, Bishamon was in effect being worshipped in certain Buddhist monasteries as a curer of sickness, and by the fifteenth century he was known as a dispenser of wealth. Bishamon wears armor and holds a spear. Often he is depicted standing on a monster he has slain. He is one of the Seven Gods of Fortune.

BLACK ELK A Lakota (Oglala) Sioux wise man whom some would call a Native American shaman, Black Elk (Hehaka Sapa) revealed much of Sioux myth and ritual to John Neihardt in the latter's *Black Elk Speaks* and to Joseph Epes Brown in *The Sacred Pipe*. Black Elk said he had fought the Indians' white enemies at Little Big Horn and at Wounded Knee Creek, that he was a cousin of the chief and holy man Crazy Horse, and that he had known many figures who have become a part of American "mythology," including Buffalo Bill, Red Cloud, and Sitting Bull. Black Elk felt a responsibility to "bring to life the flowering tree" of the Sioux. It was for this reason that he related to Neihardt his visions sent by the Great Spirit (Wakan-Tanka) and revealed to Brown the rituals of the Sioux and their central myth, that of the Great Spirit's gift to his people, through White Buffalo Woman, of the Sacred Pipe.

BLACK MADONNA The depiction of the Virgin Mary with black skin is so widespread culturally and geographically—especially in Europe—as to preclude the explanation that she is dark-skinned when a dark-skinned culture paints her and white when a light-skinned culture paints her. This race

Our Lady of Czestochowa: the Black Madonna

explanation works when we consider the generally brown-skinned Virgin of Guadalupe or various African depictions of Jesus' mother, but it does not go far enough to explain the Black Madonnas of Poland, Switzerland, France, Italy, and Spain. The black Our Lady of Czestochowa of Poland, for example, is a national symbol. Other Black Virgins such as the ones in France at Chartres and at Notre Dame du Puy are associated with pilgrimage sites. Other Black Madonnas are central to cult centers in Montserrat and Solsona, to mention only a few places in Europe. One explanation for the Virgin's dark skin is her possible ties to ancient earth-centered goddess rituals and myths. Her skin is dark because, as the mother of the resurrection god-hero, she represents the dark earth itself, where the seeds of new life are planted. In this connection, Ean Begg, in *The Cult of the Black Virgin*, suggests that the Black Madonna was related to the ancient eastern fertility goddesses such as the Ionian Artemis, the Phrygian/Roman Cyblele, and the Egyptian Isis, and that she was brought by the Crusaders to western Europe (p. 49). The goddess, whether the dark Isis in Egypt or the dark Artemis of Ephesus, represents the mystery of recreation. The ancient goddess was often the moon to her son or husband's sun, and blackness in this context, in relation to the dark face of the Madonna, might point to the dark gestative phase of the lunar cycle during which the light is temporarily hidden.

BLODEUWEDD The Welsh Celts tell the myth of the beautiful maiden Blodeuwedd ("Flower Aspect"), created out of various flowers by the great storyteller Gwydion, son of Don. Blodeuwedd became the wife of Lleu Llaw Gyffes, whose mother, Aranrhod, had sworn he would never have a human bride. When Blodeuwedd is unfaithful with Gron Pebyr, the lovers attempt to kill Lleu. Wounded, he escapes as an eagle and is later restored to human form by Gwydion. But Gron Pebyr is killed and Blodeuwedd is turned into an owl (*blodeuwedd*), an outcast among birds.

BOANN In the Celtic mythology local to Ireland, Boann ("white cattle woman") is a water goddess married to the water god Nechtan. Boann refused to accept a certain taboo associated with her husband's keeping of the sacred well known as Segais Well, the source of inspired knowledge. In defiance of the taboo, she walked around the well from right to left, and the well burst its boundaries and drowned her. The resulting river—today known as the Boyne—is named after her. Another story of Boann tells how the great god the Dagda had an illicit affair with her and thereby fathered the love god Aonghus Og.

BOAR The ancient *Taittiriya Samhita* and *Satapatha Brahmana* of India tell how the creator Prajapati became a boar and spread out the earth, which thus became Prthivi (the "extended one"), who gave birth to many gods. In the *Vishnu Purana* and *Kalika Purana*, Vishnu, as Narayana, in association with Brahma, is the earth-diver creator who, in the form of the Great Horned Boar avatar, saves earth by raising her from the primeval waters on what is, in effect, his phallic tusk.

BODHI TREE This is the sacred tree, the tree of Wisdom or Enlightenment (*bodhi*), under which the Buddha sat to gain enlightenment.

BODHIDHARMA Zen Buddhism, a Japanese version of the meditative and ecstatic form of Mahayana Buddhism, is said to have been brought to China from India by the fifth-century C.E. Bodhidharma, the twenty-eighth successor to Gautama Buddha, the Buddha Sakyamuni. There are many legends or myths associated with Bodhidharma. One story says that when he came to China, the sage crossed the Yangtse on a reed and that he spent nine years without moving in the absorbing meditation now called *zazen*. Bodhidharma became the founder of Ch'an, the Chinese version of Zen, which also owes much to the philosophy of Daoism. Another story tells how Bodhidharma was poisoned before he could return to his native India. Although he had been buried in China, he was seen walking along the road to India wearing only one sandal. When his grave was opened, there was nothing there but one sandal. In Japan, Bodhidharma is called Daruma, and doll replicas of him are given out as rewards for concentration.

BODHISATTVA Depending on the sect of Buddhism, the word "bodhisattva" has essentially two meanings. Literally, a bodhisattva is a person who is seeking enlightenment (*bodhi*). In early, Pali Buddhism, Buddhism contained in the Pali as opposed to Sanskrit texts—for example, Theravada and other forms of Hinayana Buddhism, the so-called small vehicle of India, Burma, Sri Lanka, Cambodia, and Laos—the word refers to particular beings, saints (*arhat*) in past eons who were on the path to full enlightenment or nirvana. It refers especially to the pre-enlightenment stages of Gautama Buddha, the Buddha Sakyamuni, who is commonly called simply "the Buddha." In later or Mahayana Buddhism—the "great vehicle" of Nepal, Sikkhim, Tibet, China, Mongolia, Vietnam, Korea, and Japan—the bodhisattva is the compassionate person whose life is dedicated to the salvation of others and to becoming a Buddha only in some far distant eon. The Mahayana Buddhists thus stress the possibility for many people to be on the "bodhisattva path" (in Sanskrit the *Boddhisattvayana* or *bodhisattvacarya*) leading to enlightenment, and there are many celebrated bodhisattvas who, in effect, are worshipped as divinities, as in the case of the Tibetan bodhisattvas Avalokiteshvara and Tara.

BON MYTHOLOGY Bon is the ancient indigenous pre-Buddhist religion of Tibet. It was shamanistic and animistic in nature. After the rise of Buddhism it was assimilated to some extent into the practices of the new religion and became part of a larger Tibetan mythology.

BOOK OF GOING FORTH BY DAY Toward the beginning of the Egyptian New Kingdom, a collection of funerary spells was compiled to help people negotiate the world of eternal life after death. The Egyptians called this collection on papyrus the *Book of Going Forth by Day*. Today it is generally called the *Book of the Dead* but should not be confused with the *Tibetan Book of the Dead* (*Bardo Thotrol*).

BOTA ILI In Eastern Indonesia Bota Ili was a wild woman covered in hair who had magical powers. One day she returned from hunting and tried to light a fire by striking her bottom on a rock. When the magical process failed she realized it was because she was being watched. Indeed, a

The Hindu creator god Brahma holding a page of the *Vedas*

fisherman named Wata Rian was hiding in a tree watching her. When Bota Ili discovered him she, like Artemis in the Greek myth, became furious. But unlike Artemis, Bota Ili was not committed to virginity. She calmed down and invited the man down for supper and wine. When the wine had put her to sleep Wata Rian shaved off all of her hair, revealing a beautiful woman, and eventually the two were married.

BOTOQUE The Kayapo of central Brazil say that the young Botoque brought humans fire and the bow and arrow. He had been taught about fire and the bow by a jaguar, who had adopted Botoque into his home. When, after Botoque had killed the jaguar's jealous wife, he returned to his village with the fire and the weapon, the villagers were so impressed they decided to take everything from the jaguar's cave. This they did, robbing the cat of his fire and weapons, and now the jaguar eats his meat raw and must hunt with his claws.

BRAGI The Norse god of poetry, Bragi was the son of Odin and the husband of Idun.

BRAHMA Brahma is the primary creator god in Hindu mythology. With Vishnu the "preserver" and Shiva the "destroyer," he forms a *trimurti*—a trinity of sorts. In

terms of worship, however, he does not have the importance of the other two gods. If there is a worshipped trinity in India, Devi, the "Goddess" in her many forms, makes up the third part with Vishnu and Shiva. Still, Brahma is of great mythological importance. As the creator in the *Puranas*, he is derived from the creator god Prajapati of the ancient Vedic *Brahmanas*, and sometimes he is considered the same being as Prajapati. The name "Brahma" is the masculine Sanskrit form corresponding to the neuter "Brahman"—the absolute on which the whole universe is based. But Brahma, although a creative aspect of Brahman, is not Brahman. In fact, Vishnu is more likely to be seen as a physical expression of the absolute, as in the myth of his sleeping on the primal serpent (Ananta, Vasuki, Shesha) in the primal ocean of milk—out of time and out of space. It is in this myth that Brahma appears seated, as the first conscious deity, on a lotus that emerges from Vishnu's navel. This Brahma has four faces and four arms that hold the sacred books—the *Vedas*—which existed even before creation and give him the authority to create. In the post-Vedic *Laws of Manu*, however, Brahma creates a cosmic golden egg (*arbhiranyagha*) from his seed. After a time in the primordial waters, Brahma takes form from the egg as the cosmic man Purusa. Brahma's other methods of creation are many. He copulates, masturbates, and thinks things into being. Sometimes the elements of

B

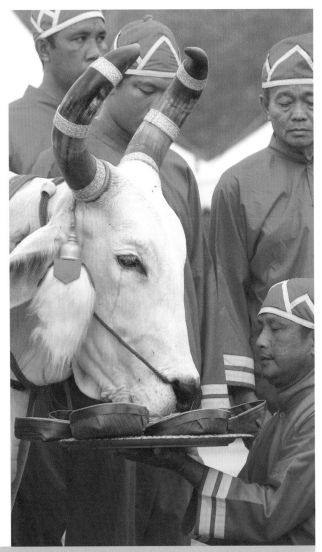

A Brahman offers food to an ox during the Royal Ploughing ceremony in Bangkok

creation develop animistically from dismembered or sacrificed parts of his body. Brahma's wife is Sarasvati, who, in the *Rig Veda*, is the primal Word or *Vac*—that is, the articulation of the Creator—in effect, his *Shakti*. She is the "mother" of the *Vedas*.

BRAHMAN Especially in the Vedanta Hindu philosophy, Brahman is the Absolute. In the Vedic hymns the neuter noun "brahman" refers to the power of the word, and a brahman is a member of the priestly caste who understands the word. In the *Upanishads* Brahman becomes the eternal first cause, present everywhere and nowhere, always and never—the ultimate unknowable mystery or riddle of the universe. The closest one can come to revealing what Brahman is is to say or write the sacred syllable Om. Brahman can be incarnated in Brahma and Vishnu, and Shiva, but when the Absolute takes no form, there is no existence. To put it another way, everything that is owes its existence to Brahman. In this sense Hinduism is ultimately monotheistic or monistic, all gods being aspects of Brahman.

BRAHMANAS These ancient Vedic texts are part of Hindu writing designated as *Shruti* or sacred knowledge. Each of the four *Vedas* is made up of poetic hymns and prayers (*Samithas*) to which are attached one or more *Brahman-*

as, theological revelations in prose. They describe certain rituals and myths and then provide explications or *artha-vadas*. The religion of the *Brahmanas* is one centered on rites of sacrifice rather than on the gods themselves. *Aranyakas* and *Upanishads* can be thought of as extensions of the *Brahmanas*.

Many versions of an incest-based creation are told in the *Brahmanas*. The *Aitareya Brahmana*, for instance, names the creator as Prajapati, who later becomes Brahma. But unlike the older *Rig Veda*, where incest also plays a role in creation, the *Brahmanas* tend to stress the importance of ritual and proper action (dharma). Not surprisingly, therefore, in the *Brahmanas*, the other gods criticize Prajapati for committing incest and he is punished, especially by the protector of rituals, Rudra.

As in the *Rig Veda*, the god of fire, Agni, plays a role in making the god's seed flow, and in the *Kausitaki Brahmana* the sons of Prajapati are involved with him in creative incest with a now seductive daughter, Ushas (Dawn). From the spilled seed of Prajapati and his sons comes the thousand-eyed god Rudra, who resembles the *Rig Veda* primal being Purusha and who attacks his father and demands to be named. Prajapati names him Bhava or "Existence." In the *Satapatha Brahmana* there is the motif of masturbation as the source of creation. Prajapati literally "milks" himself, and the butter used for rituals is churned from the milk. This process occurs after the creator produces Agni from his mouth. Agni (fire) consumes, and sacrifice must be made to him. In terms of the Brahmanic concern with proper ritual, the symbolism here has to do with the idea that, through sacrifice, Agni, who is Death, is appeased. Even in death the worshipper, who is fed to the fire, is reborn, because only the body is eaten by it.

BRAHMANISM Brahmanism refers to the whole way of life associated with the brahmans (brahmins), a caste in Hindu India. Specifically, Brahmanism is a development of earlier Vedism, which was the religion of the Indo-European Aryans, who entered India in the second millennium B.C.E. Brahmanism, like Vedism, reveres the ancient rituals and sacred texts or *Shruti*—the *Vedas* and the *Brahmanas*, *Upanishads*, and *Aranyakas* that grew out of them—but it also places a great deal of trust in the myths contained in less sacred texts or Smirti, such as the epics the *Mahabharata* and the *Ramayana*, the *Puranas*, and various books of Hindu law.

BRAHMANS The highest caste in Hindu India, brahmans (brahmins) are priests, whose primary duty is to see that proper rituals and rules—especially those spelled out in the *Brahmanas*—are followed and properly executed. The brahman is the earthly counterpart of Brhaspati, the priest among the gods.

BRAN Several characters named Bran exist in the Celtic mythologies of Ireland and Wales. One Bran, the son of Febal, is the hero of an eighth-century C.E. heroic quest tale in which Bran, with his three foster brothers and twenty-seven soldiers, leaves Ireland in search of a beautiful woman he has seen in a vision. Many adventures follow, including a dramatic meeting with the sea god Manannan Mac Lir, visits to several strange islands, and a long stay in Tir na mBan, the Land of Women. When Bran's men insist on returning to Ireland, they are informed that they have been away for hundreds of years and that once they return to the land of ordinary mortals they will immediately become ancient and die. Nevertheless, the men insist, and as the ship nears Ireland one of the men leaps ashore, only to instantly wither and turn to dust. In sadness, Bran and his remaining followers turn the ship around and continue their wanderings.

Another Irish Bran is an Otherworld god who is son of King Lir and brother of Manannan Mac Lir, the sea god met by Bran during his quest. This Bran is a cognate of the more famous Bran the Blessed of Welsh myth. His brother is Manawaydan, a cognate of the Irish Manannan, and his father is King Llyr of Britain, in all likelihood the King Lear of British legend made famous by Shakespeare. Bran the Blessed is a giant so huge that no building can contain him. He has a sister named Branwen, and with her he figures centrally in the "Second Branch" of the Welsh tales known collectively as the *Mabinogion*.

BRANWEN The sister of Bran the Blessed and daughter of King Llyr of Britain, Branwen figures strongly in the "Second Branch" of the Welsh collection of tales known as the *Mabinogion*. She marries Matholwch, the King of Ireland, and her life is marked by terrible tragedy involving a war, a magic cauldron, and a talking head.

BRER RABBIT In American and African American folklore, Brer (Brother) Rabbit is a trickster perhaps related to the Hare trickster of African slaves. He was made famous by Joel Chandler Harris in his *Uncle Remus* tales. A tale that obviously owes something to a similar tale about the African trickster Ananse and a "Gum Doll" is that of Brer Rabbit and the tar baby. The story reminds us that tricksters themselves sometimes become the victims of tricks.

Uncle Remus tells how one day Brer Fox worked out a way of catching Brer Rabbit by creating a dummy covered with tar. Brer Rabbit came along the road, saw the dummy, and thinking it was a person said "Good Morning." The dummy, of course, said nothing. After a few more attempts at politeness Brer Rabbit became angry and punched the tar baby, only to find his fist stuck to it. Now even angrier, he struck the dummy with his other hand, and that hand became stuck too. Then he kicked and butted, and finally he was totally stuck to the tar baby. Brother Fox came up, and then rolled on the ground laughing. Whether he ate Brer Rabbit we cannot be sure.

Tales such as this found receptive audiences not only among African Americans but in a white American culture addicted to the tall tale.

BRHASPATI Brhaspati might be called the chaplain of the Hindu gods. His role is that of the brahman priest in Heaven, the one who, as the "lord of sacred speech," or *mantras*, is "master of the ritual sacrifice."

BRICRIU He "of the poisoned tongue" was a troublemaker of the Red Branch warriors of Irish Ulster. He came to a bad end when he was trampled to death by the Brown Bull of Cuailgne and the White Bull of Connacht. His name is most famously associated with the myth of "Bricriu's Feast" ("Fled Bricriu"), almost certainly the source for the much-better-known fourteenth-century English Arthurian romance Sir *Gawain and the Green Knight*. Both tales make significant use of the giant theme and the theme of decapitation. In "Bricrui's Feast," several Ulster heroes claim the rights to the hero's portion of food and drink, either in King Conchobhar's hall or at Oath's Lake, where the shape shifter giant Uath Mac Imoman lived. A giant—a *bachlach*—appears and demands that a warrior behead him and that he be allowed to behead the warrior the next night. For three nights Ulster heroes take turns cutting off the giant's head, but after each decapitation the giant leaves, holding both his severed head and his axe, causing the warriors to leave the hall to avoid being beheaded themselves. Finally, Cuchulainn upholds Ulster honor by decapitating the *bachlach* and offering his own head to the axe and block on the following night. When the giant strikes he does so with the blunt side of the axe and Cuchulainn is recognized as the truest of heroes.

BRIGID Brigid (Brighid, Brigit) was an Irish Celtic triune goddess of healing, smiths, and fertility. The daughter of the father god, the Dagda, she was married to Bres, the half Fomorian, who for a while became king of the Tuatha de Danaan. Yet she is the mother of three sons by a mysterious figure named Tuireann, who is sometimes depicted as a female.

In Christian times Brigid's name was taken by Mary of the Gaels, traditionally the daughter of a druid and perhaps originally a priestess of Brigid, who became St. Bridget (St. Bride) of Kildare, the patroness of Ireland. The saint took on many of the traditions of the pagan goddess. St. Bridget's festival occurs on February 1, the same day as the pagan festival celebrating Brigid as a fertility goddess. On that day young men in various disguises visit homes to discourage evil and ensure fertility.

BRUNHILD (BRYNHILD) In Norse mythology Brynhild is a warlike but beautiful princess, a valkyrie, or attendant of Odin. In the German epic the *Nibelungenlied*, as Brunhild, she agrees to marry only the man who can accomplish certain trials. She marries the Burgundian king Gunther, for whom the hero Siegfried (Norse Sigurd) accomplishes the tasks disguised in his cloak of invisibility. Brunhild is an important figure in Richard Wagner's operas based on the *Nibelungenlied* and other stories.

BUDDHA "Buddha" or "the Buddha" is a name usually applied to the Buddha Sakyamuni, otherwise known as Gautama Buddha.

BUDDHA SAKYAMUNI Sakyamuni, "the Buddha," is, in effect, the family name of Gautama Buddha, whose father was a king of the Sakyas. The Buddha is sometimes referred to simply as Sakyamuni.

BUDDHACARITA The *Buddhacarita* ("Deeds of the Buddha") in Sanskrit (and in Tibetan and Chinese translations) is a second-century C.E. epic-like biography of Gautama Buddha by the sage Asvaghosa.

BUDDHAS A buddha is literally a person who has moved from the stage of pre-enlightenment (arhat) to that of having been enlightened, or awakened to ultimate reality. The Sanskrit/Pali term "buddhi," which is related to the term "buddha," conveys the sense of special intelligence or knowledge. The term "the Buddha" usually refers to Gautama, the Buddha Sakyamuni. But there are other buddhas. The Jains would consider their founder, Mahavira, a buddha, and the Pure Land Buddhists in Japan have their Amida Buddha.

BUDDHISM AND BUDDHIST MYTHOLOGY See Gautama Buddha, Tibetan Buddism

BULL OF HEAVEN The Bull of Heaven in the Mesopotamian mythology of the Sumerians and Babylonians is owned by the god Anu (An). In one version of the Gilgamesh story the goddess Ishtar (Inanna) sends the bull to earth to destroy Gilgamesh, who has dared to refuse her sexual advances. Gilgamesh defends himself by killing the bull, but meanwhile his friend Enkidu has been rendered blind by the beast's spit.

BULLROARER Used in the ceremonies of various cultures, especially by shamans, a bullroarer is a piece of wood containing a spirit—sometimes a literal one, as in the case of the Melanesian culture hero Tiv'r's son—that is spun around the head to activate the spirit's voice.

BULLS Gods of the Neolithic and later periods often take the form of bulls, a representation of virility and power important both in ancient fertility mythologies and later patriarchal king-dominated cultures. The Egyptian bull deity was Apis. In Iranian mythology the white bull was the first animal of creation, and the god Mithra was identified with the sacrificial bull who died for the good of humanity. His blood, like that of Jesus, became wine and his flesh a source of nourishment. The Indian god Shiva was often accompanied by a bull. The Greek god Zeus took the form of a bull to have his way with and to "fertilize" Europa. Other important bulls are the Bull of Heaven in Sumerian mythology, the Cretan Bull of the Heraklean Twelve Labors, and the great bull of the Irish *Tain Bo Cuailnge*.

BUNDAHISHN Literally, "The Book of Primordial Creation," the twelfth-century *Bundahishn* is the primary sourcebook for Zoroastrian theology and mythology in the Middle Persian or Pahlavi period. Although based in part on pre-Zoroastrian traditions, it can be considered the Zoroastrian equivalent to the Hebrew Genesis.

BURI The ancestor of the Norse gods, Buri was licked from a block of ice by themother cow Audumla.

Gautama Buddha, the founder of Buddhism

CADMUS The founder of the Greek city of Thebes and the brother of Europa, who was kidnapped by Zeus, Cadmus was the son of Agenor, perhaps originally an Egyptian, who ruled part of Canaan, later called Phoenicia, after another of his sons, Phoenix. Agenor sent Cadmus off to find Europa, and after a long search, the young man consulted the Delphic oracle, who advised him to follow a certain cow to the place where it would finally collapse. There he was to establish a new city. Cadmus followed the cow to where it collapsed, in Boetia. There he was faced by a dragon, which he killed, and the goddess Athene instructed him to sow some of the dragon's teeth in the ground. From this planting sprang an army of men who proceeded to fight each other until only five remained alive. These five (the Spartoi, or "Sown Men") became the first families of Thebes, the early acropolis of which, called the Cadmea, was founded by Cadmus after he served the god Ares for eight years as a punishment for having killed the dragon, which happened to be the god's son. The dragon teeth sowing is also present in the story of Jason, the *Argonautica*.

Zeus gave Cadmus Harmonia as a wife, and all of the Olympians attended the wedding. By Cadmus, Harmonia gave birth to Polydorus, the great grandfather of Oedipus, and Semele, the mother of Dionysos, not to mention Agave, the mother of Pentheus (whose story is told in Euripides' the *Bacchae*), and Autonoe, the mother of the unfortunate Actaeon. Eventually Cadmus and his wife were turned into serpents and moved to Elysium. It was said that Cadmus introduced to Greece an alphabet from Egypt. The Egyptian connection here suggests a further association between Egyptian Thebes and Greek Thebes.

CAIN AND ABEL The Hebrew story of these two sons of Adam and Eve continues the tragedy of the removal from the Garden of Eden, described in the Bible 's Book of Genesis. It is a story of human guilt, filial rivalry, and isolation.

According to Genesis 4, Yahweh rejected Cain's grain sacrifice but accepted the animal blood sacrifice of his younger brother Abel. Consumed by jealousy, Cain murdered Abel and was condemned by Yahweh to wander the earth with the "mark of Cain" on his forehead. In the rabbinic narratives known as the *aggadah*, the mark was said to be a pair of horns, which caused Cain to be shot by his grandson Lamech.

CALL, THE One of many universal or archetypal events in the heroic monomyth is the call—the call to adventure or specific action—literally, the vocation. Moses, the hero of the Israelites, is called to his mission by the voice of the angel in the Burning Bush. The Greek hero Theseus is, in effect, called by the existence of his father's (or foster father's) sword and sandals under a magic rock. King Arthur is called by the sword that he must pull from the rock. Often the hero refuses the call, at least temporarily. "Why me?" asks Moses, who, like most of us, would rather not be pulled away from the ordinary process of life. Sometimes the refusal of the call can have devastating consequences, as it does for Percival (Parsifal, Parzifal, Perceval) in one version of the quest for the Holy Grail.

CALLISTO An Arcadian nymph of Greek mythology, and one of Zeus's many objects of desire, Callisto was a companion of the huntress goddess Artemis. Zeus changed Callisto into a she-bear to hide her, but his jealous wife, Hera, recognized her and arranged for Artemis—or, some say, her own son, Arcas—to kill her. Zeus, however, apotheosized his beloved, turning her into the constellation called Arctos ("the Bear").

CALYPSO When in Homer's *Odyssey* Odysseus was shipwrecked on the island of Ogygia, he developed an intimate

The killing of Abel by Cain

relationship with Calypso, a beautiful nymph who lived there and was sorry to see him leave. Even her offer of immortality was not enough to distract the hero from his quest for home and his faithful wife Penelope.

CAMELOT Camelot was the castle and primary dwelling place of King Arthur, the seat of the fellowship known as the Round Table. It was at Camelot that the Holy Grail appeared to the knights of the Round Table. Many places in England to this day claim to be the site of the legendary castle. Camelot was first mentioned by Chrétien de Troyes in his twelfth-century work *Lancelot*. Supposedly Camelot was destroyed after Arthur's death.

During the early stylish and optimistic years of the American presidency of John F. Kennedy, it became customary to speak of Kennedy and his followers in the White House, and of the administration as a whole, as "Camelot."

CAMPBELL, JOSEPH Joseph Campbell (1904–1987) was perhaps the most influential American mythologist of the second half of the twentieth century, making mythology meaningful to a public beyond the classroom. Campbell was influenced by the works of psychiatrists Sigmund Freud and especially Carl Jung. Like Jung, he saw myths, whether Greek, Norse, Native American, Egyptian, or Micronesian, as cultural masks of a universal human psyche. The

Joseph Campbell (1904-1987)

patterns and universal tendencies of that psyche manifest themselves in all cultures as what Jung called archetypes. In his first truly influential book, *The Hero with a Thousand Faces*, Campbell applied archetypal theory to hero myths from around the world, revealing a universal or archetypal heroic monomyth.

CANAANITE MYTHOLOGY The middle of the second millennium had seen the flourishing of major Canaanite centers along the Mediterranean coast, centers roughly contemporaneous with those of the Mycenaeans in Greece. Some of these centers grew out of ancient Stone Age settlements. Cities such as Byblos had, by the beginning of the third millennium, long been carrying on active trade with Egyptians and Mesopotamians.

"Canaanite" is a somewhat vague term that has referred to the indigenous Semitic peoples of the "Land of Canaan," into which Hebrews migrated late in the second millennium. Numerous Canaanite tribes are listed in Genesis (10:15–20) among the Israelite conquests in the Land of Canaan. According to the Genesis (9:18–22) myth, Kan'an was the son of Noah's son Ham, who was cursed for having seen his father's genitals. It was the descendants of Kan'an who were said to have originally settled in Canaan.

We associate Canaanite culture, because of modern archeological finds, particularly with the people of the "Amorite" city of Mari on the border between modern Syria and Iraq, with the people who inhabited the Ugarit site (Ras Shamra) in the coastal region of what is now Syria, and with the coastal peoples the Greeks called the Phoenicians, who lived in what is now Lebanon. The terms "Phoenician" and especially "Ugaritic" are often used interchangeably with "Canaanite." Even the Mari-based Amorites are seen by some as Canaanites, but more often as proto-Arameans, the Arameans being the Semitic peoples who would settle around Aram (near present-day Damascus, in Syria) but who maintained a language and religion that were very different from those of other Semites in the area.

The emergence of the Hebrew people in Canaan coincided roughly with invasions all over the Middle East of the so-called Sea People, who had much to do with the deterioration of both the Hittite and Egyptian empires and who in Canaan became known as the Philistines. It is of interest to note that the events of this period are roughly contemporaneous with those of the Trojan War on the western Anatolian coast, if such a war, in fact, took place. After destroying the city of Ugarit and other Canaanite centers and establishing their own state with cities such as Gaza and Ekron in what is now southern coastal Israel-Palestine, the Philistines would gradually assimilate much of the indigenous Canaanite culture, including language and mythology. The name of their state, Philistia, would evolve still later into "Palestine," the name eventually used for all of Canaan.

Much of Canaanite mythology was adopted by the non-Semitic Philistines, who became the primary rival of the Israelites for the conquest of Canaan. When we speak of Canaanite mythology, it is important to realize that it has come down to us in a limited form gleaned from archeological sites, biblical references, and literary fragments. Still, it is fair to say that a somewhat consistent mythology does emerge.

Central to the Canaanite pantheon in its many local versions is a movement toward an understanding of deity that includes a high god associated with weather and storms who is somewhat distant from everyday life, a fertility god who is more present, and a feminine form of that fertility deity.

A Semitic word for "god" is El, or Il (thus *Elohim* and Allah, or *al-ilah*—"the god"). In second-millennium B.C.E. god lists found at Ugarit, there are several Els or versions of El. There is the El of the holy mountain Sapan (Tsafon); the Ilib (Elib), or "father god," who contains the spirits of the dead; and the El who, like so many Middle Eastern high gods, is associated with the bull. The Greeks thought of El as Kronos, the father of Zeus. Dagan (Dagon) is another vehicle for the high god concept, perhaps an early personification of the El.

It can be argued that the most important expression of the high god in Canaan, however, was Baal in his many forms. But officially Baal took second position to a father, sometimes El, sometimes Dagan. Baal was at once a weather-storm god of great power and a dying god and fertilizer of the earth. For the Philistines he was Baalzebub, a healer, whom the Greeks associated with Asclepius. In a list of Phoenician deities contained in a 677 B.C.E. treaty between the king of Assyria and the king of Tyre, he was the chief god, Baal-Shamen, the "Lord of Heaven," the El, the storm god, and Baal-Safon of the Holy Mountain, the Zeus of Phoenicia.

Among the Western Semites, goddesses played a significant and sometimes dominant mythological role. Typically, the goddess in question makes concrete the abstract reality represented by her male consort. Thus the Phoenician Ashtart, known also as Ashtoret and in Greek as Astarte, was the "name of Baal," and her equivalent in Carthage, Tinnit, was the "face of Baal." And although El was for some Canaanites the father of creation, his consort Athirat was also revered as the "Mother of the Gods." Something like this relationship between god and goddess exists in Vedic and Hindu India between the god and his Shakti, the energizing material power of the god personified as his feminine consort.

The difficulty in isolating the Western Semitic goddesses from each other is indicated by the similarity of their names, their common role as consorts to the high gods, their role as fertility goddesses, and the fact that the various cities and tribes assimilated and combined each other's mythological figures. Thus the often violent and overtly sexual Anat was the Canaanite consort of Baal and was later fused with Ashtart/Ashtoret/Astarte to become Atargatis, the goddess the Greeks associated with Aphrodite and who was known to the Romans as Dea Syria. In Hebrew she was primarily Asherah, a blend of Anat, Ashtart, and the more motherly Athirat (the Ugaritic consort of El), and was also reminiscent of the old Mesopotamian Inanna/Ishtar. It might be argued that the many Western Semitic goddesses can be seen as aspects of the one Great Goddess.

Little is known of the pre-biblical Western Semitic creation myths, but creation is suggested in various Ugaritic fragments. These texts imply that El earned the titles "creator" and "Father of the Gods" by, like the Greek Kronos, defeating his parents, Heaven and Earth. Having taken over the creator role, El became the head of the Canaanite pantheon, the source of virility without which life was not possible. One Ugaritic tablet tells how in ancient times, as El stood at the seashore, his hand (read "penis") grew as long as the sea itself. With him were two women, his wives,

Baal, the great god of Canaan

whom he kissed and impregnated simultaneously. They gave birth to Dawn and Dusk. On the other hand, as noted above, El's wife also held the title of "Mother of the gods," a title that presumably came with her role as El's consort and activating aspect.

It is in the so-called Baal cycle that we find more complex and complete stories suggesting creation, or at least the early establishment of divine order through the kind of war in heaven that also exists in Anatolian, Mesopotamian, Hebrew, Christian, and other Middle Eastern mythologies, as well as in the mythologies of Indo-Europeans. It is clear that by the late second millennium B.C.E., Baal, like Marduk in Mesopotamia, had taken over the position at the head of the pantheon, El having withdrawn from active participation in the affairs of creation. But this withdrawal was a gradual process involving a great struggle and a descent by Baal into death itself.

The Baal cycle opens with the demand of Yamm, the sea and river god ("Prince Sea," "Judge River")—perhaps a male equivalent of the Mesopotamian female Tiamat, who was destroyed by Marduk—that Baal accept his supremacy. Yamm is supported in this demand by the ancient father god El, who apparently is allied with Yamm in his attempt to prevent Baal from achieving supremacy among the gods. El commissions Yamm to fight Baal, as the Hurrian-Hittite Kumarbi had commissioned Ullikummi to fight Teshub. As Yaweh, "with his strong arm . . . cleft the sea monster . . . struck down Rahab with his skill" (Job 26:12), Baal successfully battles Yamm, using sacred thunderbolt weapons made by the craft god, and he dismembers his enemy as Marduk had dismembered Tiamat. Baal "destroys Judge River," as Yahweh caused the Sea of Reeds to part for the Hebrews. The goddess Ashtart (Astarte) proclaims Baal's new status: "Hail, the conquering Baal, Cloud-rider."

Meanwhile, Baal's sister-wife Anat has been violently subduing enemies of Baal—so violently, in fact, that Baal calls her off and tricks her into returning to his side, presumably so that she will not destroy the whole world. This situation is reminiscent of the Egyptian god Re 's having to recall the goddess Hathor-Sehkmet from her destructive rampage in the Egyptian flood myth. Upon Anat's return, Baal announces that he requires a palace commensurate with his new status. Anat agrees to help in convincing their father, El, to allow the construction of such a palace, but to obtain permission, Anat and Baal have to use bribery to gain the support of El's consort Athirat (Asherah). Ewa Wasilewska and others suggest that the building of Baal's palace, like the building of Marduk's temple and Yahweh's temple (2 Samuel 5–7, 1 Kings), is a metaphor for the creation process and for the belief that "Baal re-establishes existing principles and preserves the order of existence" (Wasilewska, p. 116).

During the building of Baal's palace, a dispute arises over the question of a window. The architect god, Kothar, wants to install one, but Baal, almost certainly because of the ancient superstition that Death enters a home through a window, refuses to have one installed. It is only after more military victories and a great celebratory banquet in the palace that the god agrees to a window. Once it is constructed, Baal proclaims his new position of dominance as the storm god and refuses to pay the tribute traditionally offered to Death.

The final episode of the cycle is concerned with the struggle between Mot (Death) and Baal (Life). Invited by Mot to descend to the underworld, Baal cannot refuse. After mating eighty-eight times with a heifer—perhaps Anat, as in the Middle East the head god is frequently depicted as a bull and the goddess as a cow—Baal enters the underworld and is, from the world's point of view, dead. Baal has taken his children and the elements of his storm-godship with him. The world thus is deprived of weather and fertility. Anat, El, and the other gods mourn and wonder what will happen to the world without the divine energy that is Baal, the "Lord of the Earth." The faithful Anat, like Isis in Egypt, springs into action. She confronts Mot, who says he has devoured Baal, and she "splits" him with her sword, "grinds" him with a hand mill, and "sows" him in the fields. The result is the return of Baal and of weather and fertility. Michael Coogan points out that in this mysterious association of death and the agricultural process we have a metaphor for the mystery of agriculture itself and for the mystery of weather, by which the dead seed is transformed into a living plant (1978, pp. 83–84).

After Anat defeats Mot, El has a dream of Baal's return and the restoration of fertility. He sends the Sun to find the lost god, who returns and reasserts his power. In seven years, however, the struggle between Death and Baal resumes, just as in nature, fertility and abundance are always under the threat of drought and devastation.

Canaanite mythology contains hero myths such as those of Danel and Aqhat and Kitra (Keret), in which fertility is a central theme. [Coogan (1978, 1987), Cooper, Gibson, Wasilewska]

CANDAINI EPIC Performed in central India (Chhattisgarh) by men of the Raut (cowherd) caste in a combination of dance and song, this epic is the story of Candaini, a raja's daughter who leaves her husband because the goddess Parvati has made him impotent. Candaini falls in love with Lorik, a local man, who fights and defeats an Untouchable who has been making unwelcome advances. Candaini and Lorik have an affair and leave home for Hardi Gahr. On the way they have many adventures. Candaini almost loses her lover in an all-female country. She does, in fact, lose him to his wife when they return to their original country.

CAO GUOJIU Cao Guojiu had become disillusioned with court life as a member of the Chinese royal family of the Song dynasty. He decided to undertake a quest for the Dao (Tao), the enlightenment "way." One day he came upon a river and showed a boatman there his imperial credentials, hoping that the man would be impressed and would take him across the water. But the boatman was in reality Lu Dongbin, one of the Eight Immortals of Daoism (Taoism). Worldly rank had nothing to do with finding the Dao, he informed Cao Guojiu. The latter, humiliated, threw his credentials into the water and so took a major step toward becoming himself one of the Eight Immortals.

CARIBBEAN MYTHOLOGY Generally speaking, Caribbean mythology is considered in two periods: the pre-Columbian and the post-Columbian. The first period is dominated by the traditions of the Island Arawak and Island Carib peoples, who migrated to the West Indies from South America in the first centuries of the Common Era. The second reflects the combined influence of Christianity and African religions on the pre-Columbian culture.

The Island Arawak lived principally in the Greater Antilles—Puerto Rico, Hispaniola (now Haiti and the Dominican Republic), Jamaica, and Cuba. The Island Carib inhabited the Lesser Antilles—Saint Christopher-Nevis, Antigua, Guadeloupe, Dominica, Saint Lucia, Barbados, Grenada, Saint Vincent, and Tobago.

Both the Island Arawak and Island Carib peoples had chief gods who were essentially uninvolved with human life. The Arawak high god was Iocauna or Guamaonocon and sometimes Jocakuvaque, Yocahu, Vaque, Maorocon, or Macrocoti. He was not himself a creator and was born of a Great Mother goddess who had various names, reflecting various functions, such as childbirth, the moon, and the tides. She was called Attabeira, Mamona, Guacarapita, Iella, and Guimazoa. There were also wind and rain goddesses and healing goddesses. The prominence of goddesses in the actual working of human life resembles the arrangements among the Native North American pueblo cultures of the Southwest, where the likes of Spider Woman and Changing Woman tended to be more important than the high gods.

The Carib high god was Akamboue or Nonuma. Nonuma was a moon god, more important than Huoiou, the sun god, who was less involved with human affairs.

Spirits played a role among both island groups. They were called variously Icheiri, Mabouia, and Zemiis. Both peoples had after-life mythologies. For some of the Arawak, there was an underworld known as Coaibai. In the absence of true creation myths from the Arawak and Carib peoples there are many origin myths. For the Arawak, the sun and moon, as well as the first people, emerged from caves or grottoes in the earth. The Arawak were taught how to live by a culture hero–trickster, Guaguigiana. As for the Caribs, their first man, Louguo, came not from caves but from the sky, and the rest of the first people emerged from his navel and thighs. Some of the early people were turned into constellations back in the sky.

With the coming of Christianity and then African slavery, such cults as Haitian Voodoo, Cuban Santeria, Trinidadian Shango, and much later (in Jamaica) Rastafarianism developed, along with ancestral cults. Voodoo owes much to European folklore about the Christian saints as well as to religions of various African peoples. Santeria grew out of the mix of Catholicism and animal sacrifice and musical traditions of the African Yoruba people. [Glazier, Simpson, George]

CARTHAGE Magna Carthago, near what is modern Tunis, is traditionally thought to have been founded by Phoenicians from Tyre 100 years before the founding of Rome. This was Carthage, the city of Hannibal, the rival city to Rome in the Punic Wars, the last of which culminated in the city's complete destruction in 146 C.E. In Roman myth, Carthage was the city of Queen Dido, visited by the Trojan hero Aeneas on his way to founding the "new Troy" (Rome). The visit, marked by love between Dido and Aeneas and ending in Dido's tragic death, is described by Virgil in his epic the *Aeneid*.

CASSANDRA The daughter of King Priam and Queen Hecuba of Troy, Cassandra was so loved by the Greek god Apollo that he gave her the gift of prophecy. When Cassandra refused the god's advances, however, he became so angry that he cursed her prophecies, condemning them never to be believed. Cassandra was taken as booty by Agamemnon to Argos after the Trojan War . In spite of her prophetic warnings—which Agamemnon, of course, did not believe—the king was killed by his wife, Clytemnestra, and her lover Aegistos. Cassandra, too, was murdered.

CASTOR AND POLYDEUCES Castor and Polydeuces (Pollux in Rome), the Greek Dioskouri (*Dioscuri*, literally, "sons of god"; the *Castorae* in Rome), were said by Homer not to have been divine, but to have been the twin sons of Leda and Tyndarios of Lacedaemon (Sparta). The more common belief was that the twins were sons of Zeus and Leda, the god having impregnated the mortal woman when he ravished her in the form of a swan. It is, of course, as Zeus's sons that they are known as the Dioskouri. What-

Dido and Aeneas in Dido's Carthage

The Gemini, Castor and Pollux

ever their parentage, they are considered to be the brothers of Helen, later to be known as Helen of Troy, whom they rescued from Athens, where she had been carried as a young woman by Theseus. The twins were part of Jason's Argonaut party and were apotheosized by their father Zeus as the stars known as the Gemini. The Dioskouri, given their Lacedaemon connections, were particularly worshipped in Sparta, and later they became important as protectors of the Romans. Like divine twins of other Indo-European cultures—the Ashvins in India, the children of the goddess Macha in Ireland, Horsa and Hengist in Britain—the Dioskouri were closely associated with horses and perhaps are ultimately rooted in the ancient Indo-European ritual of the horse sacrifice.

CATAKANTARAVANAN This is a Tamil epic of India, which owes much to the better-known *Ramayana*, but which features a woman, Rama's wife Sita, as the main character. In this epic, Sita leads the battle against the

demon called Satakantharavana (Ravana). The epic begins with Satakantharavana announcing that he will take revenge against Rama and his people for their recent defeat of his relatives in Lanka. Sita begs Rama's permission—and receives it—to lead the battle against the demon. After many days of difficult battle, with Rama as her charioteer and the Monkey King Hanuman as her general, Sita—empowered by her immortal connections— defeats the demon king and his allies.

ÇATAL HÜYÜK One of the earliest enclosed Neolithic urban-like centers, this seventh-millennium B.C.E. Anatolian settlement contains artifacts that suggest the existence of both a significant prehistoric Neolithic goddess and a bull god. Somewhat later versions of the same or similar figures have been discovered at the Anatolian settlement known as Hacilar. The Çatal Hüyük site was discovered in 1957 by archeologist James Mellaart on the Konya plateau and is arguably the most revealing of prehistoric sites anywhere. A now-familiar image from that site is the tiny terra-cotta figurine of a large woman seated between feline animals and apparently giving birth.

She is generally referred to as the Mother Goddess, and although it is convenient and probably even correct to assume that identity for her, it is important to remember that without written documents, we can know little of the specifics of her story; her genealogy and her name, if she was more than a generic entity, are a mystery. We can, of course, hypothesize about her comparatively by looking ahead to her descendants among literate cultures, figures at least somewhat recognizable as such by their association with animals and with fertility. These would include, for example, Inanna in Mesopotamia and Isis in Egypt. We can glean at least some direct knowledge of the Çatal Hüyük goddess's deeds by way of the many wall paintings in buildings obviously intended as shrines and sanctuaries at the site.

The goddess is depicted not only as a mother but as a young girl and as an old woman, indicating her association with the year and with other cycles of nature. Sometimes she is associated with a bull, clearly a representation of the male principle. The bull, like the goddess, is depicted at various stages of life, in all likelihood representing seasonal and lifetime changes in plants and humans. He is a tiny horned animal emerging in birth, and he is a mature and vibrant figure facing the goddess on a Çatal Hüyük sanctuary wall. In these roles he foreshadows later themes of the mother goddess and her son-lover.

Those who doubt a Neolithic understanding of the connection between sexual intercourse and birth would do well to consider one relief in a Çatal Hüyük shrine that depicts two figures—a male and a female—intimately embracing and immediately next to it a female figure holding an infant.

Depictions of the goddess easily outnumber those of the male entity at Çatal Hüyük. One of the most startling representations looks forward to later expressions of the necessary role of death in the fertility/regenerative process. Like the Indian goddess, Devi, in her form as the devouring Kali, the Çatal Hüyük mother goddess takes life back into her being in death, even as she delivers it to the world in birth. In many Çatal Hüyük paintings, the goddess is surrounded by plants, but in one early shrine she becomes many overpowering flying vultures who seem to have decapitated tiny humans.

CATHBHAD Cathbhad (Cathbhadh) was the druid, prophet, and teacher closely associated in Celtic mythology with the Irish king Conchobhar Mac Nessa. He was the father of Dechtire, the mother of the great Irish hero Cuchulainn, and he was the grandfather of Naoise and of Conall Cearnach ("Conall of the Victories").

CATTLE OF GERYONES The tenth of the Twelve Labors of the Greek hero Herakles is a version of the ubiquitous Indo-European myth of the cattle raid. Here the hero succeeds in killing the monstrous Geryones, the two-headed dog Orthus, and the giant Eurytion, the vicious guards of Geryones' oxen, before taking the animals to his taskmaster Eurystheus.

CATTLE RAID The theme of the cattle raid is part of a complex cattle cycle that reflects the central role of cattle to ancient economy, religion, and mythology. The theme is particularly associated with the Indo-Europeans and, therefore, with India, Iran, Greece, Rome, and the Germanic and Celtic lands. Mythologist Bruce Lincoln has developed a hypothetical proto-Indo-European cattle raid myth, based on cattle raid myths from all of the above cultures, in which an Indo-European (Aryan) hero has his cattle stolen by a three-headed serpent-monster, one perhaps representing non–Indo-European indigenous populations defeated by invading Indo-Europeans. The hero recovers his cattle with the help of the Indo-European warrior god, establishing the cattle raid as the appropriate activity for the Indo-European warrior. Lincoln relates the cattle raid myth to that of the cattle sacrifice, the original sacrifice of a man and a bull having led to the use of the sacrificed parts to create the world. The full cycle of Lincoln's myth, reflecting aspects of early Indo-European history, involves the sky god-king's first giving cattle to the Aryan people, cattle being, in fact, the central factor in the Indo-European economy. Not surprisingly, the people invaded by the Aryans stole the cattle when possible, only to have the cattle recovered in raids led by a warrior class. This class then gave cattle to the priestly caste for sacrifice that would ensure the constant flow of men and cattle from the sky king.

The best known of the extant cattle raid myths is the Celtic one contained in the Irish epic the *Tain Bo Cuailgne*.

CAULDRON OF PLENTY The Dagda, the father god of the Irish Tuatha Dé Danaan, possessed a magic cauldron that produced endless food. Another magic cauldron is taken by the hero Cuchulainn from a strange castle. A magic cauldron—the "Cauldron of Rebirth"—also plays a role in the Welsh story of Bran the Blessed and in the Welsh Arthurian tale *Spoils of Annwn*, a prototype for the later Holy Grail myth.

CELTIC MYTHOLOGY The origin of the Celts, today the smallest group of Indo-European speakers, is unclear. Some archeologists have suggested the existence of a proto-Celtic Indo-European people in the so-called Beaker and Battle-ax cultures of the third millennium B.C.E. Still others see Celtic beginnings in the Urnfield and Tumulus cultures of the second millennium. Claims with more solid basis in fact are those made for the central European Hallstatt culture of the ninth century B.C.E., a culture marked by the extensive use of iron, and especially for the fifth-century B.C.E. La Tene culture, an Indo-European aristocratic-warrior culture that existed in the European lands we generally think of as Celtic.

It is possible that Celtic peoples began their great migration from the headwaters of the Rhone, Danube, and Rhine rivers as early as the beginning of the first millennium B.C.E. We know that in the fifth century B.C.E. the Greek writers Herodotus and Hecataeus of Miletus (in western Anatolia) reported that by 500 B.C.E. the Celts lived in most areas of central and western Europe. Gaul, Spain, Italy, the Balkans, and even Sicily, Greece, and Asia Minor had all experienced a Celtic presence by then, or would soon after. Early in the fourth century B.C.E. Celtic tribes (Celtae or Galli) overran the city of Rome. In 279 B.C.E. Celts (Keltoi) attacked Delphi, and soon after that Celts (Galatae) penetrated Asia Minor, where they founded Galatia in the area around ancient Gordion, the city of King Midas, where Alexander the Great was said to have destroyed the famous Gordian knot.

A Celtic Smith God

C

C

The Centaur Chiron teaches the young Achilles

The Celtic migrations to Britain took place from the fifth century B.C.E. to the arrival of the Belgae in the first century B.C.E. Celts were in Ireland at least as early as the third century B.C.E.

In spite of the obvious importance of the Celts in Europe during a period we associate primarily with the classical cultures of Greece and Rome, we have little direct knowledge of early Celtic mythology. This is true because, although Celts had contact with the highly literate Greeks as early as 600 B.C.E. in what is now southern France, their druidic priests disdained writing as a means of transmitting sacred text. In this belief in the primacy of oral transmission, the druids resembled their Indo-European relatives in India, the brahmans, for whom works such as the *Vedas* were *Shruti*, that is, "heard" revelation rather than mere *Smirti*, or texts contaminated by human influence.

Continental Celtic myths, then, were essentially not written down until the first century B.C.E. by the Romans, including, among others, Posidonius, Diodorus Siculus, Strabo, Lucan, Tacitus, and especially Julius Caesar in his *de bello Gallico*, a history of the Roman conquest of Gaul (58–51 B.C.E.). As for the mythology of the British Isles, it was not until sometime after the advent of Christianity there—perhaps as late as the sixth century C.E.—that Irish monks

produced the manuscripts that would preserve the traditions of their homeland. Our primary access to Celtic mythology, then, is through the eyes and minds of Romans, who tended to associate the deities of the conquered with their own pantheon, and through Christian writers, who, at least to some extent, sought ways of synchronizing ancient Celtic traditions with those of the new religion.

A good example of the inevitable Roman distortion of the Gaulish pantheon is Caesar's listing of the Celtic gods with Roman rather than Celtic names. He tells us that Mercury is the most worshipped god of Gaul, that he is the god of arts, crafts, and commerce and journeys. Next in rank, he says, are Apollo, who cures disease; Mars, the god of War; Jupiter, who rules the heavens; and Minerva, who teaches the arts and crafts (vol. 6, p. 17).

If Caesar believed Mercury to be the most worshipped of the Celtic gods, it was because his terra-cotta and stone images predominated in Gaul. Sometimes he appears with three heads, reminding us of the Indo-European triad, and sometimes he has a consort called Maia or Rosemerta ("Provider"). As for Caesar's Gaulish Mars, he seems to be represented as a god of healing as well as of war. Caesar's Celtic Apollo is, in fact, a composite of several deities, including a solar god Belenus; another solar god named Grannus, whose consort was Sirona; and a god of thermal springs called Bormo, who was associated with Damona, one of the Indo-European world's many sacred cow goddesses. Caesar's Minerva was another thermal springs goddess, known as Sulis, in Gaul. But she was probably much more. Often called Belisama ("Brightest"), she was in all likelihood the Celtic Great Goddess, other versions of whom we find in Irish mythology, where she represents sovereignty and the land itself.

Various Roman interpreters provided differing versions of the Gaulish pantheon. Three figures stand out in these interpretations. Lucan mentions "harsh Teutates," "dread Esus," and "Taranis," Celtic deities or deity types. All three gods demanded brutal sacrifice. The victims of the three gods were drowned, hanged, and burned, respectively. Teutates, like Esus, was considered by the Romans to be equivalent to either Mercury or Mars, and Taranis was either Jupiter or another name for Pluto Dispater (Dis Pater), the ruler of the Otherworld (*Dis* being the Latin word for the Greek Hades, associating him with the Roman Pluto), whom, according to Caesar, the Gauls thought of as their ancestor. There may be an etymological connection here with the proto-Indo-European Dis Dyaus (sky)—thus Dis Pater ("Sky Father"). It is likely that these three gods are in reality aspects of a single triadic deity. The three-headed "Mercury" mentioned above lends credence to this interpretation. Jaan Puhvel points out that Teutates is derived from the Celtic term for "people"—thus Teutates is the "People's God"—that Esus means "Lord," and that Taranis can be associated etymologically with "thunder" (p. 169).

The Indo-European tripartite arrangement of king/priest-warrior-people is at least reflected here. Some have assumed an Indo-European triadic relationship for these gods—a Celtic trinity equivalent to the Roman Jupiter-Mars-Quirinus. Others doubt this interpretation, however, preferring to see Esus as the equivalent of Caesar's most worshipped Mercury—the high god of the Celtic pantheon. For Jaan Puhvel, Esus-Taranis-Teutates is a triad resembling not so much the Roman triad as the also sacrifice-demanding Germanic Odin-Thor-Freyr triad (pp. 169–170).

The Celts who came to the British Isles in waves beginning as early as the sixth century B.C.E. were Gaels (Goidels), the ancestors of the Celtic peoples who still inhabit Ireland and Scotland, and the Cymri, Brythons (Britons), and Belgae, whose descendants can be found in Wales and Cornwall (as well as in Brittany in France). The word "British" is a derivation of the old Breton "Brytass," a synonym for the insular Celts.

The invading Celts displaced but were certainly influenced by the religious and mythological traditions of earlier peoples, the prehistoric builders of stone circles such as Stonehenge. The Celts themselves were challenged by the tentative invasion of Julius Caesar in the middle of the first century B.C.E. and were conquered by Rome a century later. Roman influence on Celtic religion and mythology is evident in all parts of Britain. But by about 300 C.E., Roman Britain had begun to be attacked by Germanic peoples, and by the middle of the fifth century C.E., the Roman legions essentially left to fight more urgent battles. Now in a weakened position, the Celts were gradually confined by the Germanic invaders to Wales, Scotland, and Cornwall, and to Ireland—this, in spite of a possible great battle won in about 450 C.E., in which the Celtic peoples were said to have been led by the legendary King Arthur of Camelot.

The Germanic peoples, first the Angles and Saxons (the Anglo-Saxons) and later their cousins the Norsemen or Vikings from Scandinavia, of course brought their own religious traditions and accompanying myths. The Germanic peoples, like the Romans and the Celts, were Indo-Europeans, a fact that explains a certain compatibility between Celtic, Roman, and Germanic mythology, and even with Romanized Christianity, which would achieve hegemony in the British Isles by the middle of the seventh century C.E.

In a discussion of insular Celtic mythology, then, several factors need to be kept in mind. While it is true that druidic, brahmanic-like bards or *filidh* kept the ancient stories alive, there was a significant passage of time between the Celtic arrival in Britain and the compilation of the ancient sagas by Irish Christian monks in the sixth century C.E. and much later Welsh writers. And there is the peculiar mixture of traditions resulting from the contact in the British Isles between the cultures of indigenous people, the invading continental Celts, the Romans, the Germanic peoples, and the Christian missionaries. It can be argued, therefore, that Celtic-based mythology in the British Isles can be more reasonably referred to as Irish mythology and Welsh mythology rather than Celtic mythology. [Puhvel, Fee and Leeming, Leeming (2003)]

CENTAURS Inhabitants of Mount Pelion in Thessaly, these half-man, half-horse creatures of Greek mythology were the result of unnatural matings between Centauros, the son of King Ixion of the Lapiths, himself also a sexual outlaw, and the wild mountain mares of the area. Not surprisingly, the centaurs, as a race, were generally considered to be violent and sexually licentious. These characteristics are evident in the myth in which the centaur Eurytion at the wedding of Hippodamia to King Perothous of the Lapiths attempted to rape the bride. The result of the centaur's act was a much-depicted battle—the Centauromachy on the Athenian Parthenon, for example—between the centaurs and Lapiths in which the Lapiths, with the help of the Athenean hero Theseus, defeated their enemies, who were expelled to Mount Pindus.

A centaur known not for violence and sexuality but for wisdom and kindliness was Chiron, a favorite of Apollo and Artemis, who was a teacher to the heroes Jason and Achilles, among others.

CENTEOTL AND CHICOMECOATL The Aztec god and goddess of maize, these deities were naturally close to the water goddess Chalchuitlicue and her husband, the fertility god Tlaloc, as well as to Xilonen, the goddess associated with the early stages of maize plants.

CENTRAL ASIAN MYTHOLOGY The central Asian population is composed of a large variety of peoples. Siberia, for example, has long been home to the Samoyeds, the Tungus, Ostiaks, and Voguls of the Finno-Ugrian race; Altaic, Yakut, Tuvin, Buryat, and Khakass peoples of the Turko-Mongol race; and Paleo-Siberian peoples, including the Chuckchi, the Galyaks, the Koryak, the Yukaghir, and other central Asian peoples.

Not a great deal is known of pre-Buddhist, pre-Muslim central Asian mythology, but it does seem clear that creation myths were of central importance. Among these myths, the earth-diver motif seems clearly to have been predominant. The earth-diver story, also popular in Native North Ameri-

Mongolian Shamans

ca—an area of the world first populated in all likelihood by central Asians—involves a plot in which an animal is sent by the creator to find an earthly substance in the depths of the primal waters. Often a devil-trickster figure assists the creator and sometimes tries to usurp his position in the universe. There are also central Asian myths of the separation of sky and earth and the resulting loss of direct communication between humans and gods. The Samoyeds and others still have a sun god and a moon cult and many spirits. For many central Asians, the world was held up by a giant whose feet were in Hell. Hell was a place populated by spirits who sent evil to the world.

Some people living today in the Altai Mountains of Mongolia still possess a mythology that is influenced both by their own shamanistic past and their contact with Islam, Buddhism, Christianity, and even Zoroastrianism. The Turko-Mongols and Finno-Ugrians, especially, see creation as a dualistic struggle between the good work of a spirit—for example, Num or Ulgen (Ulgan)—and a competing first-man, devil-trickster figure such as Nga or Erlik. One story tells how the Erlik, created by Ulgen from clay, was, like the devil of biblical creation, flung out of Heaven for attempting to usurp the creator's position. After Erlik's expulsion, Ulgen created the earth. As in the case of Satan in the Adam and Eve story of Genesis, Erlik makes his way to earth and corrupts the first woman, bringing to us all the ills we now experience.

In another Altaic creation myth, one of the earth-diver variety, the first-man devil-trickster character tries unsuccessfully to fly higher than God, falls into the primeval waters, and begs for God's help. God orders the devil to dive into the depths to find earth, and so the world is created. When the devil tries to hide some of the earth in his mouth so as to make his own world, God discovers the trick and forces the devil to spit out the hidden material, which becomes the world's wetlands.

Among many Siberians, there is, in addition to the earth-diver creation, a cosmology centered around an egg-like universe made up of three earths—upper, middle, and lower. An Yggdrasill-like *axis mundi* world tree rises up from the lower earth through the navel of the middle earth to the pole star. The sun and the moon sit at the top of the tree and the souls of the unborn live in its branches. The sun is worshipped as a sustainer of life; the moon brings the unborn to human mothers.

The first of the Siberian earth deities seems to have been an Earth Mother who sits at the roots of the great axis tree. The ancient Mongols called her Atugan. For some peoples the Great Goddess was the wife or sister of the supreme sky god; she sometimes was said to have assisted in the creation process. Most important, the Great Mother figure was associated with the earth and nature. For some peoples there was not a single earth mother but several—each responsible for an aspect of life. The Yakuts, for instance, had the goddess Itchita, who protected health; Ynakhsyt, who protected cattle; and Ajysyt, who was connected with children and childbirth. The ancient Turks worshipped Umai (Umay), a childbirth goddess who was of primary importance and whose name meant "source." The Tungus worshipped a similar goddess. The earth was also full of lesser deities or earth spirits, avatars of the Great Mother with whom shamans communicated and who were associated with particular places and functions.

In Siberian religion, as in Native American religion, shamanism was ever present. Not only did the shaman concern himself with individual cures, with the placating of spirits who entered a body to cause disease, he was also responsible for ceremonies by which spirits can be appeased for the benefit of the whole community. Siberian shamans performed, and sometimes still perform, important rites before hunts, for example, and other rites to end droughts. In short, the shaman was the important mediator between the spirit world and the human world. It is said that shape-shifting shamans were able to travel in various forms—often as animals—into the spirit world to retrieve souls. The shamanic travel takes place during a trance or séance. As the shaman undergoes trials in the other world, his assistant describes his adventures to the people in attendance. Usually Siberian shamans were "called" to their profession by shaman ancestors in the underworld rather than appointed by the tribe. It was said that the shaman's soul enters the world in the form of his special animal—his totem—given him by the earth mother at the root of the world tree.

A Siberian underworld was thought to be somewhere below the domain of the Great Mother Goddess and was ruled over by a male king who directed its spirits and judged its inhabitants. On the other hand, it must be noted that the period of death below the earth was for many Siberians a period of gestation leading to rebirth, as is also the case, for instance, with some Hindu concepts of afterlife.

For some Tungus Siberians, the corporal soul, or *been*, takes the river to the underworld while the individual's clan soul, the *omi*, eventually goes back to the earth and enters a tent smoke hole and then the womb of a woman, producing a new clan member. Some Tungus say that the soul of an individual is attached to the Master Spirit Seveki in the upper world and that evil spirits cut the string, causing the individual to die. Still others say that the *been* goes to the underworld, ruled by the chief ancestor Mangi or Xargi, the original progenitor of shamans and the bear brother of the creator. Mangi then searches for the *omi*, which has taken the shadow form called *xanjan*. When he finds it, the soul turns into a bird and returns to earth to enter another being.

The supreme being for most Siberians was a personification of the sky, a creator who tended not to interfere in his creation but whose presence ensured harmony and order in the universe. His contact with humans was by way of messengers and shamans. The Tungus called this god Buga. Others called him Es or Turum, or Num. The sky usually had an evil brother or companion who competed with him as a creator and who could cause difficulties for humans, a figure such as Erlik. Associated with the supreme deity were lesser sky gods, such as personifications of the sun and moon, who were sometimes husband and wife, sometimes brother and sister. Often it was the moon rather than the sun who was male.

The Siberian mythological world was full of master spirits. Any given people's territory—its water, its mountains, its animals, its particular places—was ruled over by master spirits who were necessarily enemies of people of other territories. If a person died, that person went to live with the master spirit of the element responsible for his death. Often the master spirits took on animal or human shapes. Certain master spirits seem to have been ubiquitous. The master spirit of fire was one such figure, sometimes taking the form of an old woman who watches the fire. Even today the tradition of the Mother Fire persists, in which the fire is fed pieces of food in return for protecting herds. Animals are associated with the master spirit of the woods, the guardian of the hunt. The master spirit of water is an ancient man who watches over the fish and lives in waters. The Tungus have territorial master spirits known as Territory Mothers (*Dunne Enin*). And there are master spirits of the lower world who are shaman ancestors. The Buryats have spirits called *tengri*—fifty-four good ones in the west, where the god Eseg Malan is king, and fifty-five bad ones in the east, where the god of the dead, Erlik, reigns.

Turko-Mongolian mythology was essentially monotheistic. The supreme being was Tengri, the sky personified. The Yakuts called him "the white master creator." To some Tartars he was Ulgen, and it was his assistants who were called, collectively, tengri. Tengri watched over the cosmos and the human social order and later was assimilated into the Islamic concept of the one god, Allah. Other deities were aspects of Tengri, whether Odlek, the personification of time, or Umai, the embodiment of the placenta and childbirth, and sometimes the earth itself. Animals—especially the wolf, the bear (a father-man in disguise), and the eagle—were important figures. The Turko-Mongols believed in the life of the soul after death and in the power of shamans to communicate with spirits.

Origin myths are popular among the Turko-Mongols, as are myths of miraculous conceptions and births. The great Mongol conqueror Gengis Khan was deified and was said to have been a descendant of the union between the Blue Wolf and a wild doe. The ancient Turko-Mongol ancestor Alp Kara Aslan (Heroic Black Lion) was born of a woman raised by an eagle. He was adopted and suckled by a lioness. The hero Uighur Buqu Khan, parented by two trees, was born of a knothole. Other heroes and heroines were miraculously conceived by rays of light and various animal combinations. [Grimal, Bonnefoy (1991)]

CENTZON TOTOCHTIN These are the "four hundred rabbits" of Aztec mythology. They are associated with fertility and drunkenness—specifically by way of the beverage called *pulque*. Their leader is Tepoztecatl, the god of drunkenness.

CEPHALUS AND PROCRIS Cephalus, happily married to Procris, rejected the advances of the Greek goddess Eos (Latin Aurora), the goddess of dawn. Irritated by the rejection, Eos challenged Cephalus to test his wife's fidelity. When Cephalus agreed, Eos disguised him, and in his guise he almost seduced Procris with beautiful gifts before revealing himself as her husband. Procris was so humiliated that she fled to Crete. There Artemis gave her a fine dog and a spear that could never miss its mark. Eventually Procris went back to her husband disguised as a handsome youth, whom Cephalus promised to love in return for the dog and spear. When the boy revealed himself to be Procris, Cephalus became reconciled to his wife. But the jealous Procris spied on her husband, who accidentally killed her while out hunting with the ever-accurate spear.

CERBERUS Originally a monster with one hundred heads, resembling his hundred-headed father, Typhon, Cerberus later came to be depicted as a terrifying dog with three heads, the tail of a serpent, and serpent's or dragon's heads springing from his back and necks. The serpent aspect is consistent with his relationship to Echnida, a monstrous primordial half woman, half serpent. Cerberus belonged to

Cerberus sits with Hades and Persephone in the Underworld

the underworld god Hades; his job was to devour anyone who tried to escape the underworld and recross the river Styx. Only two heroes seem to have succeeded in overpowering him—Orpheus, with his beautiful music on his way to retrieving Eurydice, and Herakles, who managed to carry the beast to the upper world, thus accomplishing the last of his Twelve Labors.

CERES Ceres was probably a pre-Roman southern Italian goddess of earth, grain, and fertility. The Romans early on identified her with the Greek goddess Demeter.

CERIDWEN In Welsh mythology Ceridwen is the magician mother of Gwion Bach and Afagddu. She boils up a magic potion in a cauldron hoping to make her ugly son Afagddu the wisest of men. But a drop falls on Gwion Bach's thumb and he sucks it, thus attaining ultimate wisdom. His furious mother chases him and eventually swallows him in his disguised form as a grain of wheat. But the wheat grain becomes the source of the miraculous conception of the great and wise poet-prophet Taliesen, the reborn Gwion Bach. Ceridwen abandons the baby, placing him in a leather bag, which she throws into a river. The child is later found and adopted by Elffin and his father.

CERNUNNOS A horned Celtic god of Gaul (modern France) and parts of the British Isles, Cernunnos was a god of fertility, like the Italian goddess Ceres. He carries a club and is lord of the animals. Perhaps because of his association with planting and seeds, he was associated with the underworld. The Romans linked him to Mercury, who led souls to the underworld, and to Apollo, as he provided light for the dead in their graves. Sometimes he is equated with Dispater and the Irish Dagda

CERYNEAN HIND This golden-horned, bronze-hooved creature was captured by the Greek hero Herakles as his third of Twelve Labors.

CESAIR According to the *Book of Invasions*, Cesair (Cessair) was the granddaughter of Noah and the daughter of Bith. It was said that when her father was denied a place in the ark before the flood, she advised him to build an idol, who in turn advised the building of a second ark. In the second ark, Cesair and her people arrived in Ireland as its first "invaders," only forty days before the flood overtook the island and killed everyone there except for Cesair's husband Fintan (Finian mac Bochra), who changed himself into a salmon and survived.

CHAC Like the Aztec Tlaloc, the Mayan Chac was the god of water and fertility. He was said to have opened a primal stone that contained the first seed of maize.

CHALCHIUHTLICUE This Aztec goddess of fresh waters and the waters of childbirth was the wife of Tlaloc, the rain deity. She was the goddess who brought the fourth age to an end with a great flood.

CH'ANG O The Chinese goddess of the moon, Ch'ang O (Heng O)—the Lunar Toad—is protected by the moon after she steals and swallows an immortality herb from her husband, Yi, the Excellent Archer, who is known for shooting down nine of the ten suns that used to pass the sky one after the other each day.

CHANGING WOMAN Sometimes called White Shell Woman and White Bead Woman, Changing Woman is a major Navajo Holy Person—in effect, a goddess—who plays an important role in the female puberty myth and ritual known as the *kinaalda*. It is Changing Woman who gives female humans the capacity to give birth. The myth of Changing Woman tells how one day First Man heard a baby crying. He found the baby in a cradle made of rainbows; he took the baby to First Woman, and Talking God and House God arrived to tell them what an important event the coming of this baby was. First Man and First Woman received the baby as their own; two days the baby sat up, and in four she could walk. On the tenth day, the child was dressed in white shell and was named White Shell Woman and also Changing Woman. To the people she brought fertility and regeneration. Changing Woman became the virgin mother, by the sun, of the Navajo Twin War or Hero Gods. A ray of the sun's light had passed through the water of a waterfall and impregnated her. The twins were called Monster Slayer and Born for Water.

CHAOS Chaos is the primal void or state of uniform non-differentiation that precedes the creation of the world in most creation myths. In the Greek creation myth of Hesiod's *Theogony*, Chaos (the "Void") seems only vaguely if at all anthropomorphic, but it gave birth to Gaia ("Mother Earth"), Eros ("Desire"), Erebos ("Darkness"), and Nyx ("Night"), all aspects of existence necessary for creation.

CHARIOTEERS Charioteers often have symbolic importance, especially in Hindu mythology. As the driver of the hero's vehicle of war, the charioteer is more a guide than a servant. In fact, he sometimes represents the hero's particular source of divine guidance—his or her divine alter ego, as it were. Thus Krishna, the "yoga master," is the logical charioteer for the Pandava hero Arjuna in the *Bhagavadgita* segment of the epic the *Mahabharata*. As an incarnation or avatar of the god Vishnu, he not only drives the hero's chariot but, as his teacher, guides him along the proper divine path. In the Tamil folk epic *Catakantaravanan*, it is in his incarnation as Rama that Vishnu, in effect, guides the heroine, Rama's wife Sita, as her charioteer in her war against the demons. The significance of the charioteer is surely derived in part from the importance of the horse and chariot introduced by warrior Indo-Europeans as they moved into southern Europe, the Middle East, and the Indo-Iranian land masses during the third and second millennia B.C.E. The driver of the warrior's chariot would naturally have been an extremely important figure on whom success in war depended. The chariot was the jet fighter plane of the second and third millennia, and the charioteer was its pilot, a member of an aristocratic class. The relationship between the warrior and his driver was crucial and inevitably the subject of much lore. The list of famous Indo-European chariot pilot heroes is long. Iolas was his uncle Herakles' charioteer, and without him Herakles could not have defeated the Hydra. Patroklos was Achilles' driver in the Trojan War and was so admired that his master's immortal horses wept at his death and the previously pouting Achilles returned to the battle to seek revenge. The wind gods themselves drove the chariot of Zeus. In the epic, the *Tain*, Cuchulainn, the Irish Achilles, was served by the heroic and faithful Laig (Laeg), who drove his companion into battle fury by jeering at him and who, during the hero's final battle, purposely threw himself in front of the spear meant for Cuchulainn.

CHARON The son of Erebos ("Darkness," "Underworld") and Nyx ("Night"), Charon was the deity, always depicted as a ragged old man, assigned to ferry the dead across the underworld rivers, the Acheron and the Styx. Because he demanded payment for his services the Greeks always inserted a coin into a corpse's mouth before burial.

CHEROKEE SUN GODDESS The Cherokee Indians of North America worship the sun as a goddess rather than as a god. They tell a story about this goddess that is at once a disappearing-god myth, like that of the Hittite Telipinu, and a flood myth.

The sun goddess always visited her daughter's house in the center of the sky during her daily trip across the heavens, and while there, she often complained that her grandchildren, the people of the earth, never looked directly at her but squinted at her and then looked away. She was particularly jealous of the moon, because the people looked up lovingly at him with smiling faces. So one day the sun decided to destroy her ungrateful grandchildren by remaining for a long time at her daughter's house in the center of the sky. Her prolonged presence caused a terrible concentrated heat to parch the world below. Desperate, the earth people called on spirits known as the Little Men for help. The spirits suggested sending disguised men up to the sky to kill the goddess. Two men dressed as snakes failed miserably in that endeavor, and so did a man impersonating a horned monster. A man disguised as a rattle-snake succeeded only in biting and killing the sun's daughter. This so upset the sun that she locked herself in her house, like the Japanese sun goddess Amaterasu, and the world turned dark and impossibly cold. Again the people called on the Little Men, who advised bringing the daughter back from the ghosts in the Dark Land of the west. For this mission they chose seven men and they gave them a box to carry and gave each one a magic rod. The men traveled to the Dark Land, where they came upon ghosts dancing and quickly caught sight of the sun's daughter dancing in the outer circle. As instructed by the Little Men, each of the seven humans struck the girl with his magic rod, and after the seventh had done so the sun's daughter fell over and the men put her in the box. The other ghosts seemed not to notice, and the men were able tó carry the sun's daughter toward home. But from inside the box she complained bitterly, and finally the men let her out, making the same mistake that the Greek Orpheus did when he looked back at Eurydice just before completing his rescue of her from Hades. As soon as the box was opened the sun's daughter flew away as a redbird. The men reached home with nothing but an empty box, and now the sun, giving up hope of ever seeing her daughter again, flooded the earth

Charon crossing the River Styx

with her tears. Humans sent up dancers to placate the sun and thus stop the flood. At first the goddess ignored the dancers, but finally, when they sang a particular song, she glanced at them and was so pleased by them that she smiled, and the world went back to normal.

CHIBINDA ILUNGA The descendant of the Luba kings in Africa, Chibinda Ilunga met and married Lueji, the Lunda queen and granddaughter of the serpent king Chinawezi. Serpents are frequently closely related to goddesses. So began the history of the Luba-Lunda people.

CHIMERA One of many distorted and bestial offspring of the monsters Echnida and Typhon—also including Cerberus, Scylla, Orthus, and Gorgon—the Chimera (Chimaera _ Greek *khimaira*, "she-goat") was a fire-breathing monster with the head of a lion, the tail of a serpent or dragon, and a goat's head in the middle. Her impossibly fanciful anatomy gives us our word "chimerical," meaning unreal, imaginary, given to fantasies. The Chimera, who did terrible things to the people of Lycia, where a volcano is named after her, was killed by the hero Bellerephon.

CHINAWEZI In African mythology, Chinawezi (Chinaweji) is a name given to the primordial serpent Mother Goddess of creation whose husband for the Luba-Lunda people was Chibinda Ilunga, and for others in southern and central Africa the Sky God Nkuba ("Lightning"). Chinawezi's primary concern was the earth and its waters, the sky being the province of her husband, whose thunderous rumblings caused her waters to swell and sometimes overflow.

CHINESE EMPEROR MYTHS The stories of the ancient rulers of China are part of a Chinese mythology created by scholars at the end of the last millennium B.C.E. The myth of the Three *Huang* (Three August Ones) and the *Di*, the Five Emperors (*Sanhuang Wudi*), was the story of a golden age in which there was harmony between gods and rulers. These first eight monarchs were followed by the mythical Xia and the partly historical Yin and Zou dynasties. From the time of Quinshih Huangdi in the third century C.E., Chinese emperors took the title *Huangdi*, combining, they hoped, the power of the Three August Ones and the ancient Five Emperors (the Di), who were thought by some to have been, in fact, deities on earth. Chinese emperors, therefore, like the Japanese emperors, were in a sense descended from the gods. The August Ones were Fuxi, Shennong, sometimes the wife of Fuxi, Nuwa, and sometimes a fire god named Zhurong or Suiren. Fuxi was the inventor of the trigrams that became the hexagrams of the *I Ching* (*Yi Jing*). It is said that Fuxi

Tribal statues from the tribe of Luba-Lunda

took the form of a snake. He often is depicted holding a square. His wife, Nuwa, whose tail is that of a serpent, holds a compass. The square and compass are symbols of ongoing creation, especially of the *deus faber* sort, and of social order. The fact that the tails of the two figures are usually entwined is indicative of the necessary union of *yin* and *yang*. Shennong is depicted as a plowman, which indicates his concern with agriculture. He is also associated with healing.

Of the Five Emperors, the best known is the Yellow Emperor (Huangdi), whose real name was Xianyuan. He established crafts and guilds. Like many monomythic heroes, the Yellow Emperor was conceived miraculously. His mother, Fubao, received the energy of lightning as she walked in the countryside. The color yellow perhaps signifies a connection with the sun. It was Huangdi who defeated the monster rebel Chiyou. At the end of his life Huangdi achieved apotheosis; he and his entourage were carried up to the gods on a dragon. The Emperor Zhuanxu (Gaoyang, the "Great *yang*") also defeated a monster rebel. In this case the culprit was Gong Gong. It was he who separated Heaven and earth. The Emperor Gu had several wives, who are the sources of several royal lines. The Emperor Yao is thought by some to be historical. The Confucians consider him the model ruler and the ancestor of the Han dynasty. The Emperor Shun underwent several trials before succeeding to Yao's kingdom. When he became emperor he defeated the forces representing certain vices that threatened his own royal virtues. Yu succeeded Shun and was the son of Gun, who had attempted to stop the great Chinese Flood. Yu succeeded in ending the flood by digging channels, signifying the civilizing techniques much admired by the Confucians, who contributed to his myth. Yu was the father, in turn, of the first of the Xia emperors and stands, therefore, at the edge of Chinese history. It was at the end of the Xia dynasty and also at the end of the Yin dynasty that evil emperors effectively ended the golden age.

CHINESE MYTHOLOGY Chinese mythology, as it has developed over the ages, is a mixture of history, legend, and myth. This is most clearly seen in the mythology of the early Chinese emperors. The actual myths of ancient pre-Buddhist China are, for the most part, known to us only from later Confucian works, in which scholars have attempted to place the old stories in a historical context and to use them to illustrate moral and other social principles. In the first-millennium B.C.E. collection entitled *Shanhai jing*, for example, demons and gods were listed for the benefit of travelers. Other sources for ancient myths are the late-fourth-century B.C.E. poems of Qui Yuan. Daoists and Chinese Buddhists contributed their own perspectives to Chinese mythology as well. Daoism contributed the philosophy of a natural order, reflected in the art of *feng shui*, for instance, a system of aesthetic arrangement of space to avoid offending the spirit of that space. Buddhism, among many other things, contributed the idea of the cyclical life of the soul.

In Chinese mythology it is sometimes difficult to separate history and myth, mortals and immortals. The most important gods who have survived in today's popular culture are also considered to be the first Chinese emperors—the Three August Ones and later emperors such as Huangdi, who was also god of war. And even historical figures are well insulated by legends. Furthermore, characters who have all the supernatural qualities of deities are considered to be human.

Figure of the Chinese Goddess Guanyin

Thus Pangu, born in the cosmic egg of creation and himself the animistic source of this world, is known as the First Man. Perhaps the nearest Chinese expression of the kind of absolute godhead we find in the Brahman of Hinduism, for example, is the figure of Earth-Sky or Tiandi (Ti, T'ien), known in the Daoist tradition as the Jade Emperor so important in the story of the Chinese Flood.

Daoism suggests that an individual, through certain spiritual and physical disciplines, can achieve the state of the "immortals" (*Xianren*). Some Daoists consider their founder, Laozi, a god. In his form as the *Laojun* (Lord Lao), he is part of a divine triad presided over by the Yuanshi Tianshun and the Yuanshi's follower the Daojun (Lord of the Dao). These divinities embody Daoist principles. The role of the Yuanshi is that of father and revealer of truth to the Daojun, who passes the truth on to the Laojun, who as Laozi teaches the proper "way," the *Dao*, to human beings.

Goddesses occupy an important place in pre-Buddhist Chinese mythology. Fubao was the mother of Huangdi by way of a miraculous conception. She was the goddess of spirits and divine possession. The mother of the Emperor Yu also conceived miraculously when she swallowed the *yi-yi* seed. Yu was born when her side split open. Jiandi, the mother of the Yin dynasty, conceived miraculously by swallowing a blackbird egg. Perhaps the most important of the ancient goddesses is Nuwa, the serpent sister-wife of the August

One, the Emperor Fuxi. She was the divine matchmaker and the creator of the first humans. It was she who repaired the sky after the monster demon Gonggong smashed one of its supporting pillars.

Easily the most popular Chinese goddess, who is derived from the male Buddhist boddhisattva Avalokiteshvara, is Guanyin (the usually male Kannon in Japan), the goddess of Mercy. Guanyin is also a patron saint of Tibetan Buddhism. In ancient times of suffering and poverty, Guanyin used her breast milk to feed the rice plants and, therefore, the people.

Although there are several versions of early Chinese creation myths, which in all likelihood developed in the pre-Buddhist period, the best known is one that was written down in the third-century C.E. text the *Sanwu Liji*. According to this myth, there was once only a kind of chaos, which resembled an egg. In this cosmic egg was born Pangu (P'an-Ku), who remained in it for eighteen thousand years. When the egg finally broke, the heavy elements, called *yin*, became earth and the lighter ones, *yang*, became the sky. As the earth sank and the sky rose, Pangu grew and became as tall as the distance between yin and yang. It is written in the sixth-century C.E. *Shuyi Ji* that when Pangu died, various parts of his body became aspects of the world, as they do in the animistic creation myths of several other cultures, including several Native North American ones. In this case the eyes became the sun and moon, the body hair became trees and plants, and the head became a sacred mountain. Like most cultures, the Chinese have their flood myth. The great flood was sent by the high god Tiandi (Sky-Earth) during the reign of Yao. As is usually the case with such floods, the cause was the general wickedness of the human race. The single advocate for the human race, which was now stranded on mountaintops plagued by wild beasts, was the god Gun. Gun unsuccessfully pleaded the human case with Tiandi and finally decided, Prometheus-like, to do something on his own. Gun's de facto second creation contains aspects of the earth-diver motif that is so common in central Asia and North America. Gun told an owl and a tortoise that Tiandi had some magical earth substance that could be used to stem the flood. After managing to steal some of the material, Gun dropped it into the waters, where it became land. Although the people were happy, the high god was not, and he sent the fire god Zhurong to kill Gun and to retrieve the magic soil. The flood returned, but Gun's body, guarded by his followers, regained life. Tiandi again intervened by having Gun's body cut by a sword. But out of the cut came Gun's son, the great Dragon, Yu, who once again stemmed the flood. Gun himself became a yellow dragon and lived at the bottom of the waters.

Demons or *gui* are prevalent in the Chinese mythological world. *Gui* also refers to the secondary soul, which is separated from the higher soul (*hun*) at death. The superior soul becomes spirit (*shen*), and if not treated properly in a ritualistic sense, a *gui* can become a ghost or bad demon. Important demons are Chiyou, who fought against the Yellow Emperor, Huangdi; Gonggong, who destroyed one of the pillars of the world with his enormous horn, causing turmoil on earth; and the Four Evils, which any new sovereign had to overcome upon taking power. Chiyou had gigantic teeth, was part animal and part man, and had extra eyes and arms. He was a serpent-human combination, whose follower, the monstrous Xiangliu, ate nine mountains with his nine heads and then vomited up the swamps of the world. [Girardot, Ke, Birrell]

CHIRON A son of the ancient Greek god Kronos, Chiron was a wise and kind centaur who had the benefit of being civilized by Apollo and Artemis. Because of them he learned much about the arts, hunting, and medicine. In later years he became the teacher of heroes, most notably Achilles, Asclepios, Castor and Polydeuces, and Jason. Herakles wounded Chiron by mistake with a poisoned arrow and the good centaur died, giving up his immortality to the Titan Prometheus. Zeus apotheosized him in the constellation Sagittarius.

CHITIMUKULU The African Bemba of Zambia honor Chitimikulu as their founder. He is said to have come to the Bemba land after escaping a death sentence in his native land, where he and his brothers had built a huge tower that fell and killed many people.

CHIYOU A monster of Chinese mythology with horns and a heavily armored head, sometimes with a human body and sometimes with an animal one, Chiyou ate sand and, as a blacksmith, was the inventor of war and armaments. He was a direct descendant of Shennong, one of the so-called Three Augusts or legendary Chinese emperors. Chiyou was also a dancer and a jouster. The best-known story about him involves his fight with Huangdi, also known as the Yellow Emperor. Huangdi's army was made up of various wild animals, Chiyou's of demons. In the battle the two principals used supernatural powers and the natural elements against each other and finally Chiyou was defeated and decapitated by the Winged Dragon. The struggle between Huangdi and Chiyou reflects the cyclical aspect of Chinese mythology. One virtue is overtaken by another until another emerges to take over the previous one. This process is an aspect of the *yin-yang* of Chinese myth and philosophy.

CHRÉTIEN DE TROYES A French poet of the twelfth century C.E., Chrétien wrote metrical romances about the Welsh-British hero King Arthur and his knights of the Round Table. Most famously, he wrote *Perceval or the Story of the Grail*, about Percival (Parsifal) and the quest for the Holy Grail; and *Lancelot, or the Knight of the Cart*.

CHRISTIAN MYTHOLOGY The New Testament, or Christian section of the Bible, various non-canonical or apocryphal "gospels," and as other writings and traditions center on the person of Jesus of Nazareth, a Jewish reformer whose god and "father" was the God of the other two Abrahamic religions, Judaism and, later, Islam. For the Christians, God became a somewhat distant sky god figure whose nevertheless loving purpose was to be accomplished by Jesus, a figure eventually seen as both a human hero and an aspect of God. Christians developed the concept of God as a Trinity, reflecting the Indo-European concept of the triadic deity. God was at once God the Father or Creator, God the Son or Redeemer (Jesus) and God the Holy Spirit or Sanctifier. Yet the Father was not the Son or the Holy Spirit, the Son was not the Father or the Holy Spirit, and the Holy Spirit was not the Father or the Son. The Christian God as Father, like the god of the Jews, was popularly depicted as fully male with no feminine component. Non-Christians, observing the religion from outside, might well suggest, however, that Christians—especially of the Catholic tradition—would, over the centuries, restore something of the feminine to God through the esoteric understanding of Sophia, or Divine

Wisdom, and especially through the veneration of the person of the Virgin Mary.

As it evolved, Christian mythology was able indirectly to incorporate various aspects of Middle Eastern and Greek mythology, especially in relation to dying god and hero motifs and that of the Mother Goddess. Christianity is a religion that looks back to its Jewish roots, but in so doing it expands the possibility of redemption by extending the "kingdom" and the "Promised Land" beyond the Hebrew race, Jewish religion, or land of Canaan to the world at large. To the extent that the religion has insisted over the centuries that its way is the only way and that its myths are literal truth, it has developed a militancy and a tendency toward fundamentalism that has often placed it at odds with the actual teachings of its de facto founder by instigating or supporting violence, abuse, and repression.

Although the early Christians, given their Jewish roots, incorporated the Genesis creation into their mythology, they were also strongly influenced by Greek philosophy. This fact is evident in the prologue to the Gospel of John (1:1–18), the fourth book of the New Testament. Echoing the stoics and especially the ideas of the first-century Jewish philosopher Philo Judeas, John uses the Greek term *logos* to express the first act of creation. For Philo and the Greeks, beginning with Heraclitus in the sixth century B.C.E., the logos was the ordering force of the universe—divine wisdom or reason—the power that turned chaos into cosmos in the beginning.

John identifies Jesus with the logos (the "Word"), indicating the presence of Jesus with God and as God from the beginning of time, thus asserting Jesus' preeminence among all prophets. Genesis begins with the words "In the beginning God created the heavens and the earth." John "clarifies" this understanding with the words "In the beginning the Word [the logos] already was." And he continues, "The Word was in God's presence, and what God was, the Word was. He was with God at the beginning, and through him all things came to be; without him no created thing came into being." And later, "So the Word became flesh"; that is, was born into the world as Jesus, so that the world could, in effect, be created anew through the "flood-death" that was Jesus' sacrifice, a death symbolized by the sacrament of baptism in which the initiate "dies" in the flood of the font and is "born again" in a new creation (John 1:1–14).

The biography of Jesus is contained in the four "gospels" ("good news"), attributed to Matthew, Mark, Luke, and John; in the Acts of the Apostles, also by Luke; and in various non-canonical apocryphal gospel texts such as the Gospel of Thomas and the Gospel of Philip. Mark and Matthew were Jewish followers of Jesus, writing in the period between 70 and 90 C.E.; Luke was a gentile writing in about 90 C.E.; and the identity of John, who wrote in about 100 C.E., possibly in Ephesus, is unknown. Along with the commentaries by followers such as the extremely influential Paul of Tarsus (once Saul), these writings contain mythic elaborations of the historical life of the man Jesus, about whom little more is known than that he was an itinerant Jewish reformer with a significant following, who was crucified in the first century C.E. by the Romans.

It is the mythical or extraordinary events—the annunciation, the nativity, the temptation by the Devil, the miracles, the death by crucifixion, the descent into Hell, the resurrection, the apotheosis by ascension to Heaven—in Jesus' life that make him a particularly complete example of the heroic

A mosaic of Jesus as the Christ Pantokrator, or "Ruler of All"

monomyth and a symbolic figure around whom a major world religion was formed.

But the primary purpose of Jesus as he is depicted in the myths of the New Testament is to demonstrate symbolically the teachings of his ministry, his revised understanding of the Promised Land, and the kingdom to be established by the Messiah. This revision will also involve an assimilation of and broadening of the old Middle Eastern myths of fertility. We move from mere physical fertility and growth to the fertility and growth that are spiritual. As far as Christian theology is concerned, the new covenant expressed by the teachings and the mythic life of Jesus is one that, like the much earlier covenant with Noah, as opposed to that with the later Hebrew patriarchs, extends to all humanity.

The myth of Jesus superseded all other hero myths of the pre-Christian ages in Europe and later in other parts of the world influenced or colonized by Europe. Through Christianity, Europe became—mythologically—a de facto single entity, paying at least lip service to the new message brought by the new hero, a message that sounded more like the message of the eastern Buddha than that of the old European heroes. In terms of practice, however, from the Crusades to modern wars, and in Christian heroes such as St. George, Roland, el Cid, and even King Arthur, Europeans have tended to attach values of the old heroes—values of military

C

A statue of the Cid, hero of Christian Spain against the Moors

dominance and cultural differentiation and hegemony—to a hero who clearly decried such values and whose truer representatives were the martyrs and saints—Francis, Julian of Norwich, Patrick, and others—known more for their missionary work, self-sacrifice, and humility than for military skill. [Armstrong (1993), Pelikan, Watts (1968), Leeming (2004)]

CHRISTMAS The word "Christmas" is derived from "Christ's Mass," the church ceremony that celebrates the birth of Jesus, whom Christians see as the Christ, or Messiah. Thus, in most Latin-based languages, the word for Christmas is derived from the word for birth: *navitas*. The French term, *Noël*, however, probably comes from a word for "news." It seems likely that Christmas has origins in ancient winter solstice celebrations expressing a longing at the darkest time of the year for the return of the light, as in the case of the Roman festival of Sol Invictus. There may also be a source in the celebrations of the Iranian-Zoroastrian solar deity Mithra, who, according to some sources, was born at the winter solstice and whose birth shepherds attended.

CHUANGZI Chaungzi (Chuang tsu) may have been a contemporary of Laozi, the traditional founder of Daoism (Taoism). Like Laozi, Chuangzi was more mystical than his Confucian contemporaries, who preferred to deal with matters of this world. Chuangzi stressed the possibility of the individual's letting go of the dualities of life in favor of union with the *Dao*, the "Way," which is all of existence.

CHURNING OF THE OCEAN OF MILK The Indian *Vedas* and the epic the *Mahabharata* contain versions of a creation story in which, at the suggestion of Vishnu (Narayana), the gods (Devas) and demons (Asuras) churn the primeval ocean

or flood in order to obtain the lost *amrta* or *soma* (ambrosia), which guarantees their immortality. To churn the salt ocean, the immortals placed Mount Mandara (Mount Meru), uprooted by the serpent-demon Ananta (Vasuki), on the back of the great Tortoise, an avatar of Vishnu, who, in the tradition of the earth-diver creation myths, dove to the ocean floor so that the mountain could be placed on his back. The mountain was used as the churning stick. Ananta became the churning cord. According to the epic version of the myth, as the gods and demons churned the sea, clouds and lightning came out of Ananta's mouth and flowers came down from the spinning mountain top and formed garlands on the gods. The motion of the whole process caused a crushing of animals and great trees, and a fire resulted, which was put out by the god Indra. From the smashing of the trees and plants and the juices exuded from the process, the source of soma flowed into the sea. The sea became milk, and eventually the milk became butter, which would be used for ritual purposes. Urged on by Vishnu, the gods and demons continued churning, and beautiful elements of creation came from the waters. But out of the churning also came a terrible poison that enveloped the universe. It was Shiva who, in a ritual chant, was able to take the poison into his throat and swallow it and in so doing save the universe. This is why Shiva's throat is blue. When the soma finally emerged, the Devas and Asuras fought over it and the Devas finally won. This war in Heaven may be said to represent the necessary friction, separation, and differentiation necessary for creation.

CHU-TZU Chu-tzu (Chuti, the Grand Master) was a fourth-century B.C.E. leader of the Mohist school of Chinese philosophy, founded by Mo Ti in the fifth century B.C.E. The Mohists followed a doctrine of universal love in opposition to the formalism of Confucianism. The doctrine is contained in the text called the *Mo-tzu* and in the *Chu-tzu*. In the *Chu-tzu* we find a cosmology. The Grand Master apparently believed that the sky was made up of nine levels, one on top of the other, each divided from the other by a gate guarded by beasts. Beyond the top level there was absolute nothingness, an ultimate void or chaos.

CID, THE The hero of the early-twelfth-century medieval Spanish epic *Poema del Mío Cid* ("Poem of My Cid") was Rodrigo Díaz of Bivar (c.1043–1099), first called the Cid (the "Hero") by the Moors against whom he fought. In the anonymously composed Castillian epic, his powers were exaggerated into those of a true epic hero, and he became the symbol of early Spanish nationalism. The first part of the epic deals with the exile of the Cid by Alfonso VI and ends with his defeat of the Count of Barcelona. In Part Two, the Cid takes Valencia from the Moors and is reconciled with Alfonso. He gives his daughters in marriage to two noblemen. In the third part of the epic, the Cid overcomes his abusive sons-in-law in a trial by combat and marries his daughters to the princes of Aragon and Navarre.

CIRCE The daughter of the Greek sun deity Helios, Circe is best known as the sorceress on the island of Aeaea who, in Homer's *Odyssey*, turned several of Odysseus's crew into swine. It was the god Hermes who gave the hero a potion with which to counteract Circe's magic. Later the sorceress formed an intimate attachment with Odysseus and, no longer playing the role of femme fatale, even helped him continue his journey home. Circe was also of assistance to Jason and her niece Medea in the Argonauts' journey.

CITIES Cities are economic and cultural centers. Traditionally, for a given culture, the city represents the world center. For some ancient Egyptians creation took place when a primeval mound rose from the Nile and became the central temple of the cult center of Heliopolis. Native Americans of the western pueblos generally have emergence creation myths in which the place where the people first emerged from the lower world became their world center settlements. Most ancient cities were cult centers, with everything surrounding a temple or acropolis of the city god. Cities have often been symbolically arranged with gates, for instance, representing the four directions. Cities had gates because they were walled, the walls forming symbolic and actual barriers against the chaos of the surrounding world. So it is that feminine pronouns are often attached to cities, whose gates were in constant danger of being penetrated in war. Defeated cities were ravished. In mythology, as in real life, the "fall" of a city is high tragedy, as in the case of Troy. Cities, like humans, can be subject to deep corruption, as in the case of Thebes ruled by the incestuous, regicidal, and patricidal Oedipus. Cities can take on mythological dimensions related to the spiritual significance of particular events. Banaras was planned and created by Shiva. Jerusalem has mythical and, by extension, political significance to Jews, Christians, and Muslims. The Israelites built their Temple for the Holy of Holies there, Jesus was crucified and resurrected there, Muhammad ascended to the heavens from there. Mecca is a world center and place of pilgrimage for practitioners of Islam, as Canterbury and Rome have been for various Christians and as the world *omphalos* (navel) Delphi was for the Greeks.

Cities can be philosophical or theological entities. In the *Republic*, Plato discussed the city as an expression of our lack of self-sufficiency and our need to look for help beyond ourselves. St. Augustine wrote of the metaphorical *Civitae Dei* ("City of God"). Christians, Muslims, and Jews have all at various times thought of Jerusalem eschatologically and metaphorically: "If I forget thee, O Jerusalem," sings the biblical psalmist, sounding much like John in the Book of Revelation, who speaks of Jerusalem as a "heavenly city" of the future. In short, the city can itself become a myth.

CLYTEMNESTRA Best known as the wife and murderer of King Agamemnon of Mycenae/Argos, Clytemnestra was the daughter of Leda of Sparta, perhaps by Zeus in his form as a swan, or perhaps by King Tyndareus. She first married Tantalus, whom, in the course of feuds in the House of Atreus, Agamemnon killed. Clytemnestra and Agamemnon had three children: Iphigenia, Orestes, and Elektra. Much of the queen's story is told or referred to in the trilogy the *Oresteia*, by the great Greek dramatist Aeschylus. Before Agamemnon went off to the Trojan War, he sacrificed his daughter Iphigenia, as instructed by Artemis. In revenge, Clytemnestra had an affair with her first husband's brother Aegistus and, with him, murdered the king when he returned home. Orestes, urged on by his sister Elektra, avenged their father's murder by killing their mother and her lover.

COATLICUE Coatlicue was an important Aztec earth and mother goddess. She was the mother of the great Aztec deity

Coatlicue, Aztec Mother and Earth Goddess

C

Huitzilopochtli, the sun and war god, whom she conceived miraculously by means of a feather from Heaven. She was murdered by her already-living children, and her death was quickly avenged by her newborn son.

COFFIN TEXTS The earliest sacred funeral texts of the Egyptians were those dating from c. 2375 B.C.E., known as the Pyramid Texts. They related primarily to the death and afterlife rituals of the pharaohs. The so-called Coffin Texts coincided with a certain democratization of the Egyptian religion during the First Intermediate Period, beginning in about 2200 B.C.E. and extending into the Middle Kingdom. The protective spells, incantations, myths, and maps for the voyager in the afterlife were written inside the coffins and tombs used not only by rulers, but by other people of the upper classes as well.

CONALL In Irish mythology, Conall Cearnach (the "Victorious One") was the hero of Ulster who, out of the brain of Mac Da Tho, the king of Leinster, made the magical slingshot that was responsible for the death of King Conchobhar seven years after the shot landed in his head. It was Conall who avenged the death of Cuchulainn.

CONAN Usually known as Conan Maol (the "Bald"), this warrior follower of the Irish hero Fionn (Finn) and the brother of the great warrior Goll was not heroic in the usual sense. His gluttony, his bragging, and his comic cowardliness remind us of Shakespeare's Falstaff and also of the comic side of the gluttonous and impulsive trickster who sometimes makes a fool of himself. A story is told of Fionn and his entourage becoming stuck through sorcery on a floor in the Otherworld. Only Conan the Bald was not released; his friends tore him off the floor, leaving the skin of his buttocks behind.

CONCHOBHAR MAC NESSA In the *Tain Bo Cuailnge*, the epic of the Red Branch or Ulster Cycle of Ireland, Conchobhar was the despotic king of Ulster. Conchobhar's mother, Nessa, had promised to marry King Fergus Mac Roth if he would allow Conchobhar to sit on his throne for a year. Fergus agreed, but when he attempted to regain his throne after the year was up, Conchobhar did not relinquish it. Fergus served the new king until he defected after a particularly dishonorable act on the part of Conchobhar. Conchobhar had fallen in love with his foster daughter, Deirdre, who loved and eloped with Naoise. The king enlisted the help of Fergus to entice the couple back home, promising forgiveness and safe conduct. When they arrived, however, the king had Naoise killed.

Conchobhar won the great battle of the *Tain*, but only with the superhuman help of the hero Cuchulainn. Conchobhar was struck by the "brain ball" (made of lime and the brain of Mac Da Tho and flung by Conall) that stuck in his brain and eventually killed him when it split his head open during one of the king's rages.

CONFUCIUS AND CONFUCIANISM Confucianism is a Chinese religious philosophy that developed from the life and teachings of Confucius. Confucianism is not directly associated with mythology unless legends of the sage himself be considered mythological.

Master Kong, or Kong Fuzi (K'ung Ft-tzu), lived in the Lu state of China in the sixth century B.C.E. Legends about the great sage are contained in the conversations between Confucius and his followers in the *Analects*. Confucius was a government worker, a traveler, and a lover of the arts. Gradually gaining a reputation as a wise man, Kung attracted many disciples as he searched for balance and a better society based on an essential humanism. Although not particularly interested in religion as such or with myth, he accepted the idea of a supreme divinity which is Heaven. Although undermined by the Communist Revolution, Confucianism—the teaching of Confucius—has dominated Chinese philosophy for some two thousand years, sometimes confronting but usually interacting well enough with Buddhism and Daoism.

CONNACHT Connacht, or Connachta, was the province ruled by Queen Medb, the enemy of Conchobhar, Cuchulainn, and Ulster in the Irish epic the *Tain*.

CORN MOTHER The personification of corn in Native North American mythologies is often a figure known as Corn Mother or Corn Grandmother, who is the basis of animistic myths about the origin of corn. The New England–based Wabanaki Corn Mother had blond hair like corn silk. Certain Iroquoian speakers said that Corn Mother was also Earth Mother, the mother of the Creator, and that when she died, corn grew from her breasts, and beans and squash from the rest of her body. The Arikara people of the plains told the myth of a murdered Corn Mother from whom corn grew. The Keresan people of the Southwest say that Corn Mother planted her heart in the earth and said that corn would be the "milk" of her breasts.

A Cherokee myth concerns Kanati, a hunter who went into the woods frequently to find game for his little boy and his wife Selu, meaning "corn." One day, as Selu was washing the meat brought in by her husband, some of its blood fell on the ground and became another little boy. The miraculous conception, of course, signifies the coming of a hero into the world. One day the two boys followed Kanati into the woods to see where he got such an abundance of meat. Hiding, they watched the hunter push a great slab of rock away from a cave mouth and shoot a deer that emerged. The boys waited for several days and then returned on their own to the cave. They pushed the stone aside and were horrified to watch many game animals escape. In fact, from then on, the game animals have hidden in various places in the woods and are much more difficult to find than they were under Kanati's care.

Then the boys spied on their mother and were disgusted to see that she produced beans and corn by rubbing her stomach and armpits. Thinking their mother was a witch, they decided to kill her. Understanding this, Selu agreed to be killed and instructed the boys to bury her body and to keep watch over it for a night. The boys did this and the next day corn had grown up, ready to be harvested.

When people from far off heard of this miracle they came to visit the boys. The boys gave them kernels to plant but explained that the people must keep watch over the seeds every night during the seven days of their journey back home. Of course, the people fell asleep on the seventh night, and now corn grows much more slowly than it did for the original sons of Corn Mother Selu.

The Penobscot people of Maine say that First Mother, who was much loved by First Man, became sad when their children, the people, became so numerous that game became scarce. She told her husband that only one thing would stop her from weeping: he must kill her. The man was horrified and ran to ask advice of the Creator. All-Maker told him he must do as First Mother said. When the man, weeping bitterly, returned home, his wife instructed him to wait until the sun was at the top of the sky. Then he was to kill her and have two of their sons drag her body by her silky yellow hair back and forth over the earth until all of her flesh had been scraped away. After that, the man and his sons were to leave the place for seven moons. The man did as he was instructed and returned to find the earth filled with beautiful plants crowned by silken hair like First Mother's. On these plants was the wonderful gift of corn that would feed the people well. So it is that the people eat corn and remember the dying goddess who sacrificed herself for them.

Another corn origin myth is that of Mondawmin and the vision quest of the Ojibway youth Wunzh.

COSMIC EGG In many creation myths—including some in China, Japan, Egypt, Borneo, Finland, Greece, and Tibet, and especially India, as, for instance, in the myth of Brahma, the pre-creation void takes the form of an egg, sometimes a golden one. The analogy between cosmic birth and earthly birth is obvious here. The cosmic egg story seems to answer the perennial "chicken versus egg" argument.

COSMOGONIC AND COSMOLOGICAL MYTHS These are myths of the origins of the universe and world, respectively. A *cosmogony* is a particular culture's story of the creation; a *cosmology* is typically the way a culture sees the essential arrangement of the universe—the place of the stars, of the underworld, of Heaven and earth. The Greek roots and related roots of *cosmogony* are *genos/genea* (race, family, genealogy, genesis), *gonos* (offspring), and *kosmos* (cosmos, universe). Thus, we have *cosmo-logia*, or cosmology, the study of the cosmos, and *kosmos* + *gonos*, or *cosmogony*. In our creation myths we tell the world, or at least ourselves, who we are. We describe our ancestry, our conception, our first home, our early relations with our progenitors, our place in the first world.

COWS As the Hindu myths of Kamadhenu and the Churning of the Ocean of Milk, and ancient figures such as the Egyptian Hathor, the Sumerian Inanna, and the Greek Io all indicate, the cow holds a significant place in world mythology—especially that of the Indo-European peoples—as a symbol of the essence of life and of fertility. For the Indo-Europeans cattle were, in effect,

Confucius teaches students about filial piety

C

The cow is a holy animal in the Hindu religion

currency, and the cattle raid was a ubiquitous theme in Indo-European mythologies, especially that of the Irish. The cow was also the obvious mate of the great bull god, who plays a significant role in Indo-European and prehistoric mythology.

COYOTE A ubiquitous presence in Native American mythology, as the actual coyote is in most regions of North America, Coyote, with the SpiderAnanse in Africa and fellow Native Americans Iktome (like Ananse, the Spider) and Raven, is an example of the archetypal trickster. He is at once clever and foolish, creative and destructive, otherworldly and worldly, a community figure and a loner. His appetites for sex and food are limitless, and he recognizes no taboos. He is a braggart and sometimes the ridiculous butt of his own jokes and tricks. But he is also an amazingly powerful shape shifter, capable of changing instantly from one form to another—animate or inanimate. Occasionally, like the somewhat devilish trickster figures in many central Asian creation myths, Coyote assists the creator with his work; sometimes, like the Asian figures, he undermines the creation.

Like most tricksters, Coyote can also be a culture hero. A Papago "Noah's ark" myth tells how Coyote saved himself and Montezuma and the Indian people just after the emergence of the people into the world by warning the chief to build a huge canoe before the deluge that he, because of his closeness to the Creator, knew was coming.

Coyote's and other tricksters' positive modern-day descendants might be shamans and medicine people, his negative analogues bad witches. His constructive social and at the same time comic role is perhaps reflected in the clowns and their whipping boys in the Southwest pueblo dances, men who break religious and cultural taboos during ceremonies but who also punish members of the community who have strayed from the ceremonial path.

Literally hundreds of Coyote myths are to be found in Native American mythology. Two will serve to illustrate many of this trickster's characteristics. The first myth is a creation myth told by the Maidu people of California. They say that at the beginning of time, when there was only darkness and the primal waters, two beings arrived in a raft, Turtle and a creator figure called Earth Initiate. These two proceeded to create the world—the sun and stars, dry land, trees, and other things. Then one day, apparently out of nowhere, Coyote arrived with his pet, Rattlesnake. Coyote enjoyed watching the creators fashion animals—particularly First Man and First Woman—out of clay. In fact, Coyote thought, if they can do it so can I. But as he worked he began laughing, and his creations did not work; Earth Initiate scolded him, saying that if he avoided laughing, they might work. Immediately Coyote denied having laughed. In this way the first lie was told.

Meanwhile, Earth Initiate went on working, making a perfect world, even teaching the people to jump into a certain lake to renew their youth when they happened to get old. When Coyote, like the serpent of Genesis, came to this paradise to visit them, the people told him how wonderful life was, how they could spend their time eating and sleeping and how they could always be young. But something rankled Coyote when he heard all of this, and he told the people he could show them something, and that it would be better if sickness and death could come into the world. The people, knowing nothing of sickness and death, were fascinated and wanted to know more. So

Coyote told them about competition and suggested that they line up for a footrace. This they did, and meanwhile, Coyote's pet, Rattlesnake, hid in a hole just along the path of the race. What Coyote had not taken account of was the fact that his own son would lead the pack in the race and that when he passed the hole, Rattlesnake would bite him. When the boy fell down dead, the people thought he was only ashamed to get up because he had fallen during the race. But now Coyote came up and wept the first tears that the world had ever known. Placing the boy in the magical lake had no effect, and from that day on, when people got old they simply died.

The second myth is from the Rosebud Sioux Reservation and has a Looney Tunes kind of aspect to it. According to a storyteller named Jenny Leading Cloud, Coyote and his friend Iktome were walking along a path one day when they came upon a rock, Iya, one that Coyote knew had the power to tell a story. So he spoke respectfully to the rock and placed his own blanket on it as a gift. But later the weather turned cold and a storm came up, and Coyote had a change of heart about the gift of his beautiful blanket. In spite of Iktome's warnings, he went back to get it from Iya, only to be told by the rock that "what's given is given." Furious, Coyote ripped the blanket off and replaced it on his own back. "There, that's the end of that," he yelled. "By no means the end," murmured the rock.

So Coyote and Iktome went to a cave to rest until the storm was over and the sun came out again. They enjoyed their pemmican, fry bread, and wojapi and had settled down for a good smoke when they heard a strange rumbling noise. Suddenly they saw Iya, the great rock, rolling and crashing through the trees and underbrush and heading right toward them. "Let's run," screamed Iktome, and they did, but the rock kept gaining on them. "Let's swim across the river," shouted Iktome, and they did, but Iya rolled right along after them. The same thing happened when they fled into a forest of huge trees; the rock just pushed down the trees and kept on coming. Iktome had had enough. "This is your problem, friend," he said, and he turned himself into one of his other selves, the Spider, and fled down a hole. At that moment Iya rolled right over Coyote, flattening him out like a rug. Iya picked up the blanket and went off.

Later a man came along, looked down at Coyote, and said, "What a nice rug!" He took the "rug" home and placed it in front of his fireplace and showed it admiringly to his wife. The next morning the man's wife came into a room where her husband was and said, "I just saw your new rug running away!" Coyote, of course, has the ability to come back to life, but sometimes it takes him a while.

CREATION As the one species blessed or cursed by the sense of plot—of beginnings, middles, and ends—we are driven to tell the essential story of where we came from and why. Creation myths tell us how things began. All cultures have creation myths; they are our primary myths, the first stage in what might be called the psychic life of the species. As cultures, we identify ourselves through the collective dreams we call creation myths, or cosmogonies (*kosmos* + *gonos* = universe + offspring). Creation myths explain in metaphorical terms our sense of who we are in the context of the world, and in so doing they reveal our real priorities, as well as our real prejudices. Our images of creation say a great deal about who we are. Cosmogonies are important for the same reason that our explorations of the personal past, including our life with our parents, are important. Creation is almost always linked to the concept of deity, and creation myths reveal our sense of our relationship with and the nature of our primal parents, the deities who created us.

Naturally, creation myths are etiological in that they "explain" things during the pre-scientific age—how the world was formed, where people came from. Although each creation myth reflects its culture, basic patterns emerge when we compare creation myths from around the world. Creation myths, for example, often have flood myths attached to them. There is nearly always a creator or creatrix and a first man and first woman. Creation stories describe in various ways the essential struggle between chaos and form. In creation myths nothing becomes something; chaos becomes cosmos ordered by Logos—the ordering force of the universe. Often creation emerges from a cosmic egg, sometimes from maternal primal waters in which an earth diver finds the building material for the world creation.

The creation myth reminds us of who we are; it brings into the present time the energies of the childhood of our cultural being, and it renews us. For this reason, creation myths are typically recited during curing ceremonies. The Navajo shaman sings the creation myth as the patient sits at the center of the sacred world represented by the sand painting. Catholic and Anglican priests once read or chanted the first chapters of the Gospel of John, "In the beginning was the Word," in effect a Christian creation myth, at the end of Mass—the collective curing ceremony of Christianity. These rituals are logical, since curing means a chance to begin again, a chance for re-creation.

Creation as the Garden of Eden

C

God creates the animals

Applying the comparative method to creation mythology reveals a rich tapestry of stories, a sustained collective attempt on the part of the species to know what it is and where it came from, to make creation conscious of itself by way of an extraordinarily complex and imaginative set of metaphors. "To be sure, I wasn't there," says the collective human consciousness, "but I can use types and places and aspects of my own experience of life and society to tell you what it must have been like." The Navajo (Dine) says, "We emerged at least four times from places below the present world." A chorus of southwestern American mythmakers agree. "This is who we are," say the authors of the book of Genesis. "Yahweh created everything that is, including us, out of the void." The Christian scribe, his Muslim friend, and countless others from around the world nod in agreement. "Our world was created in a kind of dreaming," says the Australian Aboriginal representative. "Someone dove into the primordial depths for our world," says an Iroquois, echoing something similar just announced by the writer of the *Vishnu Purana* from India. And some central Asian shamans whisper, "That happened for us, too." "Akongo created a perfect world that human dissension ruined," cries a Ngombe visionary in Africa. "Yes, and he sent a great flood to punish humans," say many creation mythmakers. Some ancient Egyptians believed that the world came from the secretions of the great god—from his spit and his hand-induced semen. A Vedic god did the same thing. And so did the Boshongo creator. Chuckchee shamans tell how Raven defecated and urinated from the sky to create the mountains and the sea. Divine vomit can sometimes be a source of creation. Many creations of our world took place when first ancestors separated Sky Father and Earth Mother so that people and gods would have room in which to live and work. This is true of a Maori myth and famously true of the Egyptian myth of Geb and Nut. In Greece, according to Hesiod, the sky god cut off his father's genitals to separate him from the first mother. Many peoples, including Mesopotamians and animist groups of Africa and Native North America tell how the earth itself is the result of an ancient dismemberment. Mountains are the ancient mother's breasts, peninsulas are her fingers, the trees and the grass her hair. And then there are the cosmic egg creations of China and Tahiti and many other cultures. So-called *deus faber* believers compare the creation to some craft, such as weaving or carpentry. Others believe that creators fell from the sky.

The largest group of creation myths has roots at least as early as the Neolithic civilizations of the Fertile Crescent. These myths, from Egypt, Mesopotamia, India, Greece, and the followers of the Abrahamic God, tell of creation from nothing (*ex nihilo*) or from chaos, or from some sacred substance by a single sky god, supreme being, or father god. The group shares several dominant characteristics besides creation by the sky father. The creator is almost always male and all-powerful, and the world he creates is hierarchical. Humans—especially men—are the creator's representatives there. The supreme being mythmakers speak a great deal about special revelation. They tend to be argumentative and defensive. They ignore the likelihood that their mythic pattern displaced an older pattern in which a goddess figure representing fertility and agriculture was dominant. Particular *ex nihilo* peoples often see a special relationship between themselves and a personal god who reigns above as king of the universe.

Many of the father god people—perhaps because of their commitment to the ideal of power—have, over the centuries, tended to insist on a literal rather than symbolical understanding of their myths. As a result, they are often at odds with each other and generally unwilling to see in the myths of others representations of their own beliefs. Although the one Yahweh/God/Allah of the three Abrahamic traditions is recognized by all three as the same god, Jews, Christians, and Muslims have each—often in spite of scripture and earlier tradition—claimed exclusivity and have used that notion of exclusivity to justify the oppression of others, including each other. And even within the religions themselves scripture has often been distorted to support war against other factions and sects or the oppression or even mutilation of designated segments of the species, including children, people of different skin color, and particularly women.

Another, much smaller group of creation mythmakers represents a significant alternative to the myth pattern of the distant sky god. These are the emergers and animists—those who believe we were born of the earth, of the eternal mother, or that the earth quite simply *is* the eternal living mother. It seems likely that this group holds myths that existed before those of the father god group. And in spite of the dominance of that group, the mother people have held on to their beliefs in isolated areas such as the American Southwest, where small, often matrilineal societies still recognize the mother creatrix as the most significant divine power, even when distant sun god creators are recognized as well. In several of the Southwest cosmogonies the sun is a kind of personal creative energy that interacts with another original life force, the earth itself, often identified with a figure known as Spider Woman or Thinking Woman. In this creation pattern the first people move into successive versions of existence until they finally emerge into this world through the *sipapu*, the spider hole replicated in the kivas, or ceremonial chambers, of modern day pueblos. Once people have emerged into this world, the arrangements of life are the responsibility of the goddess or her female offspring.

Mystics of various traditions—Sufis, students of the Kabbala, some Hindus, Buddhists, and even some Christians—speak of creation by emanation from the mysterious essence of a nonpersonal being—perhaps Brahman or En Sof—an ultimate reality that is everywhere and nowhere. Brahman as referred to in the ancient *Atharva Veda* as the power within mantras. Later, in the *Upanishads*, Brahman is the ever-existing principle of creation itself. In the still later Vedanta philosophy of Hinduism, Brahman is the essence of everything that is. In the Kabbalistic understanding, En (or Ein) Sof is the transcendent god who is beyond the capacity of human thought, the essence from which all things emanate. Plato joins this group, too, if perhaps a bit tentatively, with his idea of an eternal and constant reality from which humankind has become isolated but with which reunion is possible. This understanding is revealed in the well-known myth of the Cave, in which our world is seen as merely a shadow of what Plato's follower Plotinus (205–270 C.E.) called the "one" from which existence emanates.

A good example of creation by emanation is expressed by the Turkish *faylusuf* (mystical philosopher) Abu Nasr al-Farabi (d. 980 C.E.). In what might be called his creation myth, al-Farabi followed Plato (and Aristotle) by rejecting an *ex nihilo* one-time creation in favor of a chain of being emanating from the Logos, or Divine Reason, in ten successive intellects that take form as the Ptolemaic heavenly spheres. As far as our own world is concerned, there is a Platonic chain of existence extending from lower beings to the possibility of the human being reunited with Divine Reason itself.

In modern times theologian Paul Tillich (1868–1965) has viewed creation as an emanation from "ultimate concern" or "Ground of Being." Tillich would agree with al-Farabi that God as we have understood him is one of many symbols through which humans have attempted to communicate with a god who is beyond God, beyond understanding.
[Long, Sproul, Weigle, Leeming and Leeming]

CREON The name Creon is used frequently in Greek mythology for the king of Thebes or Corinth. A famous Creon was the king of Corinth, whose daughter Glauce married the Argonaut hero Jason, who was already married to the sorceress Medea. Father and daughter died when Medea sent Glauce a magic cloak that burned them to death. A still more famous Creon was the brother Jocasta, who replaced Oedipus as king of Thebes and whose stubbornness or letter-of-the-law justice led to the death of Oedipus's daughter Antigone.

CRETAN BULL Poseidon delivered this great bull from the sea to King Minos of Crete so that he might sacrifice it, but Minos liked it so much that he decided to keep it. The Cretan (Minoan) Bull plays a significant role in the myth of Pasiphae and the Bull. The angry Poseidon drove the bull mad, and Herakles was instructed to capture it as the seventh of his Twelve Labors. This he did, carrying it back to Greece on his shoulders. The Cretan Bull is a mythological relative of the Bull of Cuailnge of the Irish *Tain Bo Cuailnge*.

CROWS AND RAVENS In Irish mythology the crow and raven are associated with the Morrigan (Badb, Nemain, and Macha), the triune goddess of war and death. Badbh means "crow." The Morrigan as a raven sits on the hero Cuchulainn's shoulder at his death. The Irish crow doubtless has relatives in other birds of prey that appear in the mythologies of various cultures.

CRUCIFIXION, THE In the Christian tradition, *the* Crucifixion, as opposed to any other crucifixion, refers to the hanging of Jesus on a cross at Golgatha in Jerusalem, an act that caused his death and provided the central symbol (the cross) of Christianity. The Crucifixion followed the Last Supper

The hero Herakles captures the Cretan Bull

and trial and preceded Jesus' Descent to harrow Hell, his Resurrection, and his Ascension.

CUCHULAINN In Ireland it is sometimes difficult to distinguish heroes from gods. But out of the Ulster or Red Branch cycle, dominated by the *Tain Bo Cuailnge*, one great hero emerges in the person of Cuchulainn (Cu Chulainn), the miraculous circumstances of whose birth, initiation, and other aspects of life place him in the company of the multitude of archetypal heroes of the monomyth, including Zoroaster, Achilles, Jesus, Herakles, and Theseus.

The mother of the hero-to-be was Dechtire, the daughter of the druid Cathbad and the love god Aonghus. During the wedding feast of Dechtire and the Ulster chieftain Sualtam, the god Lugh took the form of a mayfly and flew into the bride's drink. Dechtire fell into a deep sleep, during which Lugh came to her in a dream and instructed her to leave with him, taking fifty maidens, whom he would disguise as birds. Nine months after the disappearance of the women, a group of hunting warriors followed a flock of birds to the river Boyne, thought to be the home of the gods. There they found a palace, where they were entertained by a handsome man and a beautiful woman surrounded by fifty maidens. During the night the woman gave birth to a boy. Lugh then revealed his own and Dechtire's identities and instructed the hunters to return to Ulster with the mother and child and the maidens. There Sualtam welcomed back Dechtire as his wife and the baby as his son.

The child was first called Setanta. But one day the king, Conchobhar (Conor), noticed the boy's prodigious strength and invited him to join him at a feast being given by the smith, Culann. There the smith's huge dog attacked the child, who jammed his ball into the beast's mouth and smashed its head against a rock, killing it instantly. Culann was furious that the child had killed his favorite watchdog, but Setanta promised to find a replacement for the dog and until then to serve in its place as the "Hound of Culann," or Cuchulainn. Later, still only a seven-year-old, Cuchulainn overheard the druid Cathbad predicting that anyone who took arms that day would become the greatest of heroes but would be condemned to a short life. Cuchulainn, like the similarly doomed Achilles, immediately demanded arms of Conchobhar and went off to defeat three magical warriors who had plagued the kingdom. So the young hero joined the community of mythic children whose extraordinary boyhood deeds indicate their heroic nature.

Still a boy, Cuchulainn fell in love with the beautiful Emer, who would have nothing to do with him before he could prove himself a true hero by accomplishing certain feats. Emer's father, the chieftain Forgall Manach, placed many more barriers before the young hero, and the overcoming of those barriers became his Heraklean labors, the traditional hero's quest. With the help of training by the warrior queen Scathach on Scathach's Island (perhaps Skye), Cuchulainn grew in strength and prowess and finally returned to Ireland and, after overcoming Forgall, married Emer. In the tradition of many heroes, Cuchulainn had a famous sword, Caladin, and a magic spear, the Gael-Bolg.

Many heroic and tragic events filled the rest of Cuchulainn's short life. Like other great heroes, he traveled in the Otherworld. He lost women he loved, quarreled with Emer, and found himself in a position in which he became the killer of his own son and then his best friend. The central events in his adult life are those of the great war of the Cattle Raid, contained in the epic the *Tain Bo Cuailgne*, in which Cuchulainn is the champion of Conchobhar's Ulstermen against the Connacht armies of Queen Medb. Cuchulainn is so admired, even by his enemies, that the evil queen and the war goddess Morrigan herself desire him. But, like the ancient hero Gilgamesh, he refuses the love of the goddess and suffers for that refusal. His reputation as a hero is fully established by his defeating Medb's warriors almost single-handedly, but there is no escape from Cathbad's prophecy. In spite of Emer's pleading that he avoid his final battle and in spite of the selfless acts of his faithful charioteer Leag, Cuchulainn is slain at the famous Pillar Stone, to which the hero bound himself so that he might die standing; and as an otter drinks his blood, the goddess Morrigan sits on his shoulder as a raven, finally in possession of the man she has desired.

CULANN The smith of the Irish king Conchobhar, Culann was in reality the human form of the smith god Manannan Mac Lir. The boy Setanta, who served him as punishment for killing his hound, became known as "Culann's Hound," or Cuchulainn, the greatest of Irish heroes.

CULTURE HEROES Most cultures have culture heroes. They are particularly popular in Africa and Native North America, but they exist everywhere. Gilgamesh can be called a Sumerian culture hero; Jesus, Muhammad, Moses, and the Buddha might also be called culture heroes. Sometimes the culture hero helps the creator. More often he teaches religious rules and ceremonies and establishes the community's institutions and traditions after creation. In short, he is the hero who brings "culture." The Mbuti people of Zaire credit their culture hero Tore with, like the Greek Prometheus, stealing fire and introducing it to them. Sometimes the culture hero has trickster qualities and even introduces death, as in the case of the Maidu version of Coyote.

In matrilineal cultures the culture hero can be female. It is the sisters Iatiku (Life-Bringer) and Nautsiti (Full Basket) who teach their culture to the Acoma people of the American Southwest.

The culture hero is almost always endowed with special power as a result of divine origins. Like other monomythic heroes, the culture hero can be conceived miraculously. So the mother of the famous Manabozho of the Menomini tribe was impregnated by the wind, and the mother of the Tewa Waterpot Boy was made pregnant by a bit of clay that entered her as she stomped on material for the making of pots.

Culture heroes like the Blackfoot Kutoyis not only institute culture, they make cultures safe by killing monsters. After establishing customs and making the world safe, the culture hero usually disappears, sometimes descending to death or the underworld, like the African maiden Wanjiru or the better-known Ceramese culture heroine Hainuwele in Indonesia. The culture hero can die and be changed into food, like the Inuit Sedna or the ubiquitous Native American Corn Mother. The culture hero in one way or another nourishes the culture and in some sense literally *is* the culture.

CUMAE A town in Campania, in southern Italy, Cumae was the first settlement of the Greeks in Italy, perhaps as early as the eighth century B.C.E. It was the home of the great Sibyl, who prophesied from her oracular cave there.

CUMONG A figure whose stories figure prominently in indigenous pre-Buddhist Korean mythology is Cumong,

C

Cupid and Psyche

"the good archer." Cumong greatly resembles the Chinese Yi, also known as the "good archer." Cumong has many characteristics of the archetypal monomythic hero. In some versions of his myth, he is conceived miraculously. His mother-to-be was Ryuhwa, a virgin, sometimes seen as a daughter of the god of the waters, sometimes as the maiden daughter of a king. One day the sun, the "son of the Sky," shines on her, causing her to become pregnant and to deliver an egg. Horrified, the King tries to dispose of the egg by abandoning it, as Moses, Siegfried (Sigurd), and many other heroes were abandoned. But like other abandoned heroes, the child is protected by animals, who refuse to eat the egg. And eventually, under Ryuhwa's renewed care, a beautiful boy breaks out of it. This is Cumong, the archer.

When followers of the king plot to kill the hero, as followers of kings so often do, Cumong is saved by the power of his father, the "Emperor of Heaven," and his mother, daughter of the god of the waters. Cumong goes on the traditional hero quest journey of adventures, achieving, in his case, the shamanic powers symbolized by the mastery of the drum, the ability to cause water to dry up with his whip, and the power to conquer evil kings. As a shamanic figure, the son of the sun and a descendant of the waters, Cumong can move freely between the various worlds. He can fly into the heavens or travel under the sea. Cumong fathers a son and leaves a sign behind that the son has to find—in the manner of Theseus and King Arthur, for example—before he can be recognized as the crown prince. Eventually the son, Yuri, finds a piece of a broken sword belonging to his father and is

duly recognized. The stories of Cumong are found in many texts, especially the *Wei chou*.

CUPID Cupid is the Roman cognate of the Greek Eros. He is the son of Venus. But he tends to be depicted more often as a mischievous baby. He is popular in many parts of the world today as a symbol of love—sometimes unrequited—resulting from his magic arrows. The fact that he is often depicted blindfolded indicates the blindness of love.

CUPID AND PSYCHE In a story told by the second-century C.E. Latin writer Apuleius in *The Golden Ass*, Cupid is a young adult who falls in love with a beautiful girl named Psyche ("Soul"). Psyche, a princess, is so beautiful that people begin to ignore the most beautiful goddess of them all, Venus. Naturally angry at this neglect, Venus sends her son Cupid with his magic arrows to make Psyche fall in love with the worst character he can find. The dutiful Cupid goes forth to do his mother's bidding, but when he sees Psyche he is himself smitten and cannot make use of his arrows. As for poor Psyche, no one but Cupid falls in love with her and she can love no one either. Cupid, fearing his mother's wrath, cannot reveal his love. All he can do is ask Apollo for advice. Apollo devises a plan. When Psyche's father comes to his oracle to beg for help in finding a husband for his daughter, the oracle says he must leave her dressed in mourning clothes on a mountaintop, where a strange and powerful winged creature will come and take her for a wife. With great sadness Psyche's parents follow the instructions.

As Psyche waits on the mountaintop, a soft wind comes and carries her off to a kind of paradise, where all her wishes are fulfilled, and each night in the darkness a warm, tender, and passionate lover comes to her as a husband. One night the mysterious lover warns Psyche not to speak with her sisters, who are searching for her, bemoaning her loss. Speaking with them will lead to her ruin, he says. Eventually, however, the lover relents, saying Psyche must do what she sees fit, but above all, he says, she must not give in to their insistence that she try to see him. Seeing him will destroy their relationship forever. The sisters are brought down to Psyche by the wind and, of course, they question her about her husband. "What does he look like?" they ask. In their jealousy of their sister, they convince Psyche that her invisible husband is in fact the beast promised by Apollo's oracle and that one night he will devour her. The girl's mind is now poisoned, and she agrees to take a lamp and a knife to bed with her that night. By the light of the lamp she will finally see her husband, and if he turns out to be a beast she will kill him with the knife.

It is late at night when Psyche leaves her bed and lights the lamp. When she returns to the bed, she is moved and horrified to see not a monster but the most beautiful being she has ever seen. Entranced, and leaning over to look closely, some oil from her lamp falls on the shoulder of the young man, who is, of course, Cupid himself. Immediately

The one-eyed cyclops, Polyphemus

the god awakens and leaves. Psyche follows him, now desperate, but Cupid cries out, "Love can only exist where there is trust."

Psyche goes off in search of her husband, hoping to win him back, but now Venus learns of her son's betrayal and is even more determined to destroy her rival. When in her despair Psyche approaches Venus, begging her for forgiveness and offering to serve her, the angry goddess decides to destroy the girl's beauty and her hopes by assigning her impossible tasks—even sending her to the underworld. But with some help from others, Psyche accomplishes the tasks, and eventually Cupid finds her and appeals to Jupiter for help against his mother's rage. Jupiter agrees to help and by giving Psyche ambrosia, makes her immortal. She can then marry Cupid properly, and Venus finally puts aside her jealousy and accepts the union of Cupid and Psyche, love and soul.

CYBELE Cybele (Kybele) was the Mother goddess of Phrygia in Anatolia. She became popular in Rome as "Magna Mater" ("Great Mother") in connection with rites related to her son (some say son-lover), Attis. Cybele was the child of King Meion of Phrygia and Dindyme, but for some reason—perhaps because Meion believed she was not his child—was abandoned to the wilderness, where she was raised by wild animals. Eventually she was adopted by women of a mountainous place called Cyble, for which they named her, and she became for the people of the area a culture heroine, the "Mother of the Mountain," who taught the arts of music, medicine, and purification. Having magical powers, perhaps because of a divine father, Cybele sometimes turned herself into the Agdos Rock, on which the father god Pappas one day spilled some of his highly productive semen. The result of this union was the monstrous Agdistis. In another form, as Nana, daughter of the river god Sangarios, she picked up a pomegranate from a tree that had been fed by the blood of Agdistis, who had been castrated. A seed from the pomegranate or, some say, the pomegranate itself entered the girl, and she became pregnant and gave birth to Attis, who was exposed to the wilderness to avoid the shame the king felt because of his daughter's pregnancy. Later Attis would be assaulted sexually by Agdistis and would castrate himself rather than be disloyal to his mother, Cybele-Nana. The goddess came along and took up the dead body of her son and beloved and buried him on Mount Ida. Each year she would lament him and rebury him, and he would return as the welcome vegetation of the spring.

It is clear from similarities in the Attis and Cybele stories that the ancient mythmakers sometimes confused the two tales, taking elements from one and interjecting them in the other.

CYCLOPS The Cyclops (Cyclopes) of Greek mythology were the one-eyed sons of the first Greek Mother Goddess, Gaia, and her consort Ouranos. The next king of the gods, Kronos, imprisoned the Cyclops in Tartaros, but Kronos's son Zeus freed them to help him defeat his father and the Titans in a war in Heaven. They became the smiths who forged his thunderbolts. One tradition holds that Apollo killed the Cyclops in revenge for their making the bolts that Zeus used to kill his son Asclepius. The Cyclops with whom most readers are familiar is the terrible Polyphemus from whom Odysseus narrowly escapes after he blinds him in Homer's *Odyssey*.

DAEDALUS AND ICARUS In Greek mythology Daedalus was an Athenian sculptor and craftsman who trained his nephew in his art only to murder him when the young man became a better artist. Daedalus was condemned for his crime but managed to escape to Crete. There he impressed King Minos with his skill and was hired by Queen Pasiphae to create the wooden cow in which she hid so as to have intercourse with the Bull of Poseidon. He then created the Labyrinth/maze to enclose Pasiphae's resulting offspring, the monstrous Minotaur. In time the craftsman decided to escape from Crete with his son Icarus. As Minos would not allow him to leave by ship, Daedalus constructed wings for himself and Icarus. He attached the wings to their bodies with wax. As the pair took off, Daedalus warned his son not to fly too close to the sun, but the boy, craving adventure with his newly acquired power of flight, flew so close to the sun that the wax melted. Naturally, Icarus's wings fell off and the boy landed in the sea, where he drowned. Daedalus made his way to Sicily, where the king, Cocalus, protected him and, with his daughters, murdered Minos, who arrived with the intention of taking Daedalus back to Crete by force.

DAEVAS According to the beliefs of the reformed Iranian religion as proclaimed by Zoroaster (Zarathustra), the world is presided over by the supreme god Ahura Mazda, the Wise Lord, alone. Therefore, the ancient *daevas* (*daivas*), whose name ties them to the Hindu *devas*, or gods, have been relegated to an inferior level of being marked by unreality and even falseness. They have become, in fact, devil-demons—something like the Hindu *asuras*—who attempt to steer humans away from the supreme wisdom which is Ahura Mazda.

DAGAN Dagan (Dagon) was a form of the Canaanite high god. Perhaps a personification of El, he had fertility aspects, as his name seems to mean "grain." Dagan existed at Ebla as early as the third millennium B.C.E. and was assimilated as the high god of the Philistines in the late second millennium.

DAGDA The Dagda (the "Good One") is the father god of Irish mythology. Cognates would probably have been two other Celtic deities, the Gaulish Dis Pater and the Gaulish and British Cernunnos. The patron of druidry, the Dagda wields a gigantic club, which he carries about on wheels. He uses one end of the club to punish, the other to heal. The Dagda had a magic cauldron that had an endless supply of food. After the defeat of the Tuatha Dè Danaan by the Milesians, the Dagda arranged for his people to live in mounds called *sidhes*. After a while people thought of the Tuatha less as gods than as fairies.

DAIKOKU Mahakali in Sanskrit, Daikoku-ten is the Japanese Buddhist god known as "the Great Black One." He had once been the protector of wealth and happiness, but by the ninth century the Tendai and Shingon sects of Buddhism saw him as the protector and provider of their monasteries. Daikoku was also taken up by non-Buddhists and identified with the ancient Japanese god Okunuinushino-kami, the Great Spirit Master. Later still he was seen as part of a group called the "Seven Gods of Fortune" or Happiness. Daikoku is often depicted as a hunter who carries a sack and a rice mallet. He stands on a large bag of rice, perhaps signifying agricultural wealth.

Daedalus gives wings to his son, Icarus

DAINICHI The Buddha Dainichi Nyorai, the Buddha Mahavairocana, is known as the Illuminator. In the tradition of esoteric Japanese Buddhism (*mikkyo*) as developed in the early ninth century C.E., especially by the Shingon sect, he is the embodiment of the absolute—the supreme Buddha with whom humans may unite through proper discipline and meditation. For the Shingon Buddhist and even for many Shinto adherents, the universe is the Dainichi Nyorai in much the same way that for some Hindus, the universe is Brahman.

DAKSHA Although sometimes identified with the Indian Vedic creator Prajapati, Daksha later came to be thought of as the son of that later version of Prajapati, the creator god Brahma. He also serves as the father of Parvati, the wife of Shiva. In the *Mahabharata*, the story is told of Daksha's presiding over a sacrifice that is destroyed by Shiva. Daksha represents that aspect of the "good Hindu" who follows the proper rites and performs the sacrifice with perfection, but who is lacking in devotion (*bhakti*).

In the epic version of the myth, Daksha and the gods perform the sacrifice and dole out the offerings but fail to invite the god Rudra-Shiva or to assign him any offerings. Enraged, Shiva proves his power and comes into his own in relation to Vishnu and the other gods by destroying the sacrifice and maiming several of the gods. The gods beg him to throw the fire of his anger into the waters, and finally he does so. He then heals the maimed gods and brings back the sacrifice, and thus order, under his aegis.

In some versions of the story, Daksha is decapitated during the destruction, and his head is thrown into the fire. In the restoration of the sacrifice, Daksha is given a ram's head to replace the original. Many have seen in the destruction of Daksha's sacrifice a symbol of the destruction that will come at the end of the world under the direction of the Destroyer, Shiva. The myth also suggests, of course, that no sacrifice can be valid without the devotional aspect of Shiva, the ultimate meditative yogi.

DANAE The daughter of King Acrisius of Argos, Danae was locked up in a tower by her father, who had been warned that a son of hers would murder him. Danae, however, had attracted the amorous attention of Zeus himself, and the great god entered the tower as a shower of gold and impregnated Danae. The girl gave birth to the hero Perseus. Perseus would later kill his grandfather accidentally with a discus during games at Argos.

DANAIDES Aegyptus (Egypt) and Danaus were the twin sons of Belus, a son of Lybia and the Greek god Poseidon. The twins' mother was Anchinoe, daughter of the river god Nilus. Aegyptus conquered a land he named Egypt, for himself. He was the father of fifty sons. As to Danaus, he was given Lybia to rule. He had fifty daughters, the Danaides, or Belides. When Belus died, Aegyptus proposed that his fifty sons marry their fifty cousins, but an oracle confirmed Danaus's suspicions of foul play. So Danaus fled with his daughters to Argos. Because of various omens, Danaus was able to convince the Argives to make him their king in place of King Gelanor. The sons of Aegyptus were not to be put off, however. They were determined to marry the Danaides and then kill them, and they lay siege to Argos until Danaus apparently capitulated.

On the wedding night of the cousins, however, Danaus gave each of his daughters a hairpin with which they were to kill their husbands. Forty-nine of the daughters did as they were instructed, but one, Hypermnestra, fell in love with her husband, Lynceus, partly because he did not take her virginity during the wedding night, and she refused to kill him. Put on trial for her disobedience, Hypermnestra was saved by the advocacy of Aphrodite. Later, Lynceus avenged the murders of his brothers by murdering Danaus.

The forty-nine murderous Danaids found other husbands, and their offspring were the Greeks known to this day as Danaans. It was said that after their deaths the Danaides were condemned to carry water in jars that were, in fact, sieves. Much of the story of the Danaides was told by Aeschylus in his play the *Supplices* (the "Suppliant Women") and in the only partially extant *Egyptians* and *Danaides*.

DANCE OF SHIVA The Hindu god Shiva—at once the Destroyer and the perfect yogi—is often depicted as a dancer. Traditionally the dance is magical and trance inducing. It is a high form of cosmic yoga. Shiva is Nataraja, the Lord of the Dance, and the dance is, in a sense, the breathing of creation. As he whirls in the meditative and gentle movement called *lyasa*, the elements of the living world are the flashes of light made by his movements. These elements are destroyed in turn by the violent turnings of the *tandava*. In his dance, Shiva-Nataraja holds various symbolic objects. In his top right hand is the hourglass drum connoting the rhythm of the dance of life, which is sound, the means by which understanding is transmitted. Sound is connected in India to the essential element ether, out of which come air, fire, water, and earth, the necessary elements for creation. In the upper left hand the dancer holds fire, the agent of the destruction of creation in the sacrifice and in the cosmic cycle. The lower right hand gives the sign of peace, and the lower left hand points to the left foot raised in a sign of devotion and release. Sometimes Shiva dances on the body of a demon symbolizing human forgetfulness or ignorance.

DANEL AND AQHAT The Canaanite tale of King Danel and his son, the hero Aqhat, is contained in fragments of three Ugaritic tablets from Ras Shamra. As the tale opens, Danel is performing a seven-day ritual in hopes of being granted a son and heir. His patron god, Baal, hears his prayers and intercedes for him with the high god, El. El agrees that Danel shall have a son, and after appropriate ministrations by childbirth and marriage goddesses, Danel's wife conceives. In time, a boy, Aqhat, is born. Aqhat's conception and birth, therefore, have something of the miraculous or at least extraordinary element present at the beginning of so many hero myths, including, for instance, those of Isaac, Moses, Jesus, Sargon, and Theseus.

When Aqhat has become a young man, the craftsman of the gods, Kothar, pays a visit and presents Danel with a magical set of bow and arrows, which Danel presents to his son. The magical weapons are, again, reminiscent of other hero myths: Achilles receives a magic shield from Hephaistos, and Arthur retrieves the mysterious Excalibur.

The impetuous love and war goddess, Anat, wants the weapons for herself and attempts to bribe Aqhat with precious objects and eventually with immortality. In keeping with the heroic formula of patriarchal cultures, Aqhat refuses the bribes and does so rudely, questioning the goddess's hunting prowess and, by extension, the ability of women in general to perform masculine deeds. Gilgamesh had insulted Inanna/Ishtar in a similar manner, and several Indo-European heroes—including, for instance, the Irish Cuchulainn—act out the formula with angry goddesses. The result of the insult is usually disastrous. It leads to the hero's death and/or to the barrenness of the land. In the case of Aqhat, both catastrophes occur. There is perhaps the implication of sexuality in Anat's bribes, as there is in the similar situations in the Gilgamesh and Cuchulainn myths. This is especially so given her role as a love goddess and her connection to fertility.

Reluctantly, El agrees to his daughter Anat's demand of revenge. The goddess sends her follower, Yatpan, in the form of a bird, to accomplish her wishes, and Aqhat is bludgeoned to death as he is eating. Immediately, the land dries up, and soon Danel learns of his son's murder. Finding bits of Aqhat's body in the guts of the vultures that had been hovering ominously over his house, Danel buries them and begins a seven-year period of mourning—a metaphor for a seven-year drought.

It is left to the brave Pagat, Danel's daughter, an Ugaritic Elektra, to avenge her brother's murder. She decorates her body with rouge and a beautiful robe and makes her way to Yatpan's camp with a concealed dagger. There she seduces her enemy into a state of drunkenness, during which he boasts of killing Aqhat. Although part of the tablet is missing, we can assume that she achieves her goal of revenge, much as, ironically, Anat had avenged the death of her brother, Baal.

Pagat has a possible analogue in the Hebrew Judith, who decapitates the drunken Holofernes. Michael Coogan finds a "coincidence of themes" here. The deaths of Baal and Aqhat, as well as of Osiris in Egypt, represent "threats to fertility." It is possible that as Anat dismembered Baal's killer, Death (Mot), Pagat might well have dismembered Yatpan. In the context of Middle Eastern fertility myths, such as the Osiris myth, dismemberment often involves the scattering of the dismembered body as seed. Coogan believes that the Aqhat story continued, in the tradition of so many hero myths, with the hero's "restoration to life and the consequent return of fertility to the fields" (1978, pp. 27–31).

DANU In Irish myth the Tuatha Dé Danann are the divine race descending from the mother goddess Danu, about whom little is known. In India the goddess Diti, the mother of demons, is sometimes called Danu. In Babylon Danuna is the mother of the city god Marduk.

DAOISM Daoism (Taoism) is in some ways a religion and in others a philosophical system. The founder of Daoism, Laozi (Lao tse), was to some a god and to others the greatest of philosophers. He is said to have contributed the popular work called the *Daode Jing* (*Tao te Ching*), probably in the later years of the first millennium B.C.E. Another source for Daoist thought is the *Chuangzi*, attributed to the second of the great Daoist thinkers, Chuangzi. At the center of Daoist thought is the *Dao* (*Tao*) or "Way," the totality of existence conceived of as a whole. "In the beginning was the Tao. All

The Hindu god Shiva as "Lord of the Dance," gives life to creation in his dance

The founder of Daoism, Lao-tsu (Laozi) riding on the humble water buffalo

things come from the Tao; all things go back to the Tao," says the *Daode Jing*. The way to mystical freedom is to let go of conventional concerns and achieve union with the Dao. Once union has been achieved, such conditions as poverty and wealth become meaningless, and ordinary societal values no longer apply.

DAPHNE Daphne was the daughter of the river god, Peneus, in Greece. Although sworn to virginity, she was pursued by Apollo, who was madly infatuated by her. As Apollo was about to catch her, she prayed for deliverance and was turned by the gods into a laurel tree, forever after Apollo's favorite tree.

DASHARATHA The father of the Vishnu avatar Rama, the hero of the *Ramayana*, Dasharatha was king of the sacred city Ayodhya and, as his name in Sanskrit indicates, the owner of ten chariots.

DAVID Almost certainly a historical figure, many heroic myths and legends surround the figure of the Hebrew-Israelite king David. As a boy who emerged, like so many heroes, from obscurity, he became a giant killer, defeating the Philistine warrior Goliath with a slingshot, an event not unlike Lugh's killing of the giant Balor in Irish mythology. Like other kings of the ancient Middle East, where a tradition developed of the king's being anointed by God—that is, in some sense having the status of son of God—David was endowed with some sort of divinity. In 2 Samuel 7:14–16 of the Bible, Yahweh says of the successor to David, "I shall be a father to him, and he will be my son," and your throne [i.e., David's dynasty] will endure for all time." And in Psalm

2:7 he says, presumably to the newly anointed David, "You are my son . . . this day I become your father." For Christian mythology all of this foreshadows the belief that Jesus, of the "House of David," is the "son of God" whose dynasty will endure forever.

David mythology, however, is not always happy. Like many budding heroes, including Jesus and Zoroaster, David's life is threatened by a jealous king, in this case Saul. Like Cuchulainn in Irish mythology, he finds himself in a position where it is necessary for him to be responsible for a son's death. That son is Absalom, who murders his half brother Amnon for raping their sister Tamar, escapes from David's court, and leads a rebellion against his father. When Absalom is killed in the battle against David's army, David cries out, "Oh my son Absalom, my son, Oh Absalom, my son, my son" (2 Samuel 13–18). David could also be sinful. Like King Arthur's father-to-be, Uther, he orders a rival into battle so that he can be killed and he, David, can marry the dead man's wife, in this case Bathsheba.

DAYAK MYTHS The Dayak people of Borneo, like many people in the world, see their territory as sacred space surrounded by chaotic foreignness. They are the people of the supreme being, who has a male aspect, Mahatala, associated with the sun, and an underworld female aspect, Jata. Jata is represented by the coiled water snake biting its own tail, forming a sacred mandala that supports the Dayak world. The serpent rests on the primeval chaotic waters between the upper and lower worlds. The people can communicate with Mahatala by way of ascetic disciplines on certain sacred mountains. The supreme being created the world out of the sun and the moon. According to several so-called *bakowo* ("hiding away") myths, the universe will come to an end as a result of human failings. Following the destruction of the universe, only a maiden will remain—hidden in a rock or a tree, symbolizing the underworld. A ritual reflection of this myth is the hiding away (*bakowo*) of girls for a set time at the beginning of puberty. The annual ritual cycle of the Dayak reflects the mythological sense of the progress of the universe from beginning to end.

DAZHBOG Dazhbog, usually thought to be the son of the sky god, was a Slavic solar deity whose consort was usually the moon. Each day he rode across the sky, like so many other sun gods, in a chariot. His identity and parentage change from region to region among the Slavs.

DEATH The arrival of death in the world is a common theme in world mythology. It is usually an aspect of the creation myth and frequently, in patriarchal cultures, involves misjudgment on the part of a woman. It is Eve's sin that leads to death in the Genesis story of Adam and Eve. When Pandora opens her box, death comes into the world. In Papua, the Daribi say that the hero Souw (Sida) gave death to the people when a young woman resisted his attempt to rape her and caused his extended penis to withdraw. Abuk, the first woman of the Dinka people in Sudan, introduced death by disobeying the creator. Sometimes, however, death is brought about by the mischief or mistakes of the trickster, as in the case of several Coyote myths and central Asian myths of the trickster-devil figure who acts as a culture hero but also as an often undermining "assistant" to the creator.

Death is particularly associated with certain goddesses—the Hindu Kali, the Sumerian Ereshkigal, and the Irish Morrigan, for instance. In Polynesia, humans began to experience death after the culture hero Maui's sexual assault on the death goddess. There are also male personifications of death or the underworld. Hades (Roman Pluto) is the best-known example.

DECAPITATION Decapitation is an important theme in Celtic mythology in general and Irish and Welsh mythology in particular. The story of *Bricriu's Feast* is a decapitation myth, as is the Welsh story of Bran. The theme influenced the Arthurian myths and the medieval English romances such as *Sir Gawain and the Green Knight*. Earlier decapitation stories are found in the Bible—including the tales of David and Goliath, Judith and Holofernes, and Salome and John the Baptist. There is also decapitation in the Greek myth of Perseus and Medusa, and in the Mesopotamian myth of Gilgamesh and Humbaba.

The decapitation theme—especially when associated with a "green man" such as Gawain's Green Knight, the Aztec Corn King, or many Native North American Corn Mothers—may well have its roots in sacrificial rituals of fertility. Heads that have been cut away from the body, as in the case of Bran's head, continue to function and talk in Celtic mythology, suggesting a belief in the head's being the seat of the soul as well as of power and fertility.

DEIANEIRA Herakles and Achelous both loved Deianeira and fought for her. Not surprisingly, Herakles was victorious, and she became his second wife. Because of one of his many impulsive crimes, Herakles went into exile with Deianeira. When they came to the river Evenus, Herakles was able to ford it, but he gave his wife to the centaur Nessus to carry across. On the way Nessus attempted to rape her. Deianeira screamed, and Herakles immediately shot the centaur with a poisoned arrow. As he was dying, Nessus gave Deianeira some of his blood, claiming it could be used to keep her husband's love. When later Deianeira became jealous of what she thought was her husband's love for another woman, she steeped a cloak he wanted to wear in the centaur's blood, hoping to secure his love. Instead, the cloak, poisoned by the centaur's blood, which contained the poison of Herakles' arrow, led to the death of the hero. In despair, Deianeira hanged herself.

DEIRDRE "Deirdre of the Sorrows," as she is called in Irish mythology, was the daughter of the Ulster chieftain Felim Mac Dall. The druid soothsayer Cathbad predicted that she would grow up to be the fairest woman of all. He also said that her death would bring great tragedy to Ulster. Nevertheless, the not-always-wise King Conchobhar, in anticipation of possessing this future beauty for himself, kept the girl under his protection, intending eventually to marry her. When she was of age, however, Deirdre fell in love with Naoise (Noisu), the son of the Red Branch hero Usna, and eloped with him to Alba. After many years, Conchobhar pretended to forgive the elopement and sent the hero Fergus Mac Roth to retrieve the lovers. Trusting Fergus, they returned and were housed in the hostel of the Red Branch in the Ulster capital, Emain Macha.

Then the king made his great mistake. He had Naoise and his brothers killed and took Deirdre by force as his wife.

A Mexican breastplate representing the god of death, Mictlantecuhtli

After a year, during which Deirdre was clearly an unwilling spouse who never once smiled, Conchobhar gave her to Eoghan Mac Durthacht, the man who had actually killed Naoise. In spite of her hands being tied, Deirdre threw herself off of Eoghan's chariot and died. From her grave and Naoise's, pines grew and intertwined, bringing the two lovers together forever.

DEITY CONCEPT Deities are metaphors for—cultural dreams of—our ultimate progenitors, and psychology has taught us how important our mental depictions and memories of our parents are to any real understanding of our own identities. Humans have needed divinity to make sense of where we came from and of who and what we are. As both a species and as distinct cultures it is difficult for us to conceive of mere chance existence. The concept of divinity has apparently always been at the center of human consciousness and human life. We have indications of the concept at least as early as the cave paintings, rock carvings, and other artifacts of the Paleolithic period. Over time, divinity has taken many forms and names. There have been sky gods, mother goddesses, fertility figures, tricksters, storm-weather gods, creators, and warrior gods. Figures such as Devi, Vishnu, and Shiva have dominated the temples and landscapes of India. Hera and Zeus ruled the heavens in Greece before they were displaced by the Christian God. Spider Woman and the Great Mystery still exist in the sweat lodges, *kivas*, and mountains of Native North America. Nigerian Binis have their separated Mother Earth and Father Sky. The Japanese have their sun goddess Amaterasu, the ancestor of emperors. There are gods who become incarnated as humans—Jesus as the Christ or Messiah; Lord Krishna and the other avatars of the great god Vishnu; and, some would say, the Buddha, not to mention the pharaohs of Egypt and the emperors of Rome and Japan.

There are, of course, many explanations for the concept of deity. A significant proportion of the human race argue that divinity first revealed itself to humanity in the form of personal beings such as those just mentioned, who have been or still are in direct communication with the world. This is the divinity type of many of today's organized religions, particularly those that worship the Abrahamic god, Yahweh-God-Allah. Others have seen deities as metaphorical expressions, symbols of the mysteries of the universe, reflections of our sense of the numinous, our sense of a realm of existence that is beyond the physical, beyond our understanding. For some, gods, being immortals, are the embodiment of our instinctive drive to establish a permanent order in the universe, of which we, as the allies or offspring of deities, can be a part if we act properly.

For many, gods are as good an explanation as we have of where we and our world came from. In this light, Mircea Eliade calls gods "fecundators" of the universe, embodiments of the mysterious force that, in creating, struggles against the natural tendency toward disintegration. If there is a universal theme reflected in the archetype that becomes our many versions of divinity, it would be our need to feel that we are meaningful inhabitants of a meaningful universe. In this sense, divinity is almost always fashioned in our image and is a metaphor for the furthest extension of which the human mind is capable at any given time. Deities, therefore, change with the times, taking ever new forms, even as the essential archetype remains constant, veiled in its eternal mystery.

A generally accepted truth of psychology, the source of one of the dominant myth systems of the modern era, is that what and who we are is the product not only of our genes but also of our "background" experience, an important part of which is our parenting. Creation myths are collective stories of parenting. In these myths, our worlds, our cultures, and we ourselves were created by the original parents, our deities. When we are asked about these parents, there will inevitably be limitations on our actual knowledge but also, as the myths of psychology teach us, on what we are able to "face." And, of course, our parents—actual and cosmic—are themselves the products of a past. The study of deities, like the memory and evaluation of parents, involves a complex process of delving into the past and overcoming strong forces of what contemporary psychology would call "denial." It often means seeing our parents' limitations and the inadequacies of our visions of them as well as their positive traits.

DELPHI Delphi, located on the south slope of Mount Parnassus, was for ancient Greeks a site that was sacred from the second millennium B.C.E.—probably first as an oracular precinct of the earth goddess Gaia. Later, with the emergence of a more patriarchal religion in Greece, Delphi became the locus for the prophecies of Apollo, to whose priestess, the *Pythia*, people from all over the Mediterranean world came to seek knowledge of the future. The *Adytum*, the place where oracles were actually delivered was marked by a stone as the *omphalos* ("navel"), or center of the earth. Delphi plays an important role in the myth cycle of Apollo and also that of Dionysos, who lived there in winter, balancing controlled Apollonian ideals with some Dionysian ecstasy. Delphi remained an oracular center of importance until 390 C.E., when the emperor Theodosius shut it down.

DEMETER AND PERSEPHONE A daughter of the early Greek gods Kronos and Rhea, Demeter (Ceres in Rome) was the goddess of crops and the fertile earth. By her brother and chief Olympian, Zeus, she gave birth to the beautiful Persephone, or Kore ("the maiden," Roman Proserpina). Demeter did not know that Zeus had promised their daughter to their brother Hades (Aidoneus, Roman Pluto), the ruler of the underworld. This terrifying god took by force what he had been promised. The girl was innocently picking flowers one spring when the earth opened and Hades sprang up from below and carried her off. The poet of the *Homeric Hymns* tells it this way:

> I sing now of the great Demeter,
> Of the beautiful hair,
> And of her daughter Persephone
> Of the lovely feet,
> Whom Zeus let Hades tear away
> From her mother's harvests
> And friends and flowers—
> Especially the Narcissus,
> Grown by Gaia to entice the girl
> As a favor to Hades, the gloomy one.
> This was the flower that
> Left all amazed,
> Whose hundred buds made
> The sky itself smile.
> When the maiden reached out
> To pluck such beauty,

The earth opened up
And out burst Hades
. . .
The son of Kronos,
Who took her by force
On his chariot of gold,
To the place where so many
Long not to go.
Persephone screamed,
She called to her father,
All-powerful and high,
. . .
But Zeus had allowed this.
He sat in a temple
Hearing nothing at all,
Receiving the sacrifices of
Supplicating men.

Only Hecate in her cave and the sun heard her cries. So it was that Persephone was taken by Hades down to his home to reign there as his queen.

Persephone's mother searched the earth frantically for her daughter, until the sun told her who had carried off the girl. Demeter was, understandably, not willing to accept the rape of her daughter or the collusion of her brothers in the act. In anger and despair, she left Olympus to live on earth and to continue the search for Persephone. Wherever she went she conferred blessing or punishments, depending on how she was treated. In a place called Eleusis, not far from Athens, the king, Celeus, took in the goddess and she took care of his children. She wanted to make the king's son Demophon immortal by dipping him in fire, but the child's mother came upon the ritual and screamed, and the ritual was broken, leaving the child mortal. Demeter turned her attention to another son, Triptolemos, conferring favors on him. It was Triptolemos who, under the goddess's inspiration, invented the plough and, thus, agriculture and civilization itself. In his chariot given to him by Demeter, he traveled the earth teaching the art of agriculture. Back in Eleusis he established the worship of Demeter in the famous Eleusinian Mysteries.

But unable to find her daughter, Demeter neglected the earth to such an extent that it became barren. Things became so bad that Zeus sent Hermes to retrieve Persephone. Before allowing her to leave, however, Hades gave her pomegranate, food of the underworld, to eat, and this symbolic act, connoting a certain loss of innocence, made it necessary for Persephone to return to her husband for one-third of each year. The rest of the time she could spend with Demeter.

When Persephone left her mother each year to return to her husband and her dark palace under the earth, Demeter became sad, and the warm, fertile seasons gave way to winter. But like the seed planted in the dark earth, Persephone burst forth annually from her underground place, representing the springing forth of Demeter's bounty in the spring. It is appropriate that Demeter is often depicted wearing a garland of corn.

DEMONS In many traditions, demons (Greek *daimon*, "spirit") are evil spirits or, as in the Abrahamic tradition, devils who follow *the* Devil. In Islam they are *shaitans*; in Judaism they may be *golems*. *Asuras* can be thought of as Hindu demons. Often demons take personal and physical form to better torment humans.

DESCENT OF HERAKLES The twelfth of the Twelve Labors of Herakles involved his descending to the underworld to bring back the monstrous three-headed dog Cerberus to Eurystheus. This the hero accomplished with the help of Athena, Hermes, and Hades himself. During his descent, Herakles released Theseus from the underworld.

DESCENT TO THE UNDERWORLD In mythologies from all parts of the world, the motif of the descent to the underworld is common. Sometimes the hero—for example, the Greek Herakles, Orpheus, or Theseus—makes the descent in search of destiny or of a lost lover or relative. Jesus goes to harrow Hell and retrieve fallen humanity. In some cases a god or goddess—for example, the Sumerian-Babylonian Inanna—descends simply to "know" the world below.

As part of the traditional hero journey, the myth of the descent seems to signify several things—for instance, a return to Mother Earth in preparation for rebirth into a higher divine hero state, or the facing of death before full selfhood can be achieved. Psychologically, the descent is the "night journey" or "dark night of the soul," which points to the fact that the self, to be whole, must rule the inner world.

The motif of the descent to the underworld is perhaps not as prevalent in the Eastern world as in the Western. It is, nevertheless, clearly present there. In India there is the popular story of the beautiful Savitri, who follows Yama, the Vedic god of death, to the gates of the underworld and convinces him to release her husband Satyavan from death. In The *Upanishads* the story is told of the young brahman Naciketas, who in the underworld, manages to obtain from Yama the knowledge that beyond

The goddess Demeter longs for her abducted daughter Persephone

D

Virgil's hero Aeneas descends to the underworld with the Sibyl

death itself is the absolute, Brahman. In China, the goddess Guanyin is also a heroine who dies and returns from the underworld, where she demonstrates her powers. Having been killed by her wrathful father's servant, Guanyin rides on the back of a tiger to the Land of the Dead. There she relieves the shades of their eternal sorrow with her beautiful singing. Enraged, the king of the Land of the Dead sends her back to earth, where she lives on an island from which she sends mercy and solace to those who pray to her. In Japan, the creator god Izanagi makes a disastrous descent to the underworld in search of his wife Izanami.

DEUCALION AND PYRRHA Deucalion and his wife Pyrrha are the central figures in a Greek flood myth. Deucalion was the son of Prometheus. He and his wife were so good that Zeus spared them from death in the great deluge he sent to punish degenerate humanity. Deucalion built a ship for himself and Pyrrha, and in it they rode out the nine-day flood, landing eventually on Mount Parnassus. After the flood, Deucalion and Pyrrha went down the hill to consult Themis, the successor to Gaia as the deity of the oracle at Delphi. Themis told them to throw the bones of their mother over their shoulders. The couple decided that their mother must be Gaia and her bones must be stones. Where they threw the stones a new race of humans emerged, men from the stones of Deucalion, women from those of Pyrrha. The son of Deucalion and Pyrrha was Hellen, the ancestor of the Hellenes (Greeks).

DEUS FABER CREATION The *deus faber* (God the Maker) creation myth is one in which a deity creates the world using the methods of a craftsman. Medieval and Renaissance depictions of God the creator in the Christian context sometimes show the deity, at least metaphorically, as an architect, using a compass to mark out the new universe. In the Book of Job (38:4–5) Yahweh reminds Job that it was he who had "laid the foundation of the earth and determined its measurements." Egyptian and Polynesian creation stories sometimes involve the creator deity as a potter, making humans out of clay. The Yuki Indians of California tell a creation myth in which the creator works as if he were essentially a tent maker.

DEVAKI The mother of the Hindu Lord Krishna, Devaki was the sister or cousin of King Kamsa, who, like the Greek Kronos, killed his children as they were born because of a prophecy that one of them would kill him. Krishna was saved when he was exchanged with the daughter of the herdsman Nanda, who served as his surrogate father.

DEVAS Celestial Hindu gods, as opposed to the more demonic *asuras*.

DEVAYANA The Hindu *Upanishads* tell of the narrow bridge, the way of the gods or the wise, by which the good Hindu after death discovers Brahman. In terms of philosophy, Devayana is the path to truth. A similar bridge exists in the Zoroastrian afterlife.

DEVI Devi is the Hindu Great Goddess. Although we speak of the *trimurti* of Brahma, Vishnu, and Shiva, in fact it is Devi who, in practice, joins Vishnu and Shiva as one of the three most important bhakti, or devotional deities, in India. Some would say that she is the most important divinity, the fullest embodiment of the absolute, Brahman. In the *Markandeya Purana*, in which many of Devi's myths appear, we find the *Devimahatymya*, in which the origin of the goddess is described. It seems that the world was being threatened by a gigantic water buffalo bull monster named Mahisa. He was king of the *asuras*, who had conquered Heaven. Following Brahma, the gods take refuge with Vishnu and Shiva and, with Vishnu and Shiva, project their angry energy in the form of sheets of light, which form one light and become the eighteen-armed goddess, the perfect amalgamated personification of the power and energy of godhead. Devi emerged as the ultimate feminine principle, the Life Energy itself, the original Shakti, the psychic and spiritual energy without which even Shiva is nothing material. Devi can, in fact, be worshipped as Shakti.

Devi takes many forms. As the violent avenging warrior goddess Durga, she kills the primeval monster and saves the world. It is the world that concerns Devi; she is the key to a successful existence in this reality. Although as the bloodthirsty Kali, she brings disease, war, and destruction, it is because death and destruction are necessary to the cycle of life. For those who worship her, Devi is for the most part benevolent. Sometimes she is the wife of Shiva as Parvati, Daughter of the Mountain. As Sati, the daughter of Daksha and the husband of Shiva-Rudra, she throws herself onto her husband's funeral pyre, setting the example for Hindu wives. But Devi can also take form as Shri, or Lakshmi, the wife of Vishnu. The name Shri refers to prosperity and Vishnu to the sacrifice, indicating that prosperity cannot be separated from the necessary rituals of sacrifice. In the *Mahabharata*, Lakshmi is incarnated as Draupadi, the wife of the Pandava brothers, and in the *Ramayana* she is Sita, the loyal wife of the Vishnu avatar Rama.

Philosophically, Devi is also the yogic sleep within Vishnu—that which keeps the world within the god. When she is outside of Vishnu, she becomes not only Devi herself but Lila ("Divine Creativity") and Maya ("Divine Illusion").

DEVNARAYAN Devnarayan is the hero of the epic named for him in Rajasthan in the northwest of India. The hero is also in a sense a god. Performed by and for agricultural castes, the epic concerns twenty-four brothers who are killed by the goddess Devi, who becomes incarnated in the household of the brothers. Vishnu is incarnated there, too, as Devnarayan, and he defeats the enemies of the descendants of the twenty-four brothers. Before returning to Heaven, he establishes his own cult among the cowherds, a fact that associates him with the greatest of his avatars, Krishna.

DHARMA The Hindu concept derived from the *Vedas* of social obligation or duty and that is the basis of all Hindu social laws and ethics (see *Laws of Manu*), dharma is sometimes personified as a god and is the father of one of the Pandava brothers in the *Mahabharata*. Dharma bears some similarities to the Egyptian concept of *maat* and the Sumerian *me*.

DHOLA EPIC This popular epic of northwestern India is sung in nightly episodes at village festivals. There are fifty episodes in all, which tell the story of the Navargarh kingdom. The king, Raja Pratham, has a wife, Manja, who becomes pregnant miraculously by way of a grain of rice provided by a guru. The king's other wives convince him that Manja's son will kill him, and so begins a string of events known in fairy tales and myths in many parts of the world. The king orders a servant to kill the queen in the forest, but the servant cannot bring himself to do so and kills a deer instead, presenting the deer's eyes to the king as proof of the slaying of Manja.

Manja, of course, has a son, Nal, who, with his mother, is taken in by a merchant. The merchant and his sons are arrested when the merchant cannot present the king with more than one cowrie shell, used in gambling games. Nal arrives at court and promises to deliver more shells if the king will release the merchant and his sons. The king agrees. Nal then goes in search of the shells and is told by an old woman that they are in the possession of Motini, the daughter of a demon king called Ghumasur. After Nal meets Motini and successfully gambles with her, she agrees to marry him and turns him into a fly in order to hide him from her wicked father. Nal finally overcomes

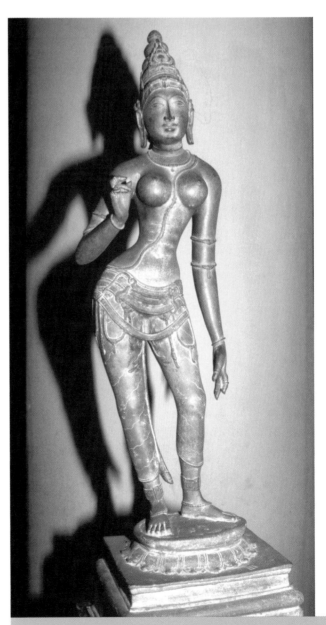

One of many incarnations of Devi, the Hindu Great Goddess

D

Pompeiian statue of Diana

Amoghasiddhi, who rides with his thunderbolt on an eagle; and the blue Aksobhya, who also carries a thunderbolt and rides on an elephant.

There is, however, little in the way of further characterization of these buddhas. We know much more about the Dhyani bodhisattvas, who result from the meditation of the buddhas. The green bodhisattva Samantabhadra is popular in Nepal. He was a companion of Gautama Buddha, and he rides on an elephant. He stands for happiness. Vajrapani was also a companion of the Buddha. His sign is a thunderbolt, and he gives kindness to true followers and pain to those who deny the Buddha. Avalokiteshvara achieved enlightenment but, in the best Mahayanist tradition, decided to remain here to bring mercy and enlightenment to other human beings. Avalokiteshvara emanates from the Amida buddha, carries a pink lotus, and works constantly to help those in need. He carries refreshment to those in Hell and converts the evil. In China he became the goddess Guanyin (Japanese Kannon).

DI JUN A name for the early Chinese supreme sky god.

DIAN CECHT As the Irish god of medicine, Dian Cecht supplied Nuada, king of the Tuatha Dè Danaan, with a silver arm after the first battle of Magh Tuired. Dian Cecht's son later supplied the king with a real arm. In fact, Dian Cecht was so jealous of his son's abilities that he killed him.

DIANA Among the pre-Roman Latins the goddess Diana was actually a more important figure than her Greek cognate Artemis. She was night to Jupiter's day. Later, among the Romans, she was somewhat reduced in importance and was, like Artemis, considered a huntress.

DIARMUID Diarmuid of the Love Spot was a warrior follower of the Irish hero Fionn (Finn). Fionn had planned to marry Grainne, the daughter of the high king, Cormac Mac Art. Unwilling to marry the aging Fionn, Grainne shamed Diarmuid into sleeping with and eloping with her. For sixteen years Fionn chased the couple all over Ulster and Connacht until, finally, Cormac and the love god Aonghus Og, who had protected the lovers, persuaded Fionn to make peace. Still, when Diarmuid was gored by his own mother's illegitimate son in the form of the magical boar of Ben Bulben, Fionn could have saved him but chose not to do so.

DIDO Virgil tells the tragic story of the Queen of Carthage in the Roman epic the *Aeneid*. Dido (Elissa) was the daughter of a chieftain in Phoenicia. Forced to flee Phoenicia, she had founded Carthage (in modern Tunisia) and was there when the hero Aeneas and his followers arrived from the defeated Troy on their way to founding the "new Troy," Rome. Dido and Aeneas became lovers, and it seems likely that Aeneas would have remained happily in Carthage as its co-ruler with Dido had the gods not reminded him of his mission. The angry and lovesick Dido killed herself when Aeneas left to continue his quest, and when Aeneas saw her during his descent to the underworld, she shunned him. In an earlier myth, Dido is said to have killed herself not because of Aeneas, but because she had been trapped into marrying a neighboring king. After that suicide, she is said to have been worshipped as a deity.

DIEVS A Baltic sky-god creator, Dievs seems to have developed from a representation of the sky, to a personification

the demon by destroying the magic duck that is the source of his strength.

When Nal returns with Motini to the merchant and his sons, the sons fall in love with Motini and throw Nal into the sea. Eventually, however, the king is offered Motini as a substitute for the promised shells, and he falls in love with her. Motini refuses to marry him until the story of Nal—the *Nal Purana*—is told. At this point, Nal himself, alive and disguised as an old man, arrives and tells his own story. The king realizes who he is, brings back Manja, and the union of Motini and Nal is celebrated. Soon Motini produces a son of her own, and he is named Dhola. What follows is the story of Nal's conflict with the god Indra over a raja's daughter, Damyanti. After many trials, Nal is able to win another raja's daughter, Maru, for his son. After more difficulties and separations, Dhola and Maru are happily united.

DHYANI BUDDHAS AND BODHISATTVAS In the Mahayana Buddhist tradition, Gautama Buddha was preceded by other buddhas in other ages. Among these are the five Dhyani ("meditation") buddhas: the white-colored Vairocana, who rides on a dragon and is particularly popular among the Shingon sect in Japan; the yellow Ratnasambhava, who rides on a horse; the red Amitabha, particularly revered in Japan, whose place is the Pure Land or *Sukhavati*; the green

of the sky, and then to a personal god. In his folkloric depiction, Dievs is a well-dressed farmer, complete with overcoat and mittens, who presides over a farm on a mountain in the heavens. True to the Indo-European tradition, he is associated with horses, which pull his chariot around his farm. Sometimes he is equated with a solar god named Usins, whose chariot, in Latvia, was said to be pulled by two white horses across the sky. Sometimes Usins was seen as one of a set of divine twins or sons of Dievs, known as the Asvinai or Dievas Deli, which were typical Indo-European horse gods, like the Vedic twins—the Ashvins—and the Greek Dioskouri ("Sons of God").

Dievs's sacred drink is beer, the mead of Baltic rituals, which has equivalents in other Indo-European cultures. In folklore, Dievs is a highly personal and domestic god who at particular times in the Baltic mythological calendar visits with and advises earthly farmers. In this domestic aspect he is unlike most Indo-European supreme deities and is perhaps reminiscent of an older, pre–Indo-European earth-centered religion. In one planting myth, Dievs spends the night with a group of farmers watching over the fire and the horses and accidentally leaves his mittens behind when he departs at sunrise.

Dievs is closely associated with and sometimes married to the goddess Saule.

DIFFUSION AND PARALLELISM Mythologists have long been aware of the fact that certain motifs or archetypes and even whole plots are found in cultures that are not geographically connected. Some thinkers—the psychiatrist Carl Jung, for example—have postulated what might be called the "parallel development" of myths as the result of a common "collective unconscious," the idea being that humans inherit certain mythic tendencies just as they inherit physical characteristics. Thus we find the motif of the hero's quest in all parts of the world because the hero is a reflection, in his various cultural clothes, of a larger psychic human need. Others have attributed the transmission of common motifs and themes to a process of diffusion, whereby ideas are carried from culture to culture by humans involved in such activities as war and trade.

DIKITHI The "Great Dikithi" is a trickster of the Bantu people in Africa. A giant with one eye, one arm, and one leg, Dikithi is an amoral thief, but he is also a culture hero who gives creatively to his people. Once Dikithi tricked an elephant into falling into a pit trap. He killed the elephant but refused to share the meat from his kill with the other villagers. Finally, he decided to take his wife and children away from the village. When he refused to allow his mother-in-law to accompany them, she followed anyway. Growing tired of his mother-in-law's relentless pursuit, Dikithi killed her; however, she revived and, now even angrier than before, continued her pursuit, threatening to catch Dikithi and cut off his manhood. Dikithi tried every means imaginable to get rid of his pursuer, finally burning her to death and

Diana the celibate huntress surrounded by her hounds

D

Dionysos in his Roman embodiment as Bacchus participating in his "bacchic rites."

making a whistle out of her leg bone. When Dikithi's father came along and asked for the whistle, Dikithi tricked him into climbing the tree where he had been hiding from his mother-in-law and then pushed him to his death.

In a kind of earth-diver act, Dikithi sent various birds down through his father's body to open its stomach and release the food he knew was there. Eventually, a small bird succeeded by traveling the alimentary canal from mouth to anus, and the stomach opened. Dikithi invited all the people to a great feast and welcomed them to live in his village.

This myth has some analogues in the myths of other cultures about male hero gods killing primeval figures representing chaos. The story of Marduk's defeat of Tiamat is such a myth, as are the myths of Ouranos being defeated by Kronos and Kronos being defeated in turn by his son Zeus.

DIOMEDES The son of Tydeus and, thus, often called Tydides, Diomedes was one of the Epigoni, or "descendants" of the warriors who failed to take Thebes in the story *Seven Against Thebes*, a version of which was told by the Greek playwright Aeschylus. Ten years after their fathers, including Diomedes' father, had died at Thebes, the Epigoni took the city, and Diomedes succeeded Adrastus as king of Argos. According to Homer in his *Iliad*, Diomedes was one of the bravest of the Greek heroes who fought in the Trojan War. Diomedes was a favorite of the goddess Athena, but Aphrodite was angry at him, and when he returned home after the war he found that his wife had betrayed him with another man.

DIONYSOS Dionysos (sometimes Zagreus, Bacchus to the Romans) was the son of the supreme Greek god Zeus. According to some, his mother was Persephone. More usually his mother is thought to have been Semele ("Moon"), who, though usually depicted as mortal, seems to have had connections with an older moon goddess, Selene. This connection is of interest in the Indo-European context given the association of the Vedic Purusha with the moon. Like Athena, Dionysos, according to Apollodorus, Apollonius of Rhodes, and others, was born directly of Zeus. This is suggested by the name Dionysos itself, which etymologically develops from sounds meaning "Zeus-like."

In the most common myth, Zeus, disguised as a mortal, had a love affair with Semele, daughter of the King of Thebes. Soon Semele was pregnant with the very son of God. It was the jealous Hera who, disguised as an old woman, advised Semele to ask her lover to allow her anything she wished. Hera suggested that when Zeus agreed—as, in the throes of passion, he surely would—Semele request that he reveal himself to her in his true form. The trick worked, and Zeus, who could never go back on his word, was forced to reveal himself to Semele. As no mortal can bear the power and brightness of the god of thunder and lightning, Semele was destroyed by her vision. Fortunately, Hermes saved the unborn baby and sewed it into Zeus's thigh, from which, three months later, the "twice born" god was born. Later, Dionysos was said to have descended to the underworld in search of his true mother, Semele.

In the Persephone version of the myth, Dionysos/Zagreus was eaten by the Titans at the request of the jealous Hera. One story says that the goddess Athena saved the boy's heart and gave it to Semele to swallow so that she could bring the child to a second birth. In still another version, Zeus plucked the baby from the dead body of Semele, and the boy transformed himself into a lion, a bull, and then a serpent (representing the three-part year). But no disguise could long fool Hera, ever jealous of Zeus's philandery, and ever vengeful. She ordered the Titans to seize the little boy. They tore him to pieces and boiled the gobbets in a cauldron.

In an Orphic version of this dismemberment myth, Dionysos is returned to life under the care of Persephone and/or Demeter. There is a strong and clear connection, as the historian Herodotus recognized, between the Dionysos-Persephone/Demeter relationship and the story of the resurrection god Osiris and his sister-wife Isis in Egypt. In the tradition of Sir James Frazer, Robert Graves, and others, the meal of the Titans and the ministrations of the goddesses can be seen as an indication of a ritual in which a king is sacrificed and his body fed to his followers as sacred food.

One of the myths tells us that where the god's blood had fallen, a pomegranate tree grew, flowered, and fruited, its luscious scarlet body holding a promising—an irresistible—profusion of seeds. In this way Dionysos's grandmother, Rhea ("Earth"), reconstituted him and brought him to life again, and he set out bearing his sacred vines, sweeping throughout Greece and the remainder of the world—even going as far as India—establishing his divinity among all people. With the world addicted to him, he later ascended into heaven as the thirteenth Olympian and sat at the right hand of Zeus.

The possibility of regeneration and rebirth that the "savior" Dionysos represents is, of course, an important path to the story of Jesus as a resurrected dying man-god, a story that would eventually give new life to the ancient Indo-European theme of the necessary sacrifice and so turn the older "religion" of Greece into "mythology."

Dionysos is in some ways the most mysterious of the gods and one of the most powerful. It is clear that, like several of the Greek gods, he has a particularly Minoan background. Like the boy Zeus of Crete, for example, Dionysos is a dying god, and he was always considered a "foreign god." Ancient writers believed that he came from Thrace, the home in the Balkans of many religiously and linguistically related tribes, including the Getae and the Dacians, who sided with Troy in the *Iliad*. In the fifth book of the *Iliad*, Homer tells how the Thracian King Lykurgos resisted Dionysos and was made insane by him, eventually committing suicide or being killed by him.

When one places this story next to that of the Thracian version of Artemis, called Cotys, a chthonic deity who made men wear women's clothes in her orgiastic rites, we cannot help but think of Euripides' the *Bacchae* and the conflict in that play between the ecstatic foreign god and the Theban King Pentheus. Pentheus, like Lykurgos, is driven mad and, dressed in women's clothes, he meets a tragic and orgiastic end. Although sometimes assimilated as an Olympian, Dionysos seems more comfortable in the company of earth-based activities such as those "mysteries" surrounding Demeter and Kore (Persephone) at Eleusis. Still, the Dionysian religion coexisted easily enough with the civic religion. The great dramatic festivals of Athens, for example, were dedicated to Dionysos, and many scholars have attributed the origins of drama itself to his myth.

DIS PATER In the Gaulish, that is, continental Celtic mythology, Dis Pater was the Roman name provided by Julius Caesar for a god claimed by the Gauls as their father god, or ultimate progenitor. The name given by Caesar suggests that the Romans saw a connection between this deity and the otherworld or underworld. As, literally, "underworld father," Dis Pater is naturally associated in Caesar's mind with the Roman Pluto. The Irish cognates would probably be the Dagda, the father god of the Tuatha Dé Danaan, and Donn, the god of the dead.

DISAPPEARING GOD The Anatolian equivalent of the dying-god motif, found in Egypt, Greece, and Canaan, is the myth of the disappearing god, a motif that also has relatives in such descent disappearances as those of Persephone in Greece, Amaterasu in Japan, and Inanna/Ishtar and Dumuzi/Tammuz in Mesopotamia. The best-known Hittite god who disappears is Telepinu, an ancient Hattic agricultural deity whose father was the dominant weather-storm god. Other Hittite-Hurrian disappearing gods included the storm god himself, the sun god, and the earth goddess, Hannahanna. The disappearing-god myths were associated with a Hittite ritual called the *mugawar* intended to appease an angry god in order to restore order to the land and its people.

DISMEMBERMENT Especially in animistic traditions, the theme of the creation from dismemberment of primal beings or first parents is common. Mesoamerican mythology contains the story of the earth goddess Coatlicue, who was pulled to earth by Quetzalcoatl and Tezcatlipoca and ripped apart to form earth and sky, her hair becoming plants and other parts of her body becoming other aspects of the natural world. The Babylonian myth of the defeat and dismemberment of the also-female primal deity Tiamat by the god Marduk is similar. In the Ceramese myth of Hainuwele, the young goddess-heroine is dismembered and planted so as to become staple crops. The emergence of crops from a dismembered and planted goddess is common in the mythologies of Native North America, as, for instance, in the many myths of the Corn Mother.

The creative dismemberment creation myth finds its way into the Indo-European tradition as well. In the Indian *Rig Veda* the primal man Purusha—in a sense the unformed universe itself—becomes the sacrifice out of whose dismemberment the rituals, the sacred words (mantras), the *Vedas*, and the world came: his mind became the moon, his eye the sun, and so forth. A Norse myth tells how the world grew from the dismembered giant Ymir. There are also aspects of dismemberment in the early creation myths of the Greeks.

Dismemberment plays a role in the myths of dying and resurrected man-gods as well. Osiris is dismembered and thrown into the Nile, for example, and the Phrygian Attis is castrated.

DITI AND THE DAITYAS In Vedic-Hindu mythology Diti (Danu), the sister and opposite of Aditi, is the mother of the

The Mayan Maize God

demonic daityas (danavas), such as Virtra and other enemies of the gods. She represents dualism and division. Aditi is universality and godliness in humans; Diti is that which is individual and mortality based.

DIVINE CHILD The divine child, or *puer aeternus*, is the hero of the monomyth or sometimes the god as a child. Typically, he or she is miraculously conceived, like Jesus, Horus, Zoroaster, Waterpot Boy, Mary, Hainuwele, or Cybele. Often the child's mother is impregnated by a divine force. Sometimes she remains a virgin after the conception. Frequently the child is abandoned, as in the cases of Moses and Siegfried. The seemingly helpless child early on experiences an initiatory act that reveals his or her essential heroism. Cuchulainn kills the hound of Culann, Herakles kills the serpent in his cradle, King Arthur pulls the sword from the rock. All of these factors point to the child as a human vehicle for divine power on earth. [Jung and Kerenyi]

DJANGGAWUL In eastern Arnheim Land in Aboriginal Australia, Djanggawul and his two sisters were primordial beings involved in the creative process known as the dreaming. The three beings traveled about the country in a bark canoe. Djanggawul had a very long, uncircumcised and decorated penis, and his sisters had exaggerated cli-

torises. Whenever these beings came to a land mass, they beached their canoe and walked around, their sex organs dragging on the ground, leaving various sacred markings still present today. The trio also left "dreamings" in the form of stories, sacred places, and ceremonies, including representations of Djanggawul's penis in the form of decorated poles. In each place Djanggawul had intercourse with his sisters, and humans were the result. Incest in the early stages of creation is a ubiquitous theme among the Australian Aborigines and many other cultures. It exists, for instance, in the creation myths of the Vedas in India. Some say that to remove some of their cumbersome genital equipment Djanggawul and his sisters instituted the tradition of circumcision.

DJUNGGUN In the western Kimberley region of Australia the people tell how a man or primordial being named Djunggun and his friend Wodoy married each other's daughters. But when Djunggun tried to possess his own daughter, Wodoy killed him, putting an end to the all-too-common practice of incestuous relationships.

DOGON CREATION The Dogon people of Mali in Africa say that the cosmic egg at the beginning of time was shaken by the stirrings of the universe and it divided into two pla-

Moses as the abandoned "divine child" found by Pharaoh's daughter

centas, each containing a set of twins engendered by the supreme god Amma. Each placenta contained a male and a female twin, each of whom also contained the essence of the opposite gender. Somehow the twin Yur ugu broke out of his placenta, a piece of which fell and became the earth. Meanwhile Yur ugu's twin joined the other set of twins in the other placenta. As for Yuyugu, he copulated with the earth—that is, with his own maternal placenta—but failed to make humans, so Amma sent the other twins down to procreate. Humans are the result of this incestuous coupling.

Other Dogon people say that it was Amma himself who had intercourse with his creation, Earth, after removing her clitoris, represented by a nest of termites obstructing his phallus. From this union came Yurugu, who brought evil and chaos into the world and later even committed incest with his mother, Earth, thus causing the birth of evil spirits and instigating menstruation in his now-impure mother. But before that happened, Amma, as fertilizing rain, would again mate with Earth, creating the Nummo ("Water") twins, who brought order and fertility to the world. The myth suggests the tradition of female circumcision.

DOMOVOI Depicted as a bearded old man, the domovoi is the "house spirit" of Slavic mythology. To ensure domestic happiness, the domovoi has to be kept happy.

DON AND THE CHILDREN OF DON The Welsh equivalent of the Irish Danu, Don is the ancient mother goddess, of the divine pantheon known in the fourth branch of the *Mabinogion* as the "Children of Don," the equivalent of the Irish Tuatha Dé Danaan. The members of the pantheon of Don represent aspects of creation. Don is the daughter of Mathonwy; the sister of Math (prosperity); the wife of Beli (death); and the mother of Gwydion (light), Aranrhod (dawn), Amaethon (agriculture), Gofannon (smith crafts), Nudd/Ludd (sky), and others. Her grandchildren include Nwyfre (space), Lleu Llaw (sun), and Dylan (sea).

DONAR The equivalent of the Norse Thor and the Anglo-Saxon Thunor, Donar is a Teutonic god of thunder, one of many Indo-European storm gods.

DONN Donn was the Irish god of the dead, who dwelt at Tech Duinn ("the House of Donn") on an island off the west coast of Ireland. He is perhaps the same as the Donn who was the son of Milesius (Mil Espaigne, leader of the Milesians), who was cursed by the goddess Eire because he did not name Ireland for her after he and the other "Sons of Mil" conquered the Tuatha Dè Danaan.

DONN CUAILGNE The Brown Bull of Cuailgne in the Irish epic the *Tain Bo Cuailgne* is the catalyst for the great war between the forces of Ulster and those of Connacht.

DRAGON KING In Vietnam, the Dragon King is Long-vuong or Thuyte. He is the lord of the seas and lives in a magnificent aquatic palace surrounded by beings of the sea. Traditionally, the Dragon King is important for giving gifts to those who release his children after unwittingly catching them in their nets or on their hooks. In one story, a student, Giap-Hai, saves a turtle from some fishermen and discovers that the shell contains a beautiful woman, who turns out to be the Dragon King's daughter. The pair is married, and, with the help of the Dragon King, Giap-Hai passes his scholarly exams with great distinction. The Dragon King also plays a role in Chinese mythology, especially in the myth of the Eight Immortals.

DRAGONS The dragon is common to many mythological traditions and is usually a giant reptilian creature who spouts fire and steam. In ancient myths, the dragon is often female and representative of chaos, as opposed to the order associated with gods of the male patriarchy. In ancient Babylonia, Tiamat was such a creature and was defeated by the god-hero Marduk. In the West the dragon has usually been a symbol of evil against whom heroes such as Sigurd (Siegfried) and Beowulf fight. For Christians, beginning from the Book of Revelation, the dragon sometimes is Satan himself, but is usually a symbol of sin or pagan ways. Christian heroes, such as Saint George, therefore, are often depicted with one foot proudly stomping on the head of the dragon.

Dragons often protect treasure, perhaps representing the value of deep understanding to be found in the chthonic depths with which the dragon is also frequently associated. For the Germanic peoples who invaded the British Isles, the dragon represented power, and on the shield of the British monarchy it represents that power and the sovereignty that goes with it.

In the Far East, the dragon tends to be a positive figure. The most important of Chinese mythological beasts, dragons are expressions of *yang*, the male principle balanced by the female *yin*, represented by the phoenix. The dragon and the phoenix were symbols of Chinese emperors and empresses from the Han dynasty on. The dragon was especially associated with the sea and other forms of water. Dragon dances mark the beginning of the Chinese lunar year.

DRAUPADI The wife of all five Pandava brothers in the Indian epic the *Mahabharata*, "fire-born" Draupadi is an incarnation of Shri (Lakshmi, "Prosperity"), the wife of the Hindu god Vishnu. The Vishnu connection is appropriate to a kingdom such as that of the Pandavas, one that follows the principles of dharma, or proper social law. Draupadi's situation as the wife of five men is not usual and occurs only because of a promise made by Kunti, the mother of the brothers. In any case, although she favors the hero Arjuna, Draupadi is a faithful wife to all five brothers and provides each with a son. When Yudishthira, the oldest brother and the king, gambles away his kingdom and his brothers and even their wife, it is Draupadi who convinces the Pandava enemies to grant the brothers their freedom. The event that leads to their release is a high point in the Draupadi myth and clearly establishes her as Shri and as the source, with Krishna, of Pandava power. When the gambling victors, the Kauravas, attempt to strip Draupadi in order to humiliate her and her husbands, Krishna intervenes and miraculously prevents the stripping. As her tormentors try to pull off her sari, they are never able to reach its end point. So Draupadi remains miraculously clothed. As always in the events of Hindu mythology, there is a symbolic meaning to this incident. It suggests that the dissolution of the universe, represented by Shri-Draupadi, will not take place yet. A cult based on Draupadi as an incarnation of the goddess (Devi) exists to this day in parts of India.

DRAUPNIR Dwarves forged Draupnir, the magical arm bracelet or arm ring of the Norse god Odin. Every ninth night, eight similar rings dropped from Draupnir, ensuring a constant supply of gold for the gods.

DRAVIDIANS Dravidians are people who speak non–Indo-European languages, primarily in southern India and northern Sri Lanka. These languages include Tamil and Malayam. When we speak of Dravidian culture, we generally refer to an indigenous pre-Hindu culture such as the one described in the Tamil *Tol kappiyam*, written in the first and second centuries C.E. Dravidian culture probably developed from Indus Valley culture in south India in the Neolithic period and, in terms of religion, was probably earth centered and possibly dominated by a goddess cult.

DREAMING, THE The original creative process, translated from Australian Aboriginal languages as "the dreaming," refers to a "dreamtime"—something like a mythological age—in which primordial beings such as Djanggawul and his sisters did "walkabouts," giving birth to people, leaving sacred markings and objects, and establishing such societal structures as clans, totems, taboos, and religious systems. A given tribe 's dreaming is its spiritual and original history.

DREAMS AND MYTH For thinkers such as Carl Jung and Joseph Campbell, myths are comparable to dreams and should be regarded as seriously as we regard dreams. Dreams provide us with important information about ourselves—information uncorrupted by conscious defense mechanisms. Myths, with their complex and often bizarre dream-like events and symbols, do the same thing for cultures; they provide direct insight to the collective psyche or the collective soul. To repress or dismiss myths as mere illusion can be as psychologically and spiritually harmful as dismissing dreams. Both are "languages" of the unconscious. In short, say Jung and Campbell, we need myths—those of our individual and cultural past and origins—and a mythical consciousness in the present time, to show us who we are. Self-knowledge and identity involve intangibles that transcend mere name, parentage, and geographical location.

DRUIDS Druids were the priestly class in early Celtic societies, especially continental Celts. They were judges and seers with great moral authority, who ranked above all other classes. As such, they were the equivalent of their Indo-European brothers, the Indian brahmans. The Romans in Gaul developed myths about the druids such as the one suggesting that they practiced human sacrifice. The Irish filidh may be said to have somewhat diminished druidic standing. The great Celtic bards Taliesen and Amairgen had druidic qualities and authority.

DUALISM Dualism is the tendency to see existence in terms of opposites—good and evil, mind and matter, body and spirit. In mythology, usually derived from theologies based on a good-versus-evil syndrome, dualism tends to take the form of cosmic figures who struggle against each other. In Zorastrianism Ahura Mazda (the "Wise Lord") is pitted against his own negative creation, Angra Mainyu, in a universal struggle for dominance. In Christian mythology, based on the Genesis story of the Jewish *Torah*, God (and later Jesus) stands as the creative force for good against the destructive tendencies of Satan. Sometimes dualism is reflected in the ubiquitous myth of the war in Heaven—God and his followers against the Devil and his fallen angels, Zeus and the Olympians against Kronos and the Titans, the Norse Aesir versus the Vanir, Vedic-Hindu gods versus demons. The concept that good and evil and

A Druid near a sacred stone circle

other opposites are inherent in creation itself is particularly well depicted in the many myths—especially among central Asians and Native North Americans—of the trickster who "assists" or copies the creator and in so doing usually undermines his work in some way.

Dualism can have a more philosophical expression in mythology, as in the case of the Chinese concept of *yin* and *yang*, or the various expressions of the sacred and profane outlined by Mary Douglas, Émile Durkheim, and Mircea Eliade.

DUMÉZIL, GEORGES Dumézil (1898–1986) was a French comparative anthropologist who specialized in Indo-European mythology and the relation between the sacred and the profane—mythological ideas and forms and earthly pursuits, fertility gods and farming, storm gods and warriors. His most provocative contribution to mythological studies was the development of the concept of the Indo-European triad or tripartite god reflecting social realities—warfare, fertility, priestly functions—as opposed to the traditional sky or father god. Dumézil's interest in the social perspective in relation to myth and religion owes a great deal to the pioneering French social scientist Émile Durkheim (1857–1917), who saw in all religions and mythologies an essentially dualistic division between the realms of the sacred and the profane.

DUMUZI The sometimes shepherd or fisherman husband of the Sumerian goddess Inanna in the fertility mythology of ancient Mesopotamia, Dumuzi (Tammuz) was in a sense a dying god, since he was condemned to take his wife's place in the underworld for part of each year. A king named Dumuzi appears on the king lists of Uruk as an actual king of the city toward the end of the third millennium B.C.E.

DURGA Durga, "the inaccessible," is the beautiful multiarmed warrior form of the Hindu goddess (Devi) and is a wife of Shiva. It is Durga who saves the gods and the universe by defeating and killing the buffalo demon Mahisa and her followers as described in the *Devimahatmya* of the *Marandeya Purana*. It seems that the demon had so threatened the gods that Durga took form from the combined anger of Vishnu and Shiva and the other gods and faced him. When Mahisa became a lion, Durga cut off his head. When he became a man, Durga stabbed him with her sword, and he became an elephant. After Durga cut off his trunk, he became a buffalo again and tried to impede Durga by throwing mountains at her. But the angry goddess leapt into his body and punctured him with her trident and then cut off his head. Until very recently, annual sacrifices of water buffalo were made to honor Durga, and to this day, she is the center of an annual festival celebrating victory over evil in many parts of the Hindu world.

DURVASAS Durvasas's name means "naked" and suggests the image of the Hindu brahman sage as ascetic. An incarnation of the god Shiva—the perfect yogi and the destroyer—he is capable of great destructive power and possesses the inner power to overcome evil. He was once given a magic garland by the goddess (Devi), whom he particularly revered.

DWARFS In mythology, dwarfs—as opposed to other "little people," such as elves and fairies—are generally chthonic, that is, associated with the mysteries of the earth. They are frequently thought of as evil and are seen as being primarily concerned with protecting their own possessions. They are master craftsmen and are always willing to bestow curses on humans who challenge them. Nowhere is all this clearer than in German and Norse mythology, where the dwarfs create the most important treasures but are motivated by lust, greed, and fear. They are relegated to a living space distant from that of the gods.

DXUI Dxui is the shape-shifting man-creator of the southwest African Bushmen (San). At the creation, he literally became each of the elements of the world—a flower, the sun, a fruit tree, a bird, an insect. When he was approached by the first woman in his form as a fruit tree with thorns, the woman was unable to get to the fruit and she died. Once when he was a man, he became the victim of a hunt and turned himself into a large bird so he could escape. In the end he died as a man but turned into a lizard.

DYAUS The Sanskrit word for the Vedic Indian personification of the sky, Dyaus is at the root of the related Indo-European terms for the sky god—for example, *Deus, Dios, Zeus.*

DYING GOD Sacrifice takes mythological form in the many stories of the dying god. This motif exists outside of the Indo-European tradition as well as within it. In Sumer Inanna herself and her consort Dumuzi enact a ritual of death and descent to the underworld, as do the goddess Hainuwele in Ceram, several African deities, and the great sacred god-king-priest Osiris in Egypt. Attis, the son of the Great Goddess Cybele of Phrygian Anatolia, was a dying god. In Europe there are several dying gods or gods who undergo a ritual of death and renewal. The Norse god Odin hangs himself on the World Tree to learn the eternal truth of the runes. The Romans imported the year god Attis from Phrygia and practiced his rites of death and renewal in the spring. In Slavic Belorussia and Russia we find the dying and reborn Iarilo, "god of heavenly light," who rides a white horse and wears a crown of flowers. Two pre-Christian dying-god myths stand out in Europe. These are the myths of the Norse god Balder—the "beautiful" god—and the Greek god Dionysos.

The dying-god motif is closely related to the even more universal myth of the hero's descent into the underworld. Nearly always the dying god's or hero's apparent death results in some kind of rebirth or resurrection. Osiris, revived by his wife Isis, returned as his son Horus and as grain and as the rejuvenated land after the annual Nilotic floods. In Ugaritic Canaan the dying god was Baal, the son of El or Dagan, who descended into the jaws of death (Mot) but who, with the help of the goddess Anat, returned and reestablished fertility for the land. In Phoenicia Melgart, the city god of Tyre, was a dying and reviving god, as was Eshmun, the city deity of Sidon and Byblos. The best known of the Canaanite dying gods was Adonis, the spring god of the Phoenicians, who also became popular in Greece and Rome as a human with whom Aphrodite/Venus fell in love.

The Middle Eastern version of the dying-god motif is fully developed in the story of Jesus, who was said to have died and then returned to life after three days—one of them in Hell—bringing the possibility of what might be called spiritual as opposed to physical fertility. [Frazer (1911–1915), Leeming (1990)]

EA Ea is the Akkadian/Babylonian name for the crafty and sometimes trickster-like Sumerian god Enki. With Anu he is one of the earliest and most important of the Mesopotamian deities. The Babylonian creation epic, the *Enuma elish*, says that out of sweet (Apsu) and salt water (Tiamat) came the gods, including Ansar and Kisar, who produced Anu (the Sumerian An) and Ea (Nudimmud), born in Anu's image. It was Ea who, like Zeus in Greek mythology, came to the rescue of the new gods, who were threatened by the old progenitor, Apsu. Using his inborn shamanic or magical powers, he disposed of Apsu and fathered, with his wife Damkina (Sumerian Damgalnuna), the great city god Marduk, who would destroy Ea's monstrous mother, Tiamat. And it was Ea, also a water god, often depicted with fish-filled streams flowing from his shoulders, who spared the flood hero Utnapishtim in the Akkadian version of the Gilgamesh epic.

EARTH A common motif in world mythologies is earth personified as a goddess. Examples include the Greek Gaia, the Incan earth mother, and any number of Native North American and African goddesses. Often Earth must be separated from Sky in order that creation can take place (*see* Sacred earth).

EARTH-DIVER CREATION In earth-diver creation myths an animal or another god is sent by the creator to retrieve substance from the depths of the primal waters. This substance, in any number of possible ways, becomes the earth. Earth-diver creations are particularly prevalent among Native American peoples, who in all likelihood originally migrated to North America across the Bering Straits from Asia. Not surprisingly, then, earth-diver creations are found in the mythology of the Ainu people of Japan and the Birhor people of India and in the *Puranas* of Hinduism. They are also found in the Chinese flood myth and especially in the creation stories of many central Asian groups—particularly the Buryat, the Samoyed, and Altaic peoples.

EASTER Easter is the Christian holiday celebrating the resurrection of Jesus three days after his crucifixion. The holiday comes in the early spring and is clearly related to ancient fertility myths of reborn heroes who sometimes take the form of grain, as in the case of the Egyptian Osiris, or other plants, as in the case of Adonis. For many, Easter is synonymous with fertility symbols such as the Easter rabbit, Easter eggs, and the Easter lily. A Germanic fertility goddess, Eostra, is perhaps a source for the term "Easter". She was said to have owned an egg-laying rabbit. A more generally accepted theory is that "Easter" comes from the German *Ostern*, which comes from the Norse *Eostur* for "spring." Romance language words for Easter are derived from the Greek *Pascha*, itself derived from the Hebrew *Pesah*, for Passover, a feast with which Easter was celebrated jointly by early Jewish Christians. As the sacrificed "Pascal Lamb" resurrected, Jesus is the center of a ritual and myth signifying for the Christian a new kind of Passover by which death gives way to eternal life.

ECHIDNE The daughter of Gaia and Tartarus, Echidne (Echnida), was the monstrous half woman, half serpent mother, by the fire-breathing giant Typhon, of several monsters in Greek mythology. Her brood included the Chimaera, the many-headed dog Orthus, the hundred-headed dragon who guarded the apples of the Hesperidies, the Colchian dragon, the Sphinx, Cerberus, Scylla, Gorgon, the Lernaean Hydra, the Nemean lion, and the Eagle that fed on the liver of Prometheus.

ECHO Because of the nymph Echo's constant chatter, Hera was unable to discover her husband Zeus's infidelities with other nymphs. The furious Hera punished Echo by condemning her to speak only when she heard others speak and then only to repeat the last few of the words spoken. In this state Echo fell in love with the beautiful self-absorbed boy Narcissus. Frustrated by her inability to communicate with or even attract him, she gradually became nothing but an echo. Some say that Echo refused the advances of Pan, who had her torn to bits by some shepherds. It is her buried remains that cause echoes everywhere.

EGYPTIAN FLOOD The Egyptian flood story resembles the Mesopotamian and Genesis flood stories in that it depicts the evil of an ungrateful humankind, the punishment for that evil, and the saving of a few in order that a new beginning might be made. A late-third-millennium B.C.E. myth of the Heraleopolitan dynasties tells how humankind plotted against the high god Re and Re called into council his Eye (the goddess Hathor) and the other important gods "who were with me in the Primeval waters," including the original god of the watery chaos, Nun himself. Re asked the advice of Nun. What was he to do about these misguided humans, the children of his Eye? Nun advised that he turn his Eye against humankind, and the other gods agreed. And so the Eye, as the now Kali-like destructive Hathor—the hot, unbridled sun—descended upon humans and killed them in the desert. Hathor returned, claiming that to destroy mankind was "pleasant to my heart." The Eye as the lion goddess Sehkmet was sent to continue the horror, but in the end Re decided to prevent total destruction. He created beer of barley and red ochre and flooded the fields of Egypt with it. Sehkmet, on her way to the slaughter, was attracted by the beer and drank so much of it that she became intoxicated and forgot about killing humans. So it was that a few were saved.

EGYPTIAN MYTHOLOGY During the development of the Sumerian culture, another civilization that would be much more enduring was rising in the southwestern region of the Middle East. It was a land populated by people speaking an Afro-Asiatic language of the Hamitic branch, distantly related to the Semitic languages. These people, who would come to be called Egyptians, were nomadic, but during what is now known as the pre-dynastic period they formed communities, especially within the Badarian culture in the south, where agriculture had become particularly important. Also present by 4000 B.C.E. were advanced agricultural tools, decorated pottery, and figurines. By the end of the pre-dynastic period Egyptians had built substantial boats, which they used for trade along the Nile and in others parts of the Middle East, including Sumer.

As in the case of other prehistoric cultures in the Middle East and elsewhere, the pre-dynastic mythology of Egypt can be surmised only by way of archeological remains. It is likely, as indicated in burial sites, where bodies are buried in a fetal position with the head south and facing west, that there was a belief in the afterlife or a sun god cult involving death and the setting sun.

By 3500 B.C.E. architectural models were buried with the dead, presumably to provide solace in the other world, indicating the continuing development of an afterlife mythology with accompanying funeral architecture and practices that would characterize ancient Egypt. During the late pre-dynastic, or Gerzean or Naquada II, period (c. 3400 B.C.E.) large, elaborately decorated and furnished tombs were built presumably to house deceased people of status.

We are on much more solid ground with Egyptian mythology when we come to the early dynastic period—specifically the first and second dynasties, beginning perhaps as early as 3100 B.C.E. During these early dynastic periods, hieroglyphic writing was developed and Upper and Lower Egypt were unified, with a capital at Memphis

(near modern Cairo) under the kingship of Narmer (c. 3110–3056 B.C.E.) or Aha, sometimes known as Menes. This was the first great nation-state of history, and its kingship seems already to have been justified by a sacred association of the king with the god Horus, represented by the emblematic falcon on one side of the slate palette—the so-called Narmer Palette—of the first monarch and the bull of kingly power on the other. The fact that kings of the second dynasty associated themselves in their titles with Horus and Seth, and in the south simply with Seth, indicates a possible early development of the Osiris cult with its dualistic antithesis between Horus and Seth. The antithesis also spoke to the historical tension between Upper and Lower Egypt. Indeed, by the end of the second dynasty north and south had once again been separated. But by about 2800 B.C.E. the kingdom was reunited with a new religion centered on the god Atum, or Re, at Heliopolis (also near Cairo). So began the period known as the Old Kingdom, in which the first of the great pyramids was built. The pyramid tomb of the third-dynasty king Djoser was built at Saqqara (c. 2650 B.C.E.), followed soon after by the even more impressive ones at Giza, most notably that of King Kahfre (2558–2532 B.C.E.). This was also the period of the great Sphinx at Giza.

It is during the Old Kingdom (dynasties 3 to 6, c. 2700–2190 B.C.E.) that an Egyptian pantheon begins to take form in the context of developed theologies. Over the centuries theologies and their particular versions of the pantheon would develop at several major cult centers. The generally dominant theology was that formulated by the priests at Heliopolis, but important interpretations came from Memphis, from Heracleopolis and Hermapolis and, briefly, Akhetaton (Amarna) further south, as well as from the major sites in deep Upper Egypt: Thebes (modern Luxor and Karnak), Abydos, Dendera, Esna, and Edfu.

The Egyptian god, Anubis, weighing the heart against the feather of truth.

The supreme Egyptian deity as the sun god, Re Harakhti or "Re-Horus of the Great Horizon," with his falcon head and solar disk

Egyptian mythology is dominated by the theme of a sacred kingship and the related theme of death and the afterlife, often in relation to the role of the Nile in a cyclical process by which the land dies and is reborn. Underlying these themes is a tension between light and darkness—between the supreme solar deities, such as Re (Ra), and the god of earth, fertility, and the underworld of death, Osiris. The Egyptians, as revealed in their myths, their rituals, their funerary writings, and their symbolic art and architecture, were preoccupied, more philosophically than the Mesopotamians, for instance, with questions of the nature of the universe and the relation of humans to the unknown. Their deities and their myths, highly symbolic vehicles for complex theologies, varied considerably in particulars according to the era and the cult center. But different centers assimilated each other's versions of deities and generally participated in what was a constant revisiting and revision of myths from very ancient times. The various local traditions had in common the central themes mentioned above and the highly philosophical and symbolic treatment of them.

The high god of Egypt was a creator god, usually associated with the sun. In Memphis, the first capital, he probably began as the falcon-headed sky-sun god Horus, the source of earthly kingship. Soon, however, he emerged in the highly complex Memphite theology as Ptah, the god of the primeval mound (Tatenen), who created by thinking things "in his heart" and then naming them with speech. His wife was the lioness goddess Sekhmet. Ptah's human form was that of a man in a cloak holding a scepter. Later he was identified with the pantheon of Khemenu, or Hermopolis (el-Ashmunein). The Hermopolitan pantheon, known as the Ogdoad ("the Eight"), was made up of four couples representing primordial chaotic forces. Amun (Amon) and Amaunet were forces of the invisible, Huh (Heh) and Hauhet (Hehet) were forces of infinity, Kuk (Kek) and Kauhet (Keket) were forces of darkness, and Nun and Naunet were the primal waters. In Memphis, Ptah was equated for a time with Nun and Naunet, out of whom was said to have come the creator god Atum. Atum, in the theology usually thought of as the most orthodox, that of Heliopolis, was "the Whole One," the creator who contained male and female. He was the head and founder of the Ennead ("the Nine"). Atum produced Shu and Tefnut (Air and Moisture), the progenitors of Geb and Nut (Earth and Sky), who were in turn the parents of Osiris and Seth and their sister wives Isis and Nephtys. Horus, as the son of Osiris and Isis, was an added, tenth member of the Ennead.

During the Old Kingdom fifth dynasty, Atum was displaced by or assimilated with the ancient sun god Re (Pre, Ra), the high god now becoming simply Re or Atum-Re or Re-Atum. As the center of the sun cult in later times, Re was Re-Harakhte ("Re-Horus of the Great Horizon"), the personification of the noonday sun, and was usually depicted as a human with the head of a hawk surmounted by a sun disk. The rising sun was Re as Khepri, the scarab. The evening sun was Re-Atum. Re assimilated the sacred king cult of Horus, as indicated by Horus's title in the so-called Pyramid Texts of the fifth Dynasty as "Son of Re." Horus's mother in this configuration was Re's consort, the cow goddess Hathor, one of the most important of the ancient line of Egyptian goddesses. The Pyramid Texts were elaborate recordings in royal tombs of hymns, prayers, and lists that reveal much about Egyptian culture at the time, especially about the dominant cult surrounding death and the afterlife, a cult centered on the god Osiris. They also reveal a further accommodation of the solar and sacred kingship cults by describing the king as a god who guards Re in his daily trip across the sky in his solar bark.

The power of the god-king was being threatened by the middle of the millennium, however, by an increase in the influence of the priests and the noble class. With a partial decentralization of royal control came the rise of a kind of feudalism. By 2250 political anarchy threatened the state. The Old Kingdom came to an end, and the country broke into two kingdoms, with capitals at Memphis or Herakleopolis in the north (near modern Cairo) and Thebes (modern Luxor) in the south. At about the turn of the millennium, roughly coinciding with the fall of Ur in Mesopotamia, Egypt was reunited by the Theban king Mentuhotep under the high god Amun, thus beginning the Middle Kingdom.

During the Middle Kingdom (2050–1756 B.C.E.), under the new rulers based in Thebes, an assimilation of gods took place that included the still powerful Re. The Theban war god Montu merged with Amun, the Hermopolitan primal force of the invisible, and with the fertility god of the Coptos, the ithyphallic Min. To this mixture Re was added, and Amun-Re came to the fore, especially at the Theban cult center of Karnak, as the sun god and King of Gods. Represented with a ram's head, Amun-Re was accompanied by his consort, the mother goddess Mut. Their son was the moon god Khonsu.

Still another expression of the high creator god was Khnum at Esna, south of Thebes. Khnum, depicted with the head of a ram, created the primal cosmic egg at his potter's wheel. He was one of the earliest of the *deus faber* (craftsman god) creators, although in some stories Ptah, too, was such a creator, molding beings out of metal.

The invasion of Egypt in about 1750 B.C.E. by an Asiatic people referred to as Hyksos, who conquered much of the country, essentially put an end to the Middle Kingdom and caused an intermediate period in Egyptian history. But with the defeat of the Hyksos in c. 1580 B.C.E. at the hands of a Theban dynasty loyal to the god Amun-Re, the New Kingdom was born and a period of Egyptian expansion and artistic achievement followed under the leadership of Thutmose I and II; the latter's wife, Hatshepsut; Thutmose III; and especially Amenhotep III (1417–1366 B.C.E.), who extended the empire into parts of Mesopotamia and most of Canaan (modern Israel-Palestine and neighboring lands).

The successor to Amenhotep III was his son Amenhotep IV (1366–1347 B.C.E.), whose reign is known as the Amarna period because the pharaoh moved his capital to a new city near present-day Amarna after disassociating himself from Amun-Re and renaming himself Akhenaton (Akhenati), in deference to Aton, the solar god he looked to for support. Akhenaton is claimed by many as the father of monotheism. It is true that the pharaoh greatly favored the god from whose name he took his new name and the name of his new capital, Akhetaton (Amarna). The new religion would not last long, however. The probable son of Akhenaton and Nefertiti, Tutankhaton (c. 1348–1339 B.C.E.), better known as King Tut, changed his name to Tutankhamun to reflect a restoration of the Amun cult.

Creation myths are central to Egyptian mythology, as they are to all mythologies. As contained primarily in the Pyramid Texts originating in Heliopolis beginning in about 2350 B.C.E., the Heliopolitan cosmogony is generally considered to be the most orthodox. Like all versions of the Egyptian creation it starts from the concept of the primeval waters—in some areas, especially Hermopolis, personified as Nun, the father of gods. Nun contained the essential energy of the dark and formless chaos out of which creation emerged. From the primeval waters arose the god Atum—later Atum-Re—as the primeval mound, symbolized by the pyramids themselves and perhaps having its source in the creative mounds left

The great Egyptian resurrection god Osiris

annually by the receding flood waters of the Nile. Atum-Re *was* Heliopolis and also the light of the rising sun and the embodiment of the conscious "Word" or Logos, the essence of life. In the somewhat later (c. 2000 B.C.E.) *Book of Going Forth by Day* ("Book of the Dead"), the emerging god, or "Becoming One," the visible form of the invisible Atum, was Khepri, the scarab, the symbol of the rebirth of the sun that looked down from the sky as the god Re.

The Egyptian god Horus making an offering

Like so many first gods in other cultures, Atum required the existence of others in order than he might become significant. As the all-encompassing "Great He-She" he had no mate but his hand—later known as the hand goddess IUshas. With that hand he masturbated "that he might obtain the pleasure of emission," and in so doing he produced the brother and sister Shu and Tefnut, Air and Moisture (Life and Order in the later Coffin Texts). In one Pyramid Text version, Atum spit Shu and Tefnut into existence. This version, conveying the idea of creation from the mouth, suggests the sense expressed in the Memphite creation, in which Ptah reated by thinking and naming "by word of mouth."

Shu and Tefnut, who were also associated with the sun and moon, gave birth to the male god Geb (Earth) and the female Nut (Sky). Geb and Nut at first lay together as one being, but were separated by their perhaps jealous father, Shu, who, as Air, provided space between Earth and Sky where other beings could be created. The theme of the separation of primordial parents to provide room for creation is a common one in world mythology. While little narrative material exists for this Egyptian version of the myth, the story is depicted in many paintings, in which Geb is shown, sometimes with an erect penis, lying on his back as his sister-wife arches over him, often held up by her father, Shu.

Separated from Geb, Nut could give birth to the stars, which rose up to her. Each day she swallowed these children so as to protect them until they could be reborn at night. Together Geb and Nut produced Osiris and Seth and their sisters Isis and Nephtys, the principles, with the god Horus—the son of Isis and Osiris—of what the Egyptians saw as the primary drama of earthly existence, that of life, death, and rebirth.

In the Hermopolitan creation, that of the Middle Egyptian city of Hermopolis (Khmun or Khemenu), emphasis was placed on the great Abyss of nothingness, out of which existence came. This primordial chaos—the primeval waters or Abyss—was made up of the four pairs that together were the Hermopolitan pantheon of eight, the Ogdoad. Huh and Hauhet, Nun and Naunet, Amun and Amaunet, and Kuk and Kauket—"the infinity, the nothingness, the nowhere, and the dark"—are the negative or undifferentiated foundation for the cosmic egg that was the immediate source of creation. In some tellings of the story it was the god Thoth in his Ibis form who laid the egg on the primeval mound formed by the Ogdoad. Another story held that it was the primeval goose, the "Great Cackler," who laid the egg. The egg was said to contain the sun god, who in another Hermopolitan myth was born as a divine child from a lotus. It was this god who would create the world.

Our source for the ancient creation myth of Memphis is a late text copied down from a much earlier one during the reign of the Nubian pharaoh Shabago during the twenty-fifth dynasty (c. 700 B.C.E.). In this document, the Memphite priests asserted the dominance of their high god, Ptah, over the gods of Heliopolis and Hermopolis. As portrayed by the Memphites, Ptah was more a spirit than an anthropomorphic being, and all the gods—those of Heliopolis and Hermopolis included—were really aspects of Ptah. Ptah here is perhaps closer to an animistic understanding of God or to the Hindu concept of the all-pervading essence of being, Brahman, than to the other Egyptian versions of the creator. Ptah was the original spirit on the primeval mound, the "self-begotten"; he contained all divine power within himself. He was Ptah-Nun (Niu)-Ptah Naunet, the primal watery abyss, the parents of Atum. In Atum's form, the heart and tongue of Ptah "came into being." The gods of the Ennead were the teeth and lips of Ptah. Horus, in this case the sun god, the god of command, represented his heart, and the moon god Thoth, the god of intelligence and wisdom, was his tongue. The gods were conceived in Ptah's heart and given their *kas*, their inner essences, by him. The gods were named, and thus given form, by Ptah's tongue. Ptah, like the Old Testament Yahweh, created *ex nihilo*, by thought and word, heart and voice. He was the Heart and Word, the Logos of the universe.

Texts dating from the New Kingdom period of Ramses II (1279–1213 B.C.E.) reveal a Theban creation dominated by Amun, later Amun-Re. Amun, we are told, was the "invisible one" of unknown origins with no parents to establish his name or *ka*. As such, he had no external identity and was invisible even to the other gods who were aspects of him. From Amun's mysterious being came the gods of Hermopolis and then those of Heliopolis. As in the case of the Memphite Ptah, the Ennead was contained by Amun's body. In fact, a later version of the Amun myth says that Amun in his form as Ptah created the primal egg in the primal waters of Nun, that he fertilized the egg, and that the other gods emerged from it. Once again, as in other Egyptian creations, especially the Memphite creation, the tendency at Thebes is toward an all-informing single god who, like the Hindu Brahman, takes many forms, a tendency furthered by Akhenaton's cult of the Aton as the only creator and, according to some, the only god.

The Egyptian theologians, in general, seem to have had little interest in the creation of humans. They were clearly more concerned with larger questions relating to cosmic arrangements, kingship, and the afterlife. There are a few texts, however, that present various ideas of our origins. In Spell Number 80 of the Coffin Texts, Shu, who is Air, is also regarded as Life itself. He literally breathes life into the nostrils of humans and other animals, completing the creative process. In both the Atum and the later Amun theologies is a bodily fluid motif associated with the creation of gods and humans. Atum was said to have created the gods out of his sweat and humans out of his tears. And in a later myth it was from Amun-Re's eyes—and presumably also tears—that "mankind came forth." In the case of Atum, the creation of humans seems to have been accidental. When Atum's eye disappeared one day, Shu and Tefnut brought it back, and when the eye was replaced in Atum he wept and people came out of his tears. The association of tears with people might suggest a certain sadness implicit in mortality.

In Esna, south of Thebes, the story of the creation of humans makes use of a universally popular motif—that of creation from clay. Here the creator is Khnum. As the ram-headed god—the word for "ram" being equivalent to the word for *ba* ("soul")—Khnum was the soul of the high god, Amun-Re. He played an important role in the myth that evolved around the usurper queen, Hathshepsut. He was said to have created the queen and her *ka* out of clay on his potter's wheel, and then to have placed her in her mother's womb to be born as Amun-Re's daughter. It was believed by some that humans in general were conceived in this manner and that, after Khnum com-

pleted the forms, the goddess Hathor would provide life by touching them with her *ankh*, the Egyptian cross-like symbol of Life itself.

As to the purpose of humans in the world, there is little information. In the "Instructions" left by the king of Heracleopolis to his son Merikare in c. 2040 B.C.E., during the period between the Old and Middle kingdoms, we learn that humans are "god's cattle" but also that they are made in his image.

Hero myths such as those found in Greece or Rome or even Mesopotamia are not common in ancient Egypt. Heroism as such seems to be inextricably tied to the themes of sacred kingship in relation to the sun's journey across the sky, and the idea of the king's and later any individual's passage after death to the underworld. At the center of what might be called the one Egyptian hero myth is Horus.

In a sense, the pharaoh, who lived as Horus, was always a god-hero who at death made the heroic journey to the sky to join Re on his solar bark and to guard him against serpents and other perils there during the daily journeys from horizon to horizon. One of Horus's titles was "Son of Re," so that the pharaoh, like Horus himself, was the son of God, to whom he returned after a sojourn on earth. The myth of Horus justifies the sacred kingship. Horus is Osiris reborn. And Osiris's resurrection as Horus represents the possibility of any individual's succeeding on the traditional heroic journey into the underworld. *The Book of Two Ways* tells us that a dead person who has learned the proper spells of the first stage of afterlife will join the moon god Thoth as a star.

Thoth also plays the traditional role of the hero's guide in the afterlife. If he knows the second stage of spells the deceased will go to the underworld palace of Osiris. And if he learns the third stage of spells he will accompany Re on his bark across the sky; in short, he will go to the "Father in Heaven." Egyptologist R. T. Rundle Clark supports this concept of the heroic pilgrimage of the soul after death when he points out that the Coffin Texts assumed "the soul's visit to Osiris at the end of the journey or a series of initiations during which the Horus soul-figure has acquired the superlative qualities of a hero—might, glory, strength, power and divinity." Clark goes on to compare Osiris to the Fisher King of Arthurian lore whose "wound" must be cured by the words—in this case the proper spells—of the Grail hero (pp. 161–162).

Osiris, the first son of Earth and Sky, was perhaps the most important of the Egyptian deities. He stands at the very center of the most characteristic themes of ancient Egyptian mythology and culture. As the first mythical king of Egypt—literally a god-king, and as the source—the father—of the king-god Horus, he was the theological basis for the eternal and sacred kingship and for the Egyptian state itself. The pharaoh died as Osiris and was resurrected as his son Horus. As the dying god who was resurrected and who became king of the underworld, Osiris was not only the dying pharaoh but, eventually, as we are told in the Coffin Texts and the *Book of Going Forth by Day*, any dying human. He was the basis for the Egyptian practice of mummification and after-life belief in general. Furthermore, Osiris's life, death, and resurrection are metaphors for the central life-giving phenomenon in Egypt, the annual death and resurrection of the land flooded by the Nile. And as the resurrection god, who was usually depicted as a mummy, sometimes in an ithyphallic state, Osiris was, quite logically, a fertility god represented by the sprouting of crops after the flood. The fertility aspect was emphasized by the association of Osiris at Memphis with the Apis bull, an association that developed in the Ptolemaic and Roman periods into the cult of Serapis, a combination of Osiris and Apis. Osiris was said to have been born at Bursiris and to have died at Abydos, his principal cult center. The sister and wife of Osiris was the great goddess Isis, a figure who would play a significant role in Egyptian mythology and resurrection theology well into Roman times.

Closely associated with Osiris is the jackal-or dog-headed Anubis (Anpu), who, in his earliest form, devoured the dead. Later, as funerary practices developed, he became the embalmer—especially of the dead Osiris—and the protector of graves. He was sometimes depicted lying on the chest containing the inner organs of the deceased. Anubis was the son of Osiris by Osiris's sister Nephtys. He served Osiris in the underworld as a judge of the dead, and he became a Hermes-like conductor of souls in the mystery cult of Isis in Roman times. [Allen, Bonnefoy (1992), Budge (1959, 1969), Leeming (2004), Lesko (1987b), Clark]

EHECATL Ehecatl was the Aztec wind god who blew on the sacrificial fire to stimulate the rising of the fifth sun and the fifth moon, the sun and moon of the present world, the fifth world. As such, Ehecatl is a creator god.

EIGHT IMMORTALS Li Xuan, Lu Dongbin, Han Zhongli, Han Xiang, Cao Guojiu, Zhang Guo, Lan Caihe, and He Xiangu are the Eight Immortals of Daoism, who traveled about the world on clouds. Once they went to the world under the sea, where the Dragon King imprisoned Lan Caihe, causing a battle between the Immortals and the Dragon King and resulting in the defeat of the king and the release of Lan Caihe. Han Xiang, led to heaven to eat at the peach tree of immortality by his teacher, the immortal Lu Dongbin, fell out of the peach tree but achieved immortality before he hit the ground. Han Zongli was taught by Li Xuan, who was the first immortal and heavenly messenger. He Xiangu was a female member of the Eight Immortals. Immortality came to her when she ate the Mother of Pearl Stone.

EIRE A name of the eponymous pre-Celtic Irish triune goddess who represented the essence of Irish spirit and sovereignty and gave her name to Ireland, as proclaimed by the bard Amairgen. The three "queens" were married to the three kings at Tara, who were defeated by the Celtic Milesians. The other aspects of the goddess, whose names were also used as synonyms for Ireland, were Banba and Fotla. Eire 's name or her mother's name is sometimes given as Eireann or Eirinn, the etymological root of Eire.

EL El was the ancient father god of the Canaanites, the husband of the goddess Asherah. The equivalent of the Mesopotamian An (Anu), he was El of the holy mountain Sapan (Tsafon), the Ilib (Elib) or "father god" who contained the spirits of the dead, and the El who, like so many Near Eastern high gods, was associated with the bull and is perhaps the creator. The Greeks thought of El as Kronos, the father of Zeus, because in various Ugaritic fragments it is suggested that El earned the title "creator"

and "Father of the Gods" by, like Zeus, defeating his parents, Heaven and Earth. Having taken over the creator role, El became the head of the Canaanite pantheon, the source of virility without which life is not possible. One Ugaritic tablet tells how in ancient times, as El stood at the seashore, his hand (penis) grew as long as the sea itself. With him were two women, his wives, whom he kissed and impregnated simultaneously. They gave birth to Dawn and Dusk.

The Semitic term "El" essentially refers to the concept of god. As such it is related to the Arabic *il* and thus *ilah* and *al ilah*—literally "the god"—and Allah and the Hebrew Elohim. It seems almost certain that the God of the Jews evolved gradually from the Canaanite El, who was in all likelihood the "God of Abraham." Karen Armstrong reminds us that in Genesis 16 and 17, an eighth-century B.C.E. text, God introduces himself as El Shaddai ("El of the Mountain") and that El's name is preserved in such words as EL-ohim, Isra-EL ("El rules"), and Ishma-EL. In Exodus 6:2–3 the deity introduces himself to Moses as Yahveh and points out that he had revealed himself to Abraham, Isaac, and Jacob as El Shaddai, and that they had not known that his name was Yahveh (1993, p. 14).

If El was the high god of Abraham—Elo-him, the prototype of Yahveh—Asherah was his wife, and there are archeological indications that she was perceived as such before she was in effect "divorced" in the context of the emerging Judaism of the seventh century B.C.E. (see 2 Kings 23:15).

ELEKTRA The daughter of Agamemnon and Clytemnestra, Elektra plays a major role in the saga of the cursed House of Atreus, urging her brother Orestes on in his avenging of their mother's murder of their father. The story is most famously told by the Greek playwrights Aeschylus in his trilogy, the Orestei, and Sophocles in his *Elektra*.

ELIADE, MIRCEA Mircea Eliade (1907–1986) was one of the twentieth century's leading scholars of religion and mythology. Like Émile Durkheim, Georges Dumézil, and their followers, he is concerned in his work with the relationship between the sacred and the profane. The sacred is revealed in symbols, myths, and rituals—archetypal structures that carry us back to *illud tempus* ("that time" or "myth time") and the essence of who we are as cultures and as a species. In the sacred we find the source of our identity, the source of whatever significance we have. As such, sacred time is "real" and effective. Through the experience of symbols, myths, and rituals, we are somehow protected against merely historical or profane time.

Among Eliade's most important works are *Cosmos and History: The Myth of the Eternal Return* (1954), *Patterns in Comparative Religion* (1958), *The Sacred and the Profane: The Nature of Religion* (1959), *Myth and Reality* (1963), and his three-volume *A History of Religious Ideas* (1978–1985).

ELEUSINIAN MYSTERIES These rituals at the town of Eleusis, near Athens, probably developed in the eighth century B.C.E. out of older fertility rituals associated with the grain goddess Demeter and her daughter Persephone, or Kore, who was kidnapped and raped by the underworld god Hades but who returned to her mother each spring. At first, the Eleusinian mysteries might have been clan initiation ceremonies. Later they were taken over by the state and became "politically correct" initiation ceremonies that transcended their earlier purposes.

According to the Demeter myth, the goddess, during her search for her lost daughter, stayed for a while in Eleusis, posing as a nursemaid for the baby, Demophon. She was discovered in a mysterious ceremony by which she was attempting to give the child immortality by dipping him in fire. Angry at being discovered and having the rite disrupted, she ordered that a temple be built for her at Eleusis. Later she revealed the mysteries of agriculture to the Eleusinians by way of the prince Triptolemos.

The mysteries remain to some extent just that. We do know that their central theme was the fertility represented by the return of the Kore, such fertility being at first related to agriculture and later to some sort of spiritual fertility or even to hopes for a blessed afterlife—the immortality that Demeter tried to give to her princely charge. The initiation rituals forming the mysteries involved acts of animal sacrifice, ceremonial purification by fire and a bath in the sea, a fast—perhaps recalling Demeter's denial of fertility during her daughter's absence—and a procession to Eleusis behind a figure of the ecstatic Dionysos. In the sanctuary of Eleusis itself, the initiates apparently reenacted the search for the Kore and performed a ceremony that involved a basket, a chest, and a mixture of grain and water, and perhaps a breaking of the fast in some sort of ritual meal. Much that occurred was in the darkness of night, but at some point—one that some Christians will recognize as similar to the events of the great vigil of Easter Eve—fire burst forth, recalling the fire of immortality in the Demeter-Demophon incident. Apparently, at this point a cry went up announcing that the mother had given birth to the divine child (*puer aeternus*), and one assumes that at this moment the initiates were full participants in the mysteries of rebirth. [Graf, Jung and Kerenyi]

ELFFIN It was the youth Elffin who, in Welsh mythology, was fishing with his father when they found the abandoned child Taliesen floating in a leather bag and adopted him. In his first poem, Taliesen, destined to be the great poetic prophet of Wales, praised Elffin, who became a part of King Arthur's court. When he boasted that his wife was the most virtuous in the land and his poet the greatest of poets, he incurred the anger of Arthur and was imprisoned. Later he would be saved by Taliesen's poetic powers.

ELYSIUM In Greek mythology Elysium is an afterlife paradise sometimes called the Elysian Fields that lies somewhere to the west of the world, where, according to Homer, certain heroes—Menelaus, for example—go without actually dying. Elysium, ruled by Rhadamanthus, is quite unlike the gloomy Land of the Dead visited by Odysseus, where most people were sent after death. The Romans—including Virgil—saw Elysium as an underworld place for blessed shades such as Aeneas's father, Anchises.

EMERGENCE CREATION The emergence creation is particularly prevalent among the Native Americans of the North American Southwest and Mesoamerica. The Aztecs, the Acoma people and other Pueblo tribes, and the Navajo, for example, all say that they originally emerged in this world from a world or worlds below the earth. Typically,

Mircea Eliade (1907-1986)

the act of emergence from one world to the next is a kind of birthing and evolving process where the people move from an insect or lower animal state to the human condition. Sometimes the people come out of a small opening in the place that becomes their home in this world. There is a sense of their having come from the womb of the earth mother, and often a female deity such as Spider Woman or Thinking Woman serves as a midwife of sorts in this birthing process, helping the people to emerge and to adjust to the ways of this world. The emergence creation myths thus eschew the dominant, male-based *ex nihilo* creation in favor of the more compatible metaphorical relationship between birth and creation. In some cases there is a male figure somewhere in the beginning, but he fades in significance with the arrival of a goddess, she who spins the universe into existence and sometimes creates two sisters who work out the details of the creation. The emergence creation myth is reflected in ritual dances and in the feminine architecture of the modest, earth-hugging hogan or the usually circular kiva, with its symbolic birth entrance or *sipapu* in the center of the floor and its equally symbolic smoke hole in the roof, out of which the dancers emerge from the otherworldly darkness into the dance plaza of this world. [Weigle]

EMMA Emma-O,' derived from the Sanskrit Yama, is the Japanese Buddhist Lord of Jigoku, or Hell. Emma judges souls and places them in hells appropriate to their crimes. In this context, there are eight hells in all. These have been described by people who were, for one reason or another, released from punishment. The hells are a popular subject for Japanese scrolls. Emma's primary enemy is Jizo, always a supporter of the dead souls against him and usually the victor over his dark adversary. As Jizo's popularity has grown and Emma's has diminished, Emma has become a demon.

EN SOF For Jewish mystics, the kabbalists, God is a mysterious entity called En (Ein) Sof. From the depths of this being came the flame of divinity at the beginning of time. The flame grew, lighting everything that had previously been hidden in the mystery that is En Sof. This was the *Bereshit*, the first word of creation, the self-revelation of En Sof, called Wisdom, which can lead to Intelligence. Elements of this kabbalist tradition have close correspondence with the thinking and mythology of the Gnostics.

ENDYMION The third-century B.C.E. poet Theocritus tells how the shepherd boy Endymion was so beautiful that the moon, Selene, fell in love with him, and as he slept came down from the heavens to kiss him and to lie with him. Selene loved him so much that she caused him to remain sleeping forever—immortal, forever hers, but unconscious of her presence each night.

ENKI Enki is the Sumerian name for the Akkadian-Babylonian Ea. Enki was one of the most important Sumerian gods. Lord (*en*) of the soil or earth (*ki*), whose home was the underground sweet waters (*abzu, apsu*), he was a god necessary to irrigation, a practice important in his home, appropriately, the city of Eridu in the southern marshlands of what is present-day Iraq. Enki was a trickster of sorts, known for his magical powers and incantations. Wise and skillful at all crafts, he was usually said to be a son of An and the mother-riverbed goddess Nammu ("Lady Vulva") and was considered third in rank among the deities after An and Enlil. Damgalnuna (Daminka), a version of the mother goddess, was his wife. Their son, Asarluhi, was later assimilated in Babylon into the god Marduk. Like most trickster gods, Enki possessed an insatiable sexual appetite, which probably was a metaphorical expression of his role as a god of fertility and irrigation.

Enki possessed the *me*, the essential elements of culture, social order, and civilization. He was a creator who placed fish in the rivers and who taught the people agriculture. As such he is etymologically related to Enkimdu, the god of farmers.

The following are unusually complete Enki myths:

ENKI AND NINMAH

To celebrate their newfound freedom and the creation of humans, the Anunnaki, the first generation of deities, had a banquet at which Enki and the goddess Ninmah drank too much. Ninmah challenged Enki to a creative contest. She would make new humans with any defects she saw fit. Enki agreed but with the idea that he would attempt to choose roles for the misfits that would negate their defects. A man with an eye problem he made a singer. A man who constantly leaked semen he cured with a magic water incantation. There were six such creations and "cures." Then the combatants changed positions:

Enki would create humans with defects for Ninmah to counteract. One of these was a being called an *umul* that was so helpless that it could neither talk, walk, nor feed itself. Taunted by Enki to solve the being's problems, Ninmah asked it questions that it could not answer, offered it food that it could not use its hands to hold, and finally gave up in disgust. Enki had won the contest. It seems likely that the *umal* was the first human infant.

ENKI AND NINHURSAGA

This is a myth that gives expression to Enki's ancient metaphorical aspect as the power behind the irrigation complexities of the southern marshlands of Mesopotamia. Enki lived in and was clearly associated with the sweet underground waters (*abzu, apsu*), which later would themselves be personified in Babylon as the god Apsu.

Enki's phallus, we are told, filled the ditches "with semen," that is "water"—the words are the same in Sumerian—in the tradition of the father god An, whose semen was life-giving rain. Married to Damgalnuna ("true wife"), one of several mother goddesses, he nevertheless "directed his semen owed to Damgalnuna . . . into the womb of Ninhursag[a]." When that goddess gave birth to the beautiful Ninmu, also a form of the mother goddess, Enki "poured semen into [her] womb." Ninmu gave birth to the goddess Ninkurra ("Mistress of the Land") and Enki fertilized her womb, causing the birth of the goddess Uttu ("Vegetation"). When Enki wished to pour his semen into Uttu, Ninhursaga advised the girl to resist unless Enki could bring her cucumbers, apples, and grapes. Enki obliged by reaching out and fertilizing more dry zones, which then produced these new products. Delighted, Uttu took Enki to "her lap," and he "poured the semen into the womb." But Ninhursaga wiped excess semen from the young goddess's body—the body of "Vegetation"—and created eight new plants. In order to name these plants—that is, to declare their "fates"—Enki had to first eat them. This act so angered Ninhursaga that she cursed Enki, saying he would die, and then she disappeared, leaving the old gods—the Anunnaki—sitting in despair "in the dust." Presumably the dust signifies that the land had dried up, deprived of Ninhursaga's fertile presence and of Enki's vital fluids, eight parts of his body now in a sense being clogged by the eight plants he had eaten. It was a little fox who determined a way of bringing the great goddess back. She returned, cured Enki by "fix[ing]" him "in her vulva" and naming eight new deities to counteract the poisoning by the plants.

ENLIL Enlil ("Lord of the Air") is the Sumerian sky god. His Akkadian-Babylonian name is Ellil. In Sumer his primary cult city was Nippur. The son of the father-sky god An (Anu) and the earth goddess Ki, Enlil, with his brother Enki, decided fate; he succeeded his father as the titular head of the gods and was wise. His area of concern was the earth itself, whereas Enki's was more with the waters on and below the earth. It was Enlil, however, from his mountain home, where he reigned as a storm god, who sent the flood to destroy wayward humanity, and it was Enki who prevented total destruction.

In a Sumerian myth from Nippur discovered in Old and Middle Babylonian and neo-Assyrian tablets, a myth that bears similarities to various Enki stories of seduction, Enlil is attracted to his natural counterpart, the young and beautiful Ninlil ("Lady of the Air"). Her mother, realizing that Ninlil is pubescent, advises her to purify herself in the river but to avoid the canal (irrigation ditch) called Inunbirdu, where Enlil will be lurking, ready to seduce and impregnate her. Naturally, Ninlil goes directly to the canal. Enlil is, in fact, waiting there, and he begins to attempt the seduction. Ninlil at first resists but later Enlil finds her at a more hidden place and rapes her, engendering the moon god Nanna (Suen or Sin). For this act, or perhaps because Ninlil had not had time for the ritual of purification, Enlil (or his son, Nanna) seems to have been expelled by the "fifty great gods," perhaps to the underworld. Enlil leaves, but is followed by Ninlil, and in various disguises he impregnates her with various gods who may possibly take his (or Nanna's) place in the underworld. In any case, the myth ends with a hymn to Enlil as the source of abundance and fertility.

In another version of the Enlil-Ninlil myth, discovered in Babylonian and neo-Assyrian fragments, Enlil, who is looking for a wife, meets the beautiful Sud. Enlil's advances are not accepted, but later he sends an envoy from Nippur to ask Sud's mother for the girl's hand. Through his agent, he gives Sud a secret love gift and promises her mother that her daughter will rule with him. At the suggestion of the mother, he sends his sister Aruru-Ninmah with a huge cache of gifts—jewels, of course, but especially fruits of the earth. In a ritual in Enlil's temple, Sud's face is anointed with holy oil, and the couple consummate the sacred marriage on the "shining bed." Finally, Enlil renames Sud—that is, he pronounces her "fates" or her essences as—Nintu ("Birth"), Asnan ("Grain"), and Ninlil ("Air"), his natural complement or queen.

ENMERKAR In a sacred marriage–related text from the Ur III period of Mesopotamia, Ensuhkesdanna, Lord of Aratta, challenges his rival, Enmerkar, King of Uruk, by claiming to be the true husband of the goddess Inanna. As Inanna is particularly the patroness of Uruk and the ritual "bride" of its king, Enmerkar takes the challenge seriously and reacts with great anger, condemning Ensuhkesdanna and asserting his right to Inanna. The King of Aratta sends a magician to Eres, a town near Uruk, where he dries up the milk of the sacred stables. The shepherds in the area beg the god Utu for help, and suddenly Sagburru, a wise crone from Eres, comes on the scene and challenges the sorcerer of Aratta to a contest involving the transforma-

Sumerian cuneiform script telling of the building of a temple such as the one described in the Enmerkar tale

tion of objects. Both magicians throw metal objects into the river. The man's turns into a carp, the woman's into an eagle that eats the carp. Then the man's ewe and lamb are eaten by the woman's wolf, and so it goes until the man gives in and the old woman throws him to his death in the river. Upon hearing the news, Ensuhkesdanna agrees that Enmerkar is the true bridegroom of Inanna.

Another story about the same rivalry dates from the Old Babylonian period. King Enmerkar of Uruk decides that the people of Aratta should come to Uruk with valuables and building materials to build temples for him there and in Erudu. Inanna, always Uruk's patroness, agrees to help and advises the king to send a messenger to Aratta, demanding the materials in question. When the Lord of Aratta refuses, claiming his own closeness to Inanna, the messenger reminds him of Enmerkar's even closer relationship and of Inanna's claim that Aratta would have to submit to Uruk.

The King agrees to submit to Enmerkar if the latter will agree to a contest. Enmerkar agrees, as his success will prove Inanna's loyalty to him. In the midst of completing several impossible tasks, Enmerkar sends a herald with a written message to Aratta. Thus he invents writ-

ing. In the message he agrees to a combat between dogs from each city, again demanding the materials for temple building and decoration, and threatens the destruction of Aratta should the conditions of the demand not be met. Although much of the text is lost, it seems likely that Enmerkar's dog wins the fight, as the story ends with the people of Aratta bringing the requested materials to Uruk.

ENNEAD In the Egyptian mythology the Ennead ("the Nine") is the name given to the pantheon of the great theological center Heliopolis. Out of the sun god Atum or Atum-Re, who emerged from the primeval waters (Nun), came Shu and Tefnut ("Air" and "Moisture"). Together they produced Geb and Nut ("Earth" and "Sky"), who in turn became the parents of four of the primary figures in a dominant Egyptian myth: Osiris, Isis, Seth, and Nephtys.

ENUMA ELISH The Babylonian creation epic, the *Enuma elish*, as we know it, is based on first-millennium B.C.E. tablet texts found at Ashur, Nineveh, Kish, and Uruk. In fact, the epic is primarily a celebration of the Mesopotamian city

A Babylonian text with map

of Babylon and its city god Marduk (Bewl, or "Lord"). It was recited at New Year festivals in Babylon (and in Assyria at Nineveh, where Ashur replaced Marduk as the protagonist). The composition of the epic probably coincides with and is intended to justify the rise of Marduk from his status as a minor Sumerian deity to chief of the Babylonian pantheon during the reign of Nebuchadrezzar I in the twelfth century B.C.E.

The rise of Marduk (and Ashur) marks a significant change in the mythology of Mesopotamia, reflecting a movement from cultural principles centered on fertility and the balance of male and female roles, to a much more patriarchal perspective.

The *Enuma elish* ("When above") begins with a description of the beginning of time: "When the skies above were not yet named / Nor earth below pronounced by name, / Apsu, the first one, their begetter / And maker [*mummu*] Tiamat, who bore them all, / Had mixed their waters together" (Dalley, p. 233). Out of this mixture of sweet (Apsu) and salt water (Tiamat) came the gods—first the ill-defined Lahmu and Lahamu ("hairy ones"), then Ansar and Kisar, who produced Anu (the Sumerian An). Ea (Nudimmud, Sumerian Enki) was born in Anu's image. The new beings made so much noise that Apsu became irritated and, encouraged by his vizier Mummu, decided to get rid of them to restore peace and quiet. Tiamat, however, could not bear to harm her offspring. In this she resembles the Greek primal mother goddesses who try to protect their offspring against their child-destroying father-god mates. It was Ea who, like Zeus in Greek mythology, came to the rescue of the new gods. Using his inborn shamanic or magical powers, he cast a spell over Apsu, sending him to sleep forever as the underground waters, the *apsu* (Sumerian *abzu*), where, with his wife Damkina (Sumerian Damgalnuna), he produced the great Marduk. Marduk was a huge, powerful god with four heads, who irritated Tiamat by causing great waves and noise, thus establishing his identity as a storm-weather god. When Anu created the winds, they added to Tiamat's noise, and Tiamat, assisted and encouraged by certain other gods, began to form an army of monsters led by her son Kingu (Quingu) to do away with Marduk and the noise. Worried about what Tiamat might do to them, the gods called on Anu and Ea for help, but they realized their powerlessness against Tiamat and refused. Ea advised Marduk to take up their cause, and he agreed, but with the stipulation that the gods recognize him as their new king. It was he who from now on would decide destinies.

Marduk approached the wild and angry Tiamat as a storm god and filled her grotesque and open mouth with wind so that she could not devour him, and then he pierced her bloated belly with an arrow and threw her dead body to the ground. When the monster-mother's army tried to escape, Marduk captured them and took the tablets of destiny away from Kingu.

Now Marduk was ready to create the world. Creation myths express the given cultures' sense of themselves, their essential identities. For several millennia, Mesopotamia had generally accepted the old Sumerian creation story, in which the female aspect is positive and important, basic to the fertility and irrigation principles so necessary for the agricultural practices of the Sumerians and Akkadians. But now the storm god Marduk, the all-dominant male, would create a world out of the dead body of the defeated feminine power that had been Tiamat. In the context of the new Babylonian national priorities—including a determination to confront threats to their hegemony by people of the so-called Sea Land in the old Sumerian territory south of them—his victory and creation signify strong hierarchical power and male reason, as opposed to a kind of irrational watery chaos represented by the female Tiamat and the old ways.

Marduk creates an animistic world by crushing Tiamat and dividing her dead body into two parts. Half of the body he sets up as the sky, the other half as the earth. Her head becomes a mountain, her eyes the Tigris and Euphrates rivers. Her breasts he turns into hills, her nostrils reservoirs. Besides this, Marduk creates the planets and stars, establishes the separation of waters, and generally gets the world operating properly. Finally, he establishes the city of Babylon as a temple home for all of the gods, thus achieving cultural and national unity and hegemony.

Marduk instructs Ea to make use of the dead Kingu's blood to create humans, who would do the work that the gods would otherwise have to do, and he prescribes functions for each of the gods. In short, he brings order to what the Babylonians had seen as the chaotic religious and social system of the past. To recognize this, the gods build the temple of Marduk as the primary temple of Babylon and celebrate him there as the supreme deity.

EOCHAIDH Irish mythology has several men named Eochaidh, a name that is related to the word for "horse." The most famous of these, whose story is told in the *Book of Invasions*, is Eochaidh Mac Erc (Eirc), the last king of the Firbolg, the fourth group of "invaders," who were defeated by the fifth group, the Tuatha Dè Danaan, at the first battle of Magh Tuireadh. Eochaidh was a just and productive ruler.

EOS In Rome this Greek goddess of the dawn was known as Aurora. She was the daughter of the Titan Hyperion and the sister of the sun god Helios, whom Homer sometimes equates with Hyperion. According to some traditions, she married Tithonus, the immortalized brother of King Priam of Troy. At the end of each night she ascended into the sky in a chariot to announce the coming of the sun. She was fond of young men, the gods having neglected to make Tithonus eternally young when they made him immortal. One of these young men was Cephalus, whose life was made wretched, and ultimately tragic, by the goddess's love. She also had an affair with the giant hunter Orion.

EPIMETHEUS The name of Epimetheus, Titan and brother of Prometheus, means "afterthought" or "hindsight" whereas his brother's means "forethought." In spite of the wise warnings of Prometheus not to accept gifts from Zeus and the Olympians, Epimetheus hastily accepted the first woman, Pandora, as a gift and wife from them. Epimetheus's naiveté made possible the presence on earth of Pandora's box, with all its evil contents.

EPONA It was primarily the continental Celts who revered Epona, the horse goddess. She was naturally adopted as a favorite by the Roman cavalry and was celebrated at an annual Roman festival. Epona has certain earth goddess aspects, such as her strong association with fertility, sexuality, and water. In Welsh mythology, Epona appears to have

E

had a cognate in the fertility-warrior goddess Rhiannon, who rode about Wales on a white horse dispensing gifts, in the traditional great goddess manner, from her bag or womb bundle.

EREBOS Erebos ("darkness" or the dark space leading to Hades) was the son of Chaos in Hesiod's Greek creation myth He mated with Nyx ("Night") to produce Aither ("Ether," "Air") and Hemera ("Day").

ERESHKIGAL The Sumerian goddess of the underworld, Ereshkigal (Akkadian-Babylonian/Hittite-Hurrian Allatum/Allatu), Ereshkigal was the sister of Inanna/Ishtar. Her most important role in Mesopotamian mythology occurs in the story of Inanna's descent. In this role she personifies the infertility that opposes her to her highly fertile sister. In later Babylonian mythology, Ereshkigal—Allata—is the goddess of copulation in her position as the wife of Nergal (based on the Sumerian Gugalanna, the "Wild Bull of Anu"), with whom she, on at least two occasions, has seven days of uninterrupted sexual activity.

ERICTHONIUS The Greek smith god Hephaistos assaulted the goddess Athena and in the ensuing struggle he ejaculated onto her thigh. The disgusted goddess flung the semen onto the earth—that is, onto the great original earth goddess, Gaia, who became pregnant and gave birth to Ericthonius (Erectheus, "Soil born"). Ericthonius was hidden from the other gods by his patroness Athena, but eventually he was discovered, and he became king of Athens. He was said to have introduced the worship of Athena there and to have built a temple in her honor on the Acropolis. After his death, he, too, was worshipped, and a temple for him, the Erechtheum, was built on the Acropolis. Ericthonius's son was Pandion, who ruled Athens until his death, when Ericthonius II became king. In a war between the Athenians and the Eleusinians, a son of Poseidon was killed by the Athenians, and the god demanded the death of one of the Athenian king's daughters as retribution. He also asked Zeus to dispose of Ericthonius II, which the king of the gods did, with a powerful bolt of lightning.

ERLIK Erlik is a sometimes first man and sometimes trickster figure frequently playing the role of either assistant to or underminer of the creator in central Asian mythologies, including those of the Siberians and Turko-Mongols.

EROS Better known by the name of his Roman cognate Cupid, popularly depicted as a baby who wields devastating love arrows, the Greek love god Eros ("Desire") was said by Hesiod to have been born at the beginning of creation, out of chaos. The more generally accepted story, however, is that he was the son of the goddess of love Aphrodite (Roman Venus) by way of her passionate and ultimately embarrassing adulterous affair with the war god Ares (Mars).

ERYMANTHIAN BOAR The wild boar on the mountain of Erymantus in Arcadian Greece was the victim of the fourth of the Twelve Labors of the hero Herakles. The boar was captured in a net.

ESCHATOLOGY Eschatology is the branch of mythology or religion that is concerned with questions such as death, judgment, heaven, and hell. Resurrection and underworld myths, for instance, are eschatological myths.

ESHU Eshu (Eschu) is a Yoruba version of the west African trickster whose cognates are such figures as Legba (Elegba) and Ananse. He is the messenger and general intermediary between the gods and humans, and, like Hermes, the Greek sometimes trickster, he is the god of thresholds. Once Eshu was sent to earth by the gods to remind humans of their obligations to them. He was told to collect sixteen palm nuts and to learn their meaning. By so doing, he would somehow be able to bring humans back to their senses. When Eshu had gathered the nuts and learned that they were the children of Ifa, the son of the high god, he instituted the religion of Ifa. But most of all, like the Native North American tricksters such as Coyote and Iktome, as well as other African tricksters, Eshu brings trouble. Once he even convinced the sun and moon to exchange places, thus instituting chaos. His tricks led to the high god's departure from earth in favor of the heavens.

ETANA A god-king of the Sumerian city of Kish, Etana, originally a mere shepherd (like the Hebrew heroes Moses and David), was appointed king by the gods. Fragments of an Akkadian-Babylonian epic tell us that as Etana and his wife were unable to produce a son, the sun god Shamash sent him to an eagle that had been captured by a serpent and instructed him to free the eagle and fly on its back to heaven, where he could petition Ishtar (Inanna) for the plant of birth. One version of the story indicates that the flight to heaven was too much for Etana, and he fell to the earth. But it seems that whatever happened, Ishtar made it possible for the king and his queen to produce a son.

ETEOCLES A son of the Greek tragic hero Oedipus and his wife-mother Jocasta, Eteocles inherited the throne of Thebes with his brother Polynices. In a struggle for the throne, Eteocles, fighting against Polynices and the "Seven against Thebes," was supported by the interim king, Creon. The two brothers killed each other in combat, leading to the confrontation over the burial of Polynices that is the basis for his sister Antigone's tragic conflict with Creon.

ETERNAL RETURN The myth of the eternal return is a concept developed by Mircea Eliade, one of the twentieth century's most influential religious scholars. Essentially Eliade differentiates between the sacred and the profane, between cyclical time and linear time, between our sense of the "real" world and the "mythic world." He suggests that by way of myths and rituals, ancient humans were able to connect with sacred time—*illo tempore*—and in so doing were able to find relief from the "terror of history" that culminates in death. By turning to the archetypes or patterns of *illo tempore*, as they return eternally in myth and ritual, modern humanity, too, enters into the sacred and is saved from the tragic end inherent in linear time. For Eliade and others, the purpose of religious traditions—the retelling of sacred stories and the reenacting of sacred events—is precisely that participation in the myth of the eternal return, participation in cyclical—that is, ever-repeating—eternal time, rather than linear, inevitably ending time.

ETIOLOGICAL MYTH Myth has always had an explanatory or etiological aspect. Myths have traditionally "explained" such phenomena as death, the changing of seasons, the passage of the sun and the moon, and the origin of the universe and life itself. The myth of Demeter and Persephone, for instance, may be seen as an etiological myth explaining the existence of the seasons.

ETRUSCAN MYTHOLOGY The people of Ertruria, which existed in the west central Italian Peninsula (modern Tuscany and Umbria) between the eighth and fourth centuries B.C.E., were non–Indo-European speakers who developed a complex civilization that included a religion and mythology that would influence the Romans. Central to that influence was the Etruscan practice of such disciplines as haruspicy (the study of entrails for prophecy), divination from lightning flashes, and various related rituals, all growing out of the mythic tradition of the prophet Tages and his sacred books. It was said that Tages appeared out of a plowed furrow as a gray-haired child with the wisdom of an ancient sage to teach the people at Tarquinia. Another source for the Etruscan divination that influenced Rome was the sibyl-like nymph, the prophet Begoia. The Romans would adopt the oracular Sibylline Books and consult them for guidance in difficult times. One story has it that the great Sibyl of Cumae sold three of her prophetic books to King Tarquin, who deposited them on the Capitoline Hill, where they were available for consultation.

Eventually, under the influence of Eastern contacts, the Etruscans would accept Astarte, the ancient Phoenician Great Goddess, whom they saw as a version of their own Uni and the Greek Hera and Roman Juno. Another important Etruscan goddess was Mernva (Minerva in Rome). It is significant, given their non–Indo-European background, that the Etruscans, who regarded women and goddesses more highly than did their Indo-European neighbors, replaced the archaic Roman and thoroughly Indo-European triad of Jupiter-Mars-Quirinus with that of Jupiter, Juno, and Minerva. The new triad was represented on a Capitoline Hill temple, and when the Roman republic replaced the Etruscan kings, the female-dominated triad remained in place.

The Etruscans, like the Romans, who often went so far as to invite the gods of their enemies to become their gods, borrowed easily from the mythologies of others—from their neighbors the Latins and, because of their maritime connections, especially from the Greeks. Foreign deities were, in effect, considered as homologues for those found in Etruria. The Etruscan name for the sovereign god (the Roman Jupiter, the Greek Zeus) was Tinia, a god known for his powerful lightning flashes. Hera was the Etruscan Uni, Aphrodite/Venus was a goddess of love, Turan. Apollo and Artemis were

Etruscan Apollo of Veio

109

Brueghel's Abduction of Europa by Zeus as a Bull

adopted as Aplu and Artumes, Poseidon was Nethuns, Hermes was Turms, Ares (the Latin Mars) was Maris, Athena/Minerva was Mernva, and the Latin Janus was the Etruscan Ani.

EUMENIDES These dreaded Greek goddesses, daughters of Earth (Gaia)—or, some say, of Night (Nyx)—who was impregnated with them by the spilled blood of the castrated father god Ouranos, were originally called the Erinyes. The Romans called them Furiae (Furies) or Dirae. ("the Avengers"). Eumenides ("Kindly Ones") was a euphemistic name meant to avoid the pronouncing of the real name of these horrifying goddesses, who came from their home in Tartarus with blood in their eyes, serpents in their hair, and wings on their backs to punish humans for various improper acts. Eumenides was also a name more appropriate for them after they were calmed by Athena and Apollo after the acquittal of Orestes for the revenge murder of his mother, Clytemnestra. Orestes' trial is described in Aeschylus's play the *Eumenides*, the final segment of the trilogy known as the *Oresteia*. As the Erinyes, they upheld the ancient revenge-based blood law of the earth. As the Eumenides, they are seen as having conformed to the more rational law represented by the wisdom of Apollo and Athena at the trial of Orestes. The Erinyes would have punished Orestes for matricide, whatever the reasons for the act—in this case, his mother's adultery and subsequent murder of her husband and king, Agamemnon. The Erinyes make inevitable the continuous vengeful history of the House of Atreus. As the Eumenides, they must take account of reasons and refrain from blind revenge.

EURIPIDES The third of the three great Greek tragic playwrights—Aeschylus and Sophocles being the other two—Euripides (480–406 B.C.E.) continued the tradition of using mythology as the source for his plots, but he did so with more skepticism and a greater tendency to divert from orthodoxy than the others. His plays are more cosmopolitan than those of Aeschylus and Sophocles, sometimes more satirical than tragic, sometimes even bordering on the comic. Of his many works, the most popular are probably the *Medea*, about the later days of the Jason-Medea relationship; the *Bacchae*, about the struggle between Dionysos (Bacchus) and the unbelieving King Pentheus; the *Hippolytus*, about the illicit love of Phaedra for Hippolytus, the son of Phaedra's husband Theseus and the Amazon queen Hippolyta; and the *Alcestis*, about the woman who gave her life for her husband Admetus but was brought back from the underworld by the hero Herakles. Euripides was said to have been a close friend of the philosopher Socrates.

EUROPA The daughter of King Agenor and Queen Telephassa of Phoenicia, the beautiful Europa caught the eye of the Greek god Zeus, who swam out of the ocean as a tame white bull and so charmed Europa, who was frolicking with her friends on the shore, that she sat on its back. The bull then swam away with Europa, and when he reached Crete, he turned himself into an eagle and had intercourse with the young woman. Europa was a descendant of an earlier Zeus conquest, Io, who had been turned by Hera into a cow. Europa gave birth to three children by Zeus: Minos, Rhadamanthus, and Sarpedon. She also gave her name to the continent of Europe (Europe = Latin "Europa"; Greek Europe = "Land of the Setting Sun," the West).

EURYDICE The wife of Orpheus and a principal in the famous myth of Orpheus and Eurydice, Eurydice died of a snakebite as she was fleeing from the unwanted advances of Aristaeus, son of Apollo and the mortal Cyrene, who gave her name to the city in Libya.

EURYSTHEUS When the Greek hero Herakles was driven mad by Hera, he killed his wife Megara and their children. The priestess of Apollo at Delphi, where Herakles went seeking purification for his deed, sent him to Tiyrns, where he was told to serve the king, Eurystheus. It was Eurystheus who imposed the famous Twelve Labors on the hero.

EX NIHILO **CREATION** Among the many kinds of creation myths in world mythology, the *ex nihilo* ("from nothing") type is probably the most common, especially if we include in the type creations from essential if not total nonexistence, such as the primal void or chaos. The deity of the *ex nihilo* myth creates by thinking, speaking, breathing, dreaming, or excreting things into existence. The biblical God speaks things into existence; the Egyptian high god in some traditions masturbates the world into existence; several Native North American creation myths involve the god or goddess thinking the elements of the material world.

EXCALIBUR Excalibur (Caliburn) was King Arthur's magic sword that came to him from a mysterious hand outstretched from under the water of a lake. Before his death, he ordered that the sword be thrown back into the lake to prevent it from falling into the wrong hands. Twice his orders were disobeyed. When the order was finally carried out, the mysterious hand appeared again to retake the sword.

EXODUS Probably written over a long period between the ninth and fifth centuries B.C.E., the second book of the Hebrew *Torah* or Christian Old Testament is the Book of Exodus. It contains the story of the misery of the Israelites (Hebrews) in their long Egyptian exile; the rise of Moses; the Passover events; the migration toward Canaan, including the parting of the Sea of Reeds; the time in the wilderness, during which Moses received the Ten Commandments; and a renewal of the ancient covenant between Yahweh and the Hebrews. Exodus contains some of the most important mythological events or sacred stories of the Jewish religion.

EYE The Eye is a common symbol for the Great Goddess in Egyptian mythology. The Eye of the high god is sometimes the god's daughter. It can sometimes be seen as the sun or moon. An angry high god can burn the world with his vengeful Kali-like Eye in the form, for instance, of the angry lion goddess Sekhmet in the Egyptian flood myth. But without the Eye, the world becomes dark and sterile. In many mythologies the Eye of heaven is simply the sun.

The story of Orpheus and Eurydice on a Greek amphora. Orpheus charms the enthroned Hades and Persephone so he can retrieve his Eurydice from the Underworld.

FAFNIR Fafnir plays a role in the Norse myth of the hero Sigurd. After the gods, the Aesir, had paid a ransom to a man named Hreimdar for having killed one of his sons, the man's remaining sons, Fafnir and Regin, fought over the ransom. One night Fafnir murdered his father and made off with the treasure. Then, under the curse of the stolen gold, he turned himself into a poison-filled dragon and devoted his life to protecting his gold and ravaging the countryside. The now-penniless brother, Regin, became a smith and eventually adopted the young hero Sigurd. As Sigurd grew

into manhood, Regin, for his own selfish purposes, tried to convince his ward to fight his dragon-brother. Sigurd agreed to the challenge on the condition that Regin forge him a powerful sword, which the smith did, using the broken parts of a sword named Gram that had belonged to the hero's father, Sigmund.

FAIRY TALE AND MYTH Any reader of fairy tales—whether those of the compilers of the Indian *Panchatantra* (c. 200 B.C.E.–1199 C.E.) or the Arab *Thousand and One Nights* (*Arabian Nights*) (c. 850–1790 C.E.); the classic European collectors, such as the Frenchman Charles Perrault (1628–1703), with his Contes de ma Mere l'Oye (*Mother Goose Stories*) or *Tales of Past Times with Lessons*; the German Grimm Brothers, Jacob (1785–1863) and Wilhelm (1786–1859), with their *Kinder un Hausmarchen*; the Englishman Andrew Lang (1844–1912), with his various *Fairy Books*; or recent collectors of tales from China, Africa, Native North America, and elsewhere—will recognize certain patterns or motifs in the tales that are also found in world mythology. Characters are miraculously conceived, heroes and heroines descend to places that resemble mythic underworlds, and young heroes go on dangerous quests and are detained by femmes fatales or challenged by monsters. Certainly these connections between myth and fairy tale suggest an archetypal and symbolic language common to the human psyche. On the other hand, they also suggest a conscious attempt on the part first of oral storytellers and later of the literary collectors who gathered and studied those oral tales to make use of the old sacred stories, motifs, and symbols in a still moralistic but generally secular context, with particular versions reflecting the moral and mannerly priorities of particular societies. It might be argued, for example, that the Cinderella story—versions of which have been told for millennia all over the world—from China to Africa, to Native America, to France, to Germany—is archetypally related to equally ubiquitous myths of transformation and sacred identifying objects. And surely the fairy tale of the young prince searching for the "water of life" or his lost father has symbolic connections not only with myths such as that of Gilgamesh in ancient Mesopotamia but with any myths in which the hero's quest is for immortality of one kind or another or for God. Often, in fact, it is difficult to differentiate between the sacred world of myth and the secular if moralistic world of the fairy tale. Is the tale of Icarus's foolish flight any more sacred or less secularly moralistic than the various tales of Red Riding Hood, who is eaten (even if, in some cases, not digested) by the wolf, or the countless tales of the person who pays dearly—if only temporarily—for his or her foibles? [Propp]

Little Red Riding Hood. A fairy tale heroine

FARO The creation myth of the Bambara people of west Africa tells how Gla and Dya, the elements of life, emerged from the void (Fu) and how the creator, Faro, then created the sky while his twin spirit Pemba made the earth. Faro then came down to earth and formed a set of twins in the wilderness. Then Faro and the twins witnessed the creation of plant life and of fish, fowl, and other animals. Faro named the elements of creation and instituted the daily and seasonal cycles. Acting as a culture hero, he established proper rituals and mores and then returned to his home in the heavens.

FATES The Greek *Moirai* ("Fates," Roman *Parcae*) were seen as three spinning crones—Clotho, Lachesis, and Atropos—who, as their names indicate, spun out life, measured it, and cut it. They are often depicted carrying various instruments of spinning. To indicate their dominion over life, they sometimes carry scepters. The Fates are sometimes thought of as goddesses of both birth and death because of the linear aspect of their spun thread of life. They present a theological problem in relation to the question of whether they or Zeus—or in modern terms, Fate or God—has ultimate control over life and death.

FAUNUS The Romans depicted Faunus, an ancient pre-Roman Italian deity of oracles, agriculture, and shepherds, with goat's feet and horns. He was said to have a voracious sexual appetite. Eventually the Romans identified him with the Greek god Pan.

FAUST Dr. Faust or Faustus (c. 1480–1540) was a German scholar of magic and arcane powers who became the center of a legend that has achieved almost mythic proportions in various literary and musical works, perhaps most famously in Wolfgang von Goethe's poetic drama *Faust*, written in two parts (1808, 1832), and in *The Tragical History of Dr. Faustus* (c. 1588), by the English playwright Christopher Marlowe. According to the Faustian legend, Dr. Faust, in search of greater magical powers, made an agreement with Mephistopheles according to which he would literally sell his soul to the Devil in return for twenty-four years of knowledge, magical power, and unlimited pleasure. In the end, of course, Faust regretted the agreement, understanding the illusory nature of that which he had apparently gained, and he was taken off to Hell.

FEMME FATALE In the heroic monomyth, the questor-hero is confronted by various barriers to the achievement of a sacred goal. Monsters can represent various human distortions; jealous kings can stand for the status quo and the resistance to growth and change. The femme fatale—the female enchantress—can also stand in the way of the male hero's quest, providing an immediate goal that distracts the protagonist from the sacred one. Because they were his sexual partners and delayed his return to Ithaca, Calypso and Circe were femmes fatales for Odysseus in Homer's *Odyssey*, though finally not very malevolent ones. Dido, queen of Carthage, was Aeneas's femme fatale in Virgil's *Aeneid*, distracting him from his future as the founder of Rome. And the Mesopotamian goddess Inanna/Ishtar played the would-be femme fatale to Gilgamesh when she tried to seduce him as he searched for eternal life. Morrigan was Cuchulainn's would-be femme fatale in the Irish *Tain*—doubly so, because he finally paid with his life for refusing her advances. The Philistine woman Delilah was a femme fatale for the Hebrew hero Samson, his attraction for her leaving him vulnerable to the removal

Methinks, a Million Fools in Choir/are Raving and Will Never Tire, illustration from Goethe's *Faust*.

of the source of his strength, his hair. In a sense Eve and Pandora, for instance, like first women in many mythologies, are femmes fatales to patriarchal societies, supposedly distracting humanity from the path outlined by the supreme deity.

FENIAN CYCLE The Fenian Cycle (Ossianic Cycle) is a series of tales related to the adventures of the Irish hero Fionn Mac Cunhail (Finn) and his followers, the Fianna, or Fenians. Although probably based on versions dating to the third century C.E., the tales were collected in the twelfth-century *Acallamh na Senorach* ("Colloquy of Ancients"). Belonging more to the popular culture than to the older religious culture preserved by the filidh, the Christian influence is apparent in these tales. In fact, the narrator of the *Acallamh*, Cailte, or sometimes Oisin (thus, Ossianic Cycle), recounts the deeds of the Fenians to St. Patrick.

FENRIR In Norse mythology, Fenrir was the terrifying giant wolf offspring of the trickster god Loki and the giantess Angrboda. This pair also produced Jormungand the serpent and a ghastly daughter, Hel. Although Fenrir lived among the gods, they knew better than to come near him. Only the war god, Tyr, could feed him, and when he did so, the wolf swallowed huge hunks of meat, bones and all. Eventually, the gods decided that they had to rid Asgard of the beast but without dishonoring their sanctuary with its blood. The only way was to bind him and remove him from their midst. Not wishing to arouse the wolf's ire, the gods decided on a plan whereby they would hide their intentions behind a contest. Appealing to Fenrir's vanity, they challenged him to break whatever bonds they could devise. The beast easily broke the first two bonds. But the gods convinced the dwarfs to make them bonds that he would not be able to break, and in time the dwarfs came up with what appeared to be a slight and silky cord. The cord was magic, however, made of the noise of a moving cat, the beard of a woman, the root of a mountain, the sinew of a bear, the breath of a fish, and the spit of a bird. Having invited Fenrir to sail out to an island in a lake, the gods again challenged him to be bound. The wolf became suspicious but at last was persuaded to be bound, on condition that Tyr place his arm in Fenrir's mouth as good-faith collateral. When the magic cord was tied around him, Fenrir struggled to get loose, but the cord only became tighter. Realizing he had been tricked, Fenrir bit down and severed Tyr's forearm. But after securing the cord with a huge chain and giant stone, the gods gagged the monster by driving a sword through his jaws.

It was believed that Fenrir would swallow Odin at the time of the world's end, known as Ragnarok, but that his victory over the high god would be avenged by Odin's son Vidar, who would rip apart the wolf's jaws.

FERDIA Ferdia (Fer Diadh) was a close friend and boyhood companion of the Irish hero Cuchulainn. Fighting on the Connacht side in the *Tain* war, he was forced by Queen Medb to enter single combat against his old friend. When the exhausted Cuchulainn finally defeated Ferdia, he fell down in despair.

FERGUS Fergus Mac Roth (Ferghus, Feargus), great warrior and lover, was an Irish king of Ulster who wished to make love with Nessa, his brother's widow. Nessa agreed on the condition that Fergus give up his throne for one year to her son Conchobhar. This Fergus did, but after a year the now-popular Conchobhar refused to return the throne. Even so, Fergus served the new king until Conchobhar undermined his honor in the betrayal of Naoise and Deirdre.

In the *Tain* war, Fergus, now the lover of Queen Medb, fought for Connacht against Ulster. But Fergus had been the foster father of Cuchulainn, and he had pledged never to fight the great Ulster hero. Fergus's refusal to fight Cuchulainn was instrumental in the defeat of Connacht. It is said that it was Fergus who first wrote down the *Tain*.

FERTILITY MYTHS Fertility deities and myths exist nearly everywhere that agriculture is important—that is, in most parts of the world. Animistic myths involving the sacrificial dismemberment and "planting" of body parts and the subsequent germination of crops are obvious fertility myths. The Hainuwele myth of the people of Ceram is an example, as are the many Corn Mother myths, such as

Echo and Narcissus, who was reborn as a plant

those we find in Native North America and in the Slavic tradition.

Myths of sacrificed and resurrected gods—the grain god Osiris in Egypt; Attis, the son of the earth goddess Cybele in Phrygia; Adonis in Phoenicia and Greece; Narcissus and Hyacinth in Greece—who die and are reborn as plants may be said to be fertility myths. The fertility aspect of many deities is indicated by their being depicted ithyphallically, as in the case of several gods in Egypt, or as bulls, as in most parts of the Middle East.

Storm or weather gods—such as Tlaloc or Chac in Mesoamerica, the Assyrian-Aramean Adad-Hadad, and several Hittite-Hurrian deities—whose power brings the new life associated with rain, are fertility deities, as are the many goddesses—the Mesopotamians Ninhursag and Inanna/Ishtar and the Canaanite Anat/Astarte—who descend and return from temporary death in the dark underworld. The many-breasted Artemis of Ephesus is a clear representation of human fertility. Other important fertility goddesses are Freya and Frigg in the Norse pantheon, Brigid in Ireland, and Demeter/Ceres and her daughter Persephone in Greece and Rome.

Whole classes of deities, such as the Vanir in Scandinavia, are fertility figures, representing female-centered agricultural societies, as opposed to later patriarchal, male-centered warrior societies represented by such groups as the Norse Aesir gods.

Farmer god myths of the Balts and Slavs are obviously fertility myths. The Nummo twins of the African Dogon creation story are fertility deities who, like many such culture hero figures, teach the people how to grow things.

In Arthurian lore, the loss of fertility is depicted in the failure of the Fisher King. In other cultures, such as those of Japan and the Hittites-Hurrians, for example, that loss is depicted by the disappearance of a sun deity.

FIANNA The Fianna (Fenians) were warrior bodyguards of the Irish high king beginning from c. 300 B.C.E. It is believed by some that the tradition of this warrior fellowship was influential in the development of the myths of King Arthur and his Round Table fellowship. The most famous leader of the Fianna was Fionn (Finn).

FILIDH A society of poets in Ireland, the filidh (fili) were official preservers of history and lore. It was they who, as sacred bards, told stories of Ireland's heroic past.

FINNO-UGRIC MYTHOLOGY The most significant and widespread of the non–Indo-European mythologies of Europe is that of the Finnic-Ugric–speaking peoples, whose original Uralic—a language spoken by peoples of the Northern Urals from at least 6000 B.C.E.—divided in about 4000 B.C.E. into Finno-Ugric west of the Urals, and Samoyed mostly, but not exclusively, to the east of them. There are those who argue from linguistic evidence that proto-Indo-European and proto-Uralic must have derived from a single proto–Indo-Uralic language (Mallory, p. 149). Be that as it may, by 3000 B.C.E. the Finno-Ugric peoples, driven by the processes of fishing, hunting, and gathering, had broken up into two primary subfamilies—Finnic and Ugric (or Ugrian)—and then into several smaller groups that would eventually develop somewhat distinct non–Indo-European mythologies and languages. The primary Ugric language and culture became what is now Hungarian. Of that culture's

mythology little is known other than the apparent dominance of shamanism, a belief in the afterlife, a high god, and a tradition of the people having descended from a female deer.

One Hungarian origin myth tells how Queen Emesu had a dream in which she was fertilized by a goshawk, much as in Buddhist lore Queen Maya was fertilized in a dream by a white elephant. Queen Emesu's resulting offspring was Almus, the founder of a line of Hungarian chiefs who would lead the Hungarians to their present land.

The Finnic peoples became Permians (Permiaks and Udmurts in Russia), so-called Volga Finns (especially Mordvians and Mari or Cheremis, also in what is now Russia), and Baltic Finns (Karelians in Russia, Estonians in the Baltics, and Finns in what is now Finland). The Lapps (Saami) in northern Scandinavia and Russia are usually included—somewhat arbitrarily, given their distinctness—in this latter group.

Many of the Volga and Permian peoples became agricultural and, not surprisingly, developed farmer-based myths that somewhat resemble those of the Balts. The Udmurt Permians had a sky god called Inmar, who was a farmer, and a weather deity. Other farmer sky gods existed among the Mordvians and the Mari. Also important for these farming peoples was the earth goddess, who in several areas was known as Corn Mother. Mordvians, known as the Ezra and the Moksha, worshipped Mastor-Ava, the earth mother responsible for the harvest. They also celebrated water goddesses.

The Lapps, who were hunters rather than farmers, were prone to totemic animal cults—especially that of the bear as animal lord, a tradition with roots in the Neolithic. Other animal spirits, popular especially among the Lapps of Finland, are the *haldi*, who watched over aspects of nature. Some Lapps also had a thunder god called Tiermes or in some places Horagalles, and other ruler sky gods such as Radien or Vearalden, whose sacred sites were marked by a *stytto*, the symbol of a world tree or pillar that reached up to the North Star. The Finns also had such a pillar. Several of the Lapp sky gods have been compared to the Samoyed sky god Num.

The Baltic Finns, especially, were directly influenced by their Indo-European neighbors, the Germans, the Slavs, and the Balts. A Finnish thunder-sky god called Ukko, with his hammer, club, and sword, resembles the Norse Thor and would later develop under Christianity into an image of the Christian God. The Finnish chief sky god was Jumala, whose name, like that of the Indo-European sky god, refers to the phenomenon of light.

Shamanism was an important influence on the mythology of most of the Finno-Ugric peoples. Thus, as sorcerers/shamans typically travel in various forms—including those of animals—between the worlds to negotiate with spirit powers, the Finno-Ugric creation myths usually involved the earth-diver pattern, in which an animal is sent by a god to bring elements of earth from the depths of primal waters so as to create our world. Also important in this connection was the concept of the great whirlpool that dragged unwary seagoing people down to the world of the water spirits. The Land of the Dead beneath the earth was also the home of spirits.

Many Finnish shamanic myths concern the Orpheus-like musician-enchanter Vainamoinen, often the creator-hero of an earth-diver or, more commonly, a cosmic egg creation. In one famous story Vainamoinen leads a group to a far land ruled by the "Woman of the North" to find the

F

A Finno-Laplander with her reindeer

sampo, a mysterious and sacred instrument that could ensure prosperity and that in some stories was forged by the smith Ilmarinen.

Another central aspect of Finno-Ugric mythology is the emphasis on astronomy. The star formations, for example, were animal spirits. Several Milky Way myths exist in the Finno-Ugric system. In one, a giant oak tree—the *iso tammi* in Finland—that had been planted by three spirit girls had grown so large that it blocked the path of the clouds across the sky and obscured the sun and the moon. A tiny figure came out of the sea and proceeded to chop down the oak, making a path for the passing of the clouds and revealing the sun and moon. This same miniature being, or one much like him, was responsible for the constellation known as the *iso harka* (Great Ox).

The astronomical myths exist in the context of a complex Finno-Ugric cosmography, in which the world is surrounded by a stream and covered by a canopy created in some versions by Ilmarinen and centered on the North Star-capped pillar mentioned above. In some stories the end of the world can occur with the collapse of the pillar. A world tree with celestial bodies in its branches exists along with a world mountain and a world navel at the center of the earth.

The most comprehensive collection of Finnic myths and legends is the national epic of Finland, the *Kalevala* ("Finland"), a late (1835, 1849) compilation of the poet Elias Lonnrot. [Honko, Siikala]

FIONN Fionn Mac Cumhail (Finn Mac Cool) was the hero of the medieval Fenian Cycle of Irish mythology and the leader in his day of the Fianna (Fenians). First named Demna (Demhne) by his parents Cumal (Cumhall) and Murna (Muirne), a druid's daughter, the young hero was so fair that he was renamed Fionn. When the druid Finegas gave him the Salmon of Knowledge to cook, Fionn burned his finger and immediately sucked on it to relieve the pain. In this way he acquired the Salmon's knowledge, much as in Germanic myth Sigurd gained powers from his ingestion of dragon blood when he burned his finger and sucked on it while roasting the dragon's heart.

The young Fionn, after a series of adventures, saved the high king, Cormac Mac Art, and was made leader of the Fianna. The group continued to pursue adventures that will remind readers of the adventures of King Arthur's knights of the Round Table. The fellowship hunted together, fought together, was confronted by magic and spells. In the Battle of Fionn's Strand, Fionn defeated the mysterious "King of the World." Fionn was also known for his love exploits and was capable of genuine mischief in connection with them, as in the story of Diarmuid.

By the goddess Sadb, he fathered the hero Oisin. Fionn had come across a fawn while hunting one day. At night the fawn took on female human form and became Fionn's lover (Sadb had been turned into a fawn by the "Dark Druid"). Later, while looking for Sadb near Ben Bulben—she had been turned back into a fawn—Fionn found a naked boy who had been brought up by a fawn. This was Oisin.

There are several tales of Fionn's death, but however he died, it is thought that one day he will return to save Ireland, just as Arthur, the "once and future king," will return to Britain.

FIRBOLG The fourth wave of "Invaders" of Ireland described in the *Book of Invasions* was a group descending from the Nemedians, who returned to Ireland as the Firbolg (Fir Bholg) or "bag men"—so named, say some, because, as slaves in distant Thrace, they had been made to carry bags of earth. The Firbolg, who could be representatives of an actual pre-Celtic people in Ireland, are credited with the division of the island into five provinces or *coiceds* ("fifths") and with the establishment of a sacred kingship based on the relationship between the king's essential integrity and the land's fertility. The five provinces, which are basic to Irish myth and history, are Ulster in the north, Connacht (Connachta, Connaught) in the west, Munster in the south, and Leinster in the east, all held together by Mide (Meath) and with Tara, the seat of the sacred high king, at its center. The age of the Firbolg was a golden age of prosperity and peace. The Firbolg were defeated, however, by the Tuatha Dé Danaan at the First Battle of Magh Tuireadh.

FIRE Learning to use fire for warmth and for cooking was obviously a huge step for ancient humans, and, not surprisingly, myths of the discovery or theft of fire from the gods are found in many parts of the world. In Greece, Prometheus stole fire for humans from Zeus and was punished. Culture heroes such as Bue in the Gilbert Islands, Tore of the Mbuti people in Zaire, and Botoque of the Brazilian Kayapo all took fire from the gods for their people. Maui in Polynesia is one of many trickster-culture heroes who stole fire.

In addition, there are fire gods in many cultures who serve as the centers of the worship of this mysteriously dangerous and useful phenomenon. Asha in Iran and Agni in Vedic India are such deities. The ancient Aryans all worshipped fire, and fire as light has been important in the symbology of many religions, including Zoroastrianism, Christianity, and Judaism.

FIRST MAN AND WOMAN Many creation myths establish the existence of a first man—for instance, Pelasgus in Greece and Erlik in central Asia. More often there are first parents, couples such as the biblical Adam and Eve, the Navajo First Man and First Woman, the Icelandic-Norse Ask and Embla, the African Dinka Garang and Abuk, the Japanese Izanagi and Izanami, and, in a sense, the Egyptian Geb and Nut, who are representative of the first couple that must be separated so that creation may take place. In India, the first man is a more philosophical concept, as demonstrated in the myths of Manu and of the Purusha.

FISH AND THE FLOOD The Indian myth of one of Vishnu's avatars, the Fish, Matsya, is related to the story of the Vishnu Boar avatar in that both animals are horned and both concern Vishnu's rescue of the world from the waters, in this case a flood. The *Satapatha Brahmana* tells a story from Vedic times of how Manu, the human progenitor, finds a small fish in the water he was using for his morning ablutions. The fish asks Manu to protect him from larger fish and promises to save his protector from a predicted flood. Manu places the fish in a jar and, when it is large enough to protect itself, into the ocean. The fish has warned Manu—now a Noah-like figure—to build a boat, and when he has done so, the Fish allows Manu to tie the boat to his horn for protection against the rising waters. Some say that the serpent Vasuki served Manu as the connecting rope. A version of the Matsya story is also told in the *Mahabharata*.

FISHER KING In the Arthurian story, the Fisher King is a somewhat ambiguous figure who is encountered in various conflicting versions by hero-knights of the Round Table—particularly Percival—during the quest for the Holy Grail. The King is in some sense wounded, a fact that affects the fertility of the land he rules. Some say that the King—Pelles, Parlan, or Pellam—was guardian of the Grail but that he had sinned and was thus unable to speak when the Grail appeared before him. The King can be cured of his wounds or his speechlessness only when certain questions are asked of him. But when Sir Percival comes to the Fisher King's castle and the Grail passes by him in procession, he fails to ask any questions about it, and the King remains under the terrible spell. [Weston]

FIVE AGES Greek mythology tells of five ages in the development or deterioration of the human race. First came the Golden Age, when humans grew out of Gaia (Earth). This was a time of paradise, when old age, work, and pain were unknown. The Silver Age was spawned by the Olympians. The people of that time were marked by pride and violence and the apron strings of their mothers. Zeus destroyed these people. The Bronze Age was the product of Zeus. The people of this age used metal to make weapons and war, and they died out. Hesiod tells of a fourth age, the Heroic Age, in which humans, fathered by gods with human women, performed heroic deeds and were eventually sent to the Elysian Fields. The fifth and current age is ours, an Iron Age of hard work and problems.

FIVE SUNS The Aztec people of Mesoamerica see creation in terms of five suns or successive worlds, the fifth being the Aztec world and the first four worlds having been destroyed successively. There are several versions of this myth. According to one, the first age was ruled by the high god Tezcatlipoca, who was defeated by Quetzalcoatl and the jaguars. The second age was destroyed by a hurricane, and Tezcatlipoca regained power. The third world was ruled by Tlaloc, but that world came to an end when Quetzalcoatl destroyed it with fire. The fourth sun was that of Chalchiuhtlicue, and it was swept away by a flood. The fifth world came about at Teotihuacan, where Nanahuatzin leapt into a fire and became the sun. This world, preserved by blood sacrifices, will end in earthquakes.

FLOOD Flood myths are found in all parts of the world, usually as aspects of creation stories. Generally the flood marks a new beginning, a second chance for a sinful humankind or for creation itself, as in Hebrew mythology in the biblical Book of Genesis. The flood waters become a second version, as it were, of the primeval maternal waters—a vehicle for rebirth as well as a cleansing element. Usually there is a human flood hero—the Hebrew Noah, the Sumerian/Babylonian Ziuasudra/Utnapishtim, the Greek Deucalion, the Indian Manu, or one of many others—who represents the human craving for

Sigmund Freud (1856-1939)

Krta or *Satya*, the *Treta*, the *Dvapara*, and the *Kali*. The first age is the golden one, the age of truth. Each following age of the dice game of life marks a deterioration of values. Thus, the Kali age—our age—finds humanity at a low ebb, which precedes the ritual sacrificial dissolution of the world by fire and resubmersion in the primal waters, in preparation for the birth of a new kalpa.

FRAOCH The hero of the Irish epic the *Tai n Bo Fraoch*, the lesser of the Irish *tains* ("cattle raids"), Fraoch falls in love with Findhair ("Fair Eyebrows"), a daughter of the *Tai n Bo Cuailnge* Ulster enemies Queen Medb and her husband Aillil, who have already arranged for their daughter to marry the hero Ferdia. Fraoch is a great fiddle player and impresses even Medb with his playing. When he tries to get Findhair to elope, she gives him her thumb ring as a token of her love but insists that he ask her parents for permission to marry her. The queen asks such a huge price for Findhair that Fraoch has to refuse. Now the parents are convinced that the couple will elope, so they decide to do away with Fraoch by having him swim in a lake inhabited by a vicious monster. Fraoch removes his clothes and enters the lake. Meanwhile, the king finds his daughter's thumb ring in the young man's clothes and, in a rage, hurls it into the lake. A salmon, always a sacred fish in Irish myth, catches it, and Fraoch, who has witnessed all of this, catches the salmon and hides the fish on the shore. Aillil insists that Fraoch swim across the lake, and halfway across, the hero is attacked by the monster. At this point, when Fraoch calls for a sword, Findhair throws off her clothes and leaps into the lake with one. When her furious father throws a spear at her, Fraoch catches it and uses it to kill the monster. Finally the king and queen decide to spare Fraoch but not their daughter, whom they would have put to death had Fraoch not produced the thumb ring from the salmon, claiming he had found it some time before and intended to give it back to Findhair. The girl's parents now agree to the wedding if Fraoch will use his large cattle herd to help in the theft of the cattle of Cuailnge.

FRAZER, SIR JAMES Sir James George Frazer (1854–1941) was the author of the thirteen-volume *The Golden Bough* (1890–1937), an early landmark work of cultural anthropology and comparative mythology. Although now somewhat out of fashion, Frazer's work on such motifs as the scapegoat and sacred kingship and the comparison between Greco-Roman myths and religions and "primitive" myths elsewhere stimulated an interest in the study of world mythology. His work would parallel that of the so-called ritualists, such as Gilbert Murray, Jessie Weston, and Jane Harrison, and psychology and mythology comparatists, such as Carl Jung and later Joseph Campbell. Frazer's most provocative writing involves the dying and resurrected gods of the Middle East—Attis, Adonis, Dionysos, Osiris, and, by implication, Jesus. His work on the Fisher King of the Arthurian tradition would deeply influence T. S. Eliot's conception of "The Waste Land."

FREUD, SIGMUND The founder of psychoanalysis, psychiatrist Sigmund Freud (1856–1939) was concerned with the psychological meaning of myth, ritual, and symbol and with the whole field known today as the psychology of religion. Although he argued in *Totem and Taboo: Resemblances between the Psychic Drives of Savages and*

life. The persistence of the flood myth in all parts of the world, even those where real floods are unlikely to have occurred, suggests a human vision of both imperfection and the possibility of redemption. A microcosmic version of the flood can be found, for instance, in various ceremonies of purification by water, including the Christian sacrament of baptism, in which the initiate "dies" to the old ways in the waters of the font and is reborn in Christ. The flood myth is the given culture's "dream" of rebirth, recreation, and renewal from the chaotic maternal waters. [Dundes (1988)]

FOMORIANS A one-armed, one-legged ancient race of gods that opposed the Tuatha Dé Danaan in Irish mythology, the violent Fomorians (Fomorii) were from "under the sea." They were proficient at agriculture and perhaps represent an older earth-based fertility religion such as that of the Vanir in Norse mythology. They were finally destroyed by the Tuatha Dé Danaan at the Second Battle of Magh Tuireadh, as the Vanir in Scandinavia were defeated by the Aesir.

FORSETI Forseti, the Norse god of justice, was the son of Balder and Nanna.

FOUR AGES OF MAN According to the Hindu *Puranas*, each eon, or kalpa, is made up of four ages or *yugas*. These ages take their names from the four essential dice throws: the

Neurotics (1913) against the validity of religions, his *Moses and Monotheism* (1939) contains a somewhat more positive view of monotheism in Western culture. Freud's interest in myth was, understandably, psychological. He saw myths and their symbols as collective, cultural dreams, and he made use of myth to gain psychic insight into cultures, using the methods by which he applied individual dreams and their symbols to the analysis of the individual psyche. Myths, he believed, were collective fantasies. His sense that myths, like dreams, revealed certain ubiquitous human concerns and thought patterns would be an important catalyst for the archetypal theories of his sometimes protègè and later rival, C. G. Jung. But whereas Jung found in myth a positive and beneficial human activity, Freud tended to see the negative "wish fulfillments" they represented. Thus, in Judaism and Christianity the father god was real only to the extent that he was a metaphor for the unconscious desire for a strong and perfect father, and the Virgin Mary was an expression of the longing for a perfect mother.

FREYA Freya (Freyja) is the primary goddess of the Norse Vanir, the old earth-based deities, as opposed to the sky-based Aesir. She is almost always associated with the fertility god Freyr, her brother or husband. She contains the magic of fecundity, the miracle of sexuality and birth. Her fertility aspect is emphasized by her many sexual liaisons. Odin lusts after her, and she is sometimes conflated with Odin's wife Frigg. The feminine aspect of the fertility triad Freyr-Freya-Njord, Freya is a goddess of both war and love and is known for her lascivious ways, even giving sexual favors to four dwarfs in return for her primary symbol of fertility, the Necklace of the Brisings.

FREYR The Norse Freyr, a god of the earth-based Vanir, as opposed to the sky-based Aesir, and his sister or wife Freya are depicted as fertility deities, forming a triad with their father, Njord. Freyr and his father are perhaps related etymologically to the old Germanic earth goddess Nerthus. In the more militantly patriarchal world of the north, Nerthus is masculinized. Freyr, the great god who regulates the sun, the rain, the produce of the land, and human fertility, is depicted, logically, with a gigantic phallus.

FRIGG The highest ranking of the Norse goddesses is Frigg, the wife of Odin. Born of Fjorgyn, an earth goddess, Frigg shares her husband's knowledge of human destiny. She is the grieving mother of the dying god Balder, and she is associated with childbirth. Suggestions of her promiscuity should probably be attributed to her role as a goddess of fertility. In the obvious fertility connection between Freya and Frigg (Freya's husband is Od, whose name relates him to Odin, and Odin often desires Freya) there is an indication of the Indo-European triune goddess, with Skadi making up the third part, or an indication of a common source in the old Germanic goddess Friia, the companion of Wodan. Frigg's association with a fish as a symbol ties her somewhat to earlier fertility goddesses such as Astarte and Aphrodite. Her role as the grieving mother of the dying god connects her with the Virgin Mary. The word "Friday" comes from Frigg—"Frigg's day."

FRIIA In old German mythology the wife of the chief god Wodan (Wotan) was Friia (Frea), who is at least partially cognate with the Norse goddesses Freya and Frigg.

FUDO The "Immovable One" at the center of the "Kings of Knowledge"—the *myoo*—Fudo was brought to Japan by the esoteric Shingon sect of Buddhism in the ninth century. He is the concrete form of the supreme buddha, the buddha Dainichi Nyorai. In the current age, Fudo is worshipped independently and is usually depicted as a blue-black or sometimes yellow or red figure. He holds a rope and a sword as weapons against evil. He stands for purity and resolution.

FUXI One of the *Sanhuang* (the "Three August Ones") in Chinese legend and myth, the Emperor Fuxi (Fu-Hsi) was the brother-husband of Nuwa. He is usually depicted in the form of a snake. Fuxi has particular connections to the *I Ching* (*Book of Changes*).

Garden statue of Fudo, Japanese Shingon God of Wisdom and Fire

GAIA The goddess Gaia (Ge, Gaea; Roman Tellus) was the Greek personification of earth, who, according to Hesiod in his *Theogony*, was the first being to emerge from Chaos or the Void of pre-creation. Gaia, in turn, gave birth to the mountains and the sea and to Sky (Heaven, Ouranos), who covered her on all sides and impregnated her with the next generation of deities, the Cyclopes, the hundred-handed giants, and the Titans—most notably Kronos and Rhea, the parents of the Olympians.

Evidence in caves near Delphi indicates goddess worship there dating at least from 4000 B.C.E. By 1400 B.C.E., Gaia seems to have been the central focus of that worship. It was not until the eighth century B.C.E. that the Gaia cult was replaced by that of the patriarchal god Apollo, a replacement symbolized by the god's killing of

Ganesh (Ganapati), the elephant-headed son of Shiva and Parvati

the goddess's natural companion and protector, the serpent Pytho. In recent years Gaia's name has been identified with an ecological scientific theory known as the Gaia hypothesis.

GAIA HYPOTHESIS A thought model devised in part by a British scientist named James Lovelock points to both the power of the old myths and the emergence of the new. Lovelock's Gaia hypothesis takes its name from the Greek creatrix, the mother earth goddess Gaia. It is a model informed, for example, by the narratives that are thermodynamics, the Big Bang, and evolution. It speaks, like most myths, to human tragedy and to what might be called universal or ultimate hope. It is a philosophical and scientific myth that expresses our era's discovered reality that the world is an ecological unity of which each aspect—including the human—can be considered something like a cell.

In this model the overall unity, earth (Gaia), is essentially a living organism, a cybernetic system that adjusts according to its thermodynamic needs. The human race, though perhaps the consciousness organ of Gaia, is not necessary for her survival and could be dispensed with by Gaia if humans become more of a detriment than an advantage to her existence. Here such conditions as the "greenhouse effect" come into play.

The Gaia hypothesis, whether true or not, is helpful in reminding us that there is more to life than merely us humans. Those who are rightly concerned with humanity must also be concerned with their "lesser" companions.

We are, Lovelock has said, bound to be eaten, for Gaia customarily eats her children. What is certain is death and decay, which seems a small price to pay for life. The price of an identity in life is mortality. Families live longer than individuals, tribes longer than families, species longer than tribes, and so on.

But all will one day go from here forever, as the sun ages and dies in a searing inferno. And life may, or may not, find another abiding place in this or another universe. [Lovelock]

GALAHAD, SIR Originally Gwalchafed in Welsh, Sir Galahad was a knight of King Arthur's Round Table in medieval Arthurian sagas. His story had strong heroic monomythic elements. Galahad was the son of Sir Lancelot and the Lady Elaine, whom Lancelot had been tricked by a potion into thinking was his beloved Guinevere. Galahad was brought up by a nun and then knighted by his father and taken to Arthur's court. He was, above all, pure, and it was this quality that made it possible for him, of all knights, to succeed in the quest for the Holy Grail.

Galahad appears in Arthurian lore in a thirteenth-century French cycle of romances, *La queste del saint graal* ("The Quest for the Holy Grail"). In Sir Thomas Malory's *Le morte d'Arthur*, Galahad achieves apotheosis; he is taken up to Heaven.

GALATEIA Galateia was a sea nymph (Nereid) who fell in love with a young shepherd named Acis. But Galateia was also loved by the terrible Cyclops Polyphemus, who killed his shepherd rival. The grieving Galateia changed her dead lover into a stream that flowed from a rock.

GANESH One of the most popular of Hindu gods, Ganesh (Ganapati), the elephant-headed son of Parvati and Shiva, is the subject of many myths. He is worshipped by Hindus called Ganapatyas, who even produced their own version of the *Bhagavadgita*, the *Ganeshgita*, in which Ganesh replaces Krishna as the source of wisdom.

The *Brhaddharma Purana* tells how Parvati, the "Daughter of the Mountain," wished for a child. Her husband, Shiva, as a yogi-ascetic and as an immortal who, therefore, had no need of descendants, heaped scorn on her desire. But when Shiva saw how unhappy he had made the goddess, he agreed to her wish. He did so, however, while preserving his own distance from the conception of the child. Tearing off a piece of Parvati's dress, he told her to make her own baby from it. This Parvati did, and soon the child was nursing at her breasts. But in this version of the story, as in many others, Shiva takes a dislike to the child. Some would even say he was jealous of it. As a result of either a curse or the evil gaze of Shiva, or a direct act of Shiva, the child is decapitated. Failing in his attempt to calm his now very unhappy wife by replacing the detached head on the body, Shiva sends Nandin, his faithful bull attendant, to take the head of Indra's elephant Airavata so that it might be attached to the body of Parvati's child. After a terrible struggle with Indra and other gods, Nandin succeeds in his mission and Shiva places the elephant's head on Parvati's son. He was now short and fat with a red face, but in some deeper sense he was very beautiful. He was named Ganesh, "Lord of his father's *ganas*" ("hosts") by Brahma and was given a rat as his mount. It is said that, directed by the poet-sage Vyasa, he wrote the *Mahabharata*. It is Ganesh who brings wealth and success in life.

In one of the many versions of his birth story, Ganesh appears in the hand of Parvati during her bath. Ganesh was, among many other things, the guardian at Parvati's door, who prevented his father Shiva from disturbing his mother. Needless to say, this only increased Shiva's jealousy.

GANGES The Ganges, or Ganga, is the sacred "white river" of purification and salvation among Hindus. In the *Mahabharata*, the personified Ganga is the mother of the hero Bhisma. Usually she is depicted as riding on a great water beast. In both the *Mahabharata* and the *Ramayana*, there are versions of the story of the descent of the sacred river from heaven to earth. The *Puranas* tell us that the source of the river is Vishnu's big toe. But in other sources it is Shiva who controls the flow of the river.

The story goes that a certain King Sagara wished to have Ganga come to earth to purify the ashes of his sixty thousand dead warrior sons. It was not until many generations later that the sage Bhagiratha, a descendant of Sagara, went to the Himalayas and succeeded in doing sufficient austerities to Ganga to convince the river to come down to earth. But in order to prevent the force of the flow from destroying the world, the sage had to

The boy Ganymede being abducted by Zeus as an eagle

do austerities to Shiva. Finally the god agreed to allow the river to fall on his head. When she did so, Ganga formed the three Himalayan rivers that in turn make up the River Ganges.

The significance of this myth lies in the relationship between the Ganges, as the "blood" of the earth, and Shiva as its heart.

GANYMEDE The Greek king of gods, Zeus, fell in love with Ganymede, the beautiful young son of Tros, king of Troy. Some say he took the form of an eagle to steal the boy from his parents. Others say he sent the eagle to fetch him. In either case, the boy was abducted for Zeus's pleasure and made both immortal and eternally young on Olympus, where he served the gods as a cupbearer.

GARDEN OF EDEN The garden paradise home of Adam and Eve in the biblical creation story of Genesis, Eden has become a word associated with innocence and pleasure, as in an "edenic" vision. Thus, the "post-edenic" state is the state of humanity after the "original sin," the "fall" from grace represented by the disobedience of the first man and woman, or perhaps any state of disillusionment.

GARDENS, GROVES, CAVES, AND HIDDEN SHELTERS
Such places are often sacred places in myth. Typically, gardens represent paradise, as in the Garden of Eden in the biblical creation myth of Genesis. In part they derive their mythic energy from their association with the earth, perhaps with the earth goddess herself. Like temples and walled cities, they are protective places, metaphors for

cosmos in the face of chaos. They are places of birth or rebirth. Jesus is born in a humble stable; the Buddha is born in a grove. Muhammad receives revelation in a cave; the Buddha finds enlightenment under a tree in a grove; Jesus prepares for his death and resurrection in the Garden of Gethsemane. As in the Adam and Eve myth, the protective, even paradisaical space that is the garden can be corrupted by outside forces, represented in Genesis by the Devil as serpent.

In older, goddess-based myths, the serpent in the maternal garden would have been the natural companion of the goddess—perhaps a trickster, perhaps a symbol of the fertilizing phallus. It might be said that generally what comes to the hero in the garden represents archetypally that which comes from within as opposed to that which comes from outside, or "above" in mountain revelations.

GARUDA Garuda is the god-bird mount of the Hindu god Vishnu. He represents both the sun and fire and is known as the enemy of the serpents (*nagas*). The *Bhagavata Purana* tells how the *nagas* present Garuda with an offering each fortnight in order to protect themselves from his tendency to devour them.

GATHAS The sacred songs attributed to Zoroaster (Zarathustra), the poet-priest and founder of Zoroastrianism, the *Gathas* stress the dualism that is at the basis of the religion—the struggle between the good Ahura Mazda and the evil Angra Mainyu.

GAUTAMA BUDDHA Gautama Buddha, the Buddha Sakyamuni, or simply "the Buddha," whose personal name was Siddhartha ("the one whose goals are achieved"), lived in northeast India during the late sixth and early fifth centuries B.C.E. He was born into the royal family of the Sakyas (thus, Sakyamuni, "wise one of the Sakyas"). Eventually he became the de facto founder of an outgrowth of Hinduism called Buddhism. Little is known about Gautama's life, but a rich mythology has developed around it. The first "biography" was not set down until about 80 C.E. in the so-called Pali Canon in Sri Lanka. Mythic narratives of the Buddha's life had developed over the centuries, however, both orally and in writing—in various *jataka*, or previous life, tales contained in Buddhist *sutras* (scriptures), for instance, and in traditional tales told at various Buddhist pilgrimage sites. As is the case with other great religious leaders—Jesus, Zoroaster, and Muhammad, for example—the Buddha's life was raised by myth to the level of the sacred and the superhuman.

The mythic Buddha's monomythic hero story begins in the heavens, where the future Buddha—the Bodhisattva—who had already lived thousands of lives, preached to the gods. When he realized that it was time for him to enter the world as the Buddha, he allowed himself to be miraculously conceived in Queen Maya of the Sakyas. He entered her womb in a dream as a beautiful white elephant, causing all of nature to rejoice. The child was born without pain or blood from the side of the queen as she stood under a saka tree in the Lumbini Garden. Upon birth, the child possessed adult qualities. He surveyed each of the four directions and thus announced his possession of the world. Soon after he received the name of Siddhartha, the Buddha's mother died of joy, her role as birth giver duly accomplished.

When Prince Siddhartha was twelve, brahman sages revealed to his worldly father, King Suddhodana, that the boy would one day be a great ascetic. As if playing out the archetypal refusal of the call for his son, the king decided he would rather that Siddhartha be a world monarch, and he provided him with sumptuous palaces, beautiful women, and riches. He was married to Yasodhara, who produced a son, Rahula. But Siddhartha's vocation was strong, and he sensed the imperfections of the world. When he asked his charioteer to take him into the city, the king first had everything ugly or unclean removed. But, miraculously, there appeared before the young prince an old man on the verge of death. On other trips he met other people marked with signs of pain, mortality, and imperfection. Finally he met an ascetic beggar who had left behind worldly pleasures in search of a deeper peace.

In spite of the efforts of his father and the love he felt for his wife and son, Siddhartha left his palace and city and became the ascetic monk Gautama. After a long period of wandering and fasting and austerities at Uruvila by the river, he accepted milk-cooked rice from the maiden Sujata and bathed in the river before moving to the central act of his life—the ordeal under the world tree, the Bodhigaya, the Bodhi Tree or fig tree of enlightenment. There he sat down to die or to achieve total enlightenment (*bodhi*).

At first, the demon Mara attempted to tempt Gautama away from his intention. He tempted him with lust, with power, and some say with the supposed enslavement of the wife and child he had left behind. Then enlightenment came to Gautama and he became a buddha. He understood death and rebirth and existence itself. After seven days of further meditation and four more weeks near the tree, the Buddha decided to put off his entering nirvana in favor of the bodhisattva's role of preaching to the world. He went first to Banaras and preached his brand of mercy and universal love there. Many miracles followed. The Buddha tamed a wild elephant sent by his cousin Devadatta to undermine his work. He converted his family, including his cousin Ananda, who became his chief disciple.

As he was dying by the river Hiranyavati, the Buddha reminded his followers that they must work for liberation from the impermanence of life. His funeral pyre caught fire of its own accord, and Gautama Buddha entered nirvana. In one popular depiction, he sits on a lotus flower between the Hindu gods Brahma and Indra and creates a vast number of lotuses each with himself seated in its center.

GAWAIN, SIR One of the greatest of the heroes of King Arthur's Round Table, Sir Gawain in Welsh mythology was the particular companion of Peredur (Percival, Parzifal). Best known as the hero of the fourteenth-century Middle English romance *Sir Gawain and the Green Knight*, Gawain's knightly quest is deeply colored by the theme of decapitation in relation to the presence of a giant figure associated with the tradition of the sacrificial green man, a fertility figure whose decapitation can be related to the ritual killings of various Corn Mother figures in world mythology. The direct source for the Gawain tale is the Irish Celtic myth of "Bricriu's Feast," in which the decapitation challenge of a giant plays a central role along with the reactions of the hero, Cuchulainn.

During a feast at the Round Table of King Arthur's court, a green giant enters on horseback and challenges any one of the knights to behead him in return for his being allowed to behead the knight in a year. After Gawain accepts the challenge and performs the deed, the green knight rises, picks up his head, and leaves. When the appointed time for the return blow approaches, Gawain makes his way toward the Green Chapel. On his way, he rests at the castle of a knight named Bercilak, whose beautiful wife tempts him. At first the pure Gawain resists Bercilak's wife, but on the third day, he accepts a green sash from her. When he arrives at the Green Chapel, the Green Knight strikes twice and misses, as Gawain had twice resisted temptation. But the third blow grazes his neck, because he had accepted the sash. The Green Knight reveals himself to be Bercilak. The whole episode had been planned by Morgan le Fay.

GAYOMART In an ancient Persian myth, Gayomart is the primal human aspect of the Zoroastrianism founder Zoroaster (Zarathustra). Zoroaster is also revealed in Saoshyant the savior. Gayomart is the sacrificial victim of Zoroastrianism. He and the great bull were created by Ohrmazd and killed by the evil Ahriman. At his death, Gayomart announced that humanity would find life in him. And, in fact, as the blood of the bull caused the earth to produce plant and animal life, the seed that was Gayomart was the source of the plant that divided into the first humans, male and female, Mashye and Mashyane.

GEB AND NUT The offspring of the Egyptian gods Shu (Air) and Tefnut (Moisture), the male god Geb (Earth) and the female Nut (Sky) at first lay together as one being but were separated by their father, Shu, who, as air, provided space between Earth and Sky where other beings could be created. The theme of the separation of primordial parents to provide room for creation is a common one in world mythology. Although little narrative material exists for this Egyptian version of the myth, the story is depicted in many paintings, in which Geb is shown, sometimes with an erect penis, lying on his back as his sister-wife arches over him, often held up by her father Shu.

Separated from Geb, Nut gave birth to the stars, which rose up to her. Each morning she consumed these children so as to protect them until they could be reborn at night. Geb and Nut were the parents of Osiris and Seth and their sister-wives Isis and Nephtys, the principals, with the god

Horus—the son of Isis and Osiris—of the central Egyptian myth of fertility, death, and rebirth.

GEFION Gefion was a Norse fertility goddess who, disguised as a beggar woman, treated with humble generosity King Gylfi of Sweden, himself disguised as an ordinary man. Gylfi, revealing himself as king, offered Gefion as much of Sweden as she could plow up in a day and a night. With the help of her four sons, whom she turned into oxen, the goddess was able to plow the land that today is known as the island of Zealand, which became her cult center.

GENESIS The creation myth of the Hebrews, sacred also to Christians and to some extent to followers of Islam (Muslims), is found at the beginning of the biblical Book of Genesis. Genesis also contains the myth of the Flood.

In Genesis 1 we learn that Elohim created the earth and the heavens, that darkness "covered" the primeval waters. As in so many creation stories, further creation required the separation of the original components of existence, so Elohim created light and separated light from darkness and named the new entities Night and Day. In the next few days of the seven first days, Elohim continued the separating or differentiating process by creating sky, seas, dry land, plants, stars, sun, moon, animals, and finally humans. In this version of the creation story, the first male and female humans were created simultaneously after the creation of plants and animals and were given guardianship of the garden at the center of creation. The seventh day was the day Elohim rested and so established the Sabbath.

Genesis 2:4–3:24 was composed under the Jerusalem monarchy, probably in about 950 B.C.E. by the so-called Jahwist author ("J"). Almost certainly based on an earlier oral account, this story is concerned primarily with the question of the creation of humans and depicts a very personal and "jealous" god, one echoed in other biblical references to creation (e.g., Job 26, Jeremiah 10, and Isaiah 45).

In this version of creation Yahweh-Elohim created Adam ("man" or "earthly being") out of the dust (*adamah* = "earth") of creation and then breathed life into him. Next he planted a garden—a place in which he strolled about like a true landowner—in Eden, somewhere in the east, and he

Geb (Earth) and Nut (Sky) being separated by Shu (Air)

placed Adam there, encouraging him to eat anything but the fruit of a particular tree; eating that fruit would bring death into the world. To keep the man company, Yahweh created animals and instructed Adam to name them. Adam did so but was still without a proper companion, so Yahweh designed a being out of one of Adam's ribs, and Adam called the new being Woman (*ishshah* = of man — *ish* = man). Adam and the woman were content in their nakedness in the garden.

But the woman was tempted by the wily serpent—mythologically speaking, a shape-changing trickster figure—to eat of the forbidden tree. The fruit of the tree, he said, would bring god-like knowledge. The woman ate some of the forbidden fruit and gave some to Adam, who also ate, and suddenly the two became aware of their nakedness—that is, of sexuality—and sewed fig leaves to cover their genitals. They then hid from Yahweh, who, of course, found them. When Yahweh learned of the disobedience, he cursed the serpent, created enmity between the woman and the serpent forever (fear of snakes), announced that women would suffer in childbirth, and made men the rulers of women. As for men, they would have to work hard to stay alive. Men and women would eventually suffer death—return to the earth (dust). Finally, Adam and the woman were expelled from the garden paradise, and the "jealous" creator placed angel guards around the Tree of Life so that humans might not eat its fruit and so become immortal like him.

Before leaving the garden, Adam named the woman Eve (*Hava* = "Mother of the Living"). Walter Beltz points out that Hava was a name of a Canaanite snake goddess whose companion, as was often the case with the early fertility god-

desses, was a serpent, a phallic figure whose name in Aramaic was *hevya* (p. 66).

What the Genesis 2–3 account does is to deprive the female once and for all of her original and positive "pagan" status and to establish a sense of sin in connection with sexuality and the life cycle itself. Christians would make use of the story as the basis for the doctrine of Original Sin that would color that religion's mythology, its strongly patriarchal treatment of women, and its negative view of sexuality. Christians took this position in spite of the fact that Original Sin is not central to the teachings of Jesus but is, in fact, negated by his role in Christian myth and theology as the "New Adam," the death-defeating fruit available to all on the new Tree of Life, the Cross.

The Hebrews, like so many ancient peoples, included in their mythology of the early period of human existence the story of a deluge, a flood, by which the high god cleansed a sinful world. The flood of Genesis 6 owes much to the flood story in the Sumerian-Babylonian story of Gilgamesh, in which the flood hero—the Noah figure—is Ziusudra/Utnapishtim. In the Hebrew account, Yahweh became disgusted with humankind and decided, in effect, to begin again with the process of creating living things. Noah, a good man, was told to build a boat (the ark) for his immediate family and representatives of the plants and animals so that they could ride out a devastating flood. When forty days had passed—the forty days that pre-figure for Christians Jesus in the wilderness—the passengers were able to leave the ark and to start over with a new life.

After the flood, God hung a rainbow in the sky as a symbol of a new covenant with humankind. In the Babylonian

The God of Genesis creates man

story the reconciling rainbow symbol was Inanna's/Ishtar's necklace, which she flung into the sky.

Of particular importance to Hebrew mythology, in addition to Noah's understanding with Yahweh, was the story that among the surviving family of the patriarch were his sons Ham, the ancestor of the Egyptians and Canaanites; Japeth, the ancestor of the Greeks and Philistines; and, most important, Shem, the source of all the Semites—Babylonians, Assyrians, Arabs, and Israelites. [Wasilewska, Beltz]

GENITAL MYTHS AND SYMBOLS In myths from many parts of the world, male genitals especially are treated as sacred or taboo objects. Ham is punished for seeing his father Noah's genitals. The loss of genitals, as in the case of Attis, Osiris, or Ouranos can be associated with fertility. In some versions of the Egyptian story, Isis plants replicas of Osiris ' genitals in Egypt's maternal earth fields, and out of these plantings comes grain. In the Greek creation myth, the ancient god Ouranos is castrated by his son Kronos, and in one story, the spilling of that "seed" in the maternal ocean results in the birth of Aphrodite. In India depictions of sex acts between Shiva or Vishnu and their mates—their *Shaktis*—are symbolic of wholeness, depictions in which the power of the male organ is emphasized. Around Hindu temples, little models of the Shiva phallus—*linga*—in conjunction with the *Shakti* vulva or *yoni* can be found. The Shiva *linga* is worshipped in his temples. In one myth, it reaches so far into the distant sky that even Vishnu cannot reach its tip. It is the *axis mundi*, the unifying force between earth and sky.

Gods are sometimes depicted ithyphallically, that is, with erections, symbolizing fertility, as in several Egyptian instances (including the god Bes), or the *herms* of the Greek god Hermes. Or, as in the case of the Australian Djanggawul, the large sexual parts may simply represent the creativity of a mythical time.

Trickster myths are frequently phallic and highly sexual in nature. The Polynesian people tell how the trickster–culture hero Maui stole the wife of the Monster Eel, Te Tuna ("The Penis"). Native North American myths of Coyote are often marked by the trickster's insatiable sexual appetite. In one myth a wagon runs over the trickster's greatly extended penis. The Sioux trickster Iktome frequently tricks women into intercourse.

A myth reflecting male ambiguity about the mysterious attracting power of female genitalia is that of the man-eating, teeth-bearing Vagina Girls in several Native North American cultures.

GERD The daughter of the frost giant Gymir in Norse mythology, Gerd attracted the Vanir fertility and sun god Freyr with her dazzling Northern Lights beauty. Freyr, in deep anguish over his love, sent his servant Skirnir to Jotunheim, the land of the giants, to bring Gerd to him. Using Freyr's great horse, Skirnir was able to penetrate the flames that protected Gerd's home. When various temptations failed to move the icy Gerd, Skirnir threatened to curse her using his magic staff. Horrible things would happen to her if she refused Freyr, not the least of which would be the wrath of Odin and the other gods. Gerd finally accepted Freyr's offer and agreed through Skirnir to meet him in the forest called Barri nine days later. There they would consummate their love, representing the fertile union of sun and frozen earth.

The ever-ithyphallic god Bes

GERMAN MYTHOLOGY In the sixth book of the *Gallic Wars* Julius Caesar spoke of a Germanic cult of the sun and fire, reminding us of other Indo-European solar and fire deities—Mitra, Surya, and Agni in Vedic India; Mithra in Iran; Apollo in Greece. At the end of the first century C.E. Tacitus outlined a German (Teutonic) pantheon following the typically Roman tendency to assimilate Roman religion with that of the enemy or conquered people. Tacitus called the primary god Mercury, a name associated with the German Wodanaz or Wodan/Wotan (related to the Anglo-Saxon battle god Woden and later the Norse Odin)—thus the Latin *Mercurii dies*, the Germanic *Wodaniztag*, and the English *Wednesday*. Following the Indo-European tripartite custom, Mercury is associated with two other gods: Mars, the German Tiwaz or Tiw (Tig for the Anglo-Saxons, Tyr among the Old Norse), and Hercules (Herakles), the Germanic Thunaraz or Thunr (the Anglo-Saxon Thunor and later the Norse Thor)—thus *Martis dies*, and the Old English *Tiwesdaeg* and our *Tuesday*; and, as the Romans also saw the Germanic Mars as Jupiter or Jove, the Latin *Jovis dies*, but the Old German *Thnrizdag* and our *Thursday*. It seems likely that this god had once been the primary German god. He would later, as Thor, be the most popular god in the Viking North.

The young David with the slain giant, Goliath

Tacitus also speaks of several Germanic tribes having descended from Mannus, a kind of "first man" in the tradition of the Indian Manu and Purusha, who like the Norse Ymir is the sacrificial victim out of which the world is born. Tacitus also tells of the earth goddess, Nerthus, one of the sacred matres or matronae, and the twins, or Alhiz. Both earth mothers and divine twins are, of course, basic to the overall Indo-European pantheon (e.g., the mother goddesses Matrona and Danu among the Celts, the Discouri in Greece, Romulus and Remus in Rome, the Ashvins in India).

During the so-called migration period of the fourth and fifth centuries C.E., Wodan remains the high god and has clearly taken on the magical poetic and ecstatic qualities later associated with the Norse Odin. Like the Indic Rudra/Shiva, who is both meditative yogi and destroyer, he is at least two-sided, and like him he demands sacrifice. Thunr, in the meantime, becomes more clearly defined as a war god. Jaan Puhvel suggests that the German Thunor and the Norse Thor took on qualities of the trustworthy warrior who balanced the volatile Wodan/Odin, as in India Vishnu balances Shiva (p. 201). Tiwaz, the third figure in the old German tripartite structure, seems to lose importance during the migration period, and fertility figures such as Friia (Anglo-Saxon Frig—thus, *Friday*—and Norse Frigg) seem to gain in importance.

Much of what we generally think of as German mythology belongs to the sagas of the *Niebelungenlied* and the hero Siegfried (Norse Sigurd). Much of this mythology has been given further exposure in the operatic works of the German composer Richard Wagner. [Todd, Fee and Leeming, Leeming (2003)]

GESAR KHAN In the pre-Buddhist religion of Tibet, Gesar ("Lotus Temple") was ordained by the gods to be born of an egg and to live a life of heroic adventure against the evils of the world caused by the curse of negative forces. In the eleventh-century Tibetan epic of the King of Ling, the story becomes the national epic of Ladakh as the *Gesar Saga* or *Kesar Saga*. At his birth, Gesar announces his identity as the Lion King. He will inevitably confront the evil Trotun, who has long ravished the kingdom. To avoid his prophecied defeat at the hand of a magical king, Trotun convinces the nobles of the land to exile Gesar, and the hero spends time wandering with his mother in the mountain wilderness. During this period, the beautiful Brougmo (Cho-cho-dogur-ma in Ladakh) is growing up in Ling. Eventually she finds the exiled hero, and together, on magical horses, they overcome evil and bring unity and prosperity to the kingdom of Ling.

Under the influence of Buddhism, Gesar was seen as an incarnation of the bodhisattva Avalokiteshvara. At the end of his life he was said to have undergone a period of meditative purification on the holy mountain of Margye Pongri before he ascended to Heaven.

GIANTS AND GIANT KILLERS Giants—huge, malevolent human-like characters—are common in folklore all over the world. In myths they stand as obstacles in the hero's path. The Mesopotamian heroes Gilgamesh and Enkidu fight the horrible giant Humbaba. In the Bible, David, representing the Israelites, kills the giant Philistine Goliath with his slingshot, thus clearing the path for Israel's defeat of its primary enemy. In Irish mythology Lugh kills the one-eyed giant Balor, also with a slingshot. Balor perhaps owes something to Homer's one-eyed giant, the Cyclops Polyphemus, whom Odysseus outsmarts in the Odyssey. Sindbad the sailor also is confronted by a Polyphemus-like giant. Beowulf, the hero of the Anglo-Saxon epic named for him, struggles with and kills the giant Grendel.

In many mythologies giants are significant first beings in a creation process. This is so, for instance, of Ymir and the other giants in Norse mythology and of the Titans in Greek mythology. Eventually these primordial, often earth-born first beings, who are unruly and dangerous—sometimes personifications of volcanoes, earthquakes, avalanches, and so forth—must be defeated in wars in Heaven by the later gods, who, in some sense, represent "civilization" and social order.

Giants are not always evil, however. Prometheus was a Titan giant who helped humanity. The Chinese giant P'an ku named Heaven and earth and gave forth rivers from his tears and wind from his breath; mountains and other earthly formations were parts of his body. And in the medieval Arthurian tale of Gawain and the Green Knight, the Green Knight is a giant of sorts whose confrontations with Gawain serve an ultimately positive purpose. The source for the Green Knight tale is probably the Irish myth of "Bricuri's Feast," in which a *bachlach*, a giant shepherd, appears and challenges the Ulster knights to what is, in effect, a decapitation contest. In American mythology Paul Bunyan is a "good giant."

In fairy tales, giants—the "Jack and the Beanstalk" giant, for example, who can smell the blood of an intruder—generally like eating humans. They tend to carry clubs and to wear animal skins.

GILFAETHWY In Welsh mythology, Gilfaethwy is a son of the mother goddess Don; his brother Gwydion helped him to gain possession of the virgin Goewin, who had the job of serving as a footstool for their uncle Math. Eventually the brothers are turned into deer by the angry Math.

GILGAMESH The most famous of Mesopotamian heroes is Gilgamesh. The mythologizing of this early dynastic Sumerian king of Unug (Uruk) had already begun by about 2400 B.C.E., when Gilgamesh, or Bilgamesh, was worshipped at several Sumerian sites. It is even possible that he was deified during his lifetime (c. 2650 B.C.E.) because of his building of the walls of Uruk and his defense of Uruk against the rival city of Kish. By the Ur III period he had become Lord of the underworld, a role that led in later years to a complex burial cult, inevitably bringing to mind the cult of the underworld lord Osiris in Egypt. Gilgamesh was always closely associated with the sun god Utu (Shamash) and was often identified with Dumuz (Tammuz), also a deified king of Uruk. It was said that his mother was the goddess Ninsun and his father the deified hero Lugalbanda. Ur III and Isin kings (c. 2100–1900) especially considered Gilgamesh their ancestor and used that connection to justify their rule. It is usually suggested that the Sumerian myths of Gilgamesh were developed during this period, perhaps including a hero birth story that does not appear in any text, however, until classical times. In that story, which has archetypal monomythic relatives in those of Etana,

Sargon, Moses, and even Jesus, a king's daughter becomes pregnant and a court magus asserts that the child will take the king's throne. This causes the king to have the child thrown from a tower. The child is saved in mid-fall by a flying eagle and is adopted and raised by an orchard worker, as Oedipus was briefly adopted by a humble shepherd and Siegfried (Sigurd) was adopted by a smith. Later, of course, the child becomes king.

There are five written stories of Gilgamesh dating from the Sumerian period, and they do not seem to have been combined in anything like the epic form of the tale that was composed later in Babylon. "Gilgamesh and Agga" or "The Man of Sumer" tells how King Gilgamesh of Uruk, besieged behind his walls by his enemy, Agga of Kish, used a distracting trick and was able to capture his enemy before generously pardoning him. "Gilgamesh and the Land of the Living," also known as "Gilgamesh and Huwawa" or "Gilgamesh and the Cedar Forest," exists in many forms and plays a role in the Babylonian epic as well. Hating the sight of death and wishing to achieve fame and immortality, Gilgamesh, with his follower Enkidu and with guidance from the sun god Utu, sets out to fight Huwawa (Humbaba), the gigantic and monstrous caretaker of the Cedar Forest sacred to the great god Enlil. When they get there, Enkidu is fearful, but Gilgamesh braves the powerful rays with which the monster plagues them and cuts down trees so as to be able to capture him. After the capture, Huwawa pleads for his life, but the angry Enkidu decapitates him. For this ungenerous act the heroes are cursed by Enlil.

"Gilgamesh and the Bull of Heaven," which exists only in fragments, probably tells how Gilgamesh disdainfully refused the advances of the beautiful goddess Inanna and how he killed the Bull of Heaven sent by the goddess to avenge the insult to her.

"Gilgamesh, Enkidu, and the Netherworld," or "Gilgamesh and the Huluppu-tree," does not follow logically from the Bull of Heaven story, as it reveals a much different relationship between the hero and Inanna. It is from the beginning of or introduction to this myth that the Sumerian creation story can be derived. After the creation, Inanna takes a windswept Huluppu-tree from the river bank and plants it in her temple at Uruk. Her plan is to make furniture from it when it is full grown, but when that time

The Mesopotamian hero Gilgamesh supporting a solar disk

The story of the flood in the epic of Gilgamesh

comes she finds that her plans are foiled by three inhabitants of the tree, the powerful and dangerous Anzu bird, the despondent maiden Lilit (Lilith), and a mean serpent. Even Inanna's brother, Utu, cannot help her dislodge the three demonic creatures, but Gilgamesh can. He successfully kills the serpent, scaring away the other demons, and the tree is cut down and used for Inanna's sacred furniture. Inanna uses part of the wood to make two mysterious objects called the *pukku* and the *mukku*, which somehow fall into the netherworld. When Enkidu offers to retrieve them, Gilgamesh cautions his friend and servant about the taboos of the underworld but allows him to go. Because Enkidu fails to follow the instructions, he is not able to return to the world above. Even Enlil and Enki are unable to help the hero retrieve his friend, but the shamanic Enki instructs Utu to burn a hole in the ground, by way of which Enkidu's ghost emerges and tells Gilgamesh about existence in the underworld.

"The Death of Gilgamesh" is a mere fragment, in which Gilgamesh expresses resentment about his death. Scholars have suggested that it might really be the story of Enkidu's death.

We know Gilgamesh best through what is probably the earliest example of an epic poem. The "Epic of Gilgamesh" certainly had oral roots but was first expressed in written—Akkadian—form in the Old Babylonian period of the early second millennium B.C.E. A more complete version was written later, in the Middle Babylonian period, supposedly by one Sin-leqeunnini, and there are neo-Babylonian, neo-Assyrian, Hittite, and other versions. The epic had gained popularity in much of the Middle East by the middle of the second millennium B.C.E. It was apparently the Middle Babylonian version that was the basis for most of the Ninevite recension, the c. 1500 line epic in twelve tablets discovered in the Assyrian Library of Ashurbanipal at Nineveh dating from the seventh century B.C.E.

Unlike the Gilgamesh of the Sumerian fragments, the hero of the Babylonian Gilgamesh epic is distinctly human rather than divine. In fact, if there is an underlying theme to the whole epic, it is Gilgamesh's discovery of his mortality in his passage from arrogance to humility in a quest for immortality. William Moran suggests that Gilgamesh's passage reflects the "ideological developments of the period that to some extent demythologized kingship and rejected the divinity that kings had been claiming for five centuries or so"; the epic emphasizes the difference between humans and deities in general, based on the fact that even a hero, a goddess's son, "must perform the very human and undivine act of dying" (p. 5:559).

The epic opens with what is essentially a hymn to the great King Gilgamesh of Uruk, builder of city walls, writer of his many experiences and journeys on tablets, son of Ninsun. This is a hymn of praise and even human arrogance that serves as the preface for the rites of passage from ignorance to knowledge that will follow. The seed of disillusionment, the existence of a significant flaw, makes itself evident even within the first tablet, when we learn that the king has tyrannized his people by demanding conjugal rights to brides. When the people complain to Anu, he instructs Aruru, the mother goddess, to create a being who can balance Gilgamesh's power. The new creation is the hairy, bestial Enkidu, who eats grass and sets free animals trapped by huntsmen. When the existence of Enkidu is reported to Gilgamesh, he follows the advice of the huntsmen and sends out the beautiful prostitute Samhat to tame him. It should be remembered that prostitutes were sacred to Ishtar (Inanna). The tactic works. Enkidu and Samhat make love for six days and seven nights until Enkidu has been humanized, told about Gilgamesh, and deprived of some of his purely animal nature. The reader here can hardly avoid a fleeting vision of the story of Samson and Delilah.

Back in Uruk, Gilgamesh dreams of Enkidu and then, recurrently, of heavy objects that have come from the sky, objects to which he feels sexually attracted. Gilgamesh's mother, Ninsun, interprets the dreams for her son, explaining that they are about a man who will become his companion and closest friend. Many critics have suggested a homosexual aspect to the Gilgamesh-Enkidu relationship, as indicated first by these dreams and then by later events.

In Tablet 2, the love of Gilgamesh and Enkidu is consummated, as it were, in a manly wrestling match, which is barely won by the king. But Enkidu's courage and power impress him, and the two become companions. The next three tablets concern the adventures of the two heroes in the Cedar Forest of Enlil, guarded by Humbaba (the Sumerian Hawawa). There, presumably, they kill the monster, as indicated in other versions of the story.

What follows, in Tablet 6, is the surprising story of Gilgamesh's refusal of Ishtar (Sumerian Inanna), based on the Sumerian story mentioned above. The heroes are back in Uruk, and the newly cleansed and adorned king is approached by Ishtar with a proposition of love and marriage and fertility for himself, his city, and its fields and animals. Gilgamesh rejects the offer outright, pointing to the tragic ends of so many of the goddess's former lovers. Furious, Ishtar has Anu send the Bull of Heaven to attack the heroes, and after the beast kills hundreds of people—perhaps representing a plague—the heroes succeed in killing him. Gilgamesh further insults his divine enemy by flinging a thigh of the beast at her.

Gilgamesh's rejection of Ishtar is difficult to understand, given the fact that she was the city goddess of Uruk and that the sacred marriage of king and goddess had been a foundation of Mesopotamian culture at least since the Old Sumerian period. There is the possibility that the incident somehow reflects the demythologizing of "divine kings" as well as a movement away from the strong goddess aspect of religion and culture to the kind of patriarchy revealed also in the Babylonian creation epic, the *Enuma elish*. But this interpretation is somewhat undermined by the existence of the earlier Sumerian version of the story. It is possible that the reaction of Gilgamesh is simply demanded by his particular character or persona, one that prefers the company of Enkidu to that of Ishtar.

In Tablet 7, Enkidu dreams that Anu, Ea, and Shamash have decided that for the killing of Humbaba and the Bull of Heaven either he or Gilgamesh must pay with his life. Enkidu fades into sickness; in Tablet 8, he dies and is lamented by the heartbroken Gilgamesh.

Tablet 9 concerns Gilgamesh's fear of death and his danger-filled journey in what is, in effect, an archetypal underworld. He must convince the horrible scorpion people to let him pass through a long, dark tunnel. And there is the relationship with the beautiful alewife Siduri in her jeweled garden. Siduri will have "sisters" in the *Odyssey*'s Calypso and Circe and the *Aeneid*'s Dido, women who, through love, would prevent the patriarchal hero from completing his mission. Like Ishtar, Siduri is a comfortable alternative that must be overcome. Still, like Circe in the *Odyssey*, she finally helps the hero on his way with advice on how to proceed, and in Tablet 10 Gilgamesh is ferried across the waters of death by the ferryman Urshanabi. On the other side, he finds the ancient flood hero Utnapishtim (Ziusudra in an older Sumerian flood myth), who reminds his visitor that only the gods determine life and death.

Tablet 11 contains the flood myth, which is remarkably similar to the one found in Genesis in the Bible. Gilgamesh asks Utnapishtim to explain how he has attained eternal life, and the old man answers by reciting the story of the flood.

Utnapishtim and his wife had lived in Suruppak. Ea had come to him there to announce that a flood was about to destroy humanity. He and his family would be spared only if they built a boat, for which the gods provided the measurements. The boat being constructed, Utnapishtim filled it with valuables, his own family, and representatives of all the species. Then came the most terrible of storms and a deluge that destroyed the earth. After seven days, the storm died down, and the ship landed on Mount Nisir. After another week, a dove was released to find land, but it returned unsuccessful to the ship. The same thing happened when a swallow was released. But when a released raven did not come back, Utnapishtim realized that he had been saved. He made offerings of thanks to the gods, and the mother goddess, in great distress, promised always to remember him. After much discussion, Enlil granted Utnapishtim eternal life.

Gilgamesh, too, longs for eternal life, but Utnapishtim is skeptical of his ability to obtain it. As a test, he challenges the hero to stay awake for six days and seven nights. Gilgamesh, exhausted, immediately falls asleep and the flood hero's wife bakes a loaf of bread for each day he remains in that state. When Gilgamesh wakes up he sees the now-moldy bread and realizes the point of Utnapishtim's challenge. He is human, with human frailties. Eternal life is beyond his powers. Before he leaves, Utnapishtim, at the urging of his wife, tells Gilgamesh about a plant under the water that can at least preserve youth. On his way home with Urshanabi, the hero dives for the plant and retrieves it. But once again, being merely human, he falls asleep, and a serpent steals the plant. So it is that serpents slough off old skin and become new again.

Gilgamesh weeps in despair, but he and Urshanabi, abandoning the latter's boat, make their way to Uruk. There Gilgamesh proudly asks the ferryman to inspect his great wall and his fine city. In a sense, the hero accepts his humanity.

Tablet 12 is a late addition to the epic, present only in the Ninevite recension. It is a retelling of the story of "Gilgamesh, Enkidu, and the Netherworld," in which the shade of Enkidu tells Gilgamesh about the underworld and the necessity of burying the dead. [Wasilewska, Kramer (1961b)]

GIRDLE OF HIPPOLYTA For the ninth of his Twelve Labors, Herakles is sent to obtain the beautiful girdle (belt) that had been given to the Queen of the Amazons by the Greek god of war, Ares. During a battle with the Amazons, Herakles, according to one version of the story, kills Hippolyta and makes off with the girdle.

GITCHI MANITOU An Algonquian term for the "Great Spirit" of Native North America, Gitchi (Kitchi) Manitou was the ancient creator.

GLA In the west African creation myth of the Bambara, Gla, or Gla Gla Zo ("Knowing"), was the first product of *Fu*, the great void. From Gla came Gla's twin, Dya, and out of the union of Gla and Dya came icy objects that filled the void and provided the potential for real creation. The twins moved about with a fiery wind that melted the objects. Gla's movements were the inner essence of creation, and his contact with Dya caused a "big bang" of sorts, out of which came the names of creation. Now Gla added human consciousness, and the world was born. The final steps in creation were taken by the twin spirits Faro and Pemba.

GLOOSKAP Glooskap was the monster-slaying trickster–culture hero of the Native North American Algonquians. Some of the people say that, using the corpse of his mother as material, he created human beings, as well as the heavenly bodies, and that he taught humans all they needed to know before he ascended into the clouds in his white canoe. Like many culture heroes, Glooskap had a twin brother—in this case Maslum—who worked against him and against his helping humans. Because of Maslum, the earthly paradise was undermined.

The bad things began one year when the people's stream dried up. The people sent a representative north to the stream's source to see what the problem was. In time, the man came to a wide part of the stream that was yellow and polluted. He nevertheless asked the people there for a drink, but they told him he would have to ask their chief upstream, who kept all of the good water for himself. The man walked on to where the chief lived. This chief was a giant who had dug a huge hole to dam up the water at its source. The man told him why he had come, and the monster opened his mouth to roar threats at him, revealing in his mouth the people and objects he had devoured. The man ran back to his people and told them what he had seen. Now Glooskap, up above in his white canoe, had seen all of this and determined to regain water for his people. He dressed himself as for war, shook the earth with his war cry and the stomping of his feet in a war dance, took up a mountain made of flint and turned it into a huge knife, and moved toward the monster chief. After a terrible fight, in which the monster tried to swallow Glooskap, the culture hero sliced open the giant's belly, thus releasing a torrent of water that turned the little dried-up stream of the first people into a mighty river. He squeezed the monster, turning him into a bullfrog, and threw him into a swamp.

Another Glooskap-giant conflict occurred when the trickster stole the beautiful maiden, Summer, to take her north to melt the giant of winter.

GNOSTIC MYTHOLOGY Generally speaking, the Gnostics were Egyptians and Essene Jews, early Christians, and certain Christian medieval "heretics" who practiced mystery cults based on the idea of "knowing" the divine. "Gnosis" is now preferred to the term "Gnosticism"—a religion of its own—as a label for this loosely connected group. An important figure for Gnosis was Hermes Trimegistos, identified with the Egyptian god Thoth, to whom is accredited the crucial saying "He who knows himself, knows the All." Many of the Christian followers of Gnosis were particularly devoted to what might seem to some to be the mysticism of John's Gospel and to his definition of "eternal life: to *know* you, the only true God, and Jesus Christ, whom you have sent" (John 17:3). The Gnostic form of the Logos was sometimes the female figure of Divine Wisdom, Sophia.

One Gnostic creation myth says that Sophia, the spirit of Wisdom, signified by the Dove that also was the sign of the Holy Spirit, was the child of the primeval Silence, and that Sophia herself was the mother of both Christ and a female spirit called Achamoth. Achamoth produced the material world and gave birth to Ildabaoth, the Son of Darkness, as well as to spirits that were emanations of Jehovah (Yahweh). It was these spirits who produced the angels and humans and who, as Jehovah, forbade humans from eating of the Tree of Knowledge. But Achamoth came to earth as the serpent Ophis and sought Christ's help in order to convince humans to disobey Jehovah by eating the forbidden fruit so as to gain knowledge—gnosis. Later Sophia sent Christ to earth as the Dove to enter the human man Jesus as he was being baptized by John the Baptist in the Jordan River. [Quispel]

GOD The god of the Hebrews dominates the myths of the Hebrew scriptures. This god, too holy to name, was expressed in the form of the tetragrammaton, YHVH (usually transliterated as Yahweh or Yahveh), based on the verb "to be." Thus he reveals himself to Moses as "I am." The name of this god was not to be spoken, since to speak the name might release its power and bring about destruction. Rather, he is addressed as Adonai ["My Lord(s)"] or Elohim ["the god(s)"]. At first he may have been, like the Moabite Chemosh or the Canaanite Baal and numerous other Middle Eastern gods of the third and second millennia, a tribal god among many gods. It seems apparent both from scriptural and historical sources that in common practice, the Hebrews assimilated the gods and goddesses of Canaan. The lack of cohesion among the early Hebrews in Canaan made monotheism—even monolatry, the exclusive worship of one god among many—an impossibility. The pull of polytheism was so strong that even the monarchy frequently succumbed to it. Monotheism, as opposed to monolatry, among the Israelites was not common until the time of the exile in Babylon and the reestablishment of Israel after the exile, that is, not until the sixth century B.C.E. And even then it can be argued that the firm establishment of monotheism in Judaism required the rabbinical or Talmudic process of the first century B.C.E. to the sixth century C.E.

Whether one among many or one alone, the god of the Hebrew Bible possessed many familiar Middle Eastern characteristics. He was a storm-weather god who could push aside the sea and lead with a pillar of fire. He was a god of war who could mercilessly kill the enemies of the Israelites. He was a fertility god who could create the world, replenish the earth after the flood, and make even the barren Sarah, the wife of Abraham, bear a child. And he was a "jealous" god of judgment who expelled Adam and Eve from the Garden, and punished his chosen people for their sins. He was the god who denied humans a common language—through which they might become too powerful—by destroying the Tower of Babel, the Babylonian ziggurat-temple, as described in Genesis 11. He was the angry god who answered the much-maligned Job "out of the tempest," asking him sarcastically, "Where were you when I laid the earth's foundations?"

It seems almost certain that the god of the Jews evolved gradually from the Canaanite El, who was in all likelihood the "God of Abraham." Karen Armstrong reminds us that in Genesis 16 and 17, an eighth-century B.C.E. text, God introduces himself as El Shaddai ("El of the Mountain") and that El's name is preserved in such words as EL-ohim, Isra-EL, and Ishma-EL (1993, p. 14). In Exodus 6, the deity introduces himself to Moses as Yahveh and points out that he had revealed himself to Abraham, Isaac, and Jacob as El Shaddai, and that they had not known that his name was Yahweh.

For Jewish mystics, the kabbalists, God is seen as a mysterious entity called En (Ein) Sof, from the innermost recesses of which the flame of divinity emerged at the beginning of time.

The early Christians in the Middle East were Jews for whom the high god was the god of the Hebrew Scriptures. In his appearances in the New Testament (the Christian books of the Bible), however, he was less of a war god than in the Old Testament, less of a weather-storm god. Rather, he was the loving and approving father of Jesus. And it was Jesus as the "Son of God" who took up much of the role of the old Jewish god who had concerned himself directly and sometimes in person with the activities of humans. As such, Jesus took on aspects of the teaching culture hero. In the Gospel of John he is seen as the Logos (the "Word"), or divine ordering principle, which had existed from the beginning of time and which was equated with God and was incarnated ("became flesh"), or took human form, as Jesus. Through Jesus and the spiritual presence of God as the Holy Spirit, the Christian god evolved in post–New Testament times into a complex philosophical construct known as the Trinity, in which God has three aspects or "persons"—Father, Son, and Holy Spirit.

In the third Abrahamic religion, Islam, God is Allah, a name derived from the Arabic for the god, al Lah (*al il-lah*).

The concept of God has, of course, continued to evolve, as is clear in the emergence in recent times of a new mythology based on a sense of interconnectedness, a mythology influenced by such diverse sources as psychology, mysticism, and science. [Armstrong (1993), Leeming and Page (1996)]

GODDESS It seems likely that our earliest sense of the numinous would have been expressed in a female metaphor reflecting the rhythms of nature. Women give birth and so does earth. So earth logically became Earth Mother and then Mother Goddess and Great Mother. Paleolithic evidence articulated by Marija Gimbutas and many others gives strong support to this scenario and to the importance and perhaps even dominance of this early female deity. The ancient peoples of Anatolia, for instance, clearly worshipped a large birthing Mother Goddess, as indicated by artifacts and excavations in places such as Hacilar and Çatal Hüyük (c. 6000 B.C.E.). Deities tend to reflect the political and social realities of those who depict them. Whether or not a dominant goddess in several forms presided over prehistoric Paleolithic and early Neolithic matriarchies is unclear. We do know that the original Great Goddess's descendants play a significant role in a deity biography of sorts that involves God and gender and the rise of the male god to prominence at her expense, and that very possibly parallels the movement from a female-centered agricultural society to a male-based warrior society.

Mythic evidence of the ancient great mother is scarce, due primarily to the nonexistence of writing. There are indications, however, in the Bronze Age cuneiform script of the Sumerians of a goddess who has retained much of the power of the hypothetical earlier figure. This goddess, Inanna (later Ishtar), descends to the underworld to confront the ravages of death in the form of her sister. It is she who performs the sacred marriage love act, the fertility ritual on which the

God with his angels in Heaven

Kali, an aspect of the Hindu Goddess (Devi)

earth's annual rebirth depends. "Who will plow my high field?" she sings. "Who will plow my wet ground?" It is her shepherd-king-lover Dumuzi (Tammuz) who provides this service, the seed bearer who "molded me with his fine hands . . . irrigated my womb" (Leeming and Page, 1994, pp. 19, 60). This fragmented myth suggests that Dumuzi is a sacrificial king, one who must die for the good of all, the seed that must be planted. As such he is the mythical companion of the Egyptian Osiris and the much later Christian Jesus, to mention only two of many dying gods.

In the Dumuzi myth Inanna has already entered the process in which the goddess will lose power to the god. Like Isis in Egypt and Cybele in Phrygian Anatolia, she is a transitional figure who has moved from dominance to a position in which she has become primarily a fertility goddess dependent on the male seed.

Other remnants of the ancient mother can be found in various societies that retain certain Neolithic lifestyle characteristics or have given them up only relatively recently. The Native North American Okanaga people of Washington State think of the earth animistically as the "Old One," a female figure whose flesh is the soil, whose hair is plant life, whose bones are rocks, and whose breath is the wind. We live on and take sustenance from her body. And we are at her mercy. When she moves, for instance, there is an earthquake. A similar belief surrounds the goddess Kunapipi among the Aboriginal people of Arnhemland in Australia. The pre-Aryan Indus Valley culture seems likely to have been presided over by a strong goddess whose descendant is the still-powerful Hindu Devi ("Goddess"), who, nevertheless, is typically subservient to her husband, usually the god Shiva. Devi wears many masks: Ma, the eternal Mother; Durga, the terrifying monster slayer; Parvati, the clever nurturing daughter of the Himalayas, wife of the yogic Shiva; and Kali, whose bloody fangs and death dance celebrate the necessary cycles of life, the eternal destruction and reconstruction—the breathing of the universe. Kali's black skin, like the skin of the later Black Madonnas of Italy, Mexico, Poland, and Chartres, is the dark fertile soil, the flesh of Earth herself.

The Yuruba Oya is another such figure—she of the "insatiable vagina, the purifying wind," as is the frightening Polynesian volcano goddess Pele.

The role of the goddess deteriorates with the invasions of so-called Indo-Europeans or Aryans into the Near and Middle East, the Indian subcontinent, and Europe during the Bronze Age (c. 3500–1000 B.C.E.). These invaders were warriors whose primary deities were almost certainly war gods associated with the sky rather than the earth, with conquest rather than nurturing, with light rather than mystery, and with stern fatherhood rather than loving motherhood. The ancient pre-Aryan goddesses had taken their power from the earth rather than from the heavens. With the emergence of cities, the domestication of animals, and the development of the technology of war, male power took precedence over female birth-giving mystery. Mystery cults, of course, continued down through the centuries and fertility rituals were important, as indicated by the continuing myths of Ishtar, Isis, Cyble, and others, but fertility goddesses increasingly came under the control of male gods. Demeter and Persephone in Greece were strong, but when Persephone was abducted by the underworld god Hades and Demeter removed her blessing from the land, causing it to wither, it was the all-powerful father Zeus who mediated the argument. And in the compromise he arranged, Hades was able to retain his victim as his wife, though she was allowed to return to her mother for part of each year.

In some cases, the goddess, clearly reflecting a pervasive male view, becomes the nagging wife who restricts her husband's freedom. The famous Zeus-Hera relationship reflects this syndrome, as do aspects of the Shiva-Parvati relationship in India. In many cases the Great Goddess seems to fade away altogether, as in the case of the Celtic mother goddess Danu in Ireland or the Greek earth mother, Gaia, about whom we hear only fragmented stories. In still other cases goddesses are masculinized or turned into dangerous seducers whose sexuality undermines male power. The well-armed Greek Athena is an example of the former, as is the virgin huntress Artemis, who in an earlier incarnation in Asia Minor had been the fertility goddess of many breasts; Aphrodite is an example of the latter. In the Babylonian epic of Gilgamesh, the male-female struggle and the superiority of the male are signaled when Gilgamesh refuses the sexual advances of the goddess Inanna/Ishtar, not wishing to fall into the femme fatale trap that destroys later heroes such as the shorn and thus emasculated Samson of the Bible, whose destructive temptress is Delilah. A case similar to that of the Gilgamesh-Ishtar conflict is that of the Irish hero Cuchulainn, who refuses the advances of and offers of help from the goddess Morrigan, claiming that as a male warrior he has no need of a woman's assistance—even that of a goddess. There is a clear belief in many of the post-Aryan invasion stories that the presence of women and of sexuality can only undermine the strength and dominance of men. The Athabascan peoples of Native North America tell the tale of the Vagina Girls, walking vaginas lined with teeth that devour men. It takes a great hero or man-god to tame these beings for proper male use by detoothing them. In all of these myths the female is dangerous because she is desirable. Therefore, the body is dangerous, something to be despised ("the flesh is weak"), and in religious traditions the intangible soul becomes an all-important counter-weight.

Myths such as those of Pandora, who, because of the female "weakness" of curiosity, releases all manner of evil into the world from her box, and Eve, who leads Adam astray with the forbidden fruit, are archetypal relatives of seducers like Ishtar and Morrigan, even though their names clearly suggest earlier more positive functions. Eve's name connotes motherhood. In a Mesopotamian form, corroborated by the Indo-European etymology of Ieva-Devi-Ma, she is a creatrix, the Mother of All Life and the consort of the serpent, himself a version of that ancient god, the often ithyphallic, genital-centered trickster, who changes shape at will and is, at least in part, a metaphor for the natural human appetites necessary for life. The trickster has many embodiments; the clever Hermes in Greece, the Spider Ananse in Africa, and Coyote and Raven in North America are just a few. As the serpent, the trickster is often the consort-companion of female deities, such as the Great Goddess of second millennium Crete, who was depicted holding snakes aloft, and the Aztec Mother Coatlicue, who was adorned with the heads of serpents.

Under the new patriarchal gods women became objects of conquest and reproductive and sexual vehicles to be owned. The cult of virginity emerged as a means of ensuring individual male ownership. Important objectives of war were the "ravishing" of city walls and of the maidens within. In ancient Sumer rape had been punishable by death; later Semitic peoples in the Fertile Crescent executed married women who were raped. The old, once sacred mysteries of womanhood were mythologically transformed into negative entities like Harpies, Sirens, and witches.

The second-millennium Babylonian creation story, the *Enuma elish*, is a landmark in the deterioration of goddess power. In that story we are told that in the land where Inanna had once reigned, the god Marduk became dominant, coming fully to power precisely by defeating and destroying Tiamat, the primeval mother of the waters, now a dangerous and mysterious monster with a horrid, venom-filled brood. So too was the goddess Ganga subdued by Shiva in India and the dragon-serpent Python by Apollo, the god of light in Greece. The sky god, now free of the earth goddess, was able to create the world, often *ex nihilo*, in his role as King of the Universe. Eventually he took form among the Semites of the Middle East as Abraham's tribal god, as Yahweh, and later as God and Allah, deities who had no female consorts.

For indications of the return of the goddess to at least something of her earlier position, we might look to the Christian myths of the Virgin Mary and the current renewed interest in the earth's ecology, represented by the ancient Gaia in the scientific Gaia hypothesis. [Leeming and Page (1994), Baring and Cashford, Preston]

GOIBHNIU The Hephaistos of Irish mythology, Goibhniu (derived from the Irish *gabha* for "smith"), was the smith god, who could make a sword or spear with only three blows of his enormous hammer. In the feast in the Otherworld known as Fled Ghobhnenn, he served a magical ale that protected the drinker from disease and death.

GOKURAKU Gokuraku is a name for paradise, as opposed to Jigoku, or Hell, in the Pure Land Buddhism of Japan.

GOLDEN FLEECE When it was arranged by his stepmother, Ino, that Phrixus and his sister Helle were to be sacrificed to the Greek god Zeus, they were saved by Hermes, who sent a flying golden ram to carry them away. During their flight, Helle fell into the Dardanelles, the strait connecting the Aegean Sea to the Sea of Marmara, which is also called the Hellespont after the drowned girl. As for Phrixus, he flew to Colchis, where King Aeetes gave him his daughter as a wife. The grateful Phrixus sacrificed the golden ram to Zeus and presented the Golden Fleece to Aeetes, who hung it from an oak tree in the Garden of Ares and placed a dragon there to guard it. Later, gaining possession of the Golden Fleece would be the goal of the hero Jason and his Argonauts, who would succeed with the help of Aeetes' daughter Medea.

GOND MYTHOLOGY The Gonds, like the Birhors, are one of many groups in central India who are outside of the traditional caste system of Hinduism and whose mythologies differ in various ways from the classical Hindu tradition. The creation story of the Gonds contains a theme common to other central Indian tribes, namely that of the brother and sister saved from the great flood, who then became the progenitors of humankind. The heroes of Gond mythology are the Pandava brothers of the *Mahabharata* and Lingal.

GONGGONG A demon deity with a serpent's body and a human head in Chinese mythology, Gonggong lost an epic

G

Jason carries the captured Golden Fleece

The Three Graces

battle to Zhurong and in his despair tried to kill himself by running into Mount Buzhou, one of the supports of the sky. This caused a tear in the sky and a subsequent flood and storm of flames. Fortunately, the goddess Nuwa restored order to things. But Gonggong's acts caused the rivers of China to run toward the east.

GOPIS In the Indian *Bhagavata Purana*, Krishna (Govinda, or "Cow Herder") is a cowherd (*gopa*) whose cows are symbolic of love and devotion to this great avatar of the god Vishnu, as is the erotic love for Krishna of the female cowherds or milkmaids, called gopis. Many stories are told of Krishna and the gopis. In one, Krishna plays a trickster role, hiding the gopis' clothes as they bathe so that he can watch them leaving the water nude.

GORGONS Stheno, Euryale, and Medusa were the terrible sisters known as the Graeae. They were usually depicted as ugly monsters with claws, wings, huge fangs, and serpents for hair. They were immortal, except for Medusa, who met her end at the hands of the Greek hero Perseus.

GOURD CHILDREN In southern China the Yao people say that humans were created by a brother and sister, the children of a certain farmer who managed to capture the storm god, thus putting an end, for the time being, to destructive storms and floods. The farmer instructed his children never to give the imprisoned god water, but they were merciful and gave him a drop. This nourishment gave the storm god the strength to escape, and he gave the kind children a tooth as he left. The children hid the tooth in the ground, and almost immediately a huge plant emerged and produced a large gourd. The released storm god went back to making floods; in fact, he made a huge flood and the children saved themselves by entering the gourd. After the flood they were the only beings still alive. Later the boy, Fuxi, and the girl, Nuwa, married, and Nuwa produced flesh, which the pair cut into pieces which they scattered in the wind. Where the pieces landed they became people.

GOVINDA Literally, the "cow herder" (*gopa, gopis*), Govinda is another name for the Lord Krishna. The *Bhagavata Purana* tells how Govinda, merely by favoring them with his ambrosia-filled glance, revived the cows and cowherds who had been killed by drinking from a pool infected by the poison of the evil snake Kaliya. Composed in about 1100 C.E. by the Bengali poet Jayadeva, the Sanskrit *Gita-govinda*, which has been called the *Song of Songs* of Hinduism, is both mystical and erotic. It celebrates the power of Krishna-Govinda as a lover. Through the *Gita*, the devoted worshipper can learn of the ecstatic love of Vishnu, whose avatar Govinda is.

GRAEAE In Greek mythology, the three sisters of the Gorgons, the Graeae ("Old Women")—Pemphredo, Dino, and Enyo—also known as the Deion ("Terrible Ones"), were born with gray hair and with only one tooth and one eye to share between them. They lived near Mount Atlas and played a significant role in the myth of the hero Perseus.

GRACES The Graces, or Charites, not to be confused with the Graeae, were offspring of the Greek god Zeus and a sea nymph, Eurynome. They were three in number—Aglaia, Euprosyne, and Thalia, personifications of splendor, cheerfulness, and joy.

GREAT MOTHER A form of the goddess who takes may forms in world mythology, Great Mother—Magna Mater in Rome—was a title often applied specifically to Cybele, the great fertility goddess of Anatolian Phrygia.

GREAT SPIRIT The Great Spirit and the Great Mystery are common translations of many Native North American concepts of a creator god who is sometimes a personification of the sun or the sky, but is more often a somewhat intangible source of life. On earth he is often assisted by a trickster–culture hero or by goddesses such as the southwestern Spider Woman. In short, since the Great Spirit tends to be withdrawn from earth and earthly things, there are few Great Spirit myths as such. It is enough to say, as in the case of the Algonquian Gitchi Manitou or the Sioux Wakan Tanka, that the Great Spirit is, animistically, like the Hindu Brahman, everywhere and in everything and neither male nor female.

GREEK MYTHOLOGY The religion or religions associated with the ancient Greeks produced one of the world's most complex and sophisticated mythologies, one that has particularly influenced the cultures of the Western world. Usually the Greek myths are read as individual stories. In fact, Greek mythology can be read as a single, gradually composed saga of the folk imagination and many talented authors, a saga in which characters and events from the beginning of conceived time are interrelated in a complex web that touches on every imaginable aspect of the human experience.

The early mythology of the land that would become Greece, the mythology of the so-called archaic and classical periods of the middle and late Iron Age, was preceded by several Bronze Age, or Helladic, stages. Linguistic evidence and the Greek historical tradition suggest that at the end of the third millennium B.C.E. Indo-Europeans intruded upon peoples whose languages and culture were primarily, if not exclusively, non–Indo-European.

These indigenous peoples are often referred to as "Aegean" or, by those who argue for an earlier pre-Greek but Indo-European intrusion, as "Pelasgian," after Pelasgus, the "first man" of the ancient Pelasgian creation story. Somewhat later arrivals in Greece are referred to as "Danaans," a name taken from the story of Danaus and his many daughters, who, according to one hypothesis, brought agriculture and the fertility mysteries of the goddess Demeter to Greece from the Middle East [see Graves (1970), vol. I, pp. 200ff]. Fragments from Apollonius of Rhodes and others suggest that the mythology of these Aegean peoples was, in fact, dominated by a mother goddess who was the source of all existence. Evidence in caves near Delphi, for instance, indicates goddess worship there dating at least from 4000 B.C.E. By 1400 B.C.E., Gaia—the personification of earth—seems to have been the central focus of worship at Delphi. It was not until the eighth century B.C.E. that the Gaia cult was replaced by that of the male god Apollo.

Two cultural systems of the pre-Greek period, systems also dominated by a goddess, are of particular interest. Burial sites dating from the Cycladic culture (the third millennium B.C.E.), named for the island group known as the Cyclades, contain a large number of nude female figurines, some with bird-like heads, many with stylized pubic triangles, all reminiscent of the fertility "goddess" figures

of the prehistoric period in continental Europe and Asia Minor. Further archeological evidence in the form of frescoes suggests the influence of a goddess cult with origins in the Minoan culture—named for the legendary King Minos—of nearby Crete, by about 2000 B.C.E., a female figure, now decorated in the Mycenaean style, is significantly present.

The Mycenaeans, a group of warlike Indo-Europeans whose language would evolve into a form of Greek and who invaded mainland Greece during the middle of the Bronze Age (c. 2000 B.C.E.), brought with them the horse and chariot, advanced weapons, and the tradition of tumulus burial as well as mythological elements of the Indo-European tradition. Sometimes called Achaeans by Homer, a name technically describing one of many groups of Hellenic peoples who migrated from Thessaly to the northern Peloponnesus, the Mycenaeans were the people of Agamemnon and Clytemnestra of Mycenae, Menelaus and Helen of Sparta, and, by association, Odysseus and Penelope of Ithaca. These are the familiar "Greek" as opposed to Trojan characters of the *Iliad* and *Odyssey* by the poet or poets we call Homer, who would live many centuries later. By 1600 B.C.E., the Mycenaeans ruled the Greek mainland.

Meanwhile, on Crete, the Minoans were building their great palaces at Knossos and for several hundred years had

G

The Olympian gods at home

possessed a form of writing we know as Linear A. We know that Greek speakers—undoubtedly the Mycenaeans—overpowered the Cretans in about 1450 B.C.E. and that they created typically Mycenaean citadels there soon afterward. By 1300 B.C.E. they had applied their own language rather awkwardly to the Linear A system and created so-called Linear B, a Greek language script useful for such things as inventories and other lists but not appropriate for literary purposes. Among the Linear B tablets, deciphered in 1953 by John Chadwick and Michael Ventris, are lists of offerings to gods. These lists indicate a radical shift away from a goddess-based mythology and religion to one presided over by the god Zeus.

In Linear B, then, we discover a pre-Homeric and pre-classical Mycenaean-Minoan version of what we think of as Greek mythology, the product of the indigenous peoples of Greece, the Minoans, the Indo-European tradition of the Mycenaeans, and the always-present influence of the Middle East. Much later this mythology would, of course, be pruned and adapted to various conditions and needs by Homer, the writers of the *Homeric Hymns*, Hesiod, Pindar, and many others, including the dramatists of fifth-century Athens. Although knowledge of the nature and deeds of these early Olympians of Linear B is sketchy, a definable and familiar pantheon does emerge.

Offerings listed on Linear B tablets for the various deities indicate the hierarchy. Zeus (Diwe) reigns supreme. Hera (Era) is present, as are Poseidon (Posedaone), Athena (Atana Potinija), Apollo (Pajawone), Artemis (Atemito), Hermes (Emaa), Ares (Are or Enuwarijo), Hephaistos (Apaitioji), Dionysos (Diwonusojo), and perhaps a form of Demeter, whose name Damater means "earth mother" and who with her daughter Persephone might be associated with the inscription Potniai ("Ladies"), the descendants of the earlier Great Mother of Crete ("Lady of the Labyrinth") and the Neolithic tradition. The missing figure here is Aphrodite, probably a post-Mycenaean arrival in Greece from Phoenicia via Cyprus, a version of many Semitic goddesses, themselves looking back to the ancient Sumerian goddess of love and fertility, Inanna (Ishtar).

Mycenaean society was characterized by a peasantry pursuing herding and relatively primitive agriculture, a society ruled over by a warrior aristocracy for whom raiding and conquest were appropriate paths to hero status. Monumental citadel architecture such as that at Mycenae itself, with its

The Goddess Pallas Athena armed

impressive Lion Gate and beehive tombs, and the celebration of heroic deeds in story were logical expressions of such a society. This feudal warrior society formed a perfect basis for works such as the Homeric epics, which were based on stories of the Mycenaean culture before its collapse, passed down by legend and myth and other word-of-mouth means over several centuries.

The Mycenaean collapse was due to many causes, including the intrusion in the twelfth century B.C.E. of a new wave of warrior-pastoralists from southwestern Macedonia called the Dorians. One of the Dorian tribes was said to have descended from the hero Herakles, and Dorian methods reflected that hero's crude power. Following the Dorian invasion there was a long "dark age" characterized by a dying out of writing and the other arts, and small, isolated colonized, often enslaved, communities eking out a living from the soil.

Homer's *Odyssey*, dominated by the sad wanderings of the old soldier Odysseus, gives some voice to the postwar disillusionment that might well have followed the Mycenaean demise, one perhaps ironically mirrored in the earlier, thirteenth-century B.C.E. fall of Troy that is the subject of the *Iliad* and other tales. But in some ways, the epic also reflects the new age of migration and advancement that began in the middle of the ninth century B.C.E., a period of developments that marked a Greek awakening from the Dark Age. A Greek alphabetic writing was established along with structural changes in the language that made it more precise and more flexible, more suited to great poetry. A revival of interest in the past took place. The migrations over the centuries of people from the lands conquered by the Dorians, especially to Athens, the city that would become the cultural center of Greece, and from there to Ionia in Asia Minor, revived a seafaring and colonizing spirit. This was the period of the legendary Homer, when the great epics took something resembling their present form and Greek mythology as we know it began to come into full literary flower. Hints of both postwar disillusionment and the cultural revival are, in fact, contained in the opening lines of the *Odyssey*:

Let me tell the tale through you, Muse,
The story of that man of all skills,
Forced to wander to the ends of the earth
Haunted by the glory days of holy Troy.

Both Homeric epics would serve the later Greeks as vehicles for the celebration of a hero cult in which figures of a mythical past, who mingled with and were often sired by the gods, were bigger, braver, and more beautiful than ordinary humans. These characters, whom the seventh-century B.C.E. poet and mythmaker Hesiod called "the divine race of heroes," became associated with particular places and societies in Asia Minor and Greece, their tombs—often on ancient Mycenaean sites—serving as unifying sacred centers.

The much-argued Homeric question makes it evident that a single poet named Homer might never have existed. The fact that so many places claim him as a son—Chios, Athens, Ionian Asia Minor, to mention only a few—makes him somehow the property of all Greece. It is likely that the work of "Homer"—especially the epic of wandering, the *Odyssey*—was at least in part a product of the Ionian migrations, with even Eastern influence, indicated by the sometimes sympathetic treatment of the Trojans in the *Iliad*.

Whether two Homers, a whole guild of Homeric bards, or one Homer composed the *Iliad* and the *Odyssey*, these works, with the seventh- and sixth-century B.C.E. *Homeric Hymns* by the Homeridae ("Sons of Homer") and the works of Hesiod—especially his creation story in the *Theogony*—are the source-books for much of what we know of Greek mythology of the pre-classical archaic period. In fact, Greeks of the later classical period used these works, almost as history sources, in schools, and the body of Greek mythology continued to grow and become more elaborate, especially in the fifth-century B.C.E. hands of the great Athenian dramatists Aeschylus, Sophocles, and Euripides and the poet Pindar. When we speak of Greek mythology we generally refer to the accumulated body of material that would have been known, for instance, to Aristotle and Alexander the Great at the beginning of the so-called Hellenistic Age in the fourth century B.C.E., with some augmentation from the later works of such literary figures as Apollonius of Rhodes and Apollodoros, whose works owe much to the stories told by the early-fifth-century B.C.E. writer Pherecydes of Leros.

It should be noted, however, that until the Hellenistic period, when Apollodorus, Hyginus, Diodorus Siculus, and others collected myths as more of an intellectual than a religious exercise, there was no single compilation of Greek mythology that could be compared, for instance, to the Bible or the *Vedas* and other collections of India. The myths were not necessarily doctrinal in any sense. They were part of a common spiritual heritage, taught in childhood by the women of the household and later interpreted and questioned by teacher-philosophers such as Socrates, Plato, and Aristotle and by the writers and dramatists such as the ones mentioned above. If there was any sense of a canonical source, it would have been centered on the ancient works of Homer, the Homeridae, and Hesiod. More important is the fact that out of this "canon," which itself reached back through earlier sources both to the ancient Indo-European myth-patterns and to some extent to the pre–Indo-European mythologies of the eastern and western Mediterranean, emerged a rich and complex mythological tradition that reflected a uniquely Greek view of humanity and of the relation of humanity to the inexplicable forces of the universe. At the center of this tradition is the pantheon known as the twelve Olympians, the family of gods and goddesses that dominates the classical Greek religion, a religion that to a great extent transcended differences between local practices and traditions.

The eventual arrangement of the Olympian gods into a relatively neat family is certainly a reflection of Mycenaean family and court arrangements. Zeus, who is associated with light, sky, and the thunderbolt, sits above all as the pater familias. As in the case of the great Mycenaean House of Atreus, for instance, his background and rise to power are marked by violent and sometimes cannibalistic taboo-breaking progenitors and cataclysmic wars, as described in the Greek creation myth of Hesiod. Zeus is a dispenser of often arbitrary justice, sometimes a doting father to his daughters, and nearly always a philanderer. His actions are based firmly in the "rights" of the Indo-European patriarchal hierarchical social system. His sister and wife Hera, the goddess of matrimony, is the forerunner of the nagging wife of later comedy who watches her philandering husband's every move and takes extreme measures to assert her wifely position.

An aspect of what the Greeks expected of women and womanhood is reflected in a sometimes Olympian, another sister of Zeus, Hestia, goddess of the hearth, who represents the patriarchal Greek ideal of the woman who says little and tends to the home. In keeping with her anonymity, there are few myths involving Hestia.

The most important of Zeus's and Hera's brothers is Poseidon, the god of the sea, who is also closely associated with horses and perhaps, therefore, with the traditional Indo-European horse mythology. Poseidon and Zeus and their non-Olympian brother Hades (he lives in the underworld, a place that shares his name) represent the three essential powers of sky, sea, and underworld. In what is a bow to the ancient pre-Indo-European tradition of earth as mother, the fourth element of the arrangement of the world, earth itself, is represented by Demeter, the sister of Zeus, whose name, in fact, suggests motherhood. But in keeping with the patriarchal essence of the Indo-European cosmos, earth and the mother are diminished in importance, and earth and earthlings have become the playthings of the sky gods. This fact is evident, for instance, in the myth of the rape of Persephone, a story most elaborately told in the first *Homeric Hymn* to Demeter.

The younger generation of the heavenly family includes several sons and daughters of Zeus by various immortals. Hermes is a trickster god who, in the Indo-European tradition, is involved in cattle raiding (as a child he stole Apollo's cows) and who leads the dead to Hades. He has a genital aspect in the stone pillars or herms set along roads and in front of houses, perhaps to mark the way or to bring fertility. These pillars often sport erect phalluses. Hermes is also a messenger for his father. His mother is Maia, the daughter of the Titan Atlas, best known for his holding up of the world. Maia's name recalls that of the Indian Maya, who represents illusion and magic, characteristics appropriate to the mother of a trickster.

Two sons of Zeus with Hera are less interesting than their more adventurously conceived siblings. Ares was the god of war. Hephaistos was the god of the crafts, a version of the typical Indo-European smith god, which we find playing more important roles, for instance, in both Celtic and Germanic mythologies. Ares and Hephaistos are sometimes treated rather comically. Hephaistos is lame as a result of his having been flung out of Heaven for attempting to protect his mother, Hera, from Zeus's physical abuse. He is married to his highly erotic and beautiful sister Aphrodite, with whom his better-looking brother Ares has an affair. Aphrodite was said to be the daughter of Zeus and the nymph Dione or, according to Hesiod, of the sea-scattered semen of the castrated Ouranos. As noted above, many scholars believe Aphrodite to be of Eastern origin, perhaps a version of the Western Semitic goddesses.

Other Olympians of probable Eastern origin were Apollo and his sometimes twin sister Artemis, born of the union of Zeus and Leto, a daughter of the Titans Coeus ("Intelligence") and Phoebe ("Moon"). Zeus and Leto coupled in the form of quails. Hera found out about this act of infidelity, and once again it was the woman who suffered the consequences. Hera had Leto chased around the world, as poor Io had been, but this time by the great Python, who would continue to be important in the Apollo myth. Artemis and Apollo were usually purported to have been born in Delos, but some say they were born in Ephesus or Lycia. It is this Asia Minor connection that makes appropriate Artemis's and Apollo's support of the Trojans in the *Iliad*. As anyone who has seen depictions of the many-breasted Artemis of Ephesus will realize, the Artemis whom the Greeks would see as a virginal huntress was at one time clearly a goddess of fertility.

Apollo was a complex god of many aspects, among them light, the sun, the arts, and, as his association with the great prophetic center of Delphi would indicate, prophecy. His motto, made so poignantly relevant in the tragic story of Oedipus, is "Know Thyself." He is a version, like the Vedic Indra and Rudra (later Shiva) and the Babylonian Marduk, of the Indo-European archer god, of the god-hero who defeats the monster—in this case, the Python. Almost always the monster/dragon/serpent is associated with the chthonic powers of the ancient great mother, whose powers are then taken over by the Indo-European patriarchy. In the case of the Greeks, this takeover is indicated not only by the replacement of the goddess cult at Delphi with that of Apollo, but by the myth of the trial of Orestes at Athens for the revenge killing of his mother Clytemnestra. At that trial, as depicted by Aeschylus in the *Eumenides*, Apollo absolves Orestes on the grounds that the mother is not the real parent, only the vessel of the seed placed there by the father.

One of the most, if not the most, prestigious of Zeus's children is the goddess Athena, patroness of Athens, goddess of wisdom, who, according to the first *Homeric Hymn*, was born, appropriately, of Zeus's painfully aching head, "bedecked in that/spangly gold war armor." With Apollo in the trial of Orestes, described in the *Eumenides*, Athena represents, in her highly masculinized form, the transformation of religious power from the mysteries of the female chthonic earth to the reason of the male-dominated sky.

Finally, there is the mysterious son of Zeus, the thirteenth Olympian, Dionysos. If we associate Apollo with the Apollonian approach to life—an approach centered in self-knowledge and moderation—we associate Dionysos with the Dionysian, the ecstatic. Both aspects are, of course, necessary to the full life (and for great art), and it is for this reason that Dionysos was said to inhabit Apollo's Delphi in the winter months.

One story says that Dionysos was the child of Zeus and Semele ("Moon") but that he was actually born of Zeus's thigh, having been sewed there after Semele 's death. Another association with Zeus is suggested by the name Dionysos itself, which etymologically develops from sounds relating him directly to Zeus—"Zeus-like" or even "Zeus's nursling."

Dionysos worship represented a "mystery" religion alternative to the official Olympian religion in Greece, as did the Eleusinian mysteries and, later, Orphism. These mystery religions and their mythologies coexisted with the civic religion. The great dramatic festivals of Athens, for example, were dedicated to Dionysos, and it was common for people of high civic stature to be associated with the Eleusinian mysteries.

Orphism, which came into its own in the Hellenistic period but which we now know existed as early as the sixth century B.C.E., was a movement that assimilated elements of the Olympian religion with those of Eleusis and Dionysos. It was not a terribly difficult step from these mystery religions to the dying-god myth that came to Greece in the first century C.E. with Paul and other Christian missionaries from the Middle East. By the time Paul and his followers made their way to the Greek colonies in Asia Minor, they found a population more than ready for the new religion. In a passage from the New Testament Acts of the Apostles (14:8–18) we are told, for instance, that when at Lystra Paul cured a man who had been "lame from birth," the people cried out, "The gods have come down to us in human form!" They called one of Paul's companions Zeus, and Paul himself "they called Hermes, because he was the spokesman"—Hermes traditionally being the messenger of the gods. The priest of

Zeus brought animals to be sacrificed, and even when Paul denied that he and his assistants were gods and attempted to preach their new religion of resurrection, "they barely managed to prevent the crowd from offering sacrifice to them." [Bonnefoy (1992), Buxton, Leeming (2003), Otto, Graves (1970), Hamilton]

GREEN MAN In European spring festivals, maypoles were set up to represent sacred trees, and a sacred marriage was enacted between a May Queen—a descendant of countless fertility goddesses reaching back to the Neolithic and the Sumerian Inanna—and a companion known as the Green Man, himself a descendant of all those ancient fertility heroes such as Dumuzi, Attis, and Adonis, many of whom were associated with sacred trees. A later relative of the Green Man was the Green Knight in the Middle English romance of *Sir Gawain and the Green Knight*, in which the theme of decapitation suggests the ancient ritual of fertile sacrifice for the good of humanity, a process reenacted in the Christian story of Jesus, who died on the "tree"-cross and was resurrected in the spring, symbolizing a new spiritual fertility.

GRENDEL Grendel was the terrifying giant-monster who was confronted and defeated by the hero Beowulf in the Anglo-Saxon epic of than name. He lived with his equally terrifying mother in an underwater lair.

GRI-GUN Before Gri-gun all kings of Tibet were immortal because of a rope that tied them to Heaven, whence they could return after their earthly deaths. However, as predicted by a shaman, Gri-gun did not return to Heaven after his death. Instead, in the confusion of a duel, he cut his magic rope, was killed, and had no way of leaving the earth.

GU The smith god of the Fon people of Africa, Gu is the son of the divine twin creators Lisa and Mawu. He was sent to earth by the twins to become the instructive culture hero to the people.

GUANYIN The most popular of Chinese female deities is Guanyin (Kuan-yin, *kuan* being the earth and *yin* being the feminine power that balances the masculine *yang*). Guanyin is a version of the Mahayana Buddhist bodhisattva Avalokiteshvara. More often than not, Guanyin is depicted in female form as a provider of children and as a compassionate mother goddess. In Japan she is Kannon. Guanyin is sometimes Nu Ka, the goddess whose signs were the dragon, the snake, and the ocean snail. Sometimes she rides a dolphin.

Many stories are told of Guanyin. It is said that, living in her father's house, the young Guanyin had no interest in marriage, asking instead to live in the temple of the White Bird. Her furious father commanded the women of the temple to treat his daughter badly so she would give up her foolish plan and decide on marriage. The plot failed; while the women of the temple slept, the impossible chores assigned to Guanyin were done by various sympathetic and magical animals.

Guanyin's father assumed he had been betrayed by the temple women, so he set the temple on fire. The fire was immediately put out when Guanyin placed her hands over it. Her hands were miraculously unburned. His fury now uncontrollable, Guanyin's father had his daughter put to death. A tiger took the girl to the Land of the Dead, where she relieved the sorrows of the shades and her own fears with her beautiful singing. This infuriated the Lord of the Dead, who exiled Guanyin from his land. Guanyin thus returned to the earth, and she continues to live in solitude on an island where she sings songs of comfort for the suffering living and dead.

GUINEVERE In the Arthurian romances, including those of Chrétien de Troyes, the Welsh historian Geoffrey of Monmouth, and Sir Thomas Malory, Guinevere (Welsh Gwenhwyfar) is the wife of King Arthur and the beloved of Sir Lancelot. There are conflicting tales of Guinevere's origins. Some traditions hold that she was the daughter of Leodegan, who gave the Round Table to Arthur when the latter married his daughter. Her love for Lancelot led to the disruption of Camelot and the fellowship of the knights of the Round Table, and eventually to Arthur's death. Some say she married Mordred after Arthur's death. More often it is said that she retired to a nunnery.

GUN Gun was a descendant of the Chinese Yellow Emperor Huangdi and the father of Yu, one of the greatest of the ancient Chinese heroes. Gun and Yu play significant roles in the ending of the Chinese flood.

GWYDION Gwydion was known as the greatest of storytellers. A son of the Welsh mother goddess Don, he was the protector, and some say father, of Lleu Llaw Gyffes, the son of his sister, Aranrhod. Gwydion had magical powers and demonstrated aspects of the trickster. In the *Mabinogion* he used trickery to make the hero Pryderi go to war, and in battle he brought about his death.

Guanyin, Chinese goddess of mercy

HACHIMAN The Japanese chronicles entitled *Kojiki* tell us that Hachiman, the Shinto god of war, was in life Ojin Tenno, a fourth-century emperor of Japan. From the late eighth century on, Hachiman was sometimes identified with Kannon or even with Amida Buddha. This last fact is in keeping with the tendency in Japan to see Shinto deities as local embodiments of Buddhist ones.

HADES Known by various names—Aides by the Greeks, and Pluto or sometimes Dis or Tartarus by the Romans—Hades was at once the name of the Greek underworld and the name of the god of the underworld, suggesting that the god Hades was originally simply a personification of the grim afterlife. In the developed Olympian mythology, Hades was the brother of Zeus and the husband of Demeter's daughter Persephone, whom he abducted and took to his forbidding home as his queen to help him rule over the unhappy dead. Hades was much feared; he did not join the other gods on Mount Olympus. Like the other gods, however, he was not a faithful husband; it was often said, for instance, that he fathered the Erinyes in an illicit relationship, but this is probably only because these unpleasant beings were believed to live under the earth. Known as the "Invisible One," Hades had a helmet

that made its wearer invisible. If Hades had a positive side, it was his metaphorical association with the gestation period of the agricultural cycle. That is, he was associated with the fertility power of the underground earth.

HAINUWELE The Wemale people of Ceram in Indonesia tell an animistic origin myth of resurrection in which the first animals and plants are the result of the sacrifice of the maiden Hainuwele. The myth's archetypal relatives are myths such as those of Corn Mother in Native North America and elsewhere.

Among the first nine families of the West Ceram people, who originally emerged from bananas in the Molucca Islands in what is now Indonesia, there was a hunter called Ameta, whose dog one night was attracted by the scent of a wild pig. The pig escaped into a pond but drowned. Ameta dragged it out of the pond and was surprised to find a coconut impaled on its tusk. Ameta was sure this coconut must be a great treasure because there were as yet no coconut palms on earth. He wrapped the coconut like a baby in a cloth, decorated it with a snake figure, and took it home. He planted it according to instructions received in a dream, and in three days a coconut palm tree had grown to full height. In three more days

A skeleton carries skulls in Mexico on the Day of the Dead to celebrate All Hallows (All Saints) Eve

it blossomed, and Ameta climbed it to retrieve some of the fruit. He cut his finger while collecting the fruit, and a baby girl emerged from the mixture of blood and sap. The dream messenger instructed Ameta to wrap the girl in the snake-decorated cloth and to bring her home. This he did, and he was amazed when, in a very few days, the girl, whom he named Hainuwele ("Coconut Branch"), was fully grown and defecating valuable things like bells and dishes.

Soon it was time for the first nine families to perform what is called the Maro dance at a place called the Nine Dance Grounds. As always, the women sat in the center of the grounds handing out betel nut to the men, who danced around them in a spiral. Hainuwele sat in the very center. On the first night she, too, handed out betel, but on the second night she gave the dancers coral, on the third fine pottery, and on each successive night something still more valuable.

The people became jealous of Hainuwele's wealth and decided to kill her. Before the ninth night's dance, they prepared a deep hole at the center of the ceremonial grounds, and during the dance they edged Hainuwele into the hole and covered her with earth.

Ameta soon missed his "daughter," and discovered through his magical skills that she had been murdered during the Maro dance. He immediately took nine pieces of palm leaf to the dance grounds and stuck them into the earth, the ninth one at the very center of the grounds. When he pulled out that piece of palm he found bits of Hainuwele's flesh and hair attached to it. He dug up the body, dismembered it, and buried the pieces, all but the arms, in various places in the dance grounds. Within minutes there grew the plants that are to this day the staples of the Ceramese diet.

Then the goddess Mulua Satene, angry at the murder of Hainuwele, an aspect of herself, struck several of the first people with an arm of the dead maiden, and these people become the first animals.

HALLOWEEN The term "Halloween" is the end product of a process by which "All Hallows Eve" became "All Hallow E'en" and then "Haloween" or "Halloween." All Hallows Eve is October 31, the eve of All Hallows Day (archaic "Allhallowmas," now "All Saints' Day"—November 1) in the Christian liturgical calendar. Something sacred is something "hallowed," and "saints" become, in this sense, "hallows." Traditionally, Catholic Christians have prayed for the souls in Purgatory on All Souls' Day, the day after All Saints' Day. In recent practice, All Saints' Day and All Souls' Day have become conflated, and many Christians remember all of the dead souls or "saints" on All Saints' Day. A secular aspect of this fascination with the dead and the return of the dead as skeletons or other ghoulish forms—now expanded to include any outlandish "costume"—has become the celebration we know as Halloween. In Mexico the All Saints'–All Souls' celebration takes the elaborate form of the Day of the Dead.

HAM In Hebrew mythology, Ham was a son of Noah, the flood hero of the biblical Book of Genesis. He was said to be the ancestor of the Egyptians and Canaanites. Ham was punished for seeing his father's genitals and thus breaking a significant taboo.

HAN XIANG A student of the immortal Lu Dongbin, Han Xiang himself became one of the Eight Immortals of Chinese Daoism. Eventually he was led by his teacher to Heaven to eat the peaches of immortality.

HAN ZHONGLI The heavenly messenger and one of the Chinese Daoist Eight Immortals, he was taught by the first of the eight, Li Xuan.

HANNAHANNA Hannahanna was one of many names attributed to the mother of the grandmother goddess of the Hattians and Hittites in Anatolia.

HANUMAN The greatest of the Hindu monkey gods, Hanuman takes his immense strength from his father, the Vedic wind god Vayu, who is also the father of Bhima, one of the Pandava brothers in the *Mahabharata*. Hanuman is worshipped as a protector to this day in shrines in many parts of India. His primary deeds are recorded in the epic *Ramayana*. In that epic, Hanuman leads the war to free Sita, the wife of Rama, an avatar of the god Vishnu, from the demon Ravana in Lanka. As the son of the Wind, he is able to make the passage from India to Lanka (Sri Lanka/Ceylon) in one leap. He demonstrates his powers of self-denial and his loyalty to Rama by not rescuing Sita himself so that Rama can have the honor of doing so.

HAOMA Haoma is the ancient Iranian version of the Vedic soma. It was the "drink of immortality," stolen in ancient times from the gods and used in ecstatic rituals by the early Indo-Europeans, including the people of the pre-Zoroastrian reforms in Iran. Zoroaster (Zarathustra) rejected the use of haoma, and it has found its way back into his religion only as a nontoxic substitute drink used in certain rituals by priests.

HARA Hara is one of the many names of the Hindu god Shiva.

HARE The Hare is a trickster in the southeastern region of Native North America. Like many tricksters, he can also be a culture hero, as in the case of the Creek Indian Great Hare who, like the Greek Prometheus and many culture heroes, stole the civilizing element fire for his people. An African American version of the rabbit trickster, probably derived from an African trickster, is Brer Rabbit. An Aztec version is the Centzon Totochtin. Hares are themselves typically promiscuous and are, therefore, appropriate representations for the nearly always sexually hungry trickster.

As a secularization of the Christian feast of Easter—a holiday celebrating a kind of ultimate fertility in the resurrection from the dead of Jesus—the notoriously fertile rabbit has played an important role. The Easter Bunny leaves its eggs everywhere for children to find, and it is closely associated with the flowers of the newly arrived spring.

HARE KRISHNA The International Society for Krishna Consciousness, or ISKCON, or Hare Krishna in the United States, is the result of the philosophy of Swami Prabhupada, the twentieth-century worshipper of the Hindu Vishnu avatar Krishna. The practitioners of the movement work toward "Krishna consciousness" as a means of salvation from the horrors and entanglements of the current age. Methods employed in this process include self-discipline, especially in connection with sexuality; specific rituals; and the singing recitation of the Krishna mantra—"Hare Krishna, Hare Krishna; Krishna, Krishna, Hare, Hare; Hare Rama, Hare Rama; Rama, Rama, Hare, Hare"—accompanied by dancing.

HARI Hari is a name of the Hindu god Vishnu. It is associated with the divinity of Vishnu and his avatar Krishna. But

H

the *Vishnu Purana* tells us that Hari is any divine presence—the vehicle by which the absolute reality, Brahman, is made known.

HARI-HARA Especially in the Advaita Vedantism branch of Hinduism, Vishnu, who is also Hari, is combined with Shiva, who is also known as Hara, to form Hari-Hara, a representation of the oneness of all things—Time being Hara and Space being Hari—united as a kind of manifestation of the absolute, Brahman.

HARIVAMSHA The *Harivamsha* is a supplement to the Hindu epic the *Mahabharata*. It is a genealogy of the god Vishnu, who is sometimes called Hari.

HARPIES Often confused with the Furies, the Harpies ("Robbers"), according to Homer, were known for kidnapping people and making them disappear. Hesiod depicted them simply as flying maidens, but later writers held that they were monsters—birds with women's heads and terrifying claws with which they tormented such unfortunates as Phineas.

HARRISON, JANE One of the leading figures in the Cambridge "myth and ritual" school of myth studies, the English scholar Jane Harrison (1850–1928) was an expert on Greek myth and ritual. With F. M. Cornford, A. B. Cook, and Gilbert Murray, she shared a particular interest in the origins of drama. She believed that myth was the narrative correlative of ritual. Her three most important works are *Prolegomena to the History of Greek Religion*, *Themis*, and *Epilegomena*.

HAUMIA The son of the Maori sky god Rangi and the earth goddess Papa, Haumia was a god of vegetation.

HAURVATAT One of the Amesa Spentas of the Mazdian pantheon of Zoroastrianism, Haurvatat represents prosperity and is associated with Amretat, or immortality. Both are grouped with the earth goddess Spenta Armaiti (Spendarmat).

HE XIANGU The eighth of the Chinese Daoist Eight Immortals, He Xiangu was female. She became immortal when she ate the "mother of pearl stone."

HEAVEN Heaven is a term used relatively loosely in many religious and mythic traditions to refer to the sky—the heavens—or more specifically to the world of the gods. As a paradise or place of rest after death, Heaven has parallels in many traditions, as, for instance, somewhat philosophically, in the Pure Land of Pure Land Buddhism or *svarga*, the Hindu Heaven of Indra, which state the worthy may hope to attain after death. In Judaism and Christianity, Heaven is where Yahweh/God lives. For Christians it is the place to which Jesus, after his resurrection, ascended and to which the Virgin Mary was bodily assumed after her death. In Christianity, Heaven is more particularly associated with the afterlife than it is in Judaism. In some Christian traditions, Heaven is where bodiless souls in a state of grace go after their sins are purged—sometimes in a place or state called Purgatory. After a general resurrection, these souls will, like the Virgin Mary, regain their bodily forms. Heaven is opposed to the concept of Hell in the Abrahamic traditions. In Islam, Heaven is *Jannat al-na'im* ("Gardens of Delight"), the joys of which are amply described in the *Qur'an*. In his ascent, Muhammad visited the "Seven Heavens."

HEAVENLY WEAVER GIRL In a Chinese stellar myth, the Weaver maiden was the daughter of the August Sun. She was obsessed by her weaving, which helped to maintain the order of the universe. When her father married her to the Heavenly Cowherd, she became obsessed with her husband rather than with her weaving, so much so that the Sun had to separate the couple. So it is that they live as stars at opposite ends of the heavenly river we call the Milky Way. On the seventh day of the seventh moon of each year, however, the Weaver Maiden crosses the Milky Way on a bridge of magpies and visits with her husband. Perhaps this myth reflects an aspect of Chinese peasant life, in which the husband often spent weeks away from home working in faraway fields while the wife attended to domestic chores at home.

HEBE Hebe was a daughter of the king and queen of the Greek deities, Zeus and Hera. As would have been common in actual Greek society, she waited on her parents and their Olympian family. Later she married the deified Herakles and bore him two sons. She had the power to convey youthfulness, and with that in mind, the Romans knew her as Juventas.

HEBREW MYTHOLOGY The development of the Hebrew-Israelite mythology, which was central to the eventual emergence of Judaism, was influenced by the mythologies of Egypt, by the mythologies of indigenous religions of Canaan, and later by the traditions of the Babylonians. The mythology, as revealed in biblical scripture (*Torah* and related texts, the Old Testament), would eventually, however, follow a highly individual course.

The late-second-millennium Hebrew influx into Canaan is shrouded in mystery. This is because at first it was too insignificant in size to have much impact compared with larger, more unified cultures such as the Assyrian, Egyptian, or Hittite. Furthermore, as in the case of earlier events, such as those surrounding the patriarch Abraham, what information we have about the exodus from Egypt is deeply imbedded in biblical tradition containing many elements that are clearly mythical rather than historical.

Bits of information do provide some clues to the migration and the religion of the migrants. During the turmoil surrounding the Akhenaton religious revolution, Egypt had gradually lost its hold on Canaan. Diplomatic letters of the period indicate a concern among Egyptians about the presence of "Habiru" or "apiru" (essentially "foreigners"). It is possible that "Habiru," which seems to have referred to several tribes, including the future Israelite Hebrews, became "Hebrew" and that in the situation surrounding these people we have the basis for the biblical story of the Exodus. It is evident that these Habiru under their jurisdiction were outsiders as far as the Egyptians were concerned. Topographical lists of Amenhotep III and Ramses II refer to "the land of nomads [of] Yahveh" to the east of the Delta in Sinai, suggesting that the religion of the early Hebrews in Canaan was probably close in spirit to the beliefs of other small neighboring clan-based tribes, such as the Moabites, Ammonites, Edomites, and Midianites. In Exodus 2 the famous story of Moses and the Burning Bush takes place in Midian, which was in the northwestern Arabian Peninsula (modern Hijaz). The Midianites have sometimes been thought to be the remnants of the Hyksos people, who had once controlled and then been expelled from Egypt, and who were said to have provided Moses not only with a wife but with important elements of the Yahweh cult.

The Hebrews pass through the parting sea

In any case, it seems likely enough that nomadic herders of various tribes, who were unified by varying degrees of kinship and common religion that left them in conflict with Egyptian culture, wandered out of northern Egypt, where Semitic non-Egyptian tribes had lived for some time. These tribes would have moved into Canaan around 1250 B.C.E. In support of this scenario are Egyptian documents suggesting that some of the Habiru were slaves who ran away and were pursued (Weinfeld, p. 484). When and how these tribes had first come to Egypt is unclear. It is possible that, as the biblical accounts suggest, they were the descendants of nomads who wandered from Mesopotamia early in the second millennium into Canaan and then to Egypt, perhaps fleeing drought and famine.

What can be said with some assurance is that the early Hebrews in Canaan, whether before or after the migration of the 1200s, would have been a loosely related group of seminomadic tribes whose livelihood came from herding and occasional farming. Kinship groups would have been ruled by male heads of family and in some cases would have worshipped family or clan deities. According to Jewish tradition, the clans as a whole traced their ancestry from Abraham to the patriarch Jacob, whose name was changed to Israel, which made the Hebrews the Children of Israel.

The Hebrews who came to Canaan would have interrelated with other Semitic migrants—Edomites, Moabites, Midianites, and Ammonites, for example—who spoke Canaanite Semitic languages related to Hebrew and who all had dominant patriarchal clan gods. The new migrants would have settled inland, as the coastal lands would have been populated by the various Canaanites, although some of the newcomers did apparently move into Canaanite cities, including the city that would become Jerusalem. It seems likely that the Hebrews both fought against and learned from the people around them. At first nonliterate, they learned the language of the Canaanites and adopted their writing skills. Canaanite religion was attractive to some of the Hebrews, but the Yahweh religion remained strong and would become the basis of what the Israelites saw as their God-given right as the nation of Israel to the land of Canaan.

It was the struggle for settlement land against the indigenous Canaanites, the smaller immigrant tribes, and especially the Philistines that led to the cohesion of the Hebrews into a military power. The earliest reference to Israel itself comes in the reign of Merneptah, the son of Ramses II. We know that at the end of the eleventh century B.C.E. the Hebrew clans united behind a monarchy. The first king of Israel was said to be Saul, who suffered several defeats at the hands of the Philistines. Saul was followed by David, of the clan of Judah, in about 1010. King David defeated the Moabites, the Edomites, the Ammonites, and the Arameans, as well as other Canaanite and Philistine rivals. He established his capital at the Canaanite (specifically Jebusite) city of Jebus (Jerusalem) and, during a forty-year reign, was greatly responsible for what is known as the golden age of Israel.

At the end of the second millennium, soon after the death of David, Solomon became the priest-king of Israel, and although tolerant of the religions of the indigenous people, he built a great temple for Yahweh in Jerusalem. In connection with Solomon, we get a glimpse of the Arab culture in the south of the Arabian Peninsula with the visit by the Queen of Saba (Sheba) to Jerusalem (2 Chronicles 9:1–12).

Soon after Solomon's death in about 922, a civil war erupted and two states emerged—Israel in the north and Judah, with Jerusalem as its capital, in the south. Meanwhile, the greater empire established by David and Solomon was already in the process of disintegration. The Arameans and Edomites had rebelled in Solomon's time, and now both Israel and Judah were threatened by the rising Assyrian power from Mesopotamia. In the middle of the ninth century, under King Ahab, Israel, in alliance with the Arameans and the Phoenicians, first defeated and then, after infighting with the Arameans, was defeated by the Assyrians.

The mythology of the *Torah*, or "Law," technically the first five books—the *Pentateuch*—of the Hebrew Bible, is traditionally attributed to Moses. Given the various versions of particular events and obvious changes in emphasis, style, and chronology in particular books, however, the actual composition of the *Torah* is now generally traced to several sources. The earliest is referred to as the Yahwist author, or simply "J" (the German Jahweh), because of his use of the name Yahweh for the creator god. "J" apparently wrote in southern Israel (Judah) during the early monarchy, that is, around 950 B.C.E. A rival document by an Elohist writer, or "E," because of the use of the name Elohim for the high god, was written in northern Israel in about 850 B.C.E., although it clearly makes use of much older oral material. The material of "J" and "E" were combined in about 750 B.C.E.

King Nebuchadnezzar of Babylon made several forays into Judah, each time setting up puppet regimes and taking away prominent Judeans into exile in Babylon. In this way, like the Assyrians before him, he hoped to prevent future rebellions and the reestablishment of hostile regimes within his empire. During the last attack on Jerusalem in 586 B.C.E. he sacked the city, destroyed the temple, and took away the rebellious puppet king and still more Judeans.

It was during the Babylonian exile that the captives from Judah emerged fully as Jews in the religious sense. Unlike earlier Israelite captives of the Assyrians, the Babylon Hebrews were not forced to become assimilated into the dominant culture. With the tenth- through eighth-century Hebrew stories as a foundation, many of the Hebrews in exile developed rules of conduct and prayers to support the exclusive Yahweh religion that gave them identity. The way was clearly paved for the development of synagogue worship and the emergence of rabbinical interpretation and authority.

Exilic and post-exilic (587–400 B.C.E.) priestly writers, usually designated as "P," assimilated and somewhat altered the "J" and "E" sources and added a great deal of material on genealogies, liturgies, temple ceremonies, and rules. And to the original stories were added eventually the other books of the Jewish Bible, probably compiled by several writers, including an eighth-century B.C.E. figure labeled by scholars as the Deuteronomic Historian or "DH." The Pentateuch and the added books—the Prophets, various Writings, and the Apocrypha—form what some refer to now as a whole as the *Torah* and what Christians call the "Old Testament," to differentiate the Jewish scriptures from the purely Christian ones ("New Testament") in the Christian Bible.

Much of the mythology of the Hebrew-Israelites was clearly intended to justify the Hebrew conquest and settlement of Canaan eventually described in Prophets, the six biblical books known as Joshua, Judges, 1 and 2 Samuel, and 1 and 2 Kings. The justification of conquest is based on the belief in a single god, who gradually emerged from the clan and tribal god of Abraham. The mythology suggests that this god, later identified as Yahweh, favored the Hebrew-Israelites, and, therefore, the Jews, above all peoples of the earth. He favored them so much that even though Canaan was heavily populated by other peoples—most of them fellow Semites—it was only right that they should take it for themselves. This was so because the Lord had promised this land to his chosen people in a covenant made with the patriarch Abram-Abraham and reaffirmed with Isaac, Jacob-Israel, and Moses. The special relationship of an "only" and "living" deity directly with a whole people marked a significant change in the religion and mythology of the Middle East. Deities such as those of the Sumerians, Assyrians, Hittites, Canaanites, and Philistines were clearly metaphorical and therefore easily assimilated by various peoples at various times (including many of the pre-exilic Hebrew-Israelites, who required the teachings and admonitions of the patriarchs, judges, prophets, and priests to turn them away from "pagan" worship). But for Judaism, as it developed, the divine was represented only by a "jealous" and not always compassionate god who had no divine rivals or companions. He was a god who reigned alone, essentially without a consort, or female counterpart, as at once a weather-storm deity, a god of judgment, and a war god, but who contained within himself aspects of the old deities who concerned themselves with fertility and life on earth. This fertility concept is indicated by the establishing by the patriarchs of altars to Yahweh specifically on sites sacred to the Canaanites and their fertility-based religion in Hebron, Bethel, and elsewhere.

In the old fertility religions, goddesses, of course, had played a significant role. But there was no place for a sexual pagan goddess consort in the concept of a god who reigned alone as the special patron of the Israelites. Even when certain kings of Israel advocated the worship of Baal or the *baalim* ("gods") for agricultural purposes, the worship of the goddess seems to have been perceived by leaders of the Yahweh cult as a threat to the community, certainly to its patriarchal arrangements (see, e.g., 1 Kings 18:17–19). In the Hebrew Bible, Asherah was the name associated with the old goddess figures. As a fertility goddess, Asherah, like the fertility god Baal, was at first attractive to the Israelites when they moved from a nomadic to an agricultural lifestyle. Represented by phallic objects called *asherim* and prayed to at particular cult places, she was seen by the Hebrew prophets as a real threat to the Yahveh religion. Jeremiah (7:44), for instance, condemned the Israelites' popular cult worship of the so-called Queen of Heaven, who was thought to ensure fecundity.

A possible indication of an earlier view of the feminine aspect of deity exists in Proverbs (8:22–31), where Wisdom, personified as a woman, is said to have been with Yahweh during the creation. The role of Wisdom in this context may be said to resemble that of the Canaanite goddesses who became the active agents of the reality of the gods, a role that bears some resemblance to that of the *Shakti* in Hinduism. Furthermore, in Jewish mysticism there is the tradition of the *shekhinah*, the feminine form of the divine. The original Hebrew word referred to the Lord's presence in the temple at Jerusalem. For some, the *shekhinah* as God's feminine aspect is thought to be present especially during the twenty-four hours of the Sabbath.

The creation myth of Judaism, also accepted by Christianity and in great part by Islam, is contained in the first two chapters of *Bere'shit* ("in the beginning"), or Genesis, the first book of the *Torah*. The story is clearly written by two writers at different times, and there are significant conflicts between the two versions, especially in connection with the creation of humans. Genesis 1:1–2:3 is generally attributed to the so-called priestly tradition that emerged in the fifth century B.C.E. during or

H

following the Babylonian exile. The creator is referred to as Elohim, the plural form including, presumably, all the Middle Eastern gods, or *els*. Furthermore, there is evident influence of the Babylonian *Enuma elish* in the vision of what might be called the early geography of the Hebrew creation story. There is also apparent Egyptian influence in the idea of Elohim speaking the world into existence.

The heroes of Hebrew mythology are many, including especially the ancient patriarchs of the mythological past, Abraham, Isaac, and Jacob (Israel), as well as Jacob's son Joseph. The great hero of developed Judaism is Moses, whose canonical story is the one contained in last four books of the Pentateuch: *Shemot* ("names"), or Exodus; *Vayiqra* ("and he called"), or Leviticus; *Bemidbar* ("in the wilderness"), or Numbers; and *Elleh hadevarim* ("these are the words"), or Deuteronomy. It is a story told from at least three perspectives, reflecting the realities of three periods in Hebrew-Jewish history. For the Yahwist writer of the "golden age" of King David, Moses is a true hero and follower of the great and often harsh king of the universe, Yahweh. The somewhat later Eloist writer, perhaps using earlier oral sources, develops the mythological aspect of Moses' biography, including his unusual birth circumstances, but stresses his talents as a military and clan leader. The post-exilic priestly writers acknowledge Moses' leadership but raise up Aaron as a priestly hero and emphasize the events that serve to justify aspects of temple-based Jewish laws and traditions. The story is an amalgamation of these three perspectives.

In Exodus we step tentatively into history, or at least into a highly mythological rendering of what was probably an actual migration of "Habiru" (Hebrew) or Semitic foreigners from Egypt to Canaan in the thirteenth century B.C.E. This is the story covering the Pharaoh's order that the too-numerous Hebrew slaves be diminished by the drowning of their newborn boy children, the rescue of Moses from the bull rushes, the message to Moses from Yahweh in the Burning Bush, the events of the Passover, the parting of the Sea of Reeds, and the leading of the "Chosen People" to the "Promised Land" of Canaan.

Perhaps the most important mythic moment of the Exodus was God's gift to Moses of the Ten Commandments and the Book of the Covenant, the *Torah*, on Mount Sinai. The tablets containing the "Law" were stored in the portable tabernacle called the Ark of the Covenant, the symbol of Yahweh himself, which led the Israelites into battle. The ark would become an important element in Jewish mythology. Its cult was officially recognized by David after his conquest of Jerusalem (for Jews the City of David on Mount Zion). The first temple housed the ark and became the principal national and religious center of the Israelites. The Ark disappeared when the Babylonians destroyed the Temple in 587 B.C.E., and it was not in the second temple of 516 B.C.E. The "lost Ark" has spawned a mythology that is both a part of Jewish religious culture and general popular culture.

The absence of the ark is of particular significance for Jewish worship. It is probable that synagogues, containing *Torah* "arks" representing the lost Ark of the Covenant, were founded in Babylon during the exile. When the required pilgrimage to the temple in Jerusalem became impossible, synagogue worship could serve as a substitute not only in Babylon but everywhere else after the temple was destroyed in 70 C.E.

The heroes of the Israelite conquest of Canaan are many, and with them we make tentative steps from myth into legend and then history. The first hero is Joshua, whose role as the leader of what in fact was a historical invasion is clearly mythical. As Joshua leads the Hebrews into Canaan, the Jordan

River, faced by the Ark of the Covenant, parts (Joshua 3–4). Amidst the blowing of ram's horns and led by the ark, Joshua leads the attack on and conquest of Jericho. Then, in the tradition of holy war, the Canaanite people are killed as a sacrifice to Yahweh. After several more victories, Joshua presides over a Covenant ceremony at Shechem, where he bids farewell to his people (23–24).

Two important heroines are Deborah, a visionary judge, and Jael, who succeeded in killing a Canaanite general single-handedly. Another hero is Gideon, who with only a small force defeated the Midianites, former friends and apparent Yahweh worshippers who had provided Moses with a wife. A popular favorite among Old Testament heroes was Samson, an ascetic or Nazirite around whose life many apocryphal tales of Herculean deeds were built. As a grown man he killed a thousand Philistines with a donkey's jawbone (Judges 15:15). But after being seduced, betrayed, and shorn of the locks that constituted his great strength by the femme fatale Delilah (the femme fatale being a traditional enemy of the patriarchal hero in myth and literature), he was captured and blinded. Eventually regaining his strength, he sacrificed his own life by causing a temple to crash down upon his Philistine captors (Judges 16, 28–30).

Many heroic legends surround the historical figure of King David. As a boy he defeated the gigantic Philistine warrior Goliath with a slingshot, and after various victories and setbacks was actually crowned King of Judah and later of a united Israel. Most important, he conquered the city of Jebus (later Jerusalem), which had long been a Canaanite religious center.

David battles Goliath

H

It was David whose armies finally defeated or expelled the Philistines and Canaanites and secured the borders promised by Abraham's god (2 Samuel, 2–20). It is said that through the prophet Nathan, Yahweh established a covenant with David; descendants of David would rule Israel forever (2 Samuel 7:2–16).

According to the story, it was through the machinations of Bathsheba, the wife stolen by David from the Hittite Uriah, that Solomon, Bathsheba's son, succeeded David as king. It was Solomon who solidified his position by murdering David's oldest son and rightful heir, who built the first temple to house the Ark of the Covenant, and who was given a special blessing of wisdom by Yahweh (1 Kings 1:1–2:25; 5:1–8:51). After Solomon's death, a rebellion of the ten northern tribes developed and they formed a separate kingdom, Israel, in the north. The Davidic dynasty, supported by the tribes of Judah and Benjamin, formed the nation of Judah, with its capital in Jerusalem.

The third major part of the Hebrew Bible is the Writings (*Kethuvim*). Perhaps the most memorable story of heroism in this section is contained in the Book of Ruth. The story goes that an Israelite and his wife Naomi escaped a famine by moving to Moab. There the couple's two sons married Moabite women, one of whom was Ruth. When both her husband and sons died, Naomi, wishing to return to Israel, suggested that her daughters-in-law remain in Moab and take new husbands. Ruth, the epitome of loyalty, who loves and respects Naomi, determines to accompany her to Israel. There, advised by Naomi, she visits the elderly Boaz, who falls in love with her. In spite of being advised by Boaz to find a younger man, Ruth proclaims her love for the old man and marries him. Ruth later gives birth to Obed, who will become the father of Jesse and the grandfather of David.

Still other biblical heroes were the prophets, who reminded the Israelites of their misguided ways before, during, and after the Babylonian exile. These include, among many others, Elisha, Isaiah, Jeremiah, and Ezekiel. One such prophet, of mythical dimensions, was Daniel (Danel), whom Yahweh protected even in the lion's den in Babylon (Daniel 6:1–28). An important heroine was Judith, a widow who in the extra-canonical Apocrypha was said to have decapitated the Assyrian general Holofernes, saving Jerusalem and bringing riches to the temple.

HECATE An earth goddess of the night and magic, Hecate was particularly associated with the dead souls of the underworld and with sorcery and witchcraft. But she was also benevolent, especially to farmers, perhaps because she understood the dark secrets of the reproductive earth. Hecate was said to have witnessed the rape of Persephone and was the crone aspect of a Greek version of the Indo-European triune goddess, of which Demeter would have been the mother and Persephone (Kore) the daughter.

HECTOR The oldest son of King Priam and Queen Hecuba of Troy, husband of Andromache, and father of Astynaz, Hector was the greatest of the Trojan heroes in Homer's *Iliad*. It was he who killed Achilles' friend Patroclos in battle and thus caused the Greek hero to give up his boycott and to return to the war. When Hector saw the infuriated Achilles approaching, he lost his nerve and fled. After running three times around the city walls he was caught and killed. Achilles dragged the body of Hector around the city in a display of pride. But directed by Zeus, he responded to the petitions of Priam and returned the body to the Trojans for burial.

HECUBA Born of Thracian or Phrygian parents, Hecuba became the wife of King Priam of Troy and the mother of Hector, Paris, Troilus, Cassandra, and others. After the Trojan War she was carried off with the other Trojan women as a slave. She was immortalized in a play named after her by the Greek playwright Euripides.

HEIMDALL The Norse god and son of nine mothers, who could hear and see all things, Heimdall was of the old Vanir race of fertility deities, specifically associated with water. His job under Odin's rule was to guard Bifrost, the flaming rainbow bridge that connected Asgard, the home of the gods, to Midgard, the human world. His enemy was Loki, who eventually killed him.

HEITSI-EIBIB Heitsi-Eibib is a first man, trickster–culture hero of the Hottentot people in Africa. Given his miraculous conception—his mother, a cow, conceived him by eating a special grass—and various heroic deeds, he qualifies as a monomythic hero.

HEL This half-dead monster offspring of the Norse trickster, Loki, rules the Niflheim land of the dead, also named Hel (just as in Greece Hades was the name of the underworld as well as of the god of the underworld). Hel's mother was the giantess Angrboda. Her brothers, also fathered by Loki, were Fenrir the wolf and Jormungang the serpent. From her waist up Hel appeared to be normal woman. But from the waist down she was all rotting flesh.

HELEN OF TROY Helen was born of the Spartan princess Leda, who had been impregnated by the Greek father god Zeus. Zeus had conducted his liaison with Leda in the form of a swan. The story goes that Leda produced two eggs as a result of the swan's act and, although the versions differ somewhat, it is usually said that one egg contained Helen and Polydeuces (Pollox), one of the sacred twins, or Dioskouri, and the other contained the future wife of Agamemnon, Clytemnestra, as well as the second of the Dioskouri, Castor. Helen was raised in the court of Leda's husband, King Tyndareus, and was renowned for her extraordinary beauty. One story has it that Theseus took her off to Athens and that the Dioskouri conquered Athens and rescued her while Theseus was on his descent to the underworld. Back home, Helen was sought after by many noblemen, and she finally chose Menelaus, the heir to Tyndareus's throne and the brother of Agamemnon. Helen's former suitors agreed on an oath to uphold the honor of Helen and Menelaus's marriage. In time Helen gave birth to Hermione, who would later marry her famous cousin Orestes, the avenging son of the murdered Agamemnon.

A Trojan prince named Paris, who had been promised Helen by Aphrodite, paid a visit to Sparta and, while Menelaus was away for a while in Crete, seduced his hostess and eloped with her to Troy. When Paris refused to return Helen to Menelaus, the oath of the suitors was activated and the Trojan War was the result. According to Homer's *Odyssey*, Helen returned to Sparta after the war and settled down as the still beautiful but now also dutiful, hospitable, and even wise wife of Menelaus.

HELIOS A Greek personification of the sun, Helios (the Roman Sol) was born of the Titans Hyperion and Theia, though Homer sometimes equates him with Hyperion. His siblings were Selene ("Moon") and Eos ("Dawn"). According to Homer, Helios rose out of Oceanus in the east each day and returned to Oceanus in the west at evening time. Others say he had a magnificent palace in the east and that each day he drove across the sky in a chariot drawn by four horses to another palace or to Oceanus in the west. His son was the unfortunate Phaethon.

HELL Hell is a place of punishment after death for many mythological traditions. In Hebrew, Hell is *Sheol* (Greek *Gehenna*). In Christianity, Hell is a place inhabited by the Devil (Satan) and his fellow "fallen angels," who traditionally rebelled against God in a war in Heaven. In Islam, Hell is *Jahannam*, a specific place that is spoken of in the *Qur'an*. It has several levels and seven gates, with punishments allotted according to the severity of sins committed during life. Hell for Christians and Muslims is traditionally associated with hellfire. Dante 's Hell or Inferno in his *Divine Comedy* more closely resembles the Muslim Hell in its details and in its correlation between particular sins and punishments than it does the more traditional Hell of Christians and Jews. Dante's vision, however, was probably more influenced by classical views of the underworld, especially those of the Roman Virgil in the sixth book of the *Aeneid*, in which Aeneas witnesses various particular sufferings of the sinful dead on his way to visit his father. Like many heroes, Jesus was said to have descended to the underworld (Hell) after his death to "harrow" it and thus to release worthy pre-Christian humans, the victims with Adam and Eve of Original Sin.

In Norse mythology, Hel is both the name of the land of the dead in Niflheim and the name of the monstrous daughter of Loki who rules over it. We find this eponymous arrangement in the Greek Hades as well.

HELLEN Hellen was the son of the Greek flood heroes Deucalion and Pyrrha. He married Orseis, who gave birth to Aeolus, Dorus, and Xuthus, the ancestors of the Hellenes (Greeks).

HEPHAISTOS The Greek version of the Indo-European smith and fire god, Hephaistos (Roman Vulcan) was said by Homer to have been lame from birth. His mother was Hera. Some say he was fathered by Zeus; others say Hera produced him without a mate in revenge for Zeus's having so produced Athena. In any case, Hera was disgusted by his lameness and his general ugliness, so she flung him off Olympus. He landed in Oceanus and was raised by the sea nymphs Eurynome and Thetis. There he apparently learned to be a great craftsman, and eventually he returned to Olympus—some say by blackmailing his mother by trapping her in a magic throne he had devised and demanding the hand of the beautiful Aphrodite as the price of Hera's release. In any case, he did return to Olympus, and he did marry Aphrodite, and he became his mother's advocate against the philandering Zeus. Once, when Hephaistos took his mother's part, Zeus became so angry that he flung poor Hephaistos for the second time from Mount Olympus. There are those who say it was this fall that made him lame. He landed on the appropriately volcanic island of Lemnos.

Even though he created wonderful palaces for the gods and weapons for heroes, Hephaistos was sometimes an object of scorn, as he was, for instance, when Ares and Hephaistos' wife, Aphrodite, were having their notorious affair. In that case, however, Hephaistos used his talents to redeem himself. He took revenge on the guilty couple by capturing them in a net during the act of love and exposing them in that position to the ridicule of all the gods.

HERA The chief goddess of the Greek Olympian family, Hera was the wife and sister of Zeus and a constant critic of his philandering tendencies. As the protector of the institution of marriage and a goddess of childbirth, she reveals remnants of the Great Mother–fertility goddess she might have been in her earlier incarnation in prehistoric Argos, the place of her special sanctuary. The classical Hera reflects her commitment to the institution of marriage in her best-known quality, her cruelty to the victims of Zeus's philandering—women such as poor Io and Semele—and to the offspring of those women, especially Herakles. In her constant losing battle against her husband's infidelities she also reflects the place of women in the aristocratic and patriarchal Greek family.

Among Hera's offspring by Zeus are Ares and Hebe. Hephaistos is her son, too, but is usually believed to have been conceived without the participation of a male.

HERAKLES The great Greek hero Herakles (Roman Hercules) was conceived heroically in a union between the disguised Zeus and a human woman, Alkmene, a granddaughter of Perseus, during a night that Zeus extended to the length of three nights in order to prolong his pleasure. Theseus, whose myths are sometimes confused with those of Herakles, was also sometimes said to have been conceived in such a union, the god in his case being Poseidon. Zeus disguised himself as Alkmene's husband during his love bout, much as Uther Pen-

The Trojan Paris abducting Helen

Hera, the protector of marriage and childbirth

dragon would be disguised as Igraine's husband in the mating that would result in the birth of King Arthur.

Hera, disapproving of her husband's infidelity with Alkmene, sent two great serpents to kill the baby, who was at that time named Alcides but who would later become Herakles, but the child gleefully strangled them both. Throughout his early life Herakles was plagued by the enmity of Hera. But at the same time he established his reputation as a hero without equal. His strength was so great and so dangerous—sometimes fatally so—to those around him that his foster father, Amphitryon, sent him away to guard his oxen around Mount Cithaeron. In that role Herakles killed and thus rid Amphitryon and his neighbors of a terrible cattle-devouring monster lion.

From then on, Herakles wore the lion's skin as clothes and placed its head on his helmet and accomplished numerous heroic deeds. He freed Alcestis from death in Hades. He fought against Lapiths, Amazons, and centaurs. He helped Jason obtain the Golden Fleece. He was an insatiable lover of women and, according to some, also took his young squire Hylas as a lover. For killing an enemy of Thebes, King Creon gave the hero his daughter Megara as a wife, and the couple had several children, all of whom Herakles killed in a mad rage caused by the meddling Hera (according to some versions of the story, he killed Megara as well). Horrified at what he had done, Herakles went into exile. There are other cases of Herakles' losing control of his strength and becoming dangerous,

as, for instance, when he killed his mentor, the centaur Chiron, while driving away other centaurs.

It was the oracle at Delphi who told Herakles he must serve Eurystheus of Tiryns to purify himself and to achieve immortality. His eventual name, which means "Hera's Glory," was an attempt to placate the goddess, and Hera agreed to allow Herakles to become a god, as predicted by the oracle at Delphi, if he could accomplish the famous Twelve Labors for Eurystheus, through which the hero earned his name and represented the glory of Greece.

The Twelve Labors are as follows:

1. *The fight with the Nemean Lion.* The hero killed the fierce lion with his bare hands.

2. *The fight against the nine-headed Lernean Hydra.* The Hydra was a favorite of his enemy Hera. Herakles burned off its eight mortal heads and buried the immortal one.

3. *The capture of the Arcadian Stag.* The stag had golden antlers and brass hooves. Herakles was instructed to take it to Eurystheus alive. The hero succeeded in wounding it and carrying it alive to Eurystheus on his back.

4. *The capture of the Erymanthian Boar.* Eurystheus also ordered that this beast be taken alive. Herakles tired it

out in a chase through the snow and then trapped it in a huge net.

5. *The cleaning of the Augean stables.* Augeas, king of Elis, had a herd of 3,000 oxen, the stables of which contained thirty years of filth. Herakles was ordered to clean the stables in a day.

6. *The killing of the Stymphalian Birds.* Sacred to Ares, these horrid birds lived in Arcadia on a lake near Stymphalus. They had brazen claws and beaks and loved to eat human flesh. Herakles frightened them with the noise of a rattle given to him by Athena, and as the birds took flight he shot them with his arrows.

7. *The capture of the Cretan Bull.* This bull had been sent to Minos on Crete as a sacrificial animal by Poseidon, but when Minos decided to keep it for himself, Poseidon drove it insane and Herakles was ordered to capture it. Herakles did this and carried it back to Greece on his shoulders.

8. *The capture of the Mares of Diomedes.* King Diomedes in Thrace had mares that ate human flesh. When Herakles, with his friend Abderus, tried to capture them, Abderus was killed by Diomedes' men and was fed to the horses. The enraged Herakles managed to kill Diomedes and feed him to the horses. After this, the horses became tame, and Herakles took them to Eurystheus.

9. *The seizing of the girdle of Hippolyta.* Hippolyta, The queen of the Amazons, had a girdle (belt) that had been given to her by the war god, Ares. Eurystheus sent Herakles to obtain the girdle for his daughter Admete. Although Hippolyta agreed to give the hero the girdle, Hera stirred up the Amazons against Herakles, and according to one version of the myth, Herakles killed the queen in the ensuing battle and made off with the girdle.

10. *The capture of the Cattle of Geryones (Geryon).* Geryones was a three-bodied monster on the island of Erythia. His oxen were guarded by a frightening giant named Eurytion and a two-headed dog, Orthus. After he built the Pillars of Herakles on each side of the Straits of Gibraltar, the overheated hero shot arrows at Helios (the Sun), an act that so impressed Helios that he gave the hero his cup (boat) in which to sail to Erythia. After successfully killing the guards and Geryones, Herakles had many adventures driving the cattle back to Eurystheus. But after some time, he managed his task, and the king sacrificed the cattle to Hera.

11. *The obtaining of the golden apples of the Hesperides.* Gaia had given Hera the golden apples as a wedding present, and Hera had entrusted them to the care of the Titan Atlas's seven daughters, the Hesperides, and the dragon, Ladon. After finally discovering where the apples were (on Mt. Atlas), Herakles asked Atlas's help in obtaining them and even held up the world for him while the Titan went for the apples. But when he returned, Atlas at first refused to retake his place in holding up the world, and Herakles resorted to trickery to gain his freedom. Finally, he had possession of the apples, and he took them to Eurystheus, who allowed Herakles to keep them. Instead, Herakles gave them to Athena, who returned them to the Hesper-ides. Increasingly, Herakles' deeds were pleasing to his arch rival, Hera.

12. *The descent to the underworld to fetch Cerberus.* With Hermes and Athena, Herakles descended to the underworld on an assigned final task, which was to bring back the terrible monster dog Cerberus. He was able to free Theseus from the clutches of Hades and to gain the underworld god's permission to take Cerberus, as long as the taking of the animal did not involve force. Herakles accomplished his task by picking up the three-headed dog, carrying it up to Eurystheus, and then returning it to Hades.

After completing the Twelve Labors, Herakles was allowed to return to Thebes, but in another mad fit he killed his friend Iphitus and had to undergo another course of purification. Part of the process involved his living as a servant to Omphale, the Queen of Lybia, spinning and wearing women's clothes. Later he accomplished many feats and even helped the gods war against the giants. Finally, he fought for the hand of Deianeira in Calydon and lived well enough there until he killed a boy by accident and once more had to go into exile, this time with his wife. When the centaur Nessus tried to rape Deianeira, Herakles shot him. Nessus gave Deianeira some of his blood, claiming that when mixed with his semen that had spilled on the ground, it could be made into a potion to ensure her husband's fidelity. In fact, when the young woman soaked her husband's shirt in it and he put the shirt on, he suffered the agonies of death and she hanged herself. Like Jesus in a much later myth, however, Herakles was taken up to Heaven on a cloud. In this apotheotic ascension he became immortal and was finally accepted even by Hera, who allowed him to marry her daughter Hebe.

Herakles defeats the Nemean Lion

HERMAPHRODITUS Named for his handsome father, Hermes, and his beautiful mother, Aphrodite, Hermaphroditus was himself such a combination of their attractiveness that a nymph, Salmacis, near Halicarnassus on the coast of Asia Minor, became so enamored of him that she embraced him suddenly while he was bathing in her fountain. As she did so she asked the gods that they never be separated. The gods granted the nymph's wish, and the result was a beautiful youth who had both the breasts of a woman and the genitals of a male.

HERMES The Greek god Hermes (Roman Mercury) was born of a liaison between Zeus and Maia, the daughter of Atlas, the Titan who was condemned to hold up the world. Maia's name recalls that of the Indian Maya, who represents illusion and magic, characteristics appropriate to the mother of the god who was said to have invented such wonders as the lyre, the alphabet, numbers, and astronomy. With his traveler's hat, winged sandals, and caduceus, Hermes was clearly marked as his father's herald and messenger. He also assisted travelers. Stone pillars, or *herms,* often sporting erect phalluses, were set along Greek roads as markers and in front of houses, perhaps to bring fertility to the inhabitants. The phallic nature of some of the herms is appropriate for a god who was able to penetrate Hades itself, leading the dead there, and who was in some ways a trickster (tricksters being known for their sexual appetite). Hermes' earliest trickster act places him squarely in the Indo-European tradition of the cattle raid. A few hours after he was born in a mountain cave in Arcadia, the baby god escaped from his cradle and made his way to Pieria, where he rounded up the prize oxen of Apollo and drove them off to Pylos. Apollo discovered the theft, angrily carried the baby off to Zeus, and demanded the restoration of his cattle. But then the angry god was so charmed by the lyre already invented by the child that he allowed Hermes to keep the cattle.

HERMIONE The daughter of Menelaus and Helen of Troy, Hermione was married to Achilles' son Neoptolemus (Pyrrhus), who had killed King Priam at the fall of Troy and who, according to most sources, was killed by Orestes. Orestes had been promised Hermione, and after the death of Neoptolemus he married her.

HERO AND LEANDER A Greco-Roman myth tells the tragic story of how Leander, a young man from Abydos, swam across the Hellespont (Dardanelles) every night to visit his beloved Hero, a priestess of Aphrodite, in a tower in Sestus. Each night Hero kept a light in the tower blazing so that her lover could find his way, but one night a storm caused the light to be extinguished and poor Leander lost his way and drowned. When Hero found Leander's body on the shore, she killed herself.

HERO QUEST The central event in the universal hero myth, the heroic monomyth, is the quest, in which a hero—the representative of a culture—seeks some significant goal or boon for his people. Often the voyage involves archetypal stages such as the search for truth or riches or a lost loved one, a struggle with monsters, and the descent to the underworld. So Jason goes in search of the Golden Fleece, Parcifal in search of the Holy Grail, and the Buddha in search of enlightenment.

HEROES Since the days when humans believed that deities might actually "come down" to interact with us in the world, we have tended to leave gods to the theologians and philosophers and to find sources for awe and wonder in heroes, those special fellow humans infused to varying degrees with divine or superhuman qualities. There have always been both religious and secular heroes. Some, to be sure, have been incarnated deities, some have been humans with at least one divine parent, some have derived their power simply from their allegiance to divine purpose, and some have performed seemingly impossible deeds in the name of entities that have nothing to do with religions. Heroes have been fictional and historical. Our heroes reflect our priorities. Usually male in patriarchal cultures, they are often the offspring of the union of deities and mortals. To varying degrees, they possess superhuman qualities, but they are also genuinely human like us. Achilles, Herakles, Odysseus, Cuchulainn, Sigurd, Moses, Beowulf, Water Pot Boy, and Arjuna are all heroes whose powers come from some connection with divinity but who suffer the agonies and joys of human life.

Heroes are our personae in the world of myth, expressions of our collective psyches—first as cultures and then as a species. Cuchulainn reflects the Irish physical and psychological experience, and Achilles could not be anything else but archaic Greek. But when we compare the heroes of these various cultures, Joseph Campbell's heroic monomyth pattern emerges and we discover a hero who belongs to the Indo-European tradition, to Europe, and ultimately to all of humanity.

HEROIC MONOMYTH Moses, Jesus, Muhammad, Theseus, Glooskap, and King Arthur are heroes to their cultures; they are, to varying extents, culture heroes. But as Joseph Campbell has demonstrated, when we consider heroes and their myths comparatively, we discover a universal hero myth that speaks to us all and addresses our common need to move forward as individuals and as a species. "The Hero," writes Campbell, "is the man or woman who has been able to battle past his personal and local historical limitations to the generally valid, normally human forms" (1949, pp. 19–20). The essential characteristic of the universal hero myth is the giving of life to something bigger than itself. By definition, the true hero does not merely stand for the status quo; he or she breaks new ground. The questing hero is our cultural and collective psyche out on the edges of knowledge and existence.

Campbell's study of the hero myth—which relies on Carl Jung, Otto Rank, Lord Raglan, and others who have made comparative studies of the archetype, presents us with what, using a word coined by James Joyce, he calls the "monomyth." The hero of the monomyth undergoes a series of transformations as significant thresholds are crossed. Three essential elements make up the heart of the monomythic life: the Departure from home, the Adventure in the unknown world, and the Return with some new understanding. These three elements are framed by an appropriately heroic beginning and ending.

The hero's life often begins with a miraculous conception and birth. Waterpot Boy is conceived when a piece of clay enters his mother. The Aztec man-god Quetzalcoatl is conceived when a god breathes on his mother Chimalman in his form as the "morning." Hainuwele is born of the combination of coconut sap and a drop of blood. In the case of the Buddha, divinity enters the world through the agency of a white elephant in Queen Maya's dream. A clot of blood is the vehicle for the Blackfoot Native North American culture hero Kutoyis. Often the hero, the divine child (the *puer aeternus*), is born of a virgin. Almost always he or she comes at a time of great need—the darkest night of the cultural year, a time of general suffering.

Even to the most rational among us, conception and birth, like the emergence of spring from winter, are miraculous. In any case, the hope for a new beginning is ubiquitous. We long for the hero who can represent all of us—as a culture and indirectly as a species—a figure who belongs not to any one family but to humanity. The hero is conceived and born mysteriously because like the first human—Adam in the Middle East, Kamunu in Zambia, or the Djanggawal in Australia—he springs from the eternal essence. The hero is our second chance. The hidden place—the stable, the grove of trees, the cave—where the hero is born and the painful times in which he emerges remind us that even the gods require the elements associated with the mother—earth, flesh, pain—to enter the world as one of us.

Not surprisingly, the newborn hero is almost immediately threatened by the first of the "guardians at the gate" of the status quo: the kings, jealous fathers, or demons who cannot tolerate the presence of a force for new understanding. Thus Herod sends soldiers to kill any child who might be what the magi have called a new king in the Jesus birth myth. And when other magi announce the birth of Zoroaster to King Duransarum, he attempts to stab the child himself. Sigurd and Moses are hidden away for their own protection. Water Pot Boy is disguised as a pot until he is ready to break out of childhood into the heroic Departure and Adventure.

As a child, the hero must somehow prove himself or herself. Signs of the divine essence must shine through. Krishna, the avatar of the god Vishnu, kills a demoness while still in the cradle. The boy Arthur removes the sword from the rock. Theseus retrieves his father's shoes and sword. The Irish hero Cuchulainn, still a mere boy, kills the giant watchdog of Culann. Jesus amazes the Elders in the Temple. As the young wife of the Pandava brothers in the Indian epic the *Mahabharata*, Draupadi reveals her inner divinity when, through Krishna's power, the evil Kauravas fail to strip her of her miraculous sari.

Once adulthood is achieved, the hero frequently undergoes a preparatory period of isolation before receiving a call to action, which the hero sometimes initially refuses. Moses, the shepherd alone in the fields, is called by the Burning Bush, and his reluctance must be overcome by Yahweh himself. The Ojibwa Hiawatha prototype Wunzh is called during his lonely vision quest, but before he can begin his adult journey he must wrestle with the corn god, with divinity itself. Jesus must be tempted in the wilderness, and the Buddha must be tempted by the fiend Mara.

All of these events are preparation for the beginning of the hero journey, the Departure. Like Odysseus, who is reluctant to accept the call of the Greeks to leave wife, child, and possessions to fight in Troy, or like Tolkien's Bilbo and Frodo, who would rather not leave the comforts of Hobbit ways, the hero must leave home precisely because he must break new ground in the overall human journey. The old ways must be constantly renewed and new understandings developed. The Blackfoot Kutoyis must search for monstrous enemies of the people, the knights of the Round Table must give up the comforts of Camelot to achieve renewal through adventure, and Gilgamesh must leave home to seek eternal life.

The adventure of the hero is marked by several universal themes. The first of these is the search. Sometimes the questing hero looks for something lost. Odysseus's son Telemachos, Theseus, and Water Pot Boy all search for the Father. Gilgamesh, Jason, the Knights of the Round Table, Moses, and the East African Kyazimba seek objects or places—often lost ones—of potential importance to their cultures: the plant

Saint George, the hero, kills the dragon

of immortality, the Golden Fleece, the Holy Grail, the Land Where the Sun Rises, the Promised Land. More overtly "religious" or philosophical heroes such as the Buddha or Jesus look to less tangible goals: enlightenment or nirvana, the Kingdom of God.

The quest always involves difficult trials. There are frightening and dangerous guardians at each threshold the hero must cross—giants, dragons, sorcerers, evil kings. And there are tests. Herakles must perform the Twelve Labors; the Grail heroes must prove themselves through various deeds and, like heroes of many cultures, are tested by a femme fatale. This enchantress, a particularly popular nemesis of the patriarchal hero—Adam's Eve, Aeneas's Dido, Samson's Delilah—is the archetypal image of the dangerous sexual and merely personal alternative to the true goal.

Many heroes must die and descend to the place of death itself, sometimes as scapegoats for the mistakes of others. Jesus and Osiris die, as do the African heroine Wanjiru and the Ceramese heroine-goddess Hainuwele. In death, the hero is planted in mother earth and during that period of dark gestation confronts the terrors and demons of the underworld.

But the hero returns, usually in the spring. He or she is resurrected, as in the case of the African Wanjiru, Hainuwele, or Jesus. Several of these heroes become sources for material or spiritual food for their people: Osiris emerges from the earth as the god of grain, Hainuwele's buried limbs become veg-

H

etables, numerous Native American corn heroes and heroines become the staple food for their people, and for the Christian the resurrected Jesus is the "bread of life." These are all versions of the boon or great gift that the hero brings upon returning from the depths of the quest. Other versions include the corn culture brought back by the Ojibwa hero from his vision quest; the curing qualities of the Grail brought back by the successful Grail hero; the "Law," brought by Moses; the knowledge of enlightenment that is the Buddha's gift; the word of Allah that is Muhammad's; or knowledge of the runes, the result of the Norse god Odin's human and heroic act of hanging himself on the tree.

As an epilogue to the Departure, the Adventure, and the Return, the hero can make a second return, this time to achieve union with the cosmic source of his or her being. Jesus and the Virgin Mary ascend to God, and a legend has it that Abraham did, too. The Buddha, King Arthur, and Moses all undergo a kind of apotheosis, a union with the ultimate mystery. Like myths of creation and deities, those of heroes all seem to lead inevitably to that very strangest and most mystical expression of the human imagination, the concept of union, which, depending on era and tradition, has been called by many names, of which nirvana, enlightenment, individuation, self-identity, and wholeness are a few.

It is important to remember that in myths, as in dreams, all of the elements belong to the culture that "dreamed" them. The hero of the myth is, of course, culturally analogous to the Ego or Persona of dream. And the given culture, with the help of experience, tradition, and environment, also dredges up the particular gate guardians, trials, and quest goals. The hero myths we have, those available to us for comparison, are primarily from strongly patriarchal societies, and it is to the patriarchal ur-hero that emerges from these myths that we must look for insight into the collective psyche of our present world, even as we watch for indications of a new hero who might be emerging from the revival of the feminine and a new planetary mythology.

In the traditional patriarchal embodiment of the archetype, the hero's adventures, even when accomplished for the good of all, are dependent on his separateness from us. In the mindset determined by our hierarchical sky god bias, as God is above and beyond us, so is mind separate from matter, soul from body, and the hero from us. Even the heroes who live humble lives and preach nonaggressive, non-hierarchical approaches to life's problems—heroes such as Jesus, the Buddha, Gandhi, and Martin Luther King, Jr.—are isolated from us, capable of deeds that are, in effect, superhuman. Whether Gilgamesh or a super-athlete, the patriarchal hero has powers greater than ours.

Although, necessarily, born of a woman, the hero quickly becomes separate from her. The Buddha's mother, like many, almost always humble, hero mothers, dies after the birthing function is completed. Mary is told by Jesus that he has more important things to think about than her or his family. Theseus's mother, like King Arthur's, is tricked into intercourse, being little more than a vessel for Poseidon's seed.

The patriarchal hero's initiation often involves a violent manly deed, such as the strangling of a monster, or the overpowering of an antihero. The quest trial, too, emphasizes physical prowess more often than not, and includes the defeat of death itself. Not surprisingly, the patriarchal myth is a celebration of stereotypically male characteristics, and specifically of male power. Sky god power is transmitted to an earthly son, and the feminine element of life is greatly diminished.

For the most part, we can relate to the traditional hero archetype to the extent that we understand the need to succeed, to persevere against seemingly impossible odds. And we can relate to the nationalistic, familial, or ethnic loyalty represented by most of these heroes. These, after all, are values we teach in our schools, homes, legislatures, and places of worship.

Archetypal patterns, however, like individual heroes, can evolve. Secular heroes, for instance, have reflected secular values and understandings of particular eras. The secular world changes more easily than the religious world. T. S. Eliot's Prufrock and Albert Camus's "stranger" are negative representatives, antiheroes of the age of existentialism who express a sense of impotence, disillusionment, and the absence of spirituality. It could be argued, however, that Prufrock and the existential heroes of the late nineteenth and twentieth centuries, as well as the heroes of popular music and sports today, are merely tangents of the old patriarchal myth. Prufrock and the "stranger" would like the old order if they could find it, and the adored singer of violent lyrics remains within the framework of the god of power. [Campbell (1949), Leeming (1998)]

The hero Achilles descends to the underworld seeking his friend Patroclus

HEROINES It would be of interest to know more of the deeds of heroic figures associated with goddess mythologies predating recorded history—if such mythologies ever existed. It is possible, for instance, that the popular motif in fairy tales of the prince's marriage to the enchanted princess, following the many trials and tests, suggests something of an older, pre-femme fatale pattern in which the princess—Joseph Campbell calls her the "Goddess-Queen" (1949, p. 120)—represented life itself. In that case the hero's marriage to her would have signified ultimate knowledge of life.

Feminine elements remain a powerful force in the matrilineal cultures of the Native North American Southwest. In the *kinaalda*, the puberty ritual of Navajo and Apache girls, the initiate becomes the creating goddess, Changing Woman, herself and attains curative powers for a time. In the Candlemas Buffalo Dance at the Pueblo of San Felipe, a maiden becomes, in effect, heroine for a day when she ascends a mountain barefooted to bring down the Buffalo King and other animal dancers, who, in the course of the ceremony that follows, symbolically allow themselves to be sacrificed as food for the tribe. The maiden is the only female in the dance, and one senses that it is her giving of herself to the Buffalo King that makes the beneficial sacrifice possible.

In these rituals we glimpse an older idea of heroism in which the ordinary individual—one of us—can be recognized as hero only in a communal act, a breaking out of the merely personal life into a sacrificing of the individual to the larger communal self. There are remnants of this communal heroism in myths such as those of Hainuwele and the African Wan-jiru, each of whom sank into the ground in the middle of a dance ground—itself the sacred symbol of a cultural "world"—and through death brought new life.

It should be noted that in the established religions of our time, heroes exist whose values seem as attuned to these hypothetical ancient goddess traditions as to those of their patriarchal cultures. The mildness and humility of Jesus and the Buddha represent attempts to bring growth and change to the older heroic traditions. Both men place less emphasis than their cultures on old patriarchal laws and hierarchy. Both attempt to break down barriers between themselves and their people. But ultimately both fail to defeat the forces in their cultures that would distort their works and words in such a way as to create out of them new hierarchies, new power-based laws of dominance. This is especially true of Christianity, in which Jesus is raised by the institution named after him to the distant level of Son of God seated on a heavenly throne—an institution in which hierarchy and power and splendid palaces and temples early on become the visual symbols of the religion. There was the rise of the Virgin Mary from folk tradition as a de facto goddess to balance the dominance of traditional male values in the Church. But the Church fathers repressed much of Mary's earth-based, nonseparate nature by emphasizing her virginity and depriving her of sexuality even as she became, through her Assumption, like the old outlawed Asherah, Queen of Heaven, a position clearly separated from ours.

HESIOD Rivaled only by Homer as a source for Greek mythology, the poet Hesiod, who lived perhaps as much as a century later than Homer, was concerned in his great work, the *Theogony*, with the origins of the gods and the world. The *Theogony* is as close as Greek mythology comes to something equivalent to a canonical creation myth such as the one found in the Hebrew Book of Genesis. The generally accepted Greek creation myth is Hesiod's version.

HESTIA Hestia was the least obtrusive of the Olympian deities of Greece. A virgin, Hestia ("Hearth") stood for the home and family and social order. She was the quiet elderly sister of her much more extroverted siblings Zeus, Hades, Poseidon, Hera, and Demeter. She is so quiet that she is sometimes left off the Olympian family tree.

Hesiod (c. 730–700 B.C.E.)

HIGH GOD "High god" is a term commonly used to indicate the head gods, such as Re, Amun-Re, Atum, Atum-Re, and Ptah, in the various Egyptian as well as other pantheons.

HINA In the Oceanic Polynesian Tongan origin myth, which has certain similarities to the Ceramese myth of Hainuwele, Hina is a virgin with whom an eel has intercourse. After her people capture and cut up the eel, Hina asks for the head, which she buries. From that "planting" comes the first coconut palm with its useful fruit. Another Polynesian myth involving Hina and the trickster Maui is somewhat different, as it is Maui who kills the eel or the Penis (Te Tuna). In a Tahitian story, Hina is the daughter of the cannibal monster Rona.

HINAYANA BUDDHISM Literally "smaller vehicle," Hinayana is the name Mahayana, or "large vehicle," Buddhists use for early forms of Buddhism, including, usually, Theravada Buddhism. It is characterized by strict adherence to the teachings of Sakyamuni—Gautama Buddha.

HINDU MYTHOLOGY Hinduism is the dominant religious system of India and of the Indonesian island of Bali. "Hindu" is a word derived etymologically from the *flowing* of a river, and Hinduism is more a flow of religious ideas than it is a religion in the usual sense of the word. Unlike Buddhism, Jainism, and Sikhism, all of which are tributaries of Hinduism, Hinduism can point to no particular founder. If there is a dominant characteristic of Hinduism, it is its ability and willingness to absorb all physical and philosophical experience

H

Brahma the Creator with four heads, symbolizing the four Vedas and the four directions

and all gods and goddesses in an apparent polytheism. It is true, however, that in practice, many Hindus tend to concentrate their worship on one of three particular deities—Shiva, Vishnu, or Devi (the "Goddess") or on lesser deities such as the always popular Ganesh. And in a mysterious way, with its all-encompassing absolute, Brahman, Hinduism for some—particularly Vedantists—might be said to be ultimately monist or even monotheistic.

The beginning of an understanding of the complexities of Hinduism requires a historical context. Perhaps the earliest source of Hinduism was the religion and mythology of the people of the Neolithic Indus Valley, which was in full bloom before the invasion of Aryan peoples from the north in the second millennium B.C.E. The Indus Valley culture is sometimes referred to as Dravidian, after the language probably spoken by the people there, or Harappan, after one of the two major cities in the area. Indus Valley archeological evidence suggests a goddess-dominated religion with composite human-animal male figures, a tradition of ritual purification in pools, and a system of ritual sacrifice. Ancient seals depict an ithyphallic yogi-like figure with buffalo horns, a figure mirrored in later Hindu representations of the great god Shiva. The dominance of the goddess is reflected in later Hinduism's emphasis on the various forms of Devi.

The Aryans, who arrived beginning in about 1500 B.C.E., brought with them an Indo-European religious system and pantheon that bears much resemblance to the patriarchal systems of other Indo-Europeans such as the Greeks and the Iranians. They also brought the beginnings of what would

become the characteristic Hindu caste system, a system that would be dominated by the two upper classes—the priestly *brahmans* and the warrior *ksatriyas*. Pre-classical Hinduism or Vedism is expressed most fully in the sacred knowledge called *Vedas*, characterized as *Shruti* ("that which is heard"). First transmitted orally, the *Vedas* were eventually transcribed—traditionally by the sage Vyasa, who was also said to have written down the great Hindu epic the *Mahabharata*. The *Vedas* and Vedic mythology developed over many centuries and are made up of several kinds of texts. Most important are the four *Samhitas* ("Collections")—the three liturgical *Vedas*, including the ancient *Rig Veda* ("Chant *Veda*"), the *Sama Veda*, and the *Yaj ur Veda*, plus the *Athara Veda* ("Atharavan's *Veda*"). Offshoots of the Vedic texts were developed by schools of Vedic priests. These texts are called *Brahmanas*, *Aranyakas*, and *Upanishads*. The *Brahmanas*, the most important of which is the *Satapatha Brahmana*, are expositions of the absolute Brahman by priests (brahmans) and are concerned with the proper practice of rituals. In the *Brahmanas*, the *Rig Veda*'s one-time-only world-forming sacrifice of the transcendent primal male, Purusha, is essentially replaced by the cyclical death and resurrection sacrifice of Prajapati, himself the source of the creator god Brahma—in a sense, a personification of Brahman. The original Purusha would evolve into the person of the god Vishnu. The theology that emerges from the *Brahmanas* is called Brahmanism.

The *Aranyakas* ("books of the forest") are more mystical texts, centering on the inner life and the universal Brahman. They precede the *Upanishads* ("mystical understandings"), which move away from Brahmanic teachings about proper ritual to a belief that the individual must seek *Moksha*, "release" from the life-death continuum or *samsara*. To achieve *Moksha* the disciple must learn—perhaps from a guru—the connection between the transcendent absolute, *Brahman*, and the inner absolute, *Atman*. It is important to understand that the concept of life and the universe as developed in Vedic philosophy is the essence of Hinduism.

During the eight or nine hundred years after the late Vedic *Upanishads*—that is, from about 500 B.C.E., the great epics the *Mahabharata*, including especially its *Bhagavadgita* section of about 200 B.C.E., and the *Ramayana* play important roles in the development of a Hinduism dominated by the concepts of *bhakti*, or "devotion," and *dharma*, or "duty." Much of the mythical material of this classical Hinduism is also contained in works called *Puranas*, or "ancient stories," written between 400 and 1200 C.E. The epics and the *Puranas* fall under the category of *Smirti*, "that which is remembered," rather than the more sacred Vedic scripture or *Shruti*. If the epics and *Puranas* take what might be called mythological liberties, they are, nevertheless, firmly based in Vedic tradition and philosophy. The epics and the *Puranas* are, like the *Upanishads*, concerned with paths to salvation, or *Moksha*. They are also primary sources for Hindu mythology, which is so important for everyday "popular" Hinduism.

Several schools of Hinduism have emerged during the many centuries in which attempts have been made to consolidate the streams of the overall tradition into one "flow." Of these schools, two have achieved a certain dominance or orthodoxy. Both base their teachings on the Vedic philosophy, but the Mimamsa school stresses the ritual tradition of the *Vedas*, while the Vedanta school (including Advaita Vedantism) emphasizes the more mystical understandings of the *Upanishads*. It must be emphasized, too, that many Hindus are particularly devoted to particular deities. It is tempting for adherents of monotheistic traditions to see all of the Hindu gods as incarnations of the one absolute, Brahman, and in a sense they are. But Brahman is not "God" in any personal sense. Still, at the level of creation there is a *trimurti* of gods that work as one being and as aspects of that one absolute. Brahma is the creator, Shiva the destroyer, and Vishnu the preserver. These three roles are important at several levels, the most important of which is the Hindu understanding of the cosmic sacrificial cycles or *yugas*, the throws of the cosmic dice of existence, whereby the universe is destroyed and re-created over and over again. It should be noted, too, that even by the last books of the *Rig Veda* the gods seem to take on the characteristics of each other, depending on the context of the hymn in question.

Hindu mythology is a network of intermingling connecting threads that, if it could be perfectly understood, would provide a clear narrative map to the rich tapestry that is Hindu thought. As in the case of the medieval cathedral, the decorations of the Hindu temple confront the viewer as a mysterious mythic story in which everything has philosophical or religious significance. The postures of the figures depicted, the objects held by them, and the way they relate to each other all have specific meanings. So it is with Hindu mythology as passed down orally and as written in the epics and religious texts. No story is told for its own sake; every myth has meaning in relation to other myths and to the Vedic tradition that is its ultimate source. This overall source is dominated by the idea of cosmic sacrifice and related human rituals, by a universe and individuals that are repeatedly sacrificed so that they might be reborn.

As Hinduism developed over the centuries from the period of the Aryan invasions, so did its mythology—the narrative expression of its religious and philosophical understandings of the universe. The complex dance of the cosmos, reflected in human life, is acted out by a variety of deities and demons and humans who, like the universe itself, possess qualities that are at once "good" and "evil," nurturing and destructive. The myths are found in many Sanskrit sources—especially the ancient *Rig Veda*, the other *Vedas*, the *Brahmanas*, the *Upanishads*, the *Mahabharata*, and the *Ramayana*, and in the *Puranas* of the Common Era.

In the Rig Veda we find a pantheon made up of the sovereigns Varuna and Mitra and the warrior Indra, as well as the two ritual deities Agni, or "Fire," and Soma, "the plant of immortality." Indra takes on a position of particular importance as upholder of cosmic order by defeating the demonic *asura* Virtra. Two sun gods are Surya and Savitr. Ushas is goddess of the dawn. Yama is god of the dead, and Vayu god of the wind. Rudra is an outsider of sorts but will develop later into the powerful god Shiva. Vishnu and Devi are present in Vedic scripture but have not yet achieved their greatest power.

A dominant creation myth of the *Rig Veda* is the animistic one of the sacrificial dismemberment of the primal man or Purusha. It is a myth that conveys the centrality of the ritual sacrifice in Hinduism. Purusha is the sacrifice out of which all things come, including the caste system. His mouth became the *brahmans*, those who teach with words; his arms became the *ksatriyas*, the warrior caste; his thighs became the ordinary populace, and his feet the servant classes. Indra and Agni were born of his mouth, Vayu of his breath.

In the *Brahmanas*, it is Prajapati who is the creator, sometimes by way of cosmic incest with his daughter, sometimes by way of masturbation, a method also employed in some Egyptian creation myths. By the time we get to the *Mahabharata*, it is Brahma who takes the place of Prajapati as creator. The presence of Agni—fire—is important in these early

creation stories. Agni "eats" even as the creator creates, and his is the appropriate element to consume the dead human, who can then be reborn, as fire eats only the body and not the soul. In the *Puranas*, Brahma creates good and evil. Eventually Brahma will lose stature in favor of the great yogi Shiva; and of Vishnu and his avatars, particularly Rama and the Lord Krishna, and the Goddess (Devi), who is at once Parvati, the wife of Shiva, Kali, the devourer, the violent Durga, and various other forms, or *Shakti*. [Bonnefoy (1991), Hiltebeitel, O'Flaherty (1975), Leeming (2001)]

HINE-HAU-ONE The Polynesian Maori people say that Hine-hau-one (Earth-born Girl) was the first human. She was created by the creator god Tane when the earth goddess Papa, the wife of the sky god Rangi, refused to give him a wife. By Tane, Hine-hau-one became pregnant and gave birth to Hine-titama, who later became Hine-nui-te-po.

HINE-NUI-TE-PO The Polynesian/Maori goddess of death and the underworld, Hine-nui-te-po, the daughter of the first human, Hine-hau-one, and the god Tane, had originally been Hine-titama ("Girl of the Dawn"). Tane was enamored of Hine-titama and became her lover, but when Hine-titama discovered that her lover was her father, she fled to the underworld now as Hine-nui-te-po ("Guardian of the Darkness") and cried out to Tane that his children—humankind—would now be mortal. The culture hero–trickster Maui attempted to overcome Hine-nui-te-po's edict by traveling through her from her genital orifice to her mouth. The goddess discovered him and killed him.

HIPPOLYTA Hippolyta was the queen of the Amazons, daughter of the Greek war god Ares. Many conflicting stories are told of her. According to one, she was killed by Herakles during one of his Twelve Labors, the one in which his goal was possession of the famous girdle given to the queen by her father. Another myth tells how Hippolyta and her Amazons invaded Attica to retrieve the queen's sister Antiope, who had been kidnapped by Theseus. According to that version of her story, Hippolyta fled to Megara and died after being defeated by Theseus. According to still another myth, made famous by Euripides in his play the *Hippolytus*, Hippolyta—or some say Antiope—produced a son, Hippolytus, by Theseus. Hippolytus would be a tragic figure in a triangle involving his father, Theseus, and his stepmother, Phaedra.

HIPPOLYTUS The son of Theseus by the Amazon queen Hippolyta or her sister Antiope, Hippolytus, a gentle and chaste young man, became the object of the lust of his stepmother, Phaedra. As described in the *Hippolytus* by the Greek playwright Euripides, he refused Phaedra's advances, and in her over-wrought emotional state, Phaedra took revenge by accusing Hippolytus of compromising her honor. This so enraged Theseus that he cursed his son, causing his divine "father," Poseidon, to send a bull from the sea to frighten the horses of the boy's chariot so badly that they overturned the chariot and dragged him to his death. When he discovered his son's innocence, Theseus was horrified, and Phaedra committed suicide. It was said that Hippolytus was restored to life at the direction of his patroness, the virgin huntress, Artemis (Roman Diana).

HITTITE-HURRIAN MYTHOLOGY Beginning early in the second millennium B.C.E. an Indo-European people, the Hittites, had ruled over a large portion of Anatolia (Asian Turkey) that had previously been occupied by the non–Indo-Euro-

The Hittite-Hurrian Sky-Storm God marries the Earth Mother Goddess

pean Hattians, a name (Hatti) used by the Hittites to identify themselves. In fact, the original Hattian culture is sometimes referred to as the proto-Hattian to distinguish it from the later Hattian-Hittite culture. The Hittite arrival in Anatolia, perhaps as early as 2300 B.C.E., coincided with that of less powerful Indo-Europeans, including the Luwians and the Palaians, and with that of the Indo-Europeans who made their way into India and Iran to the east. The Hittites quickly adapted their language to the cuneiform script learned, presumably, from the Mesopotamians, and Hittite remained the dominant language of Anatolia during the second millennium.

The Hittites were progressive rulers in the sense that they accepted the languages, religions, and other cultural traditions that existed in the lands they conquered. From the Hattians and other neighbors, the Hurrians, they borrowed and assimilated so much of both language and religion that it is almost necessary to speak of Hattian, Hurrian, and Hittite mythology as a combined entity.

The so-called Old Hittite Kingdom was centered in Hattusa (near modern Bogazköy) and by the middle of the millennium, the kingdom had formed an empire of all of Anatolia and much of Mesopotamia. During the Middle Kingdom, between 1500 and 1380 B.C.E., however, Hattusa was ruled by kings with Hurrian names. That fact suggests possible conquest by the Hurrian Kingdom of Mitanni, southwest of Lake Van in what is now the Kurdish area where Syria, Turkey, and Iraq meet. The Mitanni Hurrians (also known as Naharin), with their capital at Wassukkani, were themselves ruled by an Indo-Aryan aristocracy with some allegiance to Indian deities.

The Hurrians, or Hurri, who were neither Indo-European nor Semitic, had moved into Mesopotamia and what is now Syria at about the time of the Hittite arrival in Anatolia. By the middle of the millennium they had established major centers at Nuzi in the eastern Tigris region and Alalakh in northern Syria, and by late in the millennium there was an important Hurrian presence and influence in Canaanite Ugarit.

In the mid-fourteenth century B.C.E. Hittite kings retook the throne in Hattusa, beginning the Early Empire period, and soon conquered the Mitanni Hurrians and established control over much of the Hurrian Empire in Mesopotamia and Syria. The Hittites had always been a warlike people who both traded and fought over the centuries with their neighbors, the Hurrians and Assyrians, but also with the Babylonians and, especially, the Egyptians to the south. The Egyptians considered them barbarians who, toward the end of the millennium, stood in the way of their imperial advance to the north and east. In 1300 the armies of the Hittites and the Egyptians fought to a draw near Kadesh, and eventually a treaty between Ramses II and Hattusili III was solidified by the marriage between the Egyptian pharaoh and Hattusili's daughter.

The mythology of pre-Greek and pre-Islamic Anatolia, then, is an amalgamation of the pantheons and sacred stories of the Hattians, the Hittites, and the Hurrians. Other Mesopotamian mythic material and Canaanite stories also found their way into Anatolian mythology by way of the Hurrians.

The religiously tolerant Hittites attempted to make sense of the many deities that they accepted into their official pantheon. Near the Hittite capital of Hattusa, at a place called

Yazilikaya, is a second-millennium B.C.E. open stone gallery in which a procession of gods and goddesses is carved. These are the "Thousand Gods of Hatti," a collection of old Hattian, Hittite, and Hurrian divinities, many identified in a hieroglyphic script developed by the Luwians.

The deities assimilated by the Hittites from the indigenous Hattians are somewhat unclear to modern scholars because of our still scant knowledge of the Hattic language. The Hattian pantheon seems to have been at first a collection of personifications of aspects of nature, such as Estan ("Sun" or "Day") and Kasku ("Moon"), and expressions of life forces represented by mother goddesses (Kattahha; Hannahanna, meaning "Grandmother"; Kubaba; and Wurusemu), king–war gods (Wurrunkatte, Zababa, and Kattishabi), and a storm-weather god (Taru). Later deities derived in part from the Hurrians were, for the most part, more endowed with human characteristics, not always noble ones, than those of the Hattians and old Hittites, and were clearly influenced by Mesopotamian deities.

The old Hattian mother goddess, with roots at least as deep as the concept of the great goddess depicted in nearby Neolithic Çatal Hüyük, was the source of life and a natural mate for the Anatolian weather-storm god, himself a close mythical relative of Zeus, Indra, Thor, and other familiar Indo-European sky gods, perhaps especially those of Eastern Europe. An important function of the storm god was to constantly fight to retain his power at the top of the pantheon. In this aspect also he resembles other Indo-European high gods and storm gods.

In their specifically Hittite form, the high god and the great goddess became the sun goddess of Arina—originally Estan, later Hebat among the Hurrians—and the weather god of Hatti, sometimes called Taru in Old Hatti, Tarhunna among the Hittites, and Teshub (Tessub, Tesup) by the Hurrians. The high god, whatever his name, was symbolized, like so many Middle Eastern high gods, by the bull. His consort was always a mother goddess such as Wurusema, the wife of the Hattic Taru. At Hattusa, the weather god was the city deity. The sun goddess at first seems to have shared that honor as his consort. The patriarchal Hittites and Hurrians thought of the sun as male, however, and under them there was a definite moving away from the old Hattic understanding. The Hittites referred to "Our God Siu" (same root as Zeus, meaning "Light of Heaven"), and the Hurrians worshipped the sun as the male Simigi.

Still, the sun goddess of Arina, syncrenetized by the middle of the second millennium with the Hurrian Hebat, the "Queen of Heaven," clearly leads the procession of goddesses at Yazilikaya and might possibly have been differentiated from the male sun god by being designated a sun goddess of the underworld, an aspect supported by the Hurrian-Hittite assimilation of the Babylonian Allata or Allatum (Inanna's underworld sister, Ereshkigal) as the underworld sun goddess Allani. Certainly, in the Old Kingdom, the sun goddess was the Anatolian mother of fertility. If her ancestor was the goddess of Çatal Hüyük, her Anatolian descendants were the great Phrygian goddess Cybele, the mother of the sacrificed Attis, and the famous many-breasted Artemis of Ephesus.

The mother goddess and the storm god had two daughters: Mezulla, who served as an intermediary between the human and divine worlds, and Inara, who was enlisted by her father to help in his struggle against the chaotic forces who would overthrow him.

Another Hurrian-Hittite goddess of importance was Sausga, a mythological relative of Inanna/Ishtar in Mesopotamia. Sausga was both a warrior and a love goddess. Like Devi as Parvati in India, she had aspects of fertility, as well as of destruction, like Devi-Kali.

A goddess of magical powers was Kamrusepa, a deity of Luwian origin, who among the Hattians was Kattahziwuri and who was associated with curing spells and with the myth of the disappearing god—a myth that had many versions in Hittite-Hurrian mythology, the most important of which was the story of Telipinu.

Myths of original—pre-pantheonic—deities are present in the Hittite-Hurrian canon. The Hurrians probably equated these primeval deities with the Mesopotamian Anunnaki. They included some familiar Sumero-Babylonian gods—Anu and Enlil, for instance—and were cast aside by the weather-storm god and his associates. As in Greece, where Zeus emerged from an ancient struggle involving first Ouranos and then Kronos, the Hittite-Hurrian weather god was the end product of a process by which the original father god Alalu was overthrown by his servant or son Anu, and Anu was defeated by his son Kumarbi, who gives his name to a whole cycle of war-in-Heaven myths known as the Kumarbi cycle. The Kumarbi cycle and the Illuyanka cycle, a series of stories about the storm god and the monstrous serpent Illuyanka, provide us with the few indications we have of Hittite-Hurrian myths of creation. Both of these myth cycles are concerned with the struggle between order and chaos that is at the center of most creation myths. [Hoffner (1998), Leeming (2004), Wasilewska]

HOD Hod was the blind Norse god who was tricked by the evil trickster Loki into throwing the mistletoe dart at, and thus killing, his brother, the dying god Balder.

HOLY GRAIL The Holy Grail, or Sangreale in Old French, was an important quest object in the Arthurian tradition, particularly connected with Percival, as in the *Perceval* of Chrétien de Troyes (c. 1185) and the slightly later *Parzival* of Wolfram von Eschenbach. Whatever the original source of the legends of the Grail, Christianity associated it with one of the vessels used by Jesus at the Last Supper. It was said to have come to Joseph of Arimathea after the Crucifixion and, some say, to have been brought by him to England.

HOLY SPIRIT Along with God the Father and God the Son (Jesus), the Holy Spirit is one of three aspects of Christianity's understanding of God as a Trinity.

HOMER Homer is the name traditionally given to the composer(s) of the two great archaic Greek epics, the *Iliad* and the *Odyssey*, probably composed orally in various stages between 900 and 700 B.C.E. The existence or nonexistence of this poet or series of poets, claimed by various parts of Asia Minor and Greece, forms the basis of what scholars have long called the "Homeric question." Whether Homer existed or not, the works attributed to him have been used in schools since ancient times to teach language and Greek values. Most important, the epics in question have been a primary source for Greek mythology. Homer has long been, in fact, a part of Greek mythology himself, a mysterious blind bard.

In the blind Demodokos of Phaiakia, who sings the story of the Trojan War in the eighth book of the *Odyssey*, the poet, whoever he was, through his hero Odysseus (himself a great spinner of tales) praises the art of minstrelsy represented by Demodokos, and either paints a self-portrait or gives life to a myth that has intrigued humanity for over two thousand years: Now came the court crier, leading the

Statue of Homer

favored bard, The singer loved by the Muse, who gave him good and evil—the power of song and the absence of sight. When his thirst was quenched and his hunger fed He sang through the Muse a song of heroes, A song known by all, far and wide. Carving a piece from his chine of boar, Odysseus called out to the blind poet's guide. Pray give this meat to Demodokos, And grant him peace from unhappy me. Much honor is owed to the bards, Men loved by the Muse who gives them song. The guide took the meat, and gave it to the bard, Whose heart was full of joy.

HOMERIC HYMNS Along with Hesiod's *Theogony*, the epics of Homer, and the plays of Aeschylus, Sophocles, and Euripides, the *Homeric Hymns* are a primary source for our knowledge of Greek mythology. This collection of "hymns"—stories in verse—created in the seventh and sixth centuries B.C.E., is generally attributed to a school of poets known as the Homeridae ("Sons of Homer"). It is in the *Homeric Hymns* that we find the most complete Demeter-Persephone-Hades myth, as well as particularly important myths about Artemis, Apollo, Aphrodite, Athena, Dionysos, and the Dioscuri (Twins), as well as rare myths of Hestia.

HONIR Known for his long legs and his inability to make decisions, Honir was the Norse god sent with Mimir to the Vanir by the Aesir as a hostage to confirm a truce in the war in Heaven between the two families of gods.

HO-NO-SUSORI AND HIKO-HOHO-DEMI These are the grandsons of the Japanese sun goddess Amaterasu. Hiko-hoho-demi descended to the palace of the sea god Watatsumi-no-kami to retrieve his brother's prize fishhook, which he, Hiko, had carelessly lost. The sea god gave the young man his daughter Toyotama-hime as a wife and eventually sent him back to the upper world on the back of a crocodile

with a gift of two jewels, which when thrown into the sea would make the waters rise and fall. This is how tides came about.

HONOYETA In Melanesia, Honoyeta was a serpent deity who brought death to humans because one of his wives destroyed the skin with which he disguised himself before them.

HORUS The falcon-headed Horus, son of Isis and the dead Osiris, was one of the most important of the Egyptian gods; he also played the role of hero. Hero myths in general reflect human concerns and are expressive of that post-mythological period when the high god—in this case Re—retreats to a kind of seclusion in the heavens and no longer communicates directly with humans. Not surprisingly, then, many of the myths of Horus himself—the god who, with Isis and Osiris, had most to do with human life—have more in common with traditional hero myths than with deity myths. Like those of another man-god, Jesus, they contain all of the essential elements of Joseph Campbell's monomyth. Horus was miraculously conceived, and his quest was to restore the "kingdom" of his father in a struggle with monstrous evil represented by his nemesis, Seth.

The struggle between Horus and Seth is metaphorically related not only to the establishment of the early dynasties in Egypt and the struggle between north and south, but, in connection with Osiris, to the whole question of the sacred kingship in Egypt. The old king died as Osiris, and the new king reigned as Horus, who had defeated the disorder of Seth.

According to the myth, when Horus grew into manhood he and his followers attacked Seth, who had usurped Osiris's throne. The struggle was acutely disturbing to the universal order. Horus, like his Hittite-Hurrian cognate Kumarbi, pulled out the testicles of his uncle, and Seth took out his nephew's eye. It was up to Thoth, the god of proper order, to convince the combatants to agree to arbitration. The gods decided in Horus's favor and he was made the new king. Horus then traveled to the underworld to take his retrieved eye to Osiris as a symbol of the reestablishment of proper order. Through this visit, the soul of Osiris and, thus, fertility were revived. As Rundle Clark writes, "Osiris was nothing without Horus, just as the latter was no true king unless he was able to guarantee the fertility of the land. . . . It is Horus who fulfills the destiny for the present, undertaking the role played in other religions by the resurrected god" (p. 108). As for Seth, he became Osiris's boat or the breeze that propelled the dead king's boat on ritual voyages on the Nile.

A hauntingly familiar aspect of the Horus story exists in the so-called Delta cycle. After conceiving a child by her formerly dead but then partially revived husband Osiris, Isis retreated from the evil usurper king, Seth, into hiding in the swamps of the Delta. In this hidden and unglamorous place she gave birth to Horus. Many things happened to the divine child during his days in the Delta. While his mother was off begging for food, he was attacked and bitten by Seth disguised as a serpent. But the Pyramid Texts tell us that the holy infant "with his finger in his mouth" stamped on the serpent "with his foot," reminding us of similar acts by heroes such as the Irish Cuchculainn, the Iranian Zoroaster, and the Greek Herakles. Later, from the wilderness of the swamps, a place called Chemmis, the young man Horus went to the underworld to visit his father and then on to the great struggle.

Ultimately Horus was recognized as one of the greatest sky gods; his eyes were the sun and moon, and in art he is sometimes Wedjat, the Eye itself.

HOU JI Hou Ji was the Chinese divinity of the harvest.

HREIDMAR Hreidmar was a farmer and magician in Norse mythology. He was the father of Otter, whom Loki killed while he and the gods Odin and Honir were on a trip around Midgard. When the gods came to Hreidmar's house and asked him for lodging, they presented the dead Otter as food to be cooked for supper, not realizing that Hreidmar was the animal's father. Hreidmar and his other two sons, Fafnir and Regin, vowed to be avenged and attacked the gods, protected by Hreidmar's magic. The gods, surprised, asked for an explanation and then agreed to pay a substantial ransom. Loki, however, always the evil trickster, stole the ransom from a dwarf, who put a curse on anyone who took possession of it. This curse Loki passed on to the unfortunate Hreidmar.

HRUNGNIR Hrungnir was the strongest of the giants in the Norse world. When Odin paid him a visit, the giant did not realize who he was and argued with the god about the relative speed of their horses. Naturally, Odin's horse won, and Odin invited the giant to Valhalla for a drink. The giant became drunk and eventually challenged Thor to a duel, which ended in the giant's death.

HSI-TZU Hsi-tzu is book of the fifth-century B.C.E. *I Ching*, which was in all likelihood composed by scholars not in sympathy with prevailing Daoist thought. The book stresses mythology such as that of the Chinese emperor-god Fuxi.

HUANGDI Huangdi (Guandi) usually refers to the famous Yellow Emperor of ancient China who fought against the monstrous Chiyou. But Huangdi is the title for Chinese emperors in general. Huangdi was also a popular Chinese god who, historically, was a late-Han-dynasty warrior depicted in the Ming-dynasty *Romance of the Three Kingdoms*. As a deity, Huangdi is associated with war and with justice.

HUEHUETEOTL The Olmec-Aztec god of fire, Huehueteotl was believed to have been the first friend of humans, a Mesoamerican Prometheus who was, however, much humbler than his Greek cognate. Perhaps more a culture hero in spirit than a god, he is depicted as a toothless old man who stayed close to home.

HUITZILOPOCHTLI The most important of the Aztec deities was the sun god and war god Huitzilopochtli, who also seems to have been a culture hero of sorts. He is a god to whom human sacrifices were made. But as a hero figure he has monomythic aspects. He was miraculously conceived when his goddess mother, Coatlicue, was entered by a feather on a hill sacred to the serpent. When Coatlicue's other children, angry at her pregnancy, cut off her head and hands, she died but gave birth to the fully adult Huitzilopochtli, who took revenge against his older siblings. It was this god who, as a culture hero, led the Aztecs to Tenochtitlan, where Mexico City sits today.

HUMBABA In Tablets 3–5 of the Mesopotamian Gilgamesh epic, Gilgamesh and his companion Enkidu are in the Cedar Forest of Enlil, which is guarded by the gigantic monster Humbaba (the Sumerian Hawawa). Gilgamesh cuts down huge trees to use in capturing Humbaba, and when the monster begs for mercy, Enkidu decapitates him. The treatment of Humbaba wins the curse of Enlil and leads to later trouble for the heroes.

HUNAPHU AND XBALANQUE In the *Popul Vuh* of the Quiche Maya Indians of Mesoamerica, Hunaphu and Xbalanque are sacred twins who descend to the underworld and are reborn as the sun and moon.

HYACINTH The youth Hyacinth (Hyacinthus), probably a pre-Hellenic fertility god, was loved by both the Greek god Apollo and the wind god Zephyrus. As Apollo and the boy were playing with quoits, the jealous Zephyrus caused a quoit thrown by Apollo to strike Hyacinth on the head and kill him. From the boy's blood sprang the Hyacinth flower in the spring, suggesting a connection with such dying gods as the Phrygian Attis and the Greco-Phoenician Adonis.

HYMIR The Norse god Hymir was a giant who one day went fishing with the thunder god Thor. When Thor hooked the fierce World Serpent using the head of one of Hymir's oxen for bait, Hymir was so afraid of the dragon that he cut Thor's line, making the great god so angry at him that he threw him into the sea.

HYPERION The Titan Hyperion was, by his sister Theia, the father of Selene (Moon), Eos (Dawn), and Helios (Sun). He is sometimes confused with Helios. Hyperion's parents were Ouranos and Gaia, Heaven and Earth.

A grieving Apollo holds the dead Hyacinth

I CHING The *I Ching* (*Yijing*), or *Book of Changes*, probably composed in the fifth century B.C.E., was, according to legend, made up of elements discovered by the emperor-god Fuxi. The elements in question are the unbroken line that is *yang* and the broken line that is *yin*. *Yin* and *yang* are basic to Chinese mythology. *Yang* is the masculine principle of Heaven, light, dryness, warmth, and activity. *Yin* is the feminine principle of earth, darkness, moisture, coldness, and passivity. *Yin* and *yang* are present in everything everywhere. The whole purpose of the *I Ching*, a collection of omens and oracles, is to demonstrate how *yin* and *yang* may be related and balanced in various contexts. Particular combinations in threes of the unbroken *yang* line and the broken *yin* line form symbolic trigrams with particular meanings. It is said that the original trigrams were used by Wen, the father of Wu, the founder of the Chou dynasty, to form meaningful hexagrams. Wu's son is believed to have been the author of analyses of the hexagrams. Confucius, too, provided explanations. To use the *I Ching* as a divining source, yarrow stalks are cast to form signs, which can then be explained by referring to the *I Ching* itself and making interpretations in connection with the caster of the sticks.

IBLIS Iblis is an Islamic aspect of the Devil. Iblis in the *Qur'an* is a type, one who is without Allah (God), as opposed to another aspect of the Devil, Shaitan or al-Shaytan (Satan), the direct "enemy of God."

IBRAHIM Ibrahim is the Arabic name for the biblical Hebrew patriarch Abraham. He plays a significant role in Islamic mythology, as he does in Judeo-Christian mythology. Ibrahim was considered a prophet and the first Muslim, because in his willingness to sacrifice his own son he demonstrated *islam*, that is, total obedience to God.

IDATEN The Japanese god who protects Buddhist monastic sects, Idaten is particularly important to followers of the Zen tradition. He is known for his great speed. He wears a Chinese helmet and carries a sword.

IDUN Idun was the Norse goddess married to Bragi, the god of poetry. She was the protectress of the golden apples of youth. One day, the three gods Odin, Loki, and Honir were walking about Midgard, and Loki was tricked by an eagle—really an enemy giant in disguise—into agreeing to steal the apples of Idun from their place in Asgard. The trickster Loki then

The goddess Idun (Iduna), guardian of the Golden Apples of Youth

tricked Idun into bringing her apples to Midgard to compare them with similar apples he claimed to have found there. As soon as Loki and Idun arrived in Midgard, Idun and her apples were swept up by the eagle, really the giant Thiazi. When Thiazi had the goddess and her valuable apples locked up in his home at Thrymheim, he gloated, saying that now, without the apples of youth, the gods would grow old and could easily be defeated. And indeed, the gods began to grow old and lose their strength. In council it became evident that Loki was responsible for the kidnapping, so Odin decreed that the trickster must himself be captured and forced to get the apples back. The gods found Loki sleeping in Idun's field, tied him up, and dispatched him, disguised in Freya's falcon skin, to rescue Idun and her apples. Loki flew to the giant's home, turned Idun into a nut, and flew away with her. Thiazi in his eagle form gave chase and would have captured Idun again had the gods not set him on fire as he was about to land in Asgard.

IFA Known as Ifa among the west African Yoruba people and Fa among the Fon, this god of order has culture hero aspects. It was he who taught humans about healing. He works against the powers of the inherently disorderly trickster Eshu. Ifa is also a god of prophetic powers.

IGRAINE Igraine (Ygraine) was the mother of King Arthur.

IKTOME A popular trickster figure, especially among the Sioux Indians of Native North America, Iktome, like most tricksters, was amoral and blessed with insatiable appetites. Like his sometimes friend Coyote, he especially liked women, and there are many sexual myths about him. In a Brule Sioux myth, he disguised himself as an old woman in order to get close to a beautiful young virgin he desired. The girl was about to cross a stream, so Iktome suggested that they cross together. As Iktome lifted his skirt to keep it dry, the girl commented on the supposed old woman's hairy legs and backside. "It comes with age," answered the wily trickster. But when the water got deeper and Iktome had to hitch up his skirt further, the maiden gasped when she saw what was between his legs. "What's that?" she cried. "Oh, it 's a wart that a sorcerer put there," Iktome replied. "Then we must cut it off," said the girl. "Oh, no," cried Iktome, "but you *could* help me get rid of it if we put it in the space between your legs." According to the story, the girl allowed Iktome to do just that, and thus helped to shrink the "wart."

ILIAD Almost certainly the earlier of the two Greek epics attributed to Homer, the *Iliad* was probably composed, making use of older folk traditions, in about 750 B.C.E. or, some say, as early as 850 B.C.E. Much later it was written down and divided into sections, or "books." The *Iliad* tells a story about the war in Ilium (Troy), the famous Trojan War between the Greeks (really pre-Greeks—Mycenaeans or Hellenes, called by Homer Achaians, Argives, and Danaans), led by Agamemnon, and the people of Troy and their allies (Ionians and Aiolians), under King Priam. The Greeks have come to Troy under an alliance treaty to retrieve Helen, the wife of Agamemnon's brother Menelaus, after she had been seduced and taken to Troy by a Trojan prince named Paris. The events of the epic cover a relatively short time, beginning in the tenth year of the war with the boycotting of battle by the primary Greek warrior, Achilles.

ILLUYANKA CYCLE In Hittite-Hurrian mythology the monstrous serpent Illuyanka is the perennial enemy of the storm god. In the first Illuyanka story, the storm god is defeated in a battle at Kiskilussa (an actual place in Anatolia) by the serpent. The storm god's reaction to this defeat is to call for a feast, almost certainly representing the Hattian-Hittite Purulli festival, held in honor of the prosperity and fertility of the land and its people. The god's daughter Inara, as instructed by her father, provides the feast—including an abundance of wine and beer—symbolizing the fertility of the land. But the serpent remains a constant threat, and it seems to be up to the powerful goddess to overcome it. To accomplish her mission she apparently is in need of a human monster-tricking hero to assist her. She calls on one Hupasiya, who agrees to help in return for sexual favors. The goddess agrees, and after sleeping with Hupasiya, she hides her lover, approaches the serpent hole, and entices the monster to come out to join the feast she has prepared. The serpent and his family fall for the trick, emerge from their lair, and proceed to become so drunk that Hupasiya is able to burst out of his hiding place to tie them up. Then the storm god himself comes and kills them, and creation is preserved.

The story continues in a fairy tale–like mode. Inara is apparently fond of her human lover. One day, as she is leaving the house she has built for him, she warns him not to look out of the window. If he does, she says, he will see his neglected wife and children. Naturally, after some time, he does look out of the window and, just as predictably, sees his wife and children, whom he longs to rejoin. He begs Inara—as Odysseus had begged Calypso, for example—to be allowed to go back home and, presumably, is allowed to do so, although the existing text is unclear on that point.

The second Illuyanka tale says that the serpent defeats the storm god and steals his heart and eyes, thus threatening creation itself (and reminding us of the Horus myth in Egypt). The storm god then marries a woman of the lower classes, who provides him with a son. The son grows up and marries a daughter of the serpent, and the storm god instructs him to request the missing heart and eyes as a dowry. The son does as he is instructed, and so the storm god regains his heart and eyes. Whole again, the storm god from his position in the sky attacks the serpent in the sea and succeeds in killing him. The storm god's son announces his loyalty to his father-in-law, so the storm god kills him, too.

Ewa Wasilewska rightly points out that although these stories are apparently of proto-Hattic origin, they reflect the common Indo-European creation struggle between order and chaotic evil that would have made them popular with the Indo-European Hittites (p. 105).

ILMARINEN Ilmarinen is a major hero in the Finnic epic the *Kalevala*.

ILYAP'A Ilyap'a, the Incan storm and thunder god, was a bringer of rain. When he wanted it to rain, Ilyap'a would use his slingshot to create a crack of thunder and to break his sister's jug, which was full of water she had gathered from the Milky Way.

IMMACULATE CONCEPTION Catholic Christians claim not only that Jesus was conceived without the loss of his mother's virginity, but that the Virgin Mary was herself conceived by her mother, Anne, immaculately—that is, without the stain of sexual sin. Thus, the original sin of Adam and Eve that clings to all humans was not present in the conception

Inanna (Ishtar), the Great Goddess of Ancient Mesopotamia

handing the *me* to the goddess. After a drunken sleep, however, he realizes the enormity of what he has done, and he sends his servant to get the *me* back. But Inanna has already departed, placing the me in her "Boat of Heaven," that is, the boat of Uruk-based An, but also, perhaps, her ample genital region, a symbol of Sumerian fertility and prosperity. Enki's followers, aided by demons, chase the ship, but Inanna and her handmaiden Ninsubur hold off the pursuers with arguments and magic spells. Returning to Uruk with the *me*, the basis of what will be the well-being of the people of Uruk, a city that now perhaps has achieved dominance over Eridu, Inanna holds a celebratory feast, and Enki accepts the goddess's new, higher position among the gods.

It seems that after Inanna's gaining of the *me* and her becoming one of the four most important deities—truly a Queen of Heaven—she has yet to fulfill her destiny as a goddess of erotic love and fertility. Utu, the sun god, who watches over growth on earth, reminds his twin sister that she is now ripe for love. Inanna has two suitors, the farmer Enkimdu and the shepherd—sometimes fisherman— Dumuzi (Tammuz in Hebrew and Aramaic). Inanna at first favors the farmer but finally decides on the shepherd, who woos her with Utu's enthusiastic support. Advised by her mother, Nigal, to "open [her] house" to Dumuzi, the goddess prepares her body for her husband-to-be. When she opens the door to him they are both overcome by passion. Inanna calls on her lover to fill her with his love:

> My vulva, the horn,
> The Boat of heaven,
> Is full of eagerness like the young moon.
> My untilled land lies fallow.
> And Dumuzi, the shepherd-farmer king, obliges:
> I, Dumuzi, the King, will plow your vulva.
>
> [Wolkstein and Kramer, p. 37]

of the woman who would be the carrier of God in his sinless but human form as Jesus.

INANNA The most important of the Mesopotamian goddesses was Inanna (Ishtar), also known as Innin or Ninnin. Depending on the tradition, Inanna was the daughter of Enlil, Nanna, or Enki. In her primary center at Uruk, where dates were a staple crop, she was Ninana, "Mistress of Heaven" and "Lady of the Date Clusters." Like many fertility goddesses, she was sometimes the "Cow of Heaven." In her assimilation with the Semitic Akkadian astral goddess, Ishtar, this originally Sumerian goddess was called "Mistress of the *Me*," making her with An and Enlil among the most powerful of deities.

In a myth probably dating from the end of the third millennium B.C.E., we find an explanation for her association with the *me*, the sources of Sumerian civilized order inherent originally in the primal waters, the mother goddess Nammu. The *me* include, for example, ritual, priesthood, political power, security, crafts, animal husbandry, agriculture, sexual behavior, family, and decision making. Inanna, lacking any particular office or function among the gods, decides to visit the crafty Enki in the *abzu* at his home in Eridu with the intention of stealing the powerful elements of the *me*. The myth in question probably was enacted in a festival or cult drama, one type of which was the journey drama in which a deity traveled ritually from his or her home city to the city of another god, especially to Enki at Eridu, where great power was stored and could be obtained as a boon.

When Inanna visits him, Enki provides a grand feast at which he becomes drunk and acts impulsively, eventually

Clearly, the Inanna-Dumuzi myth was central to the ubiquitous Mesopotamian ritual of the sacred marriage. In hymns for these occasions, the goddess longs for and achieves intercourse with a king in order to bring fertility to the land. Dumuzi was represented by reigning kings in Sumerian sacred marriage rites, especially at Uruk.

The love songs that accompany the myth and ritual are more explicit than but, in tone, not unlike those to be found later in the biblical *Song of Songs*. All the senses play roles in the joyful private exploration of the physical that marks the sexual experience of Dumuzi and Inanna. But after the public consummation of the marriage, Dumuzi wishes to attend to his kingly duties and begs his wife to "set me free"; he no longer has time to make love "fifty times." This part of the myth is probably the earliest version of the universal story of conflict between love and duty.

The most famous myth about Inanna is that of her descent to the underworld ruled by her sister, Ereshkigal (Allatu). The myth of the hero's descent to the underworld is found in most cultures. The particular myth of Inanna's descent and the sacrifice of Dumuzi, which is associated with it, adds the element of resurrection that links it in varying degrees to such stories as those of the Greek Persephone, the Egyptian Isis and Osiris, and the Christian Jesus. And these stories and others like them have in common the celebration of physical or spiritual fertility related to a ritual journey to the depths, where shamanic powers are experienced or gained. There is also in Inanna's descent an implicit agricultural element involving "planting" under the earth and ultimately productive decomposition.

The Inanna descent myth tells how as "Queen of the Above," Inanna, always in search of knowledge, longs to know the Below of her sister Ereshkigal, the negative or opposite aspect of the ripe goddess of love. Inanna understands life more fully than anyone, but she knows nothing of death or of the unhealthy, unfruitful sexuality of Ereshkigal. Before leaving for the underworld, Inanna instructs her faithful helper Ninshubur to arrange official mourning for her and to approach Enlil, Nanna, and Enki, in that order, for help if she should fail to return. Inanna then abandons her seven cities and seven temples, thus stripping herself in an official sense for the ritual journey to the dead. But she takes seven of the *me*, wears them transformed into seven pieces of magnificent clothing and jewelry, and approaches the underworld in personal glory. She knocks on the great gates and demands admittance. When reasons are demanded, she first mentions her relationship to Ereshkigal and then claims to have come for the funeral of Gugalanna, the Bull of Heaven.

The Bull of Heaven is a figure traditionally linked to the generic great goddess, at least from the Neolithic period, and was important in Sumer as an animal representing the King of Uurk (in the present case, Dumuzi) as well as other kings and gods of Mesopotamia. He is also an astrological figure (Taurus), who disappears in the winter in Sumer and returns in spring. The Gugalanna theme, then, supports the descent myth's association with agriculture and beneficial sacrifice.

Neti, the guardian of the gates, informs the naked Ereshkigal of the grand visitor decked in the seven *me*. Furious at the intrusion of her opposite—of everything that she can never be—lover, mother—the queen of the underworld instructs her servant to allow Inanna through the seven locked gates of her realm, but only if she gives up one of the seven objects (the *me* as ornaments and clothing) at each gate. When Inanna arrives at her sister's throne, then, she is as naked as her host and is thus effectively stripped of her great powers. The significance seems to be that powers that function in life—sexual, familial, political, and priestly powers, for example—are useless in death. Inanna, always in search of new roles, nevertheless tries to usurp her sister's throne and is condemned by the underworld judging gods (Anunnaki) to death for her efforts. She dies and his hung up on the wall like a piece of meat.

Back in Uruk, three days and nights have passed, and the faithful Ninshubur follows her mistress's orders. The temples and cities go into deep mourning, and Ninshubur approaches Inanna's paternal grandfather, Enlil, and then her father, Nanna, for help, but both refuse, blaming the goddess for her excessive pride in going to the underworld. But Enki, the wise shamanic god, who from his home in the underground waters of the *abzu* has his ear to the underworld, agrees to help. He understands how important his granddaughter's existence is to the welfare of the living world. The effect of the goddess's absence from the world has echoes in the disappearing-god myths so prevalent among the Hittites and other peoples.

Enki creates two creatures from the mud under his fingernails. As beings apparently without sexuality or gender, these creations will not offend the infertile underworld, where Ereshkigal is screaming in pain as she gives negative birth, perhaps to the stillborn of the earth. To his two creatures, Enki gives the Plant of Life and the Water of Life and instructs them to comfort the suffering Eresh-kigal. In return, the underworld queen will offer them gifts, which they will refuse, demanding instead the body of Inanna, which they will revive with the two sacred elements. Everything happens as foreseen by Enki, but the underworld Anunnaki demand a substitute for the revived Inanna. Although she has been reborn in the underworld, she must leave a part of herself there. As Samuel Noah Kramer suggests, from the world of consciousness above, she must retain contact with the dark world of the unconscious below: "Inanna must not forget her neglected, abandoned older 'sister'—that part of herself that is Ereshkigal" (Wolkstein and Kramer, p. 161).

As Inanna leaves her sister's land, gathering up her clothing—her old *me* and power—she is accompanied by watchful demons who will ensure the payment of the sacrificial substitute. Entering her own world as once more the glorious Queen of Heaven, Inanna is greeted by Ninshubur, whose clothes of rags indicate her genuine mourning. When the demons claim the faithful servant as the sacrificial victim, Inanna refuses to give her up. Other faithful mourners—Inanna's two sons—are also spared, but when the great goddess and her underworld demons arrive at Uruk, a cheerful, well-dressed Dumuzi is acting as king, apparently unmindful of the loss of his once-

Taurus, the Bull

beloved wife. An enraged Inanna condemns him to the sacrifice. Terrified, Dumuzi begs his brother-in-law Utu for help, but even when he is turned by the sun god into a snake, he cannot escape. He, too, must experience the dark world of Inanna's other side, Ereshkigal, in order, as Kramer suggests, to become a "truly 'great' king" (Wolkstein and Kramer, p. 163). Dumuzi is taken away, but his sister Gestinanna arranges to spend six months of the year in the underworld so that he can spend those months back in the world above.

In a somewhat diminished role in later, more male-dominated Babylon, Inanna, as Ishtar, could play the role of a despised femme fatale, as in her failed attempt to seduce the hero Gilgamesh. [Wolkstein and Kramer]

INARA The daughter of the Hittite-Hurrian storm god, Inara plays a significant role in the Illuyanka cycle.

INARI Inari was the god of rice in Japan. He traveled with two messenger foxes and wore a beard.

INCAN MYTHOLOGY Incan mythology, of which little is known, comes to us indirectly from the Spanish explorers and missionaries of South America in the sixteenth century. The Incas were the most powerful and influential people of the region until their defeat by the Spanish. The Inca creator god was Viracocha (Huiracocha), who also had sun and storm god characteristics. After creating a race of giants, who became unruly, he caused a great flood to destroy all but two of them. Viracocha was married to Mamacocha (Cochamama), the sea goddess. Their son was the sun god Inti, the father of the founder and first emperor of the Incas, Manco Capac, who was also worshipped as a sun and fire god and who emerged

The Incan Viracocha Temple at Cuzco

in the Inca creation story with his brothers and sisters from a place near Cuzco known as Pacariqtambo. Manco Capac lived with these brothers and sisters at Cuzco and was married to his sister Mamaoello, a fertility goddess who taught the people spinning. One of Manco Capac's brothers was Pachacamac, who played something of the role of a devil-culture hero. He created the first people—a man and a woman—out of clay, but he forgot to give them food, and the man died. The angry woman cursed Pachacamac, and he made her fertile. She produced a son, whom Pachacamac killed and cut up into pieces that became fruits and vegetables. A second son, Wichama, escaped Pachacamac, and the angry god killed the woman, causing the even angrier Wichama to chase him into the sea.

Another Pachacamac myth tells a somewhat different story. It is said that the god created man and woman out of clay and then sent his son and daughter, born of the moon, fertility, and dragon goddess Mamapacha (Pachamama), to teach the people how to survive. The son was "the Inca" and the daughter was his queen. The Inca and his queen lived at Lake Titicaca, but they traveled around at will, following the command of their father to mark the spots of their travels with a golden rod he gave them. Where the Inca and his queen left marks, the people were to build cities. In the valley of Huanacauri, the rod disappeared into the earth, and this spot became the sun temple of the capital city of the Incas, Cuzco. The Inca and his wife functioned as culture heroes, teaching the people the ways of life.

The general themes of Incan mythology resemble those of other South American mythologies.

INDO-EUROPEAN MYTHOLOGY Beginning in the late fourth millennium or early third millennium B.C.E., Europe was gradually overrun and radically changed by people from the north—who also made their way into India and Iran to the east and eventually to Crete—so that by the end of the second millennium, all of Europe, much of Anatolia, the Fertile Crescent, Iran, and much of India were dominated by people most of whom we now refer to collectively as Indo-Europeans or, in some cases, Aryans. These peoples are the direct mythic and linguistic ancestors of much of the modern world, including Europe, with the exception of the Turks, the Basques, and peoples whose languages stem from the Finno-Ugric (Uralic) family—that is, the Finns, Hungarians, and Estonians. Not only the Indic and Iranian languages, but also the Greek, Italic, Celtic, Germanic, Baltic, and Slavic groups are all offshoots of a proto–Indo-European language.

The assumption of a proto–Indo-European culture and language out of which the Indo-European invaders sprang is based primarily on linguistic, mythological, ritualistic, and archeological correspondences. It was James Parson in his *The Remains of Japhet* (1767) who noted patterns such as similar words for numbers in Irish, Welsh, Greek, Latin, and other European languages. Sir William "Oriental" Jones, a more reputable scholar, expanded the patterns in the late eighteenth century to include Sanskrit (the ancient language of India) and Persian. Jones's position is supported by the existence of similar words for such common concepts as deity (e.g., *deus* in Latin, *dios* in Greek, *devha* in Sanskrit, and *daeva* in Persian). Nineteenth-century scholars—Rasmus Rusk, August Schleicher, Johannes Schmidt, Jacob Grimm, and others—contributed to the Indo-European hypothesis based on linguistic studies. Karl Muller, F. Max Muller, George W. Cox, and more recently Georges Dumezil, J. P. Mallory, Jaan Puhvel, and Bruce Lincoln have concentrated more on mythological patterns as well as on linguistic issues.

A Druidic grove

To better understand the sources of the Indo-European mythological patterns it is important to consider what little we know—primarily by way of archeology—of these early invaders from the north. There are many theories about the proto–Indo-Europeans. In one of the most popular theories, Marija Gimbutas refers to them as people of the "Kurgan culture." These were people of the Russian steppes, who buried their important male dead in chambers under round barrows, the Russian word for which is *kurgan*. The archeology of the burial sites and the evidence of language and myth in later Indo-European cultures suggests that these proto–Indo-Europeans were patriarchal and patrilineal, warlike, semi-nomadic pastoralists who practiced cattle herding, some small-scale agriculture, and animal husbandry and who, at least by the sixth millennium B.C.E., had domesticated the horse and trained it to pull wheeled vehicles such as chariots. The Kurgans possessed sophisticated weaponry, including the bow and arrow and metal knives and spears. Given the weaponry, the horse and chariot, and the herds, which were apparently the primary measure of wealth, it is not surprising that the military raid involving the stealing of cattle was an important activity for these peoples. A much later equivalent would be the raiding in the fifteenth century by the newly arrived, semi-nomadic pastoralist Athabascan (Navajo and Apache) peoples of the sedentary pueblo people in the Native North American Southwest.

Wherever the Indo-Europeans originated, it is clear that they brought certain mythological themes with them when they migrated south. These themes would take specific form in the mythological traditions we associate now with societies as widely diverse as those of India, Greece, Iceland, and Ireland, with religious systems as varied as Hinduism and Christianity.

The first of these themes has been called tripartization. Early in the twentieth century, sociologist Emile Durkheim postulated that myths reflected a given culture's social arrangements. Greek and Norse mythologies, for instance, reflected the patriarchal realities of the Greek and Norse cultures and their manners of governance. Following Durkheim, the French scholar Georges Dumézil argued for the existence in Indo-European mythologies of certain common forms reflecting Indo-European and, in all likelihood, proto–Indo-European cultural traditions. The dominant structure of Indo-European societies, according to Dumézil, was tripartization into classes or "functions"—religious, military, and farming/ herding. In India the three functions are represented by *brahmans* (brahmins), *ksatriyas*, and *vaisyas*, respectively; in Iran there were *athra-van*, *rathaestar*, and *vastriyo fsuyant*; in Rome *flamines* (flamens), *miletes*, and *quirites*; and in Gaulish-Celtic culture *druides*, *equites*, and *plebes*. This arrangement was clearly reflected in the pairing relationships of Indo-European mythologies, in which sovereign gods were related to priests and kings, warrior gods to warriors, and fertility gods to herder-farmers.

J. P. Mallory (pp. 130ff) outlines the Dumézil tripartite "function" theory as follows:

1. The first function embraces sovereignty and is marked by a priestly stratum of society that maintains both magico-religious and legal order. The gods assigned the sovereign function are often presented as a pair, each of which reflects a specific aspect: religious, such as the Indic Varuna or Norse Odin, and legal, such as Mitra or Tyr.

2. A second military function assigned to the warrior stratum and concerned with the execution of both aggressive and defensive force—for example, the war gods Indra, Mars, and Thor.

3. A third estate conceptualizing fertility or sustenance and embracing the herder-cultivators. Here the mythic personages normally take the form of divine twins, intimately associated with horses, and accompanied by a female figure—for example, the Indic Ashvins (horsemen) and Sarasvati, the Greek Castor and Pollox with Helen, and the Norse Frey, Freyr, and Njorth.

In relation to the third "function," Jaan Puhvel (pp. 269ff) follows an archeological and linguistic path to what he sees as a proto-Indo-European myth involving the mating of a noblewoman and a horse to produce divine twins. In support of his theory, he points to an Indic horse ceremony involving sacred intoxication and to the connection between the word for this ceremony, *asvamedha*, which can be traced back to a proto–Indo-European term meaning "horse-drunk," and forward to various later Indo-European words that are clearly related to the English *mead*. Crucial to the horse-twin myth is the sacrifice of the horse or of one of the twins, the body of whom becomes the world or is distributed to three deities.

Sacrifice, the source here of creation itself, is a primary theme in Indo-European mythology from Vedism to Christianity. An example of the sacrificed twin as what might be called the animistic material for creation occurs in the Vedic myth of the first man: Manu, who in the sacred ritual of sacrifice becomes the first priest (*brahman*), and his sacrificed twin, Yemo, who, as the essence of the world itself, becomes the first sacred king. The status of each class of being is indicated by the part of the twin's body from which it emerges: the priest from his mouth, the warrior

The Indian god Vishnu reclining on the Serpent, Sesha

from his arms, the commoner from his thighs, the servant from his feet, and so forth.

Related to the theme of sacrifice is the whole question of death and life after death. In proto-Indo-European thought, the death of an individual may well have been a reflection of the greater sacrifice that was the basis of creation. Thus, we return to the earth as a sacrifice only later to take on new life in some sense. Bruce Lincoln (1987, p. 203) outlines four essential principles behind the Indo-European death concept: (1) matter is indestructible, (2) matter is infinitely transmutable, (3) living organisms and the physical universe are composed of one and the same material substance, and (4) time is eternal. While change is thus constant, it is also meaningless, for nothing that is essentially real is ever created or destroyed. Worlds come and go, as do individuals of whatever species, but being—material being—is always there.

The individual role in the cosmic ritual of existence is represented mythologically in the person of the hero. Any reader of European and Indian mythology will be struck by the importance, for instance, of the theme of the cattle raid, a practice indicated by archeological studies of proto–Indo-European cultures. From linguistic and later Indo-European myths, including examples from India, Iran, Hittite Anatolia, Greece, and the European north, Bruce Lincoln reconstructs an essential proto–Indo-European myth of the cattle raid. The myth is dominated by a hero rather than a priest—priests being more clearly associated with the practice of sacrifice (although heroism and priesthood could be combined, as in the later cases of Jesus and the Buddha). The hero Lincoln calls Trito ("Third") possesses a significant herd of cattle that is stolen by a non–Indo-European three-headed monster. In time, Trito, assisted by the Indo-European warrior god, overcomes the monster and takes back his cattle. The point of the myth seems to be that foreigners steal while Indo-Europeans raid. The former activity is demeaning; the latter is noble. To put it in contemporary terms, bad raiders are terrorists, good raiders are freedom fighters. The cattle raid theme is important in particular cultures, especially the Irish.

A central Indo-European hero theme with probable antecedents in proto–Indo-European society is the hero's struggle with and defeat of the serpent. Whereas the serpent for Neolithic peoples seems to have been associated with fertility, the goddess, and deep earth knowledge, for the Indo-Europeans it is clearly a representation of the kind of blind, terrestrial, animal power that must be defeated by the enlightened sky god and/or his warrior-hero representative.

The ancient Indian *Bhagavata Purana* contains a myth of Krishna, the incarnation of the great god Vishnu, and his struggle with the serpent-monster Kaliya, a struggle that will be repeated in many forms by the saints and dragons, the heroes and serpents of later Indo-European cultures. Krishna's underwater struggle especially resembles the much later one between the Anglo-Saxon Beowulf and the mother of the monster Grendel. As the protector of cattle and the victor over evil represented by the serpent, Krishna also points to Jesus as the herder of human "sheep" and harrower of Hell.

Many other European mythic themes seem to have originated in some proto–Indo-European culture. Bruce Lincoln and Cristiano Grottanelli, for instance, have isolated a theme that concerns the commoner in victorious opposition to the priestly or warrior class. In one myth a humble woman, the mother of sacred twins and the symbol of earthly fertility, wins a definitive battle with warrior and kingly power [Lincoln (1987), p. 200]. Elements of this theme are found throughout European mythology, culminating, for example, in the struggles between Jesus and kingly and priestly power.

Apocalyptic battles are yet another Indo-European theme. J. P. Mallory points to "striking parallels" between the great wars between the Pandavas and Kauravas in the Indian epic the *Mahabharata*, between the Aesir and the Vanir in Norse mythology, and between the Sabines and the sacred Roman twins Romulus and Remus (p. 139). This dualism in Indo-European mythological structure is ubiquitous, indicated not only by twins such as the ones mentioned above but by twinned gods—Varuna-Mitra in Vedic India, Odin-Tyr in northern Europe. Claude Lévi-Strauss attributes the binary aspect to the human need to mediate between opposites (Mallory, p. 141).

There is much argument among scholars as to the nature of or existence of a proto–Indo-European culture. What can be said for certain is that there were several stages of conquest and migration from the north into the established cultures of the Bronze Age in Europe, Anatolia, Iran, and India; that the conquerors and migrants brought a body of myths with them; that these myths reflected the patriarchal, hierarchical, and warlike social and political structures of the conquerors; and that the new gods, goddesses, and heroes undermined but did not completely eliminate the ones found in the lands they invaded. Thus, in the mythologies that emerged from the various cultures that evolved over the centuries in the areas originally conquered by the northern invaders, we find a dominance of the proto–Indo-European themes outlined above with a lingering strain of the primary themes of the old mythology of the sedentary agriculturalists. [Dumézil, Durkheim, Gimbutas (1982, 1989), Lincoln (1986, 1987), Mallory, Puhvel]

INDO-IRANIAN MYTHOLOGY The term "Indo-Iranian" is used particularly by linguists and scholars of the Indo-European question to refer to the closeness in language and mythology of the so-called Aryan peoples who invaded India and Iran perhaps from a common culture and setting in the second millennium B.C.E.

INDONESIAN AND MALAYSIAN MYTHOLOGY Among the many indigenous peoples in Indonesia and Malaysia, there are several examples of dual gods and some of trinities. In Sumatra, the Toba Batak see the absolute, Mula Jadi na Bolon, as three persons representing the upper, middle, and lower worlds. In Nias there is a two-person divinity representing the dual nature of the universe—good and evil, light and dark. For the Ngaju people of Borneo, Jata is the feminine side of a dual godhead. She represents the lower world and the moon. Mahatala, the male aspect, is the upper world and the sun. Together Jata and Mahatala form the absolute, Tambon Haruei Bungai.

In the origin myths of insular Southeast Asia, animals, humans, and plants are interrelated players. In Kalimatan, the Indonesian section of Borneo, the first woman springs from a tree destroyed in a struggle between the male and the female hornbill. In Ceram the culture heroine–goddess Hainuwele is born of a mixture of blood and coconut sap. More generally, the first people descend from the heavenly region. Often, as in the case of Hainuwele, edible plants come from the body of a sacrificed hero or heroine. Origin myths of the overall area usually include an explanation of the prevailing social order. Clan systems, for instance, are explained by myths of the arrival of the first people at particular geographical locations. Nobility as opposed to commonness is explained by connections with particular deities.

The origin myths often include stories of the adventures of culture heroes. In the Celebes, for example, the high god Patoto'e sent his son La Toge 'langi to earth, where he took the title Batara Guru. On his way to earth, the hero traveled in a bamboo stalk, where he formed the world and its species. After a period of fasting, Batara Guru sent for his wives and servants, and thus the first human beings were categorized according to class. As his principal wife, Batara Guru took the daughter of the king of the underworld. When his first earthly daughter died, rice was formed from her body, reflecting an animistic view of reality. Descendants of Batara Guru became the culture heroes of various groups.

With the establishment of Islam in Indonesia, the indigenous myths of Java and other areas have been retained as folktales rather than as vehicles for religious truth. The first part of one of these tales, that of the hero Jaka Tarub, is reminiscent of the Indian story of Krishna and the gopis.

One evening Jaka Tarub comes across several beautiful maidens, or *bidadari* (angel-like heavenly spirits), swimming in a pond. As the spirits' winged clothes are on the bank of the pool, Jaka Tarub steals one set of them, making it impossible for the spirit Nawangwulan to fly away. Jaka Tarub and Nawangwulan marry and produce a daughter named Nawangsih. Nawangwulan feeds her family by magic, placing one grain of rice in the pot each day, which produces more than ample food, but she does so only on condition that her husband not look in the pot. Of course, when she is away one day he does look into the pot, and the magic is immediately dispelled, making it necessary for the family to use rice supplies like everyone else. Disappointed in her husband, the *bidadari* finds her winged garment and flies off to the other world.

In another folk myth, of the central Celebes in Indonesia, the people of Poso tell how the creator used to send things down to the first people by a rope from his nearby sky home. Once he sent down a stone, and the people rejected it as useless. The creator pulled up the stone and lowered a banana instead, and the people rushed to take it. Then the voice of the creator called down and scolded the people for their foolishness. Had they accepted the stone, he said, they would have achieved its solidity and immortality; but having chosen the banana, they had chosen its mortality and had introduced death into the world.

INDRA Indra of the *Rig Veda* is the king of the gods, the Vedic version of the old Indo-European warrior god Zeus/Jupiter/Odin, the god of the warrior class (*ksatriyas*). He is, in effect, the *dyaus*, the heavenly representative of the Aryan invaders of the Indian subcontinent during the second millennium B.C.E. He is the destroyer of cities—the conqueror. Like Zeus, he wields the thunderbolt and sleeps with mortal women. Like Zeus, he kills his father and is challenged by his son. One creation story tells us that Indra created the universe by separating Heaven and earth. Later, both Varuna and Vishnu will be credited with this deed. Indra is also the provider of soma, the ambrosial drug mixed with milk in the ritual sacrifice. Indra is the sun and he is fertility, represented, as Shiva would later be represented, by the erect phallus. Perhaps most important, Indra represents the new order of Vedic India. As king of the gods, Indra's primary task is to establish order. This he does in various ways. He frees the cows from the *panis*—the pre-Aryan demons of India, and he does so, above all, by killing the

Inuit statues from near the Bering Strait

dragon demon (*asura*) Virtra (the "restrainer") and Virtra's mother, calling to mind the Anglo-Saxon Beowulf's killing of the demonic Grendel and *his* mother, and Marduk's slaying of the disorderly Tiamat.

Energized by soma and using his thunderbolt to kill Virtra, who had enclosed the waters, Indra freed the waters and brought forth the sun and light and the new order. The *panis* and the dragons perhaps both symbolize the "restraining" cultures that attempted to prevent the Aryan conquest of India.

In the *Mahabharata* we find a quite different Indra and a different version of the Virtra myth. The king of the gods is now king in name only and has limited powers. Anxious that his enemy, Tvashtir, the architect of the gods, has created the three-headed son, Trisiras, to overpower him, Indra slays the demon with his thunderbolt. In revenge, Tvashtir creates the dragon Virtra, who defeats Indra—swallowing him and his whole world. It is only with the help of the great Hindu gods Vishnu and Shiva that he and the world are freed.

Even by the time of the *Brahmanas* in about 900 B.C.E., Indra's power has waned. He is now besotted with soma, and Prajapati is the supreme creator. Once the god of fertility, Indra has become a womanizer who at one point is even punished by castration. His place on the throne is dependent on the help of the now much more powerful Shiva and Vishnu.

In time Indra would become a figurehead only and sometimes the object of lessons and jokes, as in the famous myth of the "Parade of Ants."

INDUS VALLEY MYTHOLOGY In the middle of the third millennium B.C.E., an urban culture developed in the Indus Valley of western India. This culture was related, in terms of myth and religion, to the Elamite culture of southwestern Iran and to village cultures of Afghanistan, Turkmanistan, and Baluchistan. At the center of the Indus Valley culture were the cities of Harappa and Mohenjo-Daro, until a gradual decline begin-

ning early in the second millennium B.C.E. led to a movement of the culture to the Ganges-Yamuna Valley in the north and Gujarat and the Deccan Plateau in the south. After the Aryan–Indo-European invasions in the middle of the second millennium, there was an amalgamation of Indus Valley and Aryan traditions, leading to the complexities of Vedic religion and myth and to the Dravidian village culture of south India.

Archeological evidence from related cultures suggests that Indus Valley mythology was centered in the idea of female power and goddess (*Devi*) cults. There is direct evidence of goddess dominance on Indus seals, which, like the seals of ancient Sumer, bring together goddesses, sacred serpents, and such symbols of male power and virility as horned bulls and rams and mythical animals such as unicorns. There is also ample indication on the seals of rituals involving sacrifice to what appears to be a horned goddess. At the ruins at the ancient settlement of Mehrgarh, dating perhaps back to 6000 B.C.E., goddess figurines have been discovered that would seem to confirm the importance of female power during the 6000–2500 B.C.E. period.

INITIATION In the heroic monomyth the young hero performs certain acts that reveal him as the divine child (*puer Aeternus*).

INTI The primary Incan sun god, depicted as a golden disk with a shining face and extending rays, Inti was the son of the creator god Viracocha and the father of Manco Capac, the "Inca," or founder of the empire. Inti was feared because he could cause terrifying eclipses. He was worshipped particularly at the great sun temple of Cuzco.

INUIT MYTHOLOGY The Inuit (Eskimo) people live in a huge northern area that includes parts of eastern Siberia, Greenland, and northern North America. Their languages and cultures are closer to those of eastern Asian Mongolian and central Asian peoples than to those of other Native North Americans commonly referred to as "American Indians" further south. "Inuit" simply means "the people."

Inuit religion is shamanistic; shamans maintain a proper relationship between the people and the spirit world. Inuit religion and mythology are animistic; spirits inhabit all living things, including people and animals, and people all contain *anua* or *inua* (spirit-souls) that have two aspects—one that is a physical embodiment and one that goes to the underworld after death. Furthermore, every species has a particular deity who watches over rituals and taboos that ensure proper balance.

Naturally, given the huge expanse of Inuit land, Eskimos do not all have the same mythology. There are, for instance, many Inuit creation and origin myths. Some Inuit say there was once a great flood, after which two men emerged from the earth and acted as if they were man and woman. When one of the men became pregnant, the other sang a ritual song that resulted in the penis of the pregnant man becoming a vagina for the delivery of the first child.

Another myth tells how a man came to a young woman only under cover of darkness. Wishing to know who he was, the woman blacked her hands with soot and held on tightly to him during their lovemaking. The next day, by the marks on his back, she recognized her own brother as her lover and in horror fled to the sky with a bright torch, where he followed her with a dimmer one. She became the sun, he the moon.

In some areas the creator is female, as in the case of the Nunivak tribe's Sklumyoa. More often the creator is male, and sometimes he has strong trickster aspects, as is the case with the ubiquitous figure Raven, who creates the world in an earth-diver myth that involves bringing up earth from the primeval waters. Raven also makes use of more typically trickster approaches to creation, involving the expelling of excrement.

Among some of the Inuit there is an all-powerful goddess, sometimes called Sedna, who is a prime example of the deities who watch over people and animals to ensure balance.

IO The Greek father-god Zeus fell in love with the unfortunate Io, who was a priestess of Zeus's wife, Hera. When accused of infidelity by Hera, Zeus denied any inappropriate behavior and turned Io into a white cow, which Hera then had tied to an olive tree at Nemea under the watchful hundred eyes of Argus. Zeus, however, could not give up Io, so he sent Hermes to put Argus to sleep with his flute music. Hermes then killed Argus and released Io, still, of course, in her cow form. When Hera discovered what had happened, she had a gadfly chase poor Io from one end of the world to another. Various places in the ancient world took her name—for instance, Ionia, the Ionian Sea, and the Bosphorus ("Cow's Ford"). When Io got to Egypt, Zeus turned her back into a human. The offspring of their relationship was Epaphus, who ruled Egypt and who some say was the Divine Bull Apis. As is so often the case in patriarchal systems, it is the seduced woman who suffers the consequences of adultery rather than the seducer.

In one Maori myth, Io was the name of the creator god who sings the world into existence.

IOLOFATH A son of the sky god, Iolofath (Olifat) was a Micronesian trickster and culture hero. Like many culture heroes, he gave humans fire. In this case, the hero had fire brought from the sun in the beak of a bird.

IONIAN MYTHOLOGY Ionian mythology includes the myths that emerged in Greek mythology from the Hellenic people who settled in Attica and the northern Peloponnesus late in the second millennium B.C.E. and who colonized areas of the western coast of Asia Minor. The many-breasted Artemis of Ephesus is an example of an Ionian mythic figure, as is the unhappy King Midas. The Ionian Confederacy particularly admired the god Poseidon.

IPHIGENIA Iphigenia was a daughter of Clytemnestra and King Agamemnon of the cursed House of Atreus. When hunting one day, Agamemnon killed a hart sacred to the Greek goddess Artemis, who, as punishment, calmed the seas so that the king and the other Greeks could not sail off to fight the war in Troy. The seer Calchas advised Agamemnon to sacrifice Iphigenia to appease the goddess, and as the king was in the process of following that advice, the goddess substituted a hart for the girl and took her off to Tauris to be her priestess. Other versions of the story indicate that Iphigenia was, in fact, killed. In *Agamemnon*, the first play in the *Oresteia*, the trilogy by Aeschylus, Clytemnestra expresses resentment over her husband's sacrifice of their daughter. Her resentment contributes to the brutal murder of the king, described in the play.

IRANIAN MYTHOLOGY Aryans who invaded what is now Iran in the second millennium B.C.E. brought with them a patriarchal "Indo-European" mythology that was similar to that of the Aryans who invaded India at about the same time. This mythology, in both cases, replaced or assimilated religious systems in which goddesses, for example, seem to have been important. But with the reforms of Zoroaster and the development of Zoroastrianism, the mythology of Iran came to have as much in common with the strongly dualistic Abrahamic religions of the Middle East as with those of Vedic and Hindu India.

IRISH MYTHOLOGY The first point to be made about the branch of Celtic mythology associated with Ireland is that although it comes down to us in the form of manuscripts written by Christian monks, linguistic evidence suggests that the subject matter of those manuscripts was, in fact, reasonably well preserved from much earlier material. That is, the monks were committed to their Christian point of view and made certain Christian adaptations, but they were Irishmen, clearly intent on preserving Irish culture. Furthermore, Irish-Celtic culture had been less disrupted than that of the rest of the British Isles by the arrival of Romans and Christians. Essentially, Ireland escaped the Roman invasions, and Christianity seems to have had a minimal effect on the culture until Saint Patrick arrived there in the mid-fifth century. Finally, the hereditary *filidh* continued to preserve and orally transmit the ancient stories well after the establishment of Christianity.

The Irish mythological narratives were first written down in the vernacular, adapted into the Latin alphabet, by monks in the sixth century C.E. It can be argued, in fact, that by the middle of the seventh century, all or most of what we now think of as Irish mythology had been written down. The great *Tech Screpta*, in which the early manuscripts were kept, however, were gradually looted, primarily by the Viking raiders of the late eighth century, and all but fragments of the manuscripts were destroyed. Our primary sources for Irish mythology, therefore, are manuscripts written beginning in the early twelfth century.

The earliest of the twelfth-century manuscripts is the *Lebhor na hUidhre* (*Book of the Dun Cow*), primary work on which has traditionally been attributed to Mael Muire Mac Ceilchair, who was killed in a raid at the monastery of Clanmacnois in about 1106. The so-called Rawlison Manuscript B 502 in the Bodleian Library at Oxford, probably from the monastery at Glendalough or also from Clanmacnois, dates from about 1130. The *Lebhor na Nuachongbhala*, or *Lebhor Laignech* (*Book of Leinster*), is said to have been compiled by Aed Mac Crimthainn at the monastery at Terryglass in about 1150. The next two hundred years or so saw the production of the *Book of Lecan*, the *Yellow Book of Lecan*, the *Book of Ballymote*, the *Book of Lismore*, and the *Book of Fermoy*, all based on much earlier texts. A particularly important source for Irish mythology, especially the mythical history of Ireland, is a compilation known as the *Leabhar Gabhala Eireann* (*Book of the Taking of Ireland* or, more commonly, *Book of Invasions*) based on parts of various manuscripts, especially the *Book of Leinster*. The most complete version of this work is Michael O Cleirigh's, dating from the early seventeenth century. Also important are the various versions of the *Cath Maige Tuired* (*Battle of Mag Tuired* or Magh Tuireadh), especially the somewhat later account known as the *Second Battle of Mag Tuired*.

Heroic mythology in Ireland centers around a cycle of tales known as the *Ulster cycle* or *Red Branch cycle*. The sources for these sagas are primarily the *Book of the Dun Cow*, the *Book of Leinster*, and the *Yellow Book of Lecan*, out of which emerges the great Irish epic narrative the *Tain Bo*

Cuailnge (*Cattle Raid of Cuailnge*) and the lesser-known *Tain Bo Fraoch* (*Cattle Raid of Fraoch*). The twelfth-century *Acallam na Senorach* (*Colloquy of the Ancients*) is the literary form of a series of heroic tales, some of them extremely ancient in origin, known as the *Fenian cycle* or *Ossianic cycle*.

Central to Irish mythology is a mytho-historical version, derived from the many texts listed above, of the settlement of Ireland. There are conflicting versions of certain details in the story, but the essential elements are consistent. The invasions begin, according to the Christian redactors, with the arrival of Noah's granddaughter Cesair (or of Banba, one of the eponymous queens, or symbols of Irish sovereignty) before the flood. According to the Cesair myth, the flood destroyed all of these first invaders except for Cesair's husband, Fintan (the "Ancient White One"), who, according to some, saved himself by changing into a salmon. The myth claims that Fintan survived into the Christian period as a source of knowledge about the past.

Partholon and his people were the second invaders. It was Partholon who developed social customs and traditions and who began clearing land. But after fighting the simultaneously arriving Fomorians (Fomorii or Fomhoire), one-armed, one-legged, violent demons from under or "beyond" the sea, the Patholonians died of a plague.

Next came Nemed (Nemhedh) and his four women, the originators of the Nemedians, who also developed customs and crafts and cleared land. When Nemed was killed in battle with the Fomorians, his people were so mistreated by their conquerors that they revolted and emigrated to other lands. According to one version of the story, a group descending from the Nemedians returned to Ireland as the Firbolg (Fir Bholg) or "bag men"—so named, say some, because, as slaves in distant Thrace, they had been made to carry bags of earth.

The Firbolg, who could be representatives of an actual pre-Celtic people in Ireland, are credited with the important division of the island into five provinces or coiceds ("fifths") and with the establishment of a sacred kingship based on the relationship between the king's essential integrity and the land's fertility. The five provinces, which are basic to Irish myth and history, are Ulster in the north, Connaught in the west, Munster in the south, Leinster in the east, all held together by Mide (Meath) with Tara, the seat of the sacred king, at its center. The age of the Firbolg was a golden age of prosperity and peace.

The next invaders, the Tuatha Dé Danann ("People of Danu"), are the closest beings in Irish mythology to the deities of the great pantheons of the Indo-European tradition. Perhaps also descendants of the Nemedians, who in their time of exile—some say in the northern Greek islands—learned the mysteries of creation, the Tuatha had, in one way or another, become deities by the time they arrived in Ireland. They brought with them great powers of magic and druidry, symbolized by four talismans: the Fal Stone, which cried out to announce the true king when he stood on it; Lugh's Spear of Victory; Nuada's (Nuadha or Nuadhu) Undefeatable Sword; and Dagda's never-empty Cauldron.

The Tuatha Dé Danaan, as their name indicates, were descendants of the mother goddess Danu, of whom little is known. Their functions reflect a version of the Indo-European tripartite arrangement: sovereign/priest, warrior, and artisan. Many of the Tuatha have been associated with Romano-Celtic figures of the continent. In Julius Caesar's catalogue of the Celtic gods Mercury is the Irish Lugh, who contains the tripartite arrangement within himself. He is master of arts and crafts, a warrior, the source of divine kingship as druidic priest.

As sometimes king of the Otherworld, he is enthroned with a queen representing sovereignty in Ireland. The Gaulish Apollo is related to the Irish god of love, Mac ind Og or Aonghus (Oenghus), son of the "All Father" Dagda ("Good God" in the sense of "good at everything"). Dagda (Daghdah or the Dagda) is the supreme representative of the priestly class, the supreme druid. Caesar's Minerva is reflected in aspects of Dagda's daughter Brigid (Brighid), a healer and patroness of crafts and learning, who would later be assimilated by Christians as St. Brigid of Kildare and perhaps, in another context, by the British as Briganytia and then Britannia. As Brigid of Kildare, she was associated with sacred fire protected by many virgins, resembling the vestal virgins of Rome. In Scotland she was honored as the midwife of the Virgin Mary and the foster mother of Jesus. The Vulcan of Gaul has a counterpart in Goibhniu, the smith god of Ireland. Dis Pater, god of death in Gaul, has a counterpart in the mysterious Donn, the "Brown One," who can be associated with the great Bull of the *Tain Bo Cuailnge*. The Irish Ogma (Oghma) is in all likelihood a cognate for the Roman Hercules. Other important figures among the Tuatha Dé Danaan are Dian Cecht the healer, King Nuada of the Silver Arm, and his warrior queen Macha—like so many Irish deities, a triune figure who first appeared as the wife of Nemed and would later emerge as the Queen of Ulster.

When the Tuatha arrived in Ireland and established their court at Tara, they fought and defeated the Firbolg in the first battle of Mag Tuired, in which King Nuada lost his arm. Although the arm was replaced with a silver one by Dian Cecht and later with a real one by Dian Cecht's son Miach, Nuada abdicated his position as king because of his weakened condition when the Tuatha were faced with a new battle, this time against the Fomorians, who had returned to Ireland. Bres (the "Beautiful One"), the son of a Fomorian father and a Tuatha mother, was elected king, but when he proved so unsuitable as to elicit the satire of the poet Coibre—the voice of poets always carried great weight in Ireland—he was asked to resign. Instead, he turned to his enemy relatives for support, and the second battle of Mag Tuired resulted.

Before the battle, Nuada was restored to the throne, but he soon ceded his power to Lugh, who came to Tara and proved his ability to call successfully upon magical powers. Lugh led the battle, finally facing the horrid Balor, who killed both Nuada and Queen Macha and whose horrid single eye could destroy whole armies. With his sling stone, Lugh hit Balor's eye, and the stone forced the eye back through the demon's skull and turned its evil powers against the Fomorians, who were themselves destroyed and removed from Ireland forever. Bres was captured but allowed to live in return for revealing Fomorian secrets of agriculture, the Fomorians being, like the Norse Vanir and the Greek and Vedic giants against whom the gods must wage war, representatives of the powers of fertility and destruction that exist together in nature.

The next mytho-historical invasion of Ireland was that of the Gaels or Irish Celts, represented by the Milesians, or Sons of Mil Espaine ("Soldier of Spain"). There are many stories of how the Milesians eventually came to Ireland, and the Christian monks who wrote the *Book of Invasions* gave this story of Irish origins a resemblance to the biblical Book of Exodus. The Milesians, they said, journeyed from Scythia to Egypt to Spain and eventually to Ireland, where they landed, led by the poet Amairgen (Amhairghin), who used his Moses-like prophetic power and wisdom to push aside the defending cloud of mist arranged by Tuatha Dé Dan-

I

aan on the Feast of Beltene (May Day). The poet, in a sense, *sings* the new Ireland of the Celts into existence, containing within himself, like Krishna-Vishnu in the *Bhagavadgita* or the persona of the poems of Walt Whitman, all the elements of creation: "The sea's wind am I," he sings,

> The ocean's wave,
> The sea's roar,
> The Bull of the Seven Fights,
> The vulture on the cliff,
> The drop of dew,
> The fairest flower,
> The boldest boar,
> The salmon in the pool,
> The lake on the plain,
> The skillful word,
> The weapon's point,
> The god who makes fire I am

On their way to Tara, the Milesians met the triune goddess, represented by the eponymous queens Eire, Banba (Banbha), and Fotla (Fodla), who represented Irish sovereignty (sometimes together or individually they are given the name "Sovranty"). The queens tried to convince the invaders, led by Donn, to preserve their names forever as the names of the conquered island. Donn refused, and his early death was foretold by Eire. At Tara the Milesians met with the husbands of the queens, the three kings Mac Cuill, Mac Cecht, and Mac Greine, who asked for a temporary truce. It was decided by Amairgen that the Milesians should put out to sea and invade again. The second invasion was prevented by the magic wind of the Tuatha, until the stronger magic of the poet's words caused the Tuatha wind to fail. The Milesians then landed and, although Donn was killed, were able to defeat the old gods. The peace settlement left the Celts in control of the world above ground and the Tuatha in control of the land below. It was Amairgen who declared that Ireland should be named for the triune goddess. The Tuatha were said from then on to live in *sidhe*, or underground mounds, and were themselves referred to ever after as the *sidh*, the "fairies" or "little people" of legend in Ireland.

Ireland was now ready for the heroic and tragic events surrounding the lives of the likes of Cuchulainn, Conchobhar, Fergus, Queen Medb (Medbh, Maeve), Finn, Oisin, and so many others. These events, described in such works as the *Tain* and the much later *Fenian cycle*, are Irish equivalents of the Indian *Mahabharata* and *Ramayana*, the epics of the Germanic and Slavic peoples, and the more familiar epics of Homer. [Cunliffe, Ellis, Mac Cana, Green, Fee and Leeming]

ISAAC In his miraculous birth to Abraham and Sarah in their old age and his near–sacrificial death in childhood, Isaac, one of the heroes of biblical Hebrew mythology, contains familiar characteristics of other mythic heroes. He was literally the child of the covenant between Yahweh (God) and the Hebrews (Israelites, Jews), and God reestablished the covenant with him. Isaac married Rebecca (Rebekah), a distant relative of his father from Mesopotamia, and Jacob and Esau were the result of their union. His heroism was confirmed by the extraordinary length of his life; he died near Hebron at the age of one hundred and eighty and was buried there by Israel (Jacob) and Esau (Genesis 35:28–29).

ISHMAEL In the Hebrew Bible, the *Torah*, Ishmael was the son of Abraham and the slave woman Hagar. He plays a significant role in Islamic mythology as Ismail.

ISLAMIC MYTHOLOGY The word "Islam" comes from the Arabic root *slm*, meaning "to be whole and at peace." A *Muslim* is a person who surrenders to the order and peace that is the law of Allah as described in the holy book, the *Qur'an* (*Koran*). Islam was founded in Arabia by the Prophet Muhammad, the "Messenger of Allah," in the seventh century C.E. In 630 C.E. (A.H. 8), Muhammad and his followers took control of Mecca, the holy city of the Ka'bah ("cube") or "House of Allah," in the eastern corner of which is located the Black Stone. In theory, the Muslim does not pray to the stone as an idol but to God (Allah) at the stone. The Ka'bah, however, was considered a sacred place by Arabs even before the rise of Islam and probably was worshipped as a place holy to various deities of Arabian mythology.

In the Holy Book we are told of five aspects of the Muslim faith: belief in Allah, angels, the *Qur'an*, the messengers of God (prophets), and the Day of Judgment. Based on these five beliefs are the "Five Pillars of Islam": the public expression that "there is no god but Allah and Muhammad is his prophet," the obligation of prayer five times a day while facing Mecca, almsgiving, fasting during Ramadan (the ninth month of the Islamic lunar calendar), and the *hajj*, or once-in-a-lifetime pilgrimage to the Ka'bah at Mecca. Islam is a religion that is more concerned with social order than with religious ritual or myths.

Rembrandt's version of the near sacrifice of Isaac by his father Abraham

I

I

An Islamic depiction of Adam and Eve and their thirteen twins

There are, however, Islamic myths: myths of creation, myths of the afterlife, and myths of the end of the world, as in the other Abrahamic religions, Christianity and Judaism. And there are myths surrounding the Prophet Muhammad's life. But the primary concern has always been practical and rational Islamic Law in this world. Its very simplicity and directness has always made Islam a religion with great appeal. The religion has traveled easily, in Africa, for example, and, with special success, in Asia.

From the time of Muhammad's death in 632, however, Islam's history has been marked by a great schism and resulting wars. After the Prophet's death, a committee of prominent Muslim figures named Muhammad's longtime friend and father-in-law, Abu Bakr, as his successor and leader (Caliph) of the Muslims. This decision was challenged by members of Muhammad's family and their supporters. These people, the *Shi'a'Ali* ("Followers of Ali," and later simply the Shi'a Muslims, as opposed to the Sunni Muslims), believed that the Prophet had named his cousin and son-in-law Ali, who was married to his daughter Fatima, as his successor. Much violence followed, and after the murder of the Caliph Uthman in 656, Ali (for the Shi'a, the "Lion of Allah") did, in fact, become Caliph. After more wars, Ali was apparently murdered by a poison weapon. Ali's successors among the Shi'a were given the title Imam. The most important of these Imams was Ali's son Husayn, who was killed by rivals in Karbala (in Iraq) and who became, with Ali, a significant Shi'a "martyr" and focus of religious zeal. Today Shi'a Mus-

lims and the much more numerous Sunni Muslims exist in sometimes uneasy proximity in the Muslim world.

At first, Muslims maintained good relations with the older Abrahamic monotheists, fellow people "of the Book," but struggles with Christians and Jews, who shared the Islamic sense of exclusivity, were inevitable. Like that of the Jews, especially, the nationalism of the Arabs was a tribal and religious nationalism for which certain compromises were impossible. Before long, in spite of internal struggles between factions such as the Ummayids and the Abbasids, led by different Caliphs, Muslim armies, now no longer exclusively Arab, advanced in all directions, forming a great empire that would take in all of the Middle East, including Egypt and Persia. Muslim traders and settlers came to the Indian subcontinent within a generation of the Prophet's death. By the end of the seventh century C.E., Muslims had conquered parts of Afghanistan. In the early eighth century they had crossed the Straits of Gibralter into Spain and in 732 they crossed the Pyrenees into France. By the middle of the eighth century C.E. Islam dominated Turkistan, and under the Samanids in the ninth and tenth centuries Islam made inroads into the domains of the shamanistic and Christian peoples of the steppes of Central Asia. From the tenth century, Muslims began to conquer parts of the North Indian plain.

European Christians had long seen the march of Islam as both a territorial and religious threat. Holy wars against Muslims took place almost from the earliest period of Muslim expansion—in Spain, in Sicily, and in the Byzantine struggle for survival against the Turks. The fall of Jerusalem to the Selcuk Turks in 1077 set off waves of horror among Christians. Armed crusaders set out in waves to liberate Jerusalem and the "Holy Land" as a whole from the "Infidel" during the twelfth and thirteenth centuries. Several crusades led to varying degrees of success, but failure usually followed. In 1229, for instance, Frederick II of Hohenstaufen won a victory and had himself crowned King of Jerusalem, but the city was retaken in 1244. Muslims ruled essentially all of the Middle East for several centuries after that. Parts of Bengal, Assam, and Orissa were taken early in the thirteenth century, and parts of Kashmir in the fourteenth. With the invasions of the Mongols and their tolerant attitude toward Muslims in the thirteenth and fourteenth centuries, Muslims became part of the ruling class in China.

In the early sixteenth century, the Muslim Mughal dynasty was established on the ruins of the Muslim sultanate of Delhi by Babur, a descendant of Tamerlane and Ghengis Khan. The dynasty would rule northern India and eventually control most of the south as well until the last Mughal emperor was expelled by the British in 1858. Perhaps the greatest of the Mughals was Akbar, who reigned from 1556 to 1605 and was able, through tolerance and generosity, to win over his Hindu subjects. It was Akbar's grandson, Shah Janan, who built the Taj Mahal. Muslim armies would later move east and west, conquering much of the world, including parts of Christian Europe, where the Ottoman army was finally stopped at the gates of Vienna in 1683.

After the defeat of the Ottomans at Vienna, Muslim power was diminished. The advent of European colonialism occurred in the eighteenth century and continued in various degrees until the years following World War II, when a still deeper rift developed between the Muslim Middle East and the West. With the formation of the state of Israel in what Arabs saw as their land, the rift became more profound and more specifically oriented. In 1967 Jews once again took power in all of Jerusalem, and today the struggle between Semitic peoples for the city that is holy to the three Abrahamic religions and for the land that was once Canaan is still running its course.

Islam remains the dominant religion of the Middle East, Central Asia, Pakistan and Afghanistan, Indonesia and Malaysia, as well as much of Africa, and Muslims are a significant minority in India.

Islam is dominated by the person of Muhammad. Muhammad's biography is historically fairly clear, and Islam depends less on mythology than do Judaism and Christianity. Mythological tales of the Prophet did emerge from folklore, however, and two essential myths, that is, extraordinary or supernatural events, do mark his canonical life. These are the passing to him by Allah of the *Qur'an*, the holy book of Islam, making him literally God's messenger; and his Night Journey, the journey to Jerusalem (*Isra*) and the Ascension (*Mi'raj*) from there to the Seventh Heaven.

Of course, the concept of Allah, the god of Ibrahim (Abraham), worshipped also by Christians and Jews, is central to Islam. An important Islamic myth concerns the "House of Allah," the old *Ka'bah* of Mecca, taken over by Muhammad and his followers from the old pre-Islamic Arabian religions as the focal point of Islamic worship. The Ka'bah is represented by every mosque, as synagogues everywhere represent the ancient Temple of Judaism and churches represent the place of crucifixion for Christians. The Ka'bah is said to have been originally built by Ibrahim and left under the guardianship of his son Ismail (Ishmael), the founder of the Arabs. The Ka'bah remained for a time a holy place to Jews and Christians and people of other religions, too. But when the Prophet took control of Mecca, he destroyed all of the idols that surrounded the sanctuary and it became primarily a goal of the Islamic pilgrimage, the *hajj*, and the focus of the spiritual hajj that is the act of prayer.

At first, under the influence of Judaism and Christianity, and especially later, due to the teachings of Muhammad, the Arabs moved from a polytheistic mythology to what the outsider might call a hero-based monotheistic one. As in the case of the development of Judaism, there is an early struggle before and during Muhammad's career between a monolatry in which a high god presides as the most important god among many others, including important goddesses, and monotheism, which saw the high god as the only god.

It is possible that for some time before Muhammad the Meccans had associated the term *al-Lah* with the supreme divinity behind the old tribal gods of Arabia. These Meccans apparently believed that the *Ka'bah* had in the beginning been dedicated to this deity. In fact, Muhammad's first biographer, Muhammad ibn Ishaq, records the possibly apocryphal story of several of Muhammad's tribe, the Quarysh, traveling north to discover the ancient pre-Jewish, pre-Christian religion of Ibrahim. Ibrahim was considered a prophet and the first Muslim, because in his willingness to sacrifice his own son he demonstrated *islam*, total obedience to God.

Allah is identifiable as the god of Abraham and the creator god of Christians and Jews, but as he reveals himself to his messenger Muhammad—for Muslims the "Seal of the Prophets," the interpreter with the last word, as it were—he projects different emphases than the god of Moses or Jesus. Like Jews and Christians, Muslims see this god as, above all, unique: "It has been revealed to me that your god is one god" (*Qur'an* 41:6). But the

Qur'an (2:267, 4:171) specifically rejects the kind of theology that involves a divine intermediary between God and humans (e.g., a divine Jesus or "Son of God") or a God of more than one aspect (e.g., the Christian doctrine of the Trinity). Allah is less personal than in his Judeo-Christian aspect, a more mysterious power that is nevertheless behind all aspects of the universe. He is knowable only through his creation, through the signs of nature, through the metaphorical stories of the prophets, and especially through the *Qur'an*, his great gift to humankind. And though he is *al-'Azim* (the "inaccessible"), he is *al-Rahman* (the "compassionate" and the "merciful"). For the Islamic mystics or Sufis, especially, he is *al-Haqq* (the "real" and the "true") and *al-Hayy* (the "living"), in some sense the god within.

Goddesses played an important role in pre-Islamic Arabian religion and mythology. Together these goddesses were the *banat al-Lah* (the "Daughters of God") and were much revered by the Meccans. When Muhammad forbade the worship of the *banat al-Lah*, many of the first Muslims revolted. The historian Abu Jafar al-Tabari, in the tenth century, wrote that Muhammad was so upset by the split in his followers over the goddesses that he gave in and created some false or "Satanic verses," verses inspired by Satan, that allowed the *banat al-Lah* to be thought of as intercessors, like angels. Many Islamic scholars doubt that the incident of the Satanic verses ever occurred, but according to al-Tabari, the angel Gabriel instructed Muhammad to do away with the lines and to replace them with a condemnation of the worship of these "empty names" (*Qur'an* 16: 57–59, 22:52, 52:39, 53:19–26).

As for the story of creation, Muhammad essentially accepted the Genesis version of creation, with some alterations. In

The Islamic Mughal emperor Babur at the head of his army.

the *hadith* of Islam, the collection of traditional sayings, acts, and stories of Muhammad, Allah says, "I was a hidden treasure; I wanted to be known. Hence, I created the world so that I might be known." In short, humans, through an experiencing of the natural "signs" of Allah's creation, the most important of which is the *Qur'an*, would know Allah.

The *Qur'an* does not present the creation in a single unit the way it is presented in Genesis. Rather, the story comes in bits and pieces in various *sura* ("chapters"). As in Genesis, Allah created the world himself (36:81, 43:9–87, 65:12). What was once a solid mass he tore apart, and he made living things from water (21:30, 24:45). As for the creation process itself, it is said to have taken six days (7:54, 10:3, 25:59, 32:4). Allah created the dark and the light, the heavens and the earth, the astral bodies (7:54, 6:1, 21:33, 39:5). He said "Be" and it was (6:73). He created the beasts of burden and those that could be used for meat (6:142), animals and plants of all kinds (31:10–11). He created Adam in his image out of dust or clay or by a small seed (semen) and said "Be" and he was (3:59, 6:2, 15:26, 16:4, 22:5, 32:7, 35:11, 40:67). He created woman (traditionally Haiwa = Eve) out of the same material (4:1, 39:6). He also created Hell for evil spirits (*jinns*) and bad humans (7:179). Allah ordered the angels themselves to bow down to his human creation, and all did except for Iblis (the Devil), who claimed to be better than humans because he had been created from fire rather than dust (7:11–12, 15:27, 17:61, 38:75–76). For his disobedience, Iblis was banned from Paradise (7:13–18) but had permission to tempt humans (15:36–37, 17:62–63) until Doomsday, when he and his followers—that is, unbelievers, who are also *shaitans* (devils, satans)—would be sent to Hell (7:27, 26:95).

Allah made a garden—a paradise—for the man and his wife but ordered them not to eat from a particular tree (2:35). But the Shaitan (Satan, Iblis, the father of all shaitans) convinced them that the fruit of the tree contained the power that made angels and gods (7:19–22, 20:120), and the couple ate the fruit. It is noteworthy that it was the couple, not the woman first and the then the man, who committed this sin. After eating the fruit, the man and the woman became conscious of their nakedness and sexual feelings and covered their genitals (7:27). Allah scolded them for listening to his enemy, and their life became hard (20:115–121). Later, as in Genesis, God sent a great flood, during which the prophet Nuh (Noah) and his family, representing believers, were saved in an ark (11).

Islam, of course, has its heroes or prophets who existed before Muhammad. Traditionally, Ibrahim (Abraham) was thought to be the father of Islam in the sense that he "knew" the true God—*al-Lah*, the God later revealed as such to Muhammad—before there were Jews or Christians. The *Qur'an* and Islamic tradition contain many myths of this *Khalilu'llah* or "Friend of God." One story says that Ibrahim cut up a crow, a vulture, and a peacock and then revived them simply by calling to them (2:262). It is believed that Ibrahim threw stones at the devil at Mina, near Mecca, where to this day pilgrims on the *hajj* commemorate the act by throwing stones at a pillar of stone. Islamic tradition holds that Hajar (Hagar) was the first wife of Ibrahim and the mother of his first son, Ismail (Ishmael). Hajar and Ismail were sent away by the jealous second wife, Sarah, mother of Ibrahim's second son, Ishak (Isaac), also a prophet (4:163). While Hajar and Ismail were wandering in the desert, the angel Jibril (Gabriel) opened the well of Zamzam for them so that they could survive. This well is in the place now called Mecca, and pilgrims still drink from it. Pilgrims also run between two hills representing Hajar's search for water. The story says that later Ibrahim, feeling guilty about having

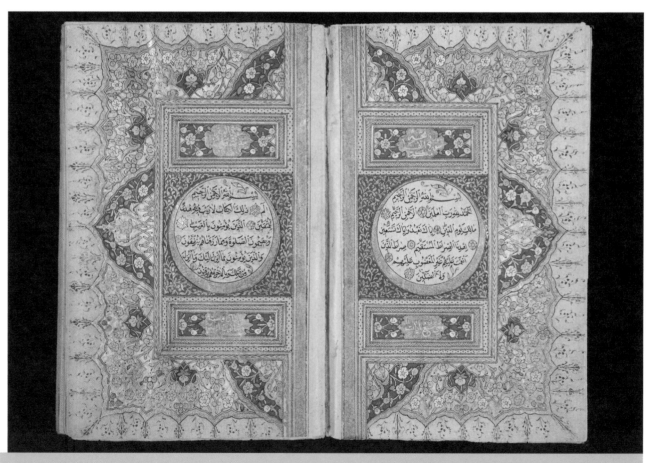

The sacred book of Islam, the Koran

expelled Hagar and Ismail, found his wife and child at the well and with Ismail built the Ka'bah (2:124–140) according to Allah's specifications, as revealed by Jibril.

In the *Qur'an*, it is Ismail who would have been sacrificed by Ibrahim had Allah not substituted a ram. When Ibrahim, his face drenched in tears, pressed the knife against his willing son's throat, it would not penetrate the flesh. In fact, the knife spoke to the distraught father, telling him that the Lord had forbidden it from cutting Ismail (37:102–107). Ismail is the symbol of the perfect Muslim child, one fully obedient to God. Not surprisingly, Muhammad was said to be a descendant of Ismail.

Another important prophet for Muslims was Musa (Moses). It is recognized that God called Musa and that he revealed the *Tawrat* (*Torah*) to him (19:52, 20:9–23, 27:7–12, 28:29–35, 79:15–16). The Quaranic stories of Musa are essentially the same as those of Moses in the Bible.

Isa (Jesus) was the penultimate prophet of Islam. He is believed to be *Al-Maih* (the Messiah) and *kalima-t-allah*, "the Word of God," but not the Son of God (3:40, 4:169, 4:171). Capable of miracles, Isa was especially successful at curing the sick (3:49, 5:30). In some sense, Isa was "raised up by God" (3:55), and many believe that he will come back.

Isa's birth was miraculous. Maryam (Mariam, Mary), for whom Sura 19 of the *Qur'an* is named, was visited by the angel Jibril (Gabriel), who lifted her dress and blew on her body, making her pregnant with the breath—the word—of God's spirit. Maryam gave birth to Isa next to a withered date palm and washed the child in a well placed there by Allah. The date palm tree suddenly flourished, and Jibril came back and advised Maryam not to make excuses for her mysterious pregnancy and birth-giving but to allow the young prophet to speak for her. Miraculously, Isa, although a newborn baby, could speak; he announced himself as a prophet, and people accepted his mother and him (3:45–46, 4:171, 19:16–27, 21:91, 23:50, 66:12).

The Islamic equivalent of Exodus, the story of the journey from lowliness to power of a people chosen of God, is the story of Muhammad. In the *hadith* and in folklore Muhammad became much more than a discontented merchant of Mecca, much more than a religious reformer; he became the world hero to whom God spoke directly and who could break the barriers of space and time in a journey to God's heaven. Muhammad is the great hero of Islam, the Prophet, the Messenger of Allah, the perfect man (*insan al-kamil*), the founder of the *ummah*, the Muslim community. This was a community that was to transcend barriers of race and ethnicity. Islam was to become, like Christianity before it, a universal religion. The *ummah* would replace the older Arabic community ideal of the *muruwab* that stressed utter and complete obedience to the clan chief and the validity of the blood feud. Muhammad replaced the loyalty of *muruwab* with the ideal of *islam*, total obedience to Allah. Not surprisingly, however, since both *muruwab* and *islam* stress the importance of the group over the individual, elements of the old *muruwab* way sometimes surface in Islam even today. [Armstrong (1993, 2000), Knappert (1985), Nasr, Rahman (1979, 1987), Renard (1998)]

ISMAIL Ismail is the Arabic name for the biblical Ishmael, the son of Abraham and the slave woman Hagar. He is much more important in Islam than in Judaism or Christianity. According to Muslims, he was the perfect Muslim child, as he (rather than Isaac) would have willingly been sacrificed by his father to Allah.

ITZAMMA The high god of the Maya, Itzamma is also a culture hero of sorts as the inventor of writing, medicine, and religion. Often he is seen as a sky serpent, the appropriate companion for his earth-based fertility goddess consort Ix Chel.

IX CHEL The Mayan goddess of fertility, Ix Chel (the "Rainbow") was the consort of the high god Itzamma. She had jaguar associations and sometimes was depicted with serpents in her hair, serpents frequently being the companions of earth goddesses.

IXION In Thessaly in Greece lived the Lapiths, an oversexed race whose king was Ixion. Ixion was so driven by lust that he even tried to rape Hera, the wife of the father-god Zeus. Hera was able to escape the unwanted intrusion by substituting a cloud for herself in her bed. The drunken Ixion had sex with the cloud and the result was Centauros, the ancestor of the centaurs, who also scorned the usual rules regarding sexuality. Insulted by Ixion's attempt to make him a cuckold, Zeus had Ixion tied to a wheel of fire, which spun forever in the underworld.

IZANAGI AND IZANAMI The *Kojiki* and the *Nihongi*, the primary sources for Japanese pre-Buddhist or Shinto mythology, tell of the mythological age that began with events surrounding the first couple, Izanagi and Izanami. When at the beginning of time, chaos was overcome by the separation of Heaven and earth, the first parents were created. The Izanagi-Izanami relationship brings to mind the *yin-yang* principle in China; Izanami was the passive principle—the "female who invites," and Izanagi was the active principle—the "male who proceeds." When the first couple thrust a jeweled spear into the maternal waters below, the central island of Japan was formed. The couple decided to marry and did so after developing a courtship ritual in which the male was dominant and in which the details of the procreative act were discussed. From their union came the islands of Japan and eventually the sun goddess, the source of all Japanese emperors, Amaterasu.

The Izanami-Izanagi cycle contains a particularly dark myth in which Izanagi goes to the Land of the Dead in search of his wife, who had been killed, in effect, by giving birth to fire. When he arrives, he finds that Izanami, like Persephone in the Greek underworld, had already eaten of the fruit of the dead and, therefore, could not return with her husband to life. Izanami ordered Izanagi not to look at her body, now deformed by death, but he disobeyed. Izanami, insulted, chased her husband to the very gates of Yomi (the underworld). Having wrongly visited the underworld, Izanagi was plagued by bad luck until he was able to wash in sacred waters, after which he isolated himself on a distant island. His wife became Queen of the Underworld.

IZUMO The Impetuous Male, Susanowo, brother to the Japanese sun goddess Amaterasu, behaved badly and was banished from the home of the gods. After his banishment, he went to Izumo across the water from Korea. There he built a palace at Suga and married the daughter of an earth spirit for whom he had killed a notorious eight-headed monster. Susanowo and his wife then became parents to many important gods—especially Okuninushi and the "Spirit Master" of Izumo.

J

JACOB The Hebrew Bible's Jacob and Esau, sons of Abraham's son Isaac, represent two nations—one urban, the other nomadic. Jacob was wily, able to trick the "hairy" Esau (the older of the two boys) out of his birthright. Rebecca (Rebekah), the mother of the two men, who preferred Jacob, perpetuated Esau's loss of his birthright by tricking the now old and blind Isaac into giving Jacob the blessing of inheritance. Esau displeased his parents by marrying Judith and Bashemath, Hittite women. Jacob pleased them by following their suggestion that he go to Mesopotamia to the family's old homeland to find wives related to him. This approach signifies the postexilic priestly tradition of marriage within the exclusive community.

On his way to Mesopotamia, near a shrine between Beersheba and Harran, Jacob lay down to sleep, using a rock for a pillow, and had a vision of a ladder rising up to Heaven and of Yahweh reasserting the Abrahamic covenant. Yahweh had confirmed the covenant earlier to Isaac as well, at Beersheba, in honor of which Isaac had built an altar and dug a well. Jacob woke up, made a sacred pillar of his stone pillow, and named the place Bethel. In Mesopotamia he fell in love with Rachel, a woman related to his family, but was tricked into marrying her older sister Leah. He had many children with Leah, and later he also married Rachel, who, though apparently barren, miraculously conceived and gave birth to Joseph. There were also children by two slave women.

After a long stay in service to his in-laws, Jacob and his wives returned to Canaan. On the way Jacob was approached by a man who wrestled with him (Genesis 32:22–30). The man was apparently Yahweh himself—"I have seen God face to face," proclaimed Jacob"—and the man blessed Jacob and changed his name to Israel ["El (God) rules"]. Rachel gave birth to another son, Benjamin, on the road to Ephrathah (Bethlehem). Benjamin and the first eleven sons of Jacob were the progenitors of the twelve tribes of Israel. As for Isaac, he died near Hebron at the age of 180 and was buried there by Israel (Jacob) and Esau, the father of the Edomites (35:28–29). Israel and his children settled in Canaan, and when Israel died he was taken, according to his instructions, to Hebron in Canaan, where he was buried with his father and grandfather. With the death of Jacob and later of Joseph, the story of the patriarchal tribal hero Abraham and his immediate family comes to an end, and the mythological stage is set for the story of the Exodus.

JAGUAR In Mesoamerica and South America, the jaguar represents the various qualities needed in supreme gods. The jaguar is particularly associated with the Aztec high god Tezcatlipoca and the Mayan solar god Ahau Kin. The jaguar qualities include fertility, power, and a knowledge of the spirit world.

JAHANGIR The oldest son of Tamerlane (Timur), Jahangir was the fourteenth-century villain/hero of the Mongolian verse epic named for him.

JAIN MYTHOLOGY Founded in part by Vardhamana Mahavira in the sixth century B.C.E., Jainism remains an important offshoot of Hinduism in India. It seems likely that Jainism came fully into being with the joining of the followers of Mahavira and those of an earlier prophet, Parsva. Over the centuries, the Jains have evolved into two primary communities, the Digambara (the sky-clad or naked) and the Svetambra (the white-clad). There are four orders of Jains—monks, nuns, laymen, and laywomen. In general, Jains practice an extreme form of the disciplines practiced by Brahmanic Hindus and certain Buddhist monks. Jain monks and nuns must, above all, practice *ahimsa*, or nonviolence to any living creature, be it man or insect. The monastic vows (*mahavratas*) are all directed toward the goal of liberation from internal and external bonds. Strict and complex rules of fasting, eating, begging, wandering, confession, and study apply. It is by means of the strictest asceticism that the Jain monk may achieve the remains of *karman* so that his soul (*jiva*), might realize its true nature and ascend to the upper world, beyond the bondage of death and rebirth.

Jains believe in a three-part cosmos, composed of the upper, middle, and lower worlds. At the bottom are seven hells for people whose lives were marked by bad *karman*. Divinities live in the upper world. The middle world (Madhyaloka) is a place where the individual can learn to be awakened and liberated. At the center of the middle world is Mount Mandara or Meru. Like the Brahmanic cosmology, which it generally resembles, the Jain system recognizes a cosmic cyclical time made up of recurring ages (*kalpas*). [Caillat]

JALAMDHARA According to a Hindu myth, Jalamdhara was a Herakles-like *asura*, born of the union of Ganga (Ganges) and Ocean. He had immense strength and was able to conquer the gods and the three worlds. Brahma had given him the gift of being able to raise the dead. He even defeated the great Vishnu in battle and perhaps would have killed him had the god's wife, Lakshmi, not intervened. He is said to have attempted to seduce Shiva's wife, Parvati. Jalamdhara was finally defeated in single combat with Shiva, who used a flaming disc to decapitate him and then instructed the goddesses to become ogresses and to drink the demon's blood before he could raise himself from death.

JANUS A Roman god always depicted with two faces, Janus was the god of comings and goings, whose face appeared, like Greek *herms*, on most entrances. He was a highly popular deity of Etruscan origin who gave his name to our month of January.

JAPANESE BUDDHISM Buddhism in Japan takes several forms but is particularly marked by a tendency toward the esoteric. The religion came into Japan during the fifth and sixth centuries C.E. in connection with the gradual influx of Sino-Korean philosophy and imagery and the adaptation of the Chinese script. When Buddhism was officially introduced to the Japanese court in the sixth century, there was strong reaction against it on the part of the conservative guardians of the ancient Shinto tradition and its divinities, or *kami*. It was the powerful Soga clan that supported Buddhism and attached it to the state. Under the regent Prince Shotoku in the late sixth and early seventh centuries, there was a bringing together of Buddhism and the indigenous Shinto religion that would color Japanese Buddhism from then on. In the eighth century, the religion flourished, especially in the capital, Nara, where many monasteries were established. The ninth century was marked by the development of the characteristic esoteric tradition that stressed enlightenment. The leaders in this movement were the Tendai and Shingon sects. The Shingon sect especially stressed the esoteric, believing that the true Buddhist could achieve union with the absolute.

Influenced by Tantrism from India, the esoteric sects gained in popularity with the Japanese people, because of the emphasis they put on the accessibility of the Buddha nature. In the tenth century, the cult of the Buddha Amitabha or Amida Buddha gained in popularity. The Tendai sect, especially, preached the idea that enlightenment through the teachings of the Buddha Sakyamuni (Gautama Buddha) was no longer possible. To achieve enlightenment, the devout person would have to be reborn in the Pure Land (*Gokurakujodo*), the land where the Buddha Amida preached. It was the monk Honen and his disciple Shinran who in the twelfth and thirteenth centuries developed this doctrine.

In reaction to Amidism the Zen sect arose. Its first master was the thirteenth-century monk Dogen. Dogen advocated the practice of ecstatic meditation and a return to the original principles of the Buddha Sakyamuni. Some sects of Zen Buddhism consider him their founder.

In the esoteric sects of Buddhism, such as the Shingon, the deities of Shinto, the *kami*, are seen as manifestations of the absolute Buddha, the Dainichi Nyorai. The theory behind this concept is called *honji suijaku*. The process by which Shinto deities were assimilated into Buddhism as *bodhisattvas*, or *bosatsu*—that is, future buddhas (*nyorai*)—and then as avatars (*gongen*), or temporary manifestations of buddhas on earth, was gradual until, by the Middle Ages, Shinto *kami* became, in effect, Buddhist *kami*—for example, Shaka, Amida, Miroku, Yakushi, Kannon, and Jizo. [Kitagawa, Tsunoda]

JAPANESE SHAMANISM In pre-Buddhist animistic Japan, shamans had the responsibility of organizing religious ceremonies and performing cures for the various clans. With the coming of Buddhism, with its magical formulae, or *mantras*, shamans participated in more secular activities as well. Furthermore, *shidoso*, monks unattached to temples, wandered the countryside practicing magic, exorcising demons, and telling the future to those who paid to know it. Certain Buddhist shamanic figures, such as one Ozuno from Mount Katsragi, were the source of legends. Ozuno walked on water, flew through the skies each evening on a multicolored cloud, and kept company with spirits.

A Jain temple in Jaipur, Rajasthan, India

JAPANESE SUN CULT The Yamato tribes—the people of the first emperor, Jimmu Tenno, were members of a sun cult in which the primary deity was the sun goddess Amaterasu. Amaterasu remains an important aspect of the Shinto emperor cult. It is said that she is the ancestor of the emperors. Her sanctuary is at Ise, near Nagoya.

JAPETH A son of the Hebrew flood hero Noah of the biblical Book of Genesis, Japeth was said to be the ancestor of the Greeks and Philistines.

JASON AND MEDEA The son of Aeson, King of Iolcus in Thessaly, the child Jason was threatened with death by his uncle Pelias, who usurped Aeson's throne. Jason escaped his uncle and grew under the care of the centaur Chiron. When Jason was fully grown he returned to Iolcus and demanded the throne as its rightful heir. Pelias, a son of Poseidon, agreed to give up the throne in return for the Golden Fleece. So began the adventures described in the *Argonautica*. After Jason returned to Iolcus with the Golden Fleece and his new wife, Medea, who had helped him obtain the prize, Pelias reneged on his promise, and Medea used her magic to kill him, convincing his daughters that by cutting him up and boiling him they would restore his youth. As he was now an accessory to a terrible crime, Jason was still not made king. In fact, he and Medea were exiled by the new king, Pelias's son Acastus.

Jason and Medea were accepted in Corinth, where they lived until the events described by Euripides in his play the *Medea*. As Euripides tells us, Jason became enamored of Glauce (Creusa), the daughter of Creon, King of Corinth and, spurred on by political reasoning, abandoned Medea for Glauce. Furious and consumed by a desire for revenge, Medea sent Glauce a beautiful but magical garment that, when the girl put it on, caused her to burst into flames. Her father, too, died in the conflagration. Then Medea killed her own children by Jason and fled to Athens in a chariot drawn by dragons. There she is said by some to have married Theseus's father, King Aegeus. There are many stories of Jason's end. Perhaps the most popular is the one of his being crushed by a falling part of the ship *Argo*.

JATAKA TALES *Jataka* literature is composed of some 550 myths and legends that have developed over the centuries about former existences of the Buddha and about his life in general. Some of the tales are clearly Buddhist in origin, and some are taken from earlier folklore. There are animal tales with morals attached, much in the tradition of Aesop or the later La Fontaine in Europe. There are tales of women who, Eve-like, prevent men from hearing the message of the Buddha. Most important, however, the *jataka* literature serves to illustrate the law of *karman*, according to which present events can be explained by those of the past. Thus the bodhisattva becomes the being he has created by his past actions.

There is a tale that perhaps owes something to the story contained in the Indian epic the *Ramayana* of the bridge made between India and Lanka by the monkey king Hanu-

Statues of stillborn and miscarried children sacred to Jizo

man. In the tale in question, the bodhisattva, who in this case was a monkey king, saved his monkey followers from archers by making a bridge, of which his own body was a segment, across the Ganges. Unfortunately, the monkey who would become the future Buddha's jealous cousin Devadatta purposely fell on the king, breaking his back. The monkey king took no revenge but died a beautiful death at Banaras, all the while advising the local king on proper governing. The moral of the tale is centered in the compassion that will become one of the primary attributes of the future Buddha.

JIGOKU A name for Hell as opposed to *gokuraku* (paradise) in Japanese Pure Land Buddhism.

JIMMU TENNO According to the *Kojiki* and the *Nihongi*, the primary sources for Japanese mythology, Jimmu Tenno was the first in the long line of Yamato emperors of Japan. His mother is said to have descended from the god of the sea and from the sun goddess Amaterasu. His wife, the first empress Ahiratsu-hime, was of the family of the storm god Susanowo. Jimmu Tenno led his people from the place where Amaterasu's grandson Ninigi had first come to earth to Yamato, which he made his capital. He lived to be well over 120 years old.

JIVA The true "life" or "soul" for the Hindu and the Jain, the *jiva*, ideally achieves freedom from deterministic *karman*—the person's past actions—so that it can be liberated rather than tied to another material incarnation.

JIZO Jizo-bosatsu, or Bodhisattva Kshitigarbha, has gradually become a popular figure in Japanese Buddhist mythology. Jizo is of the earth and of the lower world. He is traditionally the advocate for the dead in their judgment in Hell (*Jigoku*), where Emma-O rules. His fame owes much to his development by the esoteric Tendai and Shingon sects of Japanese Buddhism. Jizo's solemn vow is to stay in the world to alleviate the suffering of humanity rather than to achieve enlightenment and nirvana for himself .

JOB Traditionally, the Hebrew Bible's Book of Job was ascribed to Moses, but it now seems clear that the questions implicitly and explicitly asked by the unfortunate Job are those of a people whose god has not necessarily lived up to his promises—perhaps the people of the Babylonian exilic period. The story of Job is one of loss in spite of goodness. Ultimately it is a story that reflects humanity's exploration of our psychological relationship with divine power; it is the story of that power's responsibility for suffering.

At the beginning of the Book of Job, Job is presented as a respectable, religious, and worthy man whom even the supreme deity holds above all others. He is so good, in fact, that he is an irritant to Satan, who challenges God to test his disciple's goodness by taking away the things he values—his material possessions, his family, his status. God accepts the challenge and strips Job of everything, leaving him alone and diseased on a dung heap. Still, however, Job remains loyal to God.

During the course of a visit from three friends, who insist that Job must have done something wrong to be afflicted with such misery, the victim denies his guilt and, in effect, asks two universal questions: why must the good suffer?

The unhappy Job and his friends

And who is responsible for that suffering? Job calls on God to appear before him and to answer his questions in a human context, all the time realizing that such an appearance would be unlikely. When God responds, he does so not in the context of human justice or reason but as a terrifying blind force—a "whirlwind." "Would you dare deny that I am just, or put me in the wrong to prove yourself right?" he asks Job. "Have you an arm like God's arm; can you thunder with a voice like his?" (40:8–9). God continues with a catalogue of his powers and an air of disdain for Job's questions. Now intimidated, Job backs off in humility and misery. The message is that God is inexplicable and all-powerful, that human reason and justice do not necessarily mean anything to the god of the whirlwind. This god can bring joy or pain at his will; humanity's will has nothing to do with the matter.

So it is that God gives back a family, possessions, and a reputation to Job just as easily and inexplicably as he had taken them away.

JOCASTA The wife of the tragic king Oedipus, Jocasta commits suicide when she realizes that she is also his mother. Oedipus turns out to be not only her husband and the father of four of her children, but her son and the killer of her first husband. The myth is most famously told by the Greek playwright Sophocles in his play *Oedipus the King*.

JOHN THE BAPTIST Although the New Testament figure John the Baptist may have been historical, his biogra-

Judith's decapitation of Holfernes

phy contains elements that are clearly mythological. Like so many Old Testament heroes—Abraham and Samuel, for instance—he was conceived by an apparently barren mother. This extraordinary or miraculous conception placed him in a special category and established his credentials as a hero in the minds of Christians. Christian scripture claims that it was John's role to prepare the way for the Messiah, the king who, according to the Old Testament, would one day come from Yahweh to restore the Davidic line and glory (Matthew 3, Daniel 9:25–26). New Testament mythology nearly always exists to fulfill prophecies contained in the Old Testament. The writer of the gospel of Matthew, therefore, introduces John the Baptist by quoting the prophet Isaiah: "I am a voice crying in the wilderness, / 'Make straight the way for the Lord," and when Jesus approaches him to be baptized, John cries out, "It is I who need to be baptized by you" (Matthew 3:14). In John's gospel, even more clearly, the Baptizer recognizes Jesus as the Messiah: "There is the Lamb of God," he says (John 1: 29–37).

JONAH AND THE WHALE The Old Testament Book of Jonah is, in effect a parable of the reluctant prophet, a prime example of the archetype of the hero's refusal of the call. It contains another archetype as well in the motif of lying in the belly of the whale—a metaphor for the depths of darkness and ignorance—the dark night of the soul.

God (Yahweh) calls on Jonah to go to Nineveh, the Assyrian capital, to preach the word of God. But Jonah, fearful of such a mission, takes a ship for Spain. When a terrible storm arises at sea, the sailors reluctantly throw Jonah, the cause of the storm, overboard, and he is swallowed by a whale. From this state of abject lowliness, perhaps reflecting the state of the exilic Hebrews in Babylon, Jonah prays for deliverance and is spewed out. He now goes to Nineveh as he had been commanded to do and, also as commanded, he announces that in forty days God will destroy the city of the unworthy Assyrians. But the Assyrians are "saved"; they repent and beg for forgiveness for their evil ways. When God relents and does not destroy Nineveh, Jonah is resentful and wishes he might die. God finally asserts his right to pardon or condemn as he sees fit, and Jonah is left, in effect, in the dark as to God's reasoning.

JOSEPH The biblical Book of Genesis tells how Isaac, the son of the Hebrew patriarch Abraham, married Rebecca and how one of their sons, Jacob (renamed Israel by Yahweh), fell in love with Rachel, a woman related to his family in Mesopotamia. Jacob was tricked into marrying Rachel's older sister Leah, who then produced several children. Later, Jacob married Rachel, who, though apparently barren, conceived and gave birth to Joseph. This miraculous conception marks Joseph for the reader as a special person, a hero.

Joseph's brothers were jealous of him, as he was the obvious favorite of their father. They stripped him of a beautiful robe Jacob had given to him and threw him into a cistern. Some Midianites removed him from the well and sold him to Ishmaelites, who took him to Egypt and sold him to Potiphar, the captain of the pharaoh's guard, as a slave. But the enslaved Joseph found favor with the pharaoh and became a powerful man in Egypt.

Years later, Jacob and Joseph's brothers and their families came to Egypt looking for grain in a time of famine. Joseph revealed himself to them, and the family was reconciled. The pharaoh gave them land in Goshen in his kingdom.

When Joseph died, at age 110, he was embalmed and placed in a coffin—Egyptian style—having given instructions that at a later, proper time he should be moved to Canaan, the land promised by Yahweh to his tribe.

JOSEPH OF NAZARETH Joseph, a Jewish carpenter of Nazareth, said to be of the family line of the Hebrew king David, became the husband of the woman known to Christians as the Virgin Mary, the mother of Jesus. According to the New Testament biblical story, Mary became pregnant with Jesus before her marriage to Joseph, having been miraculously impregnated by God but left a virgin. Joseph was informed by an angel of God that he need not suspect Mary of any wrongdoing, and he married her and watched over her as she gave birth. Later, to avoid a massacre of children ordered by the jealous king Herod, he took his family to Egypt, making a biblical tie with the earlier Hebrew Joseph, who also went to Egypt. Joseph is a background figure in the Jesus myth but is a much-revered saint, especially among Catholic Christians.

JOTUNHEIM In the complex geography of Norse mythology, Jotunheim ("Giants' Home"), among the roots of the world tree Yggdrasill, was the land of the giants.

JUDITH A late biblical book, probably of the Hellenistic period (c. 150 B.C.E.), the Book of Judith is allegorical in that the name Judith, as the feminine form of Judah, may be taken to mean "Jewess." Judith is a heroine representing a nation standing against the "infidel."

Judith 1–7 tells how King Nebuchadnezzar ruled the Assyrians and sent Holofernes to punish the Israelites. Judith 8–15 contains the tale of Judith, a widow, who dressed herself beautifully and entered the Assyrian camp, flattered Holofernes, got him drunk in his tent, and then decapitated him. Judith took the head back to Jerusalem and had it displayed on the city walls. The Assyrians, seeing the head of their general, became dispirited and abandoned their camp, which the Israelites then sacked, taking the possessions of the Assyrians to Jerusalem. For a long time, thanks to the heroism of Judith, no one dared attack the Israelites.

JUNG, CARL GUSTAV The Swiss psychiatrist Carl Gustav Jung (1875–1961) broke away from his mentor, Sigmund Freud, disagreeing with him on various matters, including the importance of myth. Jung's theory of a universal collective unconscious in addition to the personal unconscious studied by Freud, has influenced many mythologists, including, most notably, Joseph Campbell, whose theory of the heroic monomyth owes much to Jung's ideas about the archetypes or universal psychic tendencies that are contained in the collective unconscious and that reveal themselves culturally in the common motifs of myth as well as in the dreams and artistic works of individuals. By studying the myths of a culture, Jung suggested, we study expressions of that culture's psyche. By the same token, comparing the myths of world mythology can tell us much about the human psyche in general.

JUNO The Roman equivalent of the Greek Hera, Juno had her origins as a pre-Roman goddess in Italy. The Etruscans associated her with Uni/Astarte, and she became part of a triad that included Jupiter and Minerva (Greek Athena). The Romans came to see her as the wife of Jupiter and the patroness of motherhood.

JUPITER Although the Romans came to see their supreme deity, Jupiter, as a cognate of the Greek Zeus, he existed in pre-Roman Italy as Jupiter Latirus and, in archaic Roman times, as part of the Roman version of the Indo-European triad of Jupiter-Mars-Quirinus, or sovereignty, power, and community.

JURUPARI The Tupi people of Brazil tell how the world was once ruled by women. But the sun did not approve of this rule, so he married the virgin Ceucy and used some cucura sap to make her miraculously conceive the culture hero Jurupari, who taught the people about male dominance, causing the death of his own mother to make his point.

J

Carl Jung (1875-1961)

181

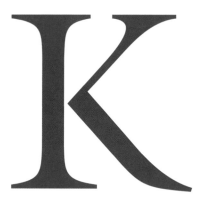

K

KA'BAH Literally the "cube," the Ka'bah is located in the Saudi Arabian city of Mecca and is called the "House of Allah." As the primary Islamic shrine, it is faced by Islamic worshippers during the five daily ritual prayers and is the pilgrimage (hajj) goal of all Muslims at least once during a lifetime. The myths surrounding the Ka'bah suggest that its cornerstone—the "Black Stone"—fell from Heaven or was brought to Mecca by angels. The stone is traditionally kissed by Muslims on their pilgrimage, as it was said to have been kissed by the Prophet Muhammad. The Ka'bah was a sacred center for pre-Islamic Ara-

bic pilgrims as well. The Ka'bah itself is said by Muslims to have been built by Adam and then rebuilt by Ibrahim (Abraham) and Ismail (Ishmael) directly under a similar structure in Heaven.

KACHINAS The Native North Americans of the Southwest—particularly the Pueblo peoples and most especially the Hopi—have spirit figures called *kachinas* (*katsinas*). These are individualized figures depicted in small doll form for religious educational (and touristic) purposes, and they are also impersonated by masked adult males in important dance ceremonies. The Hopi kachinas are said to come from their home in the San Francisco Peaks, above Flagstaff, Arizona, to visit the Indian villages for these ceremonies. They are both spirits of nature, who can bring rain, for example, and spirits of the dead, who, some say, become clouds. The Athabascan people in the same region have somewhat similar figures. These are the Navajo *yeii* and the Apache *hactin*. Some Hopis speak of the goddess Hahaiwutti as the "mother" of the kachinas. She is a goddess associated with fertility, a concern also of the kachinas in their role as clouds and, therefore, rain bringers. There are Hopis who believe that the end of Hopi ceremonies and of the world as we know it now will come when a kachina takes off his mask in a dance and/or when a Blue Star kachina dances in a plaza, signifying the coming of a blue star in the sky.

KAGUTSUCHI The Japanese Shinto god of fire, Kagutsuchi was the son of Izanagi and Izanami. During his fiery birth his mother's genitals suffered such damage that she died and went to the other world, and it was because of Izanami's fate that the furious Izanagi decapitated his son. The result of this act was an animistic emergence of deities from Kagutsuchi's blood and body parts.

KAINTANGATA This Polynesian-Maori goddess was the ancestor, by Whaitiri, a mortal cannibal chief, of the hero Tawhaki.

KALALA ILUNGA The Luba tribe of modern-day Zaire tell how the great red Rainbow King, Nkongolo, once allowed a visiting prince, Mbidi Kiluwe, to sleep with his twin sister-wives, Bulanda and Mabela. By Mbidi, Bulanda became pregnant with Kalala Ilunga and Mabela with twins—a boy and a girl. Kalala Ilunga stayed with the Rainbow King after his father went home, but the king decided to do away with him because of his prowess as a dancer and runner. After Kalala Ilunga managed, with the help of his drummer, to avoid the trap the king had laid for him on the dance grounds, he left for his father's land. Mbidi gave his son an army with which to attack Nkongolo, who fled with his sister-wives. The women betrayed their hated master, however, and Nkongolo was decapi-

A Hopi Indian kachina (katsina) doll

tated, leaving Kalala Ilunga free to become king of the Luba people.

KALAKACARYAKATHA This is a series of twelfth-century C.E. stories in India about the famous first-century B.C.E. Svetambara Jain teacher Kalaka—the "black teacher"—and about the deeds of several Jain teachers who supposedly righted wrongs, one going so far as to confront the god Indra himself.

KALEVALA The most comprehensive collection of Finnic myths and legends is found in the national epic of Finland, the *Kalevala* (Finland), a late (1835, 1849) compilation of the poet Elias Lonnrot, based to a great extent on oral traditions from Karelia and elsewhere. Central characters in the epic are Vainamoinen, Ilmarinen, the rash hero Lemmin-kainen, and Louhi, the mistress-ruler of "North Farm."

The *Kalevala* begins with an earth-diver creation myth featuring a sky maiden. A teal, searching for a nest, lands on the raised knee of the Mother of the Waters, a virgin who has descended from the sky to rest on the primal waters. The teal lays eggs, which break when the virgin moves her knee, and the earth and celestial bodies are formed. The hero Vainamoinen is also born, and the smith Ilmarinen creates the canopy of the heavens.

It is Vainamoinen who makes the wilderness fertile. After falling into the sea, he floats for a time until he is rescued and carried to North Farm, where Louhi is mistress. In return for a promise to allow the now ancient Vainamoinen to marry her daughter, Louhi asks for the creation of the *sampo*, the great tripartite mill that can grind salt, grain, and gold, and Vainamoinen promises to send the craftsman Ilmarinen to make it.

Next comes the story of the death of the wild Lemminkainen in the Land of the Dead and his resurrection through the magic of his mother.

Vainamoinen journeys back toward North Farm to ask for Louhi's daughter but discovers a rival in the form of the sampo builder Ilmarinen. Ilmarinen is favored by the daughter but is forced to perform several Herculean labors if he wishes to marry her. As Medea helped Jason, the maiden helps her lover to accomplish the tasks.

Ilmarinen's wife is killed by wild animals substituted for her cattle by the "war hero" Kullervo, and in his despair, Ilmarinen tries to craft a new wife.

Eventually Ilmarinen, Vainamoinen, and Lemminkainenen, the heroes of the *Kalevala*, put aside their differences and go off together to North Farm to capture the sampo. At first they succeed, but Louhi pursues them, and in a struggle at sea, the sampo sinks. Vainamoinen retrieves bits and pieces of the sampo and Louhi also manages to hold on to a piece of it. What follows is a long struggle between the Kalevala people and the forces of North Farm. In that struggle Louhi sends plagues against the Kalevala and hides the sun and moon, which eventually the heroes succeed in forcing her to release.

The poem ends with the departure of Vainamoinen and the baptism of a new king of Karelia. The old world has given way to the new. A poet uses the abandoned sacred harp of Vainamoinen to accompany the final song of the epic.

KALI One of several forms of the Indian great goddess (Devi), Kali is the black goddess of destruction, the logical wife for Shiva in the dance of existence, in which process Brahma is the creator, Vishnu the sustainer-preserver, and he—Shiva—the destroyer. But whereas Shiva's dance is in the cosmic realm, Kali's is in this world. Kali's name is the feminine form of the Sanskrit word *kala*, meaning "time," that which relates to the ever-devouring principle that dominates the animate world. Her name is also related to the Vedic name for one of the tongues of the sacrificial fire. Kali might be said to be the embodiment of the fact that, according to the Hindu, the world exists only by way of sacrifice; that is, the consumption of aspects of life is the source of prosperity. And it should be noted, in this connection, that "prosperity" is the meaning of Lakshmi or Shri, the wife of Vishnu, the Preserver, as Kali is the wife of Shiva, the Destroyer.

In one popular depiction of Kali, who has wild eyes, bloody fangs, and human heads as a necklace around her neck, she is standing on an apparently dead Shiva, who nevertheless has an erection. The combination of this latter genital aspect, the destructive nature of the Kali figure, and the fact that the goddess also carries a bowl overflowing with the abundance of life, would seem to suggest the necessity of death for fertility and the constant creation of life. Perhaps it could be said that Kali's rampages also represent the spiritual necessity of killing our weaknesses without mercy so that we might discover our true selves. Kali is particularly popular among the southern Tamils, for whom she is Kottavei. Kali is closely associated with the violent Durga, out of whose head she is said to spring when that goddess becomes angry. One of Kali's most famous deeds involved her assisting Durga and Durga's companions in the killing of the monster Raktabija by sucking him dry of his ever-spawning blood.

KALIYA Kaliya, the black serpent king who lived in the Yamuna River, was the incarnation of the demon Kalanemi, who had been killed by the Hindu god Vishnu. It was appropriate that Kaliya should be killed by Vishnu's incarnation, or avatar, Krishna. It is also significant that before Krishna's adventure, Kaliya insults Vishnu by taking an offering away from Garuda, the bird especially associated with the god. The *Bhagavata Purana* tells the story of how Krishna freed the waters polluted by Kaliya's poison, as Indra had once freed the waters by slaying the demon Virtra. In the Kaliya myth, the young Krishna proves himself, like so many heroes before him and after him, by vanquishing the "dragon."

KALKIN At the end of this age of evil—the *Kali yuga*—Hindus say that Kalkin, the tenth avatar of Vishnu, will arrive on a white horse or as a white horse, signifying a golden age, the *Krita yuga*.

KAMA Kama means "desire" in Sanskrit, and Kama is the Indian god of love. A well-known myth of the *Saura Purana* tells how Kama awakened the great Shiva from his meditation to call attention to the amorous Parvati, wife of the god. Shiva, as the ascetic yogi, becomes so angry that he destroys the god of love with the fire of his third eye. But when Parvati points out that without Kama there can be no love between men and women, Shiva, as the god of the *linga*, relents and allows Kama to circulate in the world.

KAMADHENU Kamadhenu or Go ("Cow") is the general name applied to the cow so sacred to Hindus. The

K

Kaliya submits to Krishna

cow stands for prosperity—as does Lakshmi, the wife of Vishnu. Kamadhenu is especially associated with brahmans and their "wealth," because she is the producer of milk and clarified butter, the offerings traditionally placed on the sacrificial fire. Cows are protected as brahmans are; the two cannot be separated. To destroy a cow would be to defy the cosmic order and to deny the need for the gifts of rain, plants, and animals that sacrifice brings to earth. In short, order can be maintained only by means of proper sacrifice, at both the cosmic and worldly levels. The cow is distinctly of the world, as she is associated with earth, and it is by her that the essential offerings are given.

KAMAMMA KATHA The Telugu people of southern India sing this epic of the young widow Kamamma, a relative of the river goddess Ganga (Ganges), who wishes to perform *sati*—self-immolation on the funeral pyre—to honor her dead husband and so to raise herself beyond her caste. By means of a miraculous projection of herself into the dream of a resisting British official, she convinces the authorities to allow her to do as she wills, and her friends congregate to watch her burn. Hers is a sacrifice that results in an apotheotic deification.

KAMI Shinto deities in Japan are known as *kami*. Shinto is literally "the way of the *kami*." For the Japanese Buddhist, the Shinto *kami* are sometimes seen as earthly representations of buddhas. In the esoteric traditions of the Shingon Buddhist sect especially, the *kami*—like everything else in the universe—were outward representations of the Buddha Dainichi. But the concept of *kami* involved more than divinities per se in the pre-Buddhist Japanese culture. That culture was animistic; that is, everything in the world was seen as "animated" by a vitality that came from the spirit realm, the realm of the five primordial deities—for example, Kamimusubi—who existed before the creation, so that all beautiful things could be worshipped as *kami*.

KAMSA In Hindu mythology, the evil king Kamsa, cousin or brother of Krishna's mother, Devaki, reminds us of the pharaoh in the Moses story, King Herod in the Christian story, or of Kronos in Greek mythology. Hearing from a prophecy that his sister's eighth child will kill him, he decrees that each of her children must be killed upon delivery. Vishnu, however, foils the king's plans by substituting embryos of demons in Devaki's womb and arranging for the baby Krishna, his own incarnation, or avatar, to be exchanged with another at birth. Eventually Krishna kills Kamsa.

KANNON Kannon (Kanzeon-bosatsu, "the one who hears the world's cries"), the Japanese version of the bodhisattva Avalokiteshvara, is perhaps the most admired of the Japanese Mahayana Buddhist bodhisattvas. Like his Chinese counterpart, the feminine Guanyin, he is, above all, compassionate. People of many sects of Buddhism in Japan make special offerings and prayers to Kannon for help with their everyday lives. Fortunately, he has one thousand hands with which to dispense his compassion and bounty. One tradition holds that Kannon can take thirty-three forms. Thus, for some thousand years, people have been making pilgrimages to the thirty-three Kannon shrines in Kyoto and Nara. Kannon is closely associated with Amida (Amitabha) in the Pure Land tradition. In Japan, as in China, this bodhisattva is sometimes portrayed in feminine form.

KANYAKA AMAVARI KATHA Like *Kamamma Katha*, this is a medieval epic of southern India. It is the story of Kanyaka, a woman and subsequent goddess of the *komati* or commercial caste. Kanyaka taught cross-cousin marrying to her people so that their women would be unattractive and therefore not be bothered by men. This was because she had been persecuted by a lustful king who had demanded her hand in marriage and vowed to win it by war if necessary. Rather than marry the king, Kanyaka led a group of the leading *komatis* to death on a funeral pyre. As she had decreed before her death, the lustful king died upon entering her city.

KARAPERAMUN In the New Hebrides of Melanesia, Karaperamun was the high god before the arrival of Christianity.

KARMAN For Hindus and Jains, *karman* (*karma* is the nominative Sanskrit form) originally referred to proper ritual actions, but the term has come to denote past actions that will affect what happens to a person in various hells or paradises after death and in the individual's particular rebirth or reincarnation. Literally, what one is now is the result of what one did in the past and, what one is now contains seeds for the future. According to the Law of Karman, then, life is a series of deaths and rebirths determined by one's past actions. To achieve true liberation from the cycle of life—*Samsara*—one must theoretically achieve total nonaction, total negation of *karman*. Buddhists, too, consider that a person's situation is determined by his or her *karman*, but that good *karman* can in some ways eliminate the results of bad *karman*.

KARNA Karna is a hero in the Indian epic the *Mahabharata*; he is allied with the Kauravas, the enemies of the Pandavas. Until late in the epic he is not aware that he is the half brother of three of the Pandava brothers, as he is the son of their mother, Kunti, and the Sun (Surya). In fact, Karna was the product of a virgin birth event. By invoking a spell taught her by the sage Durvasa, Kunti became impregnated by the "light of the universe." Karna's life is marked by several aspects of the archetypal monomythic hero's life, such as a miraculous conception and abandonment in a basket in a river. In a sense, his role in the epic is that of dark shadow to Arjuna, the righteous hero. It will be Karna's fate to be sacrificed in a climactic battle with Arjuna. It is a death that reminds us of the necessity of sacrificial destruction for redemption in the Hindu worldview, of which the *Mahabharata* is a narrative map.

KARTTIKEYA The brother of the elephant-headed Hindu god Ganesh, and the son of Shiva, adopted by Parvati, Karttikeya—also known as Skanda and, in some areas as Murugan—is essentially an opposite to his brother, as Shiva the ascetic is an opposite to Parvati the mountain mother goddess. And as Shiva and Parvati form a whole, so do Ganesh and Karttikeya. A popular myth about the two brothers has to do with the desire of their parents that they marry. As marriage is a question of the achievement of *Shakti*, or true inner energy personified by the wife, it is important to the parents to decide which of their sons should achieve this power first. A test is arranged by which the brothers are, in effect, to enter a race around the earth. Karttikeya takes the command literally and circles the earth itself. Ganesh wins, however, by simply circling his parents seven times, following a Vedic formula, or *mantra*, for the honoring of parents and symbolizing by this act that Shiva and Parvati in union *are*, in effect, the world.

Karttikeya gained his name because he was suckled by the Krittikas, the Indian version of the Pleiades. He was born in an unusual manner. During their first act of intercourse, the gods interrupted Shiva and Parvati because they feared the god's son would have too much power. Shiva's red-hot spilled semen was confined by the other deities in Ganga (Ganges), from whom the six-headed child was born and soon accepted by Parvati as her own. Later Karttikeya-Skanda, with Indra, led the army of the gods against the potentially world-destroying demon Taraka.

KATAMARAJU KATHA This medieval epic of southern India exists in a written version attributed to the fifteenth-century poet Sri-natha. The epic is concerned with a cattle-herding caste claiming descent from the Lord Krishna. A cattleman hero, Katamaraju, makes an agreement with a king in regard to grazing rights. An argument develops and leads to a war between the cattlemen and the king's army. One of the cattleman soldiers becomes afraid and deserts his comrades in battle. He is derided by his wife and mother for his cowardice and returns to battle only to be killed. When he is brought home for the ritual cremation, his wife proves her strength by joining him on the pyre.

KAURAVAS The Kauravas are the one hundred sons of the blind Dhritarastra. In the great Indian epic the *Mahabharata*, they challenge their cousins, the Pandavas, for control of the Bharata kingdom. Their leader is the jealous Duryodhana, who, in his immoral actions, takes on his father's blindness as spiritual blindness as opposed to moral duty or dharma.

KAY HUSROY According to Zoroastrian tradition, Kay Husroy is a hero king who joins the struggle against the forces of evil and reigns with Saoshyant (Saoshyans).

KEK AND KEKET In the Hermopolitan Egyptian pantheon known as the Ogdoad, made up of four couples representing primordial chaotic forces, Kek (Kuk) and Keket (Kauhet) were forces of darkness.

KERSASP Kersasp, or Sam Kersasp, is a hero king who, like Thraetona, fights the evil King Dahaka in the Zoroastrian struggle between good and evil.

KHEPRY In Egypt, Khepry is the scarab beetle pushing the sun into the sky and is thus the representation of the dawn aspect of the high god and of rebirth.

KHNUM At Esna, near Egyptian Thebes, Khnum was the creator god with the head of a ram. His was a *deus faber* (craftsman) creation. He made the primal cosmic egg at his potter's wheel, and created animals and humans out of clay there. He also controlled the all-important rising and falling of the Nile.

KHONSU In ancient Egypt, the son of the Amun-Re and Mut was the moon god, Khonsu.

KHVARENAH In the ancient Mazdian-Zoroastrian tradition of Iran, the supreme god Ahura Mazda creates the *khvarenah*, which is at once holiness and fortune. Mythologically, the concept is a deity of sorts associated with both water and fire. *Khvarenah* is essentially *charisma*, that which is the source of the power of Iranian heroes, kings, and the nation itself.

KHORI TUMED The Buryat people of central Asia tell of Khori Tumed. Khori Tumed watched one day as nine swans descended to Oikhon Island to swim in Lake Baikal. He noted that when the swans landed, they undressed, revealing themselves as beautiful young women. While the maidens were swimming, Khori Tumed stole the clothes of one, preventing her from flying away with her sisters. This maiden became his wife and bore him many sons. The day came when Khori Tumed's wife, missing her swan life, begged her husband to let her try on her old feathers. Once she had her feathers on, she flew up through the smoke hole of the family *yurt*, but before she left she named her sons, making them men, and she blessed their home.

KI The Sumerian goddess who personified the earth, Ki was the daughter of the primordial waters, Nammu. She mated with her brother An (Anu) to produce Enki, Enlil, and other Sumerian deities.

KIGWA Kigwa was the father of the culture hero and first king of Rwanda, in Africa. The story goes that the wife of the high god Nkuba (Lightning) could not have children, so she took the heart of one of her husband's cows and fed it milk in a pot for nine months until it emerged miraculously as the baby Kigwa. Later Kigwa fell from the sky to earth, where he fathered the future king Gihanga.

KIKIMORA Kikimora are small female spirits of the dead in Slavic mythology. The arrival of a kikimora can signify trouble.

KINAALDA The Athabascan Native North Americans place a great deal of emphasis on a female puberty rite that involves the young girl taking on the fertility and curing powers of the primary goddess and entering into her role as a woman. Both the Apaches (Tinde) and the Navajos (Dine) celebrate this event. The Navajos call it the kinaalda and relate a myth about how the tradition began; the myth outlines the elements of the kinaalda as it is practiced to this day.

The myth says that the young goddess who would become known as Changing Woman, the greatest of Navajo goddesses, told her parents, First Man and First Woman, that she was experiencing her first menses. The first couple decided a celebration was in order. First Woman, taking the role of a figure known as Ideal Woman, decked out the maiden in moccasins, leggings, a white dress, and jewels, and brushed her hair—all of this symbolizing the girl's taking on *hozho*, meaning beauty or harmony. During each of the four days of the ceremony, the girl ran toward the east—toward the sun and beauty—and each day Ideal Woman massaged her from head to toe, literally rubbing in the power of womanhood and the capacity later to produce the sacred twins. On the last day, after many more complex rituals, the maiden became Changing Woman.

KING ARTHUR As Saint Patrick and the stories surrounding him represent the coming of Christianity to Ireland, the Arthurian story gradually became a central aspect of the whole Christian mythological system as applied specifically to Great Britain. Connected with the Arthurian myth, for instance, is the story of Joseph of Arimathea, who provided the burial place for Jesus after his crucifixion (Luke 23), and who, according to tradition, traveled to England after Jesus' resurrection, bringing with him the Holy Grail (Sangreale), the vessel used by Jesus at the Last Supper. The Grail would be the goal of the quest of the Arthurian hero-knights and the symbol of the Christian quest in general. Joseph was said to have been responsible for the building of the church at Glastonbury, where his staff gave forth the Holy Thorn tree that is still there. It was at the great abbey at Glastonbury where King Arthur was said by the monks to have been buried. The tradition of Joseph's journey to England is related in spirit to the tradition that Jesus himself came to Britain after the resurrection, a tradition forming the basis for William Blake's words to the hymn "Jerusalem," arguably the spiritual national anthem of Great Britain:

And did those feet in ancient time
Walk upon England's mountains green?
And was the holy Lamb of God
On England's pleasant pastures seen?
And did the Countenance Divine
Shine forth upon our clouded hills?
And was Jerusalem builded here
Among these dark Satanic Mills?
Bring me my Bow of burning gold:
Bring me my Arrows of Desire:
Bring me my Spear: O clouds unfold!
Bring me my Chariot of Fire.
I will not cease from Mental Fight,
Nor shall my Sword sleep in my hand
Til we have built Jerusalem
In England's green and pleasant Land.
("Prelude" from "Milton")

At the fringes of all of this national mythology is the Arthurian Fisher King, whose wounds must be cured

MAGNUS ARTURUS REX POTENTISSIMUS ANGLIAE · DOMINUS LUNCELOT DU LAC EQUES INVICTUS

King Arthur with his knight, Sir Lancelot

before Britain can cease to be a wasteland. And not far from this myth and the Christian story itself is that of the "Once and Future King."

The Christianized Welsh hero follows the monomyth of the hero model almost ritualistically, beginning with a miraculous, or at least highly unusual, conception. In keeping with ancient tales and Geoffrey of Monmouth's *History of the Kings of Britain*, Thomas Malory, in the fifteenth-century *Le Morte d'Arthur*, has the magician Merlin tell Arthur the strange story of that conception. According to that story, when Uther Pendragon (Uthr Bendragon) was king of Britain, he was assisted in his wars against the invading Saxons by the aging Duke of Cornwall. But Uther fell madly in love with the duke's beautiful wife, Igraine, and made his love so evident that the duke became offended and took his wife away to his castle at Tintagel on the Cornish coast. As the castle was impregnable, Merlin agreed to use magic to help Uther obtain Igraine. While the duke was away fighting a battle, the magician made Uther look like Igraine's husband— so much so that the would-be lover was able to enter the castle unchallenged and was admitted to Igraine 's bed. That night Arthur was conceived and the Duke of Cornwall was killed.

Merlin predicted that Igraine's child would be the greatest of the kings of Britain. Eventually, Igraine mar-

ried Uther, and Arthur was born. It is said that elves attended the birth and that they gave the baby the gift of courage and strength as well as intelligence, generosity, and longevity. When Uther asked Igraine who the child's father was, she admitted to having slept with a stranger who resembled her husband. Delighted by her honesty, Uther revealed that he was that stranger. For his own protection, the baby Arthur was given to Merlin, who gave him to the trusted knight Sir Ector to be raised.

When Uther Pendragon died, the British kingdom was threatened by dissent and disagreement. Realizing the danger, Merlin had the Archbishop of Canterbury call together the nobles of the kingdom to decide who would be king. A stone with a sword in it suddenly appeared in a churchyard. These words were written on the stone: "Whoever pulls out this sword is the lawfully born king of Britain." At Christmas time and again at New Year's, various nobles attempted, without success, to remove the sword. At that time, Arthur arrived at the stone with Sir Ector and his foster brother Sir Kay, whom he served as squire. Sir Kay asked Arthur to return to their camp to fetch a new sword for him. Arthur returned without having found one, but while passing by he noticed the sword in the stone, and while everyone was off at a tournament, he easily removed the sword from the stone and took it to Kay. Recognizing the sword, Kay decided to claim it

187

and the throne. Sir Ector demanded to see for himself that his son could remove the sword from the stone. But when Kay replaced the sword in the stone, he could not remove it. Moved by his father's questioning, he revealed that Arthur had given him the sword. When Arthur once again removed it from the rock, Sir Ector and Sir Kay knelt before him as their king. After much resistance, the nobles accepted Arthur as the lawful monarch, and Merlin revealed the details of his parentage.

King Arthur remains the most popular of heroes in the British Isles. Associated with him is the heroic quest undertaken by his Knights of the Round Table—Percival, Gawain, and others who, among other adventures, seek the Holy Grail, the cup used by Jesus at the Last Supper. Although in all likelihood he had pagan roots, Arthur was one of many warrior heroes—Roland of the Song of Roland, Joan of Arc, and the Cid of the great Spanish national epic are other examples—who emerged from the establishment of Christianity in Europe. In fact, the pagan heroes were all assimilated in one way or another by the retelling of their stories by Christian writers such as the Beowulf poet and Snorri Sturluson in the north. Central to the King Arthur myth is his role as the "once and future king" who, although dead, would return one day. In this role, Arthur follows the monomyth model of the hero's return from the depths and, specifically, of Jesus, who went to heaven with the promise of returning one day "in glory."

5In Sicily, a story developed of Arthur's remaining forever young because he was fed from the Holy Grail. In many places Arthur was associated with the strange figure of the Fisher King, whose wounds are somehow tied to the physical and spiritual fertility of the land. In the early thirteenth century, Gervase of Tilbury supports this association by asserting that Arthur's wounds reopened each year. These and many other stories are part of the popular belief in a de facto apotheosis, or deification, of the "once and future king."

KINGU In the Babylonia creation epic, the *Enuma elish*, Kingu (Quingu) a son of Apsu, was the leader of an army of monsters enlisted by the primeval goddess Tiamat to fight against the younger generation of deities. He became her lover, and she entrusted him with the Tablet of Destinies, one of the symbols of supreme power in the world. After the defeat of Tiamat's forces, Kingu and his army were captured by Marduk, who gave the Tablet of Destinies to the god Anu (An). Kingu's blood was used to make humans.

KINTU In the African nation of Uganda, the Gandans tell of Kintu, who asked the high god for a wife and was given the god's daughter Nambi. The god warned the couple to hurry away or be taken by his brother Walumbe ("Death"). But when Nambi realized she had forgotten to ask her father for grain for her chickens, she insisted on returning to get some. Of course, Walumbe saw her return and followed her back to earth, where he lives with us all to this day.

KIRTA The Canaanite hero King Kirta (Keret), whose story is told in fragments on three Ugaritic tablets, is a good man who has lost seven wives in succession and is without children. Like the hero Aqhat, he performs a ritual, hoping for divine intervention, and his patron—possibly his father—the high god El, comes to him in a dream. El tells Kirta that after sacrificing to him and to Baal he must go to war against Pabil, the king of Udm. After laying siege to the city for seven days he must refuse Pabil's offer of gifts but must demand the hand of the king's beautiful daughter Hurriya (Huray).

When Kirta wakes up, he immediately follows the commands of the dream. On his way to Udm he stops at a shrine of the goddess Athirat/Elat (Asherah) and promises a gift to her if he succeeds in gaining the hand of Hurriya. It is at such shrines that the Hebrew patriarchs Abraham, Isaac, and Jacob would create their holy places.

Everything happens as the dream had foretold. Pabil reluctantly surrenders Hurriya and, at Baal's suggestion, El blesses the marriage, saying that Hurriya will produce eight sons for Kirta and that the first one will be nursed by Athirat and Anat. El also predicts the birth of eight daughters. But Athirat wonders threateningly why Kirta has not yet fulfilled his promise made at her shrine.

Perhaps because he has neglected the pledge to Athirat, Kirta becomes deathly ill, and Hurriya holds a feast and asks that sacrifices be made for her husband. It seems evident that the king's last hours—even if he is, in fact, the son of El—have arrived. Ilihu (Elhu), a son of Kirta, makes a speech suggesting that his father accept death. A daughter of Kitra is sent for to mourn him. Already the king's sickness—like that of the Fisher King of the Grail story—has caused the land to go barren. On Mount Zephon, the Canaanite Olympus, Baal is leading a ceremony to bring fertility back to the earth. And, just in time, El decides to intervene by way of the healing goddess Shataqat. He instructs the goddess to touch the sick king on his head with her wand and to wash his body. After this is done, Kitra revives, eats food, and returns to his throne.

But his troubles are not over. Like droughts, the king's problems are cyclical. Another cycle seems about to begin as Kirta's son Yassib complains that his father has neglected his kingdom. The clear implication is that Yassib believes he should replace his father as king. The story breaks off as Kirta curses his son. Michael Coogan compares this aspect of the myth to the story of King David and his rebellious son Absalom [2 Samuel 15; Coogan (1987), 3:54–55]. Like the myth of Danel and Aqhat, this is clearly a myth about the sacred nature of kingship and about the close relationship between the king's welfare and fertility and that of his land. [Coogan (1987), Gibson]

KISHIMO This Japanese Buddhist deity, also known as Mother Hariti (Karitei-mo), the Mother of Demons, fed on the children of Rajagriba during the days of Gautama, the Buddha Sakyamuni. The people asked for the Buddha's help against the demonness, and the Buddha hid Mother Hariti's youngest child under his alms bowl. When the demonness, in despair over the loss of her child, asked for the Buddha's help, he pointed out to her the similarity of her pain to that of the parents whose children she had devoured. So Mother Hariti was converted and became the guardian of children. A Kishimojin cult developed in China in the seventh century C.E. and later in Japan under the Shingon and Nichiren sects. Babies are still taken to shrines of the goddess to ensure their health and protection.

KOJIKI The *Kojiki* ("Record of Ancient Matters") is a product of the commands of the Japanese Emperor Temmu in the seventh century C.E. The objective was to collect and record ancient myths and legends of Japan. We are told that the storyteller Heida no Are recited the legends to the scribe O no Yasumaro. The selection of stories and the way they were written down were influenced by the political and social mores and priorities of the time. Still, the work, published in 712, is, with the *Nihongi*, the major source for our knowledge of Shinto mythology.

KOKOPELLI Kokopelli is the name generally given to the flute-playing, hunchbacked, and often ithyphallic figure found in so many pictographs and petroglyphs of the ancient Anasazi people of southwestern Native North America. It is generally believed that Kokopelli would have been a trickster.

KOREAN MYTHOLOGY The indigenous pre-Buddhist, pre-Confucian, pre-Daoist, and pre-Christian religion of the Korean Peninsula seems to have been shamanistic in nature. At the center of the religious rituals were women called *mudang*, who communicated with deities and ancestors and told fortunes. They were also knowledgeable about the afterlife. The religion of the *mudang* was polytheistic and somewhat animistic. There were several mountain gods, an earth god, and figures called Dragon King God, Good Luck God, Kitchen God, Childbirth God, and even Smallpox God. And there were—and often still are—gods for nearly every part of the house—such as toilet gods, house beam gods, and chimney gods. There were ancient myths of creation and heroes that seem to have owed something to Chinese mythology, as in the case of the hero Cumong, known as the "good archer," as the Chinese Yi was also known. In fact, a creation story tells us that after a crack appeared in chaos so that the sky and earth could be separated, an archer shot down one of two suns and one of two moons before humans were made from earth. Perhaps the archer here was Cumong. If so, he is even more directly connected with the Chinese Yi, who shot down nine of ten original suns.

An ancient petroglyph of the Anasazi trickster, Kokopelli

Lord Krishna with his beloved Radha

KOTAN UTUNNAI The indigenous Ainu people of Japan sing this epic of the hero Poiyaunpe, born on the mainland, who is raised in a place called Kotan Utunnai by a woman of the Okhotsk sea-oriented culture. As he grows up, the boy hears rumblings of the spirits of his mainland culture mingling with the rumblings of the spirits of his personal being, and he asks his adopted mother about his origins. She reveals that his parents had been killed in a struggle with her own people. Horrified, the boy asks for his father's clothes and sword, puts them on, and flies up the smoke hole. Once away, he goes on the traditional hero adventure quest, followed by his adopted mother. Together the pair kill gods and goddesses of pestilence, kill monsters, and defeat wicked chiefs, including, with the help of a brother the hero has rescued, an important one called Shipish-un-kur, whose shamanness sister, Shipish-un-mat, he abducts. Together the hero and the shamanness ravish various lands. At one point the hero is almost dead but is miraculously saved by his companion. After many other adventures, the adventurers return to Poiyanaupe's native land, where they find the hero's miraculously revived foster mother and brother.

KRISHNA Lord Krishna (Krsna), the "Dark One," is the most important avatar of the god Vishnu or Hari. The mythology of Krishna is among the richest in Hinduism. There are various versions of each part of the man-god's history, as recorded, for instance, in the *Mahabharata*—particularly in the section called the *Bhagavadgita*—in the *Harivamsha*, and in the *Vishnu* and *Bhagavata Puranas*. At times, as, for instance, in the running narrative of the *Mahabharata*, Krishna seems to be more the ideal warrior king than an avatar, but at other times, as when he miraculously saves the Pandava wife Draupadi from shame during the famous attempt on the part of the Kauravas to disrobe her, and as when he lectures the hero Arjuna in the *Bhagavadgita*, he is very much the god, the container within himself of the whole universe. Derived from various sources, the story of Krishna conforms to the basic elements of the heroic monomyth.

Both Krishna and his older brother Balarama are miraculously conceived in Devaki, through the agency of Vishnu with the help of the great goddess (Devi) as Maya ("holy illusion"). Devaki's husband and Balarama's and Krishna's surrogate father is Vasudeva. The wicked King Kamsa, fearing a prophecy of his own murder at the hands of a child of his cousin Devaki, commands that her children be killed at birth. To avoid this threat to the divine children, the goddess takes the embryo out of Devaki and places it in Vasudeva's other wife, Rohini. Krishna is born to Devaki, but at birth, to protect him from King Kamsa, he is exchanged with a child of Yasoda, the wife of the cowherd Nanda. This child, a girl born at the same time as Krishna, is an incarnation of Maya, who, when she is murdered by Kamsa, thus serves as the necessary Hindu "sacrifice" for the birth of something positive, in this case Krishna. Both Balarama and Krishna are "adopted" for their protection by Nanda and are raised along the river Yamuna among the cowherds.

As a very young child, Krishna performs miraculous initiatory feats and defeats demons (*asuras*). On one occasion, when his adopted mother looks into his mouth, she is astounded to see the whole universe there. Krishna is especially dear to the women cowherds, the gopis. Always something of a trickster, Krishna teases them. In one story he steals their clothes while they are bathing in the river and convinces them to leave the water with their hands held together over their heads, signifying worship and supplication. The gopis here embody deliverance that comes from the worship of Lord Krishna. One of the gopis, Radha, becomes his lover, a prime symbol of Krishna devotion. The erotic delight in Krishna as a representation of total devotion and joy is contained in the *Gitagovinda*, which some have compared to the Hebrew *Song of Songs*.

Another famous story of Krishna's youth is that of his struggle with the serpent monster, Kaliya. The boy Krishna went one day with his friends the gopis to the Yamuna River. The gopis and their cows were so parched by the heat of the day that they drank from the river, which had been poisoned by Kaliya, who lived beneath the water there. The gopis and the cows fainted from the pollution but were revived by a mere glance from the Lord Krishna. Deciding to take direct action against Kaliya, Krishna climbed a kadama tree and, after clapping his hands and tightening his loincloth, dove into the river. The turmoil caused by the dive, and the fact that Krishna frolicked in Kaliya's particular dwelling pool like an elephant, destroyed the monster's home and enraged him. Kaliya attacked Krishna with all his might, wrapping his horrible coils around him. Krishna appeared to have been utterly defeated by the serpent. The gopis and their herds were miserable in their grief, thinking that their lord, to whom they had dedicated their lives and possessions, was dead.

Meanwhile, back in the village, there were many portents of evil, and Krishna's foster father, Nanda, became worried, as the boy had gone off without his brother Balarama, who could always be depended on as a protector. The villagers and Krishna's other friends did not realize that Krishna was, in fact, an incarnation of Vishnu. Rushing to the river, they saw their beloved Krishna trapped in the serpent's coils, and the women went to the boy's mother and wailed over their loss. Nanda and others were about to dive into the pool to retrieve the body of their young lord, but Balarama prevented them, knowing who his brother was and aware that the monster serpent could not harm him.

Krishna now saw how unhappy his friends were, rose up out of the serpent's grip, and proceeded to dance on the beast's hundred heads, destroying each one, as poison spewed from its body. So it was that the Lord Krishna overcame the evil that was Kaliya.

In adulthood, Krishna returned to his homeland of Mathura and killed Kamsa. He also became involved in the war between the Pandavas and Kauravas depicted in the *Mahabharata*, serving as the hero Arjuna's charioteer and mentor. His lesson as expressed to Arjuna is in the *Bhagavadgita* segment of the epic. When Arjuna declares his reluctance to carry on a war of needless slaughter of friends and relatives, Krishna reminds him that as a warrior, his only proper commitment is to *dharma*, proper action or duty according to his warrior caste. To worry about the effects of action based on dharma would be wrong. Krishna-Vishnu goes on to reveal to Arjuna the proper means of achieving oneness with Brahman.

Just after the war, Krishna dies, as he had predicted he would, when, in a position of meditation, he is struck in the heel by a hunter's arrow. His apotheosis occurs when he ascends in death to the heavens and is greeted by the gods.

KRONOS AND RHEA Kronos (Cronos, Cronus), whose name may be associated with "time," was a pre-Hellenic fertility-agriculture deity who in Greek mythology was the youngest son of the original Titan sky and earth deities, Ouranos and Gaia. Kronos rebelled against his father and castrated him as he lay on Gaia, thus performing the archetypal rite of the separation of sky and earth, making full creation possible. Kronos, like his father a personification of sky, married his sister Rhea, like her mother an embodiment of earth, and Kronos and Rhea produced the older generation of Olympians, headed by Zeus, who in a war in Heaven would overthrow his father, as Kronos had overthrown his. In Rome, Kronos was thought to be the equivalent of the god Saturn.

KSHATHRA Also known as Shatevar, meaning "power," Kshathra is one of the Zoroastrian Amesa Spentas. He is a war god of sorts who uses his power in the interests of peace, religion, and the poor. He is assisted by the powers of the heavens—the Sky, the Sun, and Mithra.

KU Ku is the Hawaiian version of the Polynesian war god Tu. He is associated with war and the earth, as opposed to peace and sky, the latter represented by Lono.

KUKULKAN Kukulkan (Gucumatz) is the Mayan version of the Mesoamerican Aztec god Quetzalcoatl.

KUMARBI CYCLE The Hittites and Hurrians told a cycle of myths that parallel the war-in-Heaven myths of other Indo-European cultures, including the Greek and Vedic, a fact perhaps attributable to the mid-millennium rule of the Hurrian Mitanni kingdom by an Indo-European Aryan aristocracy. In any case, the war-in-Heaven motif is a common feature in creation myths of all parts of the world; it serves as an explanation of the way the present world order came about. It also serves, as in the case of the Hittite-Hurrian version, to express the superiority of one culture's gods over those of a rival culture.

It was said that in the distant past Alalu was king of the gods and was served by the powerful son Anu (the ancient Mesopotamian deity—sometimes An), according to some his son. But after nine years, Anu overcame his father, who fled to the darkness of earth. Anu himself reigned for only nine years, during which time he was served by his son Kumarbi. In the last year of his reign, Anu was overcome by the power of Kumarbi's eyes and hands, and he tried to flee into the sky in defeat. But

K

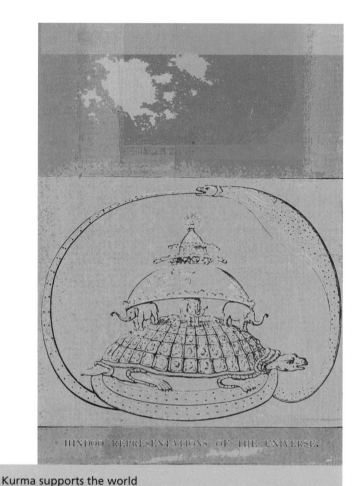

Kurma supports the world

Kumarbi reached up, pulled him back by his feet, and bit off his testicles, as the Greek Kronos had cut off those of his father, Ouranos. Kumarbi laughed at his father, who turned to him and suggested that his laughter might be foolish given the consequences of his act. By eating his father's testicles Kumarbi had been impregnated with the storm god Teshub, the Aranzah River, the "noble Tasmisu and two other frightening gods."

Teshub was born and grew to manhood, and after Kumarbi tried and failed to eat him, he became king of the gods. Later Teshub would be defeated by Ullikummi, who was for a time supported by the old primeval gods led by Ea. Later he, too, would be deposed and Teshub reinstated. This whole struggle for kingship is central to the Hurrian worldview. It is a struggle between earth and sky—Alalu having been of the earth and Anu of the sky—and is a metaphor for the cycles of nature.

KUNAPIPI The aboriginal people of Arnhem-land in Australia worship the mother goddess Kunapipi, who existed before all things and whose body is the animistic basis of earth itself. Her body—earth—contains the secret caves in which her followers worship. It was Kunapipi who, long ago in the dreaming time, brought the first ancestors to the land and, acting as a culture hero, taught them the song lines of the dreamtime songs, the lines they could follow to the sacred places of her body. Once in a lifetime, each of her worshippers goes to one of the sacred places and swings a bullroarer until Kunapipi sings and thus introduces the initiate to his or her twin soul, a soul that resides always with the goddess and, at the worshipper's death, will call its twin back to Kunapipi.

KUNDA One of several Indian Buddhist mother goddesses of compassion and knowledge, Kunda has sixteen arms or sometimes only four. Her symbols are all powerful weapons—the discus, the thunderbolt, and others—but her many hands hold prayer beads, ambrosia, and the lotus flower. She can be kind to the good and hard on the wicked.

KUNTI In the Indian epic the *Mahabharata*, Kunti is a wife of Pandu, who, because of a curse, cannot have sexual relations with his two wives. Kunti becomes the mother of the three main Pandava brothers—the heroes of the epic—by the gods Dharma, Vayu, and Indra. Because of a promise inadvertently made by Kunti, the Pandava brothers must share one wife, Draupadi. Kunti was also the mother, through miraculous conception by the sun god, of the anti-hero Karna before she became the mother of the Pandavas. It might be said, then, that the gods use Kunti as a kind of catalytic vessel for many of the events of the epic. It is perhaps for this reason that she is also called Pritha, which necessarily associates her with the primal vessel, Prithivi ("Earth"). It was to relieve the burden of Earth that Vishnu came to the world as Krishna, and it should be noted that Kunti is Krishna's father's sister.

KURMA Kurma, the Tortoise, is the second avatar of the Hindu god Vishnu. It was he who supported the world on his back while the creative churning of the ocean took place.

KUSA-NADA-HIME The wife of Susanowo, the storm-god brother of the Japanese sun goddess Amaterasu, Kusa-nada-hime ("Princess of the Rice Paddies") was the sole survivor among eight sisters of the terrible eight-headed dragon Yamato-no-orochi. When the dragon arrived to eat Kusa-nada-hime, Susanowo killed the monster and then was given the would-be victim in marriage.

KUTOYIS The Native North American Black-foot tribe hero Kutoyis was conceived and born miraculously in this way: An old man stole a big clot of blood from the catch of his wicked son-in-law. He and his wife placed the clot in a pot of boiling water to make soup and immediately heard a child crying. Upon opening the pot they found a baby and named it Kuto-yis (Bloodclot). The old couple knew that the son-in-law would kill any boy child, so they disguised it as a girl. On the fourth day Kutoyis had become a man, and soon after he killed the son-in-law before going on a heroic quest for other evil beings and monsters that tormented the people. He entered the mouth of the great Wind Sucker and killed the beast from within, freeing all the people trapped there. He allowed himself to be killed, dismembered, cooked, and eaten by the great Man-Eater. But each time he was reborn, and finally he killed the Man-Eater.

KYAZIMBA The Wachago people of Tanganyika in Africa tell how a very poor man—Kyazimba was his name—was determined to find the home of the Rising Sun. After many days of seemingly pointless travel, he was approached by a little old lady who wanted to know where he was going and why. After he told her he was looking for the home of the Rising Sun, the old woman wrapped Kyazimba in a magic cloak, which took him to the mid-point of the sky, where the Sun stops each day for a feast with his followers. The old woman presented Kyazimba to the Sun, and the great being blessed the pilgrim and sent him home to enjoy great prosperity.

LABYRINTH In Greek and Minoan mythology, the Labyrinth was a maze structure created by the master craftsman Daedalus as a living place for the Minotaur, the monstrous half-bull, half-human offspring of Pasiphae and the white bull of Poseidon. With the help of Ariadne, the hero Theseus penetrated the Labyrinth, killed the Minotaur, and was able to find his way out of it. In fact, a labyrinth is not a maze but a *mandala*, a symbolic structure with a path that leads circuitously to a center. Walking a labyrinth can represent the process of becoming spiritually centered or united with a higher reality.

LAERTES Laertes was a king of the Greek island of Ithaca, who appears in Homer's *Odyssey* as the aged husband of Anticlea and the father of the hero Odysseus.

LAIUS The king of Thebes, Laius was married to Jocasta. Laius and Jocasta had a son, later called Oedipus and made famous in plays by the Greek playwright Sophocles. Because of an oracle's prediction the couple abandoned the child in the wilderness. Later, Oedipus would kill Laius whom he did not realize was his father.

LAKSHMANA Lakshmana was the brother and loyal helper of Rama, one of the two most important avatars of the Hindu god Vishnu.

LAKSHMI A form of the Hindu goddess (Devi) as the wife of the cosmic preserver god Vishnu, Lakshmi, or Shri, stands for prosperity and good fortune in this world. In short, she is the worldly reflection of Vishnu's power, the world that emerges from the god. Lakshmi is Vishnu's *Shakti*, the energy without which he cannot be active or material. Thus, when Vishnu sleeps on the serpent Shesha (Ananta) during the cosmic night before the creation of the world, Shri is at his feet as Bhu ("Earth"), ready to be united with him when he awakens. By extension, Sita, the wife of the great Vishnu avatar Rama, is an incarnation of Lakshmi. Lakshmi is also incarnate in Draupadi, the wife of the Pandava brothers in the *Mahabharata*. Prosperity in India is associated with gold, so when a bride brings gold in some form to her marriage, she comes to the marriage as Lakshmi. To preserve Lakshmi—prosperity—proper sacrificial rituals must be performed, because, as in the cosmos, prosperity on earth depends on sacrificial destruction.

LALITAVISTARA One of several biographies of Gautama, the Buddha Sakyamuni, the *Lalitavistara* is an ancient and continually evolving Sanskrit text that is concerned with the early years of the Buddha.

LAN CAIHE Lan Caihe, sometimes seen as a woman, is one of the Daoist Eight Immortals. She (or he) was given immortality by Li Xuan, who gave her that gift after she tended to his sores when he was disguised as a beggar.

LANCELOT, SIR The son of King Ban of Benwick or Brittany, Sir Lancelot, or Lancelot of the Lake—so called because he was raised by Vivienne, the mysterious Lady of the Lake, who stole him at birth—was one of the noblest knights of King Arthur's Round Table. But his love affair with Arthur's queen, Guinevere, would lead to the downfall of Camelot and the fellowship of knights. Sir Galahad was Lancelot's son by the Lady Elaine, who tricked him into thinking she was Guinevere and so made love with him. Galahad would succeed in the quest for the Holy Grail where his father had failed.

Lancelot rescued Guinevere when she was about to be burned at the stake for adultery. When Guinevere and Lancelot fled to Brittany, Arthur followed them and his illegitimate son or nephew, Mordred, usurped his throne. This led to a war in which both Mordred and

Laokoon and his sons being killed by the sea serpents

Arthur were killed. When Guinevere retired to a nunnery, Lancelot, too, took religious vows. The Lancelot story is found in the works of Chrètien de Troyes and Sir Thomas Malory.

LAOKOON In the *Aeneid*, the epic by the Roman poet Virgil, the story is told of Laokoon, the Trojan priest of Apollo, who in vain urged the people of Troy not to allow the wooden horse "gift" of the Greeks into Troy. While the Trojans were discussing these matters, the sea god Poseidon, who was firmly on the Greek side during the war, sent two sea serpents to the place where Laokoon and his two children stood. The serpents strangled the priest and his sons, and this the Trojans took as an omen indicating that Laokoon's doubts were misguided. They took the horse, which contained Greek soldiers, into the city, thus ensuring the defeat of Troy.

LAOZI Laozi (Lao-tzu) is the quasi-historical central figure of the Chinese philosophy and religion known as Daoism. The *Daode Jing* (*Tao-te ching*)—sometimes simply called the *Laozi* or *Lao-tsu*—has been traditionally attributed to him. Known from the mid-third century B.C.E., this book, with the earlier *Chuang-tzu*, forms the basis of Daoist philosophy. By the end of the first century B.C.E., Laozi had become a deity to many of his followers.

One of the most famous legends about Laozi describes his supposed meeting with Confucius, who had come to consult the sage about ritual practices. Apparently Laozi was more interested in advocating Daoist principles, and Confucius left so impressed that he compared his "teacher" to a dragon.

Over the centuries, Laozi's life took on elements of the monomythical hero's quest biography. He was said to have been miraculously conceived by a shooting star and to have been born from his mother's side in what was, in effect, a virgin birth. Some say that Laozi lived for two hundred years before disappearing into the west and becoming the Buddha. Those who have deified him say he could change shapes at will, and that his abode is Heaven's center. Clearly, there are indigenous Chinese as well as Buddhist and even Hindu influences on this mythic biography.

LAPITHS Mythical mountain people of Thessaly in Greece, the Lapiths fought the centaurs over the inheritance of the realm of the Lapith king, who was related to the centaurs. After peace was made, the Lapiths invited the centaurs to the wedding of their king, Perithous (Pirithous), to Hippodamia. But a battle broke out when the centaurs tried to abduct Hippodamia and other Lapith women. With the help of Theseus, the Lapiths won the day. This battle, known as the centauromachy, was depicted on Parthenon metopes.

LARS The Lars (*Larae*), usually depicted as little boys, were Roman guardian divinities enshrined in homes. They were the objects of offerings on special occasions.

LAST JUDGMENT The Last Judgment, or the "Day of Judgment," at the end of historical time, is a tradition developed out of late Judaism's concept of God's final eschatological judgment of the world, when the Messiah will return. In Christian mythology, the Messiah has already arrived in the person of Jesus and will return at the Second Coming (Greek Parousia, "arrival") to judge the world, particularly the resurrected dead. There is some conflict between this millennial concept and that of the judgment of the individual soul, which is sent to Heaven or Hell (and, for some, Purgatory) at the time of death.

In Islam, both the Day of Judgment (*Yaum al-Din*) and the Day of Resurrection (*Yaum al-Qiyama*) are described in the *Qur'an* (7, 10, 17, 21, 23, 101). Judgment is based on the individual's actions during life. The division into Heaven (*janna*) and Hell (*jahannam*) will follow the Day of Judgment.

LAST SUPPER According to the Christian story, Jesus observed the Passover meal with his disciples in an "upper room" before retiring with the group to the Garden of Gethsemane, where he was arrested. Soon after that he would be tried and crucified. The meal in question, known as the "Last Supper," is analogous in Christian theology to the Old Testament story of the Passover, the last night of the Jews in Egypt. It was at the Last Supper that Jesus performed the traditional blessing of the unleavened bread and the wine but instituted a "New Covenant" by suggesting that hereafter the bread and wine be thought of as his body and blood, representing the sacrifice he was about to make on the cross. [Harris, Leeming (2004)]

LATINUS When in Virgil's Roman epic, the *Aeneid*, Aeneas arrives in Italy, he is assisted by Latinus, the king of Laurentium, in the region known as Latium. Latinus offers the hero his daughter Lavinia as a wife. The offer leads to war, however, as the young woman's fiancé, Tumus, takes issue with the new marriage arrangements. Aeneas wins the war and does marry Lavinia; he names the town of Lavinium for her.

LAWS OF MANU The Indian *Manava Dharmasastra* or *Manu Smirti*, that is, the *Laws of Manu*, composed between 200 B.C.E. and 200 C.E., is, as indicated in one of its titles, human-based *Smirti* rather than "revealed" *Shruti* literature. But the *Laws*, like all *Smirti*, are necessarily closely related to the Shruti Vedic revelations. The Laws are the first metrical Smirti treatises on dharma, the proper righteous way of orderly life for Hindus, depending on caste and status. They are the worldly laws derived from the cosmic ones of the Vedas . Their authorship is attributed to the mythical Manu Svayambhu, the first of the *manus*, or fathers of humanity. The *Laws* provide us with certain mythical constructs as well. There is, for example, an elaboration on the Vedic creation myths. We are told that Brahman—that which is "self-existent," the absolute—created the chaos and the seed out of which he was born. During his year in the cosmic egg of his own making, Brahman created existence by way of his own thoughts.

LEDA The always lustful Greek high god Zeus became enamored of Leda, the queen of Sparta, wife of Tyndareus, who would later give up his kingdom to Menelaus. Zeus came to Leda in the form of a swan and raped her as she walked along a lake. Leda had several famous children who were fathered by Zeus during the episode and/or by her husband Tyndareus. These offspring were Helen of Troy, Clytemnestra, and the famous twins, the Dioskouri, Castor and Polydeuces (Pollox).

LEGBA The Fon-Yoruba version of the west African trickster, Legba (Esu-Elegbara), like his cognates Ananse and Eshu, is a penetrator of the spirit world. As in the case of the Greek god Hermes, he stands as guardian outside of homes as a *herm*-like phallic statue. Some say he is the son of the high god. All agree that he is a rascal but that he often acts as a culture hero, committing questionable deeds for the good of the people.

One story tells how Legba in ancient days lived with his father on earth and that whereas the great god was praised for all good things, he—Legba—was blamed for bad things. Legba became tired of this situation and decided to change the situation by tricking his father. He told the high god that people were planning to steal his precious yams. This so enraged the god that he called the people together and vowed to kill anyone who touched his yams. During the night, Legba took a pair of his father's shoes and wore them into the garden and stole the yams. The next morning he announced that the yams had been stolen, but that the thief would be easy to catch since he had left footprints. But no one's footprints matched the ones in the garden. Then Legba suggested that maybe the god had been sleepwalking and had taken the yams himself. The god was furious, but he finally placed his feet on the footprints and, of course, the match was perfect. Now aware of having been tricked, the god became so exasperated that he left the earth to Legba and the people.

LEMMINKAINEN A rash and somewhat wild hero of Finno-Ugric mythology, Lemminkainen plays a role in the Finnish epic the *Kalevala*. There are many variants of the original Lemminkainen story. In many of them he is a magical or shamanic figure who dies, usually because he is shot by a herdsman who throws him into the river of death. Lemminkainen's mother retrieves the parts of his body, as the Egyptian goddess Isis retrieved the parts of the dying-god figure Osiris. Some versions of the story say that Lemminkainen descends to the Land of the Dead and is resurrected through the magic of his mother.

LERNEAN HYDRA Born of Echidne and Typhon, the Lernean Hydra was the many-headed dragon-serpent with a hound's body who died at the hands of Herakles in the first of the hero's Twelve Labors.

LESHII A forest spirit of Slavic mythology, the leshii is something of a trickster who can change his form at will and who enjoys mischievous acts. He is usually depicted as a peasant.

LETHE Lethe ("forgetfulness") is the river in the Greek underworld from which the dead must drink in order to forget their days among the living.

LETO The Titan daughter of Coeus and Phoebe, Leto (Roman Latona) became pregnant by the Greek high god Zeus. Because of this illicit relationship, she incurred the wrath of Zeus's consort, Hera, who persecuted her mercilessly, causing her to move from place to place, as poor Io, another victim of Zeus's philandering, had been forced to do. On the then-floating island of Delos (Ortygia), Leto gave birth to Apollo and Artemis, two of the most important of the Olympians.

LÉVI-STRAUSS, CLAUDE The French anthropologist and mythologist Claude Lévi-Strauss (b. 1908) is a leader of the approach to human culture—including its mythological aspect—known as structuralism. Lévi-Strauss is best known for his works *The Savage Mind, The Raw and the Cooked, The Way of the Masks,* and *The Naked Man.* In these works and many others he expresses his belief that

L

Jesus celebrates the Passover with his disciples for the last time

The sacred linga of Shiva at Angkor Wat

humans, in their language patterns and myths, express certain common structures that are basic to human life—such ultimate "binary oppositions," for instance, as male-female, life-death, and raw-cooked. In terms of myth, he attempts to demonstrate how myths "think themselves out" or are created unconsciously from certain mental structures present in the human brain. In analyzing myths, he looks for elementary units he calls *mythemes*, everyday cultural elements used to create the overall universal structure of myths. Lévi-Strauss breaks down the myths he studies until he comes to common structures mentioned above, the central opposites of our experience.

LHA-THO-THO-RI A fifth-century C.E. king who is said to have been the first worshipper of Buddhism in Tibet, Lha-tho-tho-ri "received" Buddhist texts and images when they fell out of a rainbow-filled sky. It would take three more centuries before Tibet would officially convert to Buddhism.

LI XUAN Li Xuan was the first of the Chinese Daoist Eight Immortals. He was taught the Dao by the goddess Xi

Wang, who gave him his iron crutch to compensate for his club foot.

LIBER Liber, or Liber Pater, was the name the Romans often applied to the Greek god Dionysos, also known to the Romans as Bacchus. In fact, Liber and his female cognate Libera were agriculture-fertility deities in pre-Roman Italy.

LILA Inside of the sleeping Hindu god Vishnu, the Goddess (Devi) as Lakshmi, or Shri, is the world contained within him waiting for creation. Outside of him in creation she is Maya, or the illusion of reality, Lila. That is to say, she becomes Lila ("divine play") in the created world.

LILITH A Hebrew tradition holds that Adam, Yahweh's first human creation, had a wife before Eve and that she was called Lilith. Apparently she was too arrogant to lie in the passive position under Adam and chose to leave her husband when he demanded that she do so, thereby becoming the first feminist rebel.

LIMINALITY Liminality is a term used especially by the cultural anthropologist Victor Turner (1920–1983) to refer to rites of passage or rituals that mark the crossings of thresholds between various significant stages of human life. These events all have mythic ramifications. Christian Baptism, Jewish and Muslim circumcision, and the Navajo Kinaalda, for instance, are all liminal events with mythic connotations or origins. Christians are baptized because Jesus was, Jews are circumcised because of Yahweh's command to Abraham, the Navajo girl at puberty changes from girl to the Goddess Changing Woman.

LINEAR A AND B By fairly early in the second millennium B.C.E., the Minoans on Crete possessed a form of writing we refer to as Linear A. Not long after the Greek-speaking Mycenaeans overpowered the Cretans in about 1450 B.C.E., they applied their own language rather awkwardly to the Linear A system and created so-called Linear B, a Greek language script useful for such things as inventories and other lists but not appropriate for literary purposes. Among the Linear B tablets, deciphered in 1953 by John Chadwick and Michael Ventris, are lists of Greek gods.

LINGA The *linga* (*lingam*) is the sacred phallus and principal symbol of the Hindu god Shiva. Some scholars have suggested that the genital worship aspect of Shiva indicates that he existed as a fertility god in the pre-Aryan Indus Valley culture, especially as the *linga* is nearly always presented in connection with the *yoni*, the symbolic vulva of the Goddess (Devi). In a sense, then, the *linga* united with the *yoni* symbolizes creation. This sense is supported by the fact that the linga-yoni often sits on an octagonal form representing Vishnu's jurisdiction over the cardinal directions and a square base representing Brahma and the four *Vedas*. Thus the *linga-yoni*, as a total structure, contains the Goddess (Devi) and the *Trimurti* of Shiva-Vishnu-Brahma.

Sacrifice is at the center of Hinduism; it is the price paid for prosperity or *Shri*. Traditionally, near the sacrificial altar, standing as a kind of guard over it, is the *yupa* or sacrificial column to which the sacrificial victim was once tied. The *yupa* is at once a pillar of the universe and a representation of the *linga*. The myths related to *linga* worship are found in the *Puranas* and usually involve the gods of the *Trimurti*. These myths, like the *linga*, are particularly important to the *bhakti* or special devotion associated with Shiva, whose phallus is the appropriate symbol of the destruction and regeneration, which is the essence of creation.

The following myth occurs in the *Shiva Purana*. At the beginning of an age, Shiva as destructive fire, Brahma as creative water, and Vishnu as mediating wind arose from the primal waters. Vishnu and Brahma bowed to the greater Shiva and called on him to create. Shiva agreed but dove back into the waters. Vishnu then asked Brahma to create and he gave Brahma creative energy (*Shakti*) so that he could do so. Brahma created. Now Shiva returned and was furious that Brahma had not waited for him before creating the world. In a rage, he burned up all that had been created. Impressed by this power, Brahma pleased Shiva by bowing to him. Wishing to reward Brahma for his devotion, Shiva asked him what he would like, and the creator god asked to have his creation restored and Shiva's creative energy transferred to the sun. Brahma promised to worship the Shiva *linga*, that which is past, present, and future. Shiva broke off his *linga* and flung it to the earth, where it reached down to Hell itself and then up into Heaven. Vishnu tried to find its source below and Brahma tried to find its tip on high; both were unsuccessful because the *linga* of Shiva is without end. At this point, a voice from above cried out. "Worship the *linga* of Shiva and be granted all that can be granted." So it was, say the followers of Shiva, that Vishnu and Brahma and all the gods worship the *linga*, the source of all destruction and creativity.

LINGAL Lingal is the culture hero of the Gond tribe and several other groups in central India. As always, the mythologies of the indigenous peoples of India are a mixture of Hinduism and earlier religious traditions such as those of the Dravidians, or Indus Valley people. The story is told of how the mother of the Gond gods deserted her offspring, who were taken in by Mahadeo and Parvati. These Gond gods demanded alcohol and meat and were imprisoned until Lingal and a goddess freed them. Lingal was a holy musician, who gave the gods—really the first humans—a place for homes and taught them proper social arrangements, including the clan system and rituals. On the way to the new homeland, the gods were saved from a rushing river by a monkey, or, in some related versions of the story, a tortoise.

LLEU LLAW GYFFES The Welsh equivalent of the Irish Lugh, Lleu Llaw Gyffes was particularly important in the "Fourth Branch" of the epic the *Mabinogion*. He was the son of Aranrhod, perhaps by her brother Gwydion, who acted as the child's protector. Gwydion was able to use trickery to get around his sister's proclamations to the effect that the child would have no name, never bear arms unless she provided them, and never marry a human woman. In fact, Lleu was named and he would take up arms, and he married Blodeuwedd, created from flowers by Gwydion and Math, who, however, betrayed him. Only with Gwydion's help did Lleu, in the form of an eagle, escape the attempt on his life by his wife and her lover.

LLYR Llyr (Irish Lir) was a Welsh figure featured in the "Second Branch" of the epic the *Mabinogion*. He was the father of Branwen and Bran the Blessed by Iweriadd ("Ireland") and Manawydan by Penardun, daughter of the mother goddess Don. Llyr, whose name was later spelled Leir, and who was recognized as an early British monarch, took the form of Shakespeare's King Lear.

LOGOS Logos, the "Word," is a name or title traditionally applied by Christians to Jesus as the Christ, in whom the Logos, or divine reason, was incarnate. Theologically speaking, in the context of the doctrine of God as the Trinity, Christ as Logos has always existed. So it is that the evangelist John begins his gospel with the words "In the beginning the Word already was. The Word was in God's presence, and what God was, the Word was."

LOKI The primary trickster figure in Norse mythology, Loki is the offspring of giants. Among the Aesir he is known as a mischief maker. He is lascivious and ruthless. He can change shapes at will; sometimes he looks like the other gods, sometimes he becomes a flea or a salmon or a bird. He can change sexes and even bear a child. He takes the form of a mare; mates with Svadilfari, the giant stallion; and gives birth to Odin's eight-legged horse, Sleipnir. As a male, he fathers three terrible children with the giantess Angrboda: the monstrous wolf Fenrir; the serpent Jormungard, who bites his own tail and forms a circle around Midgard; and the daughter Hel, ruler of the underworld. Loki plays a particularly evil role in the myth of the death of the much-loved Balder and in the story of the theft of Idun's apples.

L

Brahma with his four faces

After the death of Balder, Loki is bound up like the Greek Prometheus and left to be tortured until the end of the world, or Ragnarok. Sigyn is Loki's surprisingly faithful wife.

LONO The Hawaiian version of the Polynesian god Rongo, Lono is associated with the Makihiki ceremony, a four-month festival said to have been founded by a god from elsewhere known as Paao. The festival begins with the appearance of the Pleiades in the evening sky and ends with the arrival of the autumn rains. Lono is a sky god who is, nevertheless, also a god of agricultural fertility and peace. At the end of the festival in question, Lono becomes a dying god, as he is ritually killed—probably in the interest of renewed fertility—and is replaced by an earth god of war, Ku.

LOTUS OF THE GOOD LAW In 804 C.E. a Japanese Buddhist monk, Saicho (Dengyo-daishi), visited China and came back with a doctrine learned from Chinese monks on Mount Tendai. This was the beginning of the Tendai sect, a Mahayana sect that, like the Chinese Tendai monks, based its beliefs on the Hekkekyo (*Lotus of the Good Law*, or *Lotus Sutra*). This text stressed the existence of the Buddha nature and the drive for enlightenment even in inanimate

The eight immortals, along with Lu Dongbin, cross the sea

nature. The Tendai sect brought together various strands of Japanese Buddhism, including the worship of Amida Buddha. By the twelfth century a Zen monk named Nichiren reacted against what he saw as the corruption of the *Lotus* by the Tendai sect and another esoteric group, the Shin gon sect, and by Amidism in general. He called for a return to the *Lotus* and to the teachings there of the true Buddha, Gautama, the Buddha Sakyamuni.

LOUHI In the Finnish epic the *Kalevala*, Louhi is the mistress of North Farm, who struggles with various heroes for possession of the sampo.

LU DONGBIN One of the wisest of the Chinese Daoist Eight Immortals, Lu Dongbin was converted when he realized the illusory nature of worldly success and became a follower of Han Zongli. He was the particular teacher of the immortals Han Xiang and Cao Guojiu.

LUEJI The African Lunda people say that Lueji was of the family of the mother serpent Chinawezi and was married to Chibinda Ilunga, the grandson of the ancestor of all Luba Lunda kings.

LUGALBANDA In an ancient Sumero- Mesopotamian myth, the hero Lugalbanda is with his king, Enmerkar, in the mountains on the way to a war with the Lord of Aratta in the East. Suddenly he loses his ability to move, and his comrades are forced to leave him alone with some food and some weapons until they can retrieve him on their way home. The hero prays to Utu, Inanna, and Nanna. The paralysis leaves him, and good demons find him the Plant and Water of Life, which he eats and drinks. Now full of energy, he hunts for more food and captures several wild animals. In his sleep, he is told to sacrifice the animals and to offer the hearts to Utu and the blood to the mountain serpents. Lugalbanda does as he is instructed and then prepares a feast to which he invites An, Enlil, and Ninhursaga. As evening approaches, the astral deities to whom he has prayed and for whom he has made special altars reveal themselves in the night sky and chase away any evil powers.

LUGH Lugh, the Irish hero-god, whose name, like that of his Welsh cognate Lleu and the continental Celtic Lugus, means "Bright One," was the grandson of the terrible one-eyed Fomorian leader, the giant Balor. When Balor was told by an oracle that he would be killed by a grandson, he locked up his daughter, Eithne, to prevent her from having children. But she was seduced by a Tuatha Dé Danaan named Kian, and she produced triplets. Balor drowned two of the boys, but Lugh escaped and survived to lead the Tuatha against the Fomorians in the second battle of Mag Tuired. In that battle, David-like, he killed the giant Balor with his slingshot.

LUGUS His name, referring to brightness, indicates that the continental Celtic god Lugus, whom Julius Caesar equated with the Roman Mercury, was a cognate of the Irish Lugh and the Welsh Lleu. Lugus was a god of the arts.

LYNCEUS One of Jason's Argonauts, the hero Lynceus had eyesight so strong that he could see through the ground itself. Another Lynceus was an ancestor with his wife, Hypermnestra, of the Greek hero Perseus.

MAAT In Egyptian mythology, the goddess Maat (Ua Zit), the wife of Thoth, a god associated with wisdom, and daughter or aspect of the high god Atum, is at once a goddess and an idea, the personification of moral and cosmic order, truth, and justice (*maat* or *mayet*, like the Mesopotamian *me* or Indian *dharma*) that was as basic to life as breath itself, which in the Coffin Texts Maat also seems to personify. Pharaohs held small models of Maat to signify their association with her attributes. Maat gives breath itself—life—to the kings, and so is depicted holding the symbol of life, the *ankh*, to their noses. Maat represents the proper relationship between the cosmic and the earthly, the divine and the human, the earth, the heavens, and the underworld. It is she who personifies the meaningful order of life as opposed to the entropic chaos into which it might easily fall. In some stories it is the sun god Re who displaces Chaos with Maat. When a person died his heart was weighed against Maat's feather. A heart "heavy with sin" would not join the gods.

Maat was essentially in all Egyptian gods and goddesses as the principle of divinity itself. The goddess Isis acknowledges the qualities of Maat, as signified by the *maat* (ostrich feather) she wears behind the crowns of upper and lower Egypt.

Maat might be seen as a principle analogous to the Logos, divine reason and order. As Christians are told "In the beginning the Word [*Logos*] already was" (John 1:1), Atum announces that before creation, "when the heavens were asleep, my daughter Maat lived within me and around me."

MABINOGION The Welsh Mabinogion is found in two fourteenth-century manuscripts, the *White Book of Rhydderch* and the *Red Book of Hergest*. The collection, based on oral narratives, probably took literary form between the mid-eleventh to the early twelfth centuries. There are, for instance, parts of what seem originally to have been eleventh-century written versions of a few tales in an early-thirteenth-century manuscript known as *Peniarth 6*. The primary mythological material of the *Mabinogion* is contained in the four sections known as the "Four Branches." Also included in the greater *Mabinogion* are four "Independent Native Tales," so called by Lady Charlotte Elizabeth Guest, the first to translate the Welsh stories into English. This group includes the earliest known Welsh Arthurian story, "Culhwch and Olwen." The last part of the *Mabinogion* is made up of three later Arthurian romances.

The term *mabinogi* has been associated with the tradition of the mabinog, or young apprentice bard, and with the Irish *mac ind oc*, a name sometimes given to the Dagda's love-god son Aonghus—the "son of the eternal youth." As the "Four Branches" are concerned with the Children of Don, who resemble the Irish Tuatha Dé Danaan, this theory seems at least reasonable, especially since the only character to figure in all four tales is Pryderi, who in Wales was always the *mac ind oc*. Finally, the *mabinogi* has been associated with Maponos, the divine youth god popular in northern Britain and the continent, who is the Arthurian warrior and hunter Mabon in Wales. Thus, the theory goes, *mabinogi* is derived from "Mabonalia." The mother of Maponos was the mother goddess Matrona; in Wales she became Modron. In some stories we learn that Mabon was stolen from his mother soon after his birth. This theme occurs, as will be seen, in other Welsh tales as well.

The "Four Branches" of the *Mabinogi*on are independent narratives that are related, however, as certain characters appear in more than one tale.

As described in the "First Branch," Pryderi is the son of Pwyll ("Good Judgment"), lord of Dyfed, and Rhiannon.

The heart of a dead human is weighed against Maat's Feather of Truth

Dyfed is the land of the Cauldron of Plenty, perhaps the Holy Grail, and in this context Pwyll is the Arthurian Pelles, the guardian of the Grail. He is also known as "head of Annwn," Annwn being the otherworld as in the Arthurian tale *Preiddeu Annwn* (*The Spoils of Annwn*), seen by many as the prototype of the story of the quest for the Holy Grail.

While hunting in Glyn Cuch Pwyll insults another hunter, who turns out to be the mysterious King Arawn of the otherworld realm, Annwn (Annwfn). Pwyll's offense is driving away the king's hounds and substituting his own in the pursuit of a stag. To pay for his discourtesy, he is made to take Arawn's face as his own and to occupy his throne in Annwn for a year. There he sleeps in Arawn's bed, keeping a promise not to make love with his wife, and he defeats the king's enemy Hafgan, another otherworld king. Pwyll wins the fight with Hafgan only by restraining himself from administering a second blow, which would have restored power to his enemy.

Soon after his return to Dyfed, in southwestern Wales, Pwyll holds a feast at his court, Arbeth. He takes his place on the throne mound knowing full well that by so doing he will suffer pain or bear witness to something wonderful. A beautiful woman rides by on a white horse. After a fruitless chase of the woman, Pwyll begs her to stop, which she does. The woman reveals herself to be Rhiannon, and she offers herself as Pwyll's wife. Rhiannon is possibly the Welsh form of the Irish goddesses Edain Echraide ("horse riding") and Macha, who outran horses. All are figures comparable to Matrona and to the horse goddess Epona, whose legacy stretches back to early Indo-European horse-based myths and rituals.

At the wedding feast a year later, Pwyll foolishly grants a wish that results in his losing Rhiannon to Gwawl (Light), the son of the goddess Clud. But Pwyll wins his wife back at the wedding feast of Gwawl and Rhiannon. Rhiannon has given him a magic bag, which he tricks Gwawl into entering. Once there, Gwawl is badly kicked and beaten by Pwyll's followers, who thus originate the game called "Badger the Bag."

After three years of marriage, Rhiannon gives birth to Pryderi. The women who are supposed to watch over the mother and child fall asleep, and the baby is mysteriously abducted, reminding us of the story of Mabon's similar abduction. To save themselves, the women smear the blood of some killed puppies on Rhiannon so that she is accused of killing her child and is wrongly punished by her husband. After several years, the child is discovered to be alive and safe in the home of Teyrnon of Gwent and Is-Coed and is returned to his parents. The child has been named Gwri, or "Golden Hair," but Rhiannon, relieved of her worry—her care—renames him Pryderi, or "Care."

It seems that Teyrnon had amputated a giant clawed arm that had reached through a stable window on May Eve to take one of his foals. He had rushed out to give chase to the intruder but had found no one. On his return to the stable he had found a baby, and he and his wife had raised the boy, who turned out to be the lost son of Pwyll and Rhiannon.

The "Second Branch" of the *Mabinogion* concerns the children of Llyr (Irish Lir—perhaps King Lear); the gigantic Bran the Blessed, King of Britain; the gentle Branwen, sometimes thought of as a goddess of love; Manawydan, the sea god; and their half brothers Efnisien, the bringer of strife, and Nisien, the peacemaker. Efnisien is responsible for much of the tragedy in the story of Branwen's marriage to King Matholwch of Ireland. According to some sources, Llyr's first wife was Iweriadd, or "Ireland," and the mother of Bran

and Branwen. According to others, it was his wife Penardun, the daughter of the mother goddess Don, who was the mother of Bran and Branwen and certainly of Manawydan.

Matholwych comes to Harlech in Wales to ask for Branwen in marriage. All goes well at the marriage feast in Aberffraw until Efnisien, angry at not being a part of the marriage arrangements, damages Matholwych's horses. To cool the bridegroom's anger, Bran gives his brother-in-law a magic cauldron—perhaps the Cauldron of Plenty—which will bring the wounded back to life but leave them without the power of speech.

During her first year in Ireland, Branwen gives birth to a son who is named Gwern, on whom the "sovranty" of Ireland is bestowed so as to bring lasting peace between Bran and Matholwych. But the people of Ireland continue to be outraged by the behavior of Efnisien at the marriage feast in Wales, and they demand that Branwen be made to suffer. So it is that for three years she is made to work in the court kitchens and to experience the daily blows of the court butcher.

Branwen teaches a starling to speak, however, and it takes a message to her brother concerning her misery. Bran invades Ireland, his gigantic body forming a bridge between the lands by which his army can pass into Ireland. We are reminded here of the exploits of the monkey god Hanuman in the Indian epic the *Ramayana*, in which the god-hero Rama invades Ceylon (Lanka) to free his captured wife Sita.

Matholwch sues for peace to save his country, but Efnisien destroys the truce by hurling Gwern into a fire. A terrible battle ensues in which Efnisien sacrifices himself and in so doing destroys the magic cauldron that is constantly causing the resuscitation of the Irish. Bran is wounded by a poison arrow and orders his followers to decapitate him and to return his head to Britain. The severed head goes on talking and eating during a long and difficult voyage back to Britain. The prominent Celtic theme of decapitation and the talking severed head suggests a belief that the soul resides in the head and lives on after death.

Very few people survive the great war, as in the case of the Irish second battle of Mag Tuired. Only five pregnant women remain alive in Ireland and are the source for that island's future population. The survivors from Bran's forces include Manawydan, Pryderi, Taliesen, and only four others. Soon after Branwen lands in Britain with these survivors she dies of a broken heart over the destruction for which she blames herself. She is buried along the Alaw in Anglesey. The river is renamed Ynys Branwen.

At the beginning of the "Third Branch" of the *Mabinogion*, Pryderi has married Cigva (Cigfa) and succeeded his late father, Pwyll, as Lord of Dyfed. His mother, Rhiannon, marries the wise and patient Manawydan, a surviving son of Llyr. Manawydan plays the major role in the "Third Branch." Clearly he is a descendant of an earlier Celtic sea deity and a close relative of the benevolent Irish sea god who came from the Isle of Man. Like the Irish Manannan mac Lir, he is associated with rebirth, serving as lord of the land of eternal youth.

During a feast at Arbeth, the two couples sit on the magic throne mound and are covered by a mysterious mist following a huge clap of thunder. When the mist clears, they find themselves in a land empty of living things. They wander about the deserted Dyfed for two years and then go to the land of Lloegyr (England), where Pryderi and Manawydan work as saddlers, shoemakers, and shield makers.

M

The four return to Arbeth, and the impulsive Pryderi, disregarding the advice of Manawydan, allows himself to be enticed by a magic boar into an enchanted castle containing a fountain in which a golden bowl sits on a marble slab. This is perhaps the Cauldron of Plenty and/or the Holy Grail. When Pryderi tries to grasp the cauldron, he loses speech and cannot release his hands from it. When Rhiannon tries to rescue her son, she, too, loses speech and the ability to release the cup. The two now disappear into a mist.

The author of the enchantment and abduction of the hero and his mother is Llwyd, a friend of the evil Gwawl, who had once attempted to marry Rhiannon through trickery.

Manawydan, accompanied by Cigva, returns to shoemaking in England but eventually goes back to Arbeth, where he grows corn. Having discovered an army of mice carrying the corn away, he captures the slowest moving of the army and is about to hang it as a thief on the throne mound when a bishop turns up and announces that the mouse is his pregnant wife. He reveals himself as Llwyd. In return for the life of his wife, Llwyd ends forever the spells suffered by the heroic family.

The "Fourth Branch" of the *Mabinogion* is dominated by the family of Don, especially Lleu, who resembles the Irish god Lugh. The tale begins with Math of Gwynedd, son of Mathonwy. Math is a god of wealth and is possibly a cognate of the Irish Mathu. He is best known for the story of his requiring that his feet be held in the lap of a virgin when he is not at war. It is the ruse of two of the sons of Don, the magician Gwydion and Gilfaethy, that deprives him of his footstool. Gwydion also dupes Preyderi in this process, and the result is his death in a war against Gwynedd.

Gwydion attempts to substitute his sister Aranrhod for the stolen maiden. But Aranrhod drops a male child as she steps over Math's sword in a test of her virginity. And soon after the birth of the first child, the sea god Dylan, she drops an object that Gwydion takes and hides in a box, only to discover there later another child who is perhaps the incestuous offspring of Aranrhod and Gwydion. Aranrhod is ashamed and refuses to name the child, but Gwydion and the child appear in court as shoemakers, and Aranrhod inadvertently names her son by exclaiming over his brightness and skill. Thus he becomes Lleu Llawgyffes. Now the boy's mother swears that he will never bear arms unless she gives them to him, but Gwydion's magic overcomes this oath. Aranrhod also swears that Lleu will never marry into a race "now on earth," so Math and Gwydion create a woman, Blodeuwedd, or "Flower," from the blossoms of the oak, the broom, and the meadowsweet, and she becomes Lleu's wife.

Blodeuedd falls in love with Gronw Pebyr of Penllyn, however, and the lovers plot to kill Lleu. Like many femmes fatales before and after her, Blodeuwedd convinces her husband to reveal his particular weakness and learns that he can never be killed in a house or on horseback or on foot outside. Only a specially created spear can kill him. So one day when Lleu is taking a bath, he is tricked into standing with one foot on the tub and the other on a goat. In this position he is vulnerable and falls victim to Gronw's spear. He disappears as an eagle but is found by Gwydion, who gives him back his human form. Lleu returns to Gwynedd and kills Gronw. Blodeuwedd is turned into the despised owl.

The "Four Independent Native Tales" attached to the *Mabinogion* are a combination of folk history and popular themes and lack the narrative depth of the "Four Branches." The first tale, "Macsen Wledig," sometimes called "The Dream of Macsen," concerns Magnus Maximus, a Spanish Roman who came to Britain in 368 C.E. and married Helen, or Elen Lwddog. In 383 he proclaimed himself Western Emperor, crossed over into Gaul, and attacked Rome. Defeated by the Eastern Emperor Theodosius, he was put to death in 388. Elen returned to Britain and settled in what would become Wales with her children, whose offspring would be kings. The "Dream of Maxen" tells the story of Macsen's hunt, on which he was joined by thirty-two other kings, reminding us of a similar Irish story, "Bricriu's Feast," in which King Conchobhar is accompanied by thirty-two heroes to Bricriu's Hall. The number 33 is important in Indo-European mythology in general. There are, for instance, thirty-three gods mentioned in the Indian *Vedas*.

The story of "Lludd and Llefys," the second tale, is based on a Welsh translation by Geoffrey of Monmouth in the *Historia regnum Britanniae* in about 1200 C.E. Lludd (Nudd) and Llefelys were sons of the Beli, the husband of Don. With the help of the wise counsel of his brother, King Lludd of Britain puts an end to three plagues that devastated Britain. The first plague was caused by the highly knowledgeable little Coraniaids, the second by the hideous scream of a British dragon fighting a foreign dragon under the very center of Britain on May Eve. It is probably more than coincidental that it was also on May Eve that Teyrnon amputated the mysterious invasive claw in the "First Branch" of the *Mabinogion*. In any case, the dragon scream undermined fertility all over the land. The third plague was brought about by a giant who ate prodigious amounts of food. These plagues bear some resemblance to those that the Fomorians in Ireland levied on the Tuatha Dé Danaan or to the mysterious events that took place in Pryderi's Dyfed. The story is full of the fantasy of fairy tale. Some have suggested that it is a popular account of mythological invasions of Britain.

Dating from the mid-eleventh century, the third tale, that of "Culhwch (Kulhwch) and Olwen," is based on several traditional folktales and is the earliest Arthurian story in Welsh. Culhwch was the son of Cilydd and Goleuddydd, who lost her mind and ran into the woods and gave birth to Culhwch. Realizing she was about to die, she made her husband promise not to marry again until a two-headed briar grew from her grave. Cilydd respected his wife's wishes and waited the seven years until the briar grew as indicated before he married again.

The new wife hated Culhwch and put a curse on him because he refused to marry her daughter. The youth would never marry unless with Olwen, the daughter of Yspaddaden Pencawr (Benkawr), a terrifying giant. Olwen is said to be so beautiful that white flowers spring up in her tracks as she walked.

Culhwch goes to his cousin King Arthur's court to learn the arts of knighthood and to discover the whereabouts of Olwen. Stopped at the king's door, he bursts into Arthur's hall on horseback and asks that Arthur perform on him the initiatory rite of the cutting of his hair and that the king obtain Olwen for him. He asks these favors in the name of a host of Welsh heroes. Arthur agrees to help and sends out scouts to find Olwen, and when that fails Culhwch goes with several knights to find Olwen himself.

One day the party comes upon a castle near which they meet a shepherd named Custennin, who is Yspaddaden's brother and whose wife is Culhwch's mother's sister. The couple bring Olwen to meet Culhwch, and the hero asks the beautiful maiden to marry him. Olwen will agree to the marriage only if her father consents, because, according to a prophecy, he will die when his daughter marries.

M

Culhwch and his companions enter the castle, where servants hold open the giant's eyes with forks so that he can see his visitors. Culhwch asks for Olwen's hand in marriage, and the giant agrees to consider the matter, but as the knights are leaving he hurls a spear at them. Bedwyr catches it and hurls it back, wounding Ysbaddaden in the knee. The same thing happens the next day and the next, causing wounds to the giant's chest and to one of his eyes.

Finally, Ysbaddaden agrees to the marriage if the hero can complete thirteen tasks. The tasks, reminiscent of those of Herakles and of the world of fairy tales, are, in effect, preparations for the marriage that the giant hopes to prevent. Culhwch must clear a forest and prepare the land for the growing of food for the wedding feast; he must find linseed for the flax that will be used for his wife's veil; he must find perfect honey for the wedding drink, the magic cup of Llwyr to contain it, and four other magical vessels, including the famous Irish cauldron of Diwrnach for the cooking of the meat. He must even obtain a magical harp and the birds of Rhiannon so that there will be music at the feast. And he must take a tusk from Yskithrwyn, the Head Boar, to serve as Ysbaddaden's razor and the Black Witch's blood as lotion for his beard. And for the giant's hair management, he must take scissors and a comb from between the ears of Twrch Trwyth, a king who has been turned into a boar. All of these tasks and some twenty-six additional ones are accomplished with the help of the Arthurian knights, various animals, and even some gods—including Gofannon, son of Don, Gwynn, son of Nudd (Lludd), and Mabon (Maponos), son of Modron—whom Culhwch rescues from the otherworld, Caer Loyw. Finally, Ysbaddaden concedes defeat and is decapitated according to the Celtic practice, leaving Culhwch and Olwen free to marry.

Probably dating from the thirteenth century, "The Dream of Rhonabwy," the fourth tale, takes place in the context of a rebellion by Iorwerth against his brother Madawc, son of Maredudd. It is Rhonabwy who leads Madawc's troops and who one evening falls asleep on a calf's hide and remains sleeping for three nights, dreaming of King Arthur's game of chess with Owain, who has an army of three hundred ravens, and of the gathering of Arthur's forces for the great sixth-century Battle of Mount Badon in which the Celts defeated the Anglo-Saxons.

The "Three Late Arthurian Tales" of the *Mabinogion* are derived from twelfth-century romances of the French poet Chrétien de Troyes, whose sources seem to have been earlier Welsh and/or Breton versions. The theme that unites them is that of valid sovereignty and, specifically, the idea so prevalent in Irish mythology that fertility depends on the marriage of the king or hero to a goddess who represents the land in question.

In the first tale, "Owein or the Lady of the Fountain," the central figure is Owein (Owain), son of Urien, one of King Arthur's most trusted knights. We remember that in "The Dream of Rhonabwy" he plays a game of chess with the king, a game that, in a sense, can be seen as a preface to the story of his connection with the Lady of the Fountain. After he defeats the Black Knight, Owein finds himself a prisoner in the castle of the fountain until he is rescued by a ring of invisibility given to him by a beautiful young woman named Luned. Luned instructs him on how to win the love of the Lady of the Fountain, which he succeeds in doing before returning to Arthur's court. There he forgets the lady until she appears and accuses him of being a faithless knight.

Embarrassed and ashamed, Owein escapes to the wilderness, where he is saved from death by the ministrations of a noblewoman and her assistants. After killing two monstrous beasts, he saves Luned and twenty-four maidens, whom he finds imprisoned by the Black Giant. He is now worthy of the Lady of the Fountain, whom he marries.

The next tale, "Peredur Son of Efrawk," is about Peredur, the Welsh version and apparent source for the hero Percival, or Parzifal. The best-known versions of his story are Chrétien's late-twelfth-century *Perceval, ou le conte du Graal*, and Sir Thomas Malory's fifteenth-century *Morte d'Arthur*, where he is also Percival. *Per* means "bowl" in Brythonic Celtic, and Peredur-Percival-Parzival is always a hero who searches for the bowl that is the Holy Grail. In all of the tales the hero has a rough beginning, living an unmannered, unschooled life in the woods, until he arrives at Arthur's court, behaves in a bumbling sort of way, but is trained as a knight. Perhaps it is Peredur's essential innocence—even naiveté—that makes it possible for him to see the Holy Grail itself. Or perhaps his fortune is guaranteed by the young maiden relative who repeatedly guides him to the right path.

The story of "Gereint and Enid" is a romance about a lover—perhaps based on a king of Dumnonia (the Celtic area of western Britain in early Anglo-Saxon times)—who has little faith in the constancy of his beloved, Enid, the chieftain's daughter later to be made famous in the Tennyson poem named for her. Because of his doubts, Gereint treats Enid with contempt, but she proves herself in several tests, and eventually the two are reconciled, once again bringing the hero into proper relationship with the representative of sovereignty.

MABON Mabon, an Arthurian warrior and hunter, is the Welsh version of the continental Maponos. He was rescued from the otherworld by Culhwch, whom he then helps to find and marry Olwen. This is a story told in the *Mabinogion*, a title probably related to Mabon's name.

MACHA One of several Irish triune goddesses of war, Macha is the wife of the invader Nemed. But later, as the wife of the Tuatha Dé Danaan king, Nuada, she is killed at the second battle of Mag Tuired by the giant one-eyed Balor. In a third incarnation she curses the men of Ulster, causing them to suffer childbirth pangs during difficult times.

Finally, as Macha of the Reed Tresses, she is listed as the seventy-sixth monarch of Ireland.

MAEL DUIN Mael Duin (Maeldun) is the Irish hero of what probably was originally an eighth-century voyage tale. Mael Duin was the child of a nun who had been raped by Ail-lil and who died in childbirth. Aillil was murdered by foreign raiders, so Mael Duin went out into the world to find these raiders and to avenge his father's death in a series of fabulous adventures in strange lands, adventures described in the tenth-century *Immram Curaig Maile Duin*.

MAG TUIRED, BATTLES OF Mag Tuired (Magh Tuireadh or Moytura) was the place of two great battles in Irish mythology. In the first battle, the Tuatha Dé Danaan, led by Nuada, won against the Firbolg, but Nuada lost his hand, which was replaced by a silver one made by Dian Cecht. In the second battle, the Tuatha defeated the Fomorians, led by the giant Balor, whom Lugh killed with his slingshot.

The Pandava Brothers, the heroes of the *Mahabharata*

M

MAGNA MATER Magna Mater (Great Mother) was the name applied by the Romans particularly to the originally Phrygian mother goddess Cybele, the mother-lover of Attis.

MAENADS The Greek Maenads or Maenades, more commonly known as the Bacchae, were the female followers of Dionysos (Bacchus). They were often lasciviously pursued by satyrs. The Maenads played a large role in frenzied Dionysian revels or "bacchanals" that sometimes led to sacrificial dismemberments, as in the myth of Pentheus.

MAHABHARATA The Sanskrit Hindu epic the *Mahabharata* is perhaps the world's longest literary work. It is, for instance, eight times as long as the *Iliad* and *Odyssey* combined. While not considered "revealed" (*Shruti*) text, like the *Vedas*, the epic is a traditional (*Smirti*) source for many of the most popular and complex myths and legends of Hinduism and India. It is considered a reliable source for questions having to do with proper actions and social arrangements—that is, with dharma—and the relations between the human and divine worlds. *Mahabharata* means "Great (*maha*) Story of the Bharatas," the Bharatas being the legendary first Indians and, by extension, Hindus. The central issue of the epic is the war between Bharata descendants, the Pandavas and the Kauravas, which, according to tradition, took place on the sacrificial field of Kuruksetra in 3200 B.C.E. "The Epic," as it is sometimes called, continues to be performed and read all over India. There are even comic book versions widely sold. The work contains eighteen books (*parvans*) and is supplemented by the *Harivamsha*, a genealogy of Hari (Vishnu).

The legendary author of the *Mahabharata* is Vyasa, a particularly powerful sage, or *Rishi*, otherwise known as Krishna Dvaipayna—the "island-born Krishna," who is, thus, perhaps an avatar of Vishnu. The epic was said to have been dictated by Vyasa to the elephant-headed god Ganesh, who used one of his tusks as a pen. Sometimes the work is called the "Veda of Krishna," suggesting a religious connection between Vyasa and the Krishna-Vishnu figure who is so central to the epic, particularly to the highly philosophical section we know as the *Bhagavadgita*. Vyasa is also said to have brought the *Vedas* themselves to humanity. There is a tradition that holds that Vyasa was the begetter of the Bharatas, the ancestors of both the Pandavas and the Kauravas.

In fact, the authorship of the epic was collective and gradual. Much of what was transcribed by *brahmans* in the fifth century B.C.E. was based on earlier material, reaching back to ancient tribal warfare, and additions were made to the text as late as 500 C.E.

The stories of the *Mahabharata* are clearly representative of cosmic religious issues. The *Mahabharata*, as *Smirti*, is an example of particular sectarian devotion (*bhakti*) in connection with Krishna-Vishnu, as well as a reexamination of older Vedic ideas of dharma and brahmanic sacrifice.

The epic begins with the establishment of the need for sacrifice in order that true prosperity (*Shri*) might be restored. The Goddess, as earth, is oppressed by demons and general evil. Vishnu and several other gods descend to earth to relieve her. Vishnu is Krishna, friend and cousin to the Pandava brothers, who are fathered by gods for whom they become earthly vehicles or avatars. The Pandava king, Yudishthira, is fathered by Dharma, who embodies that proper order and duty that needs to be reestablished in the world. The brothers Arjuna and Bhima, whose mother, Kunti, is also the mother of Yudishthira, are fathered by the gods Indra and Vayu, representing warriors. The lesser

203

brothers, the twins Nakula and Sahadeva, whose mother is Madri, are fathered by the twin physician gods the Ashvins, who represent social welfare here. Together, the Pandavas, supported by Krishna, stand for proper action and social arrangement (dharma). Significantly, the Pandavas share one wife, Draupadi, who is an incarnation of Shri/Lakshmi, the wife of Vishnu. As such, she is "Prosperity." Opposed to the Pandavas are their hundred Kaurava cousins, led by the arrogant Duryodhana, who embodies cosmic discord and is allied with Karna, the son of the sun god Surya by Kunti. Together the Kauravas represent *adharma*, or the opposite of dharma. With the physical and philosophical opposition of the cousins, the stage is set for a war that will be the cleansing sacrifice between ages (*yugas*) and a lightening of earth's burden.

When, after political struggles and a decision to divide the kingdom, Yudishthira lays claim to universal kingship, Duryodhana challenges him to a game of dice. In this famous game, Yudishthira loses everything, including the joint Pandava wife Draupadi. He thus gambles away prosperity. The Kauravas attempt to disrobe Draupadi in order to insult and humiliate her and her husbands but are prevented from doing so by the powers of Krishna, who makes Draupadi's sari an endless garment. After losing another gambling match, however, the Pandavas are exiled for thirteen years. The religious significance of the exile is that it stands for the period of preparation (*diksa*) for a sacrifice.

The ensuing war between the Pandavas and Kauravas is prepared by Krishna, who, as the avatar of Vishnu, knows it must take place in order that Shri (Prosperity) can be restored to earth. Early in the great battle, Arjuna begins to doubt the value of the inevitable carnage and must be convinced through the divine revelations of Krishna—his charioteer—of the necessity of the sacrifice in the interest of dharma. These revelations form the *Bhagavadgita*. The war is "the war to end wars," resulting in the victory of the Pandavas but the death of almost everyone. It is the universal sacrifice that will bring to an end the age (*yuga*) that precedes our own *kaliyuga*. Vishnu has thus achieved the original goal of coming to the rescue of earth. [Bonnefoy (1993), O'Flaherty]

MAHADEVI *Maha* is Sanskrit for "great" and *devi* means "goddess." Thus, Mahadevi is "Great Goddess" or the ultimate form of Devi, *the* goddess, Mahashakti, who takes many forms. MAHAJATI The *Mahajati*, the great (*maha*) *Jataka*, is a Siamese (Thai) epic written down in the fifteenth century. It is based on certain of the *Jataka* tales of the Buddha.

MAHASHAKTI In order to relate to the physical world, the Hindu gods must give forth the power of manifestation that is called *Shakti* and that usually takes the mythological form of the god's wife or "great" (*maha*) *Shakti*, that is, Mahashakti, a form that, in turn, can take many forms—for instance, Kali or Mahakali or Parvati, in relation to the god Shiva. Vishnu's wife, Lakshmi, can be called MahaLakshmi, and Brahma's wife, Sarasvati, is also Mahasarasvati. *Mahashakti* is also a term used to refer to the totality of the divine mother, the *Shakti* of the absolute, Brahman.

MAHAVAMSA This fifth-century C.E. Pali text contains many Buddhist myths of Ceylon (Sri Lanka), based on earlier texts and oral traditions.

MAHAVASTU This is the second-century B.C.E. legendary biography of the Buddha.

MAHAYANA BUDDHISM The "Great (*maha*) Vehicle (*yana*)" Buddhism, or Mahayana Buddhism, is the reformed Buddhism that replaces the nirvana-based, monastic-based, and Gautama Buddha–oriented Hinayana (*hina* "lesser") or Theravada ("Doctrine of the Elders") Buddhism. Mahayana places emphasis on *bodhisattvas*, an all-encompassing and pervasive "Buddha nature," and the ability of lay people to achieve spiritual release.

MAHISHA The Indian goddess (Devi), as the violent Durga, kills Mahisha, the buffalo demon.

MAIA The Pleiade Maia, daughter to the Titan Atlas, had sexual relations with Zeus in a cave, and the result was the god Hermes.

MAITREYA In Mahayana Buddhist mythology, Maitreya, "the Friendly," is the Buddha of the future, the eighth Buddha, who is still the *bodhisattva* living in the heavenly paradise (*Tusita*). In Japanese Buddhism, he is Miroku.

MAKOSH A Slavic goddess of fertility, wetness, and agriculture, Makosh (Mokosh) was particularly important among pre-Christian Russians.

MALAVEYOVO Malaveyovo was a cannibal god of Papua New Guinea in Melanesia. Gifts of vegetables are traditionally left out for him so that he will eat fewer people.

MALORY, SIR THOMAS Malory is the fifteenth- century English author of *Le Morte d'Arthur*, an important compilation of Arthurian material. He is said to have created his great prose work while in prison.

MAMACOCHA Viracocha, the Incan creator god, was married to Mamacocha (Cochamama), the sea goddess. Their son was the sun god Inti, the father of the founder and first emperor of the Incas, Manco Capac.

MAMAKILYA The Incan moon goddess, Mamakilya was also the mother goddess, whose phases revealed the course of time. She was the sister-wife of the sun god Inti, the father of the first Incan emperor, Manco Capac.

MAMAPACHA The Incas believed that the creator made man and woman out of clay and then sent his son and daughter, born of the dragon goddess Mamapacha (Pachamama), to teach the people how to survive. Mamapacha was also a fertility and moon goddess who in some ways was equivalent to Mamakilya. She evolved, after the introduction of Christianity, into a version of the Virgin Mary.

MANANNAN Associated with the sea, Manannan Mac Lir was the son of the Irish sea god Lir. He encircled and guarded Ireland with his ocean. It was he who gave Lugh a horse, a boat, and a sword with which to fight the Fomorians. The Isle of Man was named for him. His Welsh cognate is Manawydan fab (son of) Llyr.

MANASA DEVI Manasa is a popular snake and childbirth goddess of the Bengali section of India. Poems about her are called *Manasa Mangals*. These are poems developed from the oral tradition, and they were transcribed in the late sixteenth century. In some of the poems Manasa appears as the offspring of the god Dharma, who mates with her. Regret-

M

ting his sin, Dharma convinces Shiva to marry the girl, who, after throwing herself on a funeral pyre, takes new form as Shiva's wife Parvati. It should be noted, in this connection, that the word *manasa* means "spiritual" and that it is also the name of a holy mountain, and that Parvati is the "Mountain Mother" or the "Daughter of the Mountain." Sometimes Manasa is Shiva's daughter. Often she is a jealous goddess who threatens people if they do not worship her. Her union with Dharma indicates her spiritual nature, as Dharma is a personification of the Hindu concept of dharma (duty).

MANAWYDAN Manawydan, known for his magical powers, is featured in the "Third Branch" of the Welsh *Mabinogion*. He is the son of Lly and is married to Rhiannon. His stepson is the hero Pryderi. In part, Manawydan is the counterpart of the Irish Manannan, son of Lir, although Manannan is a sea god and Manawydan is not.

MANCO CAPAC The father of the Incas, sometimes called simply "the Inca," was Manco Capac, who, with his sister-wife Mamaoqlyo (Mamaoello), came to the site that would become the capital, Cuzco, after emerging from the earth with his two brothers and three sisters at Pacariqtambo. He marked the site with his golden staff. The children of this first couple became the royal family of the Incas.

MANDALAS *Mandala* is Sanskrit for "circle" and the mandala used in various ways by peoples in many parts of the world—especially Asia—as a representation of sacred wholeness or significance. The serpent biting its own tail can be a mandala, as, for instance, in Dayak myth of Jata or the Norse myth of Jormun-gand. Tibetan Buddhists, or Lamists, and Native North American descendants of central Asian cul-

tures—for example, the Navajo Indians—use mandalas in sand paintings, as part of curing or initiatory ceremonies. The mandala in such cases is a representation of creation itself, an appropriate setting for the recreation of the person who is ill or not yet initiated into the "real" world of knowledge. In the same sense, a mandala can be a kind of labyrinth through which the initiate or pilgrim must pass in order to achieve union with the "center," which is the supreme deity.

Mandalas do not have to be circles. Vedic altars of various geometrical designs were arranged so that the various deities could have appropriate seats for rituals. Square mandalas are used in Buddhist and Hindu Tantric traditions and by the Jains. Temples can be arranged architecturally as mandalas, suggesting the pilgrimage to the center aspect of various communal liturgies. Mandalas, then, are in a sense dwelling places of the absolute, and they are always sources of or containers of spiritual or divine power in a given ritual. For the Buddhist, the mandala can be a potent symbol of liberation, with various gods surrounding the sacred center of enlightenment. In esoteric Japanese Buddhism, the Womb World Mandala and the Diamond World Mandala are central symbols of the process of enlightenment, elaborate designs containing deities surrounding the central figure of the cosmic Vairocana, a Buddha much revered by the Shingon sect. [Bowker]

MANICHAEISM A religious system from Iran, based on the teachings of Zoroastrianism—with some elements of Gnosticism, Buddhism, Christianity, and Hinduism—Manichaeism was the creation of the prophet Mani in the third century C.E. It is a system that stresses the dualistic nature of the universe. There is a principle of good, which is purely spiritual, and a principal of evil, which is material. These principles are represented by the Father of Light and the Prince of Darkness. The first humans were drawn into evil and would only eventually be freed by messenger-prophets from the Father.

MANIMEKHALAI A Tamil verse epic of the second century C.E., the *Manimekhalai* is attributed to Shattan. The heroine of the epic is Manimekhala, who, supported by her mother, Madhavi, has determined to enter the monastic life rather than continue the life of a dancer-prostitute in Indra's honor. The goddess of the ocean, also named Manimekhalai, comes to protect the heroine from the advances of a Chola prince. The goddess explains that the prince is a reincarnation of her husband from a former life. After many complications involving the prince and a magic bowl with which Manimekhala feeds the hungry, the heroine becomes a Buddhist nun and achieves nirvana, or release from the cycles (*samsara*) of life.

MANITOU Among the woodlands Native North Americans, *manitou* is "spirit" power. The equivalent among Plains Indians is *wakan*. The *Gitchi Manitou* is the "Great Spirit" or "Great Mystery," the supreme deity, who is neither male nor female.

MANKANAKA Born of the mind of his sage father, Kasyapa, the Indian sage (Rishi) Mananaka had immense ascetic powers. Still, once, when bathing with several beautiful nymphs, he had an orgasm. He collected his "seed" in a bowl and the seed gave birth to the seven Marut sages or storm gods who hold up the universe. One day, says the *Vamana Purana*, plant sap, the symbol of life, sprang from a wound on Mankanaka's hand, and this caused him to dance for joy. His dancing was so full of energy that the universe itself began to dance. It was then that the gods called on the god Shiva, who is also Nataraja, the "Lord of the Dance"—he whose dance is the dance of life and death, destruction and regeneration. Shiva appeared to the sage as a brahman and caused ashes of death to emanate from the blood of his thumb. Mankanaka immediately recognized the god and his superior power and bowed down before him, begging that he might keep his ascetic power. Shiva agreed and increased the sage's gifts.

MANTIS Mantis is a trickster–culture hero of the Khoisan people of southwestern Africa. It was he who stole fire for them from Ostrich, who kept the fire hidden under one of its wings. Mantis tricked Ostrich into raising his wing so that he could take the fire.

MANU Each age (*manvantara*) in the Hindu scheme of things—lasting 4,320,000 years—has a demiurge called Manu, who is the progenitor of the human race (thus "human" = *manava*). The first Manu was Svayambhuva, who produced the *Laws of Manu*. The Manu of our age is Satyavrata or Vaivasvata, son of the sun (Vivasvat). This Manu is best known for the Fish and the Flood story. The present Manu was given the *Vedas* so that he might teach the human race dharma (duty).

MANUK MANUK In Indonesian Sumatra, Manuk Manuk was the blue chicken owned by the high god in lieu of a wife. From the three eggs laid by Manuk Manuk burst the creator gods of Heaven, earth, and the underworld.

MAPONOS Maponos, son of the continental Celtic mother goddess Matrona, has a Welsh cognate in Mabon, as Matrona has one in Modron. Maponos was the divine child—the *puer aeternus*—of Celtic mythology.

MARA In Hinduism, Mara is the divine embodiment of disease and dangerous sensuality. In Buddhism, Mara the Fiend is the actual and metaphorical enemy of the Buddha and those seeking enlightenment. He directly confronts the Buddha under the Bodhi Tree with temptations of this world. In this myth he resembles Satan tempting Jesus in the wilderness in the Christian story. Often Mara is depicted with 100 arms. He rides on an elephant. Many Mara myths are found in a collection known as the *Mara-Samyutta*.

MARDUK The Babylonian city god Marduk was a gigantic and immensely powerful god with four heads, a storm-weather god who is the central figure in the Babylonian creation epic, the *Enuma elish*. His nature was associated not with fertility, in particular, but with the rise of the city-state of which he was the patron, the city of Hammurabi early in the second millennium B.C.E. Although he existed in earlier Mesopotamian texts, and was even said to be the son of Ea (Enki), Marduk was essentially created as a "new" god in Babylon. He was a popular god who was considered to be a deity accessible in prayer, one who cared about human beings and their problems. By the twelfth century B.C.E., he had risen to a position as king of the gods. His power was indicated by his depiction as a young bull.

MARES OF DIOMEDES As the eighth of his Twelve Labors, Herakles was instructed to capture the flesh-eating mares of the Thracian king Diomedes. This he did after the loss of a friend and companion to the mares and after feeding Diomedes to them. The mares became tame after eating their owner. Herakles took them home to Eurystheus.

MARICHI Marichi is one of a pantheon of Indian Buddhist goddesses. Her Hindu form is Ushas, and she is associated with the dawn. She has an eye in the middle of her forehead, and she has three frightening faces and ten arms. In Japan, she is Marishiten, who was popular among *samurai*, who placed her image on their helmets as protection. In Japan she is depicted as riding on a boar, and one of her faces is that of a boar. The esoteric Nichiren sect sees Marishiten as a male figure, Marici.

MARKANDEYA In the Indian epic the *Mahabharata*, the story is told of the sage Markandeya, who, floating on the cosmic ocean after the dissolution of the universe, took refuge inside of the mouth of a sleeping boy under a banyan tree. The boy was Vishnu, and the sage discovered within the god's mouth the entire universe. Thus, Vishnu absorbs and contains the universe. The same message is contained in a *Bhagavad Purana* myth, in which the adopted mother of Vishnu's avatar Krishna sees the universe in her son's mouth.

MARS Although usually seen as a cognate of the Greek war god Ares, Mars was a much more important deity in Rome than Ares was in his homeland. He was not only a war god but a fertility and agricultural deity as well. With Jupiter and Quirinus, he was part of the archaic Roman version of the Indo-European triad of important deities. The fact that he was seen as the father of Romulus and Venus (Greek Aphrodite) as the mother of Aeneas meant that in the story of the affair between Mars and Venus, the two origin myths of Rome were brought together.

MASSACRE OF THE INNOCENTS Related to the motif of the threat to the divine child (*puer aeternus*) in the heroic monomyth, the specific motif of the massacre of the innocents involves a jealous or insecure king trying to protect himself from a possible usurper by killing off a generation of children. The stories of Moses and Jesus contain massacre-of-the-innocents events.

MATH In the "Fourth Branch" of the Welsh *Mabinogion*, Math, the son of Mathonmy and brother of the mother goddess Don, is depicted as being able to live only if his feet can rest on a virgin's lap, except in times of war. Disaster is the ultimate result when Math's nephews, Gwydion and Gilfaethy, deprive him of his "footstool" and attempt to substitute their non-virgin sister Aranrhod for her. Math was lord of Gwynedd and was known for his magical powers.

MATRONA In the continental Celtic tradition, Matrona, whose counterpart in Welsh mythology was Modron, was the mother goddess whose son was the divine child Maponos (Welsh Mabon).

MAUI A popular figure among the Maori and other Polynesians, Maui is both a trickster and a culture hero. When he was born early, his mother threw him away into the sea, but he was protected by the sun. To help the people have more time for work, he slowed down the sun, using his dead grandmother's jawbone. He separated the primal parents to make room for the people to live; he stole fire for the people from Mahui-ike in the underworld; he fished up New Zealand. During one of his descents to the underworld he attempted to pass through his ancestress, the death goddess, Hine-nui-te-po, from her vagina to her mouth to overcome her edict against human immortality. In this incident he failed, and, in fact, died, ending humanity's hope for immortality and establishing the taboo against incest.

Many Maui myths, like those of many other tricksters, are sexual and genitally oriented. In one story, in effect a fertility myth, the beautiful Hina, dissatisfied with the ineffectual eel, Te Tuna ("the Penis"), left him in search of much-needed love. Arriving in the land of the Male-Principle Clan, Hina introduced herself as the "shameless pubic patch in search of love," but the men, fearing the wrath of Te Tuna, sent her on her way, her loins burning with desire. After some time Hina arrived at the land of the Maui Clan, named for the culture hero. At the urging of his mother, Maui took Hina as his own, and they lived passionately together for some time before the people informed the monster eel of the situation. At first Te Tuna could not have cared less, but after a while he bestirred himself, asked about Maui, and was told that he was small and that his penis was lopsided. Then the people warned Maui that Te Tuna was on his way to seek revenge against his rival. Te Tuna approached Maui's land from the sea, revealing his huge penis and causing a tidal wave. Maui's mother shouted at her son to "show him yours," and Maui did so, raising his lopsided member against the wave. The wave subsided and Maui killed Te Tuna's monster companions but spared him. For a while Te Tuna and Maui lived together with Hina, but eventually the two males decided they must fight for rights to Hina. After a struggle, in which the two entered each other, Maui cut off Te Tuna's head and buried it. Soon a huge tree grew from this "planting"; it was

The Roman god Mars, the father of Romulus

the coconut tree, from which the people gain solid and liquid nourishment to this day. Some say it was Hina who killed and planted Te Tuna.

MAYA Maya is at once a concept and a name reflecting that concept. Its Sanskrit root is *ma*, meaning to measure out or create, and *maya* is the transformation of the god's thought into the material form often represented mythologically by his wife—his particular goddess or *Shakti*, his creative energy—or by the all-encompassing goddess (*Devi*), sometimes as *Mahadevi* or *Mahashakti*. It is the principle of maya that can explain the movement from the intangible and indivisible self, which is Brahman, to the differentiated and tangible reality, which is the world. Among some Buddhist schools, maya is the source of the "illusion" that we ordinary people think of as the "real." And it should be noted that Queen Maya or Mahamaya is the mother of Gautama Buddha, the vehicle of his incarnation, of his transformation to worldly form. Maya is also the Hindu Mayadevi, the personification of delusion. In the *Bhagavata Purana* she is the girl who is exchanged in youth for Krishna; the illusion of reality is exchanged for divine reality.

The Mayan pyramid of Kukulkan at Chichen Itza

In the battle between the Hindu gods and demons described in the epic the *Mahabharata*, Maya is the evil architect of the three cities of the demons—one of gold, one of silver, one of black iron, representing Heaven, sky, and earth, respectively. The cities are destroyed by the god Shiva with the help of a chariot made by the gods' architect, Tvashtir. The chariot is made of all of the elements of the primeval creation. The myth is a kind of preface to the sacrificial destruction of the world that inevitably ends each age.

MAYAN MYTHOLOGY What we know of the mythology of the Mayans, a Mesoamerican people who achieved a particularly high level of civilization between 300 and 900 C.E. in southern Mexico and Central America, comes from a sort of hieroglyphic writing carved into stone monuments and from codices (books written on bark paper) and books from the colonial Spanish. The most important of the Spanish sources is the mid–sixteenth- century *Popol Vuh*. The mythology it contains is specifically that of the Quiche Maya of Guatemala.

Central to the *Popol Vuh* is the story of creation. Originally there was undifferentiated chaos, in which the potential for deities was also undifferentiated. At the instant of creation, the spiritual powers became separated into deities, and the universe became three quadrangular entities—the heavens, the earth itself, and the underworld. Particular colors—red, white, black, and yellow—marked the boundaries of each quarter of the world and each quarter was ruled by a chief. The chiefs were Tzakol, Bitol, Alom, and Oaholom. The four chiefs were joined by three other solar gods—Tepeu, Gukumatz, and Cabaguil—and a council of seven was thus formed. The council created plant and animal life but wanted a being that could recognize them to worship them. So it was that the council tried to create humans, at first out of mud. But the beings turned back into mud. The council members changed their names and were joined by gods who could "fabricate" and by a goddess, Chirakan-Ixmucane. The new group of gods now made humans out of wood; but these creatures were like soulless puppets with no consciousness of their creators. To put an end to them, the gods sent a universal flood, and a god of death arrived with demons to end the lives of the unwanted. Finally the gods got it right. From plant life they produced four men and then four women to go with the four corners of the world.

Other myths are intermingled with the creation stories. The sacred twins, Hunahpu and Ixbalanque, are important figures during a time before the sun had lighted the world. They are monster slayers who, with the help of their parents, two of the first deities, destroy giants such as the interfering Gukup Cakix, who pretended to be both the sun and the moon. The twins also ran the ball game, a ritual game that was ubiquitous in Mesoamerican cultures.

In other Mayan myths the earth was thought to be the back of a giant serpent that floated in primal waters. The exposed part of the back was made up of the four quarters with the familiar colors: white for north, red for east, yellow for south, and black for west. Green was the center. Heaven above and the underworld below had many levels each. An axle or world tree—a green ceiba tree—held all of the parts together.

The underworld, Xibalba, was a terrible place in Mayan mythology. It contained "houses" in which the dead were tormented: the House of Fire and the House of Bats, for example. Only rulers could escape its damp gloom. Once the sacred twins descended there and defeated the underworld lords in a game. Then, in an apotheosis, they ascended to Heaven as the sun and moon.

Particular Mayan deities, other than the original creators, included Chac, the rain god, who contained four aspects of four colors for each quarter of the world; Itzamma, a great sky god of learning; and Kinich Ahua, a version of the sun god. There were two moon goddesses—Ix Chel the young and Ix Ch'up the old, representing the phases of the moon. They were the consorts of Itzamma and Kinich Ahua. When the sun god descended into the west at night, he became the underworld king in his jaguar form.

Apparently gods could become dying gods who could be resurrected. Captured warriors were vested as gods in ritual ceremonies that culminated in their being offered as blood sacrifices so that the real god could be reborn and the good life guaranteed for the community. [R. Adams, Grimal]

M

MAZDAISM Mazdaism is a term sometimes used to indicate the ancient Iranian religion that became Zoroastrianism under the influence of Zoroaster (Zarathustra). It takes its name from the supreme god of Zoroastrianism, the Ahura Mazda.

MBOOM AND NGAAN The first gods of the Kuba people of Zaire, Ngaan and Mboon were the world creators. After an argument, Ngaan retreated to the waters and Mboom to the sky.

ME In Sumerian and other Mesopotamian mythologies, the *me* (Akkadian *parsu*) are the essential laws and offices of civilization, derived from divine order found in the primordial mother, Nammu, the first deity. They include such various aspects of human life as kingship, godship, sexual practices, power, and city destruction. In Sumerian mythology they are possessed by Enki and then taken by the goddess Inanna, probably indicting some change in the relative power of particular cults or the position of women vis-à-vis men. Some slight connections may perhaps be made between the *me*, the Egyptian *maat*, and the Indian-Hindu *dharma*.

MEDB The ruthless queen of Connacht in Irish mythology, particularly in the great war of the *Tain Bo Cuainge*, Medb (Medbh), sometimes called Maeve, was perhaps an aspect of a triune goddess. She was the enemy of the Ulstermen, led by Cuchulainn and Conchobar in the *Tain*, and was famous for her sexual appetite.

MEDUSA The only mortal member of the family of horrifying clawed and winged Gorgons, whose heads were covered in serpents, Medusa began her life as a beautiful young woman. But the Greek goddess Athena changed her hair into serpents as a punishment for her having defiled her temple by way of a relationship with Poseidon, a relationship that resulted in the birth of the winged horse Pegasus. Anyone who looked at Medusa would be turned to stone. This fact plays a role in the story of the hero Perseus.

MEGARA The first wife of the Greek hero Herakles, Megara was the daughter of the king of Thebes. Herakles killed her in a fit of madness brought about by the jealous Hera, who resented the fact that Herakles had been fathered by Zeus in an act of infidelity.

MELANESIAN MYTHOLOGY Scholars disagree about the exact geographical designation of Melanesia as opposed to Polynesia and Micronesia—the Pacific Island groups often collectively referred to by the term "Oceanic"—and there is overlapping of the mythologies of these areas. Generally, Melanesia includes New Guinea, the Solomon Islands, Vanuatu (New Hebrides), New Caledonia, the Fiji Islands, and several smaller islands. The dominant cultural groups and, therefore, mythologies of the area are the Negritos and Papuans of New Guinea and a widespread group usually referred to simply as Melanesians. The mythologies of Melanesia have in common a world full of spirits that affect humans directly. Some of these take the form of malevolent or benevolent ghosts who hope eventually, by way of proper rituals, and as a reward for proper living, to reach an underworld or otherworld that is generally a pleasant version of this world. Some of the spirits never had human form. These are sometimes called *masalia*. They take various forms and are capable of making life difficult for humans in many ways and are often associated with taboos.

Creation myths are not common in Melanesia, but there are a few. The Banks Island people say that at the beginning of time, a spirit known as Qat emerged from a rock and created living things, including three men and three women, made out of a tree.

By dancing and beating a drum, Qat woke up his human creations and taught them. A counterspirit, Marawa, like the trickster companions of creators in many societies, attempted to imitate Qat by creating his own version of humans. After he formed the bodies, he buried them in a hole and then retrieved them several days later. The bodies had decomposed, and this is why humans are not immortal. Obviously, this is an appropriate myth for an agricultural society concerned with trees, planting, and the fertilizing decomposition of matter.

Other spirits who in some ways resemble supreme deities, are Kalou-Vu, Enda Semangko, Oma Rumufa, and Ye.

In Vanatu, a Garden of Eden–like myth exists in which Avin, the mortal wife of the sun-day spirit Tortali, committed adultery in the couple's paradise-garden home with the moon-night spirit Ui and was, as a result, expelled from the garden and made to endure menstruation and work.

Culture heroes are of importance in Melanesia. Qat is such a hero, and in New Britain, two culture heroes, To-Kabinana and To-Karvuvu, emerge from the blood of a spirit and take wives who emerge from broken coconuts. People result from the union of these first beings with their wives. The culture heroes then teach the people how to live. The twin culture heroes To-Kabinana and To-Karvuvu, and Qat and Marawa, for instance, represent opposing forces in a life dominated by dualism—light and dark, good and evil. Many culture heroes do little teaching but instead leave humans on their own. At

M

The severed head of the Gorgon Medusa

Mercury in his Greek form as Hermes

this point cultural teaching seems to be taken over by totem ancestral figures. [Grimal]

MELEAGER A tragic figure in Greek mythology, Meleager was the son of King Oeneus and Queen Althaea of Calydon. At Meleager's birth, the Fates told Althaea that her son would die as soon as a particular piece of wood in the hearth had burned up. Althaea, like so many others in myths, decided to evade fate by hiding the piece of wood in a chest. When Meleager grew up, he fell in love with the speedy huntress Atalanta, while he was hunting the monstrous Calydonian Boar. After the boar was slain, Meleager gave its hide to Atalanta, infuriating his uncles, who stole it from her. Enraged, Meleager killed his uncles. This so upset his mother that she put the old extinguished and hidden log back in the fire and, fate being absolute, he died. A now-distraught Althaea killed herself.

MENELAUS A son of Atreus and the younger brother of Agamemnon, Menelaus was married to Helen, who ran off with the Trojan prince Paris and thus was the catalyst for the Trojan War. After the war and several years of wandering, Menelaus returned to his kingdom of Lacedaemon (Sparta), now, according to Homer in the Odyssey, reconciled with Helen. Menelaus and his wife were accorded the honor of life after death in Elysium. The fact that Helen's father was Zeus—her mother Leda was visited by the god as a swan—doubtless helped to bring about this ending to the Menelaus-Helen story.

MERCURY Mercurius was a Roman deity associated with trade and communication, who was identified with the Greek god Hermes. Julius Caesar tells us that Mercury—probably equated with the Celtic Lugus—was the most worshipped god of Gaul, that he was the god of arts, crafts, and commerce and journeys.

MERLIN Merlin probably has an antecedent in the legendary Scottish and/or Irish mad prophet Myrddin (Merddin). The Welsh historian Geoffrey of Monmouth, in his twelfth-century *History of the Kings of Britain*, established Merlin's position as the motivating wizard in the Arthurian legend. It was Merlin who helped arrange for the liaison between Uther and Igraine that would lead to the conception and birth of King Arthur. After Arthur's birth Merlin took the child to one Hector, this in keeping with the monomythic heroic divine child's being raised by a menial or commoner. It was Merlin who arranged for the ceremony through which Arthur would prove himself to be the king by removing a sword from a rock.

There are many versions of Merlin's life. It was said by some that he was conceived as a result of the union between a sleeping nun and a demon. In Sir Thomas Malory's *Le Morte d'Arthur*, based on many earlier sources—many of them specifically about Merlin—the magician falls in love with an enchantress, Nimuë (perhaps the Lady of the Lake), a femme fatale who imprisons him under a rock.

MERU The Mount Olympus of the Hindu gods and goddesses, Mount Meru, or sometimes Mandara, is, according to the *Mahabharata*, a golden mass of intense energy. It is the *axis mundi*, the world center.

MESOAMERICAN MYTHOLOGY The major contributors to what we think of as pre-Columbian Mesoamerican mythology were the Mayans and the Aztecs. Important influences on these cultures were the Olmec, Monte Alban (Zapotec), Teotihuacan, and Toltec groups. The Olmec people, whose culture came into its own in about 1500 B.C.E., lived in the area that is now Veracruz and Tabasco. The Olmecs built what were probably the first of the Mesoamerican pyramids, and they developed the art of large sculpture in which colossal male heads can be seen today. They also had a writing system and a calendar and a great interest in astronomy. While not a great deal is known about their religion, it seems clear that many deities came from them to later Measoamericans. By 600 B.C.E. the Olmecs had had lost much of their power.

The Zapotec people, who built the first real city in Mesoamerica on the flat top of Monte Alban, near present-day Oaxaca, gradually became the dominant southern Mexican power for some thousand years, beginning in about 500 B.C.E. Like the Olmecs, the Zapotecs built pyramids, had calendar and writing systems, and had an interest in astronomy. They worshipped a number of gods who seem to be related to those of the Olmecs and other earlier cultures.

A culture with close ties to the Monte Alban people was that of the builders of the spectacular pyramids of Teotihuacan, just northeast of present-day Mexico City. By 500 C.E., Teotihuacan was one of the largest and best appointed cities in the world, with many pyramids and squares, wide central streets, and a population of about 125,000. The pyramids were built in honor of certain gods and their astronomical cognates. There was the pyramid of the sun and that of the moon. Temples were decorated with mythological figures that resemble and suggest connections with the deities of later peoples such as the Aztecs. Both

M

the Teotihuacan and Monte Alban cultures collapsed in the mid-seventh century C.E.

Another ancient civilization of Mexico that began to fall upon bad times not long after the Teotihuacan–Monte Alban demise was that of the Mayans. The Mayans did not develop a single central city in the manner of Teotihuacan or Monte Alban. Rather, a series of smaller Mayan city-states dotted the area of southern Mexico, Guatemala, and Belize, beginning in about 600 B.C.E. These city-states and later ones grew, and Mayan civilization, as documented by the ubiquitous Mayan stone slabs that recorded events, became dominant in the area from about 300 to 900 C.E. The Mayans created what was probably the most highly developed civilization in the Americas at the time. They were advanced in their architecture, weaving, pottery, and stone carving. They built on the accomplishments of earlier Mesoamericans—especially in the fields of astronomy, mathematics, writing, architecture, and religion.

In the tenth century it was the turn of the Toltecs to come to power in Mesoamerica. A warlike and aggressively commercial people, the Toltecs established control over most of Mesoamerica and built their capital at Tollan, near present-day Tula, in Mexico. The Toltecs spoke Nahuatl and remained dominant until the late twelfth century C.E., when they fell victim to droughts and excessive warfare. Sacrifice was an important element of their religion, related to solar mythology.

In 1325 the people of the last of the great pre-Columbian Mesoamerican civilizations, the Aztecs, began to build their capital, Tenochtitlan, on land that is today Mexico City. By the early 1500s, they were a dominant power with an empire of some six million people. The Aztec culture developed naturally from that of the Toltecs. Their first ruler was descended from the Toltec rulers; like the Toltecs, they spoke Nahuatl; like the Toltecs, they were militaristic and commercial. And they shared a religious tradition based on sacrifice, solar dominance, and many of the same deities, some inherited from the Olmecs and other earlier cultures. The Aztec civilization was still developing when the Spanish, led by Cortez, conquered it in 1521.

Although each of the pre-Columbian Mesoamerican cultures had mythologies of its own, there were certain common features that can be called Mesoamerican in general. These features, common especially to the mythologies of which we have the most knowledge—those of the Mayans and Aztecs—are to some extent shared with the South American Incan civilization as well.

Certainly the Mayans and Aztecs, and presumably the Olmecs, Zapotecs, Teotihuacan people, and Toltecs, believed in a three-part universe, consisting of the heavens, the earth, and the underworld. Any given tribe occupied the earth's center. Communication between the human and divine worlds existed at these centers, marked, for instance, by pyramids reaching up to the heavens and celebrating particular deities. The deities themselves, as indicated by archeological remains, were sometimes associated with particular animals—jaguars and serpents, for example. The powers and characteristics of particular deities were often tied to their astronomical identities and the movement of their astronomical cognates in the heavens. The mythologies of Mesoamerica describe a cosmic-divine world in flux, marked by struggle. The deities generally contain opposing realities: day and night, life and death, male and female. Most gods possessed several aspects related to the four directions, represented by particular colors. The creator gods always came in pairs representing both genders. Kings were thought to have descended from deities and to have been promised

M

The Pyramid of the Sun at the Mesoamerican site of Teotihuacan

more pleasant afterlives than were available in the gloomy underworld for ordinary people.

To ensure protection of deities, especially that of the dangerous but life-giving personification of the sun, gifts were necessary. Most important, for the Toltecs and Aztecs at least, the sun had to be fed blood, and, obviously, the most valuable blood came from human sacrifice. [R. Adams, Carrasco, Heyden, H. B. Nicholson, Portilla-Leon]

MESSIAH Messiah is the king who, according to the Hebrew Bible, or Old Testament, would one day come from Yahweh to restore the Davidic line and glory to the Jews. Christians recognize Jesus as that person, extending his message and power, however, beyond Judaism to all people (see, e.g., Matthew 3, Daniel 9:25–26).

METAMORPHOSES In his *Metamorphoses*, the Roman poet Publius Ovidius Naso (43 B.C.E.–17 C.E.), better known to the world as simply Ovid, took the stories of Greco-Roman mythology and turned them into what was, in effect, an epic in some 250 tales in fifteen books, tracing world "history" from the creation to the apotheosis of Julius Caesar and a farewell from the poet himself. For centuries, somewhat expurgated versions of Ovid's often racy stories have been used by teachers to teach Latin in schools and by later poets like Boccaccio and Chaucer as sources for their own tales, so that when we think of Greek and Roman myths we, more often than not, call to mind Ovid's telling of those myths. The names we come across in the *Metamorphoses* are icons of Western culture: the Greek Olympian deities are all there using their Roman names, as are heroes and victims

Daphne is metamorphosed into a laurel tree to escape the advances of Apollo

such as Perseus, Jason, Midas, Achilles, Hercules (Herakles), Orpheus, Eurydice, and Romulus. The story of the flood is told, as are the stories of the rape of Europa, the death of Pentheus, the love affair of Venus and Adonis, and, of course, the adventures of the founder of Rome, Aeneas.

The central theme of Ovid's work is the concept of metamorphosis. His stories are of people turned by the often fickle, vindictive, or merely arbitrary gods into plants, animals, or other forms. But in a deeper sense, the poet reveals to us life itself—our life—as an experience marked primarily by flux and sometimes by our hopeless defiance in the face of powers beyond our control or understanding.

METIS Metis, the first wife of the Greek father god, Zeus, was a personification of wise counsel. She helped her husband in his war against his father Kronos. When, after the war in heaven, Metis became pregnant, the earth goddess, Gaia, predicted that she would give birth to a deity wiser than Zeus. To avoid this outcome, Zeus consumed his wife and, therefore, her wisdom, and later he gave birth to the goddess of wisdom, Athena, appropriately, from his head.

MICRONESIAN MYTHOLOGY The western Pacific islands of Oceania, known collectively as Micronesia, include the Gilbert, Marshal, Mariana, Caroline, and Pelew groups. The myths of Micronesia are influenced by the other main Oceanic cultures—those of the Polynesians and the Melanesians. Much emphasis is placed on magic, demons, nature spirits, and the journey of the soul—potentially a harmful ghost—to the underworld. Creation was undertaken by a deity who existed before anything else. This could be an earth goddess such as Ligoupup or her husband Anulap, who lived in a huge house with his brothers and sisters—most notably the wise Semenkoror; Flounder, who guards his brother; and Sandpiper, who judges souls trying to enter the world of the deities.

In some places, the earth goddess was produced from her husband's blood. Their incestuous offspring, assisted by a girl born from a boil on Anulap, then produced people. Ligoupup acted as a culture hero, teaching people proper ways of life. Other islanders say that the creator was the halffish sea god, Solal. Still others credit ultimate beginnings to Loa, who flew through the sky and spoke things into existence. For some islanders, more influenced by Polynesian ideas, Nareau (Na Areau) Areau ("Lord Spider") was the creator-trickster-culture hero. Another culture hero, who greatly resembled the Polynesian Maui, was Bue. Still another popular monomythic hero was Olo-fad, fathered by the god Lugeilan and miraculously born from the head of a mortal woman. Olofad was a dying hero who was resurrected by his father and taken up to heaven in a great act of apotheosis.

Many myths about the origins of fire exist. One story says that a boy named Te-ika ("The Fish") caught a sunbeam in the ocean. The beam caused fires that harmed the sea world, so Bakoa ("Shark"), king of the sea, exiled the boy to the land, where Tabakea, the king of Land, killed the boy with sticks that took on the power of the sunbeam. Later Tabakea revived Te-ika by rubbing the sticks together. Te-ika died out again, however. [Grimal]

MICTLAN Mictlan was the Aztec land of the dead. Many tests and trials confronted the dead soul on its way to this land, ruled by Mictlan-tecuhtli and his consort. When the god Quetzalcoatl descended to the underworld to take bones with which to create a new race of humans, he was chased by Mictlantecuhtli, and he dropped some of the bones, causing the new humans to be shorter or taller than others.

MIDGARD In Norse mythology, Midgard (the "Middle World"), the land of humans, was located between the land of the gods (Asgard) and that of the dead (Hel-Niflheim).

MILESIANS In the mythology of Ireland, the Sons of Mil or Milesius, or Mil Espaigne ("Soldier of Spain"), Milesians are the sixth race to invade the island. Their leader was Mil's son Donn. The Milesians—considered the ancestors of the Celts—defeated the Tuatha Dé Danaan and took over rulership of the land, relegating the Tuatha to the otherworld.

MILTON AND MYTH Much of what has become Christian mythology about Adam and Eve, Satan and the fallen angels, the war in Heaven between Satan and his angels, and the archangel Michael and his loyal angels comes from John Milton's *Paradise Lost* (1667) rather than from canonical texts. Milton, an Englishman of the Puritan persuasion, attempted in his great literary epic to "justify the ways of God to men." Some have argued that the literary Milton got the better of the theological Milton and made the defiant Satan in Hell the romantic hero of his work.

MIMI The *mimi* are Australian spirits among the Aborigines of western Arnhem land. For the most part, they are benign, living in the crevices of rock cliffs. They can, however, be troublesome if disturbed.

MIMIR The Norse gods, the Aesir, sent the wise god Mimir with the long-legged god Honir to their enemies, the Vanir, to secure a truce. But the Vanir became suspicious and decapitated Mimir. Odin saved the god's head and placed it at a well under the world tree, Yggdrasill, afterward called Mimir's Well. This was the Well of Wisdom.

MINAKSHI A princess in Madurai in Indian mythology, Minakshi had three breasts, was thought by her people to be a male, succeeded her father to the throne, conquered the world, and became so proud that she challenged the god Shiva. When she saw the god, however, one of her breasts fell off and she became his consort.

MINERVA The Romans worshiped Minerva as a cognate of the Greek Athena and as part of a triad inherited from the Etruscans as Jupiter-Juno-Minerva (Etruscan Mernva).

MINIA In the animistic tradition of the Sahara and Sahel areas of Africa, Minia is the serpent, whose head was the sky, whose body was the earth, and whose tail was the world underground.

MINOAN MYTHOLOGY The culture of Crete was apparently goddess centered. The name Minos, perhaps "Moon Man," seems to have been applied to all Cretan kings beginning about 2000 B.C.E., when Minoan civilization reached its highest point. It is possible that the title derives from the ritual marriage of each "priest-king" with the moon-priestess, the representative of the great Cretan goddess. Archeological evidence in the frescoes and objects found in the famous palaces of Knossos and other settlements of Crete, as well as in caves and mountain sanctuaries of the island, suggest that the goddess herself, like her probable Middle East-

Minerva in her battle clothes

ern and/or European Neolithic equivalents, was a nature deity associated with the creative essence of the earth, the cycles of nature and of life itself, including death. She is usually bare-breasted, wearing a flounced dress. Often she holds snakes; the familiar goddess companions. Her pubic area, like that of the old Neolithic goddess, is sometimes a stylized triangle. She is depicted in many contexts, leading some scholars to suppose a Cretan pantheon made up of a snake goddess, a sea goddess, a mountain goddess, a hunting goddess, and a tree goddess, all later given specific names such as Britomartis ("Sweet Virgin") or Ariadne ("the holy one") by the Greeks, who also made connections between these figures and their own goddesses, such as Demeter, Artemis, Athena, and Aphrodite. Whether one or more goddesses, the deity in question or her earthly representatives are often seen dancing in fields of flowers, accompanied by animals. A common companion is a youthful male figure whom the later Greeks associated with Zeus as a boy and who also is perhaps a form of Dionysos, a son of Zeus (*Dios* + *nusos* = Zeus-like). In Crete this figure was a dying god, perhaps related to ritual sacrifice leading to fertility and renewal. Also present in many cases is the mysterious double ax so prevalent in Minoan symbology and a tree or pillar apparently representing divinity.

An important aspect of the Cretan goddess mythology involved the bull as possibly a god and certainly as a sacrificial animal. It was said that the Cretan Zeus in the form of a bull and Europa, whose name, meaning wide-faced, was used as a synonym for the moon, were the parents of the original Minos. In the Neolithic period of the Near East, the goddess-bull association is made evident by archeological

M

213

Theseus kills the Minotaur

perhaps a form of Demeter whose name, Damater, means "Earth Mother" and who, with her daughter Persephone, might be associated with the inscription Potniai ("Ladies"), the descendants of the earlier Great Mother, of Crete ("Lady of the Labyrinth") and the Neolithic tradition. The missing figure here is Aphrodite, probably a post-Mycenaean arrival in Greece from Phoenicia via Cyprus, who is a version of many Semitic goddesses, themselves looking back to the ancient Sumerian goddess of love and fertility, Inanna (Ishtar). [Pelon, Leeming (2003)]

MINOS A common name for kings of ancient Crete, Minos is the source for the term "Minoan," referring to Cretan culture, especially before the invasion of Mycenaean Greeks in the middle of the second millennium B.C.E. The original Minos of Greek mythology was the son of Zeus, disguised as a bull, and the mortal Europa. Europa married the king of Crete, and after fighting with his brothers, Minos rose to the throne. He married Pasiphae, asked Poseidon for a special sacrificial bull, and thus unleashed the events that would lead to the Minotaur and to several major events in the life of the hero Theseus.

MINOTAUR The Minotaur was the half-bull, half-human son of Queen Pasiphae of Crete and the bull of Poseidon that had been given to King Minos for sacrifice. His home became the Labyrinth built by Daedalus, a central image in the Minoan world and a venue for one of the greatest adventures of the Greek hero Theseus.

MIRACULOUS CONCEPTION A sure sign of the monomythic hero or heroine is his or her miraculous conception, which, more often than not, does not terminate the virginity of the hero's usually mortal mother. The father of the divine child—the *puer Aeternus*—is divine. Capable of all things, he enters the world by way of the woman and envelops his divine powers in the body of the human hero, whether Jesus, Minos, Hainuwele, Kutoyis, Water Pot Boy, Quetzalcoatl, Huangdi, Karna, Sargon, or Cuchulainn. In myths from all corners of the world the divine enters the hero mother by way of sun rays, clots of blood, bits of clay, feathers, or whatever other medium seems appropriate to the landscape or customs of the particular culture. The important point is that the conception is miraculous, signifying the beginning of the hero life inspired by inherent divinity.

MIROKU The Japanese Buddhist version of the great future Buddha, the Bodhisattva Maitreya, is Miroku-bosatsu or, in his future form, Miroku-nyorai. Miroku was a popular figure among early Japanese Buddhists but was somewhat displaced by the Pure Land Buddhist emphasis on Amida Buddha and the possibility of the salvation of the individual in the Pure Land of the West.

MITHRA An ancient Iranian god corresponding originally to the Vedic Mitra, Mithra was repudiated along with other ancient gods by the prophet Zoroaster (Zarathustra) in favor of the one Wise Lord, Ahura Mazda. In this context, he was demoted to a position as judge of the dead. But the cult of Mithra remained strong and gained popularity in the first centuries C.E. in the Roman world as well as in Iran. Historically, then, Mithra is a rival to Ahura Mazda for the central place in pre-Islamic Iranian religion. His name is derived from the concept of proper arrangements or contracts. He represents loyalty, true friendship, and truth. Mithra is also

discoveries in Anatolia and sacred texts in Egypt. In Egypt, for instance, the Moon goddess Hathor was also the cowgoddess, and the god-king, or pharaoh, was the sacred bull. Much later, in the Irish epic the *Tain*, a connection is established between a great bull and a queen. In Crete a ritualized coupling of the priest-king, whose emblem was a bull, and the moon-priestess is perhaps further reflected in the story of Pasiphae, the wife of Minos, and her infatuation with a great bull.

By the mid-second millennium B.C.E., Minoans were building their great palaces at Knossos and for several hundred years had possessed a form of writing we know as Linear A. In about 1450 B.C.E., the Mycenaeans invaded and a cross-fertilization of ideas took place. By 1300 so-called Linear B, a Greek language script useful for such things as inventories and other lists, but not appropriate for literary purposes, was in use. Among the Linear B tablets, deciphered in 1953 by John Chadwick and Michael Ventris, are lists of offerings to gods. These lists indicate a shift away from a goddess-based mythology and religion to one presided over by the male god, Zeus. In Linear B, we discover a pre-Homeric and pre-classical Mycenaean-Minoan version of what we think of as Greek mythology, the product of the indigenous peoples of Greece, the Minoans, the Indo-European tradition of the Mycenaeans, and the always-present influence of the Middle East. Much later this mythology would, of course, be pruned and adapted to various conditions and needs by Homer, the writers of the *Homeric Hymns*, Hesiod, Pindar, and many others, including the dramatists of fifth-century Athens. Although knowledge of the nature and deeds of these early Olympians of Linear B is sketchy, a definable and familiar pantheon does emerge.

The Linear B tablets indicate the hierarchy. Zeus (Diwe) reigns supreme. Hera (Era) is present, as are Poseidon (Posedaone), Athena (Atana Potinija), Apollo (Pajawone), Artemis (Atemito), Hermes (Emaa), Ares (Are or Enuwarijo), Hephaistos (Apaitioji), Dionysos (Diwonusojo), and

M

a war god, a promulgator of the faith and of the Iranian "nation." And he is a solar god. Many extraordinary myths are associated with Mithra in both his Iranian and assimilated Roman form, suggesting his connection with the monomythic hero figure. There is the magical cave in which the sun god lives when he is not driving his chariot pulled by white horses across the sky. There is his miraculous birth from a rock and his ritual quest for and slaying of the primal bull, the symbol of disorder. This slaying reminds us more of the Vedic Indra, the slayer of the primal demon Virtra, than it does of the Vedic Mitra.

In the early centuries of the Common Era, Mithraism, a strong cult devoted to the god, developed in the Roman Empire. The cult was particularly important for soldiers, as it involved the ritual sacrifice of an ox and a bath of blood that would bring strength and loyalty.

MITRA The Indian Vedic god Mitra (the "friend") is the realized aspect of his twin brother Varuna, the all-encompassing infinity. He represents perfection, good judgment, proper laws, and harmony. Mitra, according to one sage, is Varuna "perfectly illumined." In classical Hinduism he becomes a sage himself rather than the powerful god he once was. A related god in the Indo-Iranian tradition is Mithra.

MJOLLNIR Mjollnir was the hammer of the Norse weather-storm-thunder god Thor. It was made by dwarfs for the god and not only became a symbol of destruction but took on a phallic aspect as a sign of fertility and renewal. A traditional Norse wedding rite involved placing a replica of Thor's hammer in the virgin bride's lap. A myth tells how the giant Thrym stole Thor's hammer and refused to return it unless he could marry the beautiful Freya. With the help of the trickster Loki, Thor disguised himself as Freya and presented himself to the giant. The giant called for the hidden hammer and placed it on the lap of the beautiful goddess, who ripped off her veil, revealing Thor. The god immediately used the hammer to dispatch Thrym.

MNEMOSYNE A daughter of the ancient Greek earth goddess Gaia and her consort Ouranos, Mnemosyne personified memory. With Zeus as the father, she produced the Muses.

MODRON The mother of the Welsh hero Mabon, Modron is the equivalent of the continental Celtic mother goddess Matrona.

MOKSHA *Moksha*—its feminine Sanskrit form is *mukti*—is the Hindu term for the much-desired release from the endless cycle of transmigration or rebirth called *samsara*. *Moksha* is central to Brahmanic Hindu thought as well as to Buddhism and Jainism.

MOMOTARO A Japanese legend tells how the hero Momotaro was born miraculously of a peach and was adopted by a childless couple. Momotaro means, in fact, "peach child." To reward his adopted parents and friends for their generosity, Momotaro, at age 15, with the help of a dog, a pheasant, and a monkey, proved himself as a divine child and true hero by defeating a band of horned demons (*oni*) who had been oppressing the people.

MONDAWMIN, WUNZH, AND THE VISION QUEST Native North Americans tell many myths of the origin of corn. Often these myths involve the Corn Mother. In an Ojibway myth a young man, on the vision quest marking his rise from boyhood to manhood, fasts in the forest waiting for a vision that might help his people. On the third day of his fast he saw a figure descend from the sky, dressed in beautiful green and yellow clothes, topped by an array of golden feathers. The strange figure praised the boy, whose name is sometimes given as Wunzh, for thinking of his people rather than himself and offered to grant him a great boon if he would wrestle with him first. Although weakened by his fasting, the boy agreed and after three wrestling sessions on three days the visitor declared himself defeated. Then he gave some mysterious instructions to Wunzh. The next day would be the seventh day of the fast. The boy was to fight him one more time, strip his clothes from him, bury his body, and clear the ground of weeds and keep it cleared from time to time. Then, after some time he was to watch carefully for the visitor's return. In time, of course, the visitor did return, as Modawmin, a beautiful plant dressed in elaborate greens and yellows, sporting a head covered in feathers and carrying beautiful clusters of yellow food that would feed Wunzh's people forever.

MONISM Monism is the belief in a unified absolute that includes all reality. A good example is the Vedantic Hindu concept of Brahman. Monism, in its sense of unity, is relatable to monotheism, but in its acceptance of the absolute's being expressed in many deities, it clearly has a polytheistic expression.

MONJU The Japanese Buddhist equivalent of the Bodhisattva Manjusri, Monju sits on a lion and holds a book and a sword. The book symbolizes his position as a source of wisdom, and the sword refers to his war against those who oppose wisdom, or enlightenment.

M

Mitra slays the Bull of Disorder

Odysseus and his companions gouge out the eye of the monster Polyphemus

MONKEY Monkey, or the Monkey King Sun Wu-k'ung, was said to have accompanied the famous Chinese Buddhist monk Xuanzang on his trip to India in search of the sacred *sutras*. Monkey was a trickster of sorts who was born miraculously from a stone egg that had been in the world since the creation. He was made King of the Monkeys and reigned for 300 years until he decided to go in search of immortality. It was the Buddhist master who taught him the path to immortality and who gave Monkey the name Sun Wu-k'ung, meaning "enlightened monkey." From the master, Sun also learned how to change forms and to fly. Back home he defeated a monster and stole a magic weapon from the Dragon King, with which he beat the emissaries from Hell who refused to believe in his immortality. He also crossed his name off of the list of the dead. When Yama, the king of the underworld, and the Dragon King complained of Monkey's arrogance, it was decided by the great Yu, the Jade Emperor himself, that Monkey should be taken to Heaven, where he could be controlled. But in Heaven, Monkey committed one arrogant sin after another. He even drank Laozi's elixir of immortality. After several attempts to destroy him, the Jade Emperor asked for Buddha's help, and eventually Monkey was imprisoned. It was 500 years later that the great Guanyin had him released on the condition that he accompany Xuanzang (sometimes called Tripitaka) on his journey to India. Monkey and Tripitaka and their companion, the worldly Pigsy, received the sacred *sutras* from the Buddha himself. After a final trial set by the Buddha, the three companions were allowed into Heaven and Monkey became the god of victory.

In general, monkeys are important figures in the mythologies of Asia, as, for instance, in the Indian epic the *Ramayana*, where another monkey king, Hanuman, is a hero. There are also monkeys in the *Jataka* tales and in the Japanese story of Momotaro.

MONOTHEISM Monotheism is the belief that there is only one god. The three Abrahamic religions are often referred to as the "monotheistic" religions. It might be argued that certain religious systems—particularly Vedantic and other schools of Hinduism, which recognize Brahman, a single absolute behind and within everything that is, seen and unseen—are, in effect, monotheistic, in spite of the incarnation of that abso-

lute in multiple deities. A better term for this sort of belief is, perhaps, monism. The acceptance of many divine expressions of the absolute gives many monistic systems—such as that of the Hindus—a polytheistic aspect.

MONSTERS All mythologies have monsters, nightmare creations that stand in the way of a hero's progress or that plague societies. The terrible Grendel and his equally frightening mother terrorize the Danes until the hero Beowulf can kill them. The Native American Kuyoyis and many heroes like him are above all monster slayers, as are the India Krishna and the Greek Herakles. Monsters can be giants like David's Goliath, the Irish Balor, or the Greek Cyclops overcome by Odysseus. They can be strange mythical beasts such as the Medusa or the Minotaur. Often they are dragons. Their main purpose is to represent impossible barriers and to instill fright—in the hero and the reader or listener.

MOON MYTHS The presence of the moon deity—usually the moon goddess—is ubiquitous in world mythology. Moonlight and moon deities are usually opposed to or related to sunlight and sun deities in some sense. The association of the moon with the feminine arises in Paleolithic times, perhaps out of a realized connection between lunar phases and those of the female body. The female figure of the famous tiny statuette, dating from c. 20,000 B.C.E., known as the "Venus of Laussel" holds up what appears to be a crescent moon in her right hand. In the cave of Abri du Roc aux Sorciers at Angles-sur-l'Anglin are three carved goddesses usually thought to represent the trinity of goddesses depicted in so many forms in human history, representing the phases of the moon and the maiden-mother-crone phases of female life. For the Greeks, for instance, there was an association of the moon with the Persephone-Demeter-Hecate and the Persephone-Artemis-Hecate trinities. It should be noted that mene is "moon" in Greek and that mensis is "month" in Latin. In Neolithic Çatal Hüyük the goddess is frequently depicted with the horns of her male counterpart, the bull, the latter's horns forming a crescent moon. The Mexican Virgin of Guadalupe, one of the world's several Black Madonnas, is clearly related to the Aztec earth and moon goddess Tonantzin and is always depicted standing on a crescent moon. Among many moon goddesses are the Greek Selene and Semele, the Incan Mamakilya, and the Egyptian Hathor.

There are moon gods as well. The Vedic primal man Purusha's mind becomes the moon, the Aramean Baal-Hadad is "Lord of the Moon," and Balts and Slavs have moon gods. Khonsu and Thoth are Egyptian gods with moon identities. The Cherokee sun goddess becomes jealous of the moon god because people stare so lovingly at him. Among the Dona of Zimbabwe, Mwetsi, the first man, was also "Moon."

Moon myths are particularly present in Chinese mythology. In the Chinese creation myth the eyes of the primal cosmic man are the sun and the moon. When the sun eye is open we have daytime, and when the moon eye is open we have night. There is also a Chinese myth about the ten suns and twelve moons—the former inhabited by crows, one of the latter by a hart and a toad. The moons stand for the annual lunar cycles. The moons have a mother, Changyi, who regularly bathes her children in a sacred lake in the west. The famous archer Yi, who destroys nine of the ten suns to save the world, takes possession of the drink of immortality, which is then stolen from him by his wife, Henge, who, having run to the moon, becomes the lunar toad. Another name for the mother of the moon is, in fact, Henge. In this connection, it is of interest that in Indian mythology, where *soma* is the ambrosial source of immortality for the gods or the means of communication with them, the moon is also its storage place and sometimes takes its name for itself. There is a Daoist tradition in China that holds that the source of immortality, or at least long life, is the cinnamon tree in the moon, a tree that no amount of chopping can fell. Finally, in China, the moon and the sun are representative of the perfect *yin* and the perfect *yang* in the well-known *yin-yang* symbol.

Something not unlike the *yin-yang* association of sun and moon and other elements occurs in the Indonesian Moluccas, where the wholeness or unity of the absolute divinity is based on the coming together of the opposite but complementary Father Sun and Mother Moon. But as in the Chinese *yin-yang* system, there is maleness in the moon and femaleness in the sun as well. Thus the moon is female in its waning and male in its waxing.

In Korea, as in China, there is a mythological archer who shoots down unwanted heavenly bodies—in this case, one sun and one moon.

The Khmer people believed that the moon protects humans by at least dimly lighting up the night world. She rides a silver chariot across the sky each night.

MORDRED In the Arthurian legends, Mordred (Modred) was the offspring of an incestuous relationship between King Arthur and his sister Anna (according to Geoffrey of Monmouth in his *Historia*) or his half sister Morgause, or Morgan Le Fay (according to Sir Thomas Malory in his *Le Morte d'Arthur*). In any case, Mordred was left in charge of Arthur's kingdom when the king went to France to fight Sir Lancelot, who had committed adultery with Queen Guinevere. Mordred attempted to take the throne, forcing a war between father and son and the death of both.

MORGAN LE FAY The shape-shifting, magical Morgan Le Fay is identified in Malory's *Le Morte d'Arthur* as King Arthur's half sister, the daughter of the king's mother, Igraine, and her first husband. Usually she is depicted as Arthur's enemy, but it is said that she led the party of women who took the mortally wounded "once and future king" off to Avalon to be healed.

MORGAUSE A half sister of King Arthur, sometimes confused with Morgan Le Fay, Morgause married Lot, sometimes called king of the Orkneys, and was the mother of Sir Gawain. She was also the mother by her brother Arthur—neither being aware of their blood relationship at the time—of Mordred.

MORMON MYTHOLOGY According to Mormons, members of the Church of Jesus Christ of Latter-day Saints, God and Jesus appeared to the young Joseph Smith as he prayed in a grove of trees in Palmyra, New York. They directed him to found the true Christian church. So began the cult of Mormonism, which developed its own rich and complex mythology, contained now in the *Book of Mormon*, first published in 1830. The mythology is based on the stories of the Bible, on Smith's many visions, and on various other apocryphal narrative traditions.

For early Mormons, America was the new Eden, the place of a new beginning, to which Jesus naturally came after his resurrection. It is said that Jesus, accompanied by Moses and other Old Testament prophets, came to Smith and another Mormon leader, Oliver Cowdrey, in the Mormon temple in Kirkland, Ohio, in 1836 and ordered them to establish a society based on Old Testament patriarchal values, including polygamy. Missionaries were sent out into the world—and continue to be sent—to preach the Mormon message.

In 1844, an angry mob murdered Smith, who had begun to preach the possibility of achieving divinity through Mormonism. After this, a split in the church developed, with Smith's son, Joseph, forming a "reorganized" branch in Independence, Missouri, and Brigham Young leading the more orthodox followers of the senior Smith to Salt Lake City, Utah.

MORRIGAN Morrigan (Morrighan, Morrigu) was the Irish triune goddess of war, death, and destruction. She was also a goddess of fertility who had intercourse with the Tuatha Dé Danaan king, the Dagda. She bears strong resemblances to the goddesses Macha, Badb, and Nemain. She can sometimes play the role of the femme fatale; as the Mesopotamian goddess Inanna/Ishtar tried to seduce the hero Gilgamesh and Dido attempted to deter the Roman hero Aeneas from his sacred duty, Morrigan attempts to seduce Cuchulainn and is rejected. The result is sworn enmity. In a fight, Cuchulainn wounds the goddess, and when he eventually is killed, Morrigan—some say Badb—sits on his shoulder as a crow (her familiar form) and watches a beaver drink the hero's blood.

MOSES The life of Moses contains elements—canonical and apocryphal—that mark him as a true mythic hero, and certainly he is Judaism's greatest hero and the central figure in Hebrew mythology. In the Book of Exodus in the *Torah*, we learn that Hebrews, serving as enslaved workers in Egypt, had become so numerous that the pharaoh ordered that all newborn Hebrew boys be thrown into the Nile to drown. This edict placed the boy who would become Moses in the position of so many representatives of the divine child (*puer aeternus*), threatened by a wicked king. As in so many of these myths, the child is, in a sense, abandoned and adopted. In the Moses story, a mother of the Levite clan placed her baby in a watertight reed basket and set him afloat in the river to avoid the massacre of the innocents. The boy's sister Miriam watched as the basket was discovered by a daughter of the pharaoh, who immediately adopted the child. Miriam quickly fetched the baby's actual mother and presented her to the pharaoh's daughter as a wet nurse. The leaving of the baby in a basket on a river ties Moses to the unusual beginnings of several mytho-

Moses displays the tablet of the Ten Commandments

logical or legendary heroes, including, for instance, Sargon of Akkad and Siegfried in Germany.

Again, as is often the case with heroes, we move directly to the stories of adulthood. Moses killed an Egyptian for mistreating two Hebrew slaves and was forced to flee for his life. He found his way to Midian, not far from Edom, the land founded by Esau, and there he married Zipporah, a daughter of a Midianite priest called Reuel (sometimes Jethro). Moses lived as a shepherd in Midian for forty years while the Hebrews continued to suffer in Egypt.

One day Moses climbed a mountain (Horeb or Sinai) and there, out of a burning bush, a voice spoke to him, revealing himself as Yahweh, the "I Am," the god of "your fathers," Abraham, Isaac, and Jacob (Exodus 3:14–15). Yahweh then placed Moses clearly at the second stage of the traditional hero journey by calling him to action. Moses was to go to Egypt to lead his people out of bondage into Canaan. At first Moses doubted his qualifications for such a role and "refused the call," as so many would-be heroes do. Through various signs, including turning Moses' staff into a serpent, Yahweh demonstrated that he would use his power to support his prophet. So Moses returned to Egypt, accompanied, according to one of the Old Testament authors, by his articulate and priestly brother Aaron, to assist in the fulfillment of the Covenant made with Abraham and confirmed with Isaac and Israel-Jacob (6:2–8).

When the pharaoh refused to let the Hebrews go, Yahweh, through Moses, sent a series of plagues to Egypt, always sparing the Hebrews. The Nile was polluted, frogs rained down, maggots and flies covered the land, the livestock all died, and locusts ate the Egyptian crops. When the pharaoh still refused to free the Hebrews, Yahweh arranged a final plague. Each Hebrew family was to mark its doorpost with the blood of a slaughtered lamb and to eat a ceremonial meal while the Angel of Death passed over the marked houses and killed the oldest male child in each Egyptian house. After this establishment of what for Jews would become the Feast of the Passover, the pharaoh was finally convinced to let the Hebrews go.

With the next great mythic event, Yahweh confirmed his identification of the Hebrews as his chosen people. As Moses and his people followed Yahweh's pillar of cloud by day and pillar of fire by night, the pharaoh changed his mind about letting them go and followed them with an army. Moses came to the apparent barrier of the Sea of Reeds and raised his staff over it, and Yahweh caused a great wind to push aside the waters so that the people could pass through. When the Egyptians pursued, the god allowed the waters to return and so drown the pharaoh's army.

A period in the wilderness followed, during which the people complained to Moses and Aaron of their plight, and Yahweh sent *manna*, sacred food, on which the Hebrews fed for forty years. Drink was provided when, as commanded by Yahweh, Moses used his staff to strike the rock at Horeb and water came from it.

Perhaps the most important mythic moment of the Exodus was God's gift to Moses of the Ten Commandments and the Book of the Covenant, the *Torah*, on Mount Sinai. The people agreed to the commandments and to other laws outlined by Yahweh, but when Moses returned to Mount Sinai for a time they began to complain. To placate them and give them something concrete to worship, Aaron made golden calves. Moses returned and in his fury at this apostasy broke the stone tablets on which God's words were recorded. Later Yahweh provided new tablets, which were stored in the portable tabernacle called the Ark of the Covenant, the symbol of Yahweh himself, that led the Israelites into battle. The ark would become an important element in Jewish mythology. Its cult was officially recognized by David after his conquest of Jerusalem (for Jews, the City of David on Mount Zion) in about 1000 B.C.E. The first temple, that of Solomon in c. 950 B.C.E., housed the ark and became the principal national and religious center of the Israelites. The ark disappeared when the Babylonians destroyed the temple in 587 B.C.E., and it was not in the second temple of 516 B.C.E. The "lost ark" has spawned a mythology that is both a part of Jewish religious culture and general popular culture.

The story of Moses continues in the three biblical books that follow Exodus. We learn how the Hebrews rebelled against Moses and Yahweh, going so far as to indulge in Canaanite fertility rites and Baal worship. Even harsh punishment by Yahweh failed to completely end the rebellions (Numbers 11–14). Deuteronomy contains the last speeches of Moses to his people, elaborating on the commandments and warning of the consequences if the Hebrews failed to honor the Covenant. Moses blessed the people and then went up to Mount Nebo in Moab, from which place Yahweh showed him the Promised Land. The leader of the Hebrews, 120 years old, then died and was buried somewhere in Moab. The last verses of Deuteronomy affirm that "there has never yet risen in Israel a prophet like Moses, whom the Lord knew face to face." These verses celebrate his "strong hand" and awesome deeds" (34:10–12).

MOT The brother and particular enemy of the Canaanite fertility god Baal, Mot is the god of death itself. His struggles with Baal represent the struggles in nature between periods of drought and those of productive growth.

MOTHER EARTH "Mother Earth" is a term typically applied in myth and folklore to the mother goddess as a personification of earth. The Greek Gaia, for instance, could be called "Mother Earth."

MOUNTAIN MYTHOLOGY In mythology, mountains serve as places where deities live—that is, as representations of Heaven—or as places on earth that are as close to the gods as we mortals can get. As such, they are places where prophets and holy people go to receive the word of divinity. In Greece, Mount Olympus was the home of the Olympian gods. In ancient Sumer and Babylon, the temples known as ziggurats represented the "holy mountain." Canaanite gods such as El and Baal were divinities of the holy mountain. The Hindu world center is Mount Meru (Mandara). The sacred center of ancient Greece was Delphi on the slopes of Mount Parnassos. The Native North Americans have many sacred mountains; the Hopi kachinas live on the San Francisco Peaks near Flagstaff, Arizona. The Phrygian mother goddess Cyble was the "Mountain Mother" from whom Moses and Jesus both received godly instructions on mountaintops. In ancient China mountains were seen as divinities who had the power to send needed rain. They were also places to which the dead were sent. Certain mountains were purely mythical. Kunlun was such a mountain and was the dwelling place of the heavenly emperor and one hundred gods. Some texts say that Kunlun is ruled by a being that is half human and half tiger. Sometimes Kunlun is seen as a kind of platonic symbol of the various levels of holiness leading to knowledge of the Supreme Ruler. For some, as the home of Xiwang Mu, the Queen of the West, Kunlun is a place of immortality.

In India, Shiva's wife Parvati is the "Daughter of the Mountain," which itself holds up the sky and makes life possible. The mountain is also the retreat of the great Shiva in his aspect as the ultimate *yogi*.

In the Japanese Shinto mythology of mountains, the influence of China is evident. Mountains contain divinity or *kami* and are sources of necessary water. They are also places of burial and the loci for festivals of the dead, such as one called *bon*.

In central Asia, Tibet, Korea, and other places in Asia, it was thought that the primal being or first king arrived on earth by landing on the summit of a mythical mountain. Mountains are the gateway to heaven.

MOYANG MELUR A negative moon spirit, the Malaysian Moyang Melur was half tiger and half man. Possessing in his bag all the proper rules of society, he watched with amusement from the moon as humans broke all these rules, of which they were ignorant. One night he leaned too far out of the moon and fell to earth. He met up with a hunter named Moyang Kapir and threatened to kill all humans if the hunter did not help him get back to the moon. This the hunter did with a rope line, and the two beings climbed to the moon. There Moyang suspected he might be killed by the moon spirit. He escaped by the rope, stealing the bag of rules on his way, reached earth, cut the rope so that Moyang Melur could not follow him, and acted as a culture hero, teaching the people proper rules of conduct found in the bag.

MUDUNGKALA The Tiwi people of the Melville and Bathurst islands of Australia say that they were separated from the mainland during the dreaming time when water followed the dreaming travel of Mudungkala, a goddess who came out of the earth with the first people.

MUROMETS, ILYA A Slavic folk hero and monster killer, Ilya was surrounded by magic—a flying horse, unstoppable weapons. After many adventures, including the slaying of a half-human, half-bird figure known as Nightingale the Brigand, he died in Kiev and turned to stone.

MURUGAN Dravidian in origin, Murugan or Murukan is an important god among the Tamils of southern India. Sometimes he seems to be a version of the war god Skanda (Karttikeya), the six-headed son of Shiva. His roots are more likely to be found in fertility worship, however. He is clearly associated with love and youthfulness, as he rides, handsome and robust, on his peacock in the company of young women. His exploits as Skanda are described in the *Mahabharata* and the *Ramayana*.

MUSES The Titan Mnemosyne by Zeus was the mother of the nine Muses, who were traditionally invoked by the poets and artists of Greece, Rome, and other parts of the world. Their patron in Greece was always the god of the arts, Apollo, who, in addition to his many other titles, was "Muse Leader" (*Musagetes*). The Muses lived on Mount

Apollo and the Muses

The Treasury of Atreus or Tomb of Agamemnon at Mycenae in Greece

Helicon or Mount Parnassos. Each was associated with a particular art: Calliope, epic poetry; Clio, history; Erato, lyric poetry; Euterpe, flute; Melpomene, tragedy; Polyhymnia, mime; Terpsichore, dance; Thalia, comedy; and Urania, astronomy.

MUT The wife of the god Amun in Thebes, this version of the Egyptian Great Goddess is strongly associated with her equivalent goddess, Sekhmet, the lioness wife of Ptah in Memphis.

MWARI The high god of the African Zimbabian Shona people, Mwari was a creator. He plays a major role in the story of the Shona first man, Mwetsi.

MWETSI Mwetsi ("Moon") was the first man in the African creation myth of the Shona in Zimbabwe. Created by the high god Mwari, he emerged from the waters to a barren earth. Mwari sent him Morning Star as a wife, and she gave birth to vegetation, which attracted rain from the sky. Then Mwari sent Mwetsi Evening Star as a wife but warned him that problems could follow if he had intercourse with her. Mwetsi and Evening Star did have intercourse, and domestic animals and human children—but already adult—were born to them. After more cohabitation they produced wild animals. Finally, Evening Star denied intercourse to Mwetsi and suggested that he mate with his daughters. This Mwetsi did, and the daughters produced offspring who became adults almost immediately. Mwetsi was their king. But Evening Star, in the ancient goddess tradition, took up with a serpent. The serpent bit and poisoned Mwetsi, and, as in the case of the Fisher King of Arthurian lore, the land became barren as he became sick. Mwetsi's children killed him so that the land would revive. So began a tradition, described by Sir James Fraser and others in various parts of the world, of the periodical ritual sacrifice of the king so that the people and land can be renewed.

MWINDO Mwindo (Mwendo, Msire) was the central hero of the Nyanga people of eastern Zaire in Africa. He is the hero of a well-known oral epic, miraculously born from his mother's palm with adult stature and magical qualities. But the chief had demanded that only female children be born, a male being, by definition, a threat to his rule, and he ordered that Mwindo be buried alive. This was done, but Mwindo rose from the grave during the night and slept in his father's hut. The king did not bury him again. Meanwhile, the hero's sister, Nyamitondo, marries Lightning, who takes her to live in the sky. The sister returns to earth from time to time and acts as a culture heroine, teaching the people how to live. But a strange bird is hatched from an egg found by Mwindo and his sister, and the bird ate all of the people, including Nyamitondo, who cut her way out of the beast, however. Mwindo and Nyamitondo then killed the bird and released the people from its stomach.

After many adventures and many good deeds, Mwindo and his people were attacked by a jealous chief. Mwindo's people were all killed, but Mwindo resurrected them. Then he decided to visit the chief god. The god attempted to trick him in many ways, but eventually Mwindo returned home with even more powers, and his father made him king.

MYCENAE Mycenae was the city in Greece founded at least as early as the third millennium B.C.E. It is a city of massive Cyclopean gates and walls that gave its name to what we now call the Mycenaean stage of Greek civilization, a stage deeply influenced by Minoan civilization. It is believed that the Mycenaeans eventually overpowered the Minoans. The great legendary king of Mycenae was Agamemnon, a member of the cursed House of Atreus and the leader of the Greek alliance that fought against Troy in the Trojan War.

NAGAS *Nagas* (or the feminine *Naginis*) are serpent figures who play a role in both Hindu and Buddhist mythology. Their source seems to lie in the pre-Aryan fertility cults of India. The *nagas* reside within the earth, in an aquatic underworld. They are personifications of terrestrial waters as well as door and gate guardians. They are beings of great power who protect the underworld and bestow fertility and wealth on the areas of the world with which they are individually associated, whether that area is a field, a place of worship, or even a whole country. If a *naga* is properly worshipped, prosperity can be the result. If ignored or slighted, the *naga* can bring about disaster. When the Buddha achieves enlightenment, he is said to have been protected by the cobra hood of the *nagaraja* Mucilinda, symbolizing the fact that the *nagas* are placing their natural powers in the service of the Buddha. Between the dissolution of one age and the beginning of another, Vishnu sleeps on what is left of the old world, the remainder of the cosmic sacrifice represented by the serpent or *naga* Shesha or Ananta. Vishnu and his avatar Krishna are both conquerors of serpents, indicating their power over the waters and over the potential chaos represented by the serpent principle.

NAMMU A Sumerian fertility goddess, Nammu, whose importance and role in association with the primal waters (Apsu) was essentially taken over by her son Enki. She was also the mother of the goddess Ninma. In some cities she was the first deity, who gave birth to An (Earth) and Ki (Sky), who in turn gave birth to the great gods, including Enki. It was she who devised the idea of creating humans to help the gods at their work.

NAMORODO Monster-like tricksters of Aboriginal Australia, the Namorodo fly about during the night and kill people with their horrible claws. They can prevent the proper repose of the souls of the dead.

NANDA The foster father of the Hindu Lord Krishna, Nanda ("Joy") was a cowherd and village elder.

NANNA In some versions of Norse mythology, Nanna was the wife of the dying god Balder, and she became so distraught over his death that her heart broke and she died, too. She was placed beside her husband on his funeral pyre.

According to some traditions, the Sumerian moon god Nanna or Nannar (Akkadian Sin), the son of Ninlil, was the father, via Ningal, of the great goddess Inanna and her twin, the sun god Utu. Nanna was known for his wisdom and, as the moon, he determined the passing of time.

NARADA Narada was a *Rishi* ("sage") with great ascetic powers. He was a creation of the Hindu god Brahma. Like the other *Rishis*, he is a messenger between humans and deities. But Narada is a notorious troublemaker. It is he who

The entwined Nagas at the royal city of Khmers

A Navajo sand painting for a curing ceremony

tells Kamsa that he will be killed by the eighth child of Devaki, causing the threat to the life of Krishna.

NARASIMHA The man-lion Narasimha is the fourth avatar of the Hindu god Vishnu. In this "descent" to the world, Vishnu comes to support a fusion of *bhakti*, in this case, specifically devotion to Vishnu, and *dharma*, the orthodox Brahmanic social order that *bhakti* sometimes appears to challenge. The association of Narashimba with Vishnu is made visually clear by the depictions of the man-lion with Vishnu's wife Lakshmi, representing "Prosperity," on his knee. The myth of the man-lion avatar is contained, with variations, in both the *Vishnu Purana* and the *Bhagavata Purana*. In the myth, Hiranya, the king of the *asuras*, is pitted against his son, a *bhakta* or yogic devotee of Vishnu. Hiranya hopes to overthrow Indra as king of the gods and to usurp even the position of Brahma. His son Prahlada, however, is a good *asura* who combines within himself the values of *bhakti* and *dharma*, signifying the fact that true *dharma* can exist, as far as Vishnu is concerned, only in conjunction with *Vishnu-bhakti*. To make this clear, Vishnu descends as the man-lion. Meanwhile, as Hiranya has been unsuccessful in his attempt to turn his son away from Vishnu, he ties him up and throws him into the sea. Instead of dying, however, Prahlada drifts into mystical union with the object of his *bhakti*, and Narasimha kills Hiranya.

NARAYANA Narayana is a name sometimes used for the Hindu god Vishnu. The *Vishnu Purana* tells us that Vishnu, who is identified with the creator, Brahma-Prajapati, and, by implication, with the idea of Brahman as the essence of the universe, is "the supreme Narayana . . . the lord of all," the source of existence without beginning or end. Vishnu is called Narayana because the waters are called *Nara* and the waters are the offspring of "the Man" (*nara*), who is presumably the primal male Purusha, who, joined with Prakti ("Nature"), became the universe and made the waters his dwelling place (*ayana*). Vishnu is the "son of the Waters" or the "Son of Man" because, in the form of his avatar the Boar, Varaha, his body composed of the *Vedas*, he used his great horn to raise the beautiful Prthivi (Earth), rescuing her from the demonic chaotic waters and re-creating the world that had been destroyed as the cosmic sacrifice at the end of the previous creation. During the time between the eras, Vishnu as Narayana sleeps on the sacrificial remnants of the old world that float on the waters as the serpent Ananata or Shesha—the "infinite." His eventual awakening is a symbol

of the spiritual awakening that comes to the one who meditates sufficiently on Vishnu-Narayana.

NAREAU The creator god of the Micronesian Gilbert Islands, Nareau used an eel to perform the necessary separation of earth and sky so that the world creation could take place.

NATARAJA As Nataraja ("Lord of the Dance") the Hindu god Shiva is the cosmic dancer whose ecstatic and liberating yogic twirling is an expression of the cyclic energy of a universe based on creation, preservation, and destruction.

NATIVE NORTH AMERICAN MYTHOLOGY The mythology of Native North America is a collection of many mythologies, illustrating the religious beliefs and traditions of several hundred tribes or "nations," many of which have inhabited North America for thousands of years. Given the fact that until very recently Native American myths were passed down orally in the absence of a writing tradition, it is difficult to tell how ancient or true to the original such myths are. Still, as different as Hopi, Sioux, Ojibwa, and Navajo mythologies, for instance, are from each other, it is possible to identify certain themes and character types that pervade the mythologies of the continent as those mythologies have come down to us. Not surprisingly, certain universal archetypal patterns are present in Native North America. There are myths of creation and creators, of primal parents such as the Zuni Sky Father and Earth Mother, of named gods and goddesses such as Great Spirit, and Spider Woman. There are many myths of the hero quest, such as the vision quest of the Ojibwa youth Wunzh in the story of Modawmin and the origin of corn. The hero quest can contain other universal motifs, including the descent to the underworld and the search for the father, as in the story of the Tewa Waterpot Boy. Other familiar monomythic hero motifs are those of the miraculous conception and birth, as in the stories of Waterpot Boy and the Blackfoot Kutoyis. Sacred twins are as familiar among the North American Indians as they are among the Mesoamericans and the Indo-Europeans. Examples are the Acoma culture-hero sister twins Iatiku ("Life bringer") and Nautsiti ("Full Basket"), and the Navajo culture-hero brother twins Nayenezgani ("Monster Slayer") and Tobadzhistshini ("Born for Water"). While recognizing the universality of Native American mythology, it can also be said that certain particular themes and characteristics are particularly ubiquitous in the mythology of the continent, perhaps because of trade and other forms of intermingling and perhaps because of the distant common ancestry of many of the groups in central Asia. This particular combination of themes and characteristics make it at least possible to speak of Native North American mythology as a whole.

The most obvious characteristic of Native American mythology and religion is the sense of the sacredness of nature. This is not a characteristic that we associate, for instance, with the Abrahamic and other "major" religions and mythologies. Native American mythology and religion belong to the animistic tradition, in which all of nature—animate and inanimate—is permeated by spirits. Whether based on a somewhat imprecise vision of the spirit world or specific myths such as those of the Okanagom Earth Mother, whose body is the earth, and the Hopi kachinas, who visit the villages from the San Francisco Peaks, the result of this sense is what skeptics might call an inordinate concern for and respect for "the earth," for such realities as holy places, totem animals, and the interrelationship of all things. Shamans and other spirit "medicine" men and women help the various peoples communicate with the spirits around them. These priestly people have mythological cognates in such figures as the Modoc trickster Kumokums, who descended to the underworld in an attempt to release his dead daughter from the spirits there.

Not surprisingly, to a great extent, the emergence of the United States in North America, one of many Abrahamic-dominated nations with dreams of expansion and development and the "conquest" of nature, has involved direct and often genocidal conflict with the animistic worldview of the cultures we call "Indian."

Supreme deities do not tend to play a central role in Native American mythology. They are present as distant creators in the sky or sometimes as the sun or, more commonly, as a form of the "Great Spirit" or "Great Mystery"—the Algonquian Gitchi Manitou or the Sioux Wakan Tanka, for instance—who is an intangible essence more like the Hindu Brahman than the Abrahamic God.

A common Indian figure is the trickster, who aids the creator in his work and/or under mines the work by introducing into the world such elements as deceit and death. He is sometimes a valuable monster-slaying culture hero such as the Blackfoot Kutoyis, sometimes a personification of unbridled appetites, like Iktome or raven or the ever-popular coyote, who is found in many parts of America. Tricksters have shape-shifting and other magical powers derived from the spirit world. They are clearly mythological relatives of the shamans and other medicine people who communicate with that world. Tricksters are everywhere in North America, as they also are in animistic Africa.

Among many Indian peoples, goddesses or female culture heroes play a more important part in the implementation of creation than do supreme deities. The Cherokee Spider Grandmother, who brings fire to the people, is such a goddess, as are the Navajo Changing Woman—so important to the puberty rite known as the kamala—the Hopi Spider Woman, and the Sioux White Buffalo Woman, all of whom loom large in the mythologies of their people.

The defining myth of most cultures is the creation myth. In Native America there are several types of creation. The Laguna Thinking Woman thinks the world into existence. The Blackfoot "Old Man" also creates *ex nihilo*, that is, alone and from nothing. Among several California tribes the creator works as a craftsman, or *deus faber*, measuring out the world like a carpenter. But by far the dominant creation patterns in North America are those of the emergence creation and the earth-diver creation.

The emergence creation is particularly central to the lives of the southwestern Indians, as it is to those of many Mesoamericans, such as the Aztecs. In the North American southwest, the Acoma people, the Hopis, and the other Keres and Tewa Pueblo people, as well as the Navajo, all say that they originally emerged in this world from a world or worlds below the earth. This is a process by which the people evolve from a lower state—for instance, insects—to the human state.

The earth-diver creation is clearly related to creation myths of central Asia—those of the Siberians, the Birhor, the Samoyeds, and the Altaic peoples. Earth-diver creations are found in other parts of Asia as well—among the Ainu and in the Indonesian myth of Batara Guru and in some of the Vedic-Hindu *Puranas*. It is also found among the Inuits. In the earth-diver pattern, the supreme being typically sends an animal into the primal waters to bring up earth from the depth. That earth then multiplies—sometimes on the back of a turtle, sometimes helped by a being—often a female

being—who has fallen from the sky. Eventually the world is formed from the original bit of earth. Such a myth is that of the Seneca Star Woman, who falls from the sky and is caught by birds, who send a toad to collect dirt from below. The dirt is placed on the turtle's back, where it grows until there is room for the Star Woman to live and propagate. [Bierhorst, Leeming and Page (1998)]

NATS *Nats*, like the *neak-ta* of Cambodia and the *phi* of Thailand, are spirits who dwell in the mountains of Burma, especially on the sacred Mount Poppa. But *nats* can also live in all aspects of nature, in people's houses and even in people. Some *nats* are troublemakers, rather like poltergeists, while some are protectors—like guardian angels. *Nats* once lived in the world as humans, many of whom were wrongly killed by evil kings. Included in the official list of thirty-seven *nats*, for instance, are a famous blacksmith and his sister who were burned alive because a king was jealous of what he saw as the smith's mysterious power.

NAUPLIUS Nauplius the elder was a son of Poseidon and the founder of the Greek city of Nauplia. Nauplius the younger was the angry and vengeful father of Palamedes, who was wrongly accused of betrayal by Odysseus and was stoned to death by his fellow Greeks in Troy during the Trojan War. Nauplius took revenge by encouraging the Greek wives at home to be unfaithful to their husbands and by other, more violent acts, such as using false beacons to force Greek ships onto rocks. Eventually the Greeks chased him out of Nauplia.

N

A buddhist monk and pagoda near Mount Poppa

NAVAJO CREATION MYTH The creation myth of the Athabascan people of the Native American Southwest known as the Navajo (the Spanish name for the Dine, meaning "the People") is an example of the emergence type of creation myth so common in the region and in the central Asian lands from which the Navajo almost certainly originally came. It is also one of the most complex and significant examples of oral narrative on the North American continent. The myth is central to the Navajo worldview and to Navajo ritual. In the most important Navajo ceremony, known as the "Blessing Way" (*Hozhoji*), a shaman, or "medicine man," gathers most of the Navajo myths into what is, in effect, a creation epic with the purpose of reestablishing *hozho*, a state of "beauty," which is "harmony" with nature, with the spirit-permeated world around us, with the people's origins. Other ceremonies, accompanied by elaborate sand paintings, addressing particular aspects of disharmony or the opposite of *hozho*, are also derived from the creation myth. The creation myth when sung at a ceremony is literally a way of getting back to the beginnings so that a new start can be made.

The creation epic and the various ceremonies contain stories of such figures as Spider Woman, the Yei ("Holy People"), and the monster-slaying holy twins, who were miraculously conceived in Changing Woman—the goddess so important to the female puberty rite, the Kinaalda—by the sun. There are many versions of the creation story—called by some the *Dine Bahane*—but the essential emergence aspect is always present.

In the beginning there was only a small, dark world with waters on all four sides, the four sides being an expression of the Navajo emphasis, like that of the Mesoamericans, on the four directions, each with a color: white for the east, blue for the south, yellow for the west, and black for the north. This First World was populated by the Insect People, who were expelled from it because of their constant arguing and other antisocial actions. The People entered the Second World from a hole in the east. There they found and made friends with the Bird People. But the first People continued behaving badly and the Bird People expelled them. So, finding an opening in the sky, the People entered the Third World. This was a world in which a male river flowed into a female river that flowed eastward. The People of the Third World were the Grasshopper People. The Insect People at first mingled with the Grasshopper People, but soon they began quarreling and doing bad things as usual, and they were once again expelled. With the help of Red Wind, they found an opening in the western sky and were able to emerge into the Fourth World. Four Grasshopper People—each one being one of the primary directional colors—went with them. The Fourth World contained four mountains marking the horizons of each of the four directions. The People traveled to the east, the west, and the south in search of life but found nothing. Finally, they went north and discovered farming village People, the Kiis 'aanii (we know them as the Pueblo People). These people taught the recently emerged People many things about farming and other life-supporting matters.

Suddenly in the first autumn, a voice—that of Talking God—called to the People from the east, and four strange gods appeared—White Body, Blue Body, Yellow Body, and Black Body. They made signs to the People that they did not understand, and eventually all but Black Body left. Black Body began talking to the People, telling them that the gods wished them to become more god-like and less insect-like in appearance and to reproduce. The People were to undergo a thorough ritual washing before the gods returned on the

twelfth day. On the twelfth day the gods did return, Blue Body and Black Body carrying holy buckskins, White Body carrying a white ear and a yellow ear of corn. On one of the buckskins, with its head facing west, the gods placed the ears of corn over similar-colored eagle feathers with the corn tips facing east. They covered the corn and feathers with the other buckskin. The gods had the White Wind from the east and the Yellow Wind from the west blow between the skins, and eight Mirage People appeared and encircled the skins four times. When the gods removed the top skin, a man lay where the white corn had been and a woman where the yellow corn had been. The blowing winds had entered them and given them what we call the breath necessary for life. These were First Man and First Woman, the Holy People. The first couple had a set of hermaphrodite twins and then several other sets of twins. The gods took the parents and then the children to the sacred mountain in the east to teach them about ceremonies, rain, agriculture, and other matters. Then the children married some of the Mirage People, some of the Klis'aanii, and some of the People who had emerged from the Third World.

After eight years Coyote and Badger arrived; they were children of contact between Sky and Earth. Coyote stayed nearby and Badger went down a hole leading to the world below.

One day First Man and First Woman had an argument when First Woman suggested that it was the sexual power of women that made men hunt. In the argument First Woman said men and their abilities were unnecessary to women. So it was that the women left the men and moved to the other side of the river along which they lived. After four years, the women agreed that they needed their husbands and recrossed the river. After a ritual bathing and dusting with sacred corn meal and a night corralled together, the women rejoined their men.

During their separation years both men and women had practiced unnatural sex. The practices of the women gave birth to the Naye'I, the monster gods who would plague the People for some time.

During the river crossing two children were found missing, so, directed by the four gods, the mother of the girls and her husband, followed by Coyote, descended into each of four rooms—the white, the blue, the yellow, and the black rooms—in the river, and in the black room of the north found the missing girls, who had been taken by Water Monster. The Monster did not resist as the parents rescued the children, and, secretly, Coyote stole the two children of Water Monster and hid them in his robe.

Soon the People noticed animals moving from east to west. They were told that a great flood was approaching. An old man and his son appeared with bits of earth from the sacred mountains, into which they planted four reeds, which grew immediately into one reed with a hole on its eastern side. The young man ushered the People into the reed as the flood surrounded it. They climbed the reed, and after Badger enlarged a hole at the top, the People emerged into the Fifth World—this world. But the water from the flood followed them and the hole had to be plugged. The People noticed something odd about Coyote and discovered the stolen children of Water Monster under his robe. These they used to plug up the hole.

An argument over corn, made worse by actions of the greedy trickster Coyote, developed between the People and the Kiis'aanii ("Pueblo People"), and they moved apart from each other in the Fifth World, a situation that prevails to this day. Now First Man and First Woman, assisted by the gods, remade the sacred mountains from the sacred earth brought by the old man and his son.

Troubles followed. Enemy monsters were devouring the People when First Man found a baby in a cradle made of rainbows and took it to First Woman. Talking God and House God appeared, and Talking God told them this was their much-wished-for baby. After four days the child—a girl—walked and was clothed in white shell. This was Changing Woman, or White Shell Woman, the source of the Kinaalda female puberty ritual. It was Changing Woman who would miraculously conceive the twin heroes Monster Slayer and Born for Water, who would kill the monsters and make the world safe for the Dine, the People, who live here in the Fifth World today. [Zolbrod, Leeming and Page (1998)]

NEAK-TA In Cambodia, the *neak-ta* are earth spirits who watch over people, places, and things, as long as they are paid proper respect. A *neak-ta* can take the name of particular places or objects with which it *is* associated. It seems that, like the *nats* of Burma, the *neak-ta* may be incarnations of people who lived long ago, sometimes dead children. Some *neak-ta* are directly associated with Hindu deities such as Ganesh and Durga, and Khmer (Cambodian) Buddhists include them in their prayers. Other Southeast Asian spirits are the Thai *phi*.

NECKLACE OF THE BRISINGS In Norse mythology, the goddess Freya is an aspect of a fertility triad. She is known for her lasciviousness, even giving sexual favors to four dwarfs in return for her primary symbol of fertility, the necklace of the Brisings. The necklace was stolen by the trickster Loki, for the furious high god Odin, who himself lusted after the beautiful goddess. Odin agreed to return the necklace to Freya only after she agreed to stir up war among humans.

NECTAR Nectar was the drink of the Greek gods. It accompanied their food, ambrosia.

NEHALENNIA Nehalennia was a Germanic and possibly continental Celtic sea goddess who protected voyagers.

NEITH One of the many forms of the Egyptian Great Goddess, known in the Delta as the "Mother of the Gods," Neith was said to have emerged from Nun, the primal waters, to have been a creatrix of gods and humans, and to have been sought out by the gods for important advice.

NEKHBET As Wadjet was the patron goddess of Lower Egypt, the vulture goddess Nekhbet was patroness of Upper Egypt. In images, her wings protected the Egyptian pharaohs.

NEMAIN Representing the madness of battle, the Irish goddess Nemain (Nemhain), one of several war goddesses, hovered over battlefields such as the one in the *Tain Bo Cuailnge*, bringing terror to the hearts of warriors.

NEMED Nemed (Nemhedh) was the leader of the Nemedians, the third people to invade Ireland. He settled in Ireland with four women and fathered the Nemedians with them. Although the Nemedians multiplied and developed Ireland, they were partially destroyed by plague and by wars with the Fomorians. After Nemed died, the Fomorians subjugated the Nemedians, and after many battles, they left Ireland, reduced to a troop of some thirty persons. According to some sources, some descendants of the Nemedians returned to Ireland as the Firbolg.

NEPHTHYS A figure in the great Egyptian resurrection myth of Osiris, Nephtys, with her husband Set (Set), her brother Osiris, and his sister-wife Isis, was born of Geb and Nut. In an adulterous relationship with Osiris she produced Anubis. She joined Isis in lamentations over Osiris when he was killed by Seth and participated with her sister in spells with which to revive the dead god.

NEPTUNE In Rome, Neptune was originally a water god, later seen as the equivalent of the Greek sea god Poseidon.

NEREUS AND THE NEREIDS A Greek sea divinity, born to Ocean (Pontus) and Gaia, Nereus lived at the bottom of the Aegean Sea. He had fifty daughters by his wife Doris. These

N

Nephthys and her sister Isis protect the winged scarab in King Tut's tomb

The centaur Nessus steals Deianeira, the wife of Herakles

were known as the Nereids, the most famous of whom was Thetis, the mother of Achilles.

NERTHUS According to the Roman historian Tacitus, Nerthus was the Earth Mother of the ancient Germanic people. She was revered in the countryside because of her power to bring fertility to the land. Nerthus's precinct was a sacred grove.

NESSUS Nessus was the centaur whose attempted rape of Deianeira and subsequent further treachery and death led to the death of Deianeira's husband, the Greek hero Herakles.

NESTOR The wise and elderly Nestor was king of Pylos in the Greek Peloponnesus. During the Trojan War he served as a counselor to his younger comrades, and after the war, in Pylos, he entertained Odysseus's son Telamachos, who, as described in the early books of Homer's *Odyssey*, was traveling about in search of his father.

NGANDJALA-NGANDJALA These are Australian Aboriginal tricksters. Essentially, they are comic troublemakers and pranksters who enjoy destroying things such as those created by the first beings during the dreaming time. In parts of Australia they are called Wurulu-Wurulu.

NIBELUNGENLIED The *Nibelungenlied* ("The Song of the Nibelungs") is a Middle High German heroic epic poem written between ca. 1191 and 1204. The term *Nibelungs* is applied at various times to the people, lands, and treasure of the Lower Rhine Germanic hero Siegfried (Sigurd in Norse mythology) and sometimes to the Worms-based Burgundian family of Siegfried's wife, Kriemhild. At the beginning of the poem Kriemhild lives under the protection of her brothers, Gunther, Cernot, and Giselher. After a dream, which her mother interprets as meaning her daughter will lose a nobleman close to her, Kriemhild vows to avoid such a situation by avoiding marriage.

Meanwhile, down the river, Siegfried, son of King Siegmund and Queen Sieglinde, travels to Worms to woo the beautiful Kriemhild. He is recognized by Gunther's vassal, Hagen, as the famous young hero who has won a huge trea-

sure by defeating the Nibelung king and hundreds of retainers, who had taken the Nibelung gold out of a cavern. After his victory, Siegfried demanded that the treasure be returned to the cavern. In the process of these adventures, the hero had obtained a cloak of invisibility and had slain a dragon. He had bathed in the dragon's blood, making himself invulnerable except for the spot on his body that a leaf had prevented the blood from touching.

Siegfried helps Kriemhild's brothers defeat the Saxons and agrees to help Gunther woo the powerful Brunhild of Iceland in return for his being allowed to marry Kriemhild. Gunther agrees to this arrangement, and using his cloak of invisibility, Siegfried accomplishes the three tasks set by Brunhild for any man who wishes to marry her. Brunhild marries Gunther, thinking it is he who has passed her test, and Siegfried marries Kriemhild.

But the suspicious Brunhild refuses the marriage bed to Gunther, tying him up in her girdle and hanging him from the ceiling, and demanding to know who Siegfried really is. Siegfried puts on the magic cloak and wrestles Brunhild for hours until she is finally subdued. She believes it is Gunther who has wrestled with her and allows the marriage to be consummated. In that act of consummation, she loses her supernatural strength.

During his wrestling with Brunhild, Siegfried has managed to steal the queen's girdle and ring, which he gives to Kriemhild as gifts. When Kriemhild and Brunhild argue over the relative importance of their husbands, Kriemhild shows her rival the ring and girdle as proof that Siegfried had slept with Brunhild before Gunther.

Although Siegfried apologizes for his wife's insult and beats her, Hagen is determined to avenge the insult for his king. He tricks Kriemhild into revealing Siegfried's one vulnerable spot and on a hunting trip kills him with a spear. King Siegmund comes to retrieve his son's body, and Kriemhild refuses to return to his kingdom with him. She remains with her brothers in Worms and Hagen gains control of the Niebelung treasure and throws it into the Rhine with the intention of retrieving it at an appropriate time.

Now missing Siegfried and her treasure and being displeased with Hagen and her family, Kriemhild, bent on revenge, agrees to marry King Etzel (Attila) the Hun. Kriemhild invites her brothers and Hagen to her castle in Hungary, and there a great battle ensues after she confronts them with their crimes. When Hagen refuses to return the treasure to her, she has Gunther's head cut off and then she herself cuts off Hagen's head. Kriemhild herself is killed and dismembered by her former ally, Dietrich of Bern, who is horrified by her treatment of Hagen and her brother.

NIGHT JOURNEY OF MUHAMMAD The myth of the Night Journey (*Isra*), the Journey to Jerusalem and Ascension (*Mi'raj*), is referred to in the *Qur'an* (17:1), where Allah is praised for bringing his Prophet from the Sacred Mosque (Mecca) to the Farthest Mosque (usually interpreted as the Al-Aqsa in Jerusalem, but for some it might refer to Allah's Heaven). This is a central myth in Islam. In tradition the story has developed from what was perhaps the reporting of a dream to a fully developed myth with several versions. It usually begins with Muhammad's rising from sleep and going during the night to the Ka'bah to worship. There he fell asleep, only to be awakened by Jibril (Gabriel) and two other angels who washed his heart with the waters of the ancient well Zamzam, thus instituting a ritual followed by Muslims and suggesting the idea of a heart cleansed of sin and idolatry. The winged

N

mule, al-Buraq, arrived and was told by Jibril to carry Muhammad on a journey. According to some, this animal possessed a human soul and had in ancient times carried Ibrahim (Abraham) to the Zamzam well to find Hajar (Hagar) and Ismail (Ishmael). As Jan Knappert suggests, the fact that Muhammad was permitted to ride on Buraq signifies that he was, in fact, continuing the mission of Ibrahim (1993, p. 163). Eventually Muhammad came to Jerusalem, where he prayed at the Temple-Mosque of the Rock as the de facto imam in front of Ibrahim, Musa, and Isa (Abraham, Moses, and Jesus), who thus recognized his supremacy among them and, in effect, trumped the events of the Transfiguration of Jesus in the New Testament. Presented with a glass of wine and a glass of milk, the Prophet chose the milk and was praised by Jibril for having chosen the "true religion." With Jibril Muhammad made the steep and difficult climb up the ladder (*mi'raj*) through the seven heavens, each with its own prophet, learning aspects of the future Islam on the way and finally reaching the place of divinity, where, according to some, Muhammad saw Allah, and according to others, he saw not Allah himself but signs of Allah. Many traditions are associated with the Night Journey. Most involve a series of symbolic events and side trips. It is said by some that, guided by Jibril, Muhammad flew on Buraq to Medina, where he was told to perform the prayers (*salat*) at the place where Islam would be established, and that Buraq took Muhammad on to Mount Sinai, where Musa had spoken with God, and to the birthplace of Isa. In most versions Muhammad passed through a series of symbolic visions representing the ignorance and sinfulness of humanity as well as the serene place of the faithful. A somewhat amusing anecdote in one version of the Night Journey tells how Allah ordered Muslims to pray fifty times a day and that when Muhammad reported this to Musa, he urged that Muhammad return to Allah to request a less demanding rule. This Muhammad did, and the number of daily praying times was reduced to five.

Another version of this incident says that Allah's order was for five praying times a day and that the Prophet rejected Musa's suggestion that he petition for fewer. There is a *mi'raj* story that tells of Musa weeping upon his realization that Muhammad had usurped his place in God's favor and that one day Muhammad's followers would outnumber his.

The ascent is a common world hero sign. It marks the lives of such religious heroes as Jela-ladin Rumi, and St. Augustine, or the character of Dante in the *Divine Comedy* and can serve, as the *mi'raj* story does for many Islamic mystics (Sufis), as a mystical metaphor for the individual's as well as the given community's ascent to wholeness or enlightenment. [Bowering, Watt]

NIHONGI Like the slightly earlier *Kojiki*, the *Nihongi* or *Nihonshoki* ("Chronicles of Japan"), published in 720 C.E., records the mythological "history" of Shinto Japan. The myths of the *Nihongi* are particularly influenced by Chinese thought, which was popular in Japan at the time, and several variants of particular myths are often given, some of them making use of actual Chinese myths.

NINGAL Ningal was the female aspect or wife of the Sumerian moon god, Nanna, in Ur. She was also the mother of the greatest of the goddesses, Inanna. In Ugaritic/Canaanite mythology she becomes the moon goddess Nikkal and is married to the moon god, Yarikh.

NINHURSAGA Ninhursaga (Belitili), with An, Enlil, and Enki, was one of the four principal deities of early Sumer. Known as "mistress of the foothills" and later "mistress of the gods," she represented fertility and birth. Ninhursaga was represented by the uterus of a cow, associating her with Neolithic cow goddesses important to agriculture and animal husbandry. Her sometimes husband Enlil was the source of fertility and abun-

N

The Dome of the Rock in Jerusalem, the place from which Muhammad ascended to the Heavens after his Night Journey from Mecca

dance as well as of storms, floods, and destruction. As Enlil's wife, she was the mother of the seasons.

In a myth sometimes called "Lugale," we get an explanation of one of Ninhursaga's attributive names. Ninurta (also Ningirsu), who in some places was the "first-born of Enlil" and son of Ninhursaga (of whom Ninlil, as a grain and birth goddess, could be a version), wages a preemptive war against his enemy Azag. Enlil sends a torrential downpour to defeat Azag, leaving Ninurta free to build a *hursag*, a natural dam (the foothills), and so to direct irrigation waters into the Tigris Valley. Ninurta-Ningirisu then honors his mother by renaming her Nin-hursaga ("Lady of the Foothills").

NINIGI Ninigi was first ruler of the Japanese islands and the grandson of the sun goddess Amaterasu.

NINLIL The Sumerian "Lady Air," Ninlil was known as Sud until her wedding with the god Enlil. She gave birth to the moon god Nanna and to the earth and agricultural god Ninurta.

NIOBE The daughter of Tantalus, Niobe had fourteen children by her husband, Amphion, King of Thebes and a son of Zeus. Amphion was a great musician, who played a lyre given to him by Hermes. His skill was so great that his music caused stones to form the wall surrounding Thebes. Niobe boasted of her children, suggesting that she be worshipped. She pointed out that Leto, who was worshipped, had only two children. This was an unwise boast, as Leto's children were the powerful Greek deities Apollo and Artemis, who killed all but one of Niobe's brood. In despair, Niobe then killed herself. Zeus turned her into a stone on Mount Sipylus in Lydia, and the stone wept in the summer months. Amphion, too, ended his own life after the slaughter of his children.

NIRVANA *Nirvana* is a Buddhist reworking of the Hindu ideal of *Moksha*, the liberation from the cycles of death and regeneration called *samsara*. It has become commonplace in the West to associate nirvana with some sort of afterlife, but, in fact, it is more an ideal or a state. Gautama Buddha achieved nirvana under the Bodhi Tree. Nirvana, then, is essentially enlightenment, but spiritual enlightenment or release in this world from the agony of the human condition. By overcoming the illusory powers of human desires, the individual can achieve nirvana, which means, literally, "no wind," or "extinction" of the sense of self, which is, in any case, illusion or delusion. For different sects of Buddhism, the paths to nirvana are different. For some it can be achieved through discipline and asceticism in this life. For others it is synonymous with immortality. For those who see *samsara* as life itself, nirvana is, in fact, sometimes "the farther shore" or almost a physical afterlife. For most Mahayana Buddhists, enlightenment is a way of living in this world, a state of mind. Thus the tradition of *bodhisattvas* developed, in which the nearly enlightened individual remains in this world to help others move toward nirvana. In this connection, there are several understandings of nirvana. There are Buddhists who see enlightenment as instantaneous, some who see it as a process taking eons, through various deaths and rebirths, and some who see it as something to be achieved gradually in this life. Among more esoteric Buddhists—especially in Tibet and Japan, ritual acts can relate the practitioner directly to the reality of the Buddha's enlightenment, so that the act of worship becomes a sacramental participation in the actual Buddha nature—perhaps a type of temporary mystical union. The Pure Land Buddhists, the Japanese followers of Amida Buddha, speak of the Pure Land or paradise—really a

The punishment of Niobe and her children by Apollo and Artemis

state of being—into which the believer must be reborn before enlightenment can be achieved. Such enlightenment can result in the individual's returning to this life as a teaching *bodhisattva*.

NITHAN KHUN BOROM This is a narrative that describes the origins of the Lao people of Laos. According to the story, an argument among the gods led to a life-destroying great flood that left only three giant gourds on the earth. When the gods (the *khun*) heard noises in the gourds, they broke them open and released animals of all kinds and a great number of people—black Kha people and light-skinned Tai Lao people. The *khun* tried to teach the people proper social arrangements, but the people were unruly, so the Phaya Then, the chief god, who was Indra, sent help in the person of his son Khun Borom, also called *Parama* (the "Lord"). Khun Borom landed in a rice paddy and began to organize the world. When a giant plant began to grow and cut off light from the world, an old man and woman who had come to the earth with Khun Borom volunteered to cut down the plant, but lost their lives in the process. These are the Lao ancestors, the Pu Ngoe Nga Ngoe, called Pu Thao Yoe (or Pu Yoe Ya Yoe), and Me Ya Ngam, who still participate in masked form in Laotian festivals.

Khun Borom had seven sons, and the territory was divided into seven areas that included parts of China, Vietnam, Thailand, Burma, and, of course, all of Laos (Lan Xang).

NJORD The father of Freyr and Freya, Njord and his family were of the old Vanir or fertility class of Norse gods, as opposed to the ruling Aesir. Njord is best known from the story of his marriage to the giantess Skadi.

Skadi was the daughter of Thiazi the giant, who, with the aid of the ever-duplicitous and self-serving Loki, kidnapped Idun, the keeper of the apples of youth precious to the gods. When Thiazi's plan was uncovered, however, the gods killed him, and his daughter approached Asgard intent on revenge. When Skadi arrived, the Aesir decided to suggest a truce. As Skadi did not have the pleasure of a husband, she announced that her price for peace was a husband and joy. She would pick a husband from among the Aesir, but she must also experience the gift of mirth. The gods agreed, but Odin applied one condition: Skadi would have to choose a mate according only to the beauty of his feet. Thinking that surely Balder, the most beautiful god, would have the most beautiful feet, Skadi agreed to Odin's condition. When the gods lined up behind a screen, with only their feet showing, the giantess chose the fine feet that turned out to belong not to Balder but to Njord, lord of the sea and its fruits. Skadi complained that she had been cheated, but it was too late, for the vow had been sworn and her choice made. Still, Skadi had not yet laughed, and she quickly reminded the gods of that part of the bargain. Odin called on Loki to make Skadi laugh. To accomplish his mission, Loki demonstrated an adventure he had had with a billy goat that morning. He took a thong and tied one end to the beard of a billy goat and the other end to his scrotum. He explained that this had been necessary, as his hands had been full and he needed to keep the goat on a leash as they walked to market. When Loki made a loud noise such as the one, he explained, that had startled the goat that morning, the present goat leaped forward, causing a tug-of-war between the goat's beard and the trickster's testicles. Finally, the goat lost his grip and fell violently into Loki, knocking him into Skadi's arms. This so

Nkongolo and other supernatural beings are channeled by Luba masks such as this one

amused the giantess that she burst into laughter and agreed to marry Skadi.

Although Skadi and Njord remained married, they went their separate ways after what might be called a trial period together.

NKONGOLO The cruel "Rainbow King" of central African mythology, Nkongolo not only committed incest with his sisters, but even tried to build a tower that would reestablish the connection between the earlier separated sky and earth. The tower, which Nkongolo hoped would restore immortality to humanity, collapsed and caused the death of many. Eventually the Rainbow King was decapitated by the army of the hero Kalala Ilunga and was buried in a termite mound, causing the ground to become red. His spirit lives on as the rainbow serpent in the sky.

NOMMO Among the Dogon people of Mali, Nommo was the creator spirit who emerged with a female twin and several more pairs of Nommos from the cosmic egg Amma.

NORN The Norse goddesses called Norns—Urd ("Fate"), Skuld ("Being"), and Verdandi ("Necessity")—were the Fates of Norse mythology. Probably members of the old fertility family, the Vanir, the Norns presumably lived near the "Well of Urd" at the base of the world tree, Yggdrasill.

NORSE FLOOD The first gods in Norse mythology killed the great frost giant Ymir and created the world out of him. The giant's spilled blood became a flood that drowned all of the frost giants with the exception of one Bergelmir and his wife, who escaped in a vessel made of a hollowed tree trunk.

A Viking stone in Sweden tells a Norse tale in runic letters

The similarity of elements of the Norse flood to those of the Sumerians, the Hebrews, and others suggests a common source, as does the familiar story of a dead primal god's body becoming an animistic world.

NORSE MYTHOLOGY Norse mythology is a term used to differentiate it from the larger body of Germanic mythology of which it is a part. The Norse people are often called Vikings. They were Swedes, Danes, and Norwegians who, between 780 and 1070, undertook wide-scale raids and, in many cases, colonization in what was, in effect, a second migration period for Germanic peoples. Vikings took much of the British Isles, found their way to Italy, Spain, and southern France and to Kiev, Constantinople, and Baghdad in the East and probably to pre-Columbian North America in the West. Most important, they colonized Iceland, where, in a somewhat isolated situation, their mythology developed and flourished well after most of Europe had become Christian. In fact, it was not until the year 1000 that the Icelandic Assembly voted to give up the old religion in favor of Christianity, and the old gods remained supreme in Sweden for longer than that. The eleventh-century German historian Adam of Bremen and many others reported eyewitness accounts of sacrifices to the Norse high god Odin at the great Temple in Uppsala as late as 1070.

Because of the persistence of Norse mythology, the Icelandic historian Snorri Sturluson (1179–1241) and the Danish historian Saxo Grammaticus (1150–1216)—two of our most important redactors of Norse mythology—were, there-fore, several centuries closer to their material than was, for instance, the author of the *Nibelungenlied* in Germany. Like the monkish collators of Irish mythology, Saxo, and especially Snorri, had a genuine desire to preserve knowledge of an ancient culture that, although relatively recent, was no longer a threat to contemporary beliefs. Saxo wrote in Latin but with real knowledge of the Norse sagas. His *Gesta Danorum* ("History of the Danes") corroborates much of the more extensive work of Snorri.

It is on Snorri that we depend most for our knowledge of Germanic or Norse mythology. His work was based on several sources. These included the *Codex Regius*, an ancient manuscript containing a collection of probably pre-Christian mythical poems of the Viking period called *Saemund's Edda* (*Edda*, in all likelihood, coming from a word meaning "poetry") after one Saemund Siugfusson, to whom they are traditionally attributed. These poems were not written down, however, until the late thirteenth century. A few other mythological poems were discovered soon after the *Codex Regius* and the whole collection is known more commonly as the *Elder Edda* or simply the *Poetic Edda*, within which the most famous poems and the ones most used by Snorri are *Voluspa* (the "Prophecy of the Seeress"), containing the great story of the beginning and end of the world; *Grimnismal*, in which the high god Odin speaks in the disguise as Grimnir (the "Hooded One"); and *Havamal*, in which is told the story of the self-hanging of Odin. Other poetic sources for Snorri and other later mythologists and historians are the highly alliterative skaldic poems (*skalds* were bards, the *filidh* of the North), known in literary circles for their extensive use of *kennings* ("namings"), compound metaphorical substitutions for the names of things (for example, "whale-road" for the sea or "Freya's tears" for gold). The skaldic form was common in Old English poetry as well as in the Old Norse. Snorri himself wrote skaldic poetry, as in *Hattatal*, a eulogy for two noblemen, and sagas based on the Icelandic sagas (the *Fornaldar Sogur*). Snorri's *Heimskringla*, compiled from poems and sagas, is a history of Norwegian kings from mythical time until 1177 and contains the *Ynglingasaga*, an important source for Norse mythology, tracing the pre-Norwegian Swedish kings and their mythological ancestors back to the god Odin.

By far, Snorri's most important work, however, is his *Edda*, or *Prose Edda*, as it is called to differentiate it from the *Poetic Edda*. Written in about 1220, his *Edda* was intended to be a handbook and guide to the old mythology for poets and scholars. The *Prose Edda* begins with an introduction called the *Gylfaginning* (the "Deluding of Gylfi"), in which a fictional Swedish king, Gylfi, disguised as a beggar called Gangleri, visits Asgard, the home of the gods, and questions the also-disguised Odin (Wotan in Germany) and two other mysterious figures about the ancient gods and mythological history. The second section of the *Prose Edda* is *Skaldskaparmal* ("Poetic Diction"), which supplies rules for traditional poetry and many myths as well. The final section is *Hat-tatal*.

More than any other European or Indo-European mythology, Germanic mythology of the Norse tradition is in tune with the ancient Indian sense of life—including that of the gods—as being part of a larger process of creation, preservation, and destruction. For many this is an essentially pessimistic mythology, reflecting the long dark days of the seemingly endless northern winters. Others might see it in the Indian way, as the natural history of birth, death, and rebirth in the cosmic context.

The mythological universe of the Norsemen, as depicted by the *Poetic Edda* and *Snorri's Edda*, was made up of three

N

levels divided by space. The top level was Asgard, where the Aesir, the race of warrior gods, led by Odin and Thor, lived. Here was the great hall Valhalla, where slain warriors fought, were killed heroically again but revived to feast on pork and mead. It was the Valkyries, Odin's maids, who summoned the warriors to Valhalla and who served them there. The warriors would fight in the great battle at the end of time. On this top level also lived the Vanir, the fertility gods who played the role of antagonists to the Aesir in one of the Norse versions of the Indo-European war in Heaven. Eventually the Aesir and the Vanir would unite into one pantheon. Light elves also lived on the top level of the universe, in Alfheim, and a place called Gimli housed the righteous dead. Midgard, the world of humans, was the middle level of the universe. This was a world surrounded by a vast ocean containing the World Serpent, Jormungand, who, according to Snorri, bit his own tail, thus forming a firm belt to hold the world together. The giants, the ultimate foes of the Aesir, lived either across the ocean or in another part of Midgard, a place called Jotunheim, protected by the fortress of the outer world, Utgard. Dwarfs and dark. elves lived in Nidavellir ("Dark Home") and Svartalfheim in the north.

The lowest level of the universe contained Niflheim, the home of the wicked dead—a place of utter darkness with a citadel called Hel, ruled over by a monstrous queen also named Hel, as the Greek Hades was a place ruled over by a god of the same name.

The axis of all three worlds was the great world tree, Yggdrasill—the cosmic ash with roots leading to Hel and to the worlds of humans and the frost giants. At the foot of the tree were various springs and/or wells, including Urd's Well, that of the Norns, and the well of Mimir ("Wisdom").

Using primarily the late-tenth-century eddaic poem the *Voluspa*, Snorri Sturlusson tells of a strange creation myth. In this myth, creation occurred between two entities that were already in existence—Muspell in the south and Niflheim in the north. Muspell was a place of fire where Black Surt, with his flaming sword, waited for his chance to destroy the world that would be created. Niflheim was a place of ice and snow, at the center of which was Hvergelmir, the spring from which the Elivagar, the eleven rivers, flowed. Between these two places was Ginnungagap, the great void into which the rivers poured, creating a desolate iciness in the north, which stood in contrast to equally desolate volcanic-like moltenness in the south. But in the middle of Ginnungagap, at the meeting of the two conflicting climates, was a mild area where melting ice became the evil frost giant Ymir. From under the left armpit of the sweating giant came a man and a woman. His legs came together to give birth to a family of frost giants. From the melting ice of the center a cow called Audumla was born, and Ymir drank the four rivers of milk that poured from her. Audumla licked the ice for three days until a man named Buri appeared. Buri's son Bor married Bestla, the daughter of the frost giant Bolthor, and Bestla gave birth to the gods Odin, Vili, and Ve. These gods killed Ymir and created the animistic world out of his body. His spilled blood was the source of the Norse flood.

Snorri tells us that there were twelve primary gods and thirteen goddesses under Odin, the "All Father," and his consort Frigg. Originally there had been two races of gods: warrior gods led by Odin and Thor called the Aesir, and fertility gods called the Vanir, the most famous of whom were Njord, Freyr, and the goddess Freya.

The Vanir, as deities of the fertile earth, were closer to humans than the sky gods of Asgard. Their concern was not social order or morality but the productivity of earth and its inhabitants. Goddesses and sexuality—even orgies—were important to ancient worshippers of the Vanir.

The Aesir were more to be feared. They were war gods and gods of social order, morality, and magic. The war between these two races of gods was as inevitable as other Indo-European wars between deities—for example, the Irish wars between the Tuatha and the Firbolg and the Tuatha and the Fomorians—and may be a distant metaphor for ancient clashes between pre–Indo-European peoples and their Indo-European warrior invaders. A later, more devastating war would be those between the giants and the gods at Ragnarok, the end of the world. Again, the Armageddon-like battles are fought in other Indo-European mythologies, as, for example, between the demons and gods of India, reflected in the human battle of the *Mahabharata*, and between the Titans and Olympians in ancient Greece.

The eventual truce between the Aesir and Vanir resulted in a valuable combination for gods and humans based on the attributes of both races. Specifically it gave rise to the powers of the imagination, or inspiration, something akin to the Vedic word power of ancient India, the poetic powers of the Celtic Amairgen and Taliesen, or the necessary ecstatic Dionysian and orderly Apollonian combination in the art of ancient Greece and perhaps all art.

A strange myth explains the powers that were born of the joining of Aesir and Vanir. To confirm their truce, the Aesir and Vanir spat into a pot, and out of the pot sprang Kvasir, the wisest of beings, who could answer any question. Soon Kvasir was made to play the role of sacrificial victim out of which new life would come. He was killed by two dwarfs, who mixed his blood with honey in two cauldrons. Kvas denotes an alcoholic beverage and, in keeping with the process of fermentation, the resulting liquid became a kind of soma-like mead, the drinking of which brought the magical fermentation we know as poetic imagination. But the mead was stolen by giants, as the Vedic *soma* had been stolen. In both ancient Indian and Norse myths the precious drink is recovered by the gods—in the Norse case by Odin—but some finds its way to human beings, giving them the godly power of imagination, or poetry.

The *Ynglinga Saga* tells another story of the truce between Vanir and Aesir. As was the Norse custom, the Vanir sent two hostages to the Aesir as a guarantee of peace. These were the gods Njord and Freyr. The Aesir sent the handsome Honir and the wise Mimir to the Vanir. Feeling that they had the worst of the exchange, the Vanir cut off Mimir's head and returned it to the Aesir, but Odin used his magic spells to make the head talk and to reveal many important secrets. Decapitation and talking heads figure also in Celtic mythology, as, for instance, in the case of the Welsh Bran, whose head went on talking long after his death.

Clearly the high god of the Norse world was Odin (Germanic Wodan, Wotan, Woden). Odin is the All Father, but not a loving one. From his place in the gods' home, Asgard, where he lives with his wife Frigg, he can see all there is to see in all the worlds of the universe. In his Zeus-like willingness to stir up trouble among those below him, he is closer to the trickster Loki than to his much-respected son Thor. In fact, shamanic qualities that associate him with the dead and with a magical knowledge of runes make him a trickster himself, as in a myth of his mysterious hanging on the world tree. Above all, Odin is a fierce god of battle.

The god Tyr, so important as the German Tiw (Tiwaz), part of the Wodan-Tiw-Thunr tripartite arrangement, plays

N

a relatively minor role in the north. He is a war god who also protects judicial assemblies and is concerned with oaths, particularly those associated with the Germanic tradition of trial by ordeal. One of the few existing myths of Tyr, known as the Binding of Fenrir, tells of a strange trial by ordeal of sorts in which the trickster Loki, the vicious wolf Fenrir, and Tyr play major roles. In this myth, Tyr, like the Irish Nuada in his battle with the Firbolg, sacrifices a hand.

Easily the most popular of the Norse gods was Thor, the northern version of the German Thunr. Thor is the god of sky and thunder, preserver of law and order in Midgard. As the son of the sky god Odin and the earth goddess Fyorgyn (Earth), he is also a god of fertility. Thor is dependable whereas Odin is unpredictable. Above all, he is steadfast in the struggle of the gods against the giants. He retains the Herculean characteristics the Romans had recognized in Thunr. Huge in size, with red beard and eyes, he has enormous appetites, and not much wit. He carries a great hammer and wears iron gloves and a girdle of power. Thor's wife is the fertility goddess Sif, whose beautiful wheat-like hair was once shaved off—that is, stolen—by Loki. His daughter is Thrud, whose name, appropriately, means "Might."

Of particular significance is Thor's hammer, Mjollnir. Flung through the sky it is a deadly weapon and is, of course, representative of lightning and thunder. Hammers representing Thor's fertile phallic power were traditionally placed in the laps of brides in Scandinavia. Such hammers were also used to hallow the newly born, perhaps to ensure fertile lives. Stories of Thor, such as one known as "Thor's Duel with Hrungnir," are among the most popular in Germanic mythology. In that myth Thor is the Indo-European giant-monster killer, the representative of good against evil, light against darkness.

The most important of the Norse fertility gods—the Vanir—belong to the family of Njord. Njord's children, Freyr and Freya, form a fertility triad with their father. Freyr, the great god who regulates the sun, the rain, the produce of the land, and human fertility, is depicted, logically, with a gigantic phallus. The feminine aspect of the fertility triad, Freya, is a goddess of both war and love, and is known for her lascivious ways, even giving sexual favors to four dwarfs in return for the necklace of the Brisings.

The highest ranking of the Norse goddesses is Frigg, the wife of Odin. Born of Fjorgyn, the earth goddess, Frigg knows human destiny and is the goddess of childbirth.

Central to many of the Norse myths is Loki, the shape-shifting trickster offspring of the giants, who is at once charming, mischievous, and evil. Nowhere is Loki's role more important than in the myth of the beautiful god Balder, son of Odin and Frigg.

With the death of Balder, Ragnarok, the end of the world, was inevitable. [Crossley-Holland, Davidson, Lindow, Page]

NORTHERN CAUCASUS MYTHOLOGY Before the rise of Islam, the people of the Caucasus—the Cherkess, the Abkhaz, the Ubyhk, the Georgians, and others—worshipped a supreme being. For many of these groups the god was divided into two aspects, one benevolent, one judgmental. The first was associated with the sky, the second with storms and with lightning, which was considered to be sacred. The Cherkess and the Abkhaz and others have a smith god linked to a sacred forge. The Blacksmith ensures fertility among women. There were also hunting gods, grain gods, and several culture heroes.

NUADA The king of the Tuatha Dé Danaan when they arrived in Ireland, Nuada lost his hand in the first battle of

Mag Tuired, against the Firbolg, and gave up his throne. He became known as "Nuada of the Silver Hand" when the medicine god Dian Cecht made him a silver replacement. Still later, Dian Cecht's son Miach made Nuada a real flesh-and-blood hand, and the former king regained the throne. He lost his life, however, in the second battle of Mag Tuired, against the Fomorians.

NUDD Nudd was a Welsh king who is a cognate of Lludd Eireint ("Ludd Silver Hand"), making him a likely equivalent of the Irish Nuada Airgedlamh (Nuada Silver Hand). This was Geoffrey of Monmouth's King Lud of Britain.

NUN In the Ogdoad pantheon of ancient Egypt, Nun is the male counterpart to Naunet. As the primeval ocean of chaos before creation, Nun, with Naunet, contained the possibility of creation and produced the primal mound on which the creator could materialize.

NUMMO TWINS The Nummos are an African version of the worldwide motif of the sacred twins. The Dogon people say that the Nummos are intermediaries between humans and the creator god, Amma. With the help of various other culture heroes, they participate in an ongoing creation. They are essentially fertility deities who, like many such culture hero figures, teach the people how to grow things.

NUT Born of Shu and Tefnut, the Egyptian sky goddess Nut was the consort of the earth god Geb. Shu, helped by the other gods of the Ogdoad, separated the ever-embracing couple so that creation could take place between them. Nut's children by Geb were the still more famous Osiris, Isis, Set, and Nephtys. Sometimes depicted as a cow, sometimes as a sow, the goddess was said to swallow the sun each evening.

NUWA Nuwa, or Nukua (Nugua), is the great Mother Goddess of Chinese mythology. The sister-wife of the August emperor-god Fuxi, she was a serpent figure, capable of changing shapes at will, who is said to have created the first humans out of yellow soil and mud, the yellow soil forming aristocrats, the mud the lower orders. It was Nuwa who defeated the Black Dragon, Gonggong, and repaired the sky after he had removed one of its support pillars.

NYAMBE The moon goddess of Ghana in Africa, Nyambe is also the primeval mother. Among the Ashanti, Nyambe is a sky deity who plays a role in the stories of the trickster Ananse.

NYIKANG Born of a crocodile by a male divinity, Nyikang was the ancestor and culture hero of the African Shilluck people of Sudan. Nyikang fought and defeated the sun himself and caused the Nile to part so that his people could cross the river.

NYMPHS Greek mythology tells many tales of nymphs—beautiful female demi-goddesses, often associated with water, who sometimes have human lovers. *Nereids* are sea nymphs; *naiads* are freshwater nymphs. There are also woodland nymphs known as *dryads*.

NYX Nyx ("Night") emerged from Chaos in the Greek creation myth as told by Hesiod. Nyx had intercourse with Erebos ("Under-world Darkness") and produced Air and Day. Nyx was the mother of Gaia and Ouranos.

OCEANIDS Daughters of the Titans Oceanus and Tethys in Greek mythology, the Oceanids were associated with the various bodies of water. They included, most famously, Poseidon's wife Amphitrite (sometimes thought to be a Nereid); Calypso, who for a while became the lover of Odysseus; and Zeus's first wife, Metis.

OCEANUS The Titan son of the original Greek deities Ouranos and Gaia, Oceanus was a personification of the river of ocean that surrounded the earth. His wife was Tethys, the mother of the Oceanids. One of their children was Styx, the spirit of the River Styx in the underworld.

ODIN Odin was the High God and "All Father" of Norse mythology. He was also a magician king, a mysterious shamanic god of runes. The strange self-sacrifice described in the *Havamal* depicts the shaman-trickster hanging on the world tree, Yggdrasill—literally Ygg's or Odin's horse—a kenning for the gallows:

> I know I hung
> on the windswept tree,
> through nine days and nights.
> I was stuck with a spear
> and given to Odin,
> myself given to myself.

In this hanging, Odin initiates rites of hanging and stabbing that were associated with his cult. The etymology of his name suggests divine inspiration, and he hangs on the tree to learn the runic mysteries guarded by Mimir's head at one of the wells at the base of Yggdrasill's roots. The *Voluspa* in the *Poetic Edda* tells how Odin sacrificed one of his eyes in return for a drink of the magical liquid of Mimir's well. Like the gigantic Balor in Irish mythology—Odin was descended from giants—his single eye had paralyzing power.

Odin is perhaps, above all, a terrifying god of battle, and he is god of the dead—a northern Dis Pater. He entertains brave fallen warriors at Valhalla (*Vaholl* = "Hall of the Slain"), and he inspires followers known as the *berserkir*—those who "go berserk" in battle, in the manner of other Indo-European warriors, such as the Indian Karna, the Greek Achilles, or the Irish Cuchulainn.

ODYSSEUS Although primarily known as the central figure of Homer's epic poem, the *Odyssey*, the Greek hero Odysseus (Ulysses) has a biography that extends beyond that work. Always known for his wiliness, Odysseus was a favorite of the wise goddess Athena. His parents were the king and queen of Ithaca, Laertes and Anticlea. As one of the Mycenaean-Greek suitors for the hand of Helen (later known as Helen of Troy), he wisely advised the woman's father, Tyndareus, to obtain an agreement from all of the suitors to abide by the family's eventual choice of a husband by signing an oath of allegiance to that man. So it was that after the Trojan prince Paris's abduction of Helen from the kingdom of her husband, Menelaus, the Greek heroes—including Odysseus—unified to make war on Troy. Meanwhile, Odysseus had married Tyndareus's niece, Penelope, who had produced a son, Telemachos. His responsibilities as a king, a husband, and a father at first led Odysseus to attempt to avoid the "draft" required by the alliance with Menelaus, but his pretended insanity was discovered, and, reluctantly, he left for the great war. During that war, as described in the *Iliad*, the *Odyssey*, and other works, Odysseus achieved greatness as a warrior and, primarily, as a strategist. His most famous act was the devising of the wooden horse full of Greek soldiers that the Trojans foolishly allowed into their city as a supposed Greek truce gift. It was this "gift" that led to the fall of Troy and allowed Odysseus to begin the ten-year voyage home that is described in the *Odyssey*.

Odysseus and the Sirens

Many stories were told about Odysseus after his return to Ithaca. One story held that to placate the god Poseidon, whom the hero had offended, he was forced to travel inland with a Poseidian trident until the trident was no longer recognized. In this way Odysseus became a missionary of the sea god.

ODYSSEY The second of the two great epics ascribed to the legendary Homer, the *Odyssey* describes the adventures of the Mycenaean-Greek hero Odysseus during a ten-year voyage home after the Trojan War, a war partly chronicled in the *Iliad*. Both epics were likely derived from earlier folk stories and legends and took something like their present form between 900 and 700 B.C.E. in the recitations and perhaps eventually the writing of bards (*rapsodes*) such as Homer. Much later, in sixth-century Athens, in what scholars call the Pisistraten Recension, the poems were edited and divided into "books" that perhaps reflected traditional recitation segments. The *Odyssey* as we know it, then, is an 11,300-line poem divided into twenty-four books.

OEDIPUS An ancient and tragic Greek hero associated closely with the city of Thebes, Oedipus is best known as the protagonist in *Oedipus Rex* and *Oedipus at Colonnus,* and as a remembered presence in *Antigone*, all plays by the fifth-century B.C.E. playwright Sophocles. The philosopher Aristotle

Oedipus answers the Sphinx's riddle

used *Oedipus Rex* as an example of the high art of tragedy. Many scholars have used the play to illustrate their theories about the mythic origins of tragedy. In the Greek myth, as essentially followed by Sophocles, Oedipus was born to Laius and Jocasta, the king and queen of Thebes. Having heard from an oracle that their child would kill his father, Laius had his newborn son abandoned on Mt. Cithaeron with his feet pierced and tied together. The child did not die, however; he was rescued by a shepherd, who handed him over to Polybus and Merope, the king and queen there. Polybus and Merope were childless and proceeded to raise the boy, now named Oedipus ("Swollen Feet"), as their own son. Years later, confused by comments by a stranger at a feast, Oedipus went to Delphi to consult the oracle there. The oracle told him he would kill his father and marry his mother. Horrified, and still believing Polybus and Merope to be his parents, Oedipus decided never to return to Corinth and headed toward Thebes. At a major crossroads between Delphi and Thebes he met up with and got into a fight with a stranger who insulted him. In the struggle Oedipus killed the man, who, unbeknownst to him, was his real father, King Laius of Thebes. Arriving at the outskirts of Thebes, Oedipus was confronted by a Sphinx who had been plaguing the city and defeated her by successfully answering her mysterious riddle. The Thebans hailed him as their savior and installed him on the now-vacant throne, arranging for him to marry the king's widow, Jocasta, who, of course, he did not realize was his own mother. Years passed, and Oedipus and Jocasta produced two sons, Eteocles and Polynices, who would later fight for control of the city, and two daughters, Esmene and Antigone. Antigone would later die in a struggle with Oedipus's successor, Creon, over his refusal to allow her to bury her brother.

In time a great plague threatened the very life of Thebes, and Oedipus sent his brother-in-law Creon to Delphi to seek understanding and help. Creon returned and informed the king that the oracle had said that the former king Laius's murderer was in the city and would have to be removed in order for the plague to end. It is here, at the beginning of Oedipus's inevitable march toward self-discovery, that Sophocles begins his play—his underlying plot, called the *mythos* by Aristotle. Within a day the Dionysian mythos of death and renewal is complete. The blind prophet Tiresias reluctantly reveals the truth of the situation, and Creon tries to be reasonable. Both are treated arrogantly with *hubris* (excessive pride) by the king. The shepherd who had originally saved Oedipus as a child appears and informs the city of the death of Polybus. Other elements of the real story become clear. Jocasta hangs herself and Oedipus blinds himself. The scapegoat cleansing is nearly complete. Life can return to Thebes. Creon becomes king and Oedipus will be exiled. Later he will die at Colonnus, blind and guided by his daughter Antigone.

OGDOAD In Egyptian mythology, the pantheon of the center at Hermopolis was known as the Ogdoad ("The Eight") and was made up of four couples representing primordial chaotic forces. Amun (Amon) and Amaunet were forces of the invisible, Huh (Heh) and Hauhet (Hehet) were forces of infinity, Kuk (Kek) and Kauhet (Keket) were forces of darkness, and Nun and Naunet were the primal waters.

OGETSU-NO-HIME The animistic source of food staples in Japan, the goddess Ogetsu once gave the god Susanowo food taken from her various orifices. This so angered the

"Impetuous Male" that he killed the food goddess. From her dead body's orifices came rice, wheat, soy beans, red beans, and millet.

OGMA Ogma (Oghma) was the Irish god of literature and eloquence. Like the Greek Hermes, he directed souls to the otherworld. He was the father of Etain, who married the medicine god Dian Cecht. Ogma was said to have invented Ogham (Ogma), the earliest Irish script. Among continental Celts he was Ogmios and was identified with Herakles; in England he was Ogmia.

OISIN The Irish warrior-hero Oisin—Ossian or Oshin in other parts of the British Isles—was the son of Fionn Mac Cumhail and the goddess Sadb. A stalwart member of the warrior society, the Fianna or Fenians, he lived for three hundred years in the other-world with the goddess Niamh. The collection of stories of the Fenians, known as the *Fenian cycle*, is also called the *Ossianic cycle*. The stories were popularized under the title *Ossian* at the beginning of the Romantic period by the Scot James MacPherson.

OKUNINUSHI This *kami*, a Japanese Shinto spirit-god, was the son of the sun goddess Amaterasu's brother Susanowo. He ruled Izumo until the arrival of Amaterasu's grandson Ninigi, who became the ruler of what would become the islands of Japan.

OLWEN In the Welsh epic the *Mabinogion*, Olwen is the daughter of the giant Ysbaddaden. She married the hero Culhwch after he successfully passed the tests set before him by her father.

OLYMPIANS The primary gods of ancient Greece—usually called the Olympians because they congregated on Mount Olympus—were the children and grandchildren of the Titans Kronos and Rhea, Sky and Earth. Although usually referred to as twelve in number, there were really fourteen Olympians, unless we discount the relatively late addition of Dionysos, the demotion of Hestia, and the designation of Hades as one of the *chthomioi*, the deities of the depths of the earth. The Olympians were sky gods, *ouranioi*—gods of the heavens, although they moved easily between the sky and the world of humans. In fact, the Olympians were heavenly representations of aristocratic families such as would have been found at places like Mycenae or Thebes. They got together from time to time for counsel of entertainment around the "high table" of Zeus above the clouds in Olympus (Olympus), but they had their own favorite homes around Greece. They were a rich and powerful family consisting of a philandering patriarch, many servants—some kidnapped—a jealous wife, and spoiled sons and daughters, who, like their parents, affected the lives of lesser beings and demanded tribute and adulation.

It was Kronos and Rhea who produced the older generation of Olympians—three sons and three daughters. These were the usurping king god Zeus of the thunderbolt and sky; Poseidon, lord of the sea; Hera, the consort of Zeus; Hades, lord of the underworld; the generally earth-based Demeter; and the little-discussed Hestia. Zeus and Hera were the parents of Hephaistos, the smith god, and Ares, the war god. Through a relationship with Leto, Zeus fathered the oracular and artistic Apollo and the virginal huntress Artemis. His relationship with Metis resulted in the warlike but wise and

also virginal Athene. Maia was the mother of the messenger and sometimes trickster Hermes by Zeus, and some believed that the goddess of love Aphrodite was not born of the "foam" resulting from the castrated Kronos but as a result of the relationship between Zeus and Dione. As for the last of the Olympians, the mysterious Dionysos, who also had *chthonioi* characteristics, was born of a liaison between Zeus and poor Semele.

OLYMPUS The snow-capped mountain between Macedonia and Thessaly in Greece, Olympus was the home of Zeus and his family of gods, known as the Olympians.

OM The Vedic Upanishads tell us that the syllable *om* (*aum*) is the "primary sound . . . the one indestructible thing (*aksara*)." Recited as a mantra, for example, at the beginning and end of prayers—something approximating the Christian "amen" but much more important—it is a sound that expresses the divine. The *Katha Upanisad* says that meditation on *om* can bring one to union with the absolute—that is, with Brahman. In a sense, *om* is Brahman and the cosmos itself. In keeping with this idea, the *Mandukya Upanisad* breaks the syllable into its contacted components, *a*, *u*, and *m*, and relates *a* to being awake, *u* to dreaming, *m* to a sleep without dream, and the whole *aum*, or *om*, to the *turiya* state—that which is Brahman. The same Upanisad speaks of the use of the *om* in meditation, the sacred syllable being the bow, the *atman*, or self, being the arrow, and Brahman being the target. Eventually the *om*, as the sound of the contraction of *a*, *u*, and *m*, was related to the *trimurti* of Brahma—*a* as creating—Vishnu—*u* as sustaining—and Shiva—*m* as dissolving.

OMAM Omam was the creator of the Yanomami people in South America. To create the people, he had intercourse with a fish woman he caught in a river. To have intercourse with her, he had to create her genital parts, as she had none.

OMETEOTL In the Aztec creation myth of Mesoamerica, Ometeotl ("Two God") was the first god. Ometeotl existed in two aspects—one male, Ometecuhtli, and one female, Omecihuatl, or Tonacatecuhtli and Tonacacihuatl. The male and female aspects of this self-created deity parented the solar deities known as the "Four Tezcatlipocas": blue Huitzilopochtli, white Quetzalcoatl, black Tezcatlipoca, and red Xipe-Totec.

ONTOLOGICAL MYTHS Ontology is the branch of philosophy concerned with being. An ontological myth is one that explores the nature of existence, of ultimate reality. It might be argued that all religious stories, or myths, are ontological in that they are archetypal records of ontological assumptions. This is a topic that particularly concerns the religious scholar Mirce Eliade, especially in connection with the eternal return.

OPHIS In Gnostic mythology, Ophis was the serpent who came to earth to seek Christ's help in order to convince humans to disobey Jehovah by eating the forbidden fruit so as to gain knowledge—*gnosis*.

ORESTEIA In 458 B.C.E. at the Festival of Dionysos in Athens, the *Oresteia*, by the playwright Aeschylus, won first prize. The *Oresteia* is a trilogy of tragic plays that includes *Agamemnon*, the *Choephoroe* ("Libation Bearers"), and the

O

The Constellation of Orion from Johann Bayer's *Uranometria*

Eumenides ("Kindly Ones"). Mythologically, the play is concerned with the story of the doomed House of Atreus from the sacrifice of Iphigenia and the return of Agamemnon from Troy to the trial of Agamemnon's son Orestes at Athens, in which Athena and Apollo settle certain issues concerned with justice and taboos.

In the opening of *Agamemnon*, we learn that Agamemnon is about to return home from Troy. The chorus discusses the war and remembers the events surrounding Iphigenia's sacrifice. Agamemnon arrives with the Trojan princess Cassandra as an unwilling concubine. After she predicts the horrors that are about to take place, Cassandra and Agamemnon are slaughtered by Agamemnon's wife, Clytemnestra, who claims revenge for Iphigenia's murder. It turns out that Aegisthos, a party in an ancient feud that pits him against Agamemnon, has participated in the murder and has been the queen's lover in her husband's absence. The chorus reminds the guilty couple that Agamemnon's and Clytemnestra's son Orestes is still alive.

In the *Libation Bearers*, Orestes in fact returns to his family's place at Argos, where Aegisthos and Clytemnestra have ruled for the ten years since Agamemnon's murder. He meets up with his sister Elektra and announces that, as ordered by Apollo, he is intent on avenging his father's murder. Orestes, encouraged by Electra, accomplishes his mission, killing Aegisthos and, more important, his own mother.

The stage is thus set for the third play, the *Eumenides*, in which the Furies (originally the Erinyes, only later renamed the Eumenides) chase Orestes—a man guilty of

matricide—from Delphi as he travels to Athens to appeal to Athena for protection. The Furies demand punishment for the matricide, Orestes claims to have been ordered by Apollo to commit the act as revenge for his mother's murder of his father. Athena determines that a trial must take place on the Areopagus hill. As the Furies question and accuse Orestes at the trial, Apollo steps in as his defender, claiming the patriarchal rights of the king and father over those of the queen and mother and thus claiming that Clytemnestra's crime is much worse than Orestes', thus justifying the latter. The Athenians as jury vote in equal numbers for Orestes and the Furies, but Athena takes Orestes' side, declares him free, and announces that from then on justice in Athens will stem from Aereopagite Court rather than from the vengefulness of the Furies. After hearing the Furies rant against her and against Athens for the court's decision, Athena convinces them to become more kindly earth deities and to submit to the new reason-based rather than blood feud–based law of Athens.

ORESTES The brother of Elektra and the son of Clytemnestra and King Agamemnon of the cursed House of Atreus, Orestes, urged on by his sister, avenges the murder of his father. His actions are best described by the Greek playwright Aeschylus in the *Orestei*.

ORIGIN MYTHS Mythologists sometimes differentiate origin myths from full-scale creation myths, or cosmogonies. Whereas creation myths tell how the *world* came into being, origin myths tell how things *in* the created world came into being. These myths can be a simple as how the leopard got its spots or as complex as how human beings or particular elements of culture emerged. Often origin myths involve the work of a culture hero or trickster, as opposed to that of the original creator deity. More often than not, creation myths proper include origin myth aspects. See, for example, Central Asian mythology, Indonesian and Malaysian mythology, and Tibetan mythology.

ORION The giant hunter Orion was the son of the Greek god Poseidon and a daughter of Minos and Pasiphae of Crete. After killing marauding beasts of the island of Chios he so offended the island's king by raping his daughter Mereope that the king, with the help of Dionysos, had the giant blinded. But with the help of Hephaistos and the sun god Helios, he regained his sight and had a relationship with Helios's sister, the dawn goddess Eos. At Delos, Orion became the hunting companion of Artemis. There are various stories of Orion's tragic death. Homer (*Odyssey* V) believed that Artemis killed Orion because of his relationship with Eos. Other traditions hold that he was killed by Artemis because he acted violently toward her. Others say that Apollo, afraid that his sister was falling in love with the giant, tricked her into shooting one of her arrows into an object in the sea, which turned out to be Orion's head. Still others say that the primal earth goddess, Gaia, sent a giant scorpion to kill him. Whatever the circumstances of his death, the gods placed him in the heavens as the constellation Orion, which is appropriately near the constellation Scorpio, named for the threatening scorpion.

ORPHEUS Son of King Oeagrus of Thrace and the epic poetry muse Calliope, Orpheus was the greatest of human musicians. He was given a lyre by the Greek god Apollo, and was trained by the Muses. All of nature delighted in his music. He traveled with Jason on the voyage of the Argonauts and even managed to overcome the Sirens with his music. Orpheus married the nymph Eurydice, who died soon after from a snake bite. Overcome by grief, Orpheus descended to the underworld in an attempt to retrieve her. With his beautiful music he charmed Hades and Persephone, the king and queen there, and it was arranged that Eurydice could follow her husband home if he refrained from looking back at her until after passing through the underworld gates. Unfortunately, at the very last moment, Orpheus did look back, and his wife once more faded away. From then on, Orpheus played music of lamentation and refused the advances of the women of Thrace until several of them became so angry at him that they dismembered him in a Bacchanal frenzy. Orpheus's head and lyre found their way to Lesbos, where it is said that they still make music.

ORPHISM In Greece, Orphism, named after its traditional founder, Orpheus, was more a philosophy than a religion, stressing a movement in the world from cosmic order, represented mythologically by an original primordial egg, to a gradually developing disorder. The possibility of reintegration is represented by an Orphic version of Dionysos, a god who is dismembered and eaten by Titans as a baby, only to be returned to life under the care of Persephone and/or Demeter. It should be noted that Orpheus, after being dismembered by Thracian women, was said by some to have continued providing music from his head and lyre. There is a strong and clear connection, as the historian Herodotus recognized, between the Dionysos-Persephone/Demeter relationship and the story of the resurrection god, Osiris, and his sister-wife, Isis, in Egypt. This connection pointed to a Hellenistic tendency to fuse Greek gods with those of the many religious traditions in the empires of Alexander and Rome. The possibility of regeneration and rebirth that the "savior" Dionysos-Osiris represents is, of course, an important path to the story of Jesus as a resurrected dying man-god, a story that would eventually give new life to the ancient Indo-European theme of the necessary sacrifice and so turn the older "religion" of Greece into "mythology."

OSIRIS AND ISIS The dominant myth in Egypt for more than three thousand years was that of the god Osiris and his sister-wife, Isis. Of all the Egyptian deities these two were the ones most closely associated with the world of human beings. As a victim and dying god, Osiris shared the human experience of mortality. This fact made him a mythological brother, as it were, of other Middle Eastern dying gods, including Dumuzi, Adonis, Attis, Dionysos, Telipinu, and, of course, Jesus. It was through Osiris and these others that humans in various cultures hoped to join the universal process of nature that involved afterlife or rebirth after apparent death. So it was that Osiris was associated with the Nile and its annual revival of the land through the death that was the flood. And it was Osiris

Osiris and Isis and their enemy Seth

237

Orpheus and his lost Euridice

retrieve the pieces of the body—all, according to Plutarch, but the penis, the symbol of fertility itself, which was eaten by a fish, another symbol of fertility.

After retrieving the pieces of her husband's body, Isis, helped by her sister (Seth's wife) Nephtys and, according to some, Anubis, repaired the body as the first Egyptian mummy and, through various spells, managed to revive it sufficiently for Isis to fly over it as a bird and to conceive Horus, presumably from the seed of the erect phallus that sprung plant-like from the dead king. Isis gave birth to Horus in the Delta and hid him away until such time as he would be ready to avenge her husband's murder. Meanwhile, Osiris descended to the underworld, where he would remain in a passive state until such time as his son could avenge his murder. In a sense Osiris was resurrected in his form as the grain god. It was said that Isis "planted" symbols of her husband's missing phallus in many burial shrines all over Egypt, thus spreading his cult and ensuring the fertility of the land.

OTHER WORLD The Other World, as opposed to the underworld of other cultures, is in Slavic cultures not so much a land of the dead as a mysterious, enchanted, and fabulously wealthy land that is literally "out of this world." It is usually beneath the earth or beneath the sea. Heroes in their quests find it by way of mountains or caves. It is a land sometimes blocked by monstrous guardians at the gate.

OTHERWORLD In the Irish and Welsh Celtic traditions, the otherworld is a land of the gods and one where rebirth takes place. During the Feast of Samhain (October 31/ November 1) the otherworld opened, and souls of people who had been offended in life could emerge and wreak their vengeance. Obviously this feast, in relation to the later Christian feasts of All Saints and All Souls, is at the basis of some of what we today celebrate as Halloween.

In Irish and Welsh mythology the other-world can also sometimes resemble the Slavic Other World as a land of fantastic pleasures where heroes can travel to and sometimes stay for a lengthy time. It can also be the goal of dangerous heroic quests. Thus King Arthur and his followers are said to have gone to the otherworld, called Annwn, to steal the King of Annwn's magic cauldron.

OURANOS Ouranos (Uranos, Uranus) was the first of the Greek supreme deities, a personification of the sky. He coupled with the First Mother, Gaia, a personification of earth. With Gaia he produces the Titans and the Cyclops and other terrifying creatures. Hating his offspring, he forced them back into Gaia until she was about to burst. Gaia became so upset that she gave her son Kronos a sickle with which to castrate his father and thus separate sky from earth, allowing for more creation.

OVID The Roman poet Publius Ovidius Naso (43 B.C.E.– 17 C.E.), better known to the world simply as Ovid, rewrote stories of Greek and Roman mythology and collected them in what became, in effect, an epic, entitled the *Metamorphoses*, composed of some 250 tales in fifteen books, tracing classical "history" from the creation to the apotheosis of Julius Caesar. This is a work that stresses the instability of life. In an earlier work, the *Heroides*, Ovid delighted his readers with dramatic monologues as love letters written between such mythological lovers as Hero and Leander and Paris and Helen.

whose revival was reflected in the grain rising from the earth. This was the god of all kinds of fertility.

Significantly, Osiris was the first pharaoh—a king in this world in a mythological Golden Age. As such he was more of a material being, more tangible than the other gods. He was an example of god become man. As the ruler at the world's beginning, Osiris gave human society—that is to say, Egypt—law and civilization. The Golden Age came to an end when Osiris's brother Seth introduced death by killing his brother and depriving the world for a time of his potency and fertility. There are many versions of the manner in which this primordial murder was accomplished. Some say that Seth became a flea whose bite poisoned Osiris. Others say Seth threw his brother into the sea. A more common story, told much later by the Greek writer Plutarch (c. 46–120 C.E.), tells how Seth tricked Osiris into lying in a special coffin, after which he and his cohorts closed the lid and flung the coffin into the water. The coffin floated to the shore of Byblos in Phoenicia, where a tree formed around it, tying the god-hero once again to other Middle Eastern figures associated in one way or another with trees. Adonis, Attis, Dionysos, and Jesus were all, in one way or another, imprisoned in or on trees.

The tree of Osiris, a symbol of renewed potency to come, was particularly sweet smelling and grew very large—perhaps like the *linga* of Shiva or the fruit tree that emerged from Dionysos' loins. It pleased the king of the region, who had it cut down for use as a column in his new palace. The column, with a herm-like erection protruding from it, was one of many symbols of Osiris. The column attracted the attention of Isis, who had traveled the world in search of her beloved husband.

It is at this point that Isis emerges as a principal figure, taking her place among the great goddesses of Egypt. Isis managed to obtain the column containing the coffin from the king, and she removed her husband's body and returned with it to Egypt. Although Isis attempted to hide her husband's body in Egypt, Seth found it and cut it into many pieces before flinging it into the Nile. Isis managed to

PABUJI EPIC This is an epic of Rajasthan in northern India. The hero is Pabuji, who is the son of a king and a nymph. His mother dies but returns to earth as a beautiful mare who is given to her son by an incarnation of the goddess (Devi). Pabuji is eventually killed in a war with a rival prince, but his son, whose mother takes him from her womb before ascending the funeral pyre in the self-sacrificial act of *sati*, lives to avenge his death.

PACARIQTAMBO In the emergence creation story of the Incas, Pacariqtambo was the place of emergence near Cuzco in Peru, from the three caves of which the original three brothers, including the Inca founder, Manco Capac, and three sisters entered this world.

PACHACAMAC In Incan mythology Pachacamac is usually thought to be one of the brothers of the Inca founder, Manco Capac, "the Inca." In other, pre-Incan stories he was the supreme creator deity and a god of prophecy, who was later given equal status to the sun god Inti. For the Incas, Pachacamac was a culture hero who created the first people—a man and a woman—out of clay. Unfortunately, he forgot to give his creations food and the man died. The angry woman cursed Pachacamac, so he made her give birth to a son, whom he killed and cut up into pieces that became fruits and vegetables. A second son, Wichama, escaped Pachacamac, and the angry god killed the woman, causing the even more angry Wichama to chase him into the sea.

Some traditions hold that Pachacamac created man and woman out of clay and then sent his son and daughter, born of the dragon goddess Mamapacha (Pachamama), to teach the people how to survive. In this version, "the Inca" was his son and the daughter was his son's queen. Although they lived at Lake Titicaca the Inca and his wife traveled at the command of Pachamac, marking the spots of their travels with a golden rod he gave them. These were the spots where Incan cities were built. In the valley of Huanacauri the rod disappeared into the earth, and this is where the Incas built their sun temple at the center of what would become their capital, Cuzco.

PADMASAMBHAVA A holy man, sometimes called the "Second Buddha," who is said to have introduced Buddhism to Tibet in 762 C.E., Padmasambhava possessed spiritual powers that gave birth to many myths about him. He is said to have been born as an eight-year-old from a lotus flower, to have overpowered and converted demons, and to have lived to be more than one thousand years old.

PAH Pah was a moon god of the Pawnee Indians of Native North America. He was sent by the great spirit Tirawa to the western sky, from which each night he rises to provide dim light.

PAHLAVI TEXTS The Zoroastrian sacred book, the *Avesta*, was translated into the Middle Iranian or Pahlavi language from the no-longer-understood older Avestan language beginning in about 250 C.E. These translations are known as the Pahlavi texts.

PALAMEDES It was the Nauplian prince Palamedes who tricked the Odysseus into admitting that he was not insane when the Greek hero of Homer's *Odyssey* attempted to evade the Trojan War "draft" by pretending to be so. Odysseus never forgave Palamedes for this insult and later accused him of spying for the Trojans, an accusation that led to Palamedes' execution.

PALE FOX The culture hero of the Dogon people of Mali, in Africa, was the trickster sometimes called Pale Fox. He stole seeds from the creator, Amma, and planted them in his mother, Earth. Because of this incestuous act, the land

The Temple of Pachacamac near Cuzco, Peru

Pan playing his pipes

lost its fertility, a problem overcome by Amma, who gave the people other seeds so that they could begin practicing proper agriculture.

PALI A form of ancient Indian non-Sanskrit or vernacular Prakrit, Pali was the language of the original southern Indian Buddhist scriptures. The terms "Pali text" and "Pali canon" refer to these ancient works of Hinayana and Theravada Buddhism.

PAN The Greek woodland and shepherd god whom the Romans identified with their gods Faunus and Silvanus, Pan was a son of Hermes. He was depicted with a goat's horns and feet and sometimes a goat's hindquarters. Pan had lecherous sexual qualities and loved frolicking and dancing with nymphs. He made noises that caused panic in woodland travelers. He also loved playing on the syrinx, or shepherd's "Pan pipes," into which a favorite nymph was changed when he chased her. According to some, Pan was the father of the ithyphallic Priapus by Aphrodite, although usually that role is assigned to Dionysos, who, especially in his Roman form as Bacchus, is sometimes associated with Pan.

PANCARATRA The name for an early sect devoted to the Hindu god Vishnu, the Pancaratra is best known for texts known as the *Samhitas*. The *Samhitas* are concerned, among other things, with creation in stages, the highest of which is pure, emanating from Vasudeva, the union of Vishnu and his *Shakti* as the goddess (Devi) in the form of Lakshmi. It is Lakshmi who gives form or realization to Vishnu's qualities in creation.

PANCATANTRA Also known as the *Fables of Bidpai*, the *Pancatantra* ("five books") is the *Grimm's Fairy Tales* and *Aesop's Fables* of India, a collection of Sanskrit tales written down between about 100 B.C.E. and 500 C.E., attributed to Vishnusaram. The stories are meant both to teach moral lessons and to entertain.

PANDAVAS The five Pandava brothers are the heroes of the Indian epic the *Mahabharata*. They fight the great battle against their cousins the Kauravas. All five brothers are married to Draupadi. Although Pandu is officially the father of the Pandavas, their parentage is said to be the result of the unions between mortal women and gods. Pandu's wife, Kunti, is the mother of the most important of the five brothers. She produces the Pandava leader Yudhishthira by Dharma, the *Bhagavadgita* hero Arjuna by Indra, and the great warrior Bhima by Vayu. The fathers of these heroes are personifications of characteristics associated with their sons. Yudhishthira, as king, is driven by a sense of *dharma* or ideal social order; Arjuna, the spiritual "king" especially close to Krishna, is represented by the ancient king of the gods; Bhima is, above all, a warrior, as is his father, the wind. The lesser Pandavas, Nakula and Sahadeva are the offspring of Pandu's second wife, Madri, and the twin gods called the Ashvins, the divine physicians.

PANDORA Angry at the theft of fire for humans by the Titan Prometheus, the high god Zeus decided to get revenge not only against Prometheus but against humans. For this purpose he asked the smith god Hephaistos, from whose forge the fire had been stolen, to fashion a woman out of clay. Athena brought this first woman—the Eve of Greek mythology—to life, Aphrodite gave her beauty, and the trickster Hermes taught her cunning. The gods named her "Pandora ("all-gifted") and gave her as a gift to Prometheus's brother Epimetheus, who accepted her even though Prometheus had warned him against accepting any gifts from the Olympians. Hesiod tells how the gods gave Pandora a box to take with her when she came with her husband into the world of humans and how, curious to know what was in the box, she opened it, releasing all of the evils that from then on have plagued humanity: work, conflict, disease, and others. Only Hope remained in the box.

Pandora and Epimetheus were the parents of Pyrrha, who, with her husband Deucalion, survived the great flood that Zeus sent to destroy humankind.

PANGU In Chinese mythology, Pangu (P'anku) the giant, the offspring of Yin and Yang and the cosmic egg and the separator of earth and sky, was the first living creature in the creation myth; his body became the animistic source of the world itself.

PANIS The Indian philosopher Aurobindo Ghose considered the myth of Panis to be the most significant of Hindu myths, one that reveals the true mystery of the sacred texts, the *Vedas*. The Panis ("misers") were an Indian race of demons, sometimes considered to represent the cattle-raiding indigenous Dravidians, who fought the invading Aryans for riches. The *Brhaddevata* and the ancient *Rig Veda* contain the story of how the Panis stole Indra's cows. Indra sent the female dog Sarama ("intuition") to bring them back, but the Panis seduced her with the milk of the cows, and when she returned to Indra, she denied that she had found his animals. Indra became so angry that he kicked Samara, who vomited up the milk. Indra followed her back to the Panis, killed them, and took back his cows. In Sanskrit the word *go* can mean "cow" or refer to illumination. When Indra retrieves the cows, guided by Sarama (intuition), he frees true illumination.

PAPA AND RANGI Papa was the earth goddess and Rangi the sky god, the mother and father of the Maori people of the Polynesian world. Earth and Sky embraced tightly, leaving no room for creation between them, so the war god Tu argued for killing his parents, but his brother Tane, the forest god, succeeded in separating them instead.

PARADE OF ANTS The Hindu *Brahmavaivarta Purana* contains a story that reveals a post-Vedic view of the ancient king of the gods, Indra, now surpassed in importance by other gods. According to the story, Indra commanded the divine architect Vishvakarman to build for him an appropriately splendid palace. As Visvarkarman worked, Indra kept demanding more and more until, in despair, the architect approached the creator Brahma to complain, and Brahma approached the still higher power Vishnu for advice. Vishnu agreed that something must be done to dampen Indra's delusory pride. One morning a brahman boy appeared before the king of gods and blessed him. Indra asked him why he had come. The boy replied that he had heard of Indra's great palace and wondered how long it would take to complete. He pointed out that no other Indra had ever succeeded in building such a place. Surprised, Indra asked how many Indras there could possibly have been. The boy then spoke to Indra as to a child, revealing himself as an ancient being who knew both Brahma and Vishnu and who had witnessed many endings and creations of the universe. When twenty-eight Indras have come and gone, said the boy, only one day and night of Brahma has passed. At this point, a parade of ants four yards wide appeared in an endless column. Each ant, said the boy, was at one time an Indra. Those Indras who pursue vain desires will become as ants. Indra thus learned a lesson about the law of *karman* and achieved humility.

PARADISE MYTHS Paradise myths exist in many religious and mythological systems in different parts of the world. Paradises are often, but not necessarily, seen as places where humans go for a blessed afterlife. The Elysian Fields is a paradise for dead Greek heroes, as is Valhalla for the Norse. But the earliest known paradise myth is that of the Sumerians, who spoke in cuneiform tablets of a place called Dilmun, a place where sickness, violence, and aging are unknown. But it seems to have been a home for the gods rather than for humans. Once Dilmun was provided with water by Utu and Enki, it became a beautiful garden. Less physical, more philosophical paradises such as the Japanese Pure Land of Pure Land Buddhism exist, but since Sumerian times, the primary image of paradise has been that of the garden, as in, for instance, the Garden of Eden, where Adam and Eve were placed by God in the tradition of the Abrahamic religions. These paradises are usually settings for a golden age at the beginning of creation rather than settings for an afterlife. Golden age paradises such as that of the Hindu age or yuga known as the *krtayuga*, or Hesiod's age when humans resembled gods, are marked by qualities that humans all long for: opulence, fertility, pleasure, freedom, peace, and full communication among all species.

Such paradises can, of course, be corrupted by invading forces such as Satan in the Genesis myth. The theme of the spoiling of a paradise that existed at the beginning of creation exists in African, Native North American, and other mythologies. Often the cause of the movement from the golden age of paradise to the world as we know it is the result of a trickster's act or the emergence of human pride or greed.

PARIS Paris (Alexander) was the son of King Priam and Queen Hecuba of Troy. As a child he was abandoned on Mount Ida because Hecuba dreamed that he would cause the destruction of Troy. But a bear suckled him, and a shepherd raised him, and he survived. Then, on a fateful day, Paris attended the wedding of Peleus and the Nereid Thetis, the future parents of the hero Achilles. The gods attended, too—all but one, Eris ("Strife"), who was not invited. Eris became so angry that she vowed to cause difficulties. She threw a golden apple into the crowd of wedding guests and marked it "for the fairest," knowing that this would cause strife. Hera, Aphrodite, and Athena each claimed to be the rightful recipient of the apple. So it was that Zeus placed Paris in the impossible position of deciding between these three powerful goddesses. Promised wisdom by Athena if he chose her, power by Hera if he chose her, Paris chose Aphrodite, who had promised him the most beautiful woman in the world. Athena and Hera thus became his enemies.

The most beautiful woman in the world was Helen, the wife of King Menelaus of Sparta. During a visit to Sparta, Helen and Paris became lovers and Paris took his conquest off to Troy. It was these events that led to the Trojan War. During the war, Aphrodite saved Paris from defeat in sin-

Pandora tempted by the "Box"

241

The most beautiful? Paris deciding between Hera, Athena, and Aphrodite

gle combat with Menelaus. It was Paris who killed Achilles by shooting him in his vulnerable heel. Paris died from a wound inflicted by a poison arrow that had once belonged to Herakles. It was shot by the famous archer Philoctetes.

PARSIS Zoroastrians in western India are called Parsis ("Persians"). According to Parsi tradition contained in the *Kisseh-e-Sanjan* ("Sanjan's Story"), a four hundred–line Persian verse narrative of 1600 written by the Parsi priest Bahman, the Parsis fled Muslim persecution in Iran, spent one hundred years hiding in the mountains, and then sailed to India. Parsis are known especially for the central place of fire in their worship. A continuous fire burns in the *agiari* or fire temple and mantras, magical formulae, are offered up to the fire as prayers to the divine presence. Also important are *dakhmas*, or "towers of silence," where the bodies of the dead are placed to be consumed by vultures.

PARTHOLON Partholon led one of the early invasions of Ireland in Irish mythology. Hoping to inherit their kingdom, he murdered his father and mother. Soon after he arrived in Ireland he went off to fight the Fomorians, who already inhabited the island. While he was away, his wife, Dealgnaid, had an affair with a household servant, Togda. Partholon blamed himself for leaving his wife alone. The Partholonians supposedly introduced agriculture to Ireland, but they all died of a plague.

PARVATI Perhaps the most popular form of the Hindu Great Goddess (Devi), Parvati ("Daughter of the Mountain") is one of several aspects of the Goddess as Shiva's wife. Others are Sati, Uma, Durga, and Kali. Parvati is depicted as a beautiful woman who characteristically sits in an embrace with her husband, signifying her position as his *Shakti*, his ener-

gizing power. Parvati is the mother of Ganapati, also known as Ganesh.

PASIPHAE Minos of Crete proclaimed himself king, thus becoming the source for the term "Minoan" for "Cretan" and justified his action by boasting that he was favored by the gods and would be given whatever he prayed for. After dedicating an altar to Poseidon, he asked that a bull come to him from the sea to serve as a sacrifice to the god. But when a beautiful white bull burst forth from the depths he so admired it that he placed it among his own herds and substituted an inferior bull for the sacrifice.

But the gods do not appreciate or ignore such duplicity. Poseidon caused Minos's wife Pasiphae, the daughter of Helios, to lust after the white bull. She became so desperate for it that she confided her passion to the master craftsman Daedalus, who lived on the island of Knossos and carved beautiful life-like dolls for the royal family of Crete. To help the queen, Daedalus carved a hollow wooden cow and placed it in the field where the great bull was grazing. Pasiphae slipped into the false cow, thrusting her legs into the cow's hollow hind legs and placing herself, back first, against an opening left under the cow's tail. The white bull soon mounted the cow and gave Pasiphae the pleasure she desired. He also impregnated her with the Minotaur, a monstrous combination of a bull's head with a human's body.

As the monster had to be kept somewhere, Daedalus created the famous Minotaur lair, the Labyrinth, which would play so important a role in the story of the Greek hero Theseus.

PASSOVER According to the Hebrew story of Moses in the Book of Exodus, when the Egyptian pharaoh refused to let the Hebrews leave his land, Yahweh, through Moses, sent a series of plagues to Egypt, always sparing the Hebrews. Finally, when the pharaoh still refused to release the Hebrews, Yahweh instructed the Hebrew families to mark their doorposts with the blood of a slaughtered lamb, to stay inside, and to eat a ceremonial meal—a *seder*—while he or his Angel of Death passed over Egypt, avoiding the marked Hebrew houses but bringing death to the oldest male child in each Egyptian house. These events are the source for the Jewish Feast of the Passover.

PATOLLO Patollo was the first member of the Baltic version of the Indo-European triad, one somewhat resembling the king-priest god, warrior god-thunder god, fertility god triad represented by the Norse Odin-Thor-Freyr. The Baltic triad was made up of Patollo (Pecullus, Pikoulis), Perkuno, and Potrimpo. Patollo was depicted as an old man with a great green beard and was associated with the skulls of humans and, in keeping with the most ancient of Indo-European traditions, cows and horses. Patollo was the Odin of the Baltics and also was, like the Celtic Dis Pater, a god of the dead. Later, in his more folkloric Christianized status as Pecullus, he became the Devil. A possible Lithuanian version of this high god is Velinus, like the Norse Odin, a terrifying one-eyed deity associated with hanging. He is also, like the Greek Hades, a kidnapper of maidens, but he sometimes favors the poor and downtrodden. For Baltic Christians Velinus was also sometimes associated with the Devil.

PATRAKLOS Patraklos (Patraclus) as a young man committed a murder, for which he was sent away from his home to the land of Peleus. There he became a close friend of Peleus's son, Achilles. Some say he and the great hero were lovers. In any case, he went with his friend to the Trojan War, where he was killed. It was his death that led Achilles back to battle in spite of his feud with the Greek leader Agamemnon.

PATRICK, SAINT Tradition has it that Saint Patrick arrived in Ireland in 432 C.E. to begin his conversion of the Irish to Christianity. Many myths are told in connection with Patrick. According to one such myth the infant Patrick was brought to the blind Gornias to be baptized, but no water was available until Gornias used the child's hand to make the sign of the cross over the dry ground. Immediately water sprung up and Gornias was cured of his blindness and given the power to speak the baptizing formulae. Another myth tells of Patrick's arrival. As Amairgen and the Milesians had arrived in Ireland on the Feast of Beltene in ancient times to proclaim a Celtic Ireland, Patrick arrived at the Feast of Beltene to claim the land for his dying and risen man-god, Jesus. Beltene refers to "bright fire" and druidic rites including purifying fires at Beltene. It is said that when Patrick arrived at Tara he set a huge bonfire, thus undermining the druidic tradition. As divine Tuatha Dé Danaan powers had overcome the Firbolg and Fomorians, and Amairgen's creation poetry had supplanted Tuatha magic, the spiritual fire of the Christian "Holy Spirit," the source of this new invader's "magic," would conquer the soul of Celtic Ireland.

PAUAHTUN A sometimes underworld god in Mayan mythology, this lecherous figure had four distinct aspects, representing the four directions. Each of these aspects held up a corner of the sky.

PEGASUS Fathered by Poseidon, this winged horse sprang out of his mother, the Gorgon Medusa, when the Greek hero Perseus cut off her head. Pegasus was tamed by the hero Bellerophon, who flew on the horse to kill the monstrous Chimera.

PELASGIAN CREATION In the beginning, according to the archaic pre-Greek Pelasgians, the Great Goddess Eurynome emerged from the void and had nothing to dance upon but the sea, which she separated from the sky. When she danced facing the south, her movement created the north wind, which she rubbed in her hands to form the great serpent Ophion. As she continued to dance, with increasing vitality, the serpent became aroused and mated with his creatrix. So it is that mares are said to become pregnant without the aid of a stallion, simply by turning their hindquarters to the north wind.

Eurynome became a dove and eventually she laid the primal cosmic egg of creation. She commanded Ophion to coil seven times around the egg to cause it to hatch. This he did, and all creation sprang forth—the sun, the moon, the mountains, the rivers—all of Eurynome's children.

The first couple moved to Mount Olympus, but Ophion resented his wife's claiming to be the creator of all things and became threatening. Eurynome would have none of this and, after bruising his head with her heel and kicking out his teeth, exiled him to the depths below earth's surface.

The goddess now created the Titans and Titanesses and the first man, Pelasgus, the source of the Pelasgians, who came from the dark earth of Arcadia and who taught his followers how to survive in the world. [Graves (1955)]

PELE A Polynesian fire and volcano goddess, particularly popular in the folklore of Hawaii to this day, Pele, a descen-

St. Patrick bans snakes from Ireland

243

Peleus seizes Thetis

dant of the earth and sky gods Papa and Rangi, was rivaled for power by her older sisters, the goddesses of the sea and the snow-capped mountains, both of whom challenged the power of her fury. Her favorite sister was Hiiaka', who had hatched from an egg kept warm by Pele under her arm on their long voyage from outer islands to the Big Island in Hawaii. There the sisters lived relatively free of external threats in the great fiery crater of Kilauea, high above the threatening sea. One day, as the two sisters were resting together, Pele heard the sound of drum beats and dancing in her dream and allowed her spirit to leave her body and to follow the sound to Kaui. There she came upon wonderful dancing and proceeded to disguise herself as a beautiful young woman participant. Before long she had attracted the attention of a handsome chief named Lohiau, and in time they became lovers.

Eventually, however, the time came for Pele to return to her sleeping body next to her sister on the Big Island; otherwise the fires of her volcano would have died out. But the lovers began to miss each other, so Pele sent her brother Lono to Hiiaka' to ask her to fetch Lohiau for her. After great difficulty with monsters and other impediments, Hiiaka' came to Kaui and succeeded in reviving Lohiau, who had died in the meantime. Stories differ as to what happened next. Some say that Pele became impatient, assuming that Lohiau and Hiiaka' were themselves having an affair and that she turned her fire on them. According to this version of the story, Hiiaka' and Lohiau ended up as a couple in spite of Pele 's anger.

PELEUS Peleus was one of the participants on the voyage of Jason and the Argonauts. He was married to the Nereid Thetis. Together they produced the hero Achilles. After his death Peleus was given immortality with his wife under the sea.

PELOPS The unfortunate Pelops was the son of the cursed Tantalus and thus the grandson of the Greek high god, Zeus. Tantalus had once dismembered his son and had him boiled up as a feast for the gods. The gods did not appreciate the feast and, after Demeter had eaten Pelops's shoulder, had the boy restored to wholeness, his shoulder replaced with an ivory one.

Having been exiled from his home in Phrygia, Pelops made his way to Elis, where he became a suitor for the hand of King Oenomaus's daughter Hippodamia. As the king had been warned by an oracle that his son-in-law would kill him, he devised what he thought was an impossible test. Any prospective suitor would have to defeat him in a chariot race or be killed. As Oenomaus had horses given to him by the gods, he had no fear of losing.

Pelops, however, devised a plan. He promised the king's charioteer, Myrtilus, a night with Hippodamia if he would throw the race. The charioteer accepted this proposal and sabotaged the king's chariot, causing a wreck in which Oenomaus died. But Pelops refused to live up to his end of the agreement and instead threw Myrtilus into the sea. As the man was drowning, he cursed Pelops and his descendants. Pelops's children were Atreus and Thyestes. Atreus was the father of Menelaus and the doomed Agamemnon. So it was that Myrtilus's curse can be said to have been the source of the horrors that surrounded the House of Atreus.

PENELOPE The wife of Odysseus, the Greek hero of Homer's *Odyssey*, and the mother of Telemachos, Penelope is the personification of wifely fidelity. During the twenty years of her husband's absence she resisted the attempts of a group of unwelcome visitors in her palace to marry her. One of her means of evading what seemed to be an inevitable fate was to promise to decide on one of her suitors after she finished weaving a garment for her father-in-law, Laertes. Each night she would unravel some of her work so as never to complete it and so never have to decide on a suitor. If Odysseus committed infidelities on his voyage, Penelope decidedly did not during her long years of waiting, years that ended with her husband's return and his killing of the suitors.

PENTHESILEA Penthesilea was the queen of the Amazons, whose army supported Troy during the Trojan War. She was the daughter of the Greek god Ares and the Amazon queen, Otrere.

PENTHEUS A king of Thebes made famous by the Greek playwright Euripides in his play, the *Bacchae*, Pentheus was the son of Echion and Agave and the grandson of Cadmus. He was dismembered by his mother and other followers of Dionysos (Bacchus) in a frenzied state after he attempted to prevent the worship of the god in Thebes.

PERCIVAL The best-known versions of the story of this virgin knight of King Arthur's Round Table are Chrétien de Troyes' late-twelfth-century *Perceval, ou le conte du Graal* and Sir Thomas Malory's fifteenth-century *Morte d'Arthur*. *Per* means "bowl" in Brythonic Celtic, and Percival-Parsifal-Parzifal is always a hero who searches for the Holy Grail. Percival arrived at Arthur's court unmannered and untutored in the ways of the courtly life. Once at the court, he behaves in a bumbling sort of way, but is trained as a knight. There are many versions of the story of Percival's quest for the Grail. In one of the most famous, he acts out the role of the hero who refuses the call. In this version, he

P

arrives at the castle of the Fisher King, who is languishing under a terrible spell with a seemingly incurable wound. For the king to be cured of his wound and his land to be freed of infertility, the questor must ask certain significant questions. But Percival, out of politeness or naiveté, fails to ask any questions about the Grail when, at a feast, it passes by him in procession. As a result of this failure, the king and his land remain under the terrible spell. But in other versions of the tale it is Percival's essential innocence and the guidance of a young maiden relative that make it possible for him to see the Holy Grail.

PEREDUR A Welsh version of Percival (Parsifal, Parzival), Peredur is the hero of the medieval tale "Peredur, Son of Efrawg," included in the *Mabinogion*.

PERIBORIWA In a South American Yanomami creation myth, Periboriwa is a moon deity whose spilled blood was the animistic source of the appropriately warlike Yanomami.

PERKUNO Perkuno was the second aspect of the original Baltic-Indo-European triad, somewhat resembling the king-priest god, warrior god–thunder god, fertility god triad represented by the Norse Odin-Thor-Freyr. The triad was made up of Patollo (Pecullus, Pikoulis), Perkuno, and Potrimpo. Perkuno—Perkunas in Lithuania, Piorun in Poland, and Perkons in Latvia—was depicted as a fully mature god with a black beard and eyes of fire. He is essentially synonymous with the Slavic Perun. A perpetual fire was apparently kept alive in connection with his worship. As his name indicates, Perkuno ("Thunder") was the thunder god, who, like his Norse relative Thor, seems to have been more popular than the nominal head god; and his cult survived the coming of Christianity, especially in times of drought, when farmers would sacrifice animals to the god as a source of fertility, drink beer in his honor, and dance around a bonfire in hopes of stimulating rain.

Perkuno, as the god of cleansing rain, was also the god of justice and moral order. So it was that he killed Jurate, goddess of the sea, because of her sexual involvement with a mortal, and broke the face of the moon god Menuo into what became the phases of the moon as a punishment for that god's desire for, and in some stories kidnapping of, Ausrine (Dawn or the planet Venus, also known as Auseklis), the daughter of Saule, the sun goddess. There is one story that suggests that the attack on Menuo (Meness) is in support of the thunder god's own affair with Ausrine. Perkuno in some places is seen as a smith god who molds the world into existence.

PERSEUS Born of the mortal Danae by Zeus, Perseus grew up to be one of the greatest of the Greek heroes. Perseus's biography begins with a miraculous conception. To prevent her from ever giving birth, King Acrisius of Argos had his daughter locked in a tower after an oracle warned him that his grandson would kill him one day. Zeus, however, had his eye on the young woman, penetrated the tower as a shower of gold, and impregnated her with the child that would be Perseus. When Acrisius discovered the child, he placed mother and child in box and abandoned them to the sea. Rescued by the fisherman Dictys, Perseus and Danae were protected by Dictys's brother, Polydectes, the king of Seriphos. In order to rid himself of Perseus, who supported his mother in her refusal of the king's relentless courting, Polydectes sent the young hero off on an apparently sure-to-fail quest to kill

the monstrous Gorgon Medusa and to return with her head. Meanwhile, he locked up Danae in a tower.

With the help of Hermes and Athena, Perseus found the three Graeae, the sisters of the Gorgons, and he took their one eye and one tooth until they agreed to tell him the way to the nymphs who could give him three magic objects he needed to accomplish his quest. These were the winged sandals, a leather sack, and a helmet (the "Helmet of Hades"; some say it was a cloak) that could render him invisible. In addition, Hermes gave the hero a magic sickle and Athena gave him a mirror or a shining shield. With the sandals he flew to the place where the Gorgons live. There he had to be careful not to look at Medusa since looking at her turned the looker into stone. He used the mirror-shield to view his victim as he cut off her head with the sickle and quickly put it into the leather bag. Then he used the cap of invisibility to evade the pursuing Gorgon sisters.

On the way back to Seriphos, Perseus had many heroic adventures, including turning the suffering Atlas into a stone mountain using the Gorgon head, and saving the beautiful Andromeda from a dragon and marrying her. On his return to Seriphos, he used the Medusa head to turn the king and his court into stone, freed his mother, and gave the head to Athena to place on her warrior's breastplate.

After Perseus, with Danae and Andromeda, returned to Argos, Acrisius fled, fearing the old oracle about his grandson. Perseus fulfilled that oracle by accidentally killing his grandfather with a discus during some public games in Larissa. Because of this accidental act, which he, nevertheless, thought of as regicide, Perseus refused the throne of Argos but became the highly successful king of nearby Tiryns.

PERUN The name of Perun, the popular thunder god of Slavic mythology, is etymologically associated with thunder as well as to the oak tree, a tree sacred to so many Indo-

Perseus rescues Andromeda

245

Aristotle and Plato, philosophical myth makers

European gods. Perun (Piorun, meaning "thunder" in Poland) is clearly related to the Baltic Perkuno (Perkunus). He seems to have been for many Slavs the most important god, as Thor was to many Germanic peoples and Perkuno was to many Balts. His animals are the bull and the goat—representing power and fertility. He carries an ax and arrows symbolizing thunder and lightning. In the Russian tradition, Perun, like the Indian gods Shiva and Indra, is a monster slayer who releases the waters of fertility. Sacrifices were made to Perun, and a sacramental communal meal following the sacrifice would blend well into the later arrival of the Christian tradition of Holy Communion.

PHAEDRE The older daughter of King Minos and Queen Pasiphae of Crete, Phaedre succeeded her sister Ariadne in the affections of the Greek hero Theseus and became his wife. Because Phaedre's stepson Hippolytus, the son of Theseus and Hippolyta or Antiope, admired the huntress Artemis over the love goddess Aphrodite, Aphrodite caused Phaedre to fall in love with her stepson. Repulsed by Hippolytus, Phaedre accused him of attempting to seduce her. This accusation led Theseus to curse his innocent son and caused the youth's death.

PHAETON Phaeton was the rash son of the Greek sun god, Helios. Helios foolishly gave in to his son's request to drive his chariot across the sky for a day. Too weak to control the massive horses of the sun, Phaeton lost control of the chariot and it hurled out of control so close to the earth that the world would have been destroyed by fire had Zeus not killed Phaeton and restored order.

PHI The *phi* are spirits in Thailand (Siam) and Laos who are known for their magical power and for their effect on everyday life. They resemble the *nats* of Burma and the *neak-ta* of Cambodia. The *phi* are, above all, associated with the land and the soil and are a link between Buddhism and pre-Buddhist animism in Thailand. There is a hierarchy of *phi* and a cult associated with them.

PHILISTINE MYTHOLOGY The Philistines came to Palestine from the Aegean region—perhaps from Crete, some time early in the twelfth century B.C.E. These warlike people were almost certainly the "Sea Peoples" who invaded Egypt and other parts of the Middle East during that period, some of whom settled in Philistia in the southern part of Palestine, a land that got its name from the Greek name for the Philistines, the *Palastinoi*. The Philistines fought the Israelites in Canaan and were defeated by King David in 950 B.C.E. Little is known of Philistine mythology. Most of their pantheon seems to have been adopted from earlier Canaanites. The chief god appears to have been Dagon as a war god. Other deities were Baalzebub, clearly related to Baal, and Ashtoret, a common form of the many-faceted Canaanite great goddess of fertility. The Philistines apparently worshipped Yahweh and several Egyptian deities as well.

PHILOSOPHICAL MYTHS An important kind of myth, at least since Plato's time, has been the metaphorical tale used to explain realities that are beyond simple logic. These "philosophical myths" differ radically from most other myths, because they are constructs of individuals rather than of collective entities such as cultures, nations, movements, and the species.

Various philosophical myths have been created to explain God, for instance. One of the most important in terms of influence on later theology is that of Aristotle. When considering Nature, Aristotle sees an orderly system motivated and directed by a substance beyond Nature—a supreme "unmoved mover"—in other words, God. Everything in Nature tries to imitate God. Aristotle's view of God did much to make Europe a fertile ground for the planting there of the later Christian concept of God.

A myth developed by the Russian mystic and philosopher Vladimir Soloviev depicts God as Ultimate Reality in gradual union with creation by way of the relationship between the Logos—the Word, or essence of active creation—and Sophia, feminine and passive divine wisdom and bride of the Christ as the Logos. Another philosophical myth of God is the eighteenth-century deistic one that saw the unmoved mover as a kind of clockmaker, who built the clock (the world) at the creation, wound it up, and left it to run on its own. This was the essentially nonpersonal God of many of the great thinkers of the Age of Reason whom we describe as deists (as opposed to theists). It was a vision that greatly affected the thinking of many of the European-bred founding fathers of the United States and perhaps contributed to the separation of Church and State that has been so important for the American social and political experience.

It could be argued that the "thought experiments" of physics are philosophical myths. There is, for instance, Einstein's space-traveling "relativity twin paradox" thought experiment. In that experiment there were two twins. One went on a round trip into outer space. When he got back home he was younger than his brother, because his heart, brain, and blood flow "clocks" had slowed down during the trip. This is because time has a material or "length" aspect. The space twin was surprised on his return to discover how much older his brother was.

It is not surprising that a science fiction writer such as Madeleine L'Engle should seize upon such narratives for the much-loved young adult series that includes *A Wrinkle in Time*, *A Wind in the Door*, *A Swiftly Tilting Planet*, and *Many Waters*, in the second of which the setting for an exciting struggle for survival is the cellular world of the human bloodstream. In so doing she is following in the path of other writers and artists who have used older mythologies as the starting point or basis for their works. The Christian story is in the background of the famous *Narnia* books by C. S. Lewis, and Norse, Finnish, and Christian mythologies clearly influenced the work of J. R. R. Tolkien.

Among the most famous of the philosophical myths is that of Plato's Cave. In the sixth book of the *Republic*, Plato suggests that we imagine some men who have lived since childhood in a place underground that can only be reached by way of a tunnel-like passage that eventually opens to the light. Since the men are chained by the neck, they can only see what lies in front of them. Above and behind them is a fire that creates light, and between them and the fire there is a track with a wall below it. The wall serves to hide people behind it, much as puppeteers are hidden in a puppet show. These people move objects that appear on the track above them. The objects are representations of animals, inanimate figures, humans, and so forth. The prisoners cannot see the fire, the wall, or the track. They can only see the shadows on the wall in front of them caused by the objects and the firelight behind them. When the people behind the wall give voices to the models they move, the prisoners hear only the echoes of those voices. Plato says that the condition of the prisoners represents our own position in relation to the light outside the cave. Like us, they are separated from the source of being and are doomed to see only shadows of being until such time as they can achieve enlightenment.

PHINEUS A Greek king in Thrace, Phineas had his two sons blinded after they were falsely accused of attempted incest with their stepmother. For this act, Zeus blinded Phineas, and until he was rescued by two of the Argonauts, he was plagued by the Harpies.

PHLEGETHON Phlegethon was a river of fire in the Greek underworld.

PHOENICIAN MYTHOLOGY "Phoenician" is a term used by some scholars interchangeably with "Canaanite" and by others to differentiate Iron Age from Bronze Age Canaanites. The Phoenicians lived in the coastal area that is modern Lebanon. They invented the alphabet in about 1500 b.c.e., not long before the Mycenaeans in Greece overpowered the old Minoan civilization of Crete. The Phoenicians established colonies and trade connections throughout the Mediterranean world. What we think of as Canaanite mythology is essentially that of the Phoenicians. Dominant among the Phoenicians was the dying-god myth so prevalent among the agricultural people of the Middle East, especially the myth of Adonis. The many goddesses of the other Canaanites play significant roles in Phoenician mythology as well.

PHOENIX A symbol of resurrection for Christians and others, the phoenix was an Egyptian bird that always lived to be 500 years old before burning itself in a sacrificial fire. Out of the ashes of that fire sprang a new, young phoenix.

PLEIADES Virgin huntress followers of the Greek goddess Artemis, these seven daughters of the Titan Atlas prayed for deliverance when they were pursued by the giant Orion.

Zeus answered their prayers by turning them into an astral constellation.

PLUTO Pluto ("Wealth-giver") was the Roman equivalent of the Greek underworld god Hades.

POETIC EDDA The Icelandic historian and mythologist Snorri Sturluson, the author of the *Prose Edda*, based his important collection of Norse mythology on several sources. The first was the *Codex Regius*, an ancient manuscript containing a collection of probably pre-Christian mythical poems of the Viking period. This collection is sometimes called *Sae-mund's Edda* (*Edda*, in all likelihood, coming from a word meaning "poetry") after one Sae-mund Siugfusson, to whom they are traditionally attributed. The poems were committed to writing in the late thirteenth century. The *Codex Regius*, when added to a few other mythological poems discovered after, is known more commonly as the *Elder Edda* or simply the *Poetic Edda*. The major sections of the *Poetic Edda*—that is, the ones most used by Snorri—are *Voluspa* (the "Prophecy of the Seeress"), in which the myths of the beginning and end of the world are told; *Grimnismal*, the vehicle for the words of Odin in his disguise as the "hooded one" (Grimnir); and *Havamal*, containing the famous myth of Odin's self-hanging.

POLYBUS Polybus was the king of Corinth who, with his wife, Merope, adopted the abandoned child Oedipus.

POLYNESIAN MYTHOLOGY Forming, with the Melanesian and Micronesian traditions what is sometimes referred to as Oceanic mythology, Polynesian mythology is that of the New Zealand Maori, the various peoples of eastern Polynesia, including Raiatea, Tahiti, and the indigenous people of the Hawaiian Islands. Legend has it that the Maori people came to New Zealand in a fleet of canoes from some Polynesian island. Like other Polynesians, their mythology is animistic, full of spirits (*atua*) who punish people for committing taboos (*tapu*). Behind everything that is, is the life force (*mauri*). For the Maori and others, the creator was Io, the "World Soul," who spoke light out of the primordial darkness and then chanted the sky, the oceans, and the earth. The people of Tahiti believe that life came from a primordial egg, Ta'aroa (Tangaroa), that split in half. This myth emphasized the dualities common to Polynesian mythology: Sky and Earth, Night and Day, Light and Darkness. Another myth says that Heaven (Sky) and Earth—the primordial gods Papa and Rangi—clung together so tightly that their offspring were in darkness. Among these offspring was Tu, later to become the god of war. He wanted simply to kill the primordial parents. The wind and storm god Tawhiri (Tawhirima-tea) wanted to leave things as they were. But Tane, the forest and birds god, and his other siblings wanted to separate their parents so that light and creation could materialize between them. Various of the offspring tried to push the first parents apart but failed. Finally, Tane-Mahuta placed his head against Papa-Earth and his feet against Rangi-Sky and pushed his parents apart, revealing a huge multitude of human-being children of Rangi and Papa. And now there was light. But the angry Tawhiri undermined the new creation, tearing things up in a rage. Finally, after a great war among the gods—Haumia, god of wild plants, Tangaroa (Ta'aroa, the primordial egg among the Tahitians), god of the sea, Rango, god of cultivated plants, and, of course, Tu—brought about peace, using all of his brothers as food for the people. The only brother he could not subdue was the storm god, who continues to plague the Maori and other Polynesians to this day. Other Polynesians say that Tane conquered Tu, created the first woman, Hine, out of earth and then made love with her, and the result of this act of incest was the release of Death into the world—because when Hine realized that Tane was also her father, she fled to the underworld, became Hine-nui-te-po, the queen there, and attracted people to her realm.

In Hawaii, several gods have special importance. Pele, the volcano goddess, is particularly present in the mythology, as are other personifications of natural phenomena. The Polynesian culture hero is Maui, a trickster figure whose sexuality and genital-based nature are emphasized by the eastern Polynesians. For Hawaiians he is mostly simply a god who, like most tricksters, is free of moral restraint. According to one Polynesian story, Maui fished up the island of New Zealand. [Grimal]

POLYNICES A son of the Greek tragic hero Oedipus and his wife-mother, Jocasta, Polynices inherited the crown of Thebes with his brother Eteocles. When Eteocles, in alliance with the interim king, Creon, seized the throne for himself, Polynices, allied with the "Seven Against Thebes," attacked Eteocles. The two brothers killed each other in combat and, once again, Creon became king. In this role, he decreed that Polynices, as punishment for his treason, not be buried. This decree was defied by Polynices' and Eteocles' sister Anti-

Poseidon in his Roman form as Neptune

gone, who ritually buried her unburied brother and finally received the ultimate punishment for that act.

POLYPHEMUS One of the one-eyed Cyclops, a son of the Greek sea god Poseidon, Polyphemus lived on an island as a shepherd and loved Nereid Galateia. In the *Odyssey*, Odysseus blinded Polyphemus during his escape from the Cyclops's island, thus angering Poseidon.

POLYTHEISM Polytheism is the belief in more than one god.

PONTOS Pontos was the personification of the sea and other waters that sprang from the Earth Mother, Gaia, at the beginning of the Greek creation.

POPOL VUH The mythology of the Mayan Indians of Mesoamerica comes to us in great part by way of the mid-sixteenth-century *Popol Vuh*, a work written in the Quiche Maya dialect but in Latin script. The mythology it contains is specifically that of the Quiche Maya of Guatemala, as remembered some two hundred years after the Christianization of the Maya.

POSEIDON Perhaps once a companion of Gaia, the personification of earth, Poseidon was originally an earthquake storm god and a fertility god representing the streams that fertilized the earth. His offspring by Gaia were monstrous. They included the giant Antaeus, who was killed by Herakles, and the terrible Charybdis, who swallowed and then threw up the sea between two great rocks and, with Scylla, thus threatened mariners such as Odysseus. In classical Greek mythology, Poseidon was among the original Olympians, a son of Kronos and Rhea. His sisters were Demeter, Hestia, and Hera. His brothers were the sky and high god, Zeus, and the underworld god, Hades. Poseidon's appointed portion of the three principal realms was the sea, where he lived with his wife, the sea nymph Amphitrite, and fathered Triton, the merman who soothed the seas with his conch trumpet. Poseidon, like his brothers, was a philanderer. With the Gorgon Medusa he had intercourse while in the form of a horse. After he dallied with the nymph Scylla, Amphritite turned the girl into the monster companion of Charybdis. Poseidon carried the trident. His animal was the horse, and it seems possible that he was at some stage worshipped as a horse, suggesting a connection with the ancient Indo-European horse cult. He was said to have taught the Greeks horsemanship. The chariot that he rode up from his undersea palace and then over the vast seas was pulled by horses with brazen hoofs and manes of gold. With Apollo, Poseidon built the walls of Troy. He did his best to prevent Odysseus from getting home in Homer's *Odyssey*, because the wily hero blinded the god's son, the Cyclops Polyphemus. As can be seen in the story of Minos and Pasiphae of Crete, bulls were sacrificed to this god, who was second only to Zeus in power.

POTRIMPO Potrimpo was the third god in the Baltic triad of Patollo (Pecullus, Pikoulis), Perkuno, and Potrimpo, a configuration that derived from the old Indo-European triad of king-priest god, warrior god–thunder god, fertility god—the triad represented, for instance, by the Norse Odin-Thor-Freyr grouping. Potrimpo is depicted as a happy, beardless youth with ears of grain. Clearly, he is a Pan-like god of fertility.

Neolithic temple ruins near Valleta, Malta

PRAHLADA Prahlada was an *asura* and a devotee of Vishnu, who became lord of the underworld after Vishnu, as the avatar Narasimha the man-lion, killed his father, the wicked *asura* king Hiranyaka.

PRAJAPATI Prajapati is the "lord of creatures," the primal being associated with creation in the Hindu *Brahmanas*. But by the time of the epic the *Mahabharata*, he has lost his position as the primal soul or first god and has become simply a god whose job is to create. From the time of the *Upanishads* on, in fact, he is frequently the same being as Brahma, the creator god in the Hindu *trimurti*, which is Brahma, Vishnu, and Shiva. There are several myths about the process by which Praja-pati created the world. The *Aitareya Brahmana* contains a story of incest that echoes the *Rig Veda* creation myth. Prajapati came to his daughter, the sky or dawn, as a stag, she becoming a doe, and had intercourse with her. But the gods disapproved, and Rudra, who later evolved into Shiva, pierced him with an arrow. Prajapati's seed flowed forth and became a lake protected by Agni (Fire), out of which came many things, including Brhaspati, the lord of the sacred speech—sometimes Indra—necessary for proper sacrifices and mantras. In the *Kausitaki Brahmana*, it is Pra-japati's sons who are seduced by his daughter. From their spilled seed, captured by Prajapati in a golden bowl, emerges the thousand-eyed Bhava or "Existence," a version of the old Vedic primal man or Purusha. In still another myth—the *Satapatha Brahmana*—Prajapati masturbates and spills his seed into Agni. The seed becomes sacred milk of clarified butter used in sacrifices. By producing progeny and making proper sacrifice, Prajapati, setting a standard for humans, saved himself and existence from the death that is Agni.

PRAKRITI In India, the Vedic Prakriti ("Nature") is the active female element with which the primal male or Purusha must unite in order to become realized as the universe. As such, Prakriti is the forerunner of the later *Shakti*.

PREHISTORIC MYTHOLOGY OF THE NEOLITHIC The first myths, those of the Paleolithic ("Old Stone Age") and early Neolithic ("New Stone Age") are, in the absence of written evidence, locked in mystery and can only be approached in a suppositional manner by way of archeology and comparison with later cultural expressions. Turning to the high Neolithic and the development of Indo-European and Middle Eastern myth, we can be more specific. And as we move into later periods we are on still more familiar ground, even as we remember that myths are often, in part, the inventions of storytellers whose particular and cultural priorities color the great sagas that are their storytelling vehicles.

The emergence in the Levant of agriculture and settlements and still more sophisticated toolmaking mark a transitional period from the Paleolithic to the Neolithic (New Stone Age) known as the Mesolithic (Middle Stone Age), Epipaleolithic, or proto-Neolithic (c. 10,000–8000 B.C.E., depending upon the location). During this period hunting and gathering remained the dominant sources of food, but agricultural practices were gradually developed, as were the storage of food, the beginning of the domestication of animals, and the building of more complex permanent settlements that were, in effect, the precursors of the truly permanent settlements of the great cultures that would emerge in the Neolithic age (c. 8000–3000 B.C.E.).

Central to the Mesolithic development in the Middle East was the Natufian culture, so named after a site north of Jerusalem. Natufian settlements for between 100 and 150

P

249

people were scattered throughout the Mesolithic Middle East. Among the best known of these are Tell ("Mound" in Arabic) Mureybat in the upper Euphrates Valley (in modern Syria), Hayonim (in modern Israel), and Tell es-Sultan (near Jericho in modern Palestine). An element of particular interest in the Natufian culture is the apparent establishment of proto-settlements even before the period of the Younger Dryas—that is to say, before the necessary advent of primitive agriculture. An example of such a settlement is Tell Abu Hureya, near Lake Assad in modern Syria, which was populated from c. 10,500 B.C.E. and which appears not to have cultivated grain until some 450 years later. Tell es-Sultan, a Natufian site near Jericho, also seems to have been settled before the development of agriculture. The urge to settle in one place may have been the result of abundant wild food resources in the immediate area. Tell Abu Hureya and other Natufian settlements were abandoned late in the Mesolithic period, perhaps because of overuse of resources or intertribal violence. When Tell Abu Huryea was reestablished, it was one of the many examples of what has come to be known as the "Neolithic revolution."

"Revolution" is perhaps not the best word to attach to a process that was gradual rather than immediate. Still, the changes that occurred during the period in question (8000–3000 B.C.E.) are comparable to other periods of radical change, such as the Industrial Revolution of the nineteenth century or the current technological revolution. What had happened in the Middle East by the end of the Neolithic was a radical change from a life based on hunting and gathering to one centered primarily on agriculture, animal husbandry, and community living based on civil and religious law and ritual, with accompanying mythology. Along with these changes came technological improvements in weaponry and tools, and the development of pottery in which to store grains and bricks to build houses.

The Neolithic period in the Middle East saw the domestication of sheep in northern Mesopotamia by 8000 B.C.E. and the cultivation of grains in Palestine and Anatolia during the eighth and seventh millennia B.C.E. Over the centuries the variety of grains and domesticated animals grew as did the size of settlements. There are indications that cult centers developed at Jericho and in Mereybet and Cayonu in the Euphrates Valley as well as in Hacilar and Çatal Hüyük in Anatolia.

In the high Neolithic or "Copper Age" (c. 8000–3000 B.C.E.), the period coinciding with the development of what are essentially the climatic conditions of our era, the turn to agriculture, as opposed to hunting and gathering, was well established. Humans in most of the world continued to hunt and to gather, but agriculture had become the primary means of subsistence. With agriculture came permanent community living places, the domestication of animals, the development of pottery, and, one assumes, more organized religious and mythological systems, including the mythologizing of the earth, the essential element of the Neolithic.

Clearly the most important metaphor for fertility itself was sexuality in connection with the birth-giving female, and as agriculture partially displaced hunting as a primary food source, the woman would have gained in stature. The emergence of polytheism, including sexually active gods—sometimes in the form of animals such as the bull or the goat—presided over by a great goddess, was inevitable. The fertility of the woman was associated with the fertility of nature, and nature itself—the earth—came to life in the metaphor of the earth mother—the earth goddess. In the Middle or Basal

Neolithic (c. 5500–4500 B.C.E.) and the High Neolithic (c. 4500–3500 B.C.E.) agriculture and animal husbandry in the context of established settlements developed still further. Pottery and weaving became important. In the Samarra and Halaf pottery of Mesopotamia, female and bull figures mingle with abstract symbols. The cult of a sacrificed and resurrected bull god related to a dominant great goddess—sometimes with a cow's head—found its way to the Egyptian Delta as well. Given the reasonably obvious analogy between the seemingly miraculous procreative aspect of females and the equally mysterious process by which earth receives seeds and produces crops, it is hardly surprising that people of the Neolithic would have built on the symbolism already present in the Paleolithic, as, for instance, in the stone "Venuses" of Laussel and Willendorf, and have developed a mythology of the earth as Mother Goddess. We can safely assume, at least, that the awe and wonder we associate with religion would have been related to the birth-giving aspect of earth as a mother and eventually on the male as a seed or seed bearer as well, and that myths would have formed around these figures and their activities. Such a mythology is evident enough in the much-discussed Neolithic ruins of the Fertile Crescent of the Near East with their images of enthroned and birth-giving goddesses and bull gods.

Leaving aside such disputed subjects as the valuation applied to male as opposed to female figures in Neolithic mythology and the question as to whether goddess religions imply matriarchal cultures, it is clear enough from archeological evidence that goddess religions, and probably mythologies, were in full flower in what Marija Gimbutas calls Old Europe at least from the seventh millennium B.C.E. "Old Europe" refers to the period before the dominance of the Indo-European invaders who came down into Europe from the Eurasian steppes between c. 4500 and c. 2500 B.C.E. Gimbutas makes a strong case for goddess-based, "gynocentric" religion and mythology in Old Europe until its gradual displacement by the patriarchal structures of the warlike invaders. The Old European religion, according to this theory, was maintained in parts of continental Europe until as late as 2000 B.C.E. and in the somewhat isolated islands of the Aegean and Mediterranean, most notably in Crete, until at least 1500 B.C.E. Gimbutas argues that in spite of the official disintegration of the Old European religion and its replacement by male-dominated pantheons, the old traditions "formed a powerful substratum that profoundly affected the religious life of European cultures that arose in the Bronze Age" (1987, p. 506) and beyond—cultures that preserve the Earth Mother and her mysteries in figures such as Gaia, in earth-based rites and mythologies such as that of Demeter at Eleusis, in the tradition of earth-centered Irish queens such as Maeve, and later in the development of the cult of the Virgin Mary.

Naturally, the development of many cultural groups in Old Europe would have resulted in a variety of specific beliefs and traditions, but archeological evidence supports the theory that a de facto universal European religion during the period in question was dominated by a Great Mother and related issues of planting, birth giving, and feminine and lunar cycles.

The archeological record of the goddess religion and mythology in Europe is extensive. Gimbutas isolates several figures from this record. There is, for instance, what Gimbutas calls a "bird goddess" from Thessaly, dating from the sixth millennium B.C.E., complete with beak, wings, and large buttocks. A "snake goddess" also appears in the early Vinca culture near Belgrade as well as in other areas. The snake goddess often has horns, which, for Gimbutas, link her to the crescent moon and lunar cycles and suggest her kinship with earlier Paleolithic Venuses. The bird and snake goddess figures, whether depicted as separate entities or as one being, are associated with life-giving water and air. The zigzagging, meandering designs signifying the snake goddess in early Vinca artifacts are similar to designs also signifying water on North American Indian pottery, designs related to a mythology that ties the serpent figure not only to the lightning of the sky but to the rivers with sources deep within the earth. A Minoan figure, dating from c. 6000 B.C.E., has a bird-like face and a snake-like lower body. She is, perhaps, the ancestor of those later Minoan goddess-priestesses with exposed breasts proudly holding snakes aloft.

It is tempting to wonder whether the story of Eve and the Serpent in Genesis is not somehow a distortion of an earlier, more compatible relationship between a goddess and her serpent companion, a companion who brings the knowledge of the under-earth to the world above.

Among the most clearly mythological of archeological goddess discoveries is that of the "white lady" or "death goddess," the ancestor of goddesses in India and elsewhere who in death take the living back to earth as part of the regenerative process of life. This death-wielding aspect is, of course, reflected in the lunar cycles or rising and dying, waxing and waning, by which goddesses have generally been symbolized. The death goddess is sometimes depicted as a nude lying stiffly with legs closed and arms close to the sides as if laid out for burial but with a clearly defined and stylized triangular pubic area signifying, as always, the life that will follow death.

Sometimes the death goddess takes the form of that ancient harbinger of death, the mysterious owl. A burial urn, dating from c. 3000 B.C.E. in Lemnos, is clearly an owl goddess complete with breasts, navel, and, most important, a prominent vulva through which, possibly, the dead may be reborn.

The best known of the Neolithic goddess depictions are perhaps the great enthroned pregnant figures of such places as Çatal Hüyük and Hacilar in Anatolia. This goddess of regeneration and procreation is also ubiquitous in Neolithic Europe. A sixth-millennium B.C.E. Vincan figurine represents the ancestor of the Grain Mother, a fertility goddess who is found in most parts of the later Neolithic world. Sprouting plants emerge from her vulva.

In a version of the great birth giver from fourth-millennium B.C.E. Malta, pregnancy is evident and the prominence of the birth passage is emphasized by means of exaggerated size. Stripes on the figure's back signify the nine months of gestation.

The Great Goddess of the Neolithic in Europe was also represented in the megalithic ("great stone") temple architecture found in many parts of the continent, including Spain, Germany, Sweden, France, and England, all perhaps expressions of the pregnant Earth Goddess. In Ireland, too, are found anthropomorphic architecture suggesting the goddess in the so-called court tombs, where the center of the structure is the uterus, again suggesting a myth of rebirth.

This is not to say that no male deities existed during the period of goddess dominance or that only gynocentric issues were present in myth and religion. Not surprisingly, we find frequent images of an ithyphallic descendant of the Upper Paleolithic shaman Animal Master, an appropriate companion to a goddess whose primary characteristic is fertility.

Sometimes these are young and ithyphallic, perhaps suggesting the renewal of life; sometimes they are clearly sad and old, indicating the death of the year or the end of life. They are usually referred to as "Year Spirits" or "Year Gods."

In the combination of these gods and goddesses of the early Neolithic we are very likely in the presence of an emerging seasonally based mythology of sacrifice, death, and renewal related to the development of the sedentary agricultural cultures beginning in the eight millennium B.C.E.—a mythology that was to take many forms, including, as in the Near East, a cult of a sacrificial bull god, and culminating in the central myth of Christianity in the Common Era.

Again, it must be emphasized that in the absence of written record we can only hypothesize as to the myths of the Paleolithic and early Neolithic. A comparison with later cultures that possess similar symbols can be helpful, but the only statement that can be made with some confidence is that archeological evidence points to the clear existence of mythic figures and mythic narratives in "Old Europe" and the Middle East.

To understand something of what these figures and their stories might have looked like, we can consider the vegetation-fertility myths of Mesopotamia, where writing was developed by about 3500 B.C.E. and at least fragments of an ancient Sumerian mythology were captured for later study. Central to this mythology are the figures of the goddess Inanna, who descends to the underworld and is revived, and her lover (perhaps brother) Dumuzi, who is chosen to take her place in the underworld for part of each year as a kind of ransom seed for Inanna's revival. It is somehow eerie to

A Neolithic "Venus" from Willendorf, c. 30000-25000 B.C.E.

P

finally have contact through words in Sumerian tablets with a previously voiceless mythology of sacrifice, fertility, and renewal that is suggested by cave paintings, burial sites, and figurines. This is the Earth Goddess speaking in her Sumerian form as Inanna. One can suppose that her European equivalents spoke in a similar way:

He shaped my loins with his fair hands,
The shepherd Dumuzi filled my lap with cream and milk,
. . .
He watered my womb.

One result of the Neolithic revolution was the establishment of cities during the fourth millennium B.C.E.—as opposed to the family-clan villages or towns of the earlier Neolithic—beginning in southern Mesopotamia. This was an age in which not only farming, but much more sophisticated metal tools and weapons replaced implements of wood and stone. An insufficiency of rainfall necessitated a strong government that could organize irrigation and other specialized activities involved in the highly interactive living of a relatively large population. The integrative aspect of the early cities was accentuated by surrounding walls meant to delineate boundaries and to protect against invaders. And organized religions with temples, a priestly cast, and highly developed mythologies provided further rationale for the existence of even larger city-states. In effect, these early cities and city-states, with their temples and ziggurats, were the foundation for what would become the religious or myth-based nationalism that is still so much a part of human life.
[Gimbutas (1987a), Srejovich]

PREHISTORIC MYTHOLOGY OF THE PALEOLITHIC It is impossible to be precise about the origins of mythology. The emergence of a tool-making proto-human being, *Homo habilis*, occurred several million years ago and was followed by the more advanced *Homo erectus*, of whom remains dating from about 800,000 B.C.E. have been found in Europe. It is not until the middle of the Paleolithic, the period marked by the development of stone tools that coincides with the geological and climatological Pleistocene or Ice Age—that is, sometime after 500,000 and before 200,000 B.C.E.—that we find in the Europe of the so-called Heidelberg man (named for the skeletal remains of a *Homo erectus* found near Heidelberg, Germany, in 1907) the first tenuous archeological hints of what might possibly have been mythological conceptualization. It was then that symmetrical tools were crafted in sizes large enough to suggest ritual use.

At the center of any mythology, of course, is story, and we cannot be certain of the details of a story without the connecting link of written or spoken language. Until the development of writing we are denied linguistic access to any mythology and must depend on such physical evidence of story as exists in burial grounds, rock carvings, cave paintings, and small artifacts. It is also possible to hypothesize the nature of the myths of preliterate periods by studying myths and rituals of peoples who continue "primitive" practices in the modern era—such examination being prompted by obvious common themes such as the sacrifice of a maiden or the presence of a serpent in a tree.

We can probably assume that in Europe, as in other parts of the world, mythology first took form when humans evolved to the point where their inherent mimetic abilities—their tendency to "make believe"—was applied to a social, even cosmic, rather than merely individual sense of identity.

Archeology suggests that proto-Paleolithic and Paleolithic humans in Europe and elsewhere created a body of symbols that formed the basis for what eventually became myths, stories with beginnings, middles, and ends—the essential elements of the Aristotelian plot or *mythos*—that were, in all likelihood, related to ritual and that expressed a sense of the nature of existence and the human place in it. The existence of such a symbolic language in a developed system of myth and ritual is strongly suggested, for instance, in connection with *Homo sapiens neanderthalensis* or *Homo neanderthalensis* (Neanderthal man), a distant predecessor or subspecies of our own species, *Homo sapiens*. "Neanderthal" refers to the Neander Valley in Germany, where skeletal remains were discovered in the mid-nineteenth century. Other Neanderthal sites have since been found in the Middle East and especially in other parts of Europe, where *neanderthalensis* represented the human species from about 250,000 B.C.E. to about 40,000 B.C.E.

Recent studies present a different view of this predecessor of our form of the species than that of the ape-like unintelligent, cannibalistic, club-wielding, woman-dragging "cave man" image with which we are all familiar. That the species was unintelligent or merely ape-like is belied by the fact of a surprisingly large brain capacity and by indications of a mythological consciousness. The primary evidence for such a consciousness—specifically for the belief in a metaphysical realm—lies in the strange and seemingly impractical but carefully arranged collections of objects in middle Paleolithic Neanderthal burial sites in Europe and elsewhere.

In excavations in the village of Le Moustier in the south of France and nearby villages of La Chapelle-aux-Saints and La Ferrassie, for instance, whole skeletons or separated skulls have been found to be surrounded or covered by valuable objects such as bits of quartz and jasper, bone plates, and tools—perhaps supplies for survival in "another world." The soil seems to have been colored by red ochre, suggesting a ceremonial approach to death. Some bodies appear to have been buried in fetal or sleeping positions, possibly indicating that death was seen as a sleeping period that might lead to new birth. It is possible that these and other Neanderthal sites in Europe—and in Israel and Iraq, for instance—suggest an early myth of the afterlife.

Joseph Campbell sees still more indication of Neanderthal's mythological character in the discovery of bear "sanctuaries" in caves of the high Alps (1969, pp. 339ff). In such caves bear skulls are set into "altar" niches, suggesting a worshipping of animal spirits and an early belief in the willing participation of animals in the life-giving process of killing and eating. In fact, bear cults would spread across northern Europe and Asia into North America. In connection with these cults, particularly in light of the fact that hibernation was a mystery for early humans—one augmented by the ability of the bear to stand and even walk upright like us—the question arises as to whether this bear "god" was the first of many dying gods who would willingly be sacrificed for the larger community. Later bear cults and myths among the Ainu, the Cherokees, and other cultures perhaps shed some light on this question.

Neanderthal humans were replaced or absorbed by about 40,000 B.C.E., during the socalled Upper Paleolithic, by a *Homo sapiens* subspecies anatomically almost identical to modern human beings. Recent discoveries suggest this subspecies emerged in Africa as early as 130,000 years ago. The European remains of our immediate ancestors were unearthed in the late 1860s in the Dordogne region of

France. This stage of *Homo sapiens* has sometimes also been referred to as Cro-Magnon man, after a place in which the archeological remains were particularly rich. Cro-Magnon man, like his significantly shorter Neanderthal predecessor, possessed a cranial capacity at least as large as that of today's humans and was a hunter-gatherer highly adept in tool invention and artistry. We know Cro-Magnon best from the rock carvings, burial grounds, and figurines from regions that span modern-day France, Germany, and parts of Eastern Europe and especially from the painted caves of France and northern Spain.

Most scholars believe that *Homo sapiens* of the Upper Paleolithic in Europe had developed religious systems. It is generally believed that ritual and associated mythology are especially indicated by the great paintings of the "cave temples" such as Les Trois Frères and Lescaux. And the existence of large numbers of rock carvings and small figurines depicting females with exaggerated breasts, buttocks, and stomachs, as well as stylized impressions of the vulva on these figures and in isolation, all suggest to Marija Gimbutas and her many followers the existence in the Upper Paleolithic of a goddess-based religion.

It is possible, of course, only to surmise the nature of the mythology associated with these various remnants of the Paleolithic. Clearly, it is the caves and the female figurines that call for the most attention.

Beginning with the caves, we are inevitably struck by the dominance in the paintings of animals, on one hand, and of beings who appear to be part animal and part human or, more likely, humans masked or disguised as animals, on the other. This "animalist" focus is not surprising for a hunting society. What is of particular interest is the impression given in the cave paintings of a ceremonial dance of sorts involving the hunters and the hunted, humans and animals. That is, we seem almost certainly to be in the presence of a ritual process through which the animal agrees to be sacrificed. Depictions of wounded bison and bear are found in the caves, as might be expected. Perhaps the most famous wounded animal is the great blood-spouting bear of Les Trois Frères, but this bear stands beneath the even more famous antlered dancing shaman or "sorcerer."

The importance of the bear—a descendant perhaps of our Neanderthal bear "god"—is further suggested by a model of a large bear in a cavern at Montespan in front of which was found a bear's skull covered by the remains of a bear's pelt. It is difficult not to agree with Campbell's assessment that a bear ceremonial rite and mythology are indicated in this altar arrangement. The bear, a kind of totem spirit or animal master, seems likely to have been the object of a "sacramental hunt."

Turning to the female figurines and rock carvings, we find still more mystery but a strong aura of mythology. It should be pointed out that generally the female depictions occur in areas meant for dwelling, whereas the ritual hunting scenes are under the earth, available only to those who venture there for ritual purposes. A visitor to Native North American pueblos in the Southwest will notice a striking similarity. Underground places called kivas are restricted places where primarily men perform secret ritual ceremonies associated with the given clan's totem animal. Kivas contain altars and various ritual objects and are themselves representative of the inner earth, the womb of the Great Mother out of whom the people once emerged. Dwelling places, on the other hand, are the precinct of the women, who, in societies that are frequently matrilineal, often own the houses where they live

with their families. For the Pueblo Indians as for the ancient people of the Paleolithic, women's "mysteries"—her cycles, apparently associated with those of the moon, her birth-giving powers—are an important source of mythology.

The best known of the European rock carvings of a female figure is the so-called Venus of Laussel, a tiny (17 cm or 7 inch) image dating from about 20,000 B.C.E. and discovered in 1911 on a ledge wall under a limestone overhang sheltering the ruins of a Paleolithic dwelling site near Lascaux.

The "Venus" is one of many images found under the Laussel overhang, all of which point to a mythology of female mysteries and, perhaps, the moon—a mythology based on such phenomena as menstruation, pregnancy, lactation, and, of course, birth. The Venus herself stands naked, her great maternal breasts reaching almost to a pronounced belly on which her left hand rests, calling attention to the navel and pubic triangle below. Meanwhile her right hand holds up what appears to be a symbolic object—an animal horn or, some have suggested, a crescent moon. "In a posture and with a gesture eloquent of some legend, the knowledge of which has been lost," writes Joseph Campbell,

> the Venus of Laussel stands before us like the figment of a dream, of which we dimly know but cannot bring to mind the meaning. The mythology of which she is the messenger remains in absolute silence behind her, like the rock out of which she is hewn. (1983, p. 66)

That the mythology of the Venus of Laussel has to do with the generative mystery of femaleness, as suggested by Marija Gimbutas and others, is further indicated by the profusion of tiny Upper Paleolithic female figurines discovered throughout most of the European continent. These figurines, made of stone, bones, and antlers, greatly outnumber male images. The most famous of the figurines is the "Venus of Willendorf"

A paleolithic "Venus" from Kostionki, c. 23,000 B.C.E.

P

in Austria, who, with her huge breasts, buttocks, and belly, has become the symbol for many of the collective ancestors of the gradually more individualized Neolithic Great Goddess.

As is the case with other parts of the world, the emergence of the human species in the Middle East is difficult to establish. There are archeological indications—primarily rough stone tools and skeletal remains—of a the presence of *Homo erectus* in the area dating from at least 300,000 B.C.E., the period known as the Lower (early) Paleolithic (c. 2 million–100,000 B.C.E.). These "people" would have been nomadic hunter-gatherers. As in Europe, crude stone carvings indicate a possible mythological or religious consciousness. But it is not until the Middle Paleolithic (c. 100,000–30,000 B.C.E.) of some 100,000 years ago that we find Middle Eastern evidence of the more advanced Neanderthal man—who was clearly moving in the direction of the kind of activity that would characterize later humans. In the archeological site of the Shanidar Cave in Iraq, for instance, graves contain bodies that appear to have been positioned ritualistically, indicating, at the very least, a sense of community responsibility that stands in opposition to the popular image of the "cave man." By about 30,000 B.C.E. Neanderthal man had been displaced in the Middle East by our own hominid species, *Homo sapiens*, who first arrived in the Middle East perhaps as early as 90,000 B.C.E. During the Upper or Late Paleolithic (c. 30,000–10,000 B.C.E.), these humans made significant strides toward the civilizations that would develop in future millennia. Excavations such as those at Kom Ombo and Jebel Sahaba in Egypt reveal a relatively sophisticated tool and weapon "industry" and clearly ritualistic burial practices. The rapid expansion of the Sahara, perhaps associated with the long drought brought about by a 1,000–1,300- year cold spell, the so-called Younger Dryas of about 12,000 years ago, seems to have forced people to remain for long periods near the Nile River, leading to the building of more or less permanent settlements. The drought in question affected the entire region of the eastern Mediterranean, in fact, and made necessary certain changes in the old hunter-gatherer cultures. [Gimbutas (1987), Narr]

PRIAM The king of Troy in Homer's *Iliad*, Priam was the father of many children—including Hector, Cassandra, and Paris by his wife Hecuba. It was Priam's abandonment of Paris in the wilderness that would lead eventually to the Trojan War with the Mycenaean Greeks. During that war, Priam was an old man. His noblest act was to enter the camp of the Greeks to ask Achilles for the body of his slain son, Hector. After the fall of Troy, Priam was executed by the now-dead Achilles' son Neoptolemus (Pyrrhus).

PRIAPUS The son of Aphrodite and, depending on the source, Dionysos, Hermes, Zeus, or Pan, Priapus, usually a fat old man, was a comically and some would say pornographically ithyphallic (always with an erect penis—thus "priapic") fertility god of the woodlands in Greece.

PRIMEVAL MOUND In Egyptian mythology of the Heliopolis theology, Heliopolis was the Primeval Mound, the first land to emerge at creation from the primeval waters. It would be the sacred space of the great solar god of light. The Primeval Mound was symbolized by sand in the pyramids of kings. The statue of the dead king was placed on the "Mound," thus symbolizing his divinity, and would cause his father, the sun god, to recognized him in the afterlife.

PRIMEVAL WATERS The primeval or primal waters are the maternal (earth mother–based) source for the creation of the world in the creation myths of many cultures, especially, but by no means exclusively, those for whom the earth-diver myth is central.

The eagle sent by Zeus picks at the liver of the bound Prometheus

PROCRUSTES An innkeeper between Eleusis and Athens, Procrustes ("Stretcher") stretched or violently shortened people who did not fit the beds of his inn. The Greek hero Theseus finally "shortened" *him* by decapitating him.

PROMETHEUS The brother of Pandora's husband, Epimetheus ("Afterthought"), and Atlas, the Titan Prometheus ("Forethought") became the enemy of the Greek Olympian high god Zeus by stealing fire from the gods and acting as a culture hero to humans, teaching them arts and survival techniques. Some accounts say that it was Prometheus who actually created the first man, Phaenon, from clay and water. Prometheus taught humans how to trick Zeus into accepting fat-covered bones rather than good cuts of meat in sacrifices. Zeus took out his anger against Prometheus and humanity by tricking Epimetheus into accepting the "gift" of Pandora and her box of evils. And he had the defiant Titan tied to a rock on Mount Caucasus, where an eagle tore out his liver every day for 1,000 years (it grew back each night), until the hero Herakles finally released him. Some of Prometheus's story is told in Aeschylus's play *Prometheus Bound*.

PROSE EDDA The Icelander Snorri Sturlusson's most important work was his *Edda*, or *Prose Edda*, as it is called, to differentiate it from the *Poetic Edda*. Written in about 1220, his *Edda* was intended to be a handbook and guide to the old mythology for poets and scholars. The *Prose Edda* begins with an introduction called the *Gylfaginning* (the "Deluding of Gylfi"), in which a fictional Swedish king, Gylfi, disguised as a beggar called Gangleri, visits Asgard, the home of the gods, and questions the also-disguised Odin (Wotan in Germany) and two other mysterious figures about the ancient gods and mythological history. The second section of the *Prose Edda* is *Skaldska-parmal* ("Poetic Diction"), which supplies rules for traditional poetry and many myths as well. The final section is *Hattatal* ("Verse Form List").

PROTEUS The Greek sea god son of the Titans Oceanus and Tethys, Proteus, sometimes called the "Old Man of the Sea," had the ability to predict the future but took myriad shapes in order to avoid having to do so. If one wanted to consult this elusive figure, it was necessary to physically capture him during his afternoon naps in the sun. Homer said he lived on the island of Pharos; Virgil placed him on Carpathos.

PRITHIVI Prithivi is the Vedic goddess associated with the earth. It is likely that she was originally an ancient earth goddess of the Indus Valley culture. Her name indicates a connection with Pritha (a name for Kunti) and Prakriti.

PRYDERI The son of Pwyll and the goddess Rhiannon, Pryderi is a major figure of the Welsh *Mabinogion*; he is the only hero to appear in all four "branches" of the epic.

PSYCHOLOGY AND MYTH It is appropriate to apply the word "myth" to psychology, just as it is appropriate to apply it to the physical sciences, because both of these approaches to the nature of existence use hypothetical models and narratives as if they were real, when, in fact, they are metaphors that merely attempt to *convey* reality. The myths of psychology have become for us an important way in which, even in common usage, we portray what and who we are. Most myths are stories with definable characters and events. These characteristics apply to the psycho-philosophical myth that perhaps had more influence on the way twentieth-century people thought

A depressed Hamlet with his friend Horatio

of themselves and regarded the world around them than the religious myths that preceded it. The myth in question, developed primarily by an Austrian Jew, Sigmund Freud, is literally a part of our vocabulary and our prevailing belief system. Freud's psyche comes with popularly accepted characters—the elemental urge-driven *Id*, the moralistic and controlling *Superego*, and the heroic *Ego*, who must achieve balance between all of the psychic elements and is constantly concerned with such mythic events as the Oedipus and Elektra complexes (which take their names from ancient myth) and concepts such as the Primal Horde, in which fathers deny their sons sexual access to the females of their clans. We speak of the psyche as if it were an actual entity, just as mystics and other religious people have always postulated an actual entity called the soul that inhabits the "inner life" and in some cases can even "fly" away at the time of the body's death. Physical scientists create what they often refer to as "elegant" models and thought experiments such as Schrödinger's Cat or Einstein's Twins to describe otherwise indescribable realities and phenomena. We cannot touch the soul or the psyche or directly experience the thought experiment, since they are myths, but as elements of a working vocabulary, as philosophical scaffolding, we accept them as real.

The psychological myth was further developed by the Swiss psychiatrist Carl Jung and others. Jung, especially, not only made extensive use of ancient myth as cultural dream in his clinical work but added a host of characters to the philosophical myth—characters such as the *Anima* and *Animus* (the projection onto the opposite sex of the individual's psychic energy or true inner self), the *Self* (the Ego-like mediator between the conscious and unconscious worlds), and the *Shadow* (the negative side of the personality). In Jung's version of the myth the individual as Self enters into something very like a heroic journey quest with the support of his Anima and the opposition of his Shadow. The goal is Self-

P

Identity or Individuation, a mythic goal in which most twentieth-century and early twenty-first–century people believe implicitly, as indicated by their willingness to pay a great deal of money for guides (psychotherapists) who can help them on their way to the quest goal.

The perils of the psychological journey-quest, whether with a Freudian, Jungian, or other sort of guide, are as real as those facing the old mythic hero. This is a "dark night of the soul" or a "night journey" fraught with monsters to be overcome, pitfalls to be avoided. In this it reminds us of Theseus's journey to his father, Odysseus's ten-year voyage from Troy to Ithaca, or the Christian philosophical journey myth contained in Dante's *Divine Comedy*, in which the human persona must descend to the depths of human sin and depravity, guided by the wise Virgil, before beginning the upward journey to God.

It is to the myth of the psyche and its universal language that we can turn to reexamine the archetypal hero myth as it is taking form in our age. Even though we recognize that particular hero myths are the stories of cultures and expressions of knowledge at a particular time, we can accept the model of the archetypal hero, who, through the comparative process, emerges in shadow form as a metaphor both for the collective human psyche and for us as individuals. Krishna and Gilgamesh, as particular expressions of the hero myth, are foreign to us, but their common characteristics are not, and through their commonality we can begin to interpret the hero as a central figure who is not separate from us but who coincides with our actual internal and even external lives. Ultimately, the unreal worlds of myth, like the unreal world of dreams, reveal psychological truths.

In terms of the psychological myth, the hero journey is that of the conscious mind into the unconscious, the search for the lost self, the ego trapped in a dark world of monsters, temptations, would-be diversions, and roadblocks. Jungian psychology, at least, suggests that to "find" him- or herself the individual must break through to transpersonal and transcultural reality. To achieve individuation or self-identity the individual must not only explore, confront, and sometimes battle personal and cultural demon guardians of the gate but must also find and bring into consciousness the Self imprisoned or denied by those guardians.

The Self is a concept derived from the *Upanishads* of India. It is the *Atman* or inner expression of *Brahman*, the Universal Life in everything. The *Chandoga Upanisad* explains it in the famous Parable of the Salt.

> Sretaketu was a proud young student of the *Vedas* who failed to answer an essential question posed by his wise father Uddalaka as to the nature of reality. The father asked his son to put a chunk of salt in some water and to report to him in the morning. This his son did, but when his father asked him to retrieve the salt it was clear that it had dissolved. So Uddalaka asked Sretaketu to take a sip from one end of the vessel and to tell him what it tasted like. "Salt," answered the young man. He then asked him to taste the middle and then the other end of the vessel. In both cases the youth tasted salt. Uddalaka ordered his son to throw away the liquid, but the salt remained salt. Uddalaka turned to his son and said, "Dear Boy, you are unable to perceive Being here, but Being is here. This Being is the Self of the entire universe. This is Reality, this is the Self that is *you*, Sretaketu."

In the tradition of the *Upanishads*, or *Vedanta*, to understand and experience this sameness between the individual's essential being and the universe's being is the basis of enlightenment or nirvana. It is the means by which the individual achieves true herohood, as it were, which has nothing to do with pride or conquest but with the realization of one's existence as an embodiment of the transpersonal universe—one's true Self.

In the terms of depth psychology, Self is the archetype of wholeness, that which orders and unifies consciousness and the unconscious. It is the essence of individuality and the means by which the identity of a culture and the species is ultimately expressed. Self can take many archetypal forms, for which the individual searches in the process of the inner quest or pilgrimage. God can refer to the Self, as can the divine child or the king. Christ, the Buddha, or Krishna can be an image or symbol of Self, and the mandala can be a non-personal embodiment. The fairy tale hero's search for the princess in the enchanted castle is a search for Self—for wholeness that is the sacred "happily ever after" marriage of the hero and his psychic energy, or *anima*. Psychologically speaking, Hamlet is a damaged hero who, in order to save himself, must journey into himself to discover kingship and the nature of kingship as Self. Willa Cather's professor in *The Professor's House* realizes that he has ruined his life by betraying the divine child, which is not only an embodiment of his youthful ideals but those somehow betrayed by humanity. His difficult quest is a search within for that lost child. In *Four Quartets* T. S. Eliot discovers wholeness in universal symbols for the Self that is a cosmic Christ: "When the tongues of flame are in-folded / Into the crown knot of fire / And the fire and the rose are one," he writes in "Little Gidding"; for Eliot this is a wholeness that can end the seemingly impossible personal and cultural dark night of the soul that had been represented by the personal and cultural "fragments I have shored against my ruin" in "The Waste Land."

It will be useful to consider the particular steps of the monomyth model in light of our general understandings or myths of the psychological journey. It might be said, for instance, that the hero's miraculous conception and birth speak to the awakening in our adult psychic lives of the imaginative capacities and adventuresome energies of childhood, which can lead us out of the psychic prison and brokenness of adulthood. The development that can follow from such an awakening often involves (as it does for the child hero of myth) the separation from parents and the conventional—one might even say unconscious—duties and activities of the world into which we were born. Indeed, there will be parental influences and social pressures that will work against the call to adventure. The psychological voyager, like the mythic hero, is "the man or woman who has been able to battle past his personal and local historical limitations" [Campbell (1972), p. 19].

Having accepted the call of the psychic adventure, the psychological voyager departs the ordinary world for a journey into the unknown in search of the lost Self, whatever form that Self might take. To be reborn, as it were, the voyager must return to the inner world. As in the case of the mythic hero's journey or the journey of the pilgrim, the passage through the unconscious will involve many significant thresholds blocked by guardians—neuroses, obsessions, and other Self-blocking factors created in the course of one's life. These guardians will demand tests and trials and will have to be fought before each threshold can be crossed, before the true "father" or "mother"—the true essence of what we are—can be attained, before the negative expressions, femmes fatales, and shadows of our beings can be replaced by clear and positive projections of our real psychic energy, before that projection or *anima/animus* can be brought to the light of consciousness for the sacred marriage of wholeness.

Many terms have been used to express mythically the seriousness of the journey of depth psychology. Psychologists have variously referred to the night journey or the dark night of the soul of the mystics. Joseph Campbell uses the constructs of Freud and those of the Bible—the return to the womb and the biblical Jonah's imprisonment in the belly of the whale—to express the sense of darkness and hopelessness, but also the possibility of gestation and rebirth, that mark the deepest part of the psychic journey. This is the stage in which we seem to die, to be lost to our old life. To face the monsters and demons of the depths is to face the most frightening forces of our inner world, those we would most prefer to ignore or deny. By now, however, it is perhaps too late to turn back, but it is also difficult to believe in the possibility of continuing. This is the period of existential disillusionment, when the journey seems both meaningless and inescapable. Should the psychological hero's journey continue, the voyager may hope to break through to a reunion with the Self. As the homecoming religious pilgrim bears the marks of spiritual revival and the mythic hero is reborn or resurrected, the psychic voyager who has mastered the inner world of darkness brings that world, now assimilated, into the light of consciousness. Having achieved at least an element of Self-realization, he or she can move on as a more truly conscious being no longer at the mercy either of conventional lethargy or the negative powers within. [Campbell (1949), Freud, Jung (1959, 1969, 1976), Leeming (2002)]

PTAH The primary creator god of the Memphite version of Egyptian mythology, Ptah was he of the Primeval Mound, the "self-begotten One" who created *ex nihilo* by way of his own thoughts followed by his words. One could say of Ptah's creation, as of the Christian vision of God and the Logos ("Word"), "In the beginning was the Word (Logos)." Ptah also established all the principles of life and existence.

PUEBLO MYTH AND RITUAL Dance rituals in the pueblos of the Native North American Southwest sometimes suggest mythological sources. This is the case at the San Felipe Pueblo in New Mexico between Santa Fe and Albuquerque at the ceremony ostensibly in celebration of the Christian Feast of Candlemas or Candelaria (the Purification of the Virgin Mary or the Presentation of Christ at the Temple). A visitor to that ceremony will come upon what is, in effect, a mystery play of the willing sacrifice of animals that gives the impression of having emerged from some ancient practice that is closer to prehistoric cave paintings than to the rituals of the Christian Church (although there is, of course, a mythological connection between the sacrificed buffalo king of San Felipe and the crucified Christ and between the maiden who dances with the buffalo and the Virgin Mary, who accepts her role as the human vessel for the divine seed). Here, as at all of the other pueblos in the area—at Christmas time or other religious holidays and pueblo feast days—men wearing great antlers or buffalo masks dance in the village square, impersonating the animals of the hunt, accompanied by medicine men and other members of the given tribe. They carry sticks that sometimes appear to represent phalluses but more often are used as forelegs on which they lean forward as they and their fellow dancers move their feet in steps eerily

reminiscent of the famous, sometimes ithyphallic masked dancers of Les Trois Frères from at least 15,000 years ago. The viewer will inevitably be moved by the dance of a village maiden with the "Buffalo King," by the "sacrifice" of the animals one by one as the ceremony progresses, and by the resurrection or "return" of the animals later in the day.

PURANAS The *Puranas* are a body of Hindu texts containing myths, legends, and ritual instructions. Of the many works designated as *puranas* ("ancient narratives"), only eighteen—the *Mahapuranas* ("Great Puranas")—are official. Even they, composed early in the Common Era, are *Smirti*, or remembered texts, rather than *Shruti*, or the revealed word. The *Puranas* are often attributed to the sage Vyasa, also said to have been the author of the *Mahabharata*. If a single theme dominates the *Puranas*, it is that of *bhakti*, or proper devotion. In the *Puranas*, two essential creation myths are developed from the myths of the *Shruti* tradition. In the first creation the primal male or Purusha is also designated as Atman or Brahman or Mahayogin ("Great Yogi"). But unlike the original Purusha, who as sacrificial victim becomes the universe, this creator uses yoga to complete the process by which existence comes about through the release of the active female aspect of

A Pueblo deer dancer

P

257

Pyramid texts from the tomb of Ramses VI

sins that have not been forgiven. At the Reformation, Protestants rejected the idea of Purgatory. A vision of it is presented by Dante in his *Purgatory* (*Purgatorio*), the second section of his *Divine Comedy*.

PURUSHA The Sanskrit for "person" or "man," Purusha in the so-called Purusha Hymn of the ancient Indian sacred text the *Rig Veda* is the "first man," who is the universe past and present and future and is the object of the first sacrifice, from which came existence. His mouth became Brahman, the moon came from his consciousness. Eventually Purusha became synonymous with the absolute—the universal "self"—Brahman or Atman. Purusha entered existence, knew himself, and exclaimed, "I am." Eventually Purusha as "consciousness" became associated in the ancient philosophical tradition of Sankhya with the idea of Prakriti ("Nature"), the creative energy necessary for the realization of materiality. With the development of Hindu mythology in the *Brahmanas*, *Upanishads*, and *Puranas*, the idea of Purusha was somewhat superseded by Brahman, Atman, and figures such as Prajapati, Brahma, and Vishnu. PWYLL A major figure in the "First Branch" of the Welsh *Mabinogion*, Pwyll married the goddess Rhiannon, who gave birth to their son Pryderi.

PYGMALION The Cypriot king of Cyprus, Pygmalion created a statue of a maiden and fell in love with it. According to the Roman poet Ovid, in his *Metamorphoses*, he prayed so hard to Aphrodite, the Greek goddess of love, that the ivory statue might come to life, that it did. Pygmalion married his now-living creation.

PYRAMID TEXTS Sacred funeral writings on the walls of the pyramids and other royal burial chambers in ancient Egypt of the Old Kingdom and the early First Intermediate Period—that is, dating from c. 2375 B.C.E.—are known as the Pyramid Texts. They precede the Coffin Texts that appear later in the coffins and tombs of the non-royal dead. The Pyramid Texts contain material that in all likelihood had been preserved orally from the prehistoric Neolithic period. The texts include protective spells, incantations, and myths meant to ensure the safe passage of the king in the afterlife. The texts, primarily of the theology of Heliopolis, establish Osiris as King of the Dead and the dominance above of the solar god Re-Atum.

PYRAMUS AND THISBE The Roman poet Ovid tells the story in his *Metamorphoses* of the star-crossed Pyramus and Thisbe, literary ancestors of Shakespeare's Romeo and Juliet. Pyramus and the Babylonian maiden Thisbe were in love and overcame their parents' prohibitions by conversing through a hole in the wall between their adjoining houses. They agreed to meet one night at a tomb. While waiting there, Thisbe was frightened away by a bloody lioness that had recently killed an ox. As she was running she dropped a piece of clothing, which became soiled by the ox's blood. When Pyramus arrived, he assumed the bloody garment meant that his beloved had been killed and he killed himself under a mulberry tree, the berries of which have forever been red because of the spilling of Pyramus' blood. Discovering her dead lover, Thisbe killed herself as well.

PYRRHA With her husband Deucalion, Pyrrha, the daughter of Pandora and Prometheus's brother Epimetheus, was a lone survivor of the great flood sent by the Greek high god, Zeus.

nature (Prakriti). In the other myth, an earth-diver creation, the Purusha Narayana, a form of Vishnu, who has been asleep on the primeval waters, awakens during the period between two *kalpas* (ages) and becomes the creator, Brahma, and then Vayu ("Wind") and then the Vishnu *avatara*, the cosmic boar, Varaha, who serves as the sacrificial diver who will bring up earth from the depths. The Puranic cosmogony also contains stories of the dissolution of existence in the cosmic fire that emerges from the breath of Rudra or Shiva. Wind and floods complete the work.

PURE LAND A pure land or "Buddha land" in Mahayana Buddhism is the land of Buddhas and bodhisattvas. We ordinary humans live in impure lands tainted by passions. The Mahayana Buddhists say that the Buddha Sakyamuni (Gautama Buddha) has his land and that other Buddhas have their own. The best known is Sukhavati, the home of Buddha Amitabha, or Amida Buddha, and the source for the name Pure Land Buddhism, so important in Japan. There the sect, called Jodoshu, was founded by a monk named Honen in the twelfth century C.E. and was based on the Chinese version called Ching-t'u. It stresses salvation through Amida Buddha, and the Amida's Pure Land can be said to be a representation of enlightenment. For some Buddhists, "Pure Land" is exclusively of the mind. For others it has a more literal quality, as in the Japanese and Chinese Tusita, or Heaven, of the Bodhisattva Maitreya. At the center of Pure Land worship is meditation and the repetition of the name of Amida Buddha.

PURGATORY In Christian theology of the Roman Catholic persuasion, Purgatory is a place or perhaps a state of being of the afterlife where people who have died and are undeserving of Hell but unready for Heaven must suffer to expiate

P

QAT Qat, or Quat, is the Melanesian spirit who created living beings. After he carved the first three men and three women from a tree, he hid them among some trees for three days and then literally enlivened them by dancing for them to a drum beat. Humans would have been immortal had the spirit Marawa not also fabricated human beings and then buried them for three days. When he dug them up they were already dead; so death came into the world. It was Qat who brought about night and day and a regular passing of time so that agriculture became possible.

QUETZALCOATL Perhaps the most important deity of the Toltec and Aztec pantheons in Mesoamerican mythology, Quetzalcoatl was the "Feathered Serpent" and at once an astral deity, a wind god, and a culture hero who taught the Aztecs their arts and crafts and the mysteries of the calendar. It was he who descended to the underworld to obtain the bones with which to create the human race. In fact, in an early incarnation, he was one of the primary creators of the world; specifically, he was the supreme deity of the second era of the Five Suns. Like the god Huitzilopochtli, Quetzalcoatl may have had hero rather than divine roots. His great enemy was Tezcatlipoca, who in the form of a jaguar chased him out of Tollan. Quetzalcoatl sailed away on a raft, but it was believed that, like King Arthur, he would return one day to save the people. Unfortunately for the Aztecs, they took this myth all too literally and mistook the conquering Cortés for their longed-for hero.

QUIRINUS Probably originally a Sabine war god—Quirinus formed a triad with Jupiter and Mars in archaic Roman mythology. The triad represented sovereignty (Jupiter), power (Mars), and community (Quirinus). Specifically, Quirinus was the embodiment of a Roman community characterized by peace and prosperity. Over the centuries, he lost his position of importance.

QUR'AN The holy scripture of Islam, the *Qur'an* is believed by Muslims to have been revealed directly to the Prophet Muhammad by way of the angel Jibril (Gabriel) gradually between 610 and 632 C.E., making Muhammad the "Messenger of Allah." The word *Qur'an* itself is derived from roots having to do with recitation and scripture. Thus Muhammad was commanded to "say" or "recite" the word of God sent to him. The book as eventually written down is made up of 114 chapters or *suras*. As literally the "word of God," for Muslims, the *Qur'an* is the basis for all proper life in all parts of the Islamic world, including Asia.

The Temple of Quetzalcoatl at Teotihuacan in Mexico

Words of the Qu'ran

Revelation came to Muhammad when he was forty. For some years he had retreated for meditation to a cave (Ghari-Hira, "the cave of learning") on Mount Hira (Jabal-an-Nur, the "Mountain of Light") during the fasting month of Ramadan. On the seventeenth day of Ramadan during his fifth such retreat, Muhammad had the first of what would be many such experiences over a twenty-two–year period, experiences reminiscent of the mountain revelations to Moses and the mountain transfiguration of Jesus.

On the seventeenth day of Ramadan, as Muhammad was sleeping, he was overpowered by the presence of divinity, apparently as represented by the angel Jibril (*Qur'an* 53:1–18). The angel recognized Muhammad as Allah's Messenger (*rasul*) through whom Allah's words would be revealed directly to humankind. The angel taught Muhammad the proper rituals of prayer and then commanded him to recite, or "say" (*iqra*), the words of Allah. Like Moses, and so many heroes, Muhammad at first refused the call, saying he was not a reciter, not a *kabin* ("soothsayer"). Then the angel squeezed him—three times—taking away his breath until finally Muhammad agreed to recite, beginning the *Qur'an* (the "recitation") with the words "Recite in the name of thy sustainer, who has created—created man out of a germ-cell! Recite—for thy sustainer is the Most Bountiful, One who has taught [man] the use of the pen—taught him what he did not know" [*Qur'an* (Asad, trans.) 96:1, Armstrong (1993), p. 137]. Shocked by his vision, Muhammad turned to his wife, Khadija, throwing himself in her lap. Khadija recognized him as a prophet and reassured him, for which reason she is much revered by Muslims. Over the next twenty-two years the Prophet would receive the *Qur'an*, the true miracle (*mu'jizah*) of Islam, bit by bit.

Q

RADHA In the twelfth-century *Gitagovinda* ("Song of Govinda" or "Song of the Cow-herd") by the Bengali poet Jayadeva, we are told the story of how Radha, a married *gopi* (female cowherd), fell madly in love with the younger Krishna (Govinda) and eventually won his love. The beautifully erotic love bouts and the obvious allegory in the work of the longing of the human soul for absolute union with Krishna, an avatar of the great god Vishnu, lead to an obvious comparison with the Hebrew Bible's *Song of Songs*.

RADISH Radish was a follower of the Buddha, who in Chinese mythology attained the enlightened status of *arhat* and was renamed Mulian. Discovering that his mother, Lady Leek Stem, had died and been sent to Hell as a result of her having kept for herself money he had given her for mendicants, Mulian begged the Buddha to return her to life. The Buddha agreed but released Lady Leek Stem as a black dog. Eventually, because of her son's goodness, she became human again and accomplished many good works.

RAGNAROK In Norse mythology Ragnarok (the "End of the Gods") is the apocalypse, the end of the world. Snorri

describes the terrible events, perhaps appropriate to the cold, dark Germanic north, in the *Prose Edda,* basing his story on that of the solemn second part of the *Vol us pa* in the older *Poetic Edda*. According to the myth, the high god Odin called up a seeress from the dead who told him how the world began and how it would end. The beginning of the end would be wars in Midgard, the land of humans. Relatives would fight each other; social order would break down. Fathers would kill their sons; incest would become common. Then would come a three-year winter, *Fimvulvetr,* recalling another Indo-European apocalyptic winter marking the end of the world in Iranian mythology. Next the wolf, Skoll, will swallow the sun, and his brother Hati will destroy the moon. The terrible wolf Fenrir and the punished trickster Loki will break their bonds and run free; earthquakes will destroy the earth. Gullinkambi, the golden cock of Asgard, will arouse Odin and his companions. Yggdrasill will tremble. The seas will overlap their shores with a violent tide as Jormungand, the great Serpent, makes his way to shore. Loki will captain the ship of the dead, Naglfar, from Hel, and Hrim will lead a host of giants. Fenrir's wide jaws will tear Asgard and Midgard, and Jormungand will spit out ven-

Krishna arriving at Radha's house

Battle between the armies of Rana and Ravana

om and poison in every corner of creation. Surt will lead the fire demons of Muspell across Bifrost the Rainbow Bridge, and it will shatter and fall beneath them; fire will envelop them, and Surt's sword will take the place of the sun. The enemies of the gods will gather on the plain of Vigrid. Called by Heimdall's mighty Gjallarhorn, the gods will gather and will march, eight hundred strong, through Valhalla's five hundred and forty doors. Resplendent in his golden helmet and shining mail, gripping his great sword, Gungnir, grimly, Odin will challenge Fenrir, and Thor beside him will look to settle his old score with Jormungand. Freyr will struggle with Surt and, after a great struggle, will fall. Tyr and Garm the Hound will kill each other, as will Loki and Heimdall. Thor will defeat Jormungand in the end, but will die himself from the serpent's poison. Fenrir will swallow Odin at the last, but his victory will be cut short by Vidar, who will avenge his father and vanquish the wolf by ripping its jaw apart. Then Surt will send his fire through the three levels and nine worlds of creation, and all will die—men and gods, dwarfs and elves, birds and beasts.

But out of Ragnarok, as out of the endings of the ancient Indian eras, a new world will be born. The earth will rise from the deeps again one day, green and blossoming, and crops will flourish again. A new sun will take the place of the old and some gods will return to the ruined Asgard, led now by Balder. Lif and Lifthrasir will survive to renew the race of humans; they will have hidden themselves securely in Yggdrasill's embrace, where Surt's fire will not have scorched them; they will have survived on morning dew and will have kept watch through the branches above them for the new sun. And thus, through its death, the world will be born again.

RAMA Rama or Ramachandra ("charming one") is one of the greatest of the avatars of the Hindu god Vishnu. Rama's wife is Sita. Their story is the story of the epic the *Ramayana*.

RAMAYANA Traditionally attributed to the sage Valmiki, the *Ramayana* is one of the two greatest Sanskrit epics of Hindu India, the other being the much longer *Mahabharata*. Popular in India and much of Southeast Asia, especially in the Indonesian Hindu-populated island of Bali, the *Ramayana* is a compilation of material dating between 500 B.C.E. and 200 C.E. It stands as a record of Hindu virtues and values. Rama, the seventh avatar of Vishnu, is the epic's hero, and he represents the perfect prince, an embodiment of *dharma*. His wife Sita, as the incarnation of Vishnu's consort Shri, or Lakshmi, is the perfect wife, who represents prosperity. Rama's faithful brother, Laksmana, is the perfect brother.

The plot of the *Ramayana*, like that of the *Mahabharata*, is highly symbolic—even allegorical—with each event representing some aspect of the Hindu spiritual journey. Rama and Sita, for example, stand as dharma and prosperity and faithfulness and the sacred sacrifice against the demonic defiler of the sacrifice, Ravana. Rama and Sita's exile in the forest is an ascetic preparation for the sacrifice and the defeat of the anti-dharma or *adharmic* forces represented by Ravana.

Rama and his three brothers grow up in the court of their father, King Dasharatha. Rama and his brother Laksmana are "borrowed" by the sage Visvamitra, to fight against the evil sacrifice-defiling *raksasas*, followers of the demon Ravana. Only Rama, he says, can defeat them. The reader knows that as an avatar of Vishnu, Rama is indeed the proper defender of the faith, and he succeeds in defeating the *raksasas*. Rama and his brother then travel on to Mithila, where Rama wins King Janaka's earth-born daughter Sita by succeeding in bending the great bow of the god Shiva, thus revealing himself as a true hero. On his way home, Rama will succeed in still another heroic trial by accepting Parashurama's challenge to bend the bow of Vishnu, a task he also accomplishes. Upon his return home, Rama's father decides to anoint him heir to the throne, but an intrigue of his stepmother forces the king to honor an old oath and to exile his son to the forest for a number of years. Sita insists on accompanying her husband to the Dandaka (the "punishment forest"). Eventually the evil Ravana abducts Sita from the forest and takes her to his fortress in Lanka. Now begins the essential aspect of the epic, Rama's quest for his Sita, mirroring Vishnu's need of his Shri, his *Shakti*, or energy source.

Rama is helped in his quest by the monkey god Hanuman and his monkey army. Magically, the monkey troops to build a bridge to Lanka, and Rama is able, during a terrible battle, to kill Ravana and thus to rescue Sita. By killing the king of the sacrifice-defiling *raksasas*, Rama has fulfilled the purpose for which he had been sent as Vishnu's avatar to earth.

Since Sita has been potentially defiled by having been abducted by Ravana, Rama allows a trial by fire in which the innocent Sita climbs upon the funeral pyre in an act of sati but is miraculously refused by the fire god Agni. Rama can now receive her again as his wife. Later his doubts about Sita revive, however, and he exiles her to the forest, where she gives birth to twin sons and stays with the sage Valmiki, who composes the Ramayana and recites it to Rama and Sita's sons. Sita returns to Rama and asks her mother, the earth (Prthivi), to take her back, as proof of her undying innocence. Immediately Prthivi rises on her throne, takes her daughter on her lap, and the earth swallows them. Rama reigns for another one thousand years.

RANGDA The evil witch-queen opponent of the Barong in Balinese mythology, Rangda has long hair and nails and is accompanied by many witch followers. In the Balinese Barong dance ceremony, as in the myth, the Barong is always victorious.

RAPE OF THE SABINE WOMEN In the mythological days of prehistorical Rome, it is said that the supposed Roman founder, Romulus, and his followers solved the problem of a shortage of women by inviting the neighboring Sabines to a feast and then seizing and raping their women. This act led to a war between the early Romans and the Sabines, a war that ended with a truce and alliance arranged by the raped women themselves, who were now Roman wives and mothers.

RAPITHWIN The god of summer in ancient Iranian mythology, Rapithwin struggled with the demon of winter, during whose time in power he retreated to the depths of the earth.

RATA A Polynesian hero, especially of the Maori, Rata and his father struggled constantly against Puna and the monster lizards. The lizards killed his father and Rata searched the world for his body, eventually finding the head in a great shark and the rest of the body with the lizards. On his way home, the lizards dismembered him as well.

RAVANA Ravana is the multi-armed, multi-headed *raksasa* (demon) of Lanka (modern Sri Lanka, formerly Ceylon), who holds Rama's wife Sita prisoner in the Hindu epic the *Ramayana*. It is said that the god Shiva imprisoned him under his mighty leg for 10,000 years as punishment for his having attempted to move the Mountain of Heaven to Lanka.

RAVEN A Native North American culture hero and sometimes creator, particularly of the northwest region, Raven, like other tricksters, such as Coyote, is often obscene, self-centered, and even foolish, as in this Chuckchee myth: In the beginning the great trickster Raven, the self-created, lived with his wife in a tiny space. Bored with her existence, the wife asked Raven to create the earth. "But I can't," he said. "Well, then," said the wife, "I shall create at least something." She lay down to sleep, with Raven watching over her. As she slept, the wife seemed to lose her feathers, and then to grow very fat, and then without even waking up she released twins from her body. Like the mother, now, they had no feathers. Raven was horrified, and when the twins noticed him they woke their mother and asked, "What's that?" She said, "It's father." The children laughed at Raven because of his strange harsh voice and his feathers, but the mother told them to stop, and they did. Raven felt he must create something since his wife had created humans so easily. First he flew to the Benevolent Ones—Dawn, Sunset, Evening, and the others—for advice, but they had none to give. So he flew on to where some strange beings sat. They were the seeds, they said, of the new people, but they needed an earth. Could Raven create one? Raven said he would try, and he and one of the man-seeds flew off together. As he flew Raven defecated and urinated, and his droppings became the mountains, valleys, rivers, oceans, and lakes. His excrement became the world we live in. The man-seed with him asked Raven what the people would eat, and Raven made plants and animals. Eventually there were many men from the original seed, but there were no women until a little spider woman appeared and made women. The men did not understand about women, so Raven, with great pleasure, demonstrated copulation.

Some tribes say that Raven was conceived miraculously by a woman who swallowed some natural object.

RE In Egyptian mythology of many regions a form of the god Re (Ra) was the supreme deity and a personification of the all-important sun. As the theologies of various centers predominated he was Atum-Re, Re-Atum, Amun (Amon)-Re, or Re Amun. As the morning sun he was Khepri, represented by the scarab. As the hot noonday sun, he was associated with the god Horus as Re-Harakhti, symbolized by a human body with the head of a falcon, topped with a solar disk. The evening sun was sometimes seen as Re-Atum wearing the Egyptian crown. Re descended to the underworld each night and was constantly attacked by his enemy, Apopis (Apep), and defended by Seth and spirits of the dead.

REBIRTH AND RETURN In the universal myth of the hero, sometimes referred to as the heroic monomyth, the major initiatory and questing events of the hero, which often include a descent into the underworld or into death itself, are usually followed by some sort of rebirth, resurrection, and/or return. Often the hero reappears in the spring, suggesting an association of the mythic theme in question with agricultural cycles, as in the case of Adonis and Attis, for example. Sometimes the hero returns as "spiritual food," as in the case of the resurrected Jesus or the revived Osiris and the reconstituted Hainuwele. With the various corn mothers of many traditions, these reborn and returning heroes are all boon bringers for their people.

The rape of the Sabine Women

R

263

RESURRECTION Resurrection is a mythic theme related to the heroic monomythic archetype of rebirth and return. It is a term and concept particularly associated with the central dogma of Christianity. Christians believe that the divinity of Jesus is irrefutably revealed in his resurrection, his literal overpowering of death by rising from the grave three days after his crucifixion.

RHADAMANTHUS Said to be a judge in the underworld, Rhadamanthus was a brother of King Minos of Crete and a son of the Greek god Zeus and the mortal Europa.

RHEA The Great Mother of the second generation of Greek gods, the Titan goddess Rhea was the wife of her brother Kronos, who had become the highest deity after he overthrew their father, Ouranos. When Rhea and Kronos's mother, Gaia, prophesied that Kronos would be overthrown by one of his children, the great god devoured each one as it was born. That is, he ate Demeter, Hades, Hera, Hestia, and Poseidon, but Rhea saved her youngest child, Zeus, by substituting a rock for him. Thanks to Rhea, Zeus was saved and later would release his siblings and become the chief god of the third generation of Greek deities, the Olympians.

RHIANNON The Welsh goddess Rhiannon ("Great Queen"), daughter of the king of the otherworld, plays an important role in the *Mabinogion*, where the story is told of her marriage to Pwyll, by whom she became the mother of the hero Pryderi. Given her association with horses, she is often seen as a cognate of the continental Celtic horse goddess Epona.

RHPISUNT People of the Native North American Northwest tell the story of a woman—sometimes named Rhpisunt—who married a bear prince and produced two bear cubs, who later removed their bear clothing and became great human hunters for a while, until they returned to the bear world. This is a totem story in which the alliance of bears and people suggests a spiritual base to the hunt.

RICE MOTHER Balinese people make models of the rice mother spirit from rice sheaves and hang them near the paddies to ensure good crops.

RIG VEDA The *Rig Veda* or *Rgveda* (after *rks*, meaning *mantra*) is the oldest of the collections (*samhitas*) of Indo-Aryan mantras and hymns, dating from about 2000–1700 B.C.E. These are hymns "revealed" directly to seers (*Rishis*) by a higher power. In short, the *Rig Veda*, like the other Vedic literature, is what is called *Shruti* or the most sacred sort of Hindu text. There are ten books or *mandalas* in the *Rig Veda*, each attributed to a privileged family of seer-sages. These books are the primary source for our knowledge of the most ancient Indian mythology, and they form the basis for the development of Hinduism. The development of mythology within the *Rig Veda* begins in the most ancient period, that dominated by the god Varuna, the fire god Agni, and the cult of *soma*; moves to the phase centered on the warrior gods led by Indra; and then to the later phase out of which Hinduism comes. In that final phase, both non-Aryan Indus Valley-Dravidian gods such as Rudra-Shiva, the Goddess (Devi), and popular Aryan figures such as Vishnu become increasingly important. The *Rig Veda* is perhaps best known for its cosmogonic or creation myths.

At the center of Vedic creation is the idea of creation as separation, or sacrifice, which leads to the ordering of chaos. Incest plays a role in creation. The *Rig Veda* tells how the unnamed creator's phallus reached out to his daughter and how during the act of union some of his seed fell onto the earth, resulting in the sacred words, or *vedas*, and the sacred rituals. Perhaps earth itself (Prthivi) may be thought of as the womb or *yoni* of the daughter.

A more complex *Rig Veda* creation story, which is further developed in the more philosophical *Upanishads* is that of the primal man, the Purusha, who must unite with the active female principle, Prakriti ("Nature"), in order for creation to be realized. In the *Rig Veda*, the Purusha himself becomes the animistic creation. Three-quarters of him is made up of the gods; one-quarter is the earthly creation. Purusha is divided up as the first sacrifice, and from that sacrifice comes the sacred chants and formulae—the *Vedas*. His breath becomes the wind (Vayu); Indra and Agni also come from his mouth, the moon from his brain, the sun from his eye, Heaven from his head, earth from his two feet, and so on.

RISHI A *Rishi* is an Indian seer or hearer and revealer of divine knowledge such as that contained in the *Vedas* and other sacred "revealed" (Shruti) Hindu texts. *Veda* means "knowledge" and the *Rishis* are, therefore, transmitters of divine knowledge, literally revealed to them in visions.

RITES OF PASSAGE Cultures practice various rites of passage—liminality or threshold rituals—marking the movement from one stage of life to another. These include such ceremonial acts as naming, circumcision, puberty rituals, marriage, and burial. The idea is that through such rituals the individual can die to one stage of life in order to be reborn to another. The Jewish *bar mitzvah* is such a ceremony, the Christian baptism is one, and the Navajo *Kinaalda* is another. Rites of passage may be said to extend to the whole community in mythology. The heroic monomyth contains a series of such rites that Joseph Campbell, Carl Jung, and others suggest reflect our individual and cultural—psychological and societal—development.

RITUAL AND MYTH A question that has long faced mythologists and anthropologists is whether myths developed to accompany rituals or whether rituals developed to accompany myths. This question has been approached by writers of the so-called Myth and Ritual School such as Jane Harrison and Sir James Frazer, and by many others in connection with such areas as the mythic origins of drama, ritual theater in general, rites of passage, and liminality. It seems at least possible that both myths and rituals developed out of human reactions to natural phenomena. The rising and setting of the sun must at one time have been mysterious events. Did humans imitate these events in rituals and then tell stories to illustrate the rituals, or did they tell stories to explain them and then act out rituals to illustrate the stories? In some cases rituals emerge directly from the stories, as in the case of the Christian ritual of Holy Communion, in which the symbolic body and blood of Jesus are consumed as bread and wine, referring back to the story of the Last Supper, the final Seder—itself a ritual growing out of the Passover story—of Jesus and his disciples, and to the story of Jesus' death and resurrection.

RITUAL THEATER Ritual theater has traditionally been a means by which mythology has been transmitted. The Egyptians and Greeks expressed myths in ritual drama. Medieval Christians developed ritual drama, as well as more secular plays, from the stories celebrated in the Mass. Ritual drama has always been particularly important for illiterate audiences

R

but has remained popular—especially in Asia—among the educated as well. There are ritual temple plays in parts of India to celebrate the life of Draupadi, for example, and any number of dramatic versions of the epics the *Mahabharata* and the *Ramayana* can be found there as well as in Java and Bali in Indonesia. One of the most elaborate ritual dramas is a Balinese one based on the *Ramayana*, where a masked version of the demon Ravana and a chorus of Hanuman's monkeys play significant roles in the quest of Rama for his Sita. In another Balinese play, a spirit king, the Barong, plays an important role in overpowering the witch-queen Rangda in a wild ritual dance.

ROAL An ancient Andean creator deity, Roal destroyed humanity with the sun when they refused his offer of divine powers.

ROD Rod was a Slavic fertility god whose cult was associated with mother goddesses. In some ways he resembles the god Svantovit.

ROLAND Roland (Orlando) was the nephew of Charlemagne and the hero of one of the greatest medieval European epics, the *Song of Roland*. Based on ninth-century French sources, the *Chanson de Roland* was traditionally first sung in 1066 by the Norman minstrel Taillefer. Like the Spanish poem *El Poema del Mio Cid*, it celebrates the Christian struggle against the Muslims, in this case called Saracens. The epic tells the story of the perfect hero, Roland, his betrayal, and his death defending Charlemagne's rear guard.

ROMAN MYTHOLOGY As Greek mythology cannot be separated from its background of indigenous pre-Greek cultures, Roman mythology is intricately influenced by ancient Italic cultures, especially those of other Latin tribes, of the non–Indo-European Etruscans, as well as by that of the Greek colonizers of Sicily and southern Italy.

By the beginning of the first millennium B.C.E. several tribes, who spoke a form of Latin, lived along the Tiber in an area known as Latium Vetus ("Old Latium") bordered by the Etruscan and Sabine territories. The Latins were united in the worship of the god Jupiter Latiaris, whose sanctuary was on Mons Albanus, and the goddess Diana Aricina, whose sacred grove was in Aricia. Jupiter Latiarus was a god to whom elaborate ritual sacrifice was made. Diana, whose name is formed from the same root as Jupiter, seems to have been just as important, representing night to Jupiter's day and also demanding significant sacrifice. Later Diana, like the great goddess of Crete and the Artemis of Anatolia, would be reduced in stature. Another element of a mythological basis for this early Latin federation is suggested by a seventh-century B.C.E. burial place at Lavinium, a grave that has traditionally been considered to be that of the hero Aeneas, the central figure in one of the myths of the founding of Rome. Lavinium was also the center of the cult of Venus, the mother of Aeneas and, therefore, of Rome. This Aeneas myth is best known to us through its treatment by the poet Virgil in his epic the *Aeneid*, written much later, during the period of the emperor Augustus.

In his *De Republica*, the Roman statesman Cicero says that it was the twins Romulus and Remus—known by the Greeks as Rhomos (Rome) and Rhomulos (Roman), sons of the god Mars and the vestal virgin Rhea Silvia—who founded Rome. Rome—the Urbs (the "City")—was, in fact, officially founded on April 21, 753 B.C.E., in a ceremony on the hill that the world knows as the Palatine.

Our sources for Roman mythology date primarily from the first century B.C.E. and the early first century C.E. and are found for the most part in the works of Cicero, Virgil, the historian Livy, the philosopher-historian Plutarch, and the poet Ovid. The supreme Roman god of the Urbs was Iup-

Moses and his people on their passage to the Promised Land

A statue of Roland with the Austrian shield

piter (Jupiter), whose name shares the Indo-European root *Iou* (*dyeu*) with the Greek Zeus (*dyeus*) and the Sanskrit *dyaus* ("the sky"). Although the early Roman gods were in some senses personal, they were generally not anthropomorphic. Many were embodiments of abstract concepts. Fides was the goddess of good faith, Ceres was the goddess of agricultural growth, Consus was the god of grain, especially in its stored form, Ops was the goddess of opulence, Janus the two-headed god of gateways or life passages, Vesta the goddess of the sacred fire. Some of the archaic deities were particularly associated with ritual celebrations. The goddesses Angerona and Mater Matuta (Aurora) were apparently known primarily through solstice activities.

At the center of archaic Roman mythology was a version of the Indo-European triad as Jupiter-Mars-Quirinus (sovereignty-power-community). Jupiter in this context is proper sovereignty, such as that belonging to the Vedic Varuna, while Mars is pure power such as that represented in Vedic India by Indra. Quirinus is a representation of peaceful Roman community marked by prosperity.

The archaic Roman triad is itself related to the Romulus and Remus myth, a crucially important Roman version of the Indo-European sacred twins theme, told by Ovid, Livy, and others. The story is that in the early days Rome experienced a shortage of women, a problem solved by Romulus in a deceitful manner. He invited the Sabines to a feast and then he and his followers seized and raped the Sabine women. After a long period of war between the Sabines and the Romans, a truce and alliance between the two peoples was arranged by the Sabine women themselves, who were now, after all, Roman wives and mothers. The Romulus-led rape of the Sabine women represents the assimilation of a rustic culture with that of Rome and Etruria, to make up an archaic Roman tripartite society. Years later Romulus disappeared in a flash of lightning and was taken to the heavens to become a god, thus establishing a precedent for the deification of Roman rulers. As the sacred king, Romulus was essential to the archaic Roman triad, as Mars was his father and Jupiter his patron, and as when he finally left this world in the thunderstorm, he was identified with Quirinus. He and his twin were referred to as the *geminos quirinos* ("twin quirini"), recalling the Greek Dioscuri ("sons of God"), Castor and Polydeuces (Pollux).

In this ancient story of Rome's founding, Remus, who after a quarrel between the brothers over which one should give his name to the new city, was killed, so Rome took its name from Romulus. In his death, Remus serves as the sacrifice out of which, it might be said, Rome was born, much as the Vedic world was born of the dead body of Manu's twin, Yama.

Eventually, in the seventh century B.C.E., Rome became the dominant force among the Latin cities, only to be overcome by the neighboring Etruscans, who ruled Rome through kings of Etruscan origin until their expulsion and the formation of the Republic in 509 B.C.E. These non–Indo-European speakers possessed the most advanced civilization in Italy from the eighth to the fourth centuries B.C.E., and their mythology influenced that of Rome significantly. Romans also accepted and over the centuries continued to make use of the "prophetic" Etruscan disciplines such as haruspicy (the study of entrails for prophecy) and divination from lightning flashes, and rituals related to the Etruscan prophet Tages and the sibyl-like Begoia. The Romans would consult the oracular Sibylline Books for guidance in difficult times. One story has it that the great Sibyl of Cumae sold three of her prophet books to the Etruscan-Roman King Tarquin, who deposited them on the Capitoline Hill for the city's use.

The non–Indo-European Etruscans gave a higher place to women and goddesses than did their Indo-European neighbors and subjects, and in Rome they substituted the Jupiter-Juno (Uni-Astarte)-Minerva triad for the archaic Roman one of Jupiter-Mars-Quirinus. The new triad was prominently worshipped in a Capitoline Hill temple, and when the Roman republic overcame the Etruscan rule, it retained its place.

Soon after the expulsion from Rome of the last Etruscan king, Tarquin the Proud, the Romans defeated the Latin tribes at Lake Regillus and formed a Latin league with them. A major setback to the development of Rome was the sacking of the city by the Gauls in the period between 387 and 390 B.C.E. The Latin alliance was dissolved after a Latin revolt in 343–341 B.C.E., and by 338 B.C.E. the Latins had simply been absorbed by Rome.

By this time the Roman pantheon was fairly well established—an amalgam of Latin, Etruscan, and absorbed Greek ideas. The Romans imported certain Greek or Greco-Etruscan deities such as Apollo, who was introduced by way of a Sibylline prophecy as a healing god early in the fifth century B.C.E., and Castor, who was imported to support the Romans in a battle. Rome brought nearly all of the major figures of its pantheon into synchronicity with those of the Greek, even to some extent accepting marriages in a divine family that in earlier times had not been thought of as a family. Temples dedicated to particular deities became more prominent, statuary became important, and the gods, understandably, became more anthropomorphic. Jupiter emerged as more Zeus-like and was now married to Juno, who took on a role as patroness of marriage. Some might see this as a promotion for Juno, but in the earlier Etruscan-Latin understanding she had been a version of Uni-Astarte, the Great Goddess, who, with Jupiter and Minerva, ruled over Rome on the Capitoline Hill. In her role as Jupiter's wife, Juno did maintain at least something of an earlier status. In the story used by Virgil in the Aeneid, it is she whose feminine powers lie behind Dido's almost preventing Aeneas from leaving Carthage to found Rome.

As for the other gods, Mars retained a greater importance than he had possessed as Ares in Greece. He was not only a martial god but an agrarian one as well. Diana became a huntress, like her Greek homologue Artemis, and lost much of her early Latin importance in the process. As in some Greek versions of her myth, she was Apollo's sister. Vesta was understood to be a version of the unimportant Greek Hestia, but she took on a great deal more significance in Rome as the embodiment not only of the hearth but of the old Indo-European fire cult, now that of the Vestal Virgins. The Roman Venus, too, may have Indo-European roots. Her name perhaps looks back to the neuter Vedic term for desire, but under the Greek influence of Aphrodite she becomes distinctly feminine. Still, as the mother of Aeneas and, therefore, a patroness

of Rome, she takes on the kind of stature that Athenians gave to Pallas Athena rather than to Aphrodite, who in Greece was something of a spoiled daughter and a vamp. Athena in Rome, however, is Minerva, once closely associated with Juno, as indicated by her place with that goddess on the Capitoline. Poseidon lives on in Rome as Neptunus (Neptune), Hermes as Mercurius (Mercury), Hephaistos as Vulcanus (Vulcan), and Dionysos as Bacchus.

A prime example of the effect of Greek mythology on Roman is that of the triad Ceres-Liber-Libera, which owes its very being to that of Demeter-Dionysos-Kore (Persephone) and the story of Hades' (the Roman Pluto) rape of Persephone (the Roman Proserpina), because of which the archaic abstract Ceres became the anthropomorphic figure depicted in a statue in her temple dedicated in 493 B.C.E. near the Circus Maximus in Rome.

A useful picture of the Roman version of the Olympians is discovered in a popular rite, the lectisternium, in which offerings of food were made to statues of gods and goddesses exposed paired in temples on great beds (lectisternia). This rite, developed through Senate-ordered consultation with the Sibylline Books during times of difficulty, was first practiced in 399 B.C.E. In this first lectisternium the purely Greek Apollo and his mother, Latona, were placed together in the most honored place in the hope that the healing god Apollo would overcome a severe pestilence that threatened the city. The historian Livy tells us that the last lectisternium, ordered in 217 B.C.E. to ward off Hannibal's attack on Rome during the Second Punic War, marked the adaptation of the Greek pattern of twelve paired deities: Juno and Jupiter, Neptune and Minerva, Mars and Venus, Apollo and Diana, Vulcan and Vesta, and Mercury and Ceres (Livy, 22.10.9). It must be pointed out that whatever the Greek meaning of these common pairs—for example, the marriage of Hera and Zeus, the erotic affair of Ares and Aphrodite, the sibling connection of Apollo and Artemis—the Romans almost certainly attached

A Roman trinity: Jupiter, Mercury, and Virtus

Augustus before the Tomb of Alexander the Great

their own meaning. We know that Juno and Jupiter had long been associated as part of the Etruscan-Roman triad in the Capitoline cult; the joining of Vulcan and Vesta referred to sacred fire, protected in Rome by the vestal virgins; and the pairing of Venus and Mars had a particularly Roman meaning, Mars being the father of Romulus and Venus the mother of Aeneas. In this pairing, the Romans succeeded in joining the two myths of the origins of Rome.

The myth of Venus as the mother of Aeneas had been augmented during the First Punic war when, during the occupation of Mount Eryx, beginning in 248 B.C.E., the Romans had recognized the Aphrodite there as Venus—specifically Venus Erycina, whose temple was later built near the summit of the Capitoline. Soon after that, another Anatolian or "Trojan" goddess, the Anatolian Cybele, the Magna Mater, the mother of the dying god Attis, later himself celebrated in Rome, was introduced to Rome and housed in a temple on the Palatine.

The extension of Roman power and language into the world beyond the Italian peninsula was marked by assimilation of other mythologies and/or the identification of foreign gods with Roman ones. This process, as we have seen, had already begun long ago in connection with Latin, Etruscan, and Greek deities and coincided with the mixture of Latin and vernacular languages that resulted, for instance, in the Romance languages: Italian, French, Portuguese, Spanish, and Romanian. Sometimes the mythic assimilation merely involved a name change, as in the case of Venus Erycina or the later Mars Lenus in Gaul or Jupiter Dolichenus from Doliche. Deities—especially eastern ones—were also directly imported as themselves. Such deities included the goddess Ma, brought from Anatolia, as the great mother Cybele already had been, and equated with Bellona. There were many examples of the Romans following their ancient tradition of enlisting the gods of

enemies to fight for them. The Greek hero Herakles, for example, became Hercules Victor in 145 B.C.E. to celebrate the Roman victory over Greece.

An important development of mythology during the imperial period was that of the emperor cult. Julius Caesar had been deified by the Senate after his death in 44 B.C.E., and Augustus, who led a religious revival, built a temple to his personal family god, Mars Ultor, as the avenger of Caesar's murder. Under Augustus's rule (31 B.C.E.–14 C.E.) the cult of the living emperor emerged, in which the emperor was thought to be guided from within by his divine element, or genius. For his work on earth he would be rewarded by Jupiter with the gift of immortality. This understanding of a divine being sent into the world to save it doubtless had an effect on the thinking of early Christians, who lived during the time of Augustus.

Early Christianity found a breeding ground in Roman thought and tradition not only because of the relatively easy transference from the emperor cult to that of the "Son of God" but because of the popularity in the first century B.C.E. and first century C.E. of mystery cults from the east, of which Christianity was one. Mithraism, imported from Persia (Iran) in the first century C.E., stressed secret communal gatherings, sacrifice, and a shared ritual meal. The Emperor Gaius built a temple to the Egyptian goddess Isis, whose mystery cult was associated with the sacrificed and resurrected king-god Osiris. Sir James Frazer's description of the Roman feast of Attis cannot help but remind us of the story of the Christian man-god whose death by hanging gave birth to a sacred ritual meal. Frazer tells us that the festival of Attis and his mother, Cybele, was celebrated in Rome in the spring. The trunk of a pine tree was brought to the sanctuary of Cybele and wrapped in cloth and decorated with flowers as if it were a corpse. An effigy of Attis was placed on it. On the third day of the ceremony—the "Day of Blood"—the priests of Attis cut themselves and dur-

R

ing a frenzied Dionysian dance splattered the "corpse" with their blood. Frazer supposes that the novices of the priestly order castrated themselves in honor of the god on the same day before the symbolic representation of the god was placed in a sepulcher. All the worshippers then mourned the death of Attis until during the night there appeared a light and the tomb was opened to reveal that the god had risen from the dead. The next day—probably on the vernal equinox, the resurrection of Attis was celebrated in a carnival-like "Festival of Joy." Associated with the mysteries of Attis were a fast, a sacramental meal, and a belief that through Attis's resurrection the worshipper would overcome death.

The replacement of Greco-Roman pagan mythology by that of Christianity was a gradual process, beginning with the missionary work of the Apostle Paul to Greece and Rome and traditionally by the arrival of St. Peter in Rome during the first century C.E. The early Christian community was adamant in its refusal to worship the Emperor and the other Roman gods. Persecution resulted, including, according to Christian tradition, the hanging of Peter and Paul, but so did the community's missionary work. When, at the Battle of Milvian Bridge in October of 312 C.E., the Emperor Constantine attributed his victory not to Apollo or Hercules or Mars but to the God of the Christians, the future dominance of Christianity in Europe was assured. Constantine would move his capital to Byzantium, the "New Rome," renamed Constantinople. In 341 pagan sacrifices were prohibited, and the closing of pagan temples followed soon after that. [Bonnefoy (1991), Dumézil, Momigliano, Schilling]

ROMULUS AND REMUS The famous twins of Roman mythology, Romulus and Remus, were born of the union of the god Mars and the mortal Rhea Silva. Rhea Silva, whose name suggests nature and the earth itself, had been forced into the role of vestal virgin by her uncle Amulius, the king, who hoped thus to keep her from producing a rival heir to the throne he had usurped from her father, Numitor. When the twins were born the evil king had them placed in an ark of sorts and left to float away in the Tiber. When the ark happened to run aground, a female wolf discovered the children and suckled them. Later the boys were adopted, as young heroes often are in such myths, by a shepherd. Romulus and Remus grew and became known for their strength, but one day Remus was overcome in a quarrel with his grandfather Numitor's followers and taken to Numitor to be punished. Hearing of this, Romulus went to his brother's rescue, and the twins were revealed as Numitor's grandsons. The reunited family now defeated the usurper Amulius and restored Numitor to his throne. Romulus and Remus went to the place along the Tiber where they had been rescued by the wolf and there they founded Rome. A quarrel between the brothers over which one should give his name to the new city resulted in the death of Remus, and so Rome took its name from Romulus.

RONA The Maori celebrate this Polynesian god as one who struggles against the moon, who has stolen his wife. Depending on the relative successes of Rongo and his opponent, the moon waxes and wanes.

In Polynesian Tahiti, Rona was a monstrous female cannibal who devoured the lover of her daughter Hina before she herself was killed.

RONGO A popular god with culture hero aspects among the Polynesian Maori, Rongo was a son of Papa and Rangi.

In Hawaii he was known as Lono, and he plays a role in the important Pele myth there.

ROUND TABLE In Arthurian lore, the Round Table is sometimes used as a term for King Arthur's court. One hundred and fifty knights sat around the actual table at Camelot, which had been made by Merlin for Arthur's father, Uther Pendragon.

RUDRA Rudra means "one who roars," and Rudra, whom some scholars see as originally a non-Aryan fertility god of the Indus valley, was a god whose symbol was the bull. He is, however, sometimes depicted in the posture of a yogi. These aspects suggest a link to the later Shiva. In the *Rig Veda*, Rudra, whose wife 's name, Prsni, means "water bag," is a bringer of life-giving rain and other boons. As a fertility god he is represented by the phallus, or *linga*, which will take on increased importance in the Shiva cult. He is also, like Shiva, a destroyer, whose arrows are to be feared by all, and sometimes he seems to deny the ancient Vedic sacrifice. Not surprisingly, he is closely associated with the god of death, Yama, with the god of fire, Agni, and with the magical drink, *soma*. "Rudra" is essentially synonymous with Bhava, Sarva, Ugra, and Mahadeva. Some of these names are attached to the Rudras, the followers of Rudra, who represent various aspects of Rudra—fear, howler, thunderbolt, arrows, and so forth. Rudras are sometimes called Maruts, who are also sometimes differentiated from Rudras as storm gods who can bring havoc.

RUKMINI Rukmini is the wife of the Hindu Vishnu avatar, Krishna. She is herself, therefore, an incarnation of Vishnu's wife, Lakshmi.

RUSALKA Rusalka were beautiful leaf-clad Siren-like femmes fatales spirits of the lakes of the northern Slavs. They enticed men to their watery graves and tickled people to death.

R

Romulus and Remus suckled by the She-Wolf

S

SACRED EARTH In animistic traditions such as those of Native North America and Africa, the earth itself is particularly sacred, as it is the embodiment of a deity or spiritual principle. In the creation myths of many peoples, the essential elements of earth—mountains, rivers, trees, oceans—are literally made of the sacrificed body of an ancient deity, as, for example, in the case of the Mesopotamian Tiamat, the Vedic Purusha, or various Native American corn mothers. Central to proto–Indo-European mythology is the idea of the creation of earth as a result of the sacrifice.

SACRED KING, SACRED QUEEN In many mythological and religious traditions, the king is an embodiment of deity on earth. In Celtic Ireland the integrity of the king at Tara was associated with the land's fertility, represented by the divine triune queen. The Sumerian kings were sacred in that they were "married" to sacred queens who represented the divine and ever-fertile Inanna. In Wales, King Arthur was the sacred once and future king as symbolized by his ability to remove the sword from the rock. Egyptian pharaohs ruled on the basis of their sacred embodiment of the essence of the dead Osiris's son Horus. Sacred kings are sometimes the founders of nations or cultures. The sacrificed Vedic twin Yemo is one such king, as is the Roman Romulus, whose sacredness is passed on to later "divine" Roman emperors.

SACRED MARRIAGE The marriage of a king to a representative of the city goddess is especially important in the mythol-

Salome presents the head of John the Baptist

ogy of ancient Mesopotamia and other areas of the ancient Middle East. Natufian artifacts of the Mesolithic period (c. 10,000–8000 B.C.E.) suggest a sacred marriage cult that would emerge clearly in the culture of the Sumerians, especially in connection with the goddess of sexuality and reproduction, Inanna. The divine marriage was the sacramental expression of what was a central fertility myth. In the ceremony, apparently ritually consummated in a chamber at the top of a ziggurat-temple, the king represented Inanna's shepherd—sometimes fisherman—husband Dumuzi (Tammuz in Hebrew and Aramaic). Presumably, a priestess took the role of the goddess in the marriage ceremony.

In the most ancient of "hymns," Inanna longs for love and intercourse with the king in order to bring her fertility to the land in question. At Uruk, Inanna's holiest city, a sacred ritual drama was enacted in which, the en or king played the role of Inanna's lover, as Amaushumgalana, the date palm god, bringing the harvest to Inanna, the "Mistress of the Date Clusters" and goddess of the storehouse-temple, who then "opened [her] door" for him, signifying a marriage that would bring prosperity to the city.

SACRIFICE Sacrifice is a universal religious act, one closely associated with the mythologies of particular traditions. Sacrifices are often offered to divinities in the name of society by priestly castes. The offerings themselves may be symbolic or literal, vegetable or animal. Abraham was instructed to offer Isaac as a sacrifice and did so. Scapegoats of various kinds may be used to substitute for living offerings that the given group is unable or unwilling to give up. An animal was substituted for Isaac, and Christians say that Christ died as an offering for us all. Sacrifices are often accomplished at sacred times of the year in certain sacred places. In Asian myth and religion sacrifice plays important roles. Japanese emperors offered sacrifices to the dead and to Shinto nature divinities (Kami). The Chinese emperor, representing his people, made winter solstice sacrifices to the gods and to the dead. Sacrifice is important in the bear cults of the Ainu and to the indigenous religions of Indonesia, as represented, for example, in the Hainuwele myth.

In the Indo-European traditions, sacrifice is the essence of existence in an endless round of dissolution and renewal. The world itself and life for the Hindu is the sacrifice—that which must continually be destroyed and recreated through the eons of history. In the Sankhya tradition, life emerges from the sacrifice of the Vedic primal male or Purusha, and the continuance of existence depends on the proper practice of ritual sacrifice, associated, for example, with deities such as Agni, Daksha, and Kali. The Purusha is the universe past, present, and future. His mouth, out of which springs the primal syllable, is Brahman, the Absolute or Universal Self, the essence that combines with nature to create reality at creation. The moon came from his consciousness, and he knew himself, exclaiming "I Am." He is also Rudra-Shiva, who

destroys the world in the ultimate sacrificial fire, and Vishnu, who reabsorbs reality into his own being. In the literal sense Vishnu becomes the Purusha in the later Hindu myth of his self-decapitation, by which he emerges as the primary god-sacrifice. Sacrifice is also central to the fire rituals of the Iranian Zoroastrians.

Norse mythology, with the story of Ymir, contains its own example of a Purusha-like creation sacrifice, as do Native North American myths of figures such as the Corn Mother.

SALOME The daughter of Herodias and of Herod, a son of Herod the Great in the first century C.E., Salome agreed to dance for her stepfather, Herod Antipas, at his birthday feast. The dance so pleased Herod that he offered to give the girl whatever she wished. At her mother's insistence, Salome demanded the head of the imprisoned John the Baptist. Herodias was furious that John had condemned her marriage to the half brother of her first husband. Herod was reluctant to kill his prisoner, but he kept his promise, and the Baptist's head was brought to Salome on a dish. Although Salome is not mentioned by name in either text, the story of her dance and John's death is told in the New Testament by Matthew (14:6–11) and Mark (6:21–28).

SAMA VEDA The *Sama Veda* is one of the four *Vedas,* or sacred *Shruti* texts of Hinduism. It is a collection of ritual hymns to the god Soma.

SAMGUK SAGI AND SAMGUK YUSA Collections of Korean myths and legends of prehistoric times, these two books were compiled by Buddhist monks. They contain epic tales of the founding of the Korean nation, sun and moon myths, and various Korean hero stories.

SAMSARA For the Hindu, *samsara* is the never-ending cycle of life or of rebirths, which seems real to those who do not understand eternal truth. To the enlightened one, *samsara* is illusion, the material of artifice or *maya.* In a sense, the union of the god and his *Shakti* represents the Absolute—the union of Eternity and Time, nirvana and *samsara.* For Buddhists, it is the teachings of the Buddha that provide the desired release from *samsara.* Through enlightenment the impurity of this world becomes the utter release, or the void, which is nirvana.

SAMSON AND DELILAH In the Book of Judges (15 and 16) of the Hebrew Bible, or Old Testament, the story is told of the hero Samson, an ascetic, or Nazirite, who was, above all, possessed of Herculean strength. It was he who killed the thousand Philistines with the jaw bone of an ass. But like many heroes he was challenged by a femme fatale—in this case, the Philistine woman Delilah—who seduced him and then betrayed him and cut off his long hair, the source of his strength. Now weakened, he was captured and blinded. But as his hair grew back, he regained strength, and eventually he sacrificed his own life by pulling down the supports of a temple, causing the death of his Philistine captors.

SANSKRIT Sanskrit (Sanscrit), a word derived from *samskrta,* meaning "perfectly formed," is the name of the ancient language of India. It is the oldest of the Indo-European languages and is used in sacred Hindu writings from the *Vedas* on.

Saturn devours one of his sons

According to myth, the language (and speech, in general) was discovered by Sarasvati, the wife of the creator god Brahma. As the creator's *Shakti*, Sarasvati was the appropriate being to create the vehicle for the articulation of creation.

SAOSHYANT Saoshyant (Saoshyans) is a Zoroastrian term for "savior." According to the Zoroastrian tradition of Iran, three great Saoshyants will come after Zoroaster (Zarathustra)—himself a Saoshyant. All later Saoshyants come from the seed of Zoroaster, saved in Lake Kansaoya and guarded by spirits until the savior's virgin mother is miraculously impregnated while bathing there. The last and greatest of the post-Zoroaster Saoshyants is to be Astvatereta—sometimes simply called Saoshyant—who will finally destroy the forces of evil aligned against those of the good in Zoroastrian theology.

SARASVATI Sarasvati means "flowing," and this Vedic goddess of India appears in the *Rig Veda* as a sacred river. She is a goddess of learning and the arts. As the wife and *Shakti* of the creator god Brahma, Sarasvati is appropriately the goddess of speech, the inventor of the sacred language, Sanskrit, the "flow" by means of which eternal creation is articulated in Time. But with the dying out of the Brahma cult Sarasvati was sometimes seen as a wife of another creator, Vishnu, and sometimes in the ancient texts she is associated, as an aspect of sacrificial fire, with the fire god Agni.

SARGON The Akkadian Semite king Sargon (Akkadian Sharrumkin, "True King") united and ruled the lands of Sumer and Akkad in Mesopotamia between c. 2335 and 2279 B.C.E. Like many of the early Mesopotamian kings, he became the source of myths and legends. Sargon was said to have been born of a virgin, hidden in a basket, released into a river, and adopted, some say by a palm grower. This sequence of events ties him to other monomythic hero stories, including those of Moses and Siegfried. Later Sargon gained the support of the goddess Ishtar (Inanna) and rose to kingship.

SARPEDON The brother of Minos and Rhadamanthus and son of Europa and the Greek high god Zeus, Sarpedon ruled Crete with his brothers until all three fell in love with the boy Miletus. When Miletus chose Sarpedon, Minos exiled both his brothers. Another story says that Sarpedon was the grandson of Bellerophon, that he became king of Lycia in Asia Minor, and that he was killed by Patroclos in the Trojan War.

SATAN In the Abrahamic traditions, Satan, meaning "enemy" in Hebrew—known as al-Shaytan (Shaitan) in Arabic, and often called the Devil in the New Testament of the Bible and other Christian writings—is the primary adversary of Yahweh-God-Allah. In Hebrew scripture *Satan* (*the satan*) is an evil entity clothed in the common noun until 1 Chronicles 21:1, when it takes on the proper name, *Satan*. The Serpent in the Book of Genesis has, of course, at least in the later Jewish tradition and in the Christian tradition, been seen as an embodiment of that Satan, as has *the satan*, the figure who, with Yahweh's permission, tests Job in the Book of Job (1 and 2).

In Christian mythology—given a romantically defiant personality by the seventeenth-century poet John Milton in his literary epic *Paradise Lost*—Satan, the Devil, who corrupted Adam and Eve in the Garden of Eden, has power in the world; tempts Jesus, much as Mara the Fiend tempted the Buddha; is over-powered by Jesus when he descends to Hell after his death; and will enter the eternal fire with his fellow "fallen angels" at the Last Judgment (Matthew 4:8–9, 13:24–30; Luke 10:18; John 14:30, 16:11; Revelation 12:7–9).

In Islamic mythology, al-Shaytan is Iblis (the "devil") and his followers, who refuse Allah's protection in favor of a path that leads to Hell (*jahannam*).

SATANIC VERSES According to Islamic tradition, al-Shaytan (Satan) caused Muhammad to utter verses in the *Qur'an* referring to ancient pre-Islamic Arabian goddesses al-Lat, al 'Uzza, and Manat as intercessors with Allah. He did so to appease the Meccans, who worshipped these deities. Through the angel Jibril (Gabriel), Allah later canceled these "Satanic" verses and substituted ones that spoke of these goddesses, the *banat al-Lah* ("Daughters of God"), as mere illusions (*Qur'an* 53:19–26).

SATI *Sati*, or *suttee*, is the Hindu custom in which wives are immolated on the funeral pyres of their husbands. Sati ("good woman") is also a name of the Great Goddess (Devi), who, as the daughter of Brahma's son Daksha and a consort of Shiva, is an embodiment of the perfect Hindu wife. The *Devibhagavata Purana* tells how Sati used the "fire of her yoga" to reveal the dharma of the practice of *sati*. Sati herself was burned in the world-destroying fire of Shiva. Shiva took her out of the fire, and Vishnu dismembered her with his arrows. Where each limb fell, a devotional area for Shiva was established.

In the Pali language of ancient Buddhist texts, *sati* ("mindfulness") is a form of meditation leading to the meaning of the word.

SATURN Saturn, or Saturnus, was a mythical king associated by the Romans with the Greek god Kronos, the father of the first-generation Olympians, and, therefore, in Rome, of their equivalents, Jupiter, Neptune, Pluto, and Juno. In fact, Saturn seems to have been an ancient Italic fertility god—possibly of Etruscan origin—of agriculture, a culture hero–like deity who introduced planting practices and social order. In that tradition, his wife was Ops, the embodiment of fertility and abundance. The feast of Saturnalia in Rome was held in Saturn's honor.

SATURNALIA The god-king Saturn's feast in Rome was a seven-day celebration in December called the Saturnalia, a term that has come to be associated with any revel-based celebration marked by licentiousness and the temporarily allowed breaking of taboos.

SATYRS In ancient Greek mythology, satyrs were male followers of the god Dionysos (Bacchus). They were part human and part goat in their physical and emotional characteristics. Usually depicted naked and in a state of sexual arousal and drunkenness, they often chased the Maenads, female followers of the god. Satyrs and Maenads represented fertility and the freedom and wildness of the woods and fields. They were sometimes identified in Rome with a species known as fauns.

SAULE A Baltic sun goddess, Saule is closely associated—sometimes in conflict—with the sky god Dievs. In places where they are not husband and wife, conflicts between Dievs and Saule arise because of things done by personifications of the stars, the Asvani, to the Saules Meitas ("Daughters of the Sun"). These actions are mirrored not only by the Baltic tradition of the ritual abduction of brides but by the theft of the brides Phoebe and Hilaeeria by the Greek Dioscuri. The conflicts between Saule and Dievs are not terribly important, however. Saule is a farming mother protecting her children, and in places where she is particularly honored she gives the world the gift of her warmth, riding, like Apollo, across the sky in her sun chariot. Saule is associated with the world oak tree, the saules koks ("sun tree"), the source of all fertility, that grows out of the heavenly mountain and has been seen by no mortal. This suggests that Saule is a relative of those pre–Indo-European great mothers of the world without whom there is no life. In Latvian folklore she walks across fields with her skirts raised as if to bring the fertility of her loins to the land.

SAVITRI Celebrated in India as, like Sati, the ideal wife, Savitri ("Daughter of the Sun") is an incarnation of sorts of Sarasvati, the wife and *Shakti* of the Hindu creator god Brahma. As Sarasvati is the founder of language and Sanskrit, Savitri is the birth giver of and sometimes, as Gayatri, a personification of the *Vedas*. Brahma felt great desire for Savitri and placed his seed in her, where it remained for a hundred years before producing the *Vedas* and many other aspects of creation—memory, the Kali age, and day and night, for example. In one of her forms Savitri saves her husband, Satyavan, from the clutches of Yama, the god of death.

SCAPEGOAT MYTHS In the Jewish tradition, the scapegoat was one of two goats used in a ritual celebration on the Day of Atonement in the Temple. While one goat was sacrificed to Yahweh, the other was thrown over a cliff to take the sins of the people with it. Sir James Frazer and others have studied the scapegoat traditions in other cultures, traditions that sometimes involved the sacrifice of a prisoner or a child, or even the symbolic or actual killing of a king or temporary "king for a day." Out of such sacrifice, it was believed, could come new life. The myths of dying gods, including those of such figures as Jesus and Osiris, may be said to be scapegoat myths, since these deaths result in physical or spiritual fertility. In the scapegoat myth the hero metaphorically carries the sins of the society away with him into the sacrificial death and leaves his people clean and ready to be reborn. [Frazer (1911–1915)]

SCATHACH Scathach nUanaind or Scathach Buanand ("the "Victorious") was an Amazon of Irish mythology, a great female warrior who trained Irish heroes such as Cuchu-

Satyrs

lainn on her island. It was she who presented Cuchulainn his famous spear, Gae-Bolg. Cuchulainn had an affair with Scathach's daughter, Uathach, and he helped Scathach in her battle against her stronger sister, Aoife, whom he defeated and then seduced, becoming the father by her of Connlai.

SCIRON Sciron was a robber who forced travelers near Corinth in ancient Greece to wash his feet before kicking them from the Scironian cliff into the sea. A giant turtle ate these fallen victims. The hero Theseus defeated the terrible Sciron and threw him off the cliff to his inevitable doom.

SCYLLA AND CHARYBDIS These terrible female nature monsters, who threatened Odysseus and other Greek heroes, guarded the straits of Messina from two large rocks between Sicily and mainland Italy. Charybdis was the daughter of Gaia by Poseidon. Scylla was a beautiful nymph who was loved by Poseidon and turned into a six-headed monster by the jealous Amphitrite. Charybdis became a whirlpool that sucked its victims into the sea to their deaths. Scylla took hold of passing sailors and ate them.

SECRET HISTORY OF THE MONGOLS The *Manghal un Niuca Tobca'an* or *Secret History of the Mongols* is an extensive narrative compiled in the thirteenth century to reveal the history of the Turko-Mongols and their attempt to achieve the vitality of mythical times in the era of Jenghiz Khan. From the time of the mythical giant Qutula, known for his enormous strength, the Mongol leaders saw themselves as descendants of the Sky, Tengri (Tangri). The narrative in question tells the story of the brutal battles for supremacy over their neighbors, battles justified by the belief in divine Mongol origins.

SEDNA Sedna (Nuliajuk) is the sea spirit of the Inuit people, the other primary spirits being of the air and of the moon. Sedna provides the animals eaten by the people. There are various stories of this spirit, but all have somewhat violent animistic aspects in which parts of Sedna herself become creatures of value to the Inuit. Some say that Sedna was once a girl who lived with her father, Anguta. One day, they say, a great sea bird, a fulmar, enticed the girl and convinced her to follow him to his home over the sea. Once she got to the fulmar's home, however, Sedna was disgusted by its foul condition and by the lack of food, and she called for her father to rescue her. Anguta took his time, arriving with the warm winds of summer a year later. He killed the fulmar and took his daughter to his boat for the trip home. But the fulmar's followers were enraged at the death of their leader and chased down Anguta's boat with violent winds. To lessen the boat's weight and to save himself, the father threw his daughter into the sea, and as she clung desperately to the side of the boat, he cut off her fingers. These became the whales, seals, and fish that the people still eat today. When the storm had passed, Sedna emerged from the depths of the sea and climbed back into the boat. As her father was asleep, she ordered their dogs to eat his hands and feet. This they did, and when Anguta woke up he was furious, causing such a great commotion that the earth swallowed him, Sedna, and the dogs and sent them to Adlivun, where Sedna now rules.

Another myth says that Sedna's father forced her to marry a dog and that after the dissolution of that marriage she married a bird. At that point the story continues in the form of the one above until the point that Sedna loses her fingers and they turn into sea animals. According to this myth, Sedna and her father and Sedna's former dog husband live in the sea.

SEKHMET In the Memphite theology of ancient Egypt, Sekhmet (the "Powerful One") was the wife of the creator god Ptah. Her form was that of a human with the head of a lioness. Sekhmet was capable of Kali-like fury and destruction. When she was sent by Re to destroy humanity, she did such a thorough job that she had to be restrained. The restraint was accomplished when she became intoxicated by the beer that was used for the world-cleansing Egyptian flood.

SELENE The sister of the sun god Helios, Selene was a Greek moon goddess.

SEMARA In Bali, Semara was the goddess of love, who resided in the heaven known as the Floating Sky.

SEMELE It is said that the Greek god Zeus, disguised as a mortal, had a love affair with Semele ("Moon"), daughter of the King of Thebes. Soon Semele was very pregnant with the son of the high god. It was the jealous Hera who, disguised as an old woman, advised the young woman to entice her lover to allow her anything she wished. The disguised goddess assured the woman that in the throes of passion Zeus would, of course, agree and Semele was then to request that he reveal himself to her in his true form. The trick worked; Zeus, who could never go back on his word, felt obligated to reveal himself to Semele. As no mortal can bear the power and brightness of the god of thunder and lightning, Semele was destroyed by her vision. Fortunately, Hermes saved the unborn baby and sewed it into Zeus's thigh, from which, three months later, the "twice-born" god was born.

SEMITES AND SEMITIC MYTHOLOGY In the ancient Middle Eastern world made up of Mesopotamia, Arabia, and the lands to which the familiar names of Iraq, Phoenicia, Lebanon, Syria, Canaan, Jordan, Israel, and Palestine have at various times been associated, Semitic peoples, with related languages, included the post-Sumerian Akkadians, Babylonians, and Assyrians; the Arameans; the Canaanites (including the Phoenicians and the people of Ugarit); the Hebrew-Israelites; and the Arabs. Abraham (Abram, Ibrahim) was a hero common to many of the Semites, as were a number of patriarchs and prophets. Out of their Abrahamic roots, the Semites produced the so-called Abrahamic religions—Judaism, Christianity, and Islam—all dedicated to the same god, known as Yahweh, God, and Allah.

SEPARATE HEAVENLY DEITIES In Japanese Shinto mythology, the five separate deities were the primal gods, the first to exist. They were Amanominakanushi, the god of Heaven; Takamimusubi; Kamimusubi; Umashiashikabihikoji; and Amanoyokotachi.

SEPARATION OF PRIMORDIAL PARENTS In the creation myths of many cultures, a common theme is the separation of primordial beings who usually represent the sky and earth. In the beginning these beings are usually locked in an embrace that leaves no room for creation between them. The significance of the primal state is that it is stagnant, lacking in the differentiation necessary for further creation. In many cases a god or several gods, sometimes offspring of the primal couple, separate the couple. In Egypt Geb (Earth) is separated from Nut (Sky); among the Polynesians various versions of the first parents are separated by their children; the Prajapati myth in the Indian *Vedas* and the Nareau myth of Micronesia have separation aspects; the central Asians have

S

a separation myth, and so do the Greeks, in whose mythology Kronos reaches a sickle in between his parents, Ouranos and Gaia, and separates them by castrating his father.

SERAPIS Serapis was a fertility god of healing introduced into Greece and Rome from Egypt in connection with the cult of the goddess Isis during the Ptolemaic period. Serapis had emerged as the "Lord of the Universe" out of the connection at Memphis between the resurrection god Osiris and the Apis Bull.

SERPENT MYTHS Serpent myths are ubiquitous in world mythology. They are phallic and they penetrate the earth, making them frequent associates of the goddess in her many forms and objects connoting fertility. Chinawezi is the serpent Mother Goddess of the Luba Linda people in Africa. In other animistic traditions in places such as Native North America and Mesoamerica the serpent, represented by symbols suggesting lightning and a zigzagging river, can signify fertility as well. The Mesoamerican god Quetzalcoatl is the "feathered serpent." In Hindu mythology the serpent is Ananta (Shesha), an embodiment of endlessness or eternity, on whose back the god Vishnu sleeps before creation. A common symbol is that of the serpent with its tail in its mouth becoming a mandala and signifying wholeness or eternity. Even a clearly negative or evil serpent such as the one in the popular myth of Adam and Eve is a fertility figure, as he in a sense seduces the first woman into partaking of forbidden fruit, an act that will lead to consciousness of sexuality. In some traditions, such as those of Babylon and Greece, the defeated serpent reflects the rise of patriarchy over the old earth-based religion. Thus Marduk defeats Tiamat and Apollo defeats the Python associated with the former dominance of Earth (Gaia) at Delphi.

SETH Trickster deities were present in Egypt as in most of the ancient world. In a very general sense the gods Seth and Thoth might be understood as negative and positive aspects of the archetypal trickster god. Seth, like so many tricksters, was amoral and was driven by Iago-like pure evil, jealousy, and greed. Also like other sometimes reprehensible tricksters—Loki in Scandinavia, Ananse in Africa, Coyote in North America, for instance—he was extremely clever and could play positive roles as well. Early in the Old Kingdom, as we have seen, he was the patron of certain dynasties. And in his positive aspect, again like several trickster gods, he assisted the high god/creator. He was sometimes shown as a guardian of Re's sun bark, using his magic spells to defend it against the serpent Apopis. Depicted with floppy ears and an erect and divided tail, he was, however, usually a negative deity, standing in the way especially of the "good" gods, Osiris and his son Horus. Seth's wife was his sister Nephtys, who helped Isis to revive Osiris. Theologically speaking, Seth performed the necessary role of death and destruction in the overall process of life. It is he who was responsible for the death of Osiris and for the loss of one of Horus's eyes—the moon—which was retrieved by Thoth.

SEVEN AGAINST THEBES Much of the story of *Seven Against Thebes* comes to us primarily by way of the 467 B.C.E. play of that title by the Greek playwright Aeschylus. The myth concerns the struggle for supremacy at Thebes between Eteocles and Polynices, the sons of the unfortunate Oedipus. Eteocles had won out over his brother and had exiled him. But Polynices returned with six comrades, including his father-in-law, Adrastus, the king of Argos. The seven invaders were defeated, and Eteocles and Polynices

killed each other, setting the stage for the second ascension of Creon to the throne and his confrontation with Oedipus's valiant daughter, Antigone. Only Adrastus managed to escape the disaster at Thebes, having been saved by the swiftness of his horse, Arion, a gift of Herakles. Ten years after the war, Adrastus led the sons of the six heroes killed during the first battle and succeeded in leveling Thebes.

SEVEN GODS OF FORTUNE In the esoteric Tendai sect of Japanese Buddhism, there developed a composite representation of good fortune made up of the god Daikoku-ten, an ancient Shinto *kami* named Ebisu, and the gods Benzai-ten and Bishamon. Joined in the sixteenth century by three deities of good fortune of Chinese origin—Hotei, Fukuroku-ju, and Jurogin—the seven deities became the Seven Gods of Fortune, or Happiness, and ever since have represented good luck, especially to people in business.

SEVEN SAGES Both Indian mythology and Sumero-Akkadian mythology contain traditions of seven sages. In India they appear frequently to impart their wisdom. In Mesopotamia, the sages (the *apkallu*) apparently irritated the gods with their advice and were banished to the Apsu. One story recounts that the seven sages acted in the role of the culture hero by teaching humanity the elements of culture.

SEVEN SISTERS The Kuungarankalpa ("Seven Sisters") are heroines of the Aboriginal Australian dreaming, the mythical creation process. As the seven sisters fled before a pursuing lecher, Nyiru, aspects of the Australian landscape followed in their path—remnants of their camping and other activities. When they reached the southern coast they fled into the sea and then into the sky, where they became the constellation known in the West as the Pleiades.

SHAH-NAMAH The *Shah-Namah* or "Book of Kings" is an epic containing the legendary and actual early history of Persia

Perseus slays the sea serpent

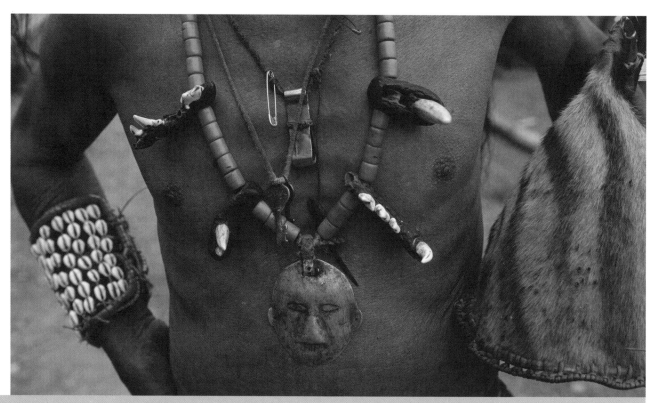

A Naga shaman ready for work in Myanmar

(Iran). Collected in the main in about 1000 C.E. by the poet Firadusi, it is a compilation of Firadusi's own work as well as later added material and ancient histories and tales composed long before Firadusi's time. In some 60,000 couplets, the epic covers the period between the rule of the invading Aryan Keyumars to the historical emergence of Islam in 651. Popular segments include the story of the rule of the evil tyrant Zahhak and his defeat at the hands of the dragon king–hero Faridun, the coming of Zoroaster (Zardosht or Zarathustra), and the tale of the giant hero Rostam, who, defending the Shah Key Kavus, unwittingly kills his own son, Sohrab. It is this story of Rostam that was used by Matthew Arnold in his poem "Sohrab and Rustam" in 1853.

SHAITAN Shaitan, or al-Shaytan, is the Islamic term for Satan and for those who are in opposition to Islam.

SHAIVAS Shaivas are Shiva Bhakti people—particular devotees of the Hindu god Shiva as the supreme god. Shaivism has many sects and is found in all parts of India.

SHAKA This is the Japanese name for the Buddha Sakyamuni, or Gautama Buddha.

SHAKAT KATHA A *katha* is a narrative performed as part of a Hindu ritual. The *Shakat Katha* is an instructive myth told in Northern India on the occasion of a festival honoring the elephant-headed Ganesh. It stresses the importance of proper fasting and proper ritual practice.

SHAKKA An incarnation of the Vedic-Hindu god Indra, Shakka was the king of the gods in the Hindu heaven known as Tavatimsa.

SHAKTAS Devotees or worshippers of the Goddess (Devi-Shakti) as ultimate power are Shaktas. Shaktism, along with the worship of Shiva (Shaivism) and Vishnu (Vais-nava), is an important element of Hinduism, especially the branch of Hinduism called Tantrism. Shaktism has roots in the pre-Aryan Indus Valley civilization. In Tantric imagery there is the tradition of the union of Shiva and Shakti as the absolute.

SHAKTI The Sanskrit for "power" or "energy," *Shakti* is the energizing material power of a given Hindu god, a power that is personified as his wife, especially the wife of Shiva. Often depicted in a state of sexual union, the god and his *Shakti* together represent the absolute, the god being non-activated Eternity, the goddess being activated Time. The Goddess, Devi, is *Shakti* or "Universal Power." As Prakriti, she is the Shakti or female energy by which the original Purusha, the primal male, becomes creation. As Lakshmi, she is the manifestation of the divine energy associated with Vishnu. Shiva's *Shakti* takes many forms—Uma, Durga, the terrifying Kali, the motherly Parvati, for instance. By extension, Sita is the Vishnu avatar Rama's *Shakti* in the *Ramayana*, and Drau-padi is the *Shakti* of the Pandavas in the *Mahabharata*. And by further extension, the Hindu wife is a manifestation of her husband's *Shakti*. By still further extension, *Shakti* lives in all women.

SHALAKAPURUSHA In the Jain mythology of India, the Shalakapurushas are saviors, heroes, and emperors in the universe's alternate periods of ascent and decline.

SHAMANISM Shamanism is a religious phenomenon involving the disciplines and the practices of shamans. Although existing in various forms in various parts of the world, shamanism in its purest form is native to Siberia and central Asia and to the indigenous peoples of Native North America—particularly the Navajos—and South America, who, in any case, seem likely to have central Asian origins. Shamans have also existed in the context of Shinto in Japan, their duties relating primarily to village rituals. In Indo-China, shamans are concerned with curing. Korean shamans communicate with the spirit world. Shamans are, in a sense, religious magicians, who typically have power over fire and are capable of achieving trance states in séances in which their souls vacate their bodies to go on curing missions to the spirit worlds above or below the earth. The shaman's primary purpose everywhere is to cure. The successful shaman controls the spirits with whom he works, and he can communicate with the dead. Thus it is that he often wears bones signifying the skeletal remains of the dead. His is a mystical vocation in that he works from an otherworldly state of ecstasy. In many cases a shaman realizes his vocation because of dreams and nonvoluntary trances. Sometimes a shaman is trained as an apprentice by a master shaman. In any case, the shaman must learn to control and use certain ritualistic paraphernalia—especially the drum, the vehicle on which he travels to the other worlds—and he must memorize the necessary ritual forms and songs. Some shamans undergo an initiation period during which they seem to die. According to these shamans they are dismembered before being given new flesh and blood. Shamans are most often male, but there are female shamans as well in many cultures.

SHANGO Shango is a deity of the western Africa Yoruba people. As a king of the Yoruba he was overthrown for his authoritarian ways, but he redeemed himself by hanging himself on a tree and making a Jesus-like ascent into Heaven, where he is now a weather god. He was married to the lake named Oja that later became the Niger River.

SHAPASH Shapash was the Canaanite (Ugaritic) sun goddess.

SHAPE SHIFTERS Tricksters and sometimes shamans are said to have the ability to change their shapes at will. The Native North American Coyote can become an old woman or a rug or a coyote. The African Ananse is sometimes a bird, sometimes a spider, sometimes a man. Magicians and wizards—shamans of sorts—such as Merlin can change shapes or cause others to change shapes in order to achieve their ends.

SHEM In Hebrew mythology, Shem was a son of Noah and the ancestor of all the Semites—Babylonians, Assyrians, Arabs, and Hebrews.

SHIH-CHING The *Shih-Ching* ("Book of Odes") is a series of collections of Chinese poetry dating from as early 1100 B.C.E. and compiled in about 600 B.C.E. Tradition has it that Confucius collected some of the poems. The collection reflects the Chou dynasty's sense of the relationship between humans and the gods. The poems were set to music and sung in praise of the gods and the ancestors and were accompanied by particular rituals.

SHINGON SECT The Shingon sect or Shingonshu of Japanese Mahayana Buddhism is the only sect today that keeps alive the esoteric or *Mikkyo* tradition centered on Dainichi Nyorai, the Buddha Mahavairocana, the cosmic illuminator, who, as the perfect expression of the ultimate truth of pure "emptiness," is the creator. The Mikkyo way is opposed to the *Kengyo* tradition, which is based on the understandings of Sakyamuni or Gautama Buddha. Shingon comes via the Chinese *Chen-yen*, meaning "true saying," itself derived from the Sanskrit term and concept *mantra*. Chen-yen was a form of Tantric Buddhism (Vajrayana). The monk Kukai (774–835) founded the Shingon sect during the Heian peri-

od. He had been introduced to the esoteric rituals and texts of Chen-yen by the Chinese monk Hui-kuo. At the center of Shingon are two Tantric *sutras*, the *Mahavairocana* and the *Sarvatathagatatatt-vasamgraha*. An essential aspect of these sutras and of Shingon is the idea that the illumination of the Dainichi nyorai exists in everyone. All beings are, therefore, capable of enlightenment, not just a perfect few. The union of the illuminator and the illumined is expressed in two complicated diagrams or sacred *mandalas* by Kukai.

SHINTO MYTHOLOGY Shinto, meaning the "*kami* way," is a term applied to the ancient religion of Japan to differentiate it from *Butsudo*, the "Buddha way" or Buddhism. Shinto is a polytheistic system that expresses the ancient Japanese worldview. There are Shinto prayers and Shinto rituals, but doctrine is minimal. Some might call Shinto a way of life rather than a religion per se. The mythic basis of Shinto is the belief in *kami*. Originally the word *kami* was used to describe any mysterious or sacred reality, anything that seemed to possess numinosity. In a sense, though, everything is potentially kami and, thus, worthy of reverence. Because of the concept of kami, Shinto at once affects the way tea is served, the way a package is wrapped, the way a war is fought, and the way an emperor is crowned. Gradually the kami concept took on concrete forms—deities who lived in natural objects or phenomena, ancestor divinities, and abstract concept divinities. Shinto shrines and rituals were at first local and agricultural in nature, but eventually they became associated with larger entities, including clans and the nation itself. The gods of Shinto are directly related to the imperial family and thus to the Japanese state. It could be argued that all Japanese are practitioners of Shinto, even if they happen to be Buddhist or Christian as well. By the eighth century, Shinto and Buddhism achieved a kind of marriage, with Shinto and Buddhist deities becoming merged and/or deities of one religion revered in the temples of the other.

Early Shinto envisioned a standard northern Asian cosmology made up of an upper world or Heaven (Takamanohara) for the gods, a middle world (Nakatsukuni) for humans, and an underworld (Yomi) for the dead. Yet simultaneously, Shinto understood the universe as the

View of a Shinto Shrine, c. 1889

Shiva, the "destroyer," shown with the Deva and Bhairava

An Indus Valley seal from the city of Harappa depicts a three-faced figure sitting cross-legged in a yogi style, suggesting the great yogi-ascetic that the god was to become in later Hinduism. In the *Vedas*, Shiva is known more as Rudra. It was not until the second century B.C.E. that the god came into his own as the equal and sometimes the superior of Vishnu and the other gods. In the epic poem the *Mahabharata*, he is even worshipped by his fellow gods. Shiva's role as god of destruction is intricately involved with his role as the god of generation. The implication is that without death there can be no life. The process of the universe is one of destruction and generation, death and renewal. It is not surprising, therefore, that Shiva is often depicted in union with his *Shakti*, or consort—his materializing power—or that he is worshipped by way of the *linga* (sacred phallus), often planted in the *yoni* (sacred female sexual organ), which can represent the Goddess, or Shakti. Shiva is worshipped in many guises. He is Nataraja, the lord of the dance, whose dance is the process of the universe itself. He is the ultimate *guru*, the model for the yogi-ascetic. He brings *Moksha* (release) to those who trust in him. There are literally thousands of myths associated with this important manifestation of Hindu godhead. Many of the myths are associated with the various forms of his consort, the Goddess, that is, embodiments of Shiva Shakti. These include the terrifying goddesses Kali and Durga, as well as the beneficent daughter of the Mountain, Parvati, the mother of the popular elephant-headed god, Ganesh. Shiva figures in countless myths, among them those of Agni, Annamar, Banaras, Daksha, the Descent of the Ganges, Durvasas, Harihara, Indra and Virtra, Jalamdhara, Karttikeya (Skanda), Mahashakti, Manasa-Mangals, Mankanaka, Maya, Mountain mythology, Murugan, Prajapati, Sati, and Shoten.

SHOTEN Shoten, or Binayakya or Daisho-kangiten, is esoteric Japanese Buddhism's version of the Indian elephant-headed god, Ganesh (Vinayaka). As in India, he came to be thought of in Japan as the son of Shiva (Daijizaiten in Japan). The cult of Shoten was brought to Japan from China and Tantric Buddhism (Vajrayana) by the founder of the Shingon sect early in the ninth century and was also taken up by the Tendai sect. Shoten is depicted as a double figure—a powerful male god in an embrace with a gentle female bodhisattva. The connection between this dual image and the embracing Shiva and his Shakti is evident. In both cases the embrace has symbolic importance, conveying wholeness. The Japanese esoteric Buddhist figure signifies, as well, the union of the individual with the Buddha. With enlightenment the double image becomes a single image.

SHRI *Shri* means "prosperity" in Sanskrit and is an honorific title for Hindus. Thus, the name of a famous guru or philosopher might be preceded by the term. Shri is also a late Vedic goddess—a personification of the idea of prosperity. The male gods were jealous of her and took over her powers. So it is that Shri is also another name for Vishnu's consort Lakshmi, who also represents prosperity.

SHRUTI AND SMIRTI Literally "that which is heard," *Shruti* is revelation, or the highest form of sacred text, for Hindus. The *Vedas* are *Shruti*, for example, while other important texts are merely *Smirti*—still sacred but only "remembered" and therefore corrupted by the human element rather than transmitted directly from the divine source. The *Mahabharata*, for instance, though much revered and considered to be "religious," is *Smirti*.

world with an adjacent eternal paradise (Tokoyo) across the sea. Under the influence of Chinese culture there was a drive to compile and standardize Shinto myths that had formerly belonged to regional and family groups. This drive for standardization coincided with the political drive for national unification and began to take concrete form during the reign of the Emperor Temmu (672–687). The culmination of the movement for mythological unity came with the creation of the two primary sacred books of Shinto, the *Kojiki* and the *Nihongi*, early in the eighth century. It is in these books and other early–eighth-century texts (e.g., the *Fudoki* and the *Sendai kujuhongi*) that the purest form of Shinto mythology is to be found. They contain the stories of and descriptions of the Shinto deities and spirits, the *kamis*), as opposed to the amalgamation of Buddhist and Shinto deities that became popular with the advent of Buddhism in Japan.

Perhaps the most important of the anthropomorphic Shinto deities is the sun goddess Amaterasu, the patroness and ancestor of the Japanese emperors. It was her relatives and descendants who founded the Japanese nation. In the beginning, when earth and Heaven separated, kamis appeared, including Izanagi and his wife Izanami, who created the natural world and various clans before their tragic separation and enmity. Their most important offspring were Amaterasu, the moon god Tsukiyomi no Mikoto, and the underworld god Susanowo. It was Susanowo's offspring, Okuninushi no Kami, who ruled Japan until the coming of Ninigi no Mikoto, the grandson of Amaterasu. This is a process described in the Izumo cycle. But it was Ninigi's grandson, Jimmu Tenno, who reigned as the first emperor. [Kitagawa, Miller, Takeshi]

SHIVA In the trinity or *trimurti* of Hinduism, Shiva, meaning "auspicious one," stands as the "destroyer" with Vishnu the Preserver and Brahma the Creator. For Shaivas, practitioners of Shiva devotion (bhakti), he is the principal manifestation of ultimate divinity (Brahman). In practice, he stands with Vishnu and the Goddess (Devi) as one of the three principal deities of Hinduism. It seems likely that Shiva, like the Goddess, has roots in the ancient pre-Aryan culture of the Indus Valley.

SHU AND TEFNUT In the Egyptian theological center of Heliopolis, Shu ("Air") and Tefnut ("Moisture") emerged out of the sun god, Atum or Atum-Re. Together Shu and Tefnut produced Geb and Nut ("Earth" and "Sky"), who in turn became the parents of four of the primary figures in a dominant Egyptian myth: Osiris, Isis, Seth, and Nephtys. It was Shu who separated his children, Geb and Nut, so that air, and the possibility of further creation, could exist between earth and sky.

SHUN One of the ancient Chinese emperors who form a part of Chinese mythology as well as history, Shun was the successor of Yao, considered by the Chinese to be the ancestor of the Han emperors. It was Yao who named the pious Shun the heir to his throne. Shun is a model of Confucian values. The myths and legends surrounding Shun are many. It is said that a blind peasant named Gu Sou dreamed of a phoenix who carried rice to him and said he would become his child and that soon after, the peasant's wife gave birth to Shun. This places Shun among other mythological heroes who are typically conceived in a miraculous or unusual manner. Shun was remarkable, too, for having two pupils in each eye. When Shun's mother died and the father remarried, this time to a woman with her own children, Shun's life became one of great suffering. Longing for his mother, the boy left home and lived in a small hut. There he sang of his lost mother and so moved the people that they gave him land and good fishing spots, and eventually he prospered and was adopted by the Emperor Yao, who gave the former peasant his two daughters as wives. With the help of heavenly magic and his loyal wives, Shun was able to overcome his family's attempts to murder him. The emperor now devised a series of tests for the man who had been recommended as his successor. Helped by his loyal wives, he succeeded in all of the tests and was named Yao's heir. After a reign in which evil was expelled from the kingdom and goodness established, Shun died and was buried in the Jiuyi Mountains.

SIBYL, THE The most famous of the Greco-Roman *sibyls* or prophetesses was the great Cumaean Sibyl, who was said to have sold her prophetic books, known as the *Sibylline Books*, to the Etruscan-Roman King Tarquin, who deposited them on the Capitoline Hill. Later, the Romans would consult these oracular books for guidance in difficult times.

One legend, popularized by the Roman writer Petronius in the forty-eighth chapter of his first-century C.E. *Satyricon*, tells how the Sibyl was given immortality but neglected to ask for eternal youth. As a result, she grew increasingly old and withered but could not die. She was said to have been kept in a bottle hung in the temple of Herakles at Cumae. T. S. Eliot made use of the Sibyl's living-death situation as an appropriate epigram at the beginning of his poem "The Waste Land."

SIDA Sida (Sido, Soido, Sosom, Souw) is a Melanesian culture hero popular in various forms among the Papua people of New Guinea. It was he who became so enraged when a young woman cried out in resistance of his very large penis that he introduced death to the world. He also gave the people various kinds of food and marked his travels, like the figures of the Australian dreaming, with various now-familiar natural landmarks. His trickster qualities, especially those expressed in genital-based myths celebrating his sexuality and particularly his penis, are similar to those of the Polynesian hero Maui.

SIDDHARTHA Siddhartha in Sanskrit (Siddhatta in Pali) is the personal name of Gautama Buddha, the Buddha Sakyamuni. The name suggests the idea of the siddha, one who has achieved perfection, namely enlightenment.

SIF Sif was the wife of the popular Norse god Thor. A fertility goddess, she was famous for her beautiful and abundant wheat-like hair. One night, as she was sleeping next to her husband, the evil trickster Loki shaved off her hair. When confronted and threatened by Thor, he convinced the dwarfs to spin a skein with which to replace the lost hair.

SIGMUND King Sigmund was the father of the hero Sigurd (Siegfried). In German mythology he figures in the *Nibelungenlied* as Siegmund. Sigmund was a direct descendant of the god Odin. He proved his status as a special hero when, as a young man, he succeeded where other warriors failed, removing the sword Gram from the tree into which Odin, disguised as a one-eyed old man, had thrust it. Having succeeded in this act, similar to the one that identified King Arthur, Sigmund went on to perform many heroic deeds. He and his wife Hjordis produced the even greater hero Sigurd.

SIGURD Sigurd (Siegfried in Germany) was the greatest of the Norse and German heroes. He figures prominently in the thirteenth-century *Volsunga Saga* in the north, in the German epic the *Nibelungenlied*, and in Richard Wagner's opera cycle *Der Ring der Nibelungen*. Sigurd was a descendant of the god Odin (Wotan) and was, as several scholars have suggested, the King Arthur of the northern world—perhaps based on a historical figure. He was mythologized in the sagas but was probably of German rather than Scandinavian origin. In the *Nibelungenlied*, he is the son of King Siegmund and Sieglinde. In the *Volsunga Saga*, he is the last of the Volsungs, the son of Sigmund, and the only one of his family who could remove Odin's sword from Branstock, the oak. His mother was Hjiordis. A tradition exists in which Sigurd/Siegfried's mother, threatened as a result of unfair accusations of infidelity, hid her newborn child in a bottle, which fell into the river and eventually broke on a shore. The child, Sigurd/Siegfried, was rescued by a doe and cared for by her for a year, by which time he had grown to the size of a four-year-old. One day he ran off into the forest, where he was rescued by the smith Mimir, who named and raised him. Before long, the boy performed miraculous deeds, revealing Herculean strength. The importance of superhuman powers and of the smith as a guardian and namer thus figures in the stories of both Cuchulainn and Sigurd and is reminiscent of similar patterns in the Greek story of Oedipus and the Roman story of Romulus and Remus.

A Scandinavian version of the story says that Sigurd, the "last of the Volsungs," was raised in his stepfather Hjalprek's court under the tutelage of the smith named Regin. Regin was the brother of Fafnir, who had killed their father, Hreimdar, to steal gold Hreimdar had obtained as ransom. Fafnir had taken the gold, including what would have been Regin's share, and transformed himself into a great venomous dragon serpent. He spent his life brooding over his cursed treasure and laying waste to the countryside all around. Regin, meanwhile, left penniless, went to the court of King Hjalprek, where he worked as smith and later as Sigurd's foster father, teaching the boy the pastimes of nobility and the mystery of runes. As Sigurd began to grow to manhood, his foster father attempted to incite in him the pride and heroic spirit necessary to confront Fafnir; eventually Sigurd agreed to do so, on the condition that Regin forge for him a magnificent sword. Regin created two lesser blades that Sigurd shattered upon the anvil, but the third time Sigurd bade him use the two pieces of Sigmund's broken blade, which Sigurd had obtained from his mother as his inheritance. This blade was named Gram and had come to Sigurd's father, Sigmund, indirectly from Odin. When Regin refashioned it, it cut easily through the anvil. Sigurd now agreed to face Fafnir, once he had avenged his own father's death.

Once Sigurd had accomplished this vengeance he returned to Regin and prepared to make good on his oath. They traveled together to the heath upon which Fafnir lived, and searched until they found the track leading from the lair of the worm to his watering hole; Regin advised Sigurd to dig a trench across this track, to lie in wait within the trench until Fafnir crossed over it, and then to thrust his sword into the serpent's heart. Sigurd asked what would happen to him if he were submerged in the dragon's blood, but Regin merely derided him for his cowardice and made off in haste. Sigurd dug a trench as he had been told, but before he had finished an old gray-beard appeared before him and noted that he should dig a series of drainage trenches so that he would not come to harm from the worm's blood. This old wanderer then vanished; it was not the first time the young hero had been helped by the disguised Odin, the all-seeing one.

Having completed his task, Sigurd hid himself at the bottom of the central trench; he had not long to wait. Soon the earth trembled with the approach of the dragon, and poison spewed all around; but Sigurd was safe in his hiding place. Just as the belly of the beast passed over him, Sigurd thrust the sword with all his might through the heart of the evil

Sinbad

one, and thus the serpent received its death blow. Fafnir asked who had slain him and why, but at first Sigurd refused to reveal his identity; finally, however, stung by the taunts of the dying beast, Sigurd foolishly revealed his name, and so the dragon was able to pass the curse of the gold along to his killer. Sigurd did not fear death, however, and so determined to take the gold anyway and be rich until the day marked out for his fall. After Sigurd had interrogated Fafnir concerning his wisdom about the gods, the dragon died.

With his vile kin safely put to rest, Regin soon appeared on the scene and made demands. Sigurd might keep all the hoard, but Regin asked of the warrior the trifle of Fafnir's roasted heart. This request Sigurd granted, and then Regin drank of the serpent's blood and fell into a deep sleep. While Regin slumbered, Sigurd roasted the dragon's heart for him. Burning his finger by accident, however, Sigurd thrust his digit into his mouth. Upon tasting the blood of the worm, Sigurd suddenly found himself able to understand the speech of birds and learned from those around him of Regin's plan to kill him. So it was that Sigurd drew Gram once more and decapitated his evil foster father. Then he ate some of the heart of Fafnir and packed the rest away. Finally Sigurd made his way to the lair of the dragon and gathered up all of the treasure he found there.

In the treasure was a golden ring that had once belonged to the dwarf Andvari, the original owner of the treasure. The dwarf had placed a curse of death on anyone who possessed the ring. Sigurd was now that possessor.

Sigurd, with his treasure, rode off to find the Valkyrie, Brynhild (German Brunhild), whom he loved and whom Odin had enchanted within a ring of flame. After a confusion of mistaken identities and deceptions, the curse against Sigurd is fulfilled through his assassination and Brynhild's immolation.

SIGYN Sigyn is the strangely faithful wife of the deceptive Norse trickster Loki. Although her husband had been condemned by the other gods for having caused the death of Balder, Sigyn saved her husband from the venom that the gods had hoped would kill him by holding a bowl up to catch it as it dripped from the snakes poised above his head.

SIKH MYTHOLOGY Sikhism is the religion of people who call themselves Sikhs, that is, "learners." The primary teacher is the one god, the ultimate *guru*, Sat-Guru. Below God are several human gurus, beginning with the fifteenth-century northern Indian Nanak Guru and including the famous sixteenth-century teacher Gobind Singh. The Sikh holy book is the *Adi Granth*, itself considered to be the guru successor of Gobind Singh. Nanak Guru chose to move away from the conflict between Hinduism and Islam by worshipping the *Nam*, the *mantra* or formula connoting God's true name. Nanak believed that, with God's help and self-discipline rather than traditional rituals, *samsara*, the endless cycle of existence, could be overcome and release achieved. The path to release involves many stages. Gradually the evil passions can be defeated and God's will achieved.

SILVANUS Silvanus was a pre-Roman Latin divinity of the fields and forests. The Romans identified him with Faunus and later with Pan, although, unlike them, he was usually depicted as an old man.

SINDBAD THE SAILOR The tales of Sindbad the Sailor are known to us as part of the collection of Indian, Persian, and

S

Arabic folktales known as The *Thousand and One Nights* or *Arabian Nights*. The Sindbad tales originate in the eighth and ninth centuries C.E. and may have been influenced by Greek tales of Odysseus. In the tales, the old sailor Sindbad tells of his seven voyages to different parts of the world. On the first voyage, Sindbad and his companions land on an island that turns out to be a whale. After the whale is awakened by the fire the travelers have built on his back, he dives into the depths. Eventually Sindbad is rescued and finds favor with a king. On the second voyage, Sindbad is marooned on an island, but with the help of a giant bird he is able to collect many diamonds before returning home. The third voyage involves confrontations with a race of wicked dwarfs and a Cyclops-like giant who reminds us of Homer's Polyphemus. The giant eats several sailors before Sindbad is rescued. During the fourth voyage Sindbad is shipwrecked in a land of cannibals, but he avoids the insanity that would have been the result of eating human flesh by avoiding the food. In the kingdom to which he escapes he is given a wife, who soon dies. The custom of the country demands that he be buried with his wife but he manages to escape from the tombs, carrying with him the treasures buried with the dead. A monster, who turns out to be the mythical Old Man of the Sea, captures the shipwrecked Sindbad on the fifth voyage and demands a ride on the sailor's back. Sindbad gets the monster drunk and kills him. Sindbad's ship sinks on the sixth voyage. The survivors are washed up on the island of Sri Lanka, where they find jewels. After his companions die, Sindbad collects the jewels and leaves for a distant land on a raft. He presents the king of that land with the jewels and is given a ship to return to his home, which is Baghdad. The final voyage is the most complex. Sindbad escapes his ship as it is being swallowed by a whale. He manages to get to an island and to build a raft. After floating down a river, he is rescued and taken to a man who gives him his daughter as a wife. When the islanders grow wings, Sindbad hopes to fly home on one of them. The winged men, including the one on which he is flying, however, turn out to be agents of the Devil, and when flying high in the sky Sindbad praises Allah, he is dropped onto a mountaintop. He returns to find his wife and then sails with her for home, having been away for twenty-seven years.

SIRENS The Sirens were three beautifully singing female monsters whose heads were human and whose bodies were avian. They seduced sailors with their singing, luring them to inevitable shipwreck on their island—sometimes thought to have been Sicily. Odysseus knew about the Sirens and, always curious, wanted to hear them. To prevent tragedy he sealed up the ears of his sailors and had himself tied to his mast as his ship sailed by the monsters. The Argonauts, too, sailed by unscathed, as Orpheus's even more beautiful music overcame that of the Sirens and, as foretold, the monsters threw themselves, defeated, into the sea.

SISUPALA A character in the Hindu *Puranas* and the epic the *Mahabharata*, Sisupala is the evil relative of the Vishnu avatar Krishna. It was said that the extra eye and extra two arms with which he was born would disappear when he first saw his future killer. The disappearance took place when, as a child, he was placed on Krishna's lap. The child's mother begged for mercy and Krishna agreed to do nothing until he had been offended by Sisupala one hundred times. The one hundredth offense took place when the Pandava king Yudhishthira honored Krishna at his coronation and Sisu-

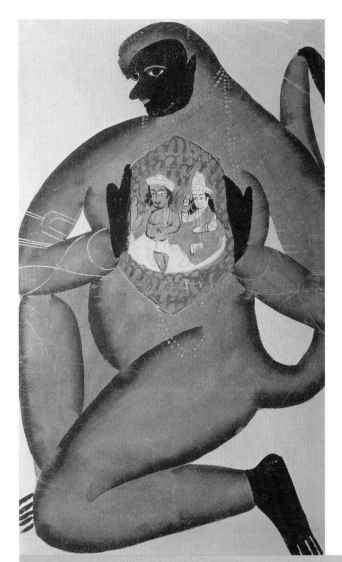

The monkey god Hanuman reveals Sita and Rama enshrined in his heart

pala objected. Krishna flung his discus at his enemy cousin, decapitating him.

SISYPHUS There are many conflicting stories about this ancient Greek king of Corinth. Homer identifies him in the *Iliad* (6:153) as untrustworthy and avaricious and in the *Odyssey* (11:593) as being punished in the underworld by having to repeatedly push a rock to the top of a hill, only to have it roll down again. Some say that Sisyphus was married to Merope, the Pleiade daughter of the Titan Atlas. The usual reason given for his punishment is that he angered Zeus by informing the river god Asopus that he had seen a god-like eagle—clearly Zeus—stealing away the river god's daughter Aegina. Another story says it was Hades he angered by not keeping his side of a bargain by which he was allowed to leave the underworld and return to life with the understanding that he would stay away only long enough to undergo the proper burial he had failed to undergo after his first death.

SITA The wife of the Vishnu avatar Rama in the Hindu epic the *Ramayana*, Sita is an incarnation of Vishnu's wife Lakshmi and is the daughter of the ancient Vedic Earth Goddess Prithivi. Sita was conceived and born miraculously. Sita's father, Janaka (the "begetter"), was plowing a field for a sacrifice when Sita emerged from a furrow in the sacred earth.

SKADI Skadi was the Norse huntress daughter of the giant Thiazi. For a while she was married to the Vanir sea god Njord, by whom she gave birth to the primary Vanir deities, Freyr and his sister Freya.

SKAN An aspect of the Native North American Lakota Great Spirit (Wakan Tanka), Skan's domain is the sky.

SKY GOD The representation of the sky as a god, like that of the earth as a goddess, is ubiquitous and ancient: Father Sky and Mother Earth is a natural prehistoric mythological metaphor. Later, in a more specific sense, sky gods, as opposed to earth deities, represent a value system or worldview in which supreme transcendent, ruling, and usually creator deities are seen as living "on high"—"Our Father who art in heaven"—out of the immediate reach of humans, whereas earth goddesses are essentially earth itself, the world we live in and depend on for nourishment. The most powerful sky gods—various solar gods, the Siberian sky gods, and Zeus and Yahweh-God-Allah, for example—tend to be male; the most powerful earth deities—Gaia and Spider Woman, for example—tend to be female. This division more often than not coincides with and reflects societal roles of and divisions between males and females. The more agricultural, matriarchal, or even merely matrilineal the culture, the more important goddesses tend to be; the more patriarchal, military, and urban oriented the culture, the more important the sky gods become.

SLAVIC MYTHOLOGY Indo-European people known collectively as Slavs, speaking proto-Slavic, were active in central and eastern Europe at least as early as 800 B.C.E. By the tenth century C.E. a long process of separation had produced a western group speaking Polish, Czech, Slovak, and Wendish; an eastern group speaking Russian, Belorussian, and Ukranian; and a southern group speaking Slovenian, Serbo-Croatian, Macedonian, and Bulgarian.

The fact that literacy, as in the case of other early European cultures, came to the Slavs only with Christianity in the ninth and tenth centuries means that relatively little is known of Slavic mythology. What we do know is derived primarily from folklore. There is also useful material in the writing of Christianized Slavs looking back at their pagan heritage. We learn something, for example, from the biographers of Otto, a twelfth-century bishop who struggled against remnants of the old religion in the north. The Byzantine historian Procopius is an important source, as is the Russian *Primary Chronicle*, dating from the early twelfth century and describing the pantheon established in Kiev in 980 by Vladimir I of Russia before his subsequent Christianization in 988.

A major Slavic god whose four heads apparently represented the four directions and the four seasons was Svantovit (Sventovit, Swiantowid), who may be a western version of the eastern Slavonic high god Svarog. In some places two of the god's heads are male, two female. Svantovit is at once a god of war and of fertility. Like many Slavic gods he has direct Iranian antecedents, as indicated by the root *svent*, which has connections with the ideas of both strength and holiness in the Iranian language.

Other many-headed Slavic gods were the seven-faced Rujevit (Rugievit, Ruevit Rinvit), perhaps an aspect of Svantovit, representing autumn and facing east; the five-headed Porevit (Turupit, Tarapita), representing summer and south; the war god Iarovit (Jarovit, Dzarowit, Gerovit, Gerovitus, and perhaps Jarilo), who represents spring and faces west;

the four-faced Porenutius (Potenut, Puruvit); and the three-headed Triglav, whose triune aspect apparently marked his watching over the three major realms—sky, earth, and underworld. Gods with more than one head are common to the Indo-European tradition.

Also present among the Slavs was Tjarnaglofi or Veles (Weles, Volos), the "Black God" or "horned god," a version of the Indo-European underworld or dark god, who may have evolved into the Slavic Christian Satan. He was essentially an earth god. His opposite was the sun god, the god of light, who takes many forms in various Slavic areas (Svantovit himself or Khors-Dazhbog). In some traditions Dazhbog-Khors is a son of Svantovit.

Marija Gimbutas points out that solar god myths are common in Slavic folklore and tells the story of the personified sun driving his golden chariot across the sky, changing from a youth to an old man as he goes. With him go two virgins, personifications of the morning and evening stars, and seven judges representing the seven planets. The solar god has a bald relative, who is the moon. Gimbutas also suggests the similarity between the Slavic opposition between gods of darkness and light and that between the Baltic Dievs and Velinus. She suggests that several of the Slavic gods represent, as noted above, like their counterparts in the Baltic tradition, the aging process of the year (1987c, p. 356).

An important Hephaistos-like smith, solar, and fire god is Svarog (Svarogu among eastern Slavs, but perhaps the same as Svantovit). Svarog is father of the sun (Dazhbog-Khors) and is highly sexual. He is sometimes identified with Swarozhicz, personified fire, whose name, however, means "Son of Svarog." Bialobog (similar to Czarnobog, his brother) is another "Black God" representing winter and north. He is a bent old man with beard and staff, resembling the common image of "Father Time" or Saturn-Kronos. Most of these names and the light-dark duality suggest Iranian influence.

Perun ("Proven"), the thunder god, who is clearly related to the Baltic Perkuno (Perkunus), seems to have been for many Slavs the most important god, as Thor was to many Germanic peoples and Perkuno was to many Balts.

A Slavic god of particular importance to the eventual emergence of Christianity was Jarilo (Iarilo), a Dionysos-like god of youth, and spring wearing a crown of flowers. This was the Slavic version of Adonis-Dionysos-Balder, the dying and resurrected god of fertility.

Another Slavic deity with European counterparts is Lada, the goddess of love, who differs from Aphrodite, however, in that she, like Jarilo, is a dying and rising deity. She is sometimes seen as one of a pair of divine twins, sometimes as the wife of the great god Svarog, as a co-creator of the world. A goddess named Dziewona is an Artemis-Diana huntress.

In the pantheon of Vladimir I, Perun is the supreme god. With him are Khursu (Khors), Dazibogu (Dazhbog), Stribogu (Stribog), Simariglu, and a single goddess, Makosh (Mokosi, Mokosh, Mokysha, Mokusha), whose name refers to wetness and is at least in part derived from the Iranian tradition. The moist goddess is sometimes Corn Mother, the spirit of grain. She is in all likelihood the same as Matka or Mata Syra Zjemlja, around whom Dionysian-like Slavic earth rituals were performed well into Christian times. As was the case with so many European goddesses of the earth, Makosh was later assimilated into the person of the Virgin Mary, perhaps especially in her earth-colored form as the Black Madonna so popular in Poland as well as in other parts of Europe.

Another popular goddess to emerge from folklore is Baba Yaga, whom Gimbutas ties to the Old European goddess of

S

death (p. 359). Baba Yaga can appear to be young or old and has the ancient prehistoric Great Goddess association with birds and snakes. She is sometimes depicted as a flying witch whose vehicle was a mortar with a pestle used as a rudder. Her turning house rested on chicken legs and was surrounded by a fence made of human bones. The keyhole of the front door contained teeth. Clearly, Baba Yaga is a Slavic version of Kali, the terrifying Indian "Black Goddess" of annihilation.

Various mythic heroes emerge from the Slavic tradition—primarily from Russian epics. These include Volkh (Volga), a major shape shifter with similarities to Odin and Sigurd, whose father was a dragon. Svjatogar is a Herculean strongman, and Mikula is a larger-than-life plowman who represents agriculture.

When Russia was officially Christianized in 988, Perun's statue was dragged through the streets tied to a horse's tail before being thrown into the river. But the god remains a folkloric fertility figure for farmers today, as do Corn Mother and many other deities. And many of the Slavic deities have been assimilated by the Christian tradition. Perun himself became Saint Il'ia, who also crosses the sky in his chariot. Veles became the Devil, as Velinus did in the Baltics, or, in some case, Saint Vlas or Blasius. [Gimbutas (1987c), Leeming (2003)]

SNORRI STURLUSON It is on the Icelander Snorri Sturluson (1179–1241) and his sources that we depend most for our knowledge of Norse mythology, primarily as contained in his *Prose Edda* of about 1220.

In 1643 in an old Icelandic farmhouse, the Bishop of Skalholt found a manuscript known as the *Codex Regius*, containing a collection of probably pre-Christian mythical poems of the Viking period, only written down, however, in the late thirteenth century. Traditionally, the compilation of these poems has been attributed to Saemund Siugfusson and thus called *Saemund's Edda*, *Edda* in all likelihood coming from a word meaning "poetry." A few other mythological poems were discovered soon after the *Codex Regius*, and the whole collection is known more commonly as the *Elder Edda* or simply the *Poetic Edda*, within which the most famous poems and the ones most used by Snorri are *Voluspa* ("Prophecy of the Seeress"), containing the great story of the beginning and end of the world; *Grimnismal*, in which the high god Odin speaks in the disguise as Grimnir (the "Hooded One"); and *Havamal*, in which is told the story of the self-hanging of the high god Odin. Other poetic sources for Snorri and other later mythologists and historians are the highly alliterative skaldic poems (*skalds* were bards, the *filidh* of the north), known in literary circles for their extensive use of *kennings* ("namings"), compound metaphorical substitutions for the names of things (for example, "whale-road" for the sea or "Freya's tears" for gold). The skaldic form was common in Old English poetry as well as in the Old Norse.

For his work, Snorri depended on his knowledge of Eddic and skaldic poetry and on his own talent as a saga writer, poet, historian, and antiquarian. His mission was to encourage Iceland poets not to lose sight of the stories and methods of skaldic and Eddic poetry. Snorri himself wrote skaldic poetry, as in *Hattatal*, a eulogy for two noblemen, and sagas based on the Icelandic sagas (the *Fornaldar Sogur*). Snorri's *Heimskringla*, compiled from poems and sagas, is a history of Norwegian kings from mythical time until 1177 and contains *Yngling-asaga*, an important source for Norse mythology, tracing the pre-Norwegian Swedish kings and their mythological ancestors back to the god Odin.

SOBEK Sobek (Sebek) was the Egyptian crocodile god of rivers and lakes sometimes associated with Osiris's enemy Seth, sometimes seen as the protector of the pharaohs. His mother was the Mother Goddess, Neith.

SOCIOLOGY AND MYTH One function of myth, as outlined by the mythologist Joseph Campbell in his *Myths to Live By* and other works, is the sociological, which has to do with reconciling people with the "social order" to which they are born—integrating "the individual organically with his group." This function coincides with the psychosocial function, the shaping of ideals and approaches of individuals to their group. Myths speak to the inner world of individuals—to their psyches—even as they validate collective social assumptions passed down through generations.

SOLAR DEITIES It is hardly surprising that from very ancient times humans have associated the sun—the source of heat and light—with a supreme deity, the master of the heavens, who drives daily across the sky in a variety of chariots and who disappears into the darkness in a blaze of glory only to reappear mysteriously in another blaze several hours later at a point directly opposite from the place where he had disappeared. The solar myths are complicated by this disappearance. Where did the sun god go—to the underworld, to death itself? Usually the solar deities are male; Re in Egypt is the sun, as is the Aton worshipped by Akhenaton. Egyptian solar gods are sometimes referred to as the "Eye of heaven."

In China, the left eye of the giant first man, Pangu, is the sun. The Chinese Yellow Emperor, Huangdi, is sometimes associated with the sun, and in India one of the primary

A sun goddess

Adityas, who are the Vedic ruling forces of the universe and themselves associated with the sun, is the sun himself, the god Surya. The svastika is a Hindu symbol of the sun. In Iran Ahura Mazda and Mithra are both solar deities. The Slavic Dazhbog is associated with the sun, as are the greatest of the Aztec and Mayan gods. The Mayan sun god Ahau Kin crosses the sky and roams the underworld as a jaguar each night. The Mesoamerican Quetzalcoatl rules one of the four suns (ages). Although sun gods are usually male, they can be female—for example, the Cherokee sun goddess and the great spiritual center of Japanese Shinto, the sun goddess Amaterasu, whose symbol of power is the rising sun. Sun goddesses can be coy, disappearing, as Amaterasu does, and causing disorder in the world.

Solar deities can be brutal with their heat as well, punishing humans with their fire power, as Re does before the Egyptian beer flood. Solar deities are usually closely associated with lunar ones, as is evident in most moon myths. Sometimes, as in the case of the Egyptian Horus, or the Chinese Pangu, one eye is the sun, the other is the moon. Usually, the moon is a goddess who is either the sister or the husband of the sun. But, as in the case of the Maori moon, it can sometimes be incarnated as a male.

SOMA The word *soma* is derived from the Sanskrit root meaning "to press." Recent scholarship suggests that the sometimes hallucinatory and psychedelic drink called soma, personified and worshipped as the god Soma in the ancient Indian *Vedas*, was, in fact, pressed from a type of mushroom called soma. The *Sama Veda* is a collection of ritual hymns dedicated to the god Soma as a source of imaginative power. Soma is much praised in the *Rig Veda* as well. A myth is told there of the discovery of the soma plant in Heaven. It was an eagle who plucked some of the plant from the heights and planted it on earthly mountains, where it was gathered by Vedic priests. The priests pressed the plant, extracting the sacred essence, which they then filtered through wool and mixed with clarified butter. They used the resulting liquid in rituals. If consumed, it would bring remarkable insights. If placed in the ritual fire as a sacrifice, it would rise up to the gods in the smoke and become their ambrosia of immortality and the source of their power. In the Persian Avestan tradition, we find a similar drink of immortality called *haoma*. Soma is also a name given to the moon, where it is said that the gods store soma.

SONG OF SONGS The *Song of Songs* or *Song of Solomon* is one of five books in the section of the Hebrew Bible known as the "Festival Scrolls" (*Megillot*). On the surface, at least, this book is a celebration of human physical love, and like the Hindu *Gitagovinda* and Mesopotamian hymns to Inanna, the eroticism contained in the book also has religious metaphorical value. The *Song* is sometimes seen by Jews as an allegory of the love of Yahweh for his people, and by Christians as an allegory of God's love for his "bride," the Church. It seems likely, however, that these beautifully erotic songs of desire, physical pleasure, and loss owe much to songs used in Mesopotamian, Israelite, and possibly Egyptian wedding celebrations. Many segments of the *Song* are particularly reminiscent of the Sumero-Babylonian myths that have correlatives in the ceremony of the sacred marriage. The book opens with the "bride," like Inanna / Ishtar, calling on her lover-"king" to "smother me with kisses." "Take me with you," she cries, "let us make haste; / bring me to your chamber, O king." make haste / bring me to your chamber." The bridegroom king's replies are just as passionate: "Your two

breasts" he says, "are like two fauns, twin fauns of a gazelle / grazing among the lilies."

SONGSTEN GAMPO Songsten Gampo (Songsen-gammpo) is a legendary-historical hero celebrated in countless folktales of the kingdom of Ladakh in India. He is said to have been responsible by way of marriage to princesses from Nepal and China, for making Tibet—and, by example, Ladakh—officially Buddhist.

SOPHIA Some Christians and Gnostics incorporated the feminine in the person of the Divine Wisdom of the Hebrew Book of Proverbs (8, 9) into their sense of deity, as Sophia—thus the great church of Saint Sophia in Constantinople (modern Istanbul).

There are many myths of Sophia. As Divine Wisdom, she was the female companion of Yahweh at the creation described in Proverbs. In the Gnostic tradition, Sophia was God's mother, the Great Virgin Mother in whom God was concealed before the beginning. For some Gnostics, Sophia was said to have been born of the female essence, Sige (Silence), and to have given birth herself to the male Christ and the female Achamoth. Achamoth produced Ildabaoth (Jehovah). When Ildabaoth denied humans access to the fruit of knowledge, Achamoth sent her own spirit as Ophis, the serpent, to teach humans to destroy Jehovah. The serpent was also seen as Christ. Later Sophia sent Christ to enter the man Jesus when he was baptized, and still later, Sophia and Jesus married in Heaven.

SOPHOCLES The most admired of the ancient Greek playwrights is probably Sophocles (495–406 B.C.E.), of whose one hundred plays only seven still exist. In 468, at the age of twenty-seven, Sophocles was the winner of the first prize over Aeschylus at the Festival of Dionysos. He remained the leading playwright until challenged by Euripides' victory over him in 441 B.C.E. Sophocles is best known for his three plays about the family of the doomed Oedipus: *Oedipus Rex* (*Oedipus Tyrannus*), *Oedipus at Colonnus*, and *Antigone*. Other plays are *Ajax*, about the insane jealousy of one of the Greek Trojan War heroes; and *Elektra*, about the daughter of Agamemnon and Clytemnestra, who urged her brother Orestes to take revenge for their mother's murder of their father. Lesser-known plays are *Women of Trachis* and *Philoctetes*.

SOUL In the general understanding of the people of many religious traditions—sometimes in spite of official theology—the soul or spirit is within the body but somehow separate from it and able to live on after death. For Jews the soul is protected when the individual follows the Torah ("Law"). For Christians, the soul remains alive after the death of the body, in which it has, in a sense, been imprisoned during life. In Christian and some animistic art, souls are depicted flying off to Heaven or Hell after the death of the body. In the modern world, the concept of soul is, understandably, sometimes confused with that of the psyche, the psychological entity that the psychology of Freud and others has led us to see as not physical but somehow within the body.

SOUTH AMERICAN MYTHOLOGY The dominant mythology that has come down to us in South America is that of the Incas of Peru, and much of the rest of South American mythology has much in common with that of the Incas.

Almost always in South America, creation is initiated by a supreme deity who may be associated with the sun. Among

S

the Witoto of Colombia, the creator himself is born of sound—of words—that is, of the ancient myths and incantations. We think, perhaps, of the east Indian Vedic Om and the divine *Vedas* themselves. The Chibcha and other Indians in Colombia say that before creation light was imprisoned in a kind of as yet undifferentiated god. When this being rose up and released the light, creation began. The primal being sent birds to spread the light around the world. For some tribes, the creator was a Mother Goddess. For the Chamacoco, this goddess is Eschetewuarha, who is married to the supreme deity but was herself the primary creative force. Sometimes the mother creatrix is a solar goddess, a personification of the sun itself, as among the Chipibo.

The creator may also be one and the same as the culture hero, who comes to earth to create and teach people. Or, he may have a culture hero assistant or, often, culture hero twins who carry out the job of teaching humans culture and sometimes—when one twin is evil or mischievous—of initiating the troubles of life, such as death. The Carib people of Guiana believe that Makunaima and his brother created the world and brought about a great flood. Other twins of Guiana are Tuminikar, a solar deity and a friend to humans, and his brother, Duid, the moon, who is a trouble-making underminer and trickster, like Erlik and so many "assistants" to the creator in central Asia, for instance.

The Onas say that the supreme being sent the culture hero–creator Kenos to the world, that Kenos created human sexual organs out of peat, and that these organs met to produce the Onas. Kenos taught the people agriculture and other things for a while but eventually turned things over to twins, who taught more things but also were responsible for the reality of death.

Sometimes the culture heroes are not altogether successful at creating. Like the Mayan creator further north, there are South American creators who botch the job at first and have to start all over again. The Taulipas say that the culture hero created humans out of wax, but they melted, so he had to recreate them out of clay.

In the agricultural societies of indigenous South America, agriculture is, of course, central, and there are many origins of plant myths. The Carin Indians say vegetables came from a sort of Tree of Life. As in the case of the Corn Mother myths of North America, there are agricultural myths that sometimes involve the archetype of the dying god who must be sacrificed so that an essential sacred "planting" and animistic transference of divine power can take place. Many of the Peruvian Indians, including the Incas, tell of the first people, who were starving until the culture hero Pachacamac caused the woman to become pregnant with a child that he cut up and planted, leading to the springing of edible vegetation from the earth.

There is an apocalyptic aspect to South American mythology. Some tribes say that the world will end in fire. Most believe in a great deluge. As is the case in most of the world, the flood is usually a punishment of humanity for one reason or another. In Peru the main reason is the failure of the people to follow the laws set down by the original culture hero. The Yaghans say that the moon caused the flood because humans knew too much about female "mysteries." Whatever the reason for the flood, at least one couple manages to escape so that the world of humans can take form again. The canaries of Ecuador tell the myth of the two boys—perhaps twins—who managed to hide from the flood and who were fed by two parrots, which turned into girls. The boys captured one and with her created a new race of people, the Canari. [Grimal]

SOUTHEAST ASIAN MYTHOLOGY Mainland Southeast Asia, made up of countries we now call Viet Nam, Cambodia, Laos, Thailand, and Burma, and populated by Austroasiatic or Austronesian peoples, lies between two cultural giants, China and India. The mythologies of the Southeast Asian area are at once indigenous and deeply influenced by the mythologies of these neighboring cultures. On the one hand, there are myths such as that of the sky-based Thens and the three earth lords, involving struggle, a flood, and the establishment of order. On the other hand, there are characters out of Indian epics and other mythological works who become characters in local myths and are changed to meet the sociological needs and concerns of the adapters. It is as if certain Brahmanic gods and traditions were pasted upon the creation and origin myths indigenous to Southeast Asia, as in the flood story, Nithan Khun Borom. And later, from China came the Buddhist influence and eventual dominance, expressed, for instance, at Angkor. Spirits (Nats, Phi, Neak-ta) play an important role in the ancient indigenous Southeast Asian mythology, controlling many aspects of daily life. Moon myths and rituals are important as well, as they are in China and India. In Cambodia, for instance, there is the tradition of the moon goddess, who is somehow associated with

A southeast Asian Shiva at Angkor with multiple heads and arms

S

the Hindu female serpent Nagi, who was married to the brahman Kasundinya. The moon goddess marries the originator of the Khmer dynasty, who is himself the sun god. There is also the story of the moon as Lord Brah Chan, who marries the mortal maiden Biman Chan. When Biman Chan asks her husband to take her farther and farther into the heavens, the wind blows her head off, and the head falls into a Buddhist monastery. When the head is restored to the body, the woman marries a mortal descendant of the sun, Suryavan. Earth goddesses, too, are important in Southeast Asia, as they are in India. The goddess Dharni owes much to the Vedic-Hindu stories of Sita and Aditi. But here the earth goddess works with the Buddha to achieve enlightenment. Many of the ancient Hindu gods survive in the Buddhist context. In Cambodia, Shiva is Brah Isvara and the *yoni-linga*/Shiva-Shakti symbol of regeneration and wholeness is found in traditional candlesticks used in Buddhist marriage ceremonies. The Temple of Angor Wat is dedicated to the Hindu god Vishnu.

The Austroasiatic and Austronesian peoples once believed that everything was created by Ndu or Adei, the most important of the *yang* (spirits, sacred beings), who, although he provides milk and rice and other particular expressions of *yang*, is, like the Hindu Brahman, a nonpersonal absolute that is everywhere and nowhere. Ndu/Adei can take form, however. There are many stories of Ndu's entering the world to assist humans. A story is told, for instance, of the culture hero the orphan Ddoi/Drit, who is refused rice by his uncle. As he wanders hungry along the road, the young man meets Ndu in the form of an old man. Ndu gives the boy magic seeds for an abundant harvest of rice and brings about the death of the uncle, and he even provides a bride.

Also important among tribes such as the Sre and the Jorai are female figures. There is a female sun and an old woman called Mother Bush or Dung-Dai, who is sometimes the wife of Adei.

The Sre people envision a world of many levels with the earth in the middle. Ndu was helped in the emergence creation by the spirit Bung, who brought up plants from the lower worlds through a hole. For the Jorai, the earth is like a basket within another, upsidedown basket that is the sky. Adei is king of the sky. The people emerged into the earth from a lower world, also by way of a small hole. Native North Americans, especially of the Southwest, have similar creation myths.

In the Jorai mythology, humans and animals conversed in ancient times and humans could fly. There was no death and humans were like *yang*. It was only when men abused their paradise that Adei left them and they had to work to live. The Sre say that Ndu offered humans the water of immortality but that they found the water too cold and therefore only dipped their hands and feet and hair in it. So it is that people die but that their hair and nails keep growing after death.

The Austrasians have a flood myth in which the only survivors of the deluge were a brother and sister who protected themselves in a drum. These two became the first human ancestors. Among the Austronesian tribes, it is a mother and son who survive. In both cases it is incest that is the basis for new life. As incest is taboo, sacrifices are necessary to purify what is essentially a flawed existence from which Ndu/Adei remains aloof and in which animals and humans are no longer in direct communication. All of the indigenous people of the Indo-Chinese region await an apocalypse or "cold darkness" at some future time.

There are many Austroasian and Austronesian myths in which the connection between the world of the *yang* and that of humans is reestablished by beings who take animal form or by spirits sent down to earth in human form. In one story the sun attracts a young man to the upper world by sending a spirit in the form of a beautiful woman to seduce him. In other stories a particular species of monkey is thought to be a remaining link between heavenly beings and earthly ones.

Shamanism is important in indigenous Indo-China, as it is in central Asia and Native North America. Shamans, like mythic heroes such as Drit, have the ability to take flight, to voyage in dreams between the worlds and to the ends of the earth. The shaman can use his dream voyage to confront tormentors of the sick in the other world and thus achieve cures.

The Vietnamese have particularly vivid creation and origin myths. [Bonnefoy (1991)]

SPHINX In ancient Egypt, the sphinx, such as the Great Sphinx of Giza, was a symbolic being rather than an individual being with a mythology attached. It had a lion-like figure with a human head. It represented the pharaoh and his divine power, and sometimes the head was meant to be that of a particular king. In Greece, the Sphinx was a particular winged female monster with a lion's body and a human head. She was the offspring of Echidne and Typhon, the parents also of the Lemean Hydra dispatched by Herakles, the Chimera, the many-headed dog Orthus, the hundred-headed dragon who guarded the apples of the Hesperides, the Colchian dragon, Cerberus, Scylla, the Gorgon, the Nemean lion, and the eagle that fed on the liver of Prometheus. The Sphinx stood on a cliff outside of Thebes and ate anyone unable to answer her riddle, effectively locking the Thebans in their city. "What being has four legs, then two legs, and then three legs?" she asked. No one knew the answer until the unfortunate Oedipus came along from Corinth and answered the riddle: A human being, he said; he crawls as a child, walks as a man, and then needs a cane as an old man. At this the Sphinx's hold on Thebes was broken; she threw herself off the cliff, and Oedipus entered the city as a "savior" and a new tragedy began.

SPIDER WOMAN Spider Woman, or Spider Grandmother, is one of the most popular Native North American goddesses. She, or figures like her, exist among most of the southwestern Pueblo cultures, especially the Hopis. The Navajos and Cherokee, too, adopted her. Spider Woman is the primary assistant of the supreme in the creative process by which the people emerge from one world to the next. Once the people arrive in this world, Spider Woman is a culture heroine who teaches them what they need to know.

One Hopi myth tells it this way: The sun god spirit, Tawa, created a world and placed in it some insect-like quarreling creatures with whom he quickly became dissatisfied. So he sent Spider Woman to lead them up to a Second World. There they took a slightly higher form but were still ignorant and improper. So Spider Woman took them to a Third World that was lighter and more hospitable. The former beings were now people, who, instructed by Spider Woman, grew corn, wove cloth, and made pots. But there were problems, including the presence of sorcerers and their evil, so Spider Woman advised the few people who remained untainted by the evil to move to the Upper World, the Fourth World. The people sent various birds to find the opening to that world and to report to them on what they saw there. They decided to go and, again advised by Spider Woman, they got a chipmunk to plant a bamboo-like tree that, assisted by songs taught to them by Spider Woman, grew up into and through

S

the hole at the top of the Third World. Spider Woman called the tree the *Sipapuni*. As it was hollow, the people could climb up through it and emerge into the Fourth World. To this day, the Hopi and other pueblo Indians have sacred places called *kivas*, in the center of the floor of which is always found a tiny spider hole or *sipapu*, representing the place of emergence into this world.

STENTOR The source of the word "stentorian," Stentor, a Greek herald in the Trojan War, had a remarkably loud voice.

STRIBOG Stribog was a Slavic wind-storm god. In folklore, he can carry off girls and destroy homes and fields.

STYMPHALIAN BIRDS These were the terrifying, human flesh–eating birds that Herakles managed to kill as the sixth of his Twelve Labors. They had brazen claws and beaks and terrorized Arcadia until the hero managed to startle them with a rattle given to him by Athena and shot them with arrows as they tried to fly away.

STYX Its name derived from the verb "to hate," the River Styx circled the Greek underworld seven times. The spirit of the river was Styx, the daughter of Oceanus and Tethys. The waters of the Styx were used by the gods to solemnize oaths.

SUALTAM Sualtam (Sualdaim) Mac Roth in Irish mythology was the human "father" of the hero Cuchulainn. The hero's mother, Dechtire, on the night before her wedding, was actually impregnated by the god Lugh. Sualtam, however, took on Cuchulainn as his own son. When, in the face of Medb's invasion, Sualtam attempted to awaken the enchanted warriors of Ulster, he turned his horse so sharply that his shield decapitated him.

SUFI MYTHS Islamic mystics (Sufis, dervishes) such as Jelaladin Rumi have traditionally used—loosely speaking—myths reminiscent of the parables of Jesus, for instance, to illustrate or capture the essence of certain sufic ideas. The stories can be serious, as in the case of the story of the destruction of a town. A Sufi cried out that he would be the cause of "this town's downfall." People paid no attention to the Sufi because he appeared to be both poor and foolish. But one day the dervish climbed a tree and fell out of it onto a reservoir wall, which broke, causing a devastating flood that destroyed the town. When the man's body was found, the people remembered his "foolish" words.

Sometimes the stories can be comic. In Aksehir, near Jelaladin Rumi's city of Konya, is a mock tomb. The tomb is that of the mythic Islamic trickster Nassredin Hodja, whose ridiculous actions can illustrate the seemingly irrational truths of mystics like Rumi. In front of the typically Islamic gravestone topped by a turban is a large gate with a gigantic padlock securing it. We can see that the stone has a little hole in it, from which, presumably, the old teacher can observe the pilgrims who visit his grave. The padlock seems to deny access to the tomb until we notice that the gate stands alone, with no fence attached to it. The pilgrim who would move beyond the merely local to the transcendence of the hodja

Herakles kills the Stymphalian birds

need merely walk around the guardian gate of conventionality and denial.

SUGRIVA Sugriva was a monkey king in India whose brother Valin usurped his throne. With the help of Rama, and the king's minister, the monkey god Hanuman, Valin was killed and Sugriva restored to his throne.

SUJATA Sujata is the heroine of a Thai myth in which she feeds the Buddha rice and milk during the process of his achieving enlightenment.

SUMERIAN MYTHOLOGY As the nation-state of Egypt was emerging to the south, in fourth millennium B.C.E., a people in Mesopotamia were creating a religious, legal, and architectural basis that would dominate the Fertile Crescent long after they faded into oblivion. The epic of Gilgamesh, the great ziggurats—stepped pyramid-like structures in honor of the gods—a complex legal system, the development of cities, and a sophisticated mythological system were inventions of these remarkable people. Their culture would be adopted to some degree by the peoples who would conquer them later, and for many centuries after their demise their language would remain the vehicle of learning and culture in Mesopotamian schools.

The people who accomplished these feats were the people of Kengir, now southern Iraq. Their later Semitic conquerors

From the treasure of the Sumerian King of Ur, c 2040 B.C.E.

called their land Sumer and we know of them as the Sumerians. The Sumerians, whose origins are a mystery, were unrelated to the Semites who would eventually conquer them. They probably arrived in Mesopotamia from central Asia in the fourth millennium B.C.E. and mixed with other non-Semitic people, called Ubaidians, who had been there from at least the fifth millennium. The Ubaidians are so called for Tell Ubaid, near the ruins of the ancient city of Ur. It was the Ubaid culture that first established proto-cities along the marshland of what is now southern Iraq. These settlements included what became the Sumerian cities of Ur, Eridu, Adab, Isin, Larsa, Lagash, Nippur, and Unug (better known by its later Semitic name, Uruk or Erech). The Ubaidians were skilled at farming, animal husbandry, pottery, and other crafts.

The period immediately following the Ubaid is generally called the Early and Middle Uruk periods (c. 4000–3500 B.C.E.). By then nomadic Semitic tribes from the northwest and Arabia had mingled with and gained considerable influence over Ubaid. Then came Sumerian dominance in the so-called proto-Literate and Late Uruk Sumerian periods (c. 3500–3100 B.C.E.). These designations vary considerably among scholars, and there are some who suggest that the Sumerians were direct descendants of the Ubaidians. The Late Uruk period coincided with the pre-dynastic period of Egypt and the proto-Elamite (Tall-i-Malyan) period in Persia (Iran).

Late Uruk, or pre-dynastic Sumer, is characterized by elements that we associate with the word "civilization." Elaborate sculpture, monumental architecture, and a governmental assembly with elected religious and civil leaders, headed by an equal among equals called the *ensi*—a system that can be contrasted with the federated government of overlords who ruled neighboring Elam until the rise of the Awan or Shustar dynasty there in c. 2700 B.C.E.—are some of these elements. But the most important contribution of the Sumerians of the late fourth millennium was writing. *Cuneiform* (Latin *cuneus* = "wedge" + *forma* = "shape") is the name given to a writing system that took the form of symbols pressed into little boxes on clay tablets.

In the face of threats from the Semitic Akkadians in the north and the Elamites to the east, the various city-states of Sumer sometimes united as a federation during what is known as their Early Dynastic period. Frequent wars had led to a more centralized leadership of the various cities. The old positions of *en*, or spouse of the patron deity, and of *lugal*, or military leader-protector, gradually merged into what was essentially a kingship by the end of the fourth millennium. And although there were general assemblies of all the states at Nippur and elsewhere, there was a strong tendency for these de facto kingdoms to fight among themselves. For a while the city of Kish under a King Etana gained dominance over Sumer and over Semitic Akkad to the north. Then Uruk under such kings as Enmerkar, Lugalbanda, and Gilgamesh, all of whom became subjects of heroic legend, took its turn as the controlling power. Uruk's day was followed by that of Ur and later that of Lagash in about 2350 B.C.E. The brief Lagash dynasty is significant for the extensive archival material it collected. Whatever the Sumerian accomplishments, the battles between the city-states left the country open to attack and eventual conquest.

King Sargon I of Akkad conquered the region sometime between 2390 and 2330 B.C.E., establishing a capital, Agade (Akkad), near Kish. The Akkadians adapted their own Semitic language to the Sumerian cuneiform script and it became the lingua franca of the region for centuries to come. The Akkadian dynasty controlled Sumer-Akkad only until about 2254, however, when the old Sumerian area regained independence, beginning what is sometimes called the neo-Sumerian period. King Naram-Sin of Akkad regained control of all of Mesopotamia soon after that, desecrating the holy city of Nippur, and he extended his territory to include the ancient Semitic kingdom of Ebla (the Eblamites being perhaps the original Amorites) that had flourished in what is now northern Syria from c. 2700 B.C.E. Ebla is near Aleppo and not far from Haran, where Abram (Abraham) is said to have lived for a while on his way to Canaan. At Tell Mardikh, the site of Ebla's center, archeologists have found important materials, including what might be called the first bilingual dictionary, cuneiform tablets combining words in several languages.

Naram-Sin was deified by the Akkadians for his successes in Ebla and elsewhere, but eventually he lost power to invading Gutian tribes from the mountains of western Iran, who were in turn confronted by Utuhegal of Uruk and by Lagash, powerful again for a brief period under the ensi Gudea. Then under Ur-Nammu of Ur Sumer became independent once again and the Third Dynasty of Ur, a renaissance period of education, literature, and elaborate law codes, dominated Sumer for about one hundred years beginning in about 2100 B.C.E. The Ur Third Dynasty ended when Ur was attacked by nomadic Semites, the Mardu, Amorites from the western desert. The Mardu settlements were looted and destroyed by Elamites from the east in about 2004 B.C.E. Ur III was followed by the Semitic dynasties of the cities Isin and Larsa (c. 2000–1763), dynasties that considered themselves to be the preservers of the now-ancient Sumerian culture.

In his landmark work *Sumerian Mythology*, Samuel Noah Kramer outlines the Sumerian creation as found in a series of fragments, some of which he calls "Gilgamesh, Enkidu, and the Nether World" (p. 30). He points out that the Sumerian term for the universe was *an-ki* (p. 41), literally the combination of An (Heaven) and Ki (Earth), which emerged as a primordial mountain from the maternal subterranean waters of the goddess Nammu. An and Ki, as male and female, conceived Enlil and, presumably, the other gods, the Anunnaki. As in many creation myths, Heaven and Earth had to be separated from each other in order that further creation could take place between them. So it was that the sky god, An, raised up the sky and the area of heaven above it and the air god, Enlil, took his mother, Earth, down, leaving the appropriate space. The goddess Ereshkigal was sent to be queen of the underworld. The gods and goddesses married, were fruitful, and took responsibility for the various aspects of agriculture. The work of farming was difficult, however, and the gods began grumbling, especially as the crafty god Enki, son of Nammu herself, lay sleeping while they worked.

Nammu had the idea of waking up her son and suggesting that he create humans (to work in the fields). Enki delegated the job to Nammu, instructing her to take some clay from the marshes (*abzu*, later *apsu*) in which he lay and to shape the clay into figures. The created humans were put to work under the watchful eyes of the goddess Ninmah-Ninhursaga.

Some of the most important Sumerian myths are those of Inanna—especially her relationship with Dumuzi and her descent to the underworld—and those of the trickster god Enki and Gilgamesh. [Black and Green, Dalley, Kramer (1961b), Leeming (2004), Wasilewska]

SUPREME DEITY Most cultures have a supreme deity, who is usually the creator and is often a sky god or high god associated with the sun. In many cases the supreme deity has little time for human concerns once the creation itself is completed. Instead of dealing directly with humans, he sends one or more culture heroes—sometimes one of his offspring—to teach humans how to live and even to complete his creation. In patriarchal societies, the supreme deity is almost always male, reflecting the social structure of the given culture.

SURABHI In India, Surabhi was the sacred cow (Kamadhenu) of prosperity who emerged from the creative churning of the ocean.

SURYA Sometimes called Savitar or Savitr, which means "he who nourishes," Surya, the Vedic god of the sun, is one of the *Adityas*, the main gods of the *Vedas*. He rules over the phenomenon of life, and as the sun, he is the great illuminator and source of life. Many of his qualities and aspects were later taken on by the god Vishnu.

SURONG GUNTING In Borneo, Surong Gunting is a culture hero who disgraced himself when he made his aunt pregnant while on a learning visit to his wise grandfather spirit. He returned home, however, and taught the people all they needed to know about agriculture, rituals, and hunting.

SUTRAS *Sutras* are the collections of the teachings of the Buddha Sakyamuni (Gautama Buddha), so important to Hinayana Buddhism. Mahayana Buddhism has also made significant use of *sutras*, as in the famous *Lotus Sutra* (Lotus of the Good Law), especially important to the Tendai sect. In Hinduism, *sutras* are essentially guides to proper ritual action.

SVANTOVIT Svantovit (Sventovit, Swiantowid) was a western Slavic god whose four heads symbolized the four seasons and the four directions. He may be the same deity as the eastern Slavonic high god Svarog. Svantovit seems to contain both male and female aspects, as two of his heads were sometimes depicted as female. In any case, he had strong fertility associations to balance his role as a war god. His name, from the Persian root *svent*, suggesting both strength and holiness, indicates Iranian antecedents, as do the names of many Slavic deities.

SVAROG Svarog (Svarogu) was the Slavic embodiment of the sky—the ultimate sky god. His offspring, in some regions, were the sun god Dazhbog, and the fire god Svarozhich.

SVAROZHICH In Slavic mythology, Svarozhich was the fire god, usually seen as the son of the sky god Svarog. In rituals connected with this god, the Slavs venerated fire and light. There is a strong Indo-European connection here with the Vedic fire god Agni.

SVASTIKA In Hinduism, what later became familiar as the hated Nazi swastika—the cross with ends bent at right angles—is a symbol of wholeness, the word literally meaning "wellness." It also refers to the sun as the ultimate source of renewal. For Buddhists, the svastika represents *dharma*, or cosmic order. It has similar meanings and represents the four directions to the Navajo of Native North America.

SYRINX The Greek god Pan played on the syrinx, or shepherd's "Pan pipes." A nymph he once loved had been turned into the pipes when he chased her.

S

TA'AROA Ta'aroa is the Tahitian name for the Polynesian god known to the Maori as Tangora. Although these are two names for essentially the same god, Ta'aroa does have his own mythological cycle and is more of a supreme deity and creator than his Maori version. According to the Tahitians, Ta'aroa ("Unique One") in the beginning lived in an egg-like shell—a version of the cosmic egg—that turned endlessly in the primal and empty darkness. But at some point Ta'aroa decided to break out of the shell. After calling out to a non-existent world he threw part of his shell home and flung it into space, where it became the sky. He used another part of the shell to make rocks and sand. Then, still enraged by the very emptiness that he found around him, he dismembered his body, the various parts of it becoming the source for an animistic creation. His spine became a mountain range; his flesh the earth; his finger and toe nails the scales of fish; his intestines lobsters, shrimp, and eels; and so forth. Yet Ta'aroa still remained Ta'aroa, and in his head he conjured up the various gods. Furthermore, his own original home, the shell, became the essential principle of a creation in which everything is contained in a shell of sorts—the space itself is a shell containing earth, sun, moon, and sky. The human body is a shell, and earth itself is a shell from which plants emerge.

TACITUS The Roman historian Publius Cornelius Tacitus (c. 55–118 C.E.), in his *Germania*, is a source for much of what we know of Roman versions of and understandings of Germanic and continental Celtic mythologies.

T'AI In Chinese, T'ai is the "supreme being," and in religious Daoism he is the ultimate god or the god within. Thus *T'ai-Tao* is the name for a form of Daoism developed by the twelfth-century sage Hsiao Pao-chen, a name that means "the path of the supreme being." And T'ai is the source of the term *T'ai-chi,* a concept of ultimate reality, that which

in the *I Ching* is the source of all being, including the *yin-yang* and the consequent four ways of combining Heaven and earth, and eventually the five elements of creation. All of this is represented in the self-defense and meditative exercise movements known as *Tai-chi-ch'üan.*

From the same "T" root, Ti or Shang-ti was the supreme creator god of the Shang dynasty of China during the second millennium B.C.E., and *T'ien* was used as early as the second millennium B.C.E. by the Chou people, meaning both Nature and supreme deity. The root meaning of these words for supreme deity is "sky"—the place where the gods live. In the Chou period (1111–256 B.C.E.), T'ien was a supreme god who interacted personally with the human world. He was also the basis of kingship. The king was T'ien's viceroy on earth and was enthroned or dethroned at his will. During the Chou period the terms *T'ien* and *Shang-ti* were used almost synonymously. In the *I Ching,* T'ien is Heaven and Ti is Earth, the father and mother gods whose union results in creation. Buddhists see Tian (T'ien) as impersonal Nature. Still another term to develop from the original root is Tiandi, literally "Heaven-earth," still another name for the supreme god of ancient China.

T'AI-HAO T'ai-hao, a version of T'ai, is the name of an ancient Chinese god who in later Han texts became confused with the god-emperor Fuxi.

TAIN BO CUAILGNE The *Tain,* the primary text of which is found in the eleventh-century *Leabhar na h-Uidhre* ("Book of the Dun Cow") and the twelfth-century *Leabhar Laighnech* ("Book of Leinster"), is the source of much Irish mythology. The epic revolves around Queen Medb's (Maeve's) attempt to capture the Brown Bull of Cuailgne and the great wars between Ulster and Connaught stirred up by that attempt. The bull itself is a highly symbolic animal in Irish myth, and cattle raids in Ireland, as in the most ancient Indo-European cultures, are a common adjunct to bull myths. The bull always stands for power and virility and is associated, in Ireland especially, with sacred kingship. According to the Book of the Dun Cow, the election of the Irish king was marked by a sacrificial ceremony in which a druid ate a bull's flesh and drank its blood and then in a deep sleep dreamed of the future king.

The great war of the *Tain* developed out of a "pillow talk" argument between Medb and Ail-ill over the relative value of their possessions. The Greek gods Zeus and Hera had such arguments, and so did the Indian god Shiva and his wife Parvati. When Medb realized that her possessions were inferior to her husband's, owing to his ownership of Finnbennach, the White-horned Bull, she determined to obtain for herself Donn Cuailgne, the great Brown Bull of Cuailgne. This bull could engender fifty calves in a day and could carry fifty boys on its back. It could shelter a hundred warriors with its body. The two bulls had once possessed human form as

The Dun Cow of the *Tain*

290

swineherds—one served the king of Connaught, the other the king of Munster. The two swineherds, once friends, had become jealous of each other and had fought over the relative values of their herds. In these fights they had taken various forms—warriors, ravens, and monsters. Finally they changed themselves into maggots, and one swam into a river in Cuailgne and was swallowed by a cow belonging to the Ulster chieftain Daire. The other swam into a Connaught stream and was consumed by one of Queen Medb's cows. The former swineherds were reborn as the White-horned Bull of Connaught and the Brown Bull of Cuailgne.

Medb asked Daire for the loan of the Brown Bull for a year, and Daire agreed until it was reported to him that the wily queen's ambassadors had boasted that if the loan had been refused she would have taken the bull by force anyway. Here the ancient Indo-European theme of the cattle theft is expressed. Daire took back his agreement to the loan, and an enraged Medb prepared for war, engaging the exiled former Ulster king Fergus as her general. Fergus hated Conchobhar because of an earlier betrayal involving Fergus's honor. But he remained loyal in spirit to his "foster son," the Ulster hero Cuchulainn, and warned him of the impending war.

Medb assumed that because of a curse that had enfeebled the Ulstermen, victory for Connaught would be a simple matter. But she had not reckoned on the fact that Cuchulainn was not by birth an Ulsterman. When Medb attacked Ulster, she was confronted by Cuchulainn in his war chariot driven by the faithful Laig (Laeg) and drawn by the greatest of war horses, the Battle Gray. The slingshot of Cuchulainn was a deadly weapon, and before long countless Connaught warriors lay dead. Amazed by the prowess of this mere seventeen-year-old, Medb determined to meet him and hoped to bring him over to her side with her charms. After much haggling, Medb and Cuchulainn agreed that from then on Cuchulainn would fight in daily single combat any warrior sent to him. The Connaught army might advance for only as long as it took him to defeat his daily enemy. While Cuchulainn defeated warrior after warrior with ease, allowing Medb's army only marginal advances, the devious queen took advantage of the hero's preoccupation by stealing the Brown Bull.

Now the gods had been watching Cuchulainn's amazing feats of battle, and the war goddess Morrigan, especially, had noticed his prowess. Appearing to the hero in a red dress and riding in a red war chariot, the goddess attempted to seduce him. She thus resembled the goddess Inanna, who practiced her wiles on Gilgamesh, the hero of the Sumero-Babylonian epic of that name. Claiming that it was she who had made his victories possible, Morrigan demanded repayment in the form of love. When Cuchulainn rashly claimed he needed no woman's help in battle and reacted disdainfully to the goddess's charms, she became his mortal enemy and made his tragic fate inevitable.

Soon Medb sent the old warrior Loch out to fight with Cuchulainn at what became ever after a famous ford. Loch was assisted by Morrigan in the form of a heifer, an eel, and a wolf, each of which Cuchulainn defeated. But Loch was able to inflict many wounds on his enemy, and the combination of warrior and goddess was about to prevail when Cuchulainn decided, reluctantly, since he considered such tactics dishonorable, to make use of his magical spear, the Gae Bolga, a weapon against which there was no defense. Loch was thus killed. The much-wounded Cuchulainn was given a strong sleeping potion by his true father, the god Lugh, and during

three days and nights of sleep was cured by the ministration of the god's powerful medicine.

Sensing impending defeat, Medb now insisted that Fergus himself fight Cuchulainn. A battle with the youth he considered his "foster son" was anathema to the former Ulster king, and he agreed to it only after Medb called him a coward. As the two friends and great warriors approached each other, they tried to find a way to avoid the fight. Finally they agreed that Cuchulainn should pretend to run from Fergus in fear on the condition that in a similar situation in the future Fergus would run from Cuchulainn. As Cuchulainn ran away after a pretend battle, the forces of Medb mocked him.

Now Medb decided to put an end to Cuchulainn. She sent the wizard Calatin with his twenty-seven sons to fight her enemy. It was only with the help of Fiacha, another Ulster exile sent by Fergus to watch the battle, that Cuchulainn was able to destroy the wizard and his children.

With her next ploy, Medb was almost successful. Against Cuchulainn she sent out Ferdia of the impenetrable skin, a childhood friend of the great hero. The two friends had sworn eternal friendship, and it was only the threats to their reputations and honor that led them to fight each other. The two fought for three days, and each night Cuchulainn demonstrated his love by sharing the medicine of Lugh to cure Ferdia's wounds. Finally, the anger of battle prevailed, and Cuchulainn once again made reluctant use of the Gae Bolga, as Karna made use of a magical weapon in the Indian epic the *Mahabharata* and King Arthur wielded the magic sword Excalibur. As Ferdia died at his feet, Cuchulainn moaned in agony at the loss of his friend.

The battle with Ferdia had left Cuchulainn badly wounded. Unable to continue the war alone, he sent his adopted father, Sualtam, who had come to nurse his wounds, to ride to Ulster on the Battle Gray to call on the Ulstermen for help. It was only when Sualtam's severed head—which was cut off by his shield as a result of the abrupt movement of Cuchulainn's horse—continued to cry out the call for help that the Ulstermen arose from their long, curse-induced stupor and sent an army to aid their hero. Decapitation and the speaking severed head is a common motif in Celtic myth.

When the forces of Conchobhar approached those of Medb, Cuchulainn revived, and he joined them. Facing Fergus, he demanded that his old friend fulfill his part of the oath of retreat, and Fergus turned and ran, causing havoc in his own army, which fled in disarray.

The battle was thus won, but the Brown Bull remained in Connaught, and his old hatred of the White-horned Bull was revived. A great battle of the bulls resulted, and eventually the Brown Bull defeated his enemy, essentially dismembered him, and with much bellowing, returned to Cuailgne, where soon his heart burst and he died.

As for Cuchulainn, his doom was manipulated by the witch daughters of the enchanter Calatin and by the young kings of Munster and Leinster, whose fathers—as well as the father of the witches—Cuchulainn had slain in battle. And, of course, the offended Morrigan was an interested party in her enemy's destruction. The witches used their magic to lure Cuchulainn out with only the horse the Battle Gray and the charioteer Laig. In spite of terrible omens, Cuchulainn insisted on venturing toward the standing Pillar of Stone. There he met the three witches and was taunted by three bards, who used threats of poetic dishonor to cause the hero to throw his three spears at them. The bards thus were killed, but Lughaid, king of Munster, and Erc, king of Leinster,

T

Davy Crockett; teller of tall tales

threw the spears back at Cuchulainn, first killing Laig and then the Battle Gray, and then wounding Cuchulainn in his guts. The dying hero struggled to the pillar and tied himself to it so that he might die standing. At this moment Morrigan arrived as a crow and sat proudly on the dying man's shoulder, and Lughaid cut off his head. The hero's falling sword severed Lughaid's arm, however, and soon Cuchulainn's friend Conall would sever Lughaid's head to avenge the unfair defeat of the greatest of Irish heroes.

TALES OF YAMATO Many tales are told in the *Kojiki* and elsewhere of the Japanese hero of the Shinto tradition, Yamato, son of the Japanese Emperor Keiko. These tales often have supernatural aspects. Yamato is a knight in search of adventures that will identify him as a hero. In various wars he defeats the "barbarians." He even defeats a god who confronts him as a white deer. But when he fights the white boar, in reality the god of the evil breath, he is overcome. After his death he becomes a white bird and flies off into the unknown.

TALIESEN Taliesen ("Shining Bow"), the Welsh equivalent of the Irish Amairgen, was said to have lived in the sixth century C.E. His prophetic poetic powers were unsurpassed. Stories in Welsh mythology identify him as the miraculously conceived and reborn Gwion Bach, who had disguised himself as a grain of wheat and been swallowed by his angry mother, the magician Ceridwen, who then gave birth to Taliesen. Taliesen overpowered King Arthur's bards, reducing their sounds to "Blerwm blerwm." His song in Arthur's

court claims his eternal power and that power liberates Elffin, the youth who, with his father Gwyddno had found the abandoned baby Taliesen in a floating leather bag and adopted him.

TALKING GOD An important figure in the Navajo creation myth of Native North America, Talking God is the leader of the spirits known as *Yei*.

TALL TALE The so-called tall tale is a folktale type common especially to American legend and myth. Its subject might be actual figures or fictional ones. All tall tales are exaggerations of the feats of American heroes—frontiersmen such as Daniel Boone and Davy Crockett, outlaws such as Billy the Kid, laborers such as John Henry and Paul Bunyan, presidents such as George Washington and Abraham Lincoln. The feats of these heroes in tall tales reflect the vastness of a new nation and its aspirations. They are reflections of ideological "myths" such as Manifest Destiny and of a sense that for Americans anything was possible. In the famous cherry tree story we learn that George Washington could never tell a lie. The African American hero John Henry could out-hammer the steam engine. Davy Crockett could plan to tear the tail off of Halley's Comet. The purely fictional Paul Bunyan could form the Grand Canyon by dragging his pick along the ground. TALOS The Greek smith god Hephaistos made a bronze giant for King Minos of Crete. The giant's name was Talos, and his job was to protect Crete from invaders by hurling huge rocks at them or using his burning hot body to hug them to death. It was Medea, accompanying the Argonauts to Crete, who killed him by drugging him and then causing him to bleed to death.

TAMI MYTHOLOGY The Tamil people, who live mostly in the southern part of India called Tamil Nadu, possess a religious and mythological tradition that is a particularly interesting mix of ancient pre-Hindu, Dravidian–Indus Valley elements and Vedic and orthodox Hindu aspects of the Sanskritic tradition. In the prehistoric Neolithic period, the Tamils were a herding, nature-oriented culture with a nature-based mythology of deities of the land. Murugan (Murakan) was a major god of the hunt who battled evil forces, and Ventan was responsible for rain and general well-being. A tradition of ecstatic worship involving sexuality and intoxication apparently existed among the early Tamils. In sacred places a linga-like pillar called a kantu represented the god in question—perhaps, more often than not, Murugan, who, like the Greek Dionysos or Hindu Krishna, was often accompanied by a following of beautiful young women. With the arrival in the south of Jains, Buddhists, and Hindu brahmans in the third century B.C.E., the myths and religious practices of the Tamils became somewhat more staid. By the eighth century the land of the Tamils had become the setting for a particularly powerful form of Hinduism marked by devotional, or bhakti, poetry, written by poet–saint followers, especially of Shiva, called Nayanars, and of Vishnu, called Alvars. Among the most famous of the Alvars was Nammalvar, who lived in the late ninth and early tenth centuries and who wrote especially about Vishnu's avatar Krishna and espoused the beliefs of Vedanta. The most notable of the Nayanars was the ninth-century Mannikavacakar, who stressed the ecstatic aspect of the worship of Shiva. The poet-saints took stories from the Sanskrit texts and gave them Tamil settings and a peculiarly Tamil sense of the closeness that can be achieved between the given deity and the worshipper. The late eighth and early ninth centuries was also the period of Sankara, who preached Advaita Vedanta, the Hinduism that stresses the absoluteness of Brahman. Also important to the mythology and religion of the Tamils is the person of the Goddess (Devi, Kali), who from ancient times had been a popular deity and who by the tenth century had regained a position of equality with Shiva and Vishnu, a position she holds to this day. Other popular deities who retain positions of importance with Shiva, Vishnu, and the Goddess are Shiva's sons Murugan and Ganesh. The twelfth century saw a flowering of Tamil literature in the Tamil version of the epic the *Ramayana*, by the poet Kampan. Since the sixteenth century, a tradition of stories about the childhoods of the gods has been a significant aspect of Tamil mythology. Finally, it can be said that Tamil mythology is among the richest and most complex narrative traditions in India, as in the epics *Annanmar, Catakantaravanan*, and *Manimekhalai*. [Clothey]

TANE The Polynesian god Tane, the tree and forest deity, plays a particularly important role in Maori mythology. He is born of Papa and Rangi, the primal parent sky and earth gods, and he succeeds in separating the tightly embracing couple so that further creation can occur. Tane's primary rival among his siblings was Tawhiri, the storm or weather god, who chased Tane's fish children from the forest to the sea, where they were ruled by the sea god, Tangaroa. According to one myth, when Tane's mother, Papa, refused his sexual advances, the god created Hine-hau-one ("Earth Girl") out of Hawaiian sand. This first human became his mate. The couple had a daughter, Hinetitami, with whom Tane also coupled. When the girl realized that her "husband" was her father, she ran off to the underworld as Hine-nui-te-po, goddess of death.

TANGAROA In the Maori and other branches of Polynesian mythology, Tangaroa was the god of the sea, one of the offspring of Papa and Rangi. His Tahitian equivalent was Ta'aroa, the creator god and supreme deity. In Tahiti he was the supreme being, Ta'aroa, and in other places simply A'a. The Maori say that Tangaroa created the things of the sea and that he is in constant struggle with his brother Tane.

TANTALUS The son of the Greek god Zeus and a nymph, and father of Niobe and Pelops, Tantalus was a king in Asia Minor or, according to some sources, of Argos or Corinth. Tantalus is best known for his punishment in the underworld. He was condemned to suffer eternal thirst and hunger there, refreshment being always just *tantalizingly* out of reach. There are several stories about the reasons for this harsh punishment. It was said by some that he revealed certain of Zeus's secrets. Others said he stole nectar and ambrosia from the gods. The most commonly held belief was that he tested the gods' powers of knowledge and perception by inviting them to dinner and serving up his dismembered and cooked son, Pelops. The gods understood immediately what the dinner was made of, brought Pelops back to life, and condemned his father.

TANTRIC MYTHOLOGY Tantra is almost always associated with the Hindu god Shiva in connection with his *Shakti*, the Goddess (Devi). In union, god and goddess represent a unified absolute. In certain Tantras and Sakta *Upanishads*, it is the Goddess who is the primary object of worship as the personified Shakti. The word "Tantra" is also applied to certain Tantric texts such as the *Lakshmi Tantra* of the *Pancaratra*,

devoted to Vishnu. Usually, however, Tantras are dialogues between Shiva and the Goddess and are especially important to Shaktism, the worship of Shakti.

With its roots in pre-Aryan, pre-Hindu India, Tantrism stands as an alternative of sorts to the orthodox Hinduism of the Vedic tradition. It emphasizes the feminine aspect of a bipolar absolute and makes use of a spiritual practice known as *sadhana*, which can lead to a unification of the two poles and liberation (*Moksha*) from our corrupt Kali age (Kali *yuga*). The body is of great importance in *sadhana*. Liberation may be achieved through bodily perfection. Thus, yoga is important as a practice in addition to more traditional worship. *Mantra Yoga* involves meditation on sounds, and *Kundalini Yoga* brings together the Shiva and Shakti within ourselves. Important to *Tantric Yoga* is the series of bodily energy points called *chakras*, which are connected by channels called *nadis*.

A form of Buddhist Tantrism—called Vajrayana—exists as well.

TARA According to Tibetan myth, in ancient times, Tara, the female counterpart to the bodhisattva Avalokiteshvara (Chenrezi) and a great Mahayana Buddhist savior goddess, sometimes called the "Mother of Buddhas," took the form of a rock demoness, mated with Avalokiteshvara in his form as a monkey, and gave birth to monkeys who gradually became the Tibetans. Another myth says that Tara was born of Avalokiteshvara's tears as he looked back at the world he was leaving for Nirvana. In Hinduism Tara is associated with the Goddess (Devi), as Parvati and Kali and other forms. There is a Tantric aspect to Tara, especially as the *Shakti* in union with Avalokiteshvara. In Tibetan Buddhism Tara takes many forms and has many functions, associated colors, and sacred formulae (mantras).

In the Irish tradition, Tara was the residence of Irish high kings. The ruins of Tara are in County Meath. Tara (Temuir, Temair) took its name from Tea, the wife of the original Milesian high king. Tara was the center of Ireland, with roads leading out like spokes of a wheel to the five provinces.

TARANIS Taranis (Taranus) was compared by Julius Caesar to the Roman god Jupiter. Taranis was the thunder and storm god of the continental Celts of Gaul. He was an aspect of the typically Indo-European triad of Esus, Taranis, and Teutates.

TARPEIA In the myths of Roman prehistory, Tarpeia was a woman who loved the enemy Sabine king and betrayed Rome for him. But when the king entered Rome in victory he treated Tarpeia with disdain and had her killed. From then on Roman traitors were thrown off the Tarpeian Rock, named after Tarpeia.

TARTAROS In the Greek epic the *Iliad*, Tartaros is described as an extra deep underworld, below Hades, reserved for the rebellious Titans.

TARTESSIAN, TURDETAN, AND IBERIAN MYTHOLOGY When the Romans, Celts, and others made their way to Spain they encountered Tartessians, non–Indo-Europeans who, influenced by Phoenician traders, had, like the Romans, adopted the goddess Astarte and who celebrated Habis, a culture hero who was responsible for the establishment of Tartessian customs. Another non–Indo-European culture in Spain was that of the Turdetans, who also wor-

T

shipped Astarte. Iberians in Spain developed a cult around the somewhat similar goddess Tanit, a figure with Greek-inspired Artemis-like qualities.

TARVAA A famous Tibetan and Mongolian shaman, Tarvaa became sick and lost consciousness as a child, and his family, according to custom, removed him from the house, where the birds plucked out his eyes. Tarvaa's soul was so upset at what had happened that it flew off to the land of the dead. There, since Tarvaa was not, in fact, dead, it was refused entrance but given a wish. Tarvaa's soul asked for knowledge of the spirit world and returned to Tarvaa. When the boy woke up he was blind but also a true shaman, that is, a wise man who could intervene for humans in the spirit world.

TATHAGATA Tathagata, perhaps meaning "discoverer of truth," is a name Gautama Buddha is said to have given himself.

TAWHAKI In the Maori mythology of Polynesia, Tawhaki was a hero whose adventures form the basis of a complex story cycle in which the hero, accompanied by his decidedly unheroic brother Kariki, undertakes many adventures, including, most important, the avenging of his father's murder. His son Rata was another Polynesian hero.

TAWHIRI The Polynesian god Tawhiri was known among the Maori as a storm god. It was he who blew down his rival brother Tane's forests and who chased the tree-dwelling fish into the sea.

TELIPINU Telipinu (Telepinu) was the most important of the disappearing gods so prevalent in Hittite-Hurrian mythology. The myth has even older Hattian origins in the Anatolian land conquered by the Hittites.

Telipinu was the son of the great storm or weather god (sometimes Teshub). His myth, like other disappearing god myths, was apparently intended to accompany rituals intended to soothe the anger of the gods—particularly that of the storm god, during times of trouble. Although an agricultural deity responsible for the care and irrigation of the fields, Telipinu had the basic characteristics of his father and was referred to as a disappearing storm god capable of great anger and destruction.

For some reason, one day Telipinu became violently angered, so he put on his shoes and disappeared. Immediately the world lost its ability to function—the gods at their altars and the domestic animals in their pens were "stifled." Animals rejected their young, all fertility ceased; the land dried up, and humans and gods alike suffered greatly. The storm god realized that his son's absence was the cause of the problem. The sun god sent out an eagle to search for Telipinu, but he could not find him anywhere—not in the sea, not on the mountains, not in the valleys. The storm god sought the advice of the ancient Hannahanna, the grandmother of goddesses. She suggested that the storm god go out himself in search of his vanished son. But in his attempt to leave his city, the storm god broke his hammer trying unsuccessfully to open the gate, so Hannahanna sent a bee to search for the god. The storm god was skeptical of the capabilities of so small a creature, but the bee departed on its mission. In time the bee found Telipinu asleep in a grove in a place called Lihzina (a famous storm god cult center). Awakened by the bee 's sting, the god became furious, demonstrating all of his storm god power, causing horrible destruction everywhere. He struck the dark earth with ferocity. In desperation, the gods turned to the magician goddess Kamrusepa for help. She used magic spells, rituals, and formulae to soothe Telipinu and to revive his benevolent spirit.

The role of Kamrusepa, who performs a mythical representation of the mugawar ritual, is similar to that of the modern therapist. She "takes his anger and his sullenness" from the disappearing god—"his soul and essence were stifled (like burning) brushwood"—and she makes that soul whole again. Under the spell of the ritual, "Telipinu let anger go"; it was "seized" by the dark earth.

Telipinu returned to his home, cleansed the destroyed land, and restored fertility and harmony. Mothers returned to the care of their children. Telipinu brought "longevity and progeny" back to the world.

TENDAI SECT Known as Tendai Shu or Hokkeshu, meaning "Lotus School," the Tendai sect is an esoteric sect of Mahayana Buddhism brought to Japan in the ninth century C.E. by the monk Saicho from China, where it had been founded in the sixth century by Chih-i. Chih-i had interpreted the Indian Buddhist sutras and arranged them according to the stages of the Buddha's career and the development of his thought. When Saicho founded his temple on Mount Hei near Kyoto, he integrated elements of the esoteric form of the Shingon school into his form of Tendai, and later, elements of Shinto were assimilated. It was Tendai's all-inclusive synthesis of various forms of Buddhism that led to the founding in the twelfth century of various new sects by monks who had been trained at the Tendai Temple. The monk Honen founded the Jodo or Pure Land School, Shinran founded Jodo Shinshu or True Pure Land sect, Eisai and Dogen founded Zen sects, and Nicheren founded the school named after him.

TENGRI Tengri was the sky god of the Turko-Mongols and other central Asian peoples, and tengri are spirit figures, particularly among certain Siberian groups.

TENGU The *tengu* are Japanese Shinto mountain demons who, like tricksters and shamans, can change shapes, have supernatural powers, and can even fly. They appear among people unexpectedly and have the power to enchant or bewitch. In the medieval period, *tengu* were sometimes thought to be proud monks—particularly the shaman-like mountain ascetics known as *yamabushi*—turned into animals. The *tengu* are depicted with wings, bird-like beaks or long noses, and sometimes red faces and the clothing of monks, especially those of the *yamabushi*. In one story, it is said that the *yamabushi* Unkei attended a meeting of *tengu* on Mount Atago, where the demons were deciding the fate of the world. This tale suggests an actual connection between these ascetic monks and the demons. *Tengu* are quite capable of evil deeds. They carry off children, change themselves into false Buddhas, kidnap novice monks, and cause anger between individuals and groups. Yet they apparently can also do some good and are venerated in shrines—either out of respect or fear of what they might do.

TEREUS Tereus was a son of the Greek war god Ares. A king in Thrace, Tereus went to the aid of Pandion, king of Attica, and, as a reward, was given the king's daughter Procne as a wife. The couple had a son, Itys. But Tereus lusted after Procne's sister Philomela and raped her on her way to visit her sister in Thrace. To prevent her from

T

exposing his crime, Tereus cut out Philomela's tongue and hid her away. Some traditions hold that it was Procne who was hidden away and that Tereus lured Philomela to Thrace as a new wife, pretending that Procne was dead. According to the Roman poet Ovid, in his *Metamorphoses*, Tereus told Procne that Philomela was dead but that from the place of her imprisonment, the tongueless Philomela wove a tapestry telling the truth of her situation and sent it to her sister. After Procne came to Philomela and freed her, the sisters avenged their wrong by killing and dismembering Itys and cooking him as a stew for his father. When the meal was over, Procne, with Philomela now present, told her husband what he had eaten, but before the furious and horrified Tereus could catch the two women, Philomela was turned by the gods into a swallow and Procne into a nightingale, whose cry "Itys, Itys" is in memory of her son.

TESHUB Teshub (Tessub, Tesup) was a Hittite storm and weather god. In a cycle of war-in-Heaven myths known as the Kumarbi cycle, after Anu deposed Alalu, Kumarbi overthrew Anu and in the process bit off and ate Anu's genitals. That act caused Kumarbi to become pregnant with and to give birth to the storm god Teshub and other frightening gods, who may be stormy aspects of Teshub. When Teshub had grown up, Kumarbi tried and failed to eat him, and Teshub took over as king of the gods. Later Teshub himself would be defeated by the giant Ullikummi. But Ullikummi's strength would be taken away by the old god Ea, and Teshub would regain his throne and renew the constant battle with Kumarbi.

TETHYS Tethys, Titan daughter of the original Greek Mother Goddess Gaia and her consort Ouranos, produced the Oceanids with her brother Oceanus.

TEZCATLIPOCA Among many Mesoamericans, including the Aztecs, Tezcatlipoca ("Dark Mirror Lord"), the jaguar, was a shadowy figure whose magic mirror showed him the future and the way into hearts and minds. He often stood in opposition to the popular Quetzalcoatl. In some versions of the Mesoamerican creation myth, Tezcatlipoca was the dominant creator god, a composite figure containing the "Four Tezcatlipocas"—the four creators and dominant gods of four of the creations, or "suns": Tezcatlipoca himself, Huitzilopochtli, Quetzalcoatl, and Xipe Totec. It was the Toltecs who developed the Tezcatlipoca myth and brought it to the Aztecs. His personality is marked by darkness and death, but he protects rulers.

THEBES Thebes was the traditional capital of upper Egypt, famous for its grandeur even in Homer's time. The Greek Thebes, in Boetia, was one of the most important venues for significant mythological events. Cadmus, the brother of Europa, founded the city, and the acropolis there was called the Cadmea, after him. The terrible story of Oedipus and his family, contained in the several plays by Sophocles, is a Theban story, as is that of Adrastus and the Seven Against Thebes, and that of Pentheus and the god Dionysos, told by Euripides in the *Bacchae*. The famous blind soothsayer Tiresias was Theban. Herakles' wife Megara was Theban. Some say that both Herakles and Dionysos were born in Thebes. Dionysos's mother, the unfortunate Semele, was Theban; Niobe's husband, Amphion, a son of Zeus, was a king of Thebes. He was so great a musician that when

Tengu the mountain god

he played on his lyre, stones moved of their own accord to form the magnificent walls of the city.

THEFT OF FIRE The theft of fire is a motif common to many mythological systems, precisely because fire has been such an important aspect of civilization. Usually the culture hero or a god steals the fire from a place protected by the supreme being and gives it to humans for their use. The Greek Titan Prometheus stole fire for humans and for doing so was brutally punished by Zeus. Culture heroes such as Bue in the Gilbert Islands, Tore of the Mbuti people in Zaire, and Botoque of the Brazilian Kayapo all took fire from the gods to be used by people. Maui in Polynesia was one of many trickster–culture heroes who stole fire.

THEIA The sister-wife of Hyperion and the mother by him of Selene (Moon), Helios (Sun), and Eos (Dawn), Theia was a Titan, a daughter of the pre-Olympian Greek gods Gaia and Ouranos.

THEMIS Themis, meaning "Order," was a Titan, the daughter of the pre-Olympian Greek deities Gaia and Ouranos. Metaphorically, her birth suggests that the union of the primal parents, Sky and Earth, created essential legal order, which Themis personified. Themis was the mother by Iapetus of several famous sons, including Prometheus, Atlas, and Epimetheus (the husband of Pandora). By Zeus she gave birth to goddesses representing various offshoots of order: Dike ("Justice") and Eirene ("Peace"). She was, according to some, also the mother of the seasons and the Fates.

THENS In Southeast Asia, especially Thailand and Laos, the Thens, at the beginning of time, were sky gods who

T

ruled the sky, which was connected to earth by a bridge. The earth was ruled by three lords as well. When the earth people refused to pay the Thens a tribute, they destroyed the earth with a great flood. But the three earth lords escaped in a houseboat and sailed up to the home of the Thens. After the receding of the flood, the Thens sent the three earth people back to earth with a buffalo. After a few years the buffalo died, but gourds grew from its nose, and when one of the earth lords, Pu Lang Seung, drilled holes in the gourds, people emerged.

The Thens returned to earth in the role of culture heroes, teaching the people how to plant, to make tools, to cook, to weave, to dance, and to sing. Finally, the Thens left, cutting the bridge between heaven and earth behind them.

THEOGONY The eighth-century B.C.E. poet Hesiod described the most widely accepted version of the Greek creation myth in his *Theogony*.

THERAVADA BUDDHISM Theravada, meaning "teaching of the elders," is a term often used synonymously with Hinayana for the early form of Buddhism that accepts only the teachings of Sakyamuni Buddha and stresses the ideal of the arhat—personal salvation through the Buddha—as opposed to the Mahayana ideal of the *bodhisattva*, who chooses to remain in this world to help others to salvation. Technically, however, Theravada, the form of Buddhism practiced primarily in Southeast Asia and Sri Lanka, is only one branch of Hinayana—albeit, practically speaking, the only extant branch. The early Hinayanas, or adherents of the ancient Pali Canon, split into two major factions, in one of which the Theravada group was dominant. Given the strict adherence to the teachings of the Buddha, mythology beyond that of the life of the Buddha does not play a major part in Theravada. In Southeast Asia, however, there is a tendency to absorb indigenous earth spirit and ancestor elements as well as a cosmology.

THESEUS There are conflicting myths about the conception of Theseus, one of the greatest of the Greek heroes. His official father was Aegeus, king of Athens, who visited Troezen and got drunk with his host, Pitteus, who gave him his daughter Aethra as a gift. According to this story, Aethra gave birth to Theseus. A more miraculous Troezenian version of the story says that the god Poseidon substituted himself for Aegeus for a time, causing Aethra to conceive Theseus. In any case, at least believing he was the child's father, Aegeus left instructions before he left Troezen that if the child were a boy, he was to be sent to Athens to find his father when he was strong enough to lift a rock, under which he would find his father's sword and sandals. In due time the boy accomplished this task and underwent the hero's ritual of initiatory, self-establishing adventures on his way to Athens. There, after Aegeus's guest and wife, the sorceress Medea, tried unsuccessfully to poison the mysterious youth, who had appeared in the king's court, Aegeus recognized the youth's sword and sandals and so identified his son and welcomed him, at the same time banishing Medea.

Theseus continued to prove himself, killing the great Bull of Marathon that had been ravishing the countryside. Some say this was the bull originally given by Poseidon to King Minos of Crete for sacrifice, the bull that the king instead kept and that his wife Pasiphae had sexual relations with, and that Herakles had brought from Crete to the mainland. The offspring of the horrendous liaison between the bull and Pasiphae had been the monstrous Minotaur, whose lair, the Labyrinth, was created by the master craftsman Daedalus.

Many versions of what follows exist, but generally it is said that Theseus volunteered to join the seven boys and seven maidens that the Athenians had been forced to agree to send each year to Minos as tribute to be fed to the Minotaur (Asterius) in his Labyrinth. Theseus sailed with the thirteen other victims to Crete. When the party arrived, Minos

Ariadne with Theseus

lusted after one of the maidens and was about to rape her when Theseus, invoking the laws of Poseidon, intervened. Minos, challenging him to prove his special relationship with Poseidon, threw his signet ring into the sea and commanded the young hero to find it. With the help of dolphins and other underwater followers of Poseidon, Theseus was able to retrieve the ring. Minos's daughter Ariadne was apparently so impressed by the Athenian that she fell in love with him and helped in what would be his battle with the Minotaur. She gave Theseus a magic ball of thread that had been given to her by Daedalus and instructed him to tie one end to the Labyrinth entrance door lintel and to unravel the thread as he worked his way to the center. Once there he was to kill the Minotaur and offer him as a sacrifice to Poseidon. When Theseus emerged victorious from the Labyrinth, he was greeted by the infatuated Ariadne, who led the Athenians to their ship and sailed away with them as Theseus's wife. After a sea battle the party found their way to the island of Naxos, where Theseus left Ariadne and sailed for Athens. Ariadne was comforted by the god Dionysos. The defeat of the Minotaur by the Greek hero Theseus can perhaps serve as a metaphorical rendering of the intrusion in about 1450 B.C.E. of the Greek-speaking Mycenaeans into Crete.

Theseus had promised his father, Aegeus, that when the Athenian ship returned to Athens, the sailors would hoist a white sail to replace the black one if he had been successful in Crete. Theseus forgot his promise and came upon Cape Sounium under black sail. Aegeus saw the sail from the cliff and in despair threw himself off. Because of this act, Theseus became King of Athens, known for wisdom and great deeds and for tolerance; it was he, for instance, who protected the outlawed Oedipus in the sanctuary at Colonnus.

Theseus continued to have significant heroic adventures as well, not always demonstrating his better qualities. He joined his friend Herakles in a fight against the Amazons, for instance. The Amazons were defeated, and Theseus took one of them as a prize and wife. According to one version of the story, his Amazon wife was queen Hippolyta who later gave birth to Theseus's son, Hippolytus. Others say he abducted Hippolyta's sister Antiope and that he defeated the Amazon army led by Hippolyta that invaded Attica in a rescue attempt. Still others say that Hippolyta and Antiope were different names for the same Amazon, and there is a story of Herakles killing Hippolyta during the course of his ninth labor, which involved the taking of her sacred belt or "girdle."

Theseus would be involved in the fight of the Lapiths against the centaurs. He joined Jason and the other Argonauts on their voyage. And he assisted in the kidnapping of Helen when she was still a young girl. He lost her, however, when her brothers, Castor and Polydeuces (Pollux), the twins known as the Dioskori, came to their sister's rescue. Theseus descended to the underworld, where he was imprisoned until, in one version of the myth, he was rescued by Herakles, who, as his twelfth labor, overcame death itself.

After the death of Antiope, Theseus had married his old friend Ariadne's sister Phaedre. When he returned home after his stay in the underworld he confronted his wife's false story that his son Hippolytus had attempted to seduce her, and he banished his son, asking Poseidon to punish him. Poseidon did so by sending a bull from the sea that so frightened the boy's chariot horses that they bolted and eventually dragged Hippolytus back to his father in a state near death. Meanwhile, the truth had become clear and

Phaedre had hanged herself. Father and son were reconciled, but Hippolytus died of his injuries, and some sources tell of Theseus ending his life in lonely self-imposed exile on an island.

THETIS Thetis was the sea nymph (Nereid) wife of the mortal King Peleus, who, instructed by the centaur Chiron, had held the nymph to the ground and won her despite her violent changing of forms. Thetis was much admired by Zeus, Poseidon, and others. She been brought up by Hera and she had received Hephaistos when Zeus had thrown him out of heaven. It was at her wedding that the uninvited goddess of Discord, Eris, threw out the golden apple that led to the contest judged by the Trojan prince Paris. In that contest, Paris was to give the apple to the most beautiful goddess, the contestants being Hera, Aphrodite, and Athena. Paris's choice of Aphrodite would lead to the Trojan War, in which Thetis's son, the Greek hero Achilles, would be killed.

THOR Thor was the most popular of the Norse gods, the northern version of the German Thunr (Thunor, Donar). He was the weather-storm god of sky and thunder who was responsible for law and order in the world of humans. His power emanated from his father, the high sky god Odin. And as the son of the earth goddess Fyorgyn ("Earth"), he was also a god of fertility. Thor was dependable and steadfast, whereas Odin was unpredictable. He retained the Herculean characteristics the Romans had recognized in Thunr. Huge in size, with red beard and eyes, he had enormous appetites, and not much wit. He always carried his huge hammer and wore iron gloves and a girdle of power. Thor's wife was the fertility goddess Sif, whose beautiful wheat-like hair was once shaved off—that is, stolen—by Loki. Their daughter was Thrud, whose name, appropriately, means "Might." Of particular significance is Thor's hammer, Mjollnir. Flung through the sky it was a deadly weapon and was, of course, representative of lightning and thunder. Hammers representing Thor's fertile phallic power were traditionally placed in the laps of brides in Scandinavia. Such hammers were also used to hallow the newly born, perhaps to ensure fertile lives. Stories of Thor, such as one known as "Thor's Duel with Hrungnir," are among the most popular in Norse mythology. In that myth Thor is the Indo-European giant-monster killer, the representative of good against evil, light against darkness.

One day while Thor was off hunting trolls and their unsavory kin, Odin became bored in Valhalla and decided to look for adventure in Jotenheim. He leapt upon the back of Sleipnir and galloped off disguised to the home of Hrungnir, the greatest, stoniest, and most dangerous of all the giants. Hrungnir saw the figure riding toward him and was full of curiosity. When his unknown visitor arrived, the giant complimented him on the lines and speed of his mount but received only boasts and insults in return. When the stranger's taunts turned to the subject of Hrungnir's own horse, Gold Mane, the giant got into his saddle and began chasing the visitor. But although Gold Mane was fast, Sleipnir was faster, and before he knew it the giant found himself no longer in pursuit but, rather, cornered, since he had somehow followed Odin right through the gates of Asgard.

Hrungnir grew anxious for himself when he realized his predicament, but it was his luck that Thor was off elsewhere that day, and Odin offered his giant adversary the sanctuary of hospitality. Soon Hrungnir was drinking from Thor's

T

own horn, repaying his hosts with boasts and curses and threatening to make love to the beautiful goddesses Sif and Freya. Quietly, Odin sent for Thor, and the thunderer soon appeared. His rage became overwhelming when he saw the drunken giant ogling his wife, Sif. When Thor reached for his hammer, however, Hrungnir reminded Thor of the sanctuary status of a guest. At this, Thor relented and agreed to Hrungnir's invitation to single combat. A date was set and a place—the House of the Stone Fence, on the border between Jotenheim and Asgard—and the drunken giant made his exit.

The other giants, although they valued the honor brought to their race by a challenge to Thor, worried about what would happen to them should Hrungnir fall. To hedge their bets, they determined to create an artificial massive giant, one even taller than their champion, but made only of clay, not of stone, and with the heart of a slaughtered mare. They named their creation Mist Calf, and they commanded him to wait for Thor at the appointed place of combat. On the chosen day the thunderer mounted his chariot with his servant, Thialfi, by his side, and as he made his way, lightning flashed and thunder crashed, sparks flew from the wheels of Thor's cart, and the earth itself seemed to buckle with the god's anger. Mist Calf was so terrified at the god's approach that urine flooded from him, and Thialfi's ax made short work of him.

Hrungnir himself was more determined, however, and he cast his mighty whetstone at Thor just as the storm god sent Mjollnir end over end toward his foe; the two weapons met in a terrible crash and Hrungnir's was turned into a thousand flying fragments that landed in Midgard and are the whetstone people still use today. But a large chunk of whetstone also knocked Thor off of his feet and left him stunned. In fact, he discovered that he had a large piece embedded in his head, leaving him with a mighty headache. And, although his hammer had ended Hrungnir's life, the giant had fallen over on him and left him pinned to the ground, unable to move. Thialfi could do nothing, so he summoned the gods, but they could not move the hulk that was the dead giant. Finally, Thor's bastard son Magni lifted the giant off of his father; for this, Thor gave Gold Mane to Magni, although Odin chafed at this gift, as he had coveted the horse for himself. So it was that Thor defeated Hrungnir, and the giants lost their greatest champion, but the whetstone remained forever lodged in the thunderer's head.

Another favorite Thor myth is that of his fishing with the giant Hymir for the World Serpent. For undermining his near success Hymir suffered Thor's wrath and was thrown into the sea where the serpent lived. The serpent and Thor would kill each other at Ragnarok, the end of the world.

THOTH Thoth was the moon god as well as the god of wisdom in Egypt. In Hermopolis, his theological home, to the dead who were initiated into his secrets he gave passage to the sky. His was the realm of the mysteries, magic, and arcane knowledge, such as that contained in the *Book of Going Forth by Day* ("Book of the Dead"). It was he who invented hieroglyphs and writing. In Hermopolis he might sometimes have been seen as a creator god. For some, Thoth was the son of Re, Re in this case being the sun, the right eye of Horus, whose moon eye

Thor chases the dwarfs

had been ripped out by Seth. His consort was Maat, the personification of the concept of truth, divine order, and justice. Thoth's head was that of a baboon or an ibis. As a funerary god, like Anubis, he weighed the hearts of the deceased. In Thoth is combined the re-creative magic of language and that of resurrection. Early in the New Kingdom, certain pharaohs chose the name Thothmose to associate themselves with this great and mysterious god. The Thothmose dynasty considered itself particularly close to divinity. When Hatshepsut, the wife of Thothmose II, usurped the throne on her husband's death, she justified her action by claiming a particularly miraculous conception and divine birth. She was, she claimed, the female version of Horus, conceived when Amun-Re took the form of her earthly father, Thothmose I, and had relations with her mother, Ahmose.

THOUSAND AND ONE NIGHTS, THE Commonly known as the *Arabian Nights, The Thousand and One Nights* is a collection of folktales, anecdotes, or fables that were originally passed on orally from the Arab lands and from Iran, India, and Egypt. The collection itself grew and developed between the 800s C.E. until it was written in its present form in Arabic in the late fifteenth century. The most popular English versions are those of Edward William Lane of the 1840s and Richard Francis Burton of the 1880s.

These are the familiar tales of "Ali Baba and the Forty Thieves," "Aladdin's Lamp," "Sindbad the Sailor," and many others not so familiar in the West. In the book, the stories are told by a Queen Scheherazade, who uses the stories to keep the cuckolded and angry sultan from marrying a new woman every night and killing her in the morning. After 1001 nights of storytelling, the sultan relents.

THRAETONA In the struggle between good and evil in Zoroastrianism, Thraetona or Feridoun is a hero called by the elements to fight against the wicked King Dahaka or Zohak, on whose shoulders are two serpents symbolizing the king's threat to the elements.

THREAT TO THE DIVINE CHILD In the archetypal monomyth of the hero, a motif of early childhood involves the threat to the divine child's (*puer aeternus*) life by a wicked king or demon. The threat signifies the unwillingness of those representing the status quo and personal power to allow the blossoming of a new vision of reality. Thus, Herod tries to kill the future "King of the Jews," Jesus, by ordering the death of baby boys; Duransarun tries to kill Zoroaster; Hainuwele 's people bury her alive; the evil Kamsa orders that Dvaki's children be killed at birth, hoping to prevent the birth of Krishna; and Moses is threatened when the pharaoh orders the death of the Hebrew children.

THREE WORLDS *Loka* is the Sanskrit for "World." In the Hindu tradition there are three *lokas*—Earth, Atmosphere, and the world of the gods. These worlds represent stages of salvation, Heaven being the *loka* of the *Vedas* . The three worlds (*trailokya* in Pali) of Buddhism are the lowly *kamaloka*, the world of Hell and desire; the *rupaloka*, the world of the gods and of form relieved of desire; and the highest or *arupaloka*, the world of perfect formlessness.

THRYM Thrym was the frost giant king in Norse mythology, who made the fatal mistake of stealing Thor's hammer, Mjollnir.

A Haida Thunderbird

THUNDERBIRD In Native North America, the Thunderbird is a personification of thunder and the destructive forces of nature. Its wings are said to create thunder, its eyes lightning. The Thunderbird appears frequently in the elaborate art of the Indians of the Pacific Northwest. Among the Sioux, the Thunderbird is an incarnation of the Great Spirit, Wakan Tanka.

TIAMAT In Mesopotamian mythology, Tiamat was the primal goddess of saltwater seas who mated with the freshwater personification, Apsu. Their offspring were Ea and the other early gods. In the Babylonian creation epic, the *Enuma elish*, Tiamat is a dragon-like demon, representing primordial chaos. She makes war on Ea and the other younger gods because Ea has killed Apsu. When she is defeated by the hero Marduk, who represents the Babylonian ideal of order, she is cut in half, becoming the animistic source of creation. Part of her becomes the sky, part the earth.

TIBETAN MYTHOLOGY When we speak of Tibetan mythology, we must differentiate between the mythology of the indigenous Bon religion and that of the later Buddhism, although the two sometimes flow together. The myths of the Bon religion are almost always associated with origins, beginning with 'Olde spurgyal, said to have been sent to rule humans by the gods above. Origin myths were told in order to make any ritual effective. If a person was sick, the curing ceremony involved a recitation of origins or creation. Marriage ceremonies included the retelling of the first marriage—that between the goddess who was daughter of the god of the world, and a human man, Lingdkar. Arguing with the reluctant god for his daughter's hand, the man suggests that the union of man and the gods should

Tibetan monks' painting of the Buddhist Wheel of Life

an incarnation of Avalokiteshvara. Finally, there are indigenous myths that see creation as coming from the struggle between the powers of light ("Radiance") and those of darkness ("Black Misery"). In this model, the black lord creates all that is anti-existence out of a cosmic egg, while the white lord creates all that is good.

Until Buddhism became dominant in Tibet in 842 C.E., the people were ruled by a dynasty of sacred kings who traced their ancestry to gNya'khri btsan-po, who came down from the land of the gods as rain that impregnates the earth. All nature celebrated his arrival. After his return to Heaven, this first king was invoked by each of his successors to ratify their divine inheritance. In a sense, the rise of Lamaism in Tibet is a continuation in a Buddhist context of this earlier practice.

Lamaism, the Mahayana Buddhism of Tibet, takes its name from the importance it attributes to *lamas*, the Dalai Lama and the Panchen Lama. The temporal (until the Chinese invasion of 1952) and spiritual leader of Tibet is the Dalai Lama. The next important figure in the Tibetan hierarchy is the Panchen Lama, an emanation of the Buddha Amitabha (Amida Buddha). The closeness of the two *lamas* is indicated by the fact that Avalokiteshvara is himself an emanation of the Buddha Amitabha.

Lamaism is deeply influenced by the Tantric aspect of Buddhism (*Vajrayana*), which is itself tied to the tradition of *Sutrayana*, in which one identifies with the suffering of others and works toward the liberation not only of the self but of others. Vajrayana stresses the possibility of liberation in this life and is a much faster process than *Sutrayana* alone.

It is said that Buddhism was introduced to Tibet by the Chinese and Nepalese wives of King Songsten Gampo (Song-sen-gam-po), who reigned in Tibet in the seventh century C.E. He was, in a sense, the first Dalai Lama, as he is considered to have been, like the Dalai Lamas of later periods, an incarnation of Avalokiteshvara, the most important of Tibetan bodhisattvas. But it was later in the century that King Trisong Detsen actually adopted Buddhism as the state religion. Later kings turned against Buddhism and persecuted its adherents. It was not until the eleventh century that Buddhism returned in force to Tibet, very much under Indian rather than Chinese influence and with a character all its own, brought about by its *Vajrayana* characteristics and its partial assimilation of the indigenous shamanistic and animistic Bon religion.

One of the most obvious aspects of Tibetan Buddhism is its reliance on works of art. At the center of this tradition is the depiction of the endless cycle of birth and death known as *samsara* in the Wheel of Life. The wheel is held up by Shinje, the Lord of Death and, therefore, the determiner of Life. The "machine" that turns the wheel is made of ignorance, desire, and hatred, represented by a pig, a cockerel, and a snake. Contained in the Wheel of Life paintings is a rich symbolism depicting the causes of existence and the various possibilities of existence—god, part god, human, animal, ghost, Hell. The Wheel suggests symbolically that it is only through birth as a human that the individual can move beyond Hell, ghost, and animal and begin to achieve liberation from the domain of Death.

As noted above, the Bon and Buddhist traditions openly blend together in certain myths. One such myth sees the Tibetans as descendants of a monkey and an ogress. The monkey was sent to Tibet by the Bodhisattva Avalokiteshvara. There, as he meditates on the virtues of the bodhisattva, he is confronted by an ogress who takes the form of a

mean worship for the gods and protection for humans. Upon leaving Heaven, the goddess is given a third of her parents' inheritance (her brother, as a male, receives two-thirds). Her father gives her the masculine arrow and her mother gives her the feminine spindle. In actual Bon wedding ceremonies each action is tied to this origin myth. For instance, the priest presents the groom with a piece of gold and the bride with a piece of turquoise, and then the priest and the couple sing the story of the arrow and the spindle. They sing of how at the beginning of time the union of two immortals resulted in three eggs. From a golden one came a golden male "arrow of life" with turquoise feathers. From a turquoise egg came a turquoise arrow of the female with golden feathers. From a white egg came a golden spindle. And from the sky and the ocean mist came Bon.

There are many variations of Tibetan myths of creation via a cosmic egg or eggs. One tells how in the beginning the elements became a giant cosmic egg. On its shell was the white cliff of the gods, and within it was a lake with a yolk containing the six classes of life. Out of this center came eighteen smaller eggs, one of which was a white one that produced of its own accord the various parts of a being who became a man who named himself King Yesmon.

Other cosmogonic themes in Tibet include an animistic one of creation from the actual body of a primordial goddess. It is said that the Klu Queen who made the world was a child of the Void, that the sky came from her head, the planets from her teeth, the moon from her right eye, the sun from her left, and so forth. It was day when she opened her eyes and night when she closed them. Her voice was thunder, her breath clouds, her tears rain.

Some Tibetan myths say the original being was the "uncreated blue toad of turquoise"; some say it was a tigress. In some stories, creation comes from the killing of a primordial being by a young hero, sometimes, especially in Ladakh, named Gesar, whom Buddhists would see as

woman and asks him to marry her. If he refuses, she will unite with a demon and produce a race of life-destroying demons. The monkey returns to Avalokiteshvara and asks for advice. The bodhisattva, with the assent of the goddess Tara, releases his disciple from his vows of chastity and orders him to marry the ogress, prophesying the coming of Buddhism to Tibet. The union of monkey and goddess results eventually in a tribe of monkeys who then become so populous that they are starving, until Avalokiteshvara, from the sacred Mount Meru, digs grains that he scatters in the world of monkeys, providing crops. Gradually the monkeys lose their tails and learn to walk upright, to talk, and to wear clothes. Their descendants are the Tibetans. In some versions of this myth, the first monkey's name is Ha-lu-ma-da, which could well be related to the Indian monkey god Hanuman. In any case, the monkey is sometimes associated with Avalokiteshvara and worshipped himself as a *bodhisattva*. There is also a Buddhist tradition that Gautama Buddha had been a monkey in one of his former lives. [Bonnefoy (1993)]

TINTIYA The cosmology of Bali contains six heavens poised over earth. The highest heaven is ruled by the supreme being, Tintiya.

TIRESIAS The famous Greek soothsayer, Tiresias (Teiresias) was closely associated with the city of Thebes. He revealed to Oedipus in Sophocles' *Oedipus Rex* that it was he who was the cause of the city's problems and to Pentheus in Euripides' the *Bacchae* that he was wrong to deny Dionysos. Tiresias also prophesied to Homer's Odysseus in the underworld. Although physically blind, Tiresias had prophetic sight and insight. There are various versions of the story of how he became blind and how he gained the power of prophecy. It was most widely reported that one day Tiresias saw two snakes copulating and hit the female one with his stick. For this sin he was made a woman. When years later he hit a male snake copulating, he became a man again. So it was that Tiresias, alone among the Greeks, had sexual experience as both a woman and a man, and so it was that Zeus and Hera called upon him to settle an argument between them. Zeus claimed that intercourse was more enjoyable for women than for men, Hera claimed it was more pleasurable for men. When Tiresias took Zeus's side, Hera became so furious that she blinded Tiresias. Zeus could not take away the blindness, but he gave Tiresias the power of insight—of prophecy—a dubious gift since people tended to rail against the soothsayer for his prophecies or to deny their validity.

TISHTRYA In ancient Iran (Persia), Tishtrya was a rain god, who, as a white horse, fought Apaosha, the demon god of droughts. When Apaosha won, the earth dried up. But after Tishtrya appealed to the high god, Ahura Mazda, for more strength, he was given that strength, and he defeated his enemy, and once again released the life-giving rains.

TITANS The offspring of the original Greek deities Ouranos (Heaven) and Gaia (Earth), the Titans, urged on by Gaia and led by Kronos (Saturn), rebelled against their father and Kronos became king. Later, Zeus, supported by his mother, Rhea, led his Olympian brothers and sisters in a rebellion—a war in Heaven—against Kronos and some of the Titans. When they were defeated by the Olympians, the rebels were thrown into a place below Tartarus. Among the best known of the Titans were Oceanus, Themis, and Hyperion. Among the most important offspring and other descendants of the Titans were Prometheus, Atlas, Hecate, Selene, and Helios.

TITHONUS When the Greek goddess of dawn, Eos, asked Zeus to give her human lover Tithonus immortality, she forgot to ask that he be granted eternal youth. Tithonus, who was the brother of the Trojan king Priam, eventually withered up so badly that Eos hid him away in her palace.

TIV'R A Melanesian culture hero in Papua New Guinea, Tiv'r retrieved his son, the first bullroarer, from his wife's womb when he heard him rumbling there.

TIW Tiw (Tig) was the Anglo-Saxon version of the German Tiwaz and the Norse Tyr.

TIWAZ The war god in ancient Germany, Tiwaz became Tyr in Norse mythology. The Romans identified him with their Mars.

TLALOC Tlaloc was an important pre-Aztec, Aztec, and general Mesoamerican deity whose elements were mountains and rain. He sometimes had storm god characteristics, bringing devastating rather than life-giving rainstorms. Tlaloc's wife was Chalchiuhtlicue. Tlalocan was the earthly paradise of the Aztecs.

TONANTZIN An Aztec version of an ancient Mesoamerican goddess, Tonantzin was a mother goddess closely associated with the moon. The pyramid of this goddess stood on the spot where the basilica of the Virgin of Guadalupe now stands in Mexico City, and it seems likely that first goddess merged into the "goddess" of the Christianized Mexicans.

TOOTHED VAGINA In various mythologies around the world are found myths of male-devouring femmes fatales who clearly represent a male view of the feminine. Particularly vivid among the genital-based myths is this Native North American one told by the Jicarilla Apaches and in slightly different versions by other Athabascan tribes such as the Navajo.

In ancient times a monster known as Kicking Monster roamed the earth causing destruction and pain. He had four daughters who looked like women but were really walking and talking vaginas with teeth. At that time, only these beings possessed vaginas. And they lived in a house with lots of vaginas hanging on the walls. The news of these vagina girls spread, and men from the world below this one came up to look for them. When he saw them, Kicking Monster kicked them into the vagina house, where they were devoured. Fortunately, one of the twin heroes, Monster Slayer or "Killer-of-Enemies," came along and managed to evade Kicking Monster and enter the vagina house. There he was set upon by the four vagina girls, who were hungry for intercourse. Monster Slayer held them off and asked about the whereabouts of all the men who had entered the house previously. "We have eaten them," answered the girls. Again the vagina girls lunged for Monster Slayer, but he again pushed them away, saying he would do what they wanted, but only after they had taken a certain sour berry-based medicine that would improve their vaginas, that is to say, the girls themselves. The women took the medicine and soon their teeth wasted away and their mouths—that is, their vaginas—became puckered and capable only of swallowing.

The Tower of Babel (Babylon)

Vaginas were from then on toothless and more friendly, as they are now.

TOWER OF BABEL In Genesis 11:1–9 in the Hebrew Bible (*Torah*) the story is told of how there was a time when all the people of the world spoke the same language, and some Mesopotamian people came to a place and decided to build a city with a tower that would reach up to the heavens. This city would be Babel (Babylon) and the tower was a ziggurat. The people 's object in building the tower was to make a name for themselves. When Yahweh saw what they were doing, he realized that they had aspirations that might be endless. Not wishing to be so challenged by humans, he dispersed them all over the earth and made them speak different languages so that their attempts at communication would be mere "babble" and they would not be able to achieve unity in their attempts to reach up to his level.

TREES Trees play important roles in mythology as natural objects rooted in the earth and reaching up to the sky. They become symbols of communication between the world of humans and that of divinity, as in the case of the world tree, Yggdrasill. Trees are also places of sacrifice. Thus Jesus hanging on the cross (often referred to as a tree) becomes the new fruit to replace the sinful fruit of the forbidden tree in the Garden of Eden, the effigy of Attis is hung on a tree, symbolizing death and resurrection, and Odin hangs willingly on the world tree to learn the mysteries of the runes. The body of the murdered Osiris is discovered in a column that had been a tree, the Buddha finds enlightenment through resisting temptation under a tree.

TRIADS Indo-European mythology is marked by the concept of threes, as in the tripartism of certain deity combinations and in the tri-une arrangement of the goddess as maiden, mother, and crone. In the Celtic world—particularly in Ireland and Wales—the concept is revealed in depictions of three-headed figures. It is also expressed in Ireland in the ubiquitous concept of the triune goddess: Morrigan, who is also Badb, Nemain, and Macha; or the "three queens, who are Eire, Banba, and Fotla.

TRICKSTER A common character in mythology is the trickster. Typically male, the trickster usually has extreme appetites—for food, but also for women. According to the given society's mores, he is immoral, or at least amoral, and he is frequently a thief. Yet he often uses his inventiveness, even his closeness to the creator, to help human beings as a de facto culture hero. Often his inventiveness interferes with creation, however, and results in such realities as pain and death. The trickster can change shapes at will and is perhaps a mythological relative of the shaman.

Raven, Coyote, and Iktome are popular Native North American tricksters. In Africa some of the best-known tricksters are Ananse, Legba, Eshu, and Dikithi. In ancient Sumer, Enki had trickster qualities, as did Hermes in ancient Greece. The often wicked and destructive Norse trickster was Loki. A particularly phallic-oriented trickster is the Polynesian Maui. Erlik is a ubiquitous trickster-devil in central Asia. Tricksters can be noble figures. The India Vishnu avatar Lord Krishna is a trickster whose pranks usually can be interpreted metaphorically for moral purposes.

TRIKAYA In Sanskrit, *trikaya* means "Three Forms," and in Mahayana Buddhism the term refers to the three forms taken by the Buddha: the human form, the transcendent enlightened form, the supernatural *yogin* form.

TRIMURTI In India the *trimurti* is that of Brahma the creator, Vishnu the preserver, and Shiva the destroyer. Devi (the Goddess), sometimes is a de facto substitute for the less important Brahma.

TRINITY Christian theology sees God in three aspects: Creator, Redeemer, and Sanctifier—Father, Son, and Holy Spirit, the Son being Jesus as the Christ, or Messiah. In this mystery, the father is God, the Son is God, and the Holy Spirit is God, but the Father is not the Son or the Holy Spirit, the Son is not the Father or the Holy Spirit, and the Holy Spirit is not the Father or the Son. Non-Christians see this as a form of polytheism. Christians insist that the three aspects are expressions of one god.

TRIPARTISM Early in the twentieth century, the French scholar Georges Dumézil pointed to a pervasive Indo-European tradition of a tripartization made up of religious/legal, military, and fertility (farming/herding) "classes" or functions. In India these functions were represented by *brahmans* (brahmins), *ksatriyas*, and *vaisyas*, respectively; in Iran there were *athravan*, *rathaestar*, and *vastriyo fsuyant*; in Rome, *flamines* (flamens), *miletes*, and *quirites*; and in Gaulish-Celtic culture, *druides*, *equites*, and *plebes*. This arrangement was clearly reflected in the pairing relationships of Indo-European mythologies, in which sovereign gods were related to priests and kings, warrior gods to warriors, and fertility gods to herder-farmers. This tripartization is reflected in religious and mythological constructs. The first function, the religious and legal one, is reflected in gods presented as a pair, each member of which reflects a specific aspect—religious such as the Indic Varuna or Norse Odin, and legal such as Mitra or Tyr. The second function, the military one, is represented by the war gods, such as Indra, Mars, and Thor. The third function, the fertility one, is represented by divine twins, sometimes associated with horses, and accompanied by a female figure, for example, the Indic Ashvins (horsemen) with Sarasvati, the Greek Castor and Pollux with Helen, and the Norse Frey and Freyr with Njorth.

TRISIRAS The son of Tvashtir, Trisiras was a three-headed demon killed by the Vedic god Indra. Trisiras read the *Vedas* with one head, ate with another, and stared into space with the third. Indra became concerned that this powerful ascetic might absorb the whole universe, so he killed him with a thunderbolt. But even in death the body gave off power, so Indra had a woodcutter cut off the demon's heads.

TRISTAN AND ISEULT The romance of Tristan (Trystan) and Iseult (Esyllt, Ysolt, Isolde) appears in many versions in medieval Europe. A twelfth-century French version is attributed to an unknown writer named Beroul, who seems to have been translating from a Celtic—specifically, Breton—source. The first Celtic version is in a Welsh manuscript of the sixteenth century. A later Cornish version also exists. The myth type is clearly Celtic—one of many stories of elopement such as those of Diarmuid and Grainne and of Noisu and Deirdre in Irish mythology.

Tristan was a warrior, poet, musician, storyteller, and great lover, who was the nephew of King Mark (March) of Cornwall. Tristan was ordered to travel to Ireland to escort Mark's wife, Iseult, to Cornwall. Depending on the version of the tale, various circumstances lead to the couple swallowing a magic potion that caused Tristan and Iseult to fall in love with each other. A disastrous love affair leads to their banishment and death. The best-known versions of the story are those told by Wagner in his opera *Tristan und Isolde* and in the Arthurian legends told by Malory and others.

TROJAN WAR The Trojan War was waged by a Mycenaean Greek alliance led by King Agamemnon of Mycenae-Argos against the Asia Minor city of Troy and its allies. The war took place after the Trojan prince Paris "abducted" Helen, the beautiful wife of King Menelaus of Sparta. The Greek allies went to Troy to avenge this act and to retrieve Helen. The story of the war and much of its aftermath is told by Homer in his epics, the *Iliad* and the *Odyssey*. The Greek playwright Aeschylus also tells of events leading to and following the war. Among the primary Greek warriors were Agamemnon, Menelaus, Achilles, Ajax, Diomedes, and Odysseus. The most famous of the Trojans were King Priam and his son Hector. The war ended when the famous wooden horse, devised by Odysseus and containing a large part of the Greek army, was allowed into the city of Troy as a parting "gift" of the Greeks. At night, the Greek soldiers exited the horse and laid waste to the city.

TSUKIYOMI Tsukiyomino-Mikoto was the moon god born of the right eye of the Japanese Shinto creator god Izanagi. He was the brother of the sun goddess Amaterasu and the storm god Susanowo. According to some, Tsukiyomi killed the food goddess Ukemochi (Ogetsunohime) for serving food from her various orifices. Amaterasu was so angry over this deed that she vowed never to look at her brother again. Thus the sun and moon remain separate from each other. Other sources say that it was Susanowo who killed the food goddess.

Tristan and Isolde about to drink the love potion

TU The Maori war god, this Polynesian figure was the son of earth and sky—Papa and Rangi. Tu fought with his brothers and advocated killing his parents rather than separating them when it became apparent that their embrace was undermining creation. According to some Polynesians, he used his brothers as food for the people.

TUATHA DÉ DANAAN The Tuatha Dé Danaan, the "People of Dana"—Dana being the original Mother Goddess of Irish mythology—were the gods, who, under their leader Nuada, inhabited Ireland from the north long before the arrival of the Milesians. Although they defeated other pre-Celtic races, the Firbolg and the Fomorians, they were themselves overcome and reduced by the Celtic Milesians to their present position as fairies, *sidhe*—"people of the hills"—under which the Milesians drove them. The Tuatha Dé Danaan were positive figures, though, like many divine families, sometimes marred by human-like foibles.

TU'CHUEH The Tu'chueh—also known as Kok Turks or Blue Turks—were worshippers of Tengri, the sky god, who inhabits both Heaven and Hell, where good and evil souls, respectively, live. The world between Heaven and Hell is for living humans. The Blue Turks also worshipped Umai, the goddess of child-birth, a popular figure in Turko-Mongol mythology of central Asia. Tradition has it that the founder of the Blue Turks, like the founders of Rome, was suckled by a she-wolf with whom he eventually mated and produced the first Tu'chueh. The greatest Tu'chueh hero was Bumin, who formed a marriage alliance with the Chinese and defeated the Mongols.

TVASHTIR The great architect of the gods in the ancient Indian *Rig Veda*, the demiurge Tvashtir resented the Vedic king god Indra's killing of his pious son, Trisiras. To avenge his son's death, Tvashtir created the gigantic demon Virtra, who challenged Indra's authority. The fight was earth-shattering, and eventually the demon swallowed Indra. Horrified, the other gods induced a yawn in the monster, Indra leapt out of the gaping mouth, and the war resumed. When Indra was put to flight, the other gods convinced Vishnu to intervene until such time that Indra was able to kill his foe.

TWINS The sacred twins are ubiquitous, not only in Indo-European mythology, where they first appear as the Vedic Ashvins and later as the Greek Diskouri and the Roman Romulus and Remus, but also in African mythology among, for instance, the Dogon and Fon peoples. They are particularly important in the Americas, too, as in the cases of the Mayan Hunaphu and Xbalanque, the Acoma culture hero sister twins Iatiku ("Life Bringer") and Nautsiti ("Full Basket"), and the Navajo culture hero brother twins Nayenezgani ("Monster Slayer") and Tobadzhistshini ("Born for Water"). Twins play significant roles in many tribal mythological histories. In some cases, one twin is good and one bad. Sometimes, as in the Romulus and Remus story, one must die—in effect, serve as a sacrifice—to benefit the people in question.

TYR One of the Aesir in Norse mythology, Tyr was the war god who bound the great wolf, Fenrir, and lost part of his arm in the process. His German equivalent was Tiwaz. Tyr was a god of judicial assemblies and of oaths. In Anglo-Saxon he was Tiw or Tig.

Persian sacred twins

T

UKEMOCHI Ukemochi no kami is the Japanese Shinto goddess of food. According to the *Nihongi*, the goddess was created by the first parent gods, Izanagi and Izanami, and was sent down to earth by the sun goddess Amaterasu. It is said that boiled rice poured forth from her mouth when she faced the land, seafood when she faced the sea, and game when she faced the mountains. She served up her food first to the moon god Tsukiyomi. The moon god was disgusted by being fed things that had come from the mouth of the goddess, so he killed his hostess. In anger, Amaterasu refused to look at him again, so to this day the sun and moon avoid each other. But out of the dead body of Ukemochi came all of the things that humans now eat. According to other sources, the food goddess—in this case Ogetsu—was killed by Susanowo.

ULGEN Ulgen is a creator god in many central Asian mythologies, including those of the Altaic and Turko-Mongol peoples.

ULL A Norse god famous for hunting, Ull, whose name is associated with "brilliance," was known for hunting and skiing and was a stepson of Thor. When, according to one story, Odin was dethroned for an immoral act of seduction, Ull became king of Asgard for ten years, until Odin returned and deposed him.

ULLIKUMMI In Hittite-Hurrian mythology, Ullikummi was the giant son of the coupling of Kumarbi and the Sea (Chaos). Ullikummi took on the great storm-weather god Teshub and forced him to abdicate his throne. But eventually Ullikummi was deposed when, at Teshub's bidding, the old primal god Ea took away the giant's strength.

UMA An early but post-Vedic Hindu personification of divine wisdom, Uma is, like Parvati, with whom she is identified, the wife of Shiva. Thus, Shiva is sometimes called Umpati (the "Spouse of Uma"). As the daughter, like Parvati, of Himavat, the king of the Himalayas, Uma represents a high state of spiritual being. In the *Kena Upanishad*, it is Uma who, as true wisdom, explains to the other gods that the "supreme spirit" is Brahman.

UMAI Umai was a popular central Asian-Turko-Mongol goddess of childbirth.

UNDERWORLD Underworlds, as opposed to paradises, otherworlds, or even punishment-based hells, are ubiquitous in afterlife myths. They tend, like the Greek underworld depicted in Homer's *Odyssey*, or the place called Hades, ruled by Hades and his wife Persephone, to be places where souls live after death, almost regardless of their earthly deeds. Such underworlds are dark, gloomy, and predominantly boring for their inhabitants.

In ancient Egypt, however, the underworld was an intricate and important element of a complex theology and an afterlife belief and ritual. It was ruled by the great resurrection god–king Osiris and was a place of judgment. The Roman underworld, too, at least as depicted by Virgil in his *Aeneid*, was a place related to judgment. It was the ancestor of the underworld described in the much later *Divine Comedy* by the late medieval Christian and Italian poet Dante.

UPANISHADS An extension of early Vedic thought, or Vedanta (the "end of the Vedas"), but to some extent a reaction against what their eighth- to fourth-century B.C.E. compilers thought of as the somewhat closed-mindedness and action-oriented approach of the *Brahmanas*, the *Upanishads* are sacred Hindu *Shruti* texts that are marked by a free-ranging search for the essence of reality. For the *Upanishad* writers, meditation on rituals and thought rather than on rituals and right actions was the true path to salvation. Their emphasis is on inwardness and the spiritual life, a differentiation between the self of

A vision of the Underworld

the body (*jiva*) and the true self, or *atman*. Understanding that the true self within must identify, as followers of Advaita Vedanta say, with *Brahman*, the ultimate cosmic reality or essential basis of the universe, the goal of the thinkers in the *Upanishads* is *Moksha*, or release from the world of physical phenomena. The *Upanishads* use myths as teaching tools, as in the famous parable of Prajapati—or Vairocana—leading the god king Indra along the way of truth to the understanding of Atman as both formless and ultimately real.

The *Brhadaranyaka Upanishad* tells this creation story. The universe began as Self or Atman in the body of the primal man, Purusha. Looking about and seeing only himself, Purusha said "I am." At first, Purusha was afraid but stopped fearing when he realized he was alone and that one could only be afraid of another. Still, he wished for another, and being of two parts in one body, he caused himself to become two—man and woman. The result of the union of the man and the woman was humankind. But the woman was ashamed of incest, of having united with a man who had created her from himself, so she hid from him as a cow. But the man became a bull and mated with the cow, and soon cattle were born. The same thing happened when the woman hid as an ass, as a goat, and so forth. In this way, the world was populated.

URASHIMA In Japan, the story is told of the fisherman Urashima who captured a sea tortoise that turned into a young woman. The woman took Urashima to a kingdom under the sea where she was a princess. Urashima and the princess fell in love and were married, and Urashima forgot about his old home and family for many years until one day he missed them. The princess sent him home and gave him a box that she forbade him to open. If he opened it he would never see her again. Suddenly Urashima was home, but in the many hundred earth years that had passed during his three sea kingdom years, he had become a legend of the distant past. Disturbed by the situation, Urashima opened the box and a white mist flew out bearing the diminishing voice of his princess. Urashima then became a wrinkled old man.

USHAS Ushas is the ancient Vedic Indian *Rig Veda* goddess of dawn. She restores life and creates consciousness.

UTNAPISHTIM Utnapishtim (Ziusudra in Sumerian) was the hero of the flood myth in Mesopotamian mythology. Like the Hebrew Noah, whose story this myth doubtless influenced, he survived the deluge sent by an angry Enlil by following divine advice—usually from Ea (Enki)—and building a boat in which to ride it out. After sending out a dove, a swallow, and a raven to find dry land, Utnapishtim left his boat and offered sacrifice to the gods. He was then granted eternal life by the Enlil.

The most complete version of the Utnapishtim flood myth exists in the Babylonian version of the Gilgamesh epic. In that epic, the hero Gilgamesh journeys to the flood hero in search of immortality.

UTU The Sumerian version of the Mesopotamian sun god (Akkadian Shamash), Utu was the brother of the goddess Inanna (Ishtar) and the son of the moon god Nanna (Sin)

U

A Japanese fishing boat is overtaken by a wave

VAINAMOINEN The Orpheus-like musician-enchanter Vainamoinen is a major hero of the Finnic epic the *Kalevala* and a popular figure in Finnic mythology in general. He is often the creator-hero of an earth-diver or more commonly a cosmic egg creation. Vainamoinen is born miraculously of a teal's egg, in effect a cosmic egg. It is he who makes the wilderness fertile, and it is he who leads the quest for the sacred mill instrument known as the *sampo*. Vainamoinen becomes a rival of another hero, Ilmarinen.

VAIROCANA Literally, "one who is sun-like," or "illuminator," Vairocana (Virocana) is an *asura*, who, in the Vedic-Hindu *Upanishads*, attempts with the god Indra to find the essence of self or *atman*. In Buddhism, he becomes one of the transcendent Buddhas and is called Mahavairocana ("Great Vairocana") among Mahayana Buddhists in Tibet and elsewhere in Asia. In Japan he plays a central role in the Shingon sect as the Dainichi-Nyorai.

VAISHNAVISM Hindus particularly devoted to Vishnu as the supreme god are Vaishnavas, followers of Vaishnavism, one of the three major forms of Hindu *bhakti*, devotion to a single god—the others being Shaivism and Shaktism. For many Vaishnavas, Vishnu is the manifestation of Brahman. He is popularly worshipped through his avatars, especially Rama and Krishna.

VAISHRAVANA Also called Kubera, Vaishravana is associated in Hinduism with wealth and is a guardian of the north, one of the four cardinal directions. He is also king of the *Yakshas*, the spirits of nature. His evil brother Ravana, who plays a major role in the epic the *Ramayana*, stole his home in Lanka, causing him to move to Mount Kailasa to be near the god Shiva.

VALHALLA In Norse mythology, Valhalla ("Hall of the Dead Heroes") was the great hall in Asgard, presided over by the high god Odin. There fallen warriors put on their armor each morning and fought each other to the death, rising again to feast with the great god. The hall was built partly of shields and spears and a wolf guarded the western door, one of Valhalla's five hundred and forty doors. At the end of the world, Ragnarok, eight hundred warriors would march out of each door to fight the terrible wolf Fenrir.

VALI Vali was the son of the Norse high god Odin. His mother was the giant Rind. He was conceived for the purpose of killing Hod, the blind god who played a role in the killing of his own brother, Balder. Vali was also the name of one of the sons of the evil trickster Loki. Angry at Loki's role in the murder of Balder, the gods turned Vali into a wolf who ripped apart his brother Narvi.

VALMIKI Valmiki was one of the Homers of ancient India, the legendary author of the *Ramayana*, and the inventor of poetry. When he saw a hunter's arrow kill a mating bird he felt deep sorrow, and out of this sorrow came poetry. A brahman who went wrong, he was restored to holiness by the sage Narada. It is said that Valmiki, who may, in fact, have been one of many bards who composed the *Ramayana*, saw the epic within the sacred texts, the *Vedas*. Like Homer, Valmiki has a community of followers; they are known as Balmiki or Valmiki.

VAMANA Vamana, the Dwarf, is the fifth avatar of the Hindu god Vishnu. He tricked the demon Bali out of the world the demon had stolen from the gods. Seeing a mere dwarf before him, Bali agreed to give Vamana the land he could cover in three steps. Immediately Vamana changed into a giant so huge that his first two steps encompassed Heaven and earth. He took Bali's head as payment for the third step.

Vishnu, the god of Vaishnavism

Statue of Vlad Tepes, otherwise known as the vampire Dracula

VAMPIRE In Slavic mythology, vampires are the evil dead who leave their graves at midnight to ravish the living and suck their blood.

VANIR In Norse mythology, the Vanir were ancient fertility deities associated with earth and the waters who perhaps represent an earlier earth-based religion that was superseded by that of the more sky god–like Aesir, led by Odin. Although the Vanir and Aesir struggled in a war in Heaven, the two groups eventually intermarried and, in effect, became an integrated pantheon. The Vanir spent time at Asgard with the Aesir, but their own home was Vanaheim, in the under-earth world. Famous among the Vanir were Freyr and Freya, the offspring of the sea god Njord and the giantess Skadi.

VARAHA Varaha was the name of the great boar, the third incarnation, or avatar, of the Hindu god Vishnu. In a kind of earth-diver creation, the boar lifted earth—in her form as a woman (Prithivi)—out of the primal ocean on his tusk.

VARUNA In the Indian *Vedas,* Varuna takes the place of the ancient Indo-European sky god Dyaus. He seems likely to have been a chief god of the Aryans, who invaded the Indian subcontinent in the second millennium B.C.E. He may be related to the Greek sky god Ouranos. Blessed with one thousand eyes, Varuna watched over humanity for evildoers and was associated with the concept of social order (*dharma*). With the development of Vedism and Hinduism, Varuna's importance dwindled. He would become the god of the night sky and of the waters and the guardian of the dark west. Varuna is closely related to the Iranian Ahura Mazda. He is referred to in the *Vedas* as an *asura.* As an *asura,* in the Indian as opposed to Iranian sense, Varuna is to some extent a demon who possesses the illusory magic of maya. With this

power, he makes the night dark. Furthermore, the Mithra of the Persian *Avesta* is related to Ahura Mazda just as in the *Vedas* Mitra is related to Varuna. Mitra's eye is the sun, and, with Varuna, he becomes the sky god who replaces the older Dyaus. In a sense, Varuna, as king of the Adityas, is replaced in the *Vedas* by Indra. Both are called "king" or "emperor."

VASUDEVA Vasudeva is the earthly father of the Hindu Vishnu avatar Krishna and Balarama. As the name of the creative union of the Hindu god Vishnu and his *Shakti,* Lakshmi, Vasudeva is also another name for Krishna.

VASUKI As told in the Hindu Indian epic the *Mahabharata,* Vasuki serves as the rope used to spin the world axis Mount Mandara, the land mass resting on Vishnu in his form as the avatar, the Tortoise, in the depths of the primal Ocean of Milk. The churning of the ocean brings about aspects of the world's creation and the nectar of immortality called *soma.*

VAYU In the India *Rig Veda,* Vayu is the god of the wind, a personification of the breath of the fire god Agni. Vayu is the father of the Pandava hero Bhima in the epic the *Mahabharata* and of the monkey god Hanuman, an important figure in Hindu mythology, especially in the *Ramayana.*

VE AND VILI Ve and Vili were brothers of the Norse high god Odin. Together the three brothers created the world from the body of the frost giant Ymir.

VEDANTA Literally meaning "end or culmination of the *Vedas,*" Vedanta is essentially a Hindu religious tradition based on the *Upanishads.* Vedanta stresses the inner spiritual life, the presence of Brahman as the absolute that is everywhere and nowhere and yet present in the material and personal world as the eternal Self, or *Atman.* Vedanta also relies on the wisdom contained in the *Brahma Sutra,* or *Vedanta Sutra,* and the great philosophical book of the *Mahabharata* known as the *Bhagavadgita.* In the latter, Krishna, as the Pandava hero Arjuna's charioteer, explains the relationship between the material world and Brahman and other philosophical aspects of Vedantic thought. One of the greatest of Vedanta philosophers was Sankara, who lived in the late eighth and early ninth centuries C.E. and who advocated the approach to Vedanta known as *Advaita Vedanta.* In 1896, the Vedanta Society, emphasizing the use of yoga and the belief in the essential divinity of human nature, was founded in the United States by Swami Vivekananda, a disciple of Shri Ramakrishna.

VEDAS Technically the *Vedas* are the four ancient Indian collections of hymns and ritual formulae of the Samhita period (c. 2000–1100 B.C.E.)—works known as the *Rig Veda,* the *Atharva Veda,* the *Sama Veda,* and the *Yaj ur Veda.* But the word *veda* itself means "knowledge," and the *Veda,* as a collective noun, has come to mean not only the four *Vedas* themselves, but the commentaries on them as well. These include the *Brahmanas* and *Aranyakas* of the period between c. 100 and c. 800 B.C.E., the *Upanishads,* compiled between 800 and 500 B.C.E., and various *sutras* and *Vedangas,* the latter being technically *Smirti*—that is, less sacred texts—rather than sacred *Shruti.*

VEDIC MYTHOLOGY The first thing that must be said about Vedic mythology, the source of Hindu mythology, is that it is not an organized corpus of myths moving in a lin-

V

ear path as a "history" of a people. Rather, it is a collection of sometimes confusing and even contradictory fragments in which one deity seems to become another and one action resembles another. The purpose of the brief narratives seems to be more symbolic than historic. Each event suggests many possible interpretations having to do with the centrality of sacrifice and the nature of the absolute in its multitudinous forms. Still, certain specific figures and events do emerge in fairly clear narrative form from the *Vedas*—especially the *Rig Veda*. There is the Rig Vedic creation story in its several forms, involving the primal man Purusha and Prajapati, and there are the developing gods of later Hinduism. Among these are the Adityas, who were perhaps the sun and planets, but who, in the persons of Varuna, Mitra, and Aryaman, were also associated with rulership and social order. Varuna, especially, was the guardian of essential truth. But the fact that Varuna also contained a dark *asura*, or demonic aspect, meant that he had to be dethroned and replaced by Indra as king of the Vedic gods. While not technically an Aditya, Indra is often associated with that group of deities. A somewhat erratic thunder-warrior god, he sometimes goes astray, as in the Parade of Ants myth. Indra is famous for his defeat—with help—of the monstrous demon Virtra. Other Vedic gods include the Maruts and Vayu, the storm and wind gods; Rudra, who will develop later into Shiva; an early form of Vishnu, who, with Shiva and Devi, will eventually dominate Hindu mythology; and the ritually important gods Agni and Soma, who, as fire and the ambrosial and hallucinatory soma, are so important to the ritual sacrifices. An interesting aspect of Agni mythology is the god's tendency to hide—as fire hides—and the necessity of finding him. As fire he is central to the life of any home and also to the death of any individual who on the funeral pyre is a sacrifice that will lead to reincarnation. Soma is also the god of the waters, making

him a kind of opposite associate of Agni. Among the female deities of the *Vedas*, there is Ushas, who, as Dawn, seduces the creator into materializing the universe—bringing it into the light of day, as it were, through union with her. Less individualized forms of this feminine force are Earth, known as Prithivi, and Nature, in the person of Prakti. These goddesses, as the materializing vehicles of the creative energy of the male force of the creators, are the forerunners of the later concept of *Shakti*. [Heesterman, O'Flaherty]

VEDISM Vedism refers to the schools of Hinduism that base their beliefs on *Shruti*, the sacred texts and rituals of the ancient Vedic tradition—that is, the *Vedas* and their offspring: the *Brahmanas, Aranyakas,* and *Upanishads.* This branch of Hinduism grows directly out of the religion brought by the Aryan Indo-Europeans who invaded India in the second millennium B.C.E. As the invaders moved farther south into India, Brahmanism developed as an outgrowth of Vedism and became what we think of as classical Hinduism.

VELES A Slavic earth deity associated with the underworld and the dead, Veles perhaps evolved into the Christian idea of Satan. Some say he evolved into Saint Vlas or Blasius.

VENUS The Romans equated Venus with the Greek Aphrodite, but she was less sexual and less frivolous than that goddess. Indo-European roots for this goddess are indicated by the fact that her name perhaps has connections with the neuter Vedic term for desire. But as the mother of Rome's founder, Aeneas, and, therefore, a patroness of Rome, she takes on the kind of serious stature that Athenians gave to Pallas Athena rather than to Aphrodite. Venus in Rome was traditionally paired with Mars, the father of Romulus and Remus, and the god whom the Romans saw as a cognate

The seashell birth of Venus/Aphrodite

V

of the Greek Ares. But whereas the Greek pairing of Aphrodite and Ares was based on a highly comic and sexual myth, the pairing of Venus and Mars in Rome served a more theological and nationalistic purpose, bringing together the two myths of the founding of Rome.

VESSANTARA Vessantara was a prince who was an incarnation of the buddha preceding Gautama Buddha.

VIDAR Vidar was a son of a giantess named Gird and the Norse high god Odin. It was said that at Ragnarok—the end of the world—after Odin would be killed by Fenrir the wolf, Vidar would avenge his father's death by tearing apart the jaws of Fenrir, thus killing him.

VIETNAMESE MYTHOLOGY Vietnamese mythology is particularly rich in colorful tales, some of them influenced by Chinese mythology. According to a Vietnamese creation myth, there was chaos in the beginning until Kung Lo, a great giant, appeared and separated the sky and the earth with his head before creating a pillar to maintain the separation. At first the giant was creation itself, his breath the wind, his voice the thunder. When the separation of the sky and earth seemed to be holding, he broke up the pillar and threw the pieces around him to form islands and mountains. Where he had dug out the earth to build the original pillar, oceans were formed, and a giant turtle's breathing caused the tides. When a giant female figure came into being, Kung Lo fell in love with her, but the female resisted him and was the larger and stronger of the two. Before she would agree to marry her suitor, she challenged him to several contests and always won. It was in the course of these frequently earth-changing contests that much of the world as we know it—mountains, rivers, and so forth—were formed. Finally, the giantess accepted the giant and they were married. On the way to the wedding ceremony, the giant stretched his phallus across a river to serve as a bridge for his companions. When one of the friends dropped hot ashes on the penis, the giant jumped, and half of the men fell into the water, only to be rescued by the giantess, who hid them under her dress to dry.

Other stories tell how it was the Ngoc Hoang—the Vietnamese version of the Chinese Jade Emperor (Yu)—who, after the separation of Heaven and earth, created animals out of rough pieces of the sky and earth and humans out of the original chaos. With the humans he had the help of the twelve heavenly Midwives. The Sun and Moon, daughters of the creator, were assigned to give light and warmth to the world. At first there was a perfect golden age when people were immortal and rice and warmth were plentiful. But when the people became lazy and forgot the commands of the creator, it became necessary to work to achieve shelter and sustenance. As for immortality, it was denied humans only because a messenger, who was sent by the creator to tell humans they could live forever by shedding their skins when they became old, was convinced by snakes to allow them rather than the humans that privilege.

Sometimes the supreme deity is Ong Troi, Lord Sky—the sky itself. Sometimes he is Thuongde. As such, he is the patriarch of a pantheon made up of his family and assistants. Among the most popular members of the pantheon is the goddess Lieu Hanh, who was sent to earth to interact with humans.

The origin of Vietnam is told in several legendary and sometimes quasi-historical epic tales of great antiquity, which were written down in the thirteenth century. In the tale of *Lac Long Quang and Au Co*, we are told of the founding of the nation. It is said that a king called De Minh, who was a descendant of a Chinese emperor-god, fathered Kinh Duong Vuong, king of the Red Demons, with a mountain spirit. Kinh Duong Vuong fathered Lac Long Quang with a princess of the family of the Dragon King of the Sea. Lac Long Quang, also called the Dragon King, is known as the first Vietnamese king. For political reasons, the king married the immortal Au Co, daughter of the enemy Chinese emperor, Lai. This union of dragon and immortal blood resulted in one hundred eggs and one hundred sons, half of whom went away as immortals with Au Co to the mountain lands while the other half remained as mortal dragon people of the lowlands ruled by Lac Long Quang. Eventually Lac Long's son Vuong was named king (Hung—thus Hung Vuong), and it is he who stands at the beginning of the dynasty that was to rule over the land called Van Lang, "home of the tattooed."

In the epic known as *A War between the Gods*, the story is told of a conflict during the third-century B.C.E. reign of the last king of the Hung Vuong dynasty, Hung Vuong XVIII. This is a conflict between relatives and is said to be the source of Vietnamese monsoons. Son Tinh, the mountain god, one of the immortal sons of Lac Long Quang and Au Co, joins a fisherman who is talking about an extraordinary fish he has caught. The god buys the fish from the fisherman to save it and returns it to the water. Later a handsome youth comes to Son Tinh in his home on the Vietnamese Olympus and reveals himself as Thuy Tinh, Lord of the Waters, who had lost his immortal powers when he changed himself into a fish. The grateful Thuy Tinh invites his relative to visit him in his sea kingdom. Son Tinh is impressed by Thuy Tinh's world and he is given a gift of an old book that he discovers has the power to turn dreams into reality.

When the king, Hung Vuong, holds a contest for the hand of his daughter My Nuong, both Son Tinh and Thuy Tinh compete and become finalists. A final test is assigned to determine the winner. The winner will be the first to bring to the king ten white elephants, ten tigers, ten green pearls, and several other gifts—half from the mountain world, half from the sea world. Thuy Tinh gathers the assigned gifts gradually, but Son Tinh makes use of the magical book given him by Thuy Tinh and assembles the gifts long before Thuy Tinh returns to Hung Vuong's palace. When he discovers Son Tinh's trick, Thuy Tinh becomes so angry that every year he pours as much water as he can, from the sea and the sky, on his rival. Son Tinh lives high in the mountains, however, and remains immune to the monsoons and floods.

Another aspect of the Vietnamese cycle tells the quasi-historical story of An Duong Vuong, one of the hundred sons of Lac Long Quang and Au Co who ruled Au Lac, a part of what would later become the Vietnamese nation. Au Lac is being threatened by the Chinese general Trieu Da (Chao T'o), so the king tries to build a fortress. But each night evil spirits under the rule of an evil thousand-year-old chicken tear down the walls. It is only with the defeat of the chicken by the golden turtle Kim Quy that the walls get built. The turtle gives An Duong Vuong one of his toenails as a trigger for a new crossbow made under the turtle's directions. The use of the new crossbow with the toenail will make it possible for the king to kill many enemies in any given shot. Using the magic bow, An Duong Vuong prevails over his Chinese enemies. But the king is tricked by Trieu Da, who sends his son Trong Thuy as an emissary to Au Lac to find out

V

Vikings in their ships

the source of An Duong Vuong's power. Trong Thuy falls in love with and marries the king's daughter Mi Chau, and she unwittingly destroys her father by revealing the secret of the bow. Trong Thuy substitutes an ordinary bow for the magic one and returns with the latter to his father. Before he leaves, however, he instructs his bride to leave a trail of feathers if for any reason she is forced to leave the palace while he is away. She is forced to leave with her father when Trieu Da attacks Au Lac with the magic crossbow. She leaves the trail of feathers behind, a trail that the enemy army can easily follow. When An Duong Vuong prays to the Golden Turtle for help, Mi Chau's treachery is revealed, and her father cuts off her head. When Trong Thuy, with the pursuing Chinese army, finds the decapitated body of his wife, he buries her and then throws himself into a well. Tieu Da's victory in 207 B.C.E. did, in fact, mark the beginning of a long period of Chinese rule in Vietnam. [Bonnefoy (1993)]

VIKINGS The terms "Norse" and "Viking" are often used interchangeably. These were people from Scandinavia—specifically, Sweden, Denmark, and Norway—who between 780 and 1070 undertook wide-scale raids and in many cases colonization. Vikings conquered much of the British Isles and ranged as far as Italy, Spain, and southern France and even Kiev, Constantinople, and Baghdad in the east. It is probable that they found their way as well to pre-Columbian North America in the west. Most important, they colonized Iceland, where their mythology, which we now think of as Norse mythology, developed after most of Europe had become Christian.

VIRACOCHA Viracocha (Huiracocha) was the Inca creator god. He was a solar deity with storm god characteristics. Viracocha created a race of giants who became unruly, causing him to send a cleansing flood. He then created a new race of humans out of clay and lit up the world by commanding the sun, moon, and stars to emerge from Lake Titicaca. Viracocha's wife was Mamacocha (Cochamama), the sea goddess. Their son was the sun god Inti, the father of the Inca founder and first emperor, Manco Capac.

VIRGIL Publius Virgilius (Vergilius) Maro (70 B.C.E.–19 C.E.) was the Roman poet commissioned by the emperor Caesar Augustus to write a Roman epic. The result was the *Aeneid*, modeled on the Greek Homeric epics.

VIRGIN BIRTH The idea of conception and birth occurring without the loss of virginity is an offshoot of the story of the monomythic hero's miraculous conception. In Christianity, the motif becomes an aspect of dogma. It is said in the New Testament that God came to Mary as the Holy Spirit and conceived God the Son in his earthly form as Jesus without depriving Mary—ever after known as the "Virgin Mary"—of her virginity. The symbolic importance of the virgin birth motif and of the general motif of the miraculous conception and/or birth seems to lie in the importance it confers on the born hero, who is at once human and somehow divine, both a result of the mortal procreative process and divine immortality that is beyond that process.

V

311

The Virgin Mary with the Christ Child

VIRGIN MARY In Christian scripture and tradition, a Hebrew maiden named Mary was engaged to marry a Nazareth carpenter, Joseph, when the angel Gabriel appeared to her and announced (the Annunciation) that she was to be the birth giver of the Messiah, who would be Jesus. Mary protested that she had never had intercourse, but the angel explained that she was pregnant by way of the Holy Spirit aspect of God. When she gave birth to Jesus in Bethlehem, Mary was still a virgin.

In scripture the early Church had made Mary a symbol of proper obedience—perhaps feminine obedience. "Be it unto me according to thy word," she replied to the angel's announcement of her pregnancy. This is one of the few statements attributed to her in the New Testament. But throughout the Middle Ages and the Renaissance and down to our own age, the people, in effect, have demanded the recognition of Mary as an incarnation of the Great Goddess. To a great extent this demand was made possible by the scriptural claim of Jesus' virgin birth. Later, Christians began to believe that as Jesus had been conceived "without sin," the mother of Jesus must have been so conceived. This belief emerged into the late Catholic dogma of Mary's own immaculate conception. Another late dogma states that Mary, like her son, was bodily assumed into Heaven (the Assumption). In effect, if not theologically, Catholic Christians gradually restored the "Queen of Heaven" to her ancient position. In so doing they made Mary their chief intercessor with God in Heaven. Yet this new incarnation of the ancient goddess was deprived of the sexuality once associated with other Western Semitic goddesses such as Asherah and Ishtar. Mary was assumed into heaven to reign there as immaculate intercessor queen, but decidedly not as God's wife.

In spite of official Church doctrine to the contrary, Mary, celebrated in countless works of art and especially in the thousands of great churches dedicated to her, gives every impression of having become a goddess. This status is emphasized in her many appearances to Christians in the ages since her dormition (a kind of sleep rather than actual death). Her appearance as the Virgin of Guadalupe is one of many examples.

VIRGIN OF GUADALUPE On December 9, 1531, a Christianized Indian peasant of the Mexican village of Tolpetlac heard a beautiful voice singing and saw a golden cloud on a hill in Guadalupe once sacred to the Aztec fertility-moon goddess Tonantzin. A voice from the cloud called to Juan Diego, and he climbed the hill to find there a dark-skinned woman who announced that she was the Virgin Mary. She promised to help the Indian people if Juan Diego could persuade the local bishop to build a shrine in her honor on the hill. The peasant went immediately to report these events to the bishop, but the bishop did not believe the story. Juan Diego returned to the woman on the hill and told her what had happened. She insisted that he try again the next day. Again the bishop was skeptical but the lady remained insistent. But the next day, Juan Diego had to take care of his dying uncle and so avoided the hill. But the woman appeared to him on a path and told him that his uncle was cured and that he should climb the hill, where he would find some roses, and bring them back to her. Juan Diego did as he was told and when he returned with the roses, the woman arranged them into a beautiful cloak and told him to take it to the bishop. When Juan Diego presented the cloak to the bishop a painted depiction of Our Lady of Guadalupe appeared. The amazed bishop agreed to build the shrine. The dark-skinned Virgin of Guadalupe is always pictured standing on a crescent moon. She is one of the world's several Black Madonnas and, as such, is clearly related to the dark earth and moon goddess Tonantzin. It might be noted that in Neolithic Çatal Hüyük and other prehistoric sites goddesses are frequently depicted with the horns of a male counterpart, the bull, its horns forming a crescent moon.

VIRTRA Meaning "storm cloud" or "one who restrains" in Sanskrit, Virtra is the demon personification of negativity and darkness in Vedism and Hinduism. In the *Vedas* the demon is killed by the king of the gods, Indra.

VISHNU The Hindu god Vishnu is the "pervader" and preserver; he pervades all things and preserves the order of the universe. He is known by his four arms, his conch, his powerful flaming discus weapon, and the lotus. He rides on the eagle Garuda and is accompanied by the embodiment of his *Shakti*-consort, Shri (Lakshmi). For his particular worshippers (Vaishnavas), he is the source of the elements of creation, the supreme god who becomes incarnate when his presence is required, whether as Krishna, Rama, or one of several other avatars. He contains the universe in his being and is, ultimately, the universal absolute, Brahman, as indicated in the *Vishnu Purana*. As he is the creator, his consort Lakshmi is the creation, the manifestation of Vishnu's energy. Vishnu is infrequently mentioned in the ancient *Vedas*, but in the *Rig Veda* it is he who, as Vamana, takes the giant steps by which Heaven and earth are established. Thus, already in the *Rig Veda*, he is the pervasive one, the axis of the cosmos whose ritual pillar—like the *linga* of Shiva in other myths—reaches from the navel of the earth to the highest heavens. Vishnu is the essential sacrifice, he who in the *Mahabharata* raises up the world in the manner of the earlier version of the creator as Prajapati, and saves it from overcrowding. In fact, as Vaishnavism developed, Vishnu assimilated other early creator forms, including the Purusha of the *Rig Vedic* cosmogony and the creator god Brahma as the Brahman within all things, or Atman, and, therefore, as the personification of creative energy itself or Narayana. Finally, it is Vishnu who, as sun, wind, and rain, will absorb the universe at the end of the current age. The mythology of Vishnu is a rich one. One important myth of the *Jayakhya Samhita* tells how two demons steal the *Veda*, plunging the world into disorder. Vishnu restores the *Veda* by way of his own knowledge and kills the demons with sacred formulae or mantras, which reflect his creative energy or *Shakti*. One creation story tells how Vishnu and Lakshmi sleep on eternity embodied by the thousand-headed primal serpent Shesha (or Ananta). During his sleep, the world is unrealized—is, in fact, only Vishnu's "thought." When the god awakens he meditates and begins the process of re-creation. When a lotus springs from his navel, Brahma appears from it and becomes the actual creator of the world that Vishnu will preserve until the next destruction.

VISHNU PURANA The *Vishnu Purana* is a work of the late third or early fourth century C.E. It is a work dedicated essentially to the greatness of the Hindu god Vishnu and is, therefore, particularly sacred to Vaishnavas, worshippers of Vishnu. In the *Vishnu Purana*, Vishnu is the omnipotent deity. In fact, he is synonymous with the ultimate absolute, Brahman, as he is in the *Bhagavadgita*. The *Vishnu Purana* tells of the creation of the universe by Vishnu. The great god is the navel of the universe; he reaches from its heavens to its depths. The *Purana* tells of Vishnu's incarnation as the avatar Lord Krishna and of the way the universe will be absorbed into Vishnu at the end of the age. According to the Vishnu Purana, Brahman is one and the same with Brahma as he creates, Vishnu as he preserves, and Shiva as he destroys. All are elements of the same universal sacrifice, or process of creation, life, and the destruction that leads to new life.

VISHVAKARMAN Meaning "all creating" in Sanskrit, Vishvakarman appears in the Indian *Rig Veda* as the creative power that holds the universe together. In the *Satapatha Brahmana*, he sacrifices himself, and his sacrifice becomes the model for all order-sustaining sacrifices to follow. It is clear, then, that Vishvakarman, who is later associated with the divine architect Tvashtir, is also a name for the Vedic creator Prajapati and the first sacrifice, the primal male, Purusha.

VOHUMAN One of the Amesa Spentas of Iranian mythology, Vohuman (Vohu Manah) is the personification of the wisdom of the great god Ahura Mazda. It was he who led Zoroaster in his dream visions to the source of divine power. And it is he who leads good souls to Heaven.

VOLSUNG Volsung was a Norse warrior who was descended directly from the high god Odin. He was the father of Sigmund, who in turn fathered the great hero Sigurd.

VOLSUNGA SAGA The late-thirteenth-century C.E. Scandinavian work the *Volsunga Saga* contains the story of the Volsung family and its adventures. The dominant figure in the saga is the hero Sigurd (Germanic Siegfried). The *Volsunga Saga* was one of the primary sources for Snorri Sturlusson's *Prose Edda*.

VOODOO MYTHOLOGY A tradition that comes to America from Africa, primarily by way of the West Indies and Haiti, Voodoo is a spirit-based religion. These spirits (*nanchon* or "nations") are elaborately celebrated in various rituals. Two important *nanchons* are the sweet *rada* and the hot *petro*. An important element in Voodoo is death. The spirits known as *gede* are spirits of death—and of sexuality—suggesting a connection with the West Indian trickster Gede, who is, in fact, a god of death and sexuality, capable, like most tricksters, of penetrating the depths.

VYASA Vyasa was the legendary semi-divine dark-skinned sage, or *Rishi*, who is said to have transmitted the Indian epic the *Mahabharata*. According to the story, he dictated the epic of the two families, the Pandavas and Kauravas, of whom he was himself the progenitor, to the elephant-headed god Ganesh, who wrote it down with one of his tusks. Thus, the story of the Bharatas (India) can be said to have flowed literally from the mind and body of Vyasa. Like Valmiki, the *Ramayana* poet, he was one of the Homers of ancient India. He is said to have been the miraculously conceived son of Satyavati, herself the child of a fish. *Vyasa* is also the Sanskrit for "collector," and the word can refer, in general, to collectors of Hindu *Vedas* and other sacred works. Sometimes the collectors are condensed into one Vyasa, said to have been an incarnation of Vishnu as Narayana and to have been the transmitting vehicle for the *Puranas* as well as the *Mahabharata* and the Vedas.

A Voodoo mask

WAKAN TANKA Usually translated as the "Great Spirit" or the "Great Mystery," Wakan Tanka is the supreme deity and creator god of the Native North American Sioux Indians. Wakan Tanka is less a personal god than an all-encompassing spirit or Brahman-like essence that pervades all things. Wakan Tanka's ritual is that of the sacred pipe. In the beginning Wakan Tanka was four aspects—Rock, Earth, Sky, and Sun. Later Wakan Tanka created all the other deities—aspects of himself and personifications of other elements of nature, beginning with Moon, Wind, Falling Star, and Thunderbird. Next came aspects of himself known as Kindred Gods: Two-Legged Beings (such as humans and bears), Buffalo, Four-Winds, and Whirlwind. Finally he created aspects of himself that are spirits: Spirit of the Dead, Spirit-Like, Life's Breath, and Spirit Power.

WANDJINA Among the Australian Aboriginal people, a *wandjina* is a tribe-protecting spirit being of the mythical age the Dreamtime. A *wandjina* has a particular totem animal aspect.

WANJIRU Wanjiru was a central African heroine whose death is, in effect, a sacrificial ritual undergone for the renewal of her people. Her story contains the descent to the underworld motif and the death and resurrection motifs that are common to many cultural expressions of the heroic monomyth.

For three years there had been no rain and the people 's fields were dry. The people met in a large open place to dance for rain, but the shaman told them rain would not come unless the people bought the maiden Wanjiru. Each family would have to pay a goat for the girl. The families brought the goats to the dance ground, and Wanjiru came there with her family. As the object to be sold, she was placed in the middle of the circle, but, mysteriously, she began to sink into the ground. Both she and her relatives cried out in horror, but Wanjiru continued to sink, crying out, "There will be rain." As various people stepped forward to try to save the maiden they were paid off with goats. "My own people have done this to me," Wanjiru cried out, as she disappeared, like the Ceramese heroine Hainuwele, into the earth. Immediately the rains came.

Then one night a young man who had been deeply in love with Wanjiru decided to follow her—Orpheus-like—into the underworld. He stood on the spot in the center of the dance circle and sank quickly to the world below. There he followed a path until he found his lost Wanjiru. Joyfully he carried her out into our world again.

When Wanjiru appeared again at the dance circle the people were astounded. The young man who had brought her back married her.

WAR IN HEAVEN As, for instance, in the case of the Titans and Olympians in Greek mythology, Tiamat's followers and Marduk in Babylon, the Aesir and Vanir in Norse mythology, or the struggle between the angels who were loyal to God and those who were loyal to Satan in Judeo-Christian lore, the early mythical history of the world's various depictions of Heaven often involves a war between powerful forces. These forces represent good and evil, as in the Christian myth, or primordial "chaotic" earth forces and sky gods dedicated to order and control, as in the Babylonian myth of the *Enuma elish* or the Norse myths of the sagas. The war in Heaven can also have an end-of-the-world, apocalyptic aspect, as it does in the Ragnarok story of Norse mythology, in the Armageddon or the Christian Book of Revelation, or the great final battle of the Indian *Mahabharata*.

WATATSUMI-NO-KAMI In Japanese Shinto mythology, Watatsumi was the spirit (*kami*) of the sea. His daughter Toyotama-hime married Hiko-hoho-demi, brother of Ho-no-susori and a grandson of the Japanese sun goddess Amaterasu. When Ho-no-susori lost his prize fishhook in the sea, Hiko-hoho-demi descended to the palace of the sea god Watat-sumi- no-kami to retrieve it. The sea god gave the young man his daughter Toyota-ma-hime as a wife. This couple became the grandparents of the first Japanese emperor, Jimmu Tennu.

WATER OF LIFE In many traditions the "Water of Life" is a life-saving or life-preserving potion. In the Christian Bible's Book of Revelation, the Christ offers the Water of Life, perhaps signifying baptism. In the Mesopotamian myth of Lugalbanda, good demons give the Water of Life to the endangered hero. In another Mesopotamian myth cycle—that of the goddess Inanna—the god Enki sends Water of Life to comfort the suffering goddess Ereshkigal. In a medieval fairy tale, retold by the Grimm Brothers, a young prince seeks the Water of Life to save his dying father.

WATER POT BOY Certain Tewa Indians of the Native North American West tell a hero story that has many monomythic elements, including miraculous conception, virgin birth, the quest (in this case, the search for the father), the descent to the underworld, and rebirth.

A woman at Sikyatki had a beautiful daughter who refused to get married. The mother spent her days making water pots, and one day she asked the daughter to help mix some clay while she went for water. The girl put some clay on a flat stone and stamped on it to smooth it out. Somehow some of the clay entered her and she became pregnant. Her mother was angry about her daughter's condition and was horrified when her daughter gave birth to a water pot boy instead of a regular baby. But the girl's father was pleased, and he greatly enjoyed watching his "grandson" grow. In about twenty days Water Pot Boy was big enough to play with the other children of the village, who became quite fond of him. But his mother cried a lot because he had no arms or legs—just eyes and ears and a mouth for feeding at the top of the pot.

One day Water Pot Boy begged his grandfather to let him go rabbit hunting like other boys, but his grandfather said he couldn't, as he didn't have any arms or legs. The boy pleaded so hard that his grandfather finally gave in and let his grandson roll along next to him while he searched for rabbits down under the mesa. Suddenly Water Pot Boy spied a rabbit and rolled quickly after it, out of sight of his grandfather. As he rolled along he hit a large rock and broke, and out of the broken pieces sprang a fine boy, beautifully dressed with lots of turquoise, good leather, and feathers. Delighted to be free of his old "skin" and now extremely skillful and fleet of foot, he caught four rabbits before rejoining his grandfather at the foot of the mesa. Naturally the grandfather did not recognize his grandson. "Who are you?" he asked the boy. "Have you seen my Water Pot Boy?"

"That's me!" said the boy, but at first his grandfather didn't believe him. Finally, after the boy explained about the rock the old man accepted him as his grandson and they went home. When they got home the boy's mother thought he was a suitor being brought to marry her, and she became upset. But when her father explained that the handsome boy was in fact Water Pot Boy, everything was OK and the boy went off to play with his old friends.

One day Water Pot Boy asked his mother who his father was. "I don't know," his mother said.

"Well, I'm going to find him."

"You can't—I've never been with a man, so there 's no place to look."

"Well, I think I know where he must live," said Water Pot Boy, and after his mother fixed him a pack of dried meat and some water, he left, walking southwest toward Horse Mesa Point. There, near a spring, he came upon a man, who asked him where he thought he was going. "I'm going to see my father," answered the boy.

"You'll never find him," said the man. "Who is he, anyway?"

"I think you're my father," said Water Pot Boy.

Now the man glared at the boy, trying to scare him, but the boy held his ground and stared right back." Yes, I am sure you are my father," he said. Finally the man smiled and embraced the boy and took him over to the spring and then directly into it. Down in the water he found all of his father's dead relatives, who ran up and hugged him. The next day he left the spring and went back to the village to tell his mother what had happened.

Not long after that, his mother got sick and died, and the boy decided to go back to the spring. There he found his mother down with the other relatives. His father greeted him, revealing that he was Red Water Snake and that he had made the boy's mother die so that she and Water Pot Boy, too, would come over to the spring to live with him.

And that's where they still live.

WAWILAK SISTERS The Wawilak sisters were heroines of an Australian Aboriginal myth. Like most Dreamtime figures, they traveled about, creating objects and places as they went. The sisters each had an infant boy. One day one of the sisters somehow spilled some of her menstrual blood into the serpent Yurlunggur's pool, and this so enraged the serpent that he caused a flood and swallowed the sisters and the boys before himself becoming a rainbow, signaling the end of the flood. Later the serpent returned to the ground and vomited up the sisters and the boys.

WAYANG THEATER AND MYTHS Wayang is a myth-based ritual shadow puppet theater tradition of Bali and Java in Indonesia. Manipulated by a man called a *dalang*, the figures in the dramas are familiar characters from the Hindu epics the *Mahabharata* and the *Ramayana*. There is some Islamic influence—especially in Java. The *dalang* recites the familiar epic episodes accompanied by a gamelan orchestra and some singers. The most popular

Water poured into the Fountain of Life

W

Pandava Brothers as puppets in a wayang play in Indonesia

divine *wayang* characters are the four-armed Betara Guru or Manikmaya and his old potbellied brother Semar. The main heroes are those of the *Mahabharata*, the Pandavas and the Kauravas, the former, not surprisingly, being much favored.

WEATHER GODS In nearly all mythologies there are gods who can be called more or less interchangeably thunder gods, storm gods, or weather gods. They are frequently, like the Norse Thor, the German Donar, and the Celtic Taranis, associated with lightning and thunder. Among the Sumerians and later Western Semites we find weather-storm gods who play important roles in the rain-drought fertility alternations so important to agricultural peoples. The Babylonian Tiamat is a chaotic storm goddess who is subdued by a more powerful but more positive storm god, Marduk. The Mesopotamian Adad (Had-dad) and the Canaanite Dagan are such gods, as is the Canaanite Baal in such aspects as Baal Karmelos, who sends his storms from the top of Mount Carmel in Palestine. The Hittite-Hurrian Taru or Teshub plays a dominant role in Hittite-Hurrian narratives. The Sumerian Enlil is a flood-causing storm god and was almost certainly an influence on the Hebrew Yahweh, also a master of the flood. Storm-weather gods can be generally destructive in an arbitrary way, for no particular moral reason. The African Yuruba Shango is a god of this type, as is the Polynesian Tarhiri and the Japanese Susanowo.

WELSH MYTHOLOGY Welsh mythology has come to us from various sources, all much more directly affected and distorted by time and non-Celtic elements than is the case in the much more isolated Ireland. There are the two Latin texts especially concerned with the Arthurian legends—the early-ninth-century *Historia Brittonum* by Nennius and the twelfth-century *Historia Regum Britanniae* by Geoffrey of Monmouth—and there are, of course, oral sources, including, traditionally, poems questionably attributed to the semi-mythic sixth-century poet-prophet Taliesin, whose Irish equivalent was Amairgen, the poet-warrior. But Welsh mythology, including the remnants of a pre-Christian Welsh pantheon, is more essentially contained in the "four branches" of a collection of eleven medieval tales known in modern times as the *Mabinogion* (*Mabinogi*) and in the various traditions associated with King Arthur.

WHITE BUFFALO WOMAN White Buffalo Woman is a goddess or goddess-like figure in the Native North American mythology of the Lakota Sioux. It is said that long ago the Sioux called a council to discuss the lack of game for food. A group under Chief Standing Hollow Horn went out to hunt one morning and noticed something approaching them, but the figure was floating rather than walking, so they realized it must be a spirit (*wakan*). Eventually they saw that the spirit was a beautiful woman with two round red dots on her face and powerful shining eyes. She was beautifully clothed in marvelously decorated white buckskin. One strand of the woman's deep black hair was tied with a piece of buffalo fur. She carried a large bundle and some dried sage. The woman was White Buffalo Woman (Ptesan-Wi).

W

The amazed men stared at her and one reached for her with lust in his heart. He immediately burned up in a flash of lightning. Lust is destructive. White Buffalo Woman instructed another young man to return to his chief and to instruct him to set up a sacred medicine tent with twenty-four poles. She would follow with great gifts.

When the spirit woman arrived she told the people to set up an altar of red earth within the medicine tent. They were also to place on the altar a buffalo skull and a rack for a sacred object. When all was ready White Buffalo Woman circled the tent several times and then stopped before the chief and opened her bundle. In it was the sacred pipe (*chanunpa*) that would forever after be the central object of Sioux ritual. She showed the people how to grasp the stem with the left hand and to hold the bowl with the right. This is how the sacred pipe is always held and passed. The chief offered White Buffalo Woman all they had for nourishment, water. They dipped sweet grass into a skin bag full of fresh water and handed it to her. This act, too, is still a part of the Sioux ritual life.

Now White Buffalo Woman showed the people how to fill the pipe with red willow bark tobacco and to walk around the tent four times in the pattern of the great sun. This was the endless circle, what in Asia would have been called a *mandala* and what the Sioux call the Sacred Hoop or the Path of Life. Like a true culture hero, White Buffalo Woman continued her teaching, showing the people how to use the pipe, how to pray, how to sing the proper pipe-filling song, and how to lift the pipe up to "Grandfather Sky" and point it down to "Grandmother Earth" and then to the four directions. "The Sacred Pipe will hold all things together," she said, "the sky, the earth, the world, the people. The ritual of the pipe would please Wakan Tanka, the Great Spirit." She went on to tell them much more about the meaning of the pipe and about the buffalo. Then she got up to leave, but promised to come back in every cycle of ages. The ages of creation were within her, she said. She walked off into the bright red sun that was setting. As she went she rolled over four times. The first time she turned into a black buffalo, the second time into a brown one, the third time into a red one. When she rolled the fourth time she became a pure white female buffalo calf. So it is that a white buffalo is the most sacred of beings under the sky.

Now the buffalo came and allowed themselves to be killed so that the people would have meat to eat, skins for clothes, and bones for tools. The people always wait for White Buffalo Woman to return.

WHITE GODDESS, THE *The White Goddess: A Historical Grammar of Poetic Myth*, by Robert Graves, is a controversial work, popular among Wiccans and those who think of themselves as modern "Pagans." It is concerned with the relationship between literature, myth, and goddess worship. Influenced by Sir James Frazer's *The Golden Bough* and ancient Celtic bardism and mythology, Graves, in *The White Goddess*, speaks particularly to those who see the goddess as the center of true spirituality.

WILDERNESS PASSAGE A time in the wilderness occurs in many versions of the heroic monomyth. If it takes place during childhood, the wilderness is a place where the hero-to-be is abandoned by those who do not understand his importance or fear his potential power and his undermining of the status quo. In this situation, the hero is usually adopted by menials or animals, as in the Remus and Romulus myth or the Siegfried myth. In some cultures—for example, those of many Native North Americans—the wilderness passage serves as an initiatory period in preparation for greater things to come. In Native North America, the vision quest is an acting out of this myth and, in turn, the vision quest ritual gives birth to myths such as those of the boy Wunzh wrestling with the corn spirit, Mondawmin, or the Cherokee youth who is entertained for a year by a bear in his cave. Related to this initiatory motif is the wilderness passage of adult heroes who go to the wilderness to be tempted by evil forces and so overcome them, and/or to "talk to God." Moses, Jesus, and the Buddha all fit this pattern.

WODAN Wodan (Wotan, Wodon, Woton, Woden) was the Germanic antecedent of the Norse Odin and of our name for Wednesday. He was married to Freya (Norse Frigg). The Romans thought of him as a cognate of their Mercury, probably because he guided the dead to the underworld. Wodan was a warrior god and a sky god. Like Odin, he was associated with mysteries—with magic, soothsaying, and runes. He was Woden among the Anglo-Saxons.

WODEN Woden was the Anglo-Saxon name for the German Wodan (Wotan) and the Norse Odin.

WOLF Among the Native North American Shoshoni and others, Wolf was a form taken by the creator in myth time. Coyote was his sometime mischievous companion in those days. Wolf wanted people to be immortal, but Coyote argued with Wolf about that so Wolf killed Coyote's son, and death has existed ever since.

Wodan strides through the world

WOMAN AS SOURCE OF SORROW The depiction of women as a curse finds expression in many Indo-European myths, the Pandora story being an example, as well as the Hebrew biblical story of Adam and Eve. In this connection it is significant that the Judeo-Christian God had no wife, unless Sophia, the sometimes female embodiment of Wisdom, described by Gnostics and some philosophically minded Christians as God's eternal partner, be considered his wife. In any case, Sophia, particularly revered as Holy Wisdom by Eastern Christianity, as indicated by the great cathedral of Saint Sophia in ancient Constantinople, was never a sexual being. In Western Christianity her role as Divine Wisdom was, in effect, taken over by the third aspect of God, the Holy Spirit.

WOMAN OF POI-SOYA This *Taming of the Shrew*–type Ainu epic takes place in Hidaka, Japan. The hero, Otsam-Un-Kur, has been raised by his two beautiful sisters, who represent all that is valued in Ainu women. But news comes to him of a manly woman named Poi-Soya-Un-Mat, who dresses in men's clothing and hunts, fishes, and steals the game caught by others. When the hero goes hunting and shoots a deer, the bad woman attacks him with her servants. Enraged, the hero kills them all, including Poi-Soya-Un-Mat. But the man-woman is revived by servants. It is then that Otsam-Un-Kur is informed that he and Poi-Soya-Un-Mat had been betrothed in childhood. Meanwhile, the newly revived heroine goes on a trading trip, and when approached by would-be suitors, she fights and defeats them to uphold the honor of her fiancé. This manly behavior, however, enrages Otsam-Un-Kur. The epic continues with numerous episodes revealing the inappropriate actions of the heroine and the violent anger of the hero. In the end, the hero finds a submissive wife who is willing to cook for him and care for him without complaint.

WOMAN'S EPIC: REPUNNOT-UN-KUR The *Woman's Epic: Repunnot-Un-Kur* is an Ainu work. In the Ainu tradition, as in *Woman of Poi-Soya*, the epic is told in the first person by the heroine, Shinutapka-Un-Mat. The heroine, who has been raised by her foster brother, is chosen by him as a wife. The brother leaves for a trading trip to Japan, but not before he captures a bear cub for a bear ceremony. The bear cub comes to Shinutapka-Un-Mat in a dream and warns her that her foster brother and future husband, Repunnot-Un-Kur, is a villain who had in fact stolen her in childhood and whose jealousy has now been aroused by a rival woman who is claiming that she and the bear are having an unnatural relationship. The villain is on his way home with plans of killing his betrothed and the bear. The bear defends the heroine and takes her away to her real brothers. After the bear is sacrificed during the bear ceremony, he returns as a god and marries Shi-nutapka-Un-Mat.

WOOT Among the Kuba people of Africa, Woot is the name of nine culture heroes born to the creator Mboom, each of whom had a role in creating the world. One story says that one of the Woots committed incest with his sister and was expelled from his land, on which he left a curse. With some of his followers he went elsewhere and founded the Kuba tribe.

WORKS AND DAYS *Works and Days* is a source of Greek myths. It was written by the eighth-century B.C.E. poet Hesiod.

WORLD NAVEL Delphi, the ancient Greek seat of the famous oracle, was thought of as the navel of the world, the world center. In some cultures the world tree grows out of the world navel.

WORLD TREE The tradition of the cosmic world tree, sometimes called the Axle Tree or Axis Mundi, is found in many parts of the world. In insular Southeast Asia the cosmic tree unites the sky with the earth and symbolizes wholeness. In the Korean myth of Cumong, the hero's legitimate son is recognized when he is able to find half of his father's sword at the base of a pine tree growing out of a heptagonal stone. Also in Korea, it was believed that a sacred tree connected the three worlds of existence. Among the Turko-Mongol peoples of central Asia, cosmic trees are of great importance. For the Tartars, a giant pine tree grows out of the navel of the earth and reaches to the home of the supreme ruler in heaven. Without the cosmic tree the world above would not be able to communicate with the world below and without it the shaman would be unable to make his journeys to the spirit world. The most famous of European world trees is Yggdrasill, a central element in Norse mythology.

WULBARI Wulbari is a name of the sky god ruler of the heavens of the Krachi people of Africa. In myths he is often at odds with the spider trickster Ananse, who sometimes out-smarts him.

W

XARGI In Siberia, it was said that the chief ancestor, Mangi or Xargi, ruled the underworld to which certain souls went in the afterlife. Xargi was the original progenitor of shamans and the bear brother of the creator.

XBALANQUE AND HUNAHPU Xbalanque and Hunahpu were the holy twins of the Quiche Maya of Mesoamerica. According to the *Popul Vuh*, the underworld (Xibalba) gods challenged the twins to a ball game in the underworld. After descending to the underworld, Hunahpu was decapitated in the House of Bats, but his brother replaced his head with a turtle and then, during the game, managed to replace the turtle with the original head. The twins then fooled the underworld gods by dismembering themselves and taking shape again. The gods of Xibalba asked the twins to show them how to do this and the twins did so, but only halfway, leaving the gods in a dismembered state. The twins came out of the underworld as the sun and the moon.

XEGLUN Xeglun is the Elk of the heavens, who in Siberian Tungus mythology is chased on skis by the great hunter Mangi (Xargi), whose tracks formed the Milky Way.

XIBALBA Xibalba is the dark and fearful underworld of the Mayans of Mesoamerica. Made up of several stages, known as "houses," Xibalba presented a terrible prospect for the Mayans. When they died they would have to face such "houses" as those of knives, fire, bats, and jaguars. In a famous myth the twins Xbalanque and Hunaphu descended there and overcame the ruling gods.

XIHE Originally a Chinese goddess of the ten suns, Xihe came to be thought of as a dual god of Time.

XILONEN Xilonen was a corn goddess of the Aztecs of Mesoamerica.

XIPE TOTEC An early Mesoamaerica fertility god, Xipe Totec was presented with flayed sacrificial victims. The Aztecs worshipped him as the ruler of the first "sun" or creation age and the bearer of new life.

XOCHIPILLI AND XOCHIQUETZAL In the Aztec mythology of Mesoamaerica, the male Xochipilli and the female Xochiquetzal were horticultural deities. The god was associated with summer and pleasure, but also with the sometimes painful results of illicit pleasure. His consort was a goddess of pregnancy and childbirth.

XUANZANG Xuanzang was the Chinese Buddhist monk of the seventh century C.E. who was the historical source for the legendary traveling master of the *Tripitaka* ("Three Collections of the Buddhist Dharma"); thus Xuanzang is also known as "Tripitaka." In the legend, he was accompanied by the Monkey King Sun Wu-k'ung, as narrated in the *Hsi-yu chi* or *Xi you ji* ("Journey to the West").

A mask representing Xipe Totec

YAJUR VEDA The *Yajur Veda* is one of the four *Vedas,* or sacred *Shruti* texts of Vedism and the Hinduism that emerged from Vedism.

YAKSHAS The *Yakshas* are divine beings in Hindu myth; they can be either benevolent or demonic. They are led by Vaishravana, also known as Kubera.

YAKUSHI A former bodhisattva, who after long years of practice achieved enlightenment and the status of buddha, Yakushi-nyorai, the Japanese Mahayana Buddha, Bhaisajy Aguru, made twelve vows early on his path to enlightenment. One of the vows was to become a bright beryl that would illumine the world. So it is that he stands in the east, opposite the Amida Buddha, the Pure Beryl World. He also vowed to cure illnesses and is called the "King of Medicines."

YAM Yam, the Ugaritic-Canaanite sea god of chaos and disorder, periodically battled the weather-storm god Baal for supremacy. When Baal succeeded in killing his arch enemy, he scattered his remains as fertilizing rain.

YAMA In both Hinduism and Buddhism, Yama is the Lord of Death. In the Indian *Rig Veda* he is Lord of the Ancestors, and in the *Upanishads* he is the bestower of ultimate knowledge, teaching that god and truth are achieved through meditation on the *Atman*, the god within. In the *Rig Veda*, he is also the son of the Sun (Vivasvat), and he becomes the first human, a fact that associates him with both the Purusha and Manu. In later Hindu mythology, Yama is the more recognizable Lord of the Land of the Dead—a figure to be feared. In Buddhism he is also Lord of the Underworld, sometimes the same as the fiend Mara, who tempted Gautama Buddha under the Bodhi Tree. In Tantric (Vajrayana) and Tibetan Buddhism, Yama is a terrifying deity who judges the dead, holding the mirror of *karma* in his left hand and the sword of justice and wisdom in his right. In Japanese Buddhism, Yama is Emma-O', the demon lord of the underworld who judges the dead. In China he was Yanlou, who represented the Jade Emperor (Yu) as ruler in Hell.

YAMA NO KAMI In Japanese Shinto, *Yama no kami* is the mountain deity who comes down from the mountain and becomes *ta no kami*, the god of the fields, who brings crops.

YAMABUSHI These shaman-like Japanese mountain ascetics, the Yamabushi, are associated with spirits (kami); their nature is ambiguous. They are similar to if not identical with the Tengu.

YAMI The twin sister of Yama, the Vedic-Hindu god of Death, Yami in the *Rig Veda* proposes an incestuous relationship with her brother and is refused.

YAMUNA The Yamuna, or Jumna, is a sacred river of the Hindus. It is often personified as Yami, the daughter of the Sun and the twin of Yama, the god of Death. It flows from the Himalayas into the Ganges.

YAO The legendary Chinese Emperor Yao, said to be the Han ancestor, was unpretentious and diligent, and remains of great importance to Confucianists. He wore simple clothes, and during times of starvation and a great flood, he stood firmly with his suffering people. The gods supported Yao, making rice out of his horses' straw and leading him to inventions such as the calendar. In this latter endeavor he had the help of the deities Xi and his two brothers and He (Xihe). Each of these figures was assigned a cardinal direction and a season. Through his organization of time and space, Yao brought about a balance of *yin* and *yang*. Many stories are told of the great Yao, including that of the bird with double eyeballs given him by one of his provinces. The bird looked like a rooster but sounded like a phoenix. It was capable of shedding its feathers and flying without them and it could defeat evil spirits. Yao lived for a century. Instead of choosing his evil son Dan Zhu to succeed him, Yao chose the wise Shun.

YARIKH Yarikh was a Ugaritic-Canaanite moon deity.

YASHTS *Yashts* are hymns in the Zoroastrian *Avesta*, containing much of what we know of Iranian mythology.

YASNA In the Zoroastrian sacred book of Iran, the *Avesta*, the *Yasna* is the collection of the seventeen "songs" (*gathas*) of Zoroaster and other, longer hymns. The *Yasna* is the part of the *Avesta* used during sacred sacrifices.

YEI The Yei are Native North American creator spirits or deities of the Athabascan tradition, particularly of Navajo mythology. Their Apache equivalent are the Hactin. The Yei and the Hactin resemble the Hopi Kachina. The Yei appear in sand paintings and in rituals as masked dancers. They are personifications of natural powers and they play important roles in the Navajo creation myth. Their leader is Talking God.

YGGDRASILL In Norse mythology Yggdrasill was the world tree, the *axis mundi* that linked the various "worlds" of the universe. It was the cosmic ash with roots reaching down to Hel and to the worlds of humans and the frost giants. The great god Odin hanged himself on Yggdrasill—literally Ygg's or Odin's horse, a kenning for the gallows—for nine days and nights to learn the runic mysteries. At the foot of the tree were various springs and wells, including Urd's Well, that of the Norns, and the well of Mimir ("Wisdom").

YI Known as the "Excellent Archer," Yi lived during the time of the Chinese Emperor Yao, when ten suns suddenly rose in the sky, causing a total destruction of crops and great misery for the people. The suns were the offspring of the god of the east, Di Xun, sometimes confused with the Emperor Shun, and the goddess Xihe. Ordinarily, the suns lived in the solar Mulberry Tree or Fusang and took turns appearing at the top of the tree. But on the day in question, all of the suns went to the top of the tree. Things became so bad that Yao had no choice but to ask the archer, Yi, to shoot down all but one sun. This he did, and from that time on, the remaining sun crossed the sky each day in a chariot driven by his mother.

Another story of Yi concerns the theft by his wife Henge of the elixir of immortality, which Yi had obtained. After the theft, Henge fled to the moon and became a toad there. Thus, the moon contains immortality and is a perpetual body.

After he shot down the suns, Yi followed the traditional hero's Herculean quest path and rid the world of various evil beings.

YIMA Yima was an ancient Iranian king of the mythological period. He is related to the Vedic Yama. Like Yama, Yima was associated with death, as he agreed to become subject to that condition as the first human in the Zoroastrian flood myth.

YIN-YANG In Chinese philosophy, which stresses an organic universe, *yin* ("shadow") and *yang* ("brightness") are opposite energies that interact in such a way as to produce *wu-hsing* (the five elements), which in turn bring about the material world and space and time. *yin* and *yang* are the opposite boundaries of the absolute source of being, *t'ai-chi*. The famous *yin-yang* symbol represents the intermingling of the opposites, which leads to what is essentially the creation of the universe. The interaction is continuous, as indicated by the dark spot that is, in the light, *yang* and the light spot that is, in the dark, *yin*. Each contains the seed of the other and creates a renewed version of the other. In keeping with this sense of necessary interacting opposites, *yin* is that which is feminine, passive, and accommodating. It is the moon, earth, and wetness. Yang is masculine, active, and firm. It is the sun, the heavens, and dryness. The *yin-yang* model is first mentioned in the first millennium B.C.E. (See *I Ching*.)

YMIR The animistic source of the world in Norse mythology, Ymir was the giant who emerged at the creation at the meeting place of fire and ice. As an androgyne, he gave birth to the first man and woman from under his left armpit. His legs came together to form the frost giants. Ymir drank from the four rivers of milk that came from the cow called Audumla. Audumla licked the ice for three days, and finally a man named Buri appeared. Buri's son Bor married Bestla, the daughter of the frost giant Bolthor, and Bestla gave birth to the gods Odin, Vili, and Ve. These gods killed Ymir and created the world out of his body. His skull became the sky; his spilled blood became the Norse flood.

YOGA The term *yoga* is derived from the Sanskrit for "joining" or "yoking." As a discipline, it takes many forms leading to extreme focusing of one's physical and mental powers and to consciousness raising and liberation (*Moksha*) from *samsara* or—ultimately and ideal-

A man fishes in the Yamuna near the Taj Mahal

Y

ly—to a "joining" with Brahman. A *yogi*, or *yogin*, is one who practices yoga or who, in a more general sense, is a Hindu ascetic. Yoga seems likely to have been practiced long before the Vedic period in India. There is archeological evidence suggesting its sources or at least its presence in Indus Valley civilization, where the practice was perhaps associated with the deity who became Rudra-Shiva, himself known as the greatest of yogis. A successful yogi is expected to achieve mental control by way of various types of disciplined movement and breathing. The third-century C.E. *Yoga Sutra* established yoga as a bona fide Hindu philosophical system, developing ideas originally found in the *Rig Veda* and the *Upanishads*. In the *Bhagavadgita*, Krishna becomes the object of meditation for the yogi. The clear implication here is that yoga can be a form of devotion (*bhakti*), or worship.

YOMI-NO-KUNI In the early Japanese Shinto tradition, Yomi was the gloomy afterlife.

YONI In Sanskrit, *yoni* means "womb" or "source" and also "vulva," "nest," and even "caste" and "race." Its root meaning, like that of *yoga*, is the idea of joining or uniting. In Hinduism and Tantrism, the *yoni* is the generative organ of the Goddess (Devi). Often it is worshipped in conjunction with the *linga*, the genital organ of the god, particularly Shiva. Small models of the joined *linga* and *yoni* are found in all parts of India. It is thought that *yoni* worship stretches back to the pre-Vedic, Indus Valley period in India, the period from about 4000 to 1000 B.C.E. Archeological evidence in the south of India suggests a myth in which Shiva takes the form of a buffalo and is sacrificed to the Goddess and reborn from her *yoni*. In southern India there are numerous places where stones with cleavages are worshipped as the Goddess *yoni*. A popular symbol of the *yoni* is the triangle.

YORIMITSU A Japanese samurai of the tenth and early eleventh centuries C.E., Yorimitsu is said to have accomplished many heroic deeds, which place him in the category of a legendary-mythic figure. He defeated a giant who thrived on human blood. He was victorious even though the decapitated giant's head continued to fight after it was detached from its body. Yorimitsu also defeated a supernatural spider and performed miraculous feats with his bow and arrows.

YU Many mythological tales are told in China of The Great Yu, sometimes called Gaomi or Yuhuang, the man considered to be the first Xia emperor. As a prime example of intelligence, leadership, and adherence to duty, Yu was the epitome of the Chinese ideal of the hero. It was he who would end the great flood. Sometimes Yu is considered a dragon. There are several myths of his miraculous conception and birth. According to one, the mother of Yu, after seeing a shooting star, swallowed a magic pearl and became pregnant. Her chest broke open to release Yu. In another version, the mother picked up a seed on a mountain, ate it, became pregnant, and gave birth to Yu from her side. Some say Yu, like his son and successor, was born from a rock. Still others say that Yu sprang as a great dragon from the body of his father, Gun, who had been put to death for failing to stop the flood. Gun and his father were associated with mythical aquatic animals. It was they who organized the fields and waterways for agriculture and generally organized the world. In effect, Yu became a high god—the god of the soil. He married the daughter of the Earth Mountain, Tushan. When she made the mistake of watching her husband turn into a bear, she became a stone, and it was then that Yu had to cut her open to release his son, Qui. Sometimes Yu is known as the Jade Emperor.

YUDISHTHIRA Yudishthira was the leader of the Pandavas in the Indian epic the *Mahabharata*. His father was the personified Dharma, the embodiment of that proper order and duty much needed in the corrupt world. He was by no means a perfect hero. In fact, it was he who gambled away the faithful Pandava wife Draupadi, an act that led to the temporary exile of the Pandavas by their cousins and arch rivals, the Kauravas.

YURLUNGGUR Yurlunggur was a rainbow serpent of the Yolngu in Australian Arnhem mythology.

YURUPARY The Barasana people of Colombia in South America tell of a culture hero named Yurupary who stole fire for humans from the underworld.

The Emperor Yu

ZEN BUDDHISM Zen Buddhism is said to have come to Japan by way of Ch'an, a form of Mahayana Buddhism brought to China from India by Bodhidharma, the twenty-eighth successor to Gautama Buddha, the Buddha Sakyamuni, in the fifth century C.E. Ch'an was a version of what in India was called *dhyana*, a meditative and ecstatic form of Buddhism—influenced also by Daoism when it got to China and various esoteric forms of Buddhism when it got to Japan, where it eventually flourished in the Rinzai and Soto sects. The monk Dogen is said to have been responsible in the thirteenth century for the rise of Soto Zen. The monk Hakuin led a major Rinzai form of Zen in the eighteenth century. Ch'an and Zen emphasize the possibility for the individual to discover, through concentration and meditation, the Buddha nature underlying all things, including the self. Zen means literally recognizing the truth that is already there. For the Zen Buddhist, the wisdom to be gained from meditation or from a master who has achieved enlightenment is more important than anything that can be gained from ritual or scripture. Therefore, mythology plays a minimal role in this form of Buddhism.

ZEUS When Indo-European Hellenes invaded the land we now call Greece, they brought with them a chief sky god, who personified light and sky and who, as also a storm and weather god, replete with thunderbolt, brought forth rain and fertility. His fertility aspect is reflected in the many myths of his relationships with mortal women: Europa, Leda, and Semele, for example. Associated early with the chief god of Crete, Zeus gained a particular personality as his mythology developed in Greece through Homer, Hesiod, and others. He was said to be one of several children of the ancient gods Kronos and Rhea. When Kronos was overthrown by Zeus and his siblings, Zeus, as the primary facilitator of that revolt, became the leader of his family of gods, known now as the Olympians, since they lived on Mount Olympus. The eventual arrangement of the Olympian gods into a relatively neat family in Greek myth is a reflection of Mycenaean family and court arrangements. Zeus reflected the person of the pater familias, the ultimate decision maker. Zeus dispensed often-arbitrary justice, could be a doting father to his daughters, and was, above all, a philanderer. His actions are based firmly in the "rights" of the Indo-European patriarchal hierarchical social system. Over time, Zeus had three wives: Metis, who conceived Athena; Themis, the Titan, who gave birth to the Fates; and, most important, the Queen of Olympus, Hera, the understandably jealous spouse who was the mother of Ares and Hephaistos. By his many other sexual conquests, Zeus was the father of many gods and heroes, including, among others, Herakles, Perseus, Persephone (by his sister Demeter), Minos, Castor and Polydeuces,

Helen of Troy, Clytemnestra, Apollo, Artemis, Hermes, the Muses, and Dionysos.

ZHANG GUO Zhang Guo was the sixth of the Chinese Daoist Eight Immortals. He was known for his magical powers and for his white mule, which could be folded up when it was not being used.

ZHURONG In ancient China, Zhurong was the God of Fire, the "Brilliant One of the Forge." It was he who defeated Gonggong in an epic battle of the gods, a Chinese version of the war in Heaven.

ZIGGURATS In the Ubaid culture of southern Mesopotamia the ziggurat temples were first built at the site that would become Sumerian Ur. The ziggurats were capped by sanctuaries that apparently were used for the celebration of rites representing the sacred union of the earth goddess and the human descendant of the ancient bull god, now the city god of Ur and of later cities where these temples were built, not only by the Sumerians but by their Semitic replacements, the Akkadians and Babylonians. The earthly representatives of this couple would have been a queen and a king of a hieratic city or city-state. This tradition of the sacred marriage is a central element in the religion and mythology of the Mesopotamian civilizations.

Zeus

323

A Mesopotamian Ziggurat

ZIUSUDRA Ziusudra (Ziusura) was the Sumerian name for the Mesopotamian flood hero of the Gilgamesh myth. In the Babylonian tradition he was Utnapishtim.

ZONG BELEGT BAATAR Zong Belegt is the hero (*baatar*) of this central Asian Turko-Mongol epic. He is a rich and powerful king who must confront a terrible monster called Khuiten Tomor, who, like so many ogres before him, enjoys eating children and laying waste to the land of the good—especially that of heroes like Zong Belegt, whom he dreams of destroying. After two marathon struggles—one lasts four years, the other seven days—Zong Belegt kills and dismembers the ogre.

ZOROASTER Zoroaster, or Zarathustra, was one of the great prophets of the ancient world. He lived in northeastern Iran, probably late in the second millennium B.C.E. His concern as a Mazdian priest was the reinterpretation of the ancient Iranian religion and a reestablishment of "good religion" as opposed to the corruption he saw around him. The result of his having "seen God" (Ahura Mazda) and having interpreted the old teachings was the religious system we now call Zoroastrianism, based, as it is, on Zoroaster's preaching in the books called the *Gathas*. Central to Zoroaster's work was the belief in an essential dualism in the universe, represented by the Wise Lord Ahura Mazda and the evil Angra Mainyu. Eventually, many myths developed around the life of the prophet, placing him clearly among those heroes we associate with the heroic monomyth. It was said that his mother, Dughda, dreamt that good and evil spirits were fighting for the baby in her womb. At birth the baby laughed. Wise men warned the wicked king Duransarun that the child

was a threat to his realm, and the king set off to kill the baby Zoroaster. Miraculously the would-be murderer's hand was paralyzed. When demons stole the child, they also failed to kill him; his mother found him peacefully sleeping in the wilderness. Later, the king sent a herd of oxen to trample his enemy, but the cattle took care not to hurt Zoroaster. The same thing happened when horses were sent to trample him. Even when the king had two wolf cubs killed and had the baby Zoroaster put in their place in the den, the mother wolf's anger was quieted by God, and sacred cows were sent to suckle the child. In adulthood, Zoroaster was resented by followers of the old tradition, but he convinced many with his miraculous cures, and even though he was killed at an advanced age by soldiers while he was carrying out a ritual sacrifice, it is said that Zoroaster will one day return as a final prophet or *saoshyant*.

ZOROASTRIAN MYTHOLOGY Zoroastrianism is a religion that takes its name from the late-second-millennium B.C.E. Iranian prophet Zarathustra, traditionally called Zoroaster by people in the West. Believing that he had spoken to the ancient Iranian high god Ahura Mazda, Zoroaster undertook a reform of the old Indo-European, Indo-Iranian religion of the Aryan invaders of India and Iran. At the center of his reformation is an essential dualism that places the good Ahura Mazda and his heavenly followers, the *asuras*, against the evil Angra Mainyu and the *daevas*, who in their old Indo-Iranian context were not particularly evil but who in Zoroastrianism become demons bent on war and destruction. After long years of struggle against the followers of the old religion, Zoroastrianism became the state religion of Iran under Cyrus the Great in the sixth century B.C.E. and remained so until the rise of Islam in the seventh century C.E. In India Zoroastrians are called Parsis.

Important aspects of Zoroastrianism are the belief in the prophet (Zoroaster), a past and future savior (Saoshyant), an afterlife, a Last Judgment and apocalypse, and the resurrection of the body. A central aspect of Zoroastrian ritual is fire and fire temples, a tradition that reaches back to ancient Indo-Iranian roots and resembles the fire emphasis in Indian Vedism, where the fire sacrifice is important. An offshoot or "heresy" of Zoroastrianism is Zurvanism, in which Zurvan, or Time, in a sense supplants Ahura Mazda as ultimate reality.

Zoroastrians believe that too few people follow the right path, that the evil ones at present outnumber the good. But they also believe that one day the Wise Lord will rectify things at the Great Renewal at the end of the present age. Fire, the son of Ahura Mazda, will flow like a river over the universe as an ultimate sacrifice, destroying all before it—including even Hell—and separating the good from the evil at a "Last Judgment." Then, through ceremonies presided over by the savior, Saoshyant, the resurrection of the bodies of the good will take place and a new Golden Age will follow. In some stories it is said that the castle of the primal man, the flood survivor and sacred king Yima, is Paradise and that at the Great Renewal, Yima's dominion will encompass the earth itself as the basis of the new Golden Age.

Several stories of creation exist in the Iranian tradition. One story tells how Yima, the primal human, king of the Golden Age, and later a solar deity, pierced the earth with a golden arrow, making it pregnant. Yima, who resembles the Indian Vedic god Yama, had been created by the sun god Vivahant, a servant of Ahura Mazda. In the *Avesta*, we are told that there was only Light—an essential purity—in the beginning. In the Light was the Word and the power of Nature. It was the creator, usually seen as Ahura Mazda himself, who joined together the Word and Nature to make the world. When the world had become overwhelmed by the constant multiplication of its all immortal beings, Ahura Mazda decided that the earth must be enlarged and a new beginning made. He warned the faithful king Yima that a great flood was coming to cleanse the world and that Yima had to protect himself and two of each species in his castle on top of the highest mountain. The deluge arrived, and the world, except for Yima's castle and its inhabitants, was destroyed. When the waters receded, Yima opened his doors and the world was inhabited again.

According to the twelfth-century text the *Bundahishn*, in the beginning only the essential duality existed: the good Ahura Mazda and the evil Angra Mainyu. At first Ahura Mazda created a spiritual world rather than a physical one in order to foil the evil intention of his adversary. Only 3,000 years later did he create the tangible world (*getig*), a perfect place with a perfect beast and a perfect human, Gayomart. Instinctively, the evil Angra Mainyu reacted against this perfection. Break-

ing through the great cosmic shell that encompassed the world and its cosmic sea, he caused so much vibration that the sun began to rotate rather than stand still, causing day and night, and mountains and valleys were formed. And as in Genesis, the interference of evil in the stillness and perfection of original creation led to death, work, and pain for humans. It is interesting, then, that Angra Mainyu, like many trickster and devil figures of other creation myths—many, for instance, in central Asia and Native North America—contributes to the creative process. It is also important to note that in the Zoroastrian myth there is the understanding that creation contains the means to defeat Angra Mainyu's evil. When the first beast and the first human died, they released sperm, from which more life emerged, instituting a process by which death could always be overcome. This is why people must always support the goodness of creation by farming the land and creating children.

In his reform of the old Mazdian religion, Zoroaster, in theory, did away with mythology. The early Aryan idea of a pantheon of amoral immortals was discarded in favor of the essential duality that lay at the source of existence. The choice for humanity and for individuals was between the two sides of the duality. [Gnoli]

ZUNI CREATION The Zuni people of the Native North American Southwest have an elaborate creation and cosmology myth. In the womb of the world, all earthly life was conceived when Earth Mother and Sky Father lay together on the primeval waters. Earth Mother grew so large in pregnancy that she had to push Sky Father away from her. She was so large with progeny that she began to sink into the world waters. But fearing that evil might befall her offspring, she kept avoiding giving birth to them. She and Sky Father discussed the problem. They decided to take the form of the first man and woman.

Suddenly a great bowl filled with water appeared nearby, and Earth Mother realized that each place in the world would be surrounded by mountains like the rim of the bowl. She spat in the water and, as foam formed, she said, "Look, sustenance will come from me." Then she blew her warm breath over the foam, and some of the foam lifted, sending down mist and spray in great abundance. This was the origin of clouds. Earth Mother said that Sky Father's colder breath would make the clouds drop their waters onto her lap as rain, the water of life falling down to fertilize the earth. Earth would be the place where Earth Mother's children would nestle, be nurtured, and thrive in her warmth.

ZURVAN In Zoroastrianism, Zurvan is the concept of Time. In a Zoroastrian offshoot cult, Zurvan was considered to be the ultimate reality, the power behind even Ahura Mazda and Angra Mainyu and thus the source of what was seen as predestination. This "heresy," known as Zurvanism, was at odds with orthodox Zoroastrianism, with its emphasis on the possibility of choice between good and evil.

Z

EGYPTIAN-HELIOPOLIS SYSTEM

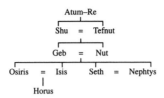

GREEK SYSTEM

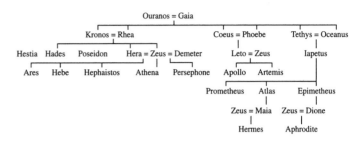

BABYLONIAN SYSTEM

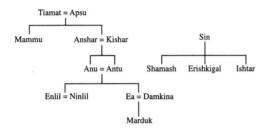

NORSE SYSTEM

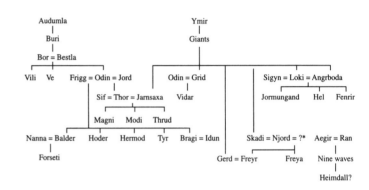

JAPANESE SYSTEM

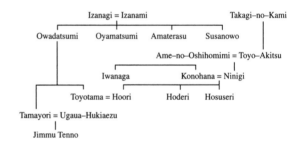

SUMERIAN-BABYLONIAN EQUIVALENT DEITIES

Sumerian	Babylonian
Abzu	Apsu
An	Anu
Dumuzi ("sacred son")	Tammuz
Enki	Ea
Enlil	Enlil or Ellil
Ereshkigal	Ereshkigal
Geshtinanna ("Lady of the Vine")	
Gugalanna (Bull of Heaven)	Nergal
Imdugud bird ("heavy rain")	Anzu or Zu bird
Inanna	Ishtar
Namtar	Namtar
Nammu	Tiamat
Nanna	Sin
Ninhursag (Nintu)	Mami, Belet-ili, Aruru
Ninurta (Ningirsu)	Ninurta
Utu	Shamash
Ziusudra, Atrahasis	Utnapishtim

GREEK-ROMAN EQUIVALENT DEITIES

Greek	Roman
Zeus	Jupiter
Hera	Juno
Poseidon	Neptune
Demeter	Ceres
Hades	Pluto
Aphrodite	Venus
Athena	Minerva
Apollo	Apollo
Artemis	Diana
Hermes	Mercury
Ares	Mars
Hephaistos	Vulcan
Hestia	Vestia
Dionysos	Bacchus
Eros	Cupid
Kronos	Saturn
Gaia	Tellus
Rhea	Ops
Persephone	Proserpina

Bibliography

ABRAHAMS, ROGER D. *African Folktales*. New York: Pantheon, 1983.

ADAMS, CHARLES J. "*Qur'an*: The Text and Its History." *In* Mircea Eliade, ed. *The Encyclopedia of Religion*, vol. 12, pp. 156–176. New York and London: Macmillan, 1987.

ADAMS, RICHARD E. W. *Prehistoric Mesoamerica*, rev. ed. Norman: University of Oklahoma Press, 1991.

ALBRIGHT, WILLIAM F. *Yahweh and the Gods of Canaan*. Garden City, NY: Doubleday, 1968.

ALLEN, J. P. Translations of Egyptian texts. In W. W. Hallo, ed. *The Context of Scripture*, vol. I: *Canonical Compositions from the Biblical World*. Leiden, New York, and Cologne: Brill, 1997.

ALLOUCHE, ADEL. "Arabian Religions." *In* Mircea Eliade, ed. *The Encyclopedia of Religion*, vol. 1, pp. 363–367. New York and London: Macmillan, 1987.

APOLLODORUS. *The Library*. James G. Frazer, trans. London: Heinemann, 1921.

APOLLONIUS OF RHODES. *The Voyage of the Argo*. E. V. Rieu, trans. Baltimore: Penguin, 1959p.

ARBERRY, A. J. *The Koran Interpreted*. London: Oxford University Press, 1964.

ARMSTRONG, KAREN. *Muhammad: A Biography of the Prophet*. San Francisco: Harper, 1992.

——. *A History of God: The 4000-Year Quest of Judaism, Christianity, and Islam*. New York: Knopf, 1993.

——. *Islam: A Short History*. New York: Modern Library, 2000.

ARTIGAS, MARIANO. *The Mind of the Universe: Understanding Science and Religion*. Philadelphia: Templeton, 2000.

ASAD, MUHAMMAD, trans. *The Message of the Qur'an*. Gibraltar: Dar Al-Andalus, 1980.

ASHTON, W. G., trans. *Nihongi*. Tokyo: Charles Tuttle, 1972

BACKMAN, LOUISE. "Saami Religion." *In* Mircea Eliade, ed. *The Encyclopedia of Religion*, vol. 12, pp. 497–499. New York and London: Macmillan, 1987.

BARBOUR, IAN G. *Issues in Science and Religion*. New York: Prentice-Hall, 1966.

——. *Religion in an Age of Science*. San Francisco: Harper, 1990.

BARING, ANNE, and JULES CASHFORD. *The Myth of the Goddess: Evolution of an Image*. New York: Viking, 1991.

BASHAM, A. L. *The Wonder That Was India*. London: Sidgwick and Jackson, 1954.

BATESON, GREGORY. *Steps to an Ecology of the Mind*. New York: Ballantine Books, 1972.

BEGG, EAN. *The Cult of the Black Virgin*. London: Arkana, Routledge and Kegan Paul, 1985.

BEIER, ULLI. *The Origin of Life and Death: African Creation Myths*. London: Heinemann, 1966.

BELTZ, WALTER. *God and the Gods: Myths of the Bible*. Peter Heinegg, trans. Middlesex, UK: Penguin, 1983.

BENTLY, PETER, ed. *The Dictionary of World Myth*. New York: Facts on File, 1995.

BERMAN, MORRIS. *The Reenchantment of the World*. Ithaca, NY: Cornell University Press, 1981.

BIERHORST, JOHN. *The Mythology of North America*. New York: William Morrow, 1985.

BIERLEIN, JOHN FRANCIS. *Parallel Myths*. New York: Ballantine Books, 1994.

BIEZAIS, HARALDS. "Baltic Religion." *In* Mircea Eliade, ed. *The Encyclopedia of Religion*, vol. 2, pp. 49–55. New York and London: Macmillan, 1987.

BIRRELL, ANNE. *Chinese Mythology: An Introduction*. Baltimore: Johns Hopkins University Press, 1993.

BLACK, JEREMY, and ANTHONY GREEN. *Gods, Demons and Symbols of Ancient Mesopotamia*. Austin: University of Texas Press, 2000.

BLACKBURN, SIMON. *Think*. Oxford: Oxford University Press, 1999.

BLAZQUEZ, JOSE M. "Basque Religion." Erica Melzer, trans. *In* Mircea Eliade, ed. *The Encyclopedia of Religion*, vol. 2, pp. 80–81. New York and London: Macmillan, 1987a.

——. "Iberian Religion." *In* Mircea Eliade, ed. *The Encyclopedia of Religion*, vol. 6, pp. 547–551. New York and London: Macmillan, 1987.

BLOCH, RAYMOND. "Etruscan Religion." Carol Dean-Nassau and Marilyn Gaddis Rose, trans. *In* Mircea Eliade, ed. *The Encyclopedia of Religion*, vol. 5, pp. 182–185. New York and London: Macmillan, 1987b.

BOER, CHARLES, trans. *The Homeric Hymns*. Chicago: Swallow Press, 1970.

BONNEFOY, YVES. *Roman and European Mythologies*. Chicago: University of Chicago Press, 1991.

——. *Greek and Egyptian Mythologies*. Chicago: University of Chicago Press, 1992.

BONNEFOY, YVES, with WENDY DONIGER, trans., ed. *Asian Mythologies*. Chicago: University of Chicago Press, 1993.

BORNKAMM, GUNTHER. *Jesus of Nazareth*. New York: HarperCollins, 1976.

BOROWITZ, EUGENE B. "Judaism: An Overview." *In* Mircea Eliade, ed. *The Encyclopedia of Religion*, vol. 8, pp. 127–149. New York and London: Macmillan, 1987.

BOWERING, GERHARD. "Mi'raj." *In* Mircea Eliade, ed. *The Encyclopedia of Religion*, vol. 9, pp. 552–556. New York and London: Macmillan, 1987.

BOWKER, JOHN, ed. *The Oxford Dictionary of World Religions*. Oxford and New York: Oxford University Press, 1997.

BRANDON, S. G. F. *Creation Legends of the Ancient Near East*. London: Hodder and Stoughton, 1963.

BRANSTON, BRIAN. *Gods of the North*. New York: Thames and Hudson, 1955 and 1980.

BROWN, JOSEPH EPES. *The Sacred Pipe: Black Elk's Account of the Seven Rites of the Oglala Sioux*. Norman: University of Oklahoma Press, 1953.

BRYCE, T. *The Kingdom of Hittites*. Oxford: Clarendon Press, 1998.

BUCK, WILLIAM, trans. *The Ramayana*. Berkeley: University of California Press, 1976.

BUDGE, E. A. W. *Egyptian Religion*. New York: Bell, 1959.

——. *The Gods of the Egyptians or Studies in Egyptian Mythology*. New York: Dover, 1969.

BULFINCH, THOMAS. *Bulfinch's Mythology*. 2 vols. New York: Mentor, 1962.

BUXTON, RICHARD. *The Complete World of Greek Mythology*. New York: Thames and Hudson, 2004.

CAESAR, JULIUS. *See* Hammonds.

CAILLAT, COLETTE. "Jainism." *In* Mircea Eliade, ed. *The Encyclopedia of Religion*, vol. 7, pp. 507–514. New York and London: Macmillan, 1987.

CAMPBELL, JOSEPH. *The Hero with a Thousand Faces*. Princeton, NJ: Princeton University Press, 1972 (1949).

——. *The Masks of God: Oriental Mythology*. New York: Viking, 1962.

——. *The Masks of God: Occidental Mythology*. New York: Viking, 1964.

——. *The Masks of God: Creative Mythology*. New York: Viking, 1968.

——. *The Masks of God: Primitive Mythology*. New York: Viking, 1969.

——. *Myths to Live By*. New York: Viking Press, 1970.

——. *The Way of the Animal Powers*. London: Summerfield Press, 1983.

CAMPBELL, JOSEPH, with BILL MOYERS. *The Power of Myth*. New York: Doubleday, 1988.

CAPRA, FRITJOF. *The Tao of Physics*. San Francisco: Shambhala, 1975.

CARLYLE, THOMAS. *On Heroes, Hero Worship, and the Heroic in History*. Lincoln: University of Nebraska Press, 1966 (1841).

CARRASCO, DAVID. *Ancient Mesoamerican Religions*. New York: Holt, Rinehart, and Winston, 1990.

CASSIRER, ERNST. *Language and Myth*. Susanne Langer, trans. New York: Dover, 1946.

CHADWICK, NORA K., ed. *The Celts*, new ed. New York: Penguin Books, 1997.

CICERO. *See* Rudd.

CLARK, R. T. RUNDLE. *Myth and Symbol in Ancient Egypt*. London: Thames and Hudson, 1959.

CLARKE, LINDSAY. *Essential Celtic Mythology*. San Francisco: HarperCollins, 1997.

CLOTHEY, FRED. "Tamil Religion." *In* Mircea Eliade, ed. *The Encyclopedia of Religion*, vol. 14, pp. 260–268. New York and London: Macmillan, 1987.

COFFIN, T. P., ed. *Indian Tales of North America*. Philadelphia: American Folklore Society, 1961.

COHEN, MARK R. "Judaism in the Middle East and North Africa to 1492." *In* Mircea Eliade, ed. *The Encyclopedia of Religion*, vol. 8, pp. 148–157. New York and London: Macmillan, 1987.

COHN, N. *Noah's Flood: The Genesis Story in Western Thought*. New Haven, CT, and London: Yale University Press, 1996.

COOGAN, MICHAEL DAVID. *Stories from Ancient Canaan*. Louisville, KY: Westminster Press, 1978.

——. "Canaanite Religion: The Literature." *In* Mircea Eliade, ed. *The Encyclopedia of Religion*, vol. 3, pp. 45–58. New York and London: Macmillan, 1987.

——. *The Oxford History of the Biblical World*. Oxford and New York: Oxford University Press, 1998.

COOPER, ALAN M. "Canaanite Religion: An Overview." *In* Mircea Eliade, ed. *The Encyclopedia of Religion*, vol. 3, pp. 35–45. New York and London: Macmillan, 1987.

CROSS, F. M. *Canaanite Myth and Hebrew Epic: Essays in the History of the Religion of Israel*. Cambridge, MA: Harvard University Press, 1973.

CROSSLEY-HOLLAND, KEVIN. *The Norse Myths*. New York: Pantheon, 1980.

CULIANO, IOAN PETRU, and CICERONE POGHIRC. "Thracian Religion." *In* Mircea Eliade, ed. *The Encyclopedia of Religion*, vol. 14, pp. 494–497. New York and London: Macmillan, 1987.

CUNLIFFE, BARRY. *The Ancient Celts*. New York: Oxford University Press, 1997.

CURRID, J. D. *Ancient Egypt and the Old Testament*. Grand Rapids, MI: Baker Books, 1997.

DALLEY, STEPHANIE. *Myths from Mesopotamia* (World's Classics series), rev. ed. Oxford and New York: Oxford University Press, 2000.

DAVIDSON, HILDA RODERICK ELLIS. *Gods and Myths of Northern Europe*. Harmondsworth, UK: Penguin, 1964.

——. *Roles of the Northern Goddess*. New York: Routledge, 1998.

DAVIDSON, HILDA RODERICK ELLIS, with PETER FISHER, trans. *Saxo Grammaticus: The History of the Danes*. Woodbridge, UK: Boydell & Brewer, 2001.

DAVIES, PAUL, ed. *The New Physics*. New York: Cambridge University Press, 1989.

——. *The Mind of God: The Scientific Basis for a Rational World*. New York and London: Simon & Schuster, 1993.

DAVIES, PAUL, and JOHN GRIBBIN. *The Matter Myth*. London: Penguin, 1992.

DE VORAGINE, JACOBUS. *The Golden Legend*. London: Longmans, Green, 1941.

DEL RE, GIUSEPPE. *The Cosmic Dance: Science Discovers the Mysterious Harmony of the Universe*. Philadelphia: Templeton, 2000.

DOMOTOR, TEKLA. "Hungarian Religion." *In* Mircea Eliade, ed. *The Encyclopedia of Religion*, vol. 6, pp. 530–531. New York and London: Macmillan, 1987.

DOTY, WILLIAM G. *Mythography: The Study of Myths and Rituals*. Tuscaloosa: University of Alabama Press, 2nd ed. 2000.

——. *The Times World Mythology*. New York: Times Books, 2002.

——. *Myth: A Handbook*. Westport, CT: Greenwood Press, 2004.

DOUGLAS, MARY. *Purity and Danger: An Analysis of Concepts of Pollution and Taboo*. New York: Praeger, 1966.

——. *Natural Symbols: Explorations in Cosmology*. New York: Pantheon, 1970.

DOWNING, CHRISTINE R. *The Goddess: Mythological Images of the Feminine*. New York: Crossroad, 1981.

DUMÉZIL, GEORGES. *L'idéologie tripartite des Indo-Européens*. Brussels: Latomus, 1958.

——. *Archaic Roman Religion*. 2 vols. Philip Krapp, trans. Chicago: University of Chicago Press, 1970.

DUNDES, ALAN. "Earth-Diver: Creation of the Mythopoeic Male." *American Anthropologist* 64(1):95–105, 1962.

——. *The Flood Myth*. Berkeley: University of California Press, 1988.

DURKHEIM, EMILE. *The Elementary Forms of Religious Life*. J. W. Swain, trans. London: Allen & Urwin, 1915.

ELIADE, MIRCEA. *Patterns in Comparative Religion*. Cleveland: Meridian, 1963 (1958).

——. *Myth and Reality*. New York: Harper & Row, 1963 (1962).

——. *The Myth of the Eternal Return*, rev. ed. Princeton, NJ: Princeton University Press, 1965 (1949).

——, ed. *Essential Sacred Writings from Around the World*. San Francisco: HarperCollins, 1977.

——, ed. *The Encyclopedia of Religion*. 16 vols. New York and London: Macmillan, 1987.

ELIOT, T. S. *The Complete Poems and Plays*. New York: Harcourt, Brace, 1952.

ELLIS, PETER BERRESFORD. *Dictionary of Celtic Mythology*. New York: Oxford University Press, 1992.

ERDOES, R., and A. ORTIZ, eds. *American Indian Myths and Legends*. New York: Pantheon, 1988.

FAULKNER, R. O. *The Ancient Egyptian Book of the Dead*. C. Andrews, ed. London: British Museum, 1985.

FEE, CHRISTOPHER, with DAVID LEEMING. *Gods, Heroes, and Kings: The Battle for Mythic Britain*. New York: Oxford University Press, 2001.

FOSTER, B. O., trans. *History of Rome* (by Livy). Cambridge, MA: Harvard University Press, 1988.

FOX, MATTHEW. *The Coming of the Cosmic Christ*. San Francisco: Harper, 1988.

——. *Sins of the Spirit, Blessings of the Flesh*. New York: Harmony Books, 1999.

——. *One River, Many Wells*. New York: Putnam, 2000.

FRANKFORT, H. *Kingship and the Gods: A Study of Ancient Near Eastern Religion as the Integration of Society and Nature*. Chicago: University of Chicago Press, 1948.

FRAZER, SIR JAMES. *The Golden Bough.* 12 vols. London: Macmillan, 1911–1915; abridged 1922; volume 13, 1936.

———. *The New Golden Bough.* Theodor Gaster, ed. New York: Criterion Books, 1959.

FREUD, SIGMUND. *Totem and Taboo: Resemblances between the Psychic Lives of Savages and Neurotics.* A. A. Brill, trans. New York: Moffat, Yard, 1918.

FREY-ROHN, LILIANE. *From Freud to Jung.* New York: Putnam, 1974.

FRYE, NORTHROP. *Anatomy of Criticism: Four Essays.* Princeton, NJ: Princeton University Press, 1957.

———, ed. *Myth and Symbol: Critical Approaches and Applications.* Lincoln: University of Nebraska Press, 1963.

FRYMER-KENSKY, TIKVA. "Enuma Elish." *In* Mircea Eliade, ed. *The Encyclopedia of Religion,* vol. 5, pp. 124–126. New York and London: Macmillan, 1987.

———. *In the Wake of Goddesses: Women, Culture and the Biblical Transformation of Pagan Myths.* New York: Free Press, 1992.

FULCO, WILLIAM J. "Anat." *In* Mircea Eliade, ed. Th*e Encyclopedia of Religion,* vol. 1, pp. 262–263. New York and London: Macmillan, 1987a.

———. "El." *In* Mircea Eliade, ed. *The Encyclopedia of Religion,* vol. 5, pp. 73–74. New York and London: Macmillan, 1987b.

FULLER, REGINALD H. "God in the New Testament." *In* Mircea Eliade, ed. *The Encyclopedia of Religion,* vol. 6, pp. 8–11. New York and London: Macmillan, 1987.

GARDET, LOUIS. "God in Islam." *In* Mircea Eliade, ed. *The Encyclopedia of Religion,* vol. 6, pp. 26–35. New York and London: Macmillan, 1987.

GARDNER, JOHN, and JOHN MAIER, eds. *Gilgamesh.* Translated from the Sin-Legiunninni version. New York: Knopf, 1984.

GASTER, THEODOR H. *The New Golden Bough. See* Frazer.

———. *Thespis: Ritual, Myth, and Drama in the Ancient Near East.* Garden City, NY: Doubleday, 1961.

———. "Heroes." *In* Mircea Eliade, ed. *The Encyclopedia of Religion,* vol. 6, pp. 302–305. New York and London: Macmillan, 1987.

GERBER, JANE S. "Judaism in the Middle East and North Africa Since 1492." *In* Mircea Eliade, ed. *The Encyclopedia of Religion,* vol. 8, pp. 157–164. New York and London: Macmillan, 1987.

GIBSON, J. L. C. *Canaanite Myths and Legends.* Edinburgh: T. & T. Clark, 1978.

GIMBUTAS, MARIJA. *The Balts.* London: Thames & Hudson, 1963.

———. *The Goddesses and Gods of Old Europe: Myths and Cult Images,* rev. ed. Berkeley: University of California Press, 1982.

———. "Megalithic Religion." *In* Mircea Eliade, ed. *The Encyclopedia of Religion,* vol. 9, pp. 336–344. New York and London: Macmillan, 1987a.

———. "Prehistoric Religions: Old Europe." *In* Mircea Eliade, ed. *The Encyclopedia of Religion,* vol. 11, pp. 506–515. New York and London: Macmillan, 1987b.

———. "Slavic Religion." *In* Mircea Eliade, ed. *The Encyclopedia of Religion,* vol. 13, pp. 353–361. New York and London, 1987c.

———. *The Language of the Goddess.* San Francisco: Harper & Row, 1989.

GIRARDOT, N. J. "Chinese Religion: Mythic Themes." *In* Mircea Eliade, ed. *The Encyclopedia of Religion,* vol. 3, pp. 296–305. New York and London: Macmillan, 1987.

GLAZIER, STEPHEN D. "Caribbean Religions: Pre-Columbian Religions." *In* Mircea Eliade, ed. *The Encyclopedia of Religion,* vol. 3, pp. 81–90. New York and London: Macmillan, 1987.

GNOLI, GHERARDO. "Zoroastrianism." *In* Mircea Eliade, ed. *The Encyclopedia of Religion,* vol. 15, pp. 579–591. New York and London: Macmillan, 1987.

GOETZ, DELIA, and SYLVANUS G. MORLEY, trans. *Popol Vuh: The Sacred Book of the Ancient Quiche Maya.* From trans. of Adrian Recinos. Norman: University of Oklahoma Press, 1950.

GRAF, FRITZ. "Eleusinian Mysteries." *In* Mircea Eliade, ed. *The Encyclopedia of Religion,* vol. 5, pp. 83–85. New York and London: Macmillan, 1987.

GRAVES, ROBERT. *The Greek Myths.* 2 vols. London and New York: Penguin, 1955.

———. *The White Goddess: A Historical Grammar of Poetic Myth,* rev. ed. New York: Farrar, Straus and Giroux, 1966.

GRAY, ELIZABETH A. *Cath Maige Tuired: The Second Battle of Mag Tuired.* London: Irish Texts Society, 1982.

GREEN, MIRANDA. *Celtic Myths* (Legendary Past series). London: British Museum Press, 1993.

GREENE, BRIAN. *The Elegant Universe.* New York: W.W. Norton, 1999.

GRIBBON, JOHN. *In Search of Schrödinger's Cat.* New York: Bantam, 1984.

GRIFFITHS, SIAN. *Predictions.* Oxford and New York: Oxford University Press, 1999.

GRIMAL, PIERRE, ed. *Larousse World Mythology.* London and New York: Hamlyn, 1974.

GURNEY, O. R. *The Hittites.* London and New York: Penguin, 1990.

HADAS, MOSES, ed. *Complete Works of Tacitus.* New York: McGraw-Hill, 1964.

HALLO, WILLIAM. W. *The Context of Scripture,* vol. I: *Canonical Compositions from the Biblical World.* Leiden, New York, and Cologne: Brill, 1997.

HALLO, WILLIAM W., and WILLIAM KELLY SIMPSON. *The Ancient Near East: A History,* 2nd ed. Fort Worth, TX: Harcourt Brace, 1998.

HAMILTON, EDITH. *Mythology.* Boston: Little, Brown, 1940.

HAMMONDS, CAROLYN, trans. *The Seven Commentaries on the Gallic War* (by Julius Caesar). New York: Oxford University Press, 1998.

HARAKAS, STANLEY SAMUEL. "Christianity in Eastern Europe." *In* Mircea Eliade, ed. *The Encyclopedia of Religion,* vol. 3, pp. 372–379. New York and London: Macmillan, 1987.

HARRIS, STEPHEN L. *Understanding the Bible,* 2nd ed. Palo Alto, CA, and London: Mayfield, 1985.

HARRISON, JANE. *Epilegomena to the Study of Greek Religion and Themis: A Study of the Social Origins of Greek Religion.* Hyde Park, NY: University Books, 1962.

HART, G. *Egyptian Myths.* London: British Museum. 1990.

HARVEY, ANDREW. *The Way of Passion: A Celebration of Rumi.* Berkeley, CA: Frog, Ltd., 1994.

———. *Son of Man: The Mystical Path to Christ.* New York: Tarcher/Putnam, 1998.

HEESTERMAN, JAN C. "Vedism and Brahmanism." *In* Mircea Eliade, ed. *The Encyclopedia of Religion,* vol. 15, pp. 217–242. New York and London: Macmillan, 1987.

HESIOD. *Theogony.* Norman O. Brown, trans. Indianapolis, IN: Bobbs-Merrill, 1953.

HEYDEN, DORIS. "Mesoamerican Religions: Classical Cultures." *In* Mircea Eliade, ed. *The Encyclopedia of Religion,* vol. 9, pp. 409–419. New York and London: Macmillan, 1987.

HICK, JOHN, ed. *The Myth of God Incarnate.* London: Westminster John Knox Press, 1977.

HILTEBEITEL, ALF. "Hinduism." *In* Mircea Eliade, ed. *The Encyclopedia of Religion,* vol. 6, pp. 336–360. New York and London: Macmillan, 1987.

HINNELS, J. R. *Persian Mythology*. London: Hamlyn, 1975.

HOFFNER, HARRY A., JR. "Hittite Religion." *In* Mircea Eliade, ed. *The Encyclopedia of Religion*, vol. 6, pp. 408–414. New York and London: Macmillan, 1987.

——. *Hittite Myths*, 2nd ed. Atlanta: Scholars Press, 1998.

HOLLANDER, LEE M., trans. *The Poetic Edda* (by Snorri Sturluson). Austin: University of Texas Press, 1962.

HOMER. *Iliad*. Richard Lattimore, trans. Chicago: Phoenix Books, 1961.

——. *The Odyssey of Homer*. Robert Fitzgerald, trans. Garden City, NY: Doubleday, 1963.

HONKO, LAURI. "Finno-Ugric Religions: An Overview." *In* Mircea Eliade, ed. *The Encyclopedia of Religion*, vol. 5, p. 335. New York and London: Macmillan, 1987.

HOOKE, S. H. *Babylonian and Assyrian Religion*. New York: Hutchinson's University Library, 1953a.

——. *Middle Eastern Mythology*. Harmonsworth, UK: Penguin, 1953b.

HOYLE, FRED. *Frontiers of Astronomy*. New York: Harper, 1955.

HYNES, WILLIAM J., and WILLIAM G. DOTY. *Mythical Trickster Figures: Contours, Contexts, and Criticisms*. Tuscaloosa: University of Alabama Press, 1997.

JACKSON, GUIDA M. *Encyclopedia of Traditional Epics*. Santa Barbara, CA: ABC-CLIO, 1994.

JACOBSEN, THORKILD. *The Treasures of Darkness: A History of Mesopotamian Religion*. New Haven, CT, and London: Yale University Press, 1976.

——. "Mesopotamian Religions." *In* Mircea Eliade, ed. *The Encyclopedia of Religion*, vol. 9, pp. 447–469. New York and London: Macmillan, 1987.

JONES, GWYN. *A History of the Vikings*, rev. ed. Oxford: Oxford University Press, 1984.

JONES, GWYN, and THOMAS JONES, trans. *The Mabinogion*, rev. ed. Rutland, VT: Charles E. Tuttle, 1993.

JUNG, CARL GUSTAV. *Modern Man in Search of a Soul*. W. S. Dell and Cary Baynes, trans. New York: Harcourt, Brace and World, 1933.

——. *The Undiscovered Self*. R. F. C. Hull, trans. New York: Mentor, 1957.

——. *The Archetypes of the Collective Unconscious*. R. F. C. Hull, trans. Princeton, NJ: Princeton University Press, 1959 (1934/54).

——. *Answer to Job*. R. F. C. Hull, trans. Cleveland: Meridian, 1960 (1954).

——. *Memories, Dreams, Reflections*. Richard and Clara Winston, trans. New York: Vintage, 1963.

——. *Four Archetypes: Mother/Rebirth/ Spirit/Trickster*. R. F. C. Hull, trans. Princeton, NJ: Princeton University Press, 1969.

——. *Symbols of Transformation*. R. F. C. Hull, trans. Princeton, NJ: Princeton University Press, 1976 (1956).

JUNG, CARL GUSTAV, and C. KERENYI. *Essays on a Science of Mythology: The Myth of the Divine Child and the Mysteries of Eleusis*. R. F. C. Hull, trans. Princeton, NJ: Princeton University Press, 1963.

KE, YUAN. *Dragons and Dynasties: An Introduction to Chinese Mythology*. London: Penguin, 1993.

KERENYI, C. *The Gods of the Greeks*. London: Thames and Hudson, 1951.

——. *The Heroes of the Greeks*. New York: Grove Press, 1960.

KERRIGAN, MICHAEL, ALAN LOTHIAN, and PIERS VITEBSKY. *Epics of Early Civilization: Myths of the Ancient Near East*. London: Duncan Baird, 1998.

KINSELLA, THOMAS, trans. *The Tain*. Oxford: Oxford University Press, 1970.

KITAGAWA, JOSEPH M. "Japanese Religion: An Overview." *In* Mircea Eliade, ed. *The Encyclopedia of Religion*, vol. 7, pp. 520–538. New York and London: Macmillan, 1987.

KNAPPERT, JAN. *Islamic Legends*. 2 vols. Leiden: Brill, 1985.

——. *The Encyclopedia of Middle Eastern Mythology and Religion*. Shaftesbury, Rockport, Brisbane: Element, 1993.

KRAMER, SAMUEL NOAH, ed. *Mythologies of the Ancient World*. Garden City, NY: Doubleday, 1961a.

——. *Sumerian Mythology*, rev. ed. New York: Harper & Row, 1961b.

KRAMER, SAMUEL NOAH, and JOHN MAIER. *Myths of Enki: The Crafty God*. New York and Oxford: Oxford University Press, 1989.

LAMBERT, W. G. "A New Look at the Babylonian Background of Genesis." *Journal of Theological Studies* 16:1965.

LANSING, J. STEPHEN. "Balinese Mythology." *In* Mircea Eliade, ed. *The Encyclopedia of Religion*, vol. 2, pp. 45–48. New York and London: Macmillan, 1987.

LARRINGTON, CAROLYNE, ed. *The Feminist Companion to Mythology*. London: Pandora, 1992.

LEEMING, DAVID. "Quests." *In* Mircea Eliade, ed. *The Encyclopedia of Religion*, vol. 12, pp. 146–152. New York and London: Macmillan, 1987a.

——. "Virgin Birth." *In* Mircea Eliade, ed. *The Encyclopedia of Religion*, vol. 15, pp. 272–276. New York and London: Macmillan, 1987b.

——. *The World of Myth*. New York: Oxford University Press, 1990.

——. *Mythology: The Voyage of the Hero*. New York: Oxford University Press, 1998.

——. *A Dictionary of Asian Mythology*. New York: Oxford University Press, 2001.

——. *Myth: A Biography of Belief*. New York: Oxford University Press, 2002.

——. *From Olympus to Camelot: The World of European Mythology*. New York: Oxford University Press, 2003.

——. *Jealous Gods and Chosen People: The Mythology of the Middle East*. New York: Oxford University Press, 2004.

LEEMING, DAVID, with MARGARET LEEMING. *A Dictionary of Creation Myths*. New York: Oxford University Press, 1994.

LEEMING, DAVID, and JAKE PAGE. *Goddess: Myths of the Female Divine*. New York: Oxford University Press, 1994.

——. *God: Myths of the Male Divine*. New York: Oxford University Press, 1996.

——. *Myths, Legends, and Folktales of America*. New York: Oxford University Press, 1999.

——. *The Mythology of Native North America*. Norman: University of Oklahoma Press, 1998.

LEICK, GWENDOLEN. *A Dictionary of Ancient Near Eastern Mythology*. London and New York: Routledge, 1991.

LESKO, LEONARD. "Atum." *In* Mircea Eliade, ed. *The Encyclopedia of Religion*, vol. 1, p. 519. New York and London: Macmillan, 1987a.

——. "Egyptian Religion: An Overview." *In* Mircea Eliade, ed. *The Encyclopedia of Religion*, vol. 5, pp. 37–54. New York and London: Macmillan, 1987b.

——. "Isis." *In* Mircea Eliade, ed. *The Encyclopedia of Religion*, vol. 7, p. 302. New York and London: Macmillan, 1987c.

——. "Osiris." *In* Mircea Eliade, ed. *The Encyclopedia of Religion*, vol. 11, pp. 132–133. New York and London: Macmillan, 1987d.

——. "Ptah." *In* Mircea Eliade, ed. *The Encyclopedia of Religion,* vol. 12, p. 81. New York and London: Macmillan, 1987e.

——. "Re." *In* Mircea Eliade, ed. *The Encyclopedia of Religion,* vol. 12, pp. 222–223. New York and London: Macmillan, 1987f.

——. "Seth." *In* Mircea Eliade, ed. *The Encyclopedia of Religion,* vol. 13, p. 178. New York and London, 1987g.

——. "Thoth." *In* Mircea Eliade, ed. *The Encyclopedia of Religion,* vol. 14, pp. 493–494. New York and London: Macmillan, 1987h.

LÉVI-STRAUSS, CLAUDE. *The Savage Mind.* Chicago: University of Chicago Press, 1966.

——. *The Raw and the Cooked.* John and Doreen Weightman, trans. New York: Harper & Row, 1969.

——. *Myth and Meaning.* New York: Harper & Row, 1979.

LINCOLN, BRUCE. *Myth, Cosmos, and Society: Indo-European Themes of Creation and Destruction.* Cambridge, MA: Harvard University Press, 1986.

——. "Indo-European Religions." *In* Mircea Eliade, ed. *The Encyclopedia of Religion,* vol. 7, pp. 198–204. New York and London: Macmillan, 1987.

LINDOW, JOHN. *Norse Mythology: A Guide to the Gods, Heroes, Rituals, and Beliefs.* New York: Oxford University Press, 2002

LIVY. *See* Foster.

LONERGAN, ANNE, and CAROLINE RICHARDS. *Thomas Berry and the New Cosmology.* Mystic, CT: Twenty-third Publications, 1988.

LONG, CHARLES. *Alpha: The Myths of Creation.* New York: George Braziller, 1963.

LOVELOCK, JAMES E. *Gaia: A New Look at Life on Earth.* New York: Oxford University Press, 1979.

LURKER, M. *The Gods and Symbols of Ancient Egypt.* London: Thames and Hudson, 1980.

MAC CANA, PROINSIAS. *Celtic Mythology.* London: Hamlyn, 1970.

——. "Celtic Religion." *In* Mircea Eliade, ed. *The Encyclopedia of Religion,* vol. 3, pp. 148–166. New York and London: Macmillan, 1987.

MACALISTER, R. A. S. *Lebor Gabala Erenn (Book of Invasions).* 5 vols. Dublin: Irish Text Society, 1956.

MACQUEEN, J. G. *The Hittites and Their Contemporaries in Asia Minor.* New York: Thames and Hudson, 1996.

MAHABHARATA. *See* van Buitenan.

MALLORY, J. P. *In Search of the Indo-Europeans: Language, Archaeology and Myth.* London: Thames and Hudson, 1989.

MCLEAN, ADAM. *The Triple Goddess: An Exploration of the Archetypal Feminine.* Grand Rapids, MI: Phanes Press, 1989.

MELLAART, JAMES. *Çatal Hüyük: A Neolithic Town in Anatolia.* New York: McGraw-Hill, 1967.

MENDELSOHN, ISAAC, ed. *Religions of the Ancient Near East: Sumero-Akkadian Religious Texts and Ugaritic Epics.* New York: Liberal Arts Press, 1955.

MERTON, THOMAS. "Symbolism: Communication or Communion?" *New Directions* 20:1–12, 1968.

MILLER, ALAN A. "Japanese Religion: Popular Religion." *In* Mircea Eliade, ed. *The Encyclopedia of Religion,* vol. 7, pp. 538–545. New York and London: Macmillan, 1987.

MITCHELL, STEPHEN, trans. *Tao Te Ching.* New York: Harper & Row, 1988.

MOMIGLIANO, ARNALDO. "Roman Religion: The Imperial Period." *In* Mircea Eliade, ed. *The Encyclopedia of Religion,* vol. 12, pp. 462–471. New York and London: Macmillan, 1987.

MONTGOMERY WATT, WILLIAM. *Companion to the Qur'an.* London: Allen and Unwin, 1967.

MORAN, WILLIAM L. "Gilgamesh." *In* Mircea Eliade, ed. *The Encyclopedia of Religion,* vol. 5, pp. 557–560. New York and London: Macmillan, 1987.

MORFORD, MARK P. O., and ROBERT J. LENARDON, eds. *Classical Mythology.* New York and London: Longman, 1985.

MOSELEY, MICHAEL E. *The Incas and Their Ancestors.* London: Thames and Hudson, 1992.

MOYNE, JOHN, and COLEMAN BARKS. *Unseen Rain: Quatrains of Rumi.* Putney, VT: Threshold Books, 1986.

MUDROOROO. *Aboriginal Mythology.* Scranton, PA: Thorson's, 1995.

MULLER, HERBERT. *Science and Humanism.* New Haven, CT: Yale University Press, 1943.

MURRAY, GILBERT. *Five Stages of Greek Religion.* Garden City, NY: Doubleday, 1955 (1951).

NARR, KARL J. "Paleolithic Religion." Matthew J. O'Connell, trans. *In* Mircea Eliade, ed. *The Encyclopedia of Religion,* vol. 11, pp. 149–159. New York and London: Macmillan, 1987.

NASR, SEYED HOSSEIN. *Islamic Spirituality.* 2 vols. New York: Crossroads, 1987, 1991.

NEIHART, JOHN G. *Black Elk Speaks.* Lincoln: University of Nebraska Press, 1988.

NEUMANN, ERICK. *The Great Mother: An Analysis of the Archetype.* Princeton, NJ: Princeton University Press, 1955.

NICHOLSON, ERNEST W. *God and His People.* New York: Oxford University Press, 1986.

NICHOLSON, H. B. "Mesoamerican Religions: Postclassical Cultures." *In* Mircea Eliade, ed. *The Encyclopedia of Religion,* vol. 9, pp. 419–428. New York and London: Macmillan, 1987.

NIGG, JOSEPH. *The Book of Fabulous Beasts: A Treasury of Writings from Ancient Times to the Present.* New York: Oxford University Press, 1998.

NILSSON, MARTIN. *The Mycenaean Origin of Greek Mythology.* New York: W.W. Norton, 1963 (1932).

——. *A History of Greek Religion.* F. J. Fielden, trans. New York: W.W. Norton, 1965.

NORWOOD, GILBERT. *Greek Tragedy.* New York: Hill and Wang, 1960.

O'COLLINS, GERALD. "Jesus." *In* Mircea Eliade, ed. *The Encyclopedia of Religion,* vol. 8, pp. 15–28. New York and London: Macmillan, 1987.

O'FLAHERTY, WENDY DONIGER. *Hindu Myths: A Sourcebook Translated from the Sanskrit.* Harmondsworth, UK: Penguin, 1975.

OHNUKI-TIERNEY, EMIKO. "Ainu Religion." *In* Mircea Eliade, ed. *The Encyclopedia of Religion,* vol. 1, pp. 159–161. New York and London: Macmillan, 1987.

OKPEWHO, ISADORE. *Myth in Africa.* London: Cambridge University Press, 1983.

OLCOTT, WILLIAM TYLER. *Myths of the Sun.* New York: Capricorn Books, 1914.

OTTO, WALTER F. *The Homeric Gods: The Spiritual Significance of Greek Religion.* London: Thames and Hudson, 1954.

OVID. *Ovid's Metamorphoses.* Charles Boer, trans. Dallas, TX: Spring Publications, 1989.

PAGE, R. I. *Norse Myths* (Legendary Past series). London: British Museum Press, 1990.

PAGELS, ELAINE. *Adam, Eve, and the Serpent.* New York: Random House, 1988.

PANIKKAR, RAIMUNDO. "Deity." *In* Mircea Eliade, ed. *The Encyclopedia of Religion,* vol. 4, pp. 264–276. New York and London: Macmillan, 1987.

PARRINDER, GEOFFREY. *African Mythology.* London: Hamlyn, 1982.

PATAI, RAPHAEL. "The Goddess Asherah." *Journal of Cuneiform Studies,* 1965.

——. *The Hebrew Goddess.* New York: Ktav, 1967.

——, ed. *Arab Folktales from Palestine and Israel.* Detroit: Wayne State University Press, 1998.

PELIKAN, JAROSLAV. "Christianity: An Overview" *In* Mircea Eliade, ed. *The Encyclopedia of Religion,* vol. 3, pp. 348–362. New York and London: Macmillan, 1987a.

——. "Christianity in Western Europe." *In* Mircea Eliade, ed. *The Encyclopedia of Religion,* vol. 3, pp. 379–387. New York and London: Macmillan, 1987b.

PELON, OLIVIER. "Aegean Religions." Anne Marzin, trans. *In* Mircea Eliade, ed. *The Encyclopedia of Religion,* vol. 1, pp. 32–39. New York and London: Macmillan, 1987.

PHILIPPI, DONALD L. trans. *Kojiki.* Tokyo: University of Tokyo Press, 1968.

POLOME, EDGAR C. "Germanic Religion." *In* Mircea Eliade, ed. *The Encyclopedia of Religion,* vol. 5, pp. 520–536. New York and London: Macmillan, 1987.

PORTILLA-LEON, MIGUEL. "Mesoamerican Religions: Pre-Columbian Religions." *In* Mircea Eliade, ed. *The Encyclopedia of Religion,* vol. 9, pp. 390–406. New York and London: Macmillan, 1987.

PRESTON, JAMES. *Mother Worship: Theme and Variations.* Chapel Hill: University of North Carolina Press, 1982.

PRITCHARD, JAMES B. *Ancient Near Eastern Texts Relating to the Old Testament,* 3rd ed. Princeton, NJ: Princeton University Press, 1969.

PROPP, VLADIMIR. *Morphology of the Folktale.* Austin: University of Texas Press, 1968.

PUHVEL, JAAN. *Comparative Mythology.* Baltimore: Johns Hopkins University Press, 1987.

QUISPEL, GILLES. "Gnosticism: From Its Origins to the Middle Ages." *In* Mircea Eliade, ed. *The Encyclopedia of Religion,* vol. 5, pp. 566–574. New York and London: Macmillan, 1987.

RAGLAN, LORD FITZROY. *The Hero: A Study in Tradition, Myth, and Drama.* New York: Vintage, 1966 (1937).

RAHMAN, FAZLUR. *Islam.* Chicago: University of Chicago Press, 1979.

——. "Islam." *In* Mircea Eliade, ed. *The Encyclopedia of Religion,* vol. 7, pp. 303–322. New York and London: Macmillan, 1987.

RAMAYANA. See Buck.

RANK, OTTO. *The Myth of the Birth of the Hero.* New York: Knopf, 1959 (1936).

RAUF, M. A. *The Life and Teaching of the Prophet Muhammad.* London: Longman, 1964.

READ, HERBERT. *The Philosophy of Modern Art.* London: Faber and Faber, 1953.

REDFORD, DONALD B. "Egyptian Religion: The Literature." *In* Mircea Eliade, ed. *The Encyclopedia of Religion,* vol. 5, pp. 54–65. New York and London: Macmillan, 1987.

——, ed. *Oxford Essential Guide to Egyptian Mythology.* New York: Berkley Books, 2003.

REES, ALWYN, and BRINLEY REES. *Celtic Heritage: Ancient Tradition in Ireland and Wales.* London: Thames and Hudson, 1961.

RENARD, JOHN, ed. *Windows on the House of Islam: Muslim Sources on Spirituality and Religious Life.* Berkeley: University of California Press, 1998.

——. *Responses to 101 Questions on Buddhism.* New York: Paulist Press, 1999a.

——. *Responses to 101 Questions on Hinduism.* New York: Paulist Press, 1999b.

RHIE, MARYLIN M., and ROBERT A. F. THURMAN, eds. *Worlds of Transformation: Tibetan Art of Wisdom and Compassion.* New York: Tibet House, 1999.

ROBINSON, MAXINE. *The Arabs,* 2nd ed. Chicago: University of Chicago Press, 1981.

ROSENBERG, DONNA. *World Mythology: An Anthology of the Great Myths and Epics.* Lincolnwood, IL.: National Textbook Co., 1986.

RUDD, NIALL, and JONATHAN POWELL, eds., trans. *The Republic & the Law by Cicero.* New York: Oxford University Press, 1998.

RUSSELL, J. R. "Armenian Religion." *In* Mircea Eliade, ed. *The Encyclopedia of Religion,* vol. 1, pp. 417–419. New York and London: Macmillan, 1987.

SANDARS, N. K., trans. *The Epic of Gilgamesh.* Harmondsworth, UK: Penguin, 1973.

SANTILLANA, GIORGIO DE, and HERTHA VON DECHEND. *Hamlet's Mill: An Essay on Myth and the Frame of Time.* Boston: David R. Godine, 1977.

SAXO GRAMMATICUS. *See* Davidson and Fisher.

SCHILLING, ROBERT. "Roman Religion: The Early Period." Paul C. Duggan, trans. *In* Mircea Eliade, ed. *The Encyclopedia of Religion,* vol. 12, pp. 445–461. New York and London: Macmillan, 1987.

SCHWARTZ, HOWARD. *Tree of Souls: The Mythology of Judaism.* New York: Oxford University Press, 2004.

SHARIATI, ALI. *Hajj.* Laleh Bakhtiar, trans. Bedford, OH: Free Islamic Literatures, 1978.

SIIKALA, ANNA-LEENA. "Finnic Religions." Susan Sinisalo, trans. *In* Mircea Eliade, ed. *The Encyclopedia of Religion,* vol. 5, pp. 323–330. New York and London: Macmillan, 1987.

SIMPSON, GEORGE. "Caribbean Religion: Afro-Caribbean Religions." *In* Mircea Eliade, ed. *The Encyclopedia of Religion,* vol. 3, pp. 90–98. New York and London: Macmillan, 1987.

SIMPSON, JACQUELINE, ed. *European Mythology.* London: Hamlyn, 1987.

SMITH, WILLIAM. *Smaller Classical Dictionary.* New York: E.P. Dutton, 1958.

SOYINKA, WOLE. *Myth, Literature & the African World.* Cambridge: Cambridge University Press, 1976.

SPERLING, S. DAVID. "God in the Hebrew Scriptures." *In* Mircea Eliade, ed. *The Encyclopedia of Religion,* vol. 6, pp. 1–8. New York and London: Macmillan, 1987.

SPROUL, BARBARA. *Primal Myths: Creation Myths around the World.* New York: HarperCollins, 1991.

SREJOVICH, DRAGOSLAV. "Neolithic Religion." Veselin Kostic, trans. *In* Mircea Eliade, ed. *The Encyclopedia of Religion,* vol. 10, pp. 352–360. New York and London: Macmillan, 1987.

STANNARD, RUSSELL, ed. *God for the 21st Century.* Philadelphia: Templeton, 2000.

STETKEVYCH, JAROSLAV. *Muhammad and the Golden Bough: Reconstructing Arabian Myth.* Bloomington and Indianapolis: Indiana University Press, 1996.

STURLUSON, SNORRI. *See* Hollander, Young

SUGGS, M. JACK, KATHERINE DOOB SAKENFELD, and JAMES R. MUELLER, eds. *The Oxford Study Bible.* New York: Oxford University Press, 1992.

SWANTON MICHAEL, ed. *The Dream of the Rood.* New York: Barnes and Noble, 1970.

SWIMME, BRIAN. *The Universe Is a Green Dragon: A Cosmic Creation Story.* Santa Fe, NM: Bear and Co., 1984.

TACITUS. *See* Hadas.

TAKESHI, MATSUMAE. "Japanese Religion: Mythic Themes." *In* Mircea Eliade, ed. *The Encyclopedia of Religion,* vol. 7, pp. 545–552. New York and London: Macmillan, 1987.

TEIXIDOR, JAVIER. "Aramean Religion." *In* Mircea Eliade, ed. *The Encyclopedia of Religion,* vol. 1, pp. 367–372. New York and London: Macmillan, 1987.

THOMAS. *The Gospel According to Thomas.* Leiden: Brill, 1959.

THOMPSON, STITH. *Motif-Index of Folk Literature.* Bloomington: Indiana University Press, 1971.

TODD, M. *The Early Germans.* Oxford: Blackwell, 1992.

TSUNODA, RYUSAKU, and WILLIAM THEODORE DE BARY. *Sources of Japanese Tradition.* New York: Columbia University Press, 1958.

TURVILLE-PETRE, E. O. G. *Myth and Religion in the North.* New York: Holt, Rinehart and Winston, 1964.

ULANOV, ANN, and BARRY ULANOV. *Religion and the Unconscious.* Philadelphia: Westminster Press, 1975.

VAN BUITENAN, J. A. B., trans. *The Mahabharata.* Chicago: University of Chicago Press, 1973–1978.

VAN SETERS, JOHN. "Abraham." *In* Mircea Eliade, ed. *The Encyclopedia of Religion,* vol. 1, pp. 13–17. New York and London: Macmillan, 1987a.

——. "Moses." *In* Mircea Eliade, ed. *The Encyclopedia of Religion,* vol. 10, pp. 115–121. New York and London: Macmillan, 1987b.

VAN VOSS, M. HEERMA. "Anubis." *In* Mircea Eliade, ed. *The Encyclopedia of Religion,* vol. 1, pp. 330–331. New York and London: Macmillan, 1987.

VASQUEZ, JUAN ADOLFO. "South American Religions: Mythic Themes." *In* Mircea Eliade, ed. *The Encyclopedia of Religion,* vol. 13, pp. 499–506. New York and London: Macmillan, 1987.

VERGIL (VIRGIL). *Aeneid.* Robert Fitzgerald, trans. New York: Vintage, 1990.

VERNANT, JEAN-PIERRE. "Greek Religion." Anne Marzin, trans. *In* Mircea Eliade, ed. *The Encyclopedia of Religion,* vol. 6, pp. 99–118. New York and London: Macmillan, 1987.

——. *Myth and Society in Ancient Greece.* Janet Lloyd, trans. New York: Zone Books, 1990.

WALKER, BARBARA G. *The Woman's Encyclopedia of Myths and Secrets.* San Francisco: Harper & Row, 1983.

WASILEWSKA, EWA. *Creation Stories of the Middle East.* London and Philadelphia: Jessica Kingsley, 2000.

WATT, V. MONTGOMERY. "Muhammad." *In* Mircea Eliade, ed. *The Encyclopedia of Religion,* vol. 10, pp. 37–148. New York and London: Macmillan, 1987.

WATTS, ALAN. *Myth and Ritual in Christianity.* Boston: Beacon Press, 1968.

——. *The Spirit of Zen.* New York: Grove, 1958.

WEIGLE, MARTA. *Creation and Procreation: Feminist Reflections on Mythologies of Cosmogony and Parturition.* Philadelphia: University of Pennsylvania Press, 1989.

WEINFELD, MOSHE. "Israelite Religion." *In* Mircea Eliade, ed. *The Encyclopedia of Religion,* vol. 7, pp. 481–497. New York and London: Macmillan, 1987.

WESTON, JESSIE L. *From Ritual to Romance: An Account of the Holy Grail from Ancient Ritual to Christian Symbol.* Garden City, NY: Doubleday, 1957.

WHITE, LYNN, JR. "Christian Myth and Christian History." *In Machina ex Deo: Essays in the Dynamism of Western Culture.* Cambridge, MA: MIT Press, 1969.

WHITTAKER, CLIO, ed. *An Introduction to Oriental Mythology.* London: Grange Books, 1995.

WOLKSTEIN, DIANE, and SAMUEL NOAH KRAMER. *Inanna: Queen of Heaven and Earth.* New York: Harper & Row, 1983.

YOUNG, JEAN I., trans. *The Prose Edda of Snorri Sturluson: Tales from Norse Mythology.* Berkeley: University of California Press, 1954.

ZERRIES, OTTO. "South American Religions: An Overview." *In* Mircea Eliade, ed. *The Encyclopedia of Religion,* vol. 13, pp. 486–499. New York and London: Macmillan, 1987.

ZIMMER, HEINRICH. *Myths and Symbols in Indian Art and Civilization.* Princeton, NJ: Princeton University Press, 1972 (1946).

ZOLBROD, PAUL G. *Dine Bahane: The Navajo Creation Story.* Albuqueque: University of New Mexico Press, 1984.

ZUESSE, EVAN M. "African Religions: Mythic Themes." *In* Mircea Eliade, ed. *The Encyclopedia of Religion,* vol. 1, pp. 70–82. New York and London: Macmillan, 1987.

Index